Founders

The People Who
Brought You a Nation

Ray Raphael

THE NEW PRESS

NEW YORK
LONDON

Requests for permission to reproduce selections from this book should be mailed to:
Permissions Department, The New Press, 38 Greene Street, New York, NY 10013.

First published in the United States by The New Press, New York, 2009
This paperback edition published by The New Press, New York, 2010
Distributed by Perseus Distribution

LIBRARY OF CONGRESS CATALOGING-IN-PUBLICATION DATA
Raphael, Ray.
Founders : the people who brought you a nation / Ray Raphael.
p. cm
Includes bibliographical references and index.
ISBN 978-1-59558-327-7 (hc.)
ISBN 978-1-59558-417-5 (pb.)
1. United States—History—Revolution, 1775–1783. 2. Revolutionaries—United States—
History—18th century. 3. United States—History—Revolution, 1775–1783–Social aspects.
4. United States—History—Revolution, 1775–1783—Biography. I. Title
E208.R248 2009
973.3—dc22
2008052745

The New Press was established in 1990 as a not-for-profit alternative to the large,
commercial publishing houses currently dominating the book publishing industry.
The New Press operates in the public interest rather than for private gain, and is committed
to publishing, in innovative ways, works of educational, cultural, and community value
that are often deemed insufficiently profitable.

www.thenewpress.com

Composition by NK Graphics
This book was set in Adobe Caslon

Printed in the United States of America

2 4 6 8 10 9 7 5 3 1

Contents

List of Images

Introduction

We know them well: George Washington, James Madison, Benjamin Franklin, Thomas Jefferson, Alexander Hamilton, John Adams. Collectively, they were *the* Founders, a small cadre of very special individuals who bequeathed us a nation.

That's not how people at the time saw it, however. They recognized a host of personages, rarely mentioned today, as indispensable to the task at hand—revolution and nation building. All patriots knew, for instance, that a wealthy merchant named Robert Morris offered his personal credit to save the embryonic nation from financial ruin. Some called him "The Great Man," others "The Dictator"; but nobody disputed the awesome power and influence of "The Financier," whose "reign" lasted for three years as the Revolutionary War drew to a close.

More in the spirit of those tumultuous times, common farmers, artisans, and laborers were fully aware of their own collective participation and sacrifice, their defeats and triumphs. The body of the people, as they were called at the time, acted "out of doors" or "out of chambers," gathering by liberty poles and liberty trees in the open air, or within taverns and meetinghouses, to oppose British authority and push for self-governance. The new nation would bear the robust genetic imprint of this grand multitude.

Today, few Americans know of Robert Morris or appreciate the revolutionary impact of the body of the people. The reality of our nation's founding, wide and encompassing as it was happening, has narrowed in the decades and centuries since. Through successive filtrations of the historical record, actual events have been simplified, and truth diminished.

Can we now call back a distant time, to view it more fully and accurately? Can we embrace a wider array of Revolutionary actors, views, and visions?

Historians who have tried to do this in recent years have run into a problem: with so many actors, scenes, and perspectives, the story grows too big. That in part is why popular history writers have returned once again to the limited cast of recognizable figures, who touch us on a personal level. Fortuitously, since *the* Founders were inveterate writers, historians can mine and re-mine their letters, diaries, and political tracts, fashioning them into cohesive stories with wide audience appeal. The plot remains direct and clear, the stars familiar and attractive.

But history based on this select crew, if left to stand on its own, has a serious shortcoming. The basic principle of the American Revolution was that government should be firmly rooted in the will of the people; four score and seven years later, Abraham Lincoln gave poetic voice to this message by boasting that our original patriots had established a nation "of the people, by the people, and for the people." When we say our nation was created by a mere handful of Founding Fathers, we lose a key component of this democratic trinity. "Of the people, for the people, but by a few wise men" doesn't have the same ring.

So whom should we feature: the great men we know, or the many others we do not?

The answer is both.

This book focuses on the lives of seven individuals drawn from a representative sampling of Revolutionary Americans. The traditional Founding Fathers are not the only ones capable of providing narrative direction, and because they come from a narrow stratum of society with a restricted range of life experiences, they should not be our only selections. That's why I venture to more varied echelons as well. There, by consulting the original historical records, I find fresh individuals who can be tracked through the entire period of our founding. These people also affected events of the times, and because we have not heard much from them before, they produce unexpected twists and turns in the dramatic action. Appearing together and complementing each other, they encompass the full sweep of the Founding era. Along with a sampling of their better-known contemporaries, whom I have not neglected, they shape an authentic, engaging, and coherent drama.

My first lead character, George Washington, will be familiar, but others might not. Readers will also meet:

- Joseph Plumb Martin, a private in Washington's army, who chronicled his wartime experiences with heart and wit

- Mercy Otis Warren, the most political woman of the Revolutionary generation and author of one of the earliest American histories
- Robert Morris, undoubtedly the most powerful civilian in Revolutionary America, but strangely neglected today
- Timothy Bigelow, a small-town blacksmith who helped engineer the first overthrow of British authority, the year *before* Lexington and Concord
- The conservative Henry Laurens, South Carolina's most unlikely rebel and Britain's most improbable prisoner
- Thomas Young, a country doctor turned peripatetic revolutionary, who fomented rebellion in seven states

Directing the story, such characters expand it. While ensuring the tale's cohesion, they confirm its rich diversity.

If particular individuals focus our narrative, so do specific scenes. A sequence of live dramas occurring in set locations at definite times grounds this history. In these pages readers will travel from the Ohio backcountry in 1754 to Philadelphia's Independence Hall in 1787, with stops along the way in the streets of Boston, plantation mansions and slave quarters in South Carolina, and a host of towns, taverns, and battlefields throughout the land.

Step by step, the narrative moves forward along a chronological line that starts with the first hints of patriotic unrest, when British colonists in North America sensed that something was wrong but did not yet dream of creating a separate nation. From there it proceeds through the declaring of independence, the war that was fought to preserve it, and the establishment of a nation based on a firm and lasting constitution. By proceeding in a linear fashion, I try to re-create each moment as it appeared to contemporary revolutionaries, who had no cognizance of what the future would bring. And by following the course of events over several decades, I hope to reveal that our nation was created not in a single epiphany, but through an extended and collaborative process that involved an entire generation of American patriots.

Without limiting its breadth and extent, I also contain this vital story by focusing on five key themes, central to both the founding of our nation and the way we think of America today.

1. *Popular sovereignty.* From the Revolution's inception, one core tenet of the eighteenth-century Enlightenment was uppermost in the minds of American patriots: all government must be rooted in the will of the people.

They embraced this belief fervently and on a grand scale. If their aim was to root government in a collective entity—the people—the Revolution itself reflected that aim. At each and every turn it was a people's affair. The Revolutionary generation founded a nation on the ideal of popular sovereignty, without any vestige of monarchical power or aristocratic privilege, and this was certainly its supreme achievement.

2. *Inclusion and exclusion.* Though popular sovereignty was the people's battle cry, questions of access to power remained. How far did popular sovereignty extend? Who was included and who was not? Should the power derived from sovereignty be distributed widely, or were certain inequalities inevitable and perhaps even desirable? Although nearly all Americans embraced the general notion that governmental authority resided in "the people," this basic premise was interpreted in numerous and competing ways. Outsiders wanted in but were often denied. In the evolving order, internal struggles between groups and individuals assumed new significance.

3. *Exchanges of power.* During the Revolutionary era, power traveled both up and down social and political hierarchies, from inside chambers to the population at large, and from the people outside to the men within. Sometimes the so-called leaders led, as we commonly assume, but at other times they received their directives from the people and had little choice but to follow. Our two most sacred documents demonstrate these opposite trajectories in the political process. The Declaration of Independence resulted from an immense outpouring of popular sentiment, as commoners drove their representatives forward. The Constitution, on the other hand, was conceived in secret behind closed doors, and then sold to the people.

4. *Constraining authority.* As they cast off British rule, patriots resisted the undue concentration of military, economic, or political power. In their minds, standing armies, monopolistic corporations, and intrusive governments interfered with the people's right to self-government, and they deliberately instituted various check and balances in their new governments (both state and national) to guard against it. Today, in a nation that boasts the largest concentration of military, economic, and political power in the world, and perhaps in history, this component of our national heritage appears anachronistic, but, for that very reason, we should highlight the fears that weighed so heavily upon the Founders.

5. *Expansion.* American patriots, in forming a new nation, looked west as well as east. Even as they defied British control, they struggled to extend their own control over the vast American interior. Victory in the Revolutionary War doubled the area claimed by the United States, while Native Americans lost more land in the Revolution than in any other war. The desire to move west was a major cause of the Revolution and moving west a major result. In the emerging American ethos, expansion was often linked to popular sovereignty. Because they possessed the most progressive form of government, many Americans felt they had a right and even a duty to spread it. Like the fundamental belief in popular rule and the struggles over inclusion and access to power, expansion of American influence has been a major component of our national experience from the outset.

These, in brief, are the characters, settings, and themes. This history, like all high drama, abounds with grand purpose, stalwart effort, and human foibles. The lead characters evolve as our country does, and in the end, their spirited stories become our country's chronicle—inclusive and in that sense patriotic, for if the American nation is all about "the people," our national narrative must be too.

Act I

Resistance

1

Facing East and West

May 28, 1754: A Forest Glen in Ohio Country, Deep in the Colonial West

"In a heavy rain, and in a night as dark as pitch, along a path scarce broad enough for one man," twenty-two-year-old George Washington wrote in his diary, forty militiamen from Virginia "were frequently tumbling one over another, and often so lost that 15 or 20 minutes search would not find the path again." They clung together in this strange and ominous land, not wishing to lose touch, since they had no sight.[1]

The following morning, May 28, 1754, Washington ordered his militiamen to fire the shots that triggered not just one war, but two—the French and Indian War and its successor, the American Revolution.

The purpose of Washington's mission was to establish a military presence west of the Appalachian Mountains, in Ohio country. A few years earlier, Virginia Governor Robert Dinwiddie, Lawrence Washington, and members of prominent families such as the Lees, Mercers, and Masons had organized the Ohio Company of Virginia, which intended, as its name implies, to speculate in large tracts of land located in the Ohio Valley. The previous fall, Dinwiddie had dispatched the company's young surveyor—George Washington, in fact—with a "summons" to French officers who were building military forts along the upper reaches of the Ohio River: cease and desist, the governor wrote, for Virginia has already claimed the region. To which the French replied bluntly: we will not. Dinwiddie concluded that Virginia would have to build some forts of its own in the neighborhood.[2]

To this end, Dinwiddie invited George Washington to make another trip westward. Washington could have declined the offer and remained at his Mount Vernon plantation, which he had just inherited upon the death of his older half brother, Lawrence. That would have been the safe and comfortable way, but not the ambitious way—for a young man just setting out on life's path, safe and comfortable would not suffice. Lawrence had also bequeathed to George a salaried rank in the colonial militia and an interest in the Ohio Company, both of which tempted the aspiring surveyor to undertake ventures far afield. The younger Washington had already achieved some degree of renown for his published report of his first expedition, and perhaps this small taste of fame gave him the desire to acquire more. In any case, some soupy mix of fortune, fame, glory, honor, duty, and devotion to king and country fed the young officer's appetite for adventure. He was not at that moment prompted by notions such as home rule and republican virtue, which would gain currency at a later date.

After accepting the commission, Washington attempted to gather recruits for the risky mission. This did not prove easy. "You may, with almost equal success, attempt to raise the dead to life again as to raise the force of this county," Washington wrote to Dinwiddie. In the end, the promise of land in Ohio was able to lure a few recruits. These were men with few options, or, as Washington described them, "loose, idle persons, that are quite destitute of house, and home; and many of them cloathes." Eager for at least the appearance of respectability, Washington requested uniforms, but Dinwiddie, lacking both time and funds, denied him. The young commander had to take the men as is; it was "very fatiguing," he reported, "to manage a number of selfwill'd, ungovernable people."[3]

So it was that Washington and his ragged contingent found themselves traipsing through the forest in the dead of the night. They were headed to meet with Tanacharison, an Iroquois warrior known to whites as the Half-King, who had just sent word that a French party was camping nearby in a hidden ravine. The militiamen reached the Iroquois camp shortly before sunrise, and after a brief confab, Washington and the Half-King decided to take the French by surprise.

The battle was brief, no more than fifteen minutes. Although the wounded French officer, the Sieur de Jumonville, tried to surrender, he was soon killed, as were several of his company. Accounts differ as to how this happened, as they often do when some men kill others, and as they always do when such actions initiate a war. Here is one recent telling of the story:

Tanacharison decided to take matters into his own hands. He stepped up to where Jumonville lay, in French declared, "Thou art not yet dead, my father," then sank his hatchet into Jumonville's head, split his skull in half, pulled out his brain, and washed his hands in the mixture of blood and tissue. His warriors fell upon the wounded French soldiers, scalped them all, and decapitated one and put his head on a stake. All this happened under the eyes of the shocked and hapless commanding officer, Lieutenant Colonel Washington.[4]

This is certainly the version Governor Dinwiddie would have preferred. He did not wish to be perceived as the aggressor. In order to relieve himself, Washington, the Ohio Company, and Virginia of any responsibility for shedding first blood, he pointed to the Indians. "This little skirmish was by the Half-King & their Indians," he wrote. "We were auxiliaries to them, as my orders to the commander of our forces [were] to be on the defensive."[5]

The French commanding officer, who had given the camping party its orders, told a very different story. The men he had sent forth were on a diplomatic mission and nothing more, he claimed, when they were surrounded and massacred. After two volleys of fire by the Virginians, Jumonville "asked them to desist, that he had something to tell them." He then stepped forward to read the message he had been sent to deliver. As Jumonville spoke, unarmed and defenseless, he "was killed by a musket-shot in the head." The entire French party would have been slaughtered in a like manner "had not the Indians who were present, by rushing between them and the English, prevented their design."[6]

Washington himself described the event with less hyperbole and greater candor. He believed the French party was concerned with espionage, not diplomacy. Indian informers had told him as much, and the fact that the French were camping in a secluded place confirmed it in his mind. Had they been true diplomats instead of spies, they would have stayed on the main trails and made their presence known. He had to take decisive action, he felt, so these spies would not be able to report on his strength and position, in preparation for a major French offensive. Unlike Dinwiddie, Washington did not try to pass off all responsibility. "We were advanced pretty near to them, as we thought, when they discovered us; whereupon I ordered my company to fire," he stated flatly, although he did note that after ten men had been killed, "The *Indians* scalped the dead, and took away the most part of their arms."[7]

Whether or not the French were actually spies, the key point is that Washington believed they were. He decided to attack rather than wait and let the French attack him. It was a preemptive strike.

Any preemptive strike, by its very nature, raises a worrisome question: how can anybody be certain, even in retrospect, that the other side was also picking a fight? This troubled people at the time, causing Washington to proclaim over and over that the victims had been part of a military mission. Perhaps, judging from his defensive posture, it troubled Washington as well, although he certainly did not express any Hamlet-like torment. Instead, the young officer confessed to being titillated by his first actual military encounter: "I can with truth assure you," he wrote to his half brother three days later, "I heard bulletts whistle and believe me there was something charming in the sound."[8]

One spark kindled a conflagration. Predictably, the French struck back at the Virginians, with Jumonville's brother leading the troops. The imperial government in London, France's enemy for the better part of a century, then ordered its Regulars to come to the aid of the Virginians. Indians joined the fray on this side or that, and before long the shots fired at Jumonville Glen, as it came to be called, had resonated across a good portion of two continents. Several years later, Great Britain and her colonies argued among themselves over who should pay for the war and who should have access to the immense territory they had acquired in the interior of the continent. Those arguments led directly, almost seamlessly, to a war between the British imperial government in London and thirteen of Britain's colonies in North America.

All this was set in motion by George Washington's preemptive strike, twenty-two years before the United States of America declared its independence from Great Britain. Many of the intervening events, although certainly not predetermined, flowed in a normal sequence, each following the next in a somewhat rational fashion, if the discrete elements of war can ever be considered in that light.

An astute observer in 1754, by carefully calculating the likely responses of all interested parties, might have predicted that victory in the French and Indian War would lead to a serious dispute between Britain and her colonies. Even so, few reasonable people could foresee the coming union of thirteen disparate colonies based on the progressive notion that all government is rooted in the collective will of the people, and not even a soothsayer could have prophesized that ordinary citizens, acting in concert, would play critical roles in that union's creation.

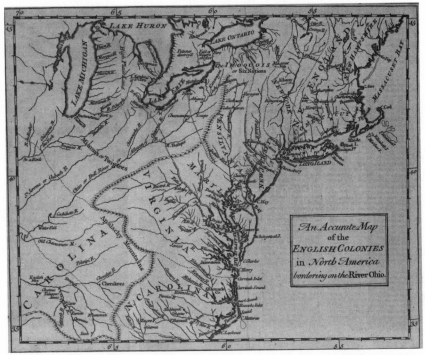

Figure 1. Britain's North American colonies in 1754, when George Washington attacked French scouts at Jumonville Glen. Britain, France, and various Native American nations claimed the area west of the Appalachian Divide, featured prominently here. This map appeared in the *Universal Magazine of Knowledge and Pleasure,* December 1754.

November 21, 1760: British Colonies in North America

Mount Vernon, Virginia. One month after retiring from service in the French and Indian War, George Washington married the wealthy widow Martha Custis, and by combining their fortunes, primarily in the form of land and slaves, George and Martha created one of Virginia's most impressive estates. (According to law, because a married woman could not possess her own property, one-third of Martha's wealth passed to George for the duration of his life; the other two-thirds went in trust to her son John, with George as the administrator.) Buying out his neighbors, Washington more than doubled his Mount Vernon plantation and expanded his mansion.[9]

The Washingtons inaugurated their union by purchasing all the finest clothing and home furnishings that their factor in London, Robert Cary, could locate, but by November 21, 1760, after a two-year spending spree, George Washington's dowry was nearly gone. The former military man, unaccustomed to private life, was beginning to notice a serious discrepancy between the money he made (the season's yield from tobacco, his main source of income, had been very low due to a wet summer) and the money he spent (the fall shopping list he sent to Cary included hundreds of separate items, ranging from "1 pair crimson velvet breeches" to "1 dozn stone chamber pots").[10] Clearly upset by his dependent relationship with British merchants in general and with Robert Cary in particular, Washington started to complain. The clothes Cary sent him didn't fit, he grumbled, and worse yet, they were dated. "Instead of getting things good and fashionable . . . we often have articles sent us that coud only have been used by our forefathers in the days of yore," he wrote to Cary. "'Tis a custom . . . with many shop keepers, and tradesmen in London when they know goods are bespoke for exportation to palm sometimes old, and sometimes very slight and indifferent goods upon us, taking care at the same time to advance 10, 15 or perhaps 20 prct upon them."[11]

Such grievances, however petty, would engender others. At the age of twenty-eight, George Washington took no special issue with imperial policies of the mother country, but at least he was complaining about something, and that was a start. In time, he would begin to perceive a link between the state of his own private affairs and the political economy of the British Empire in North America.

The Carolina backcountry. Although the French and Indian War was winding down in the North, it had yet to reach its climax in the South, and that is why, on November 21, 1760, Henry Laurens was scrambling through the backcountry looking for farmers willing to fight the Cherokees. Unlike many Anglo-Americans, Laurens did not wish to kill Indians or even remove them from their homes. He had been buying deerskins from the Cherokees for years and sending the hides to Europe, where they fetched a handsome price, and he hoped to stabilize the borderland so business could resume.

Laurens, one of the South's leading merchants, had recently been commissioned a lieutenant colonel for the South Carolina Provincials. Unlike Washington, he had no particular military ambitions, and he would not likely have fired the first shot of any war, but he believed in duty to his country, and his country had called.

Henry Laurens was deeply conservative—politically, socially, and personally. Within South Carolina politics, he favored the status quo and did the king's bidding, whatever that might be. Looking down from his position at the top of the social and economic hierarchy, he accepted the world as it was, even though the world he inhabited was predicated upon human slavery. Laurens did express some qualms about placing people in chains for life, but any misgivings remained no more than inconsequential musings, trumped by his inherent belief that what is must be. "I have often reflected with much concern on the same subject [slavery] & wished that our economy & government differ'd from the present system," he wrote, "but alass—since our constitution is as it is, what can individuals do?"[12]

Henry Laurens, like any true conservative, believed the role of the individual was not to challenge the established rules but to work as best one can within them. Those who didn't should be brought into line.

The Tower of London, reserved for the most treacherous traitors in the British Empire, would have seemed an unlikely home for Henry Laurens, had anybody at the time bothered to entertain such a preposterous prospect.

Philadelphia, Pennsylvania. On November 21, 1760, Philadelphia merchant Robert Morris was much richer than he had been at the outset of the French and Indian War. Morris and his partner, Thomas Willing, had benefited from the conflict in several ways: selling provisions and military supplies to both the British Army and provincial soldiers, sending forth privateering vessels (these bore "letters of marque," which granted permission from the government to raid enemy ships for private gain), and importing slaves, much in demand to replace indentured servants who had marched off to war. The wartime activities of the firm of Willing and Morris can be tracked through their advertisements in the *Pennsylvania Gazette*:

> To be sold by WILLING and MORRIS, Barbados and Jamaica Rum, Muscovado Sugar, Coffee, the best Madeira and white Wines. Also sundry Naval and Military Stores, such as Canvas, Cordage, Cables, 9, 4 and 3 Pound Cannons, Swivel Guns, Muskets, and Fusees, with bayonets, Scymeters, Cutlasses, Iron and Lead Bullets, &c.

> For BARBADOS directly, The Ship CARRINGTON, SAMUEL AP-POWEN master, Is a fine letter of Marque Ship, mounting ten Carriage Guns between decks, is well provided with Close Quarters, an excellent Sailer, and will carry thirty Men. For Freight or Passage, apply to Willing and Morris, at their Store in Front street, or to the said Master on board at Stamper Wharff. Ten or twelve able bodied Landsmen will be wanted on board said Ship about a Fortnight hence.

To be sold by WILLING and MORRIS, At their store in Front street, near Walnut street, A Negroe Man, a goldsmith by trade, blows the French horn or trumpet, and is very fit either to follow his trade, or for an armourer of a privateer. A likely [attractive] young Negroe woman. Also Barbados rum, muscovado sugar, &c. They have likewise a parcel of cambricks and lawns; an assortment of Manchester goods, silks, anvils, beck irons, sailcloth, anchors, &c. &c. all which will be sold at the lowest prices.[13]

At the tender age of twenty-five, Robert Morris was already on a trajectory that would make him the richest person in America. By inclination a man of business, he could not at that moment imagine a situation in which the public good would trump private gain. At this point in his career, if asked to bankroll an army or bail out a bankrupt nation, Morris would not likely have parted with his cash or volunteered his credit. Wealth was to be pursued and enjoyed, the hunt to be followed by the feast.

Plymouth, Massachusetts. On November 21, 1760, Mercy Otis Warren was between babies. She had borne two sons, ages one and three, with three more yet to come. We do not know precisely what she was doing on that autumn day, but we can safely assume that, like other women of her times and her class, she disciplined her children, performed her chores, and prayed. Mrs. Warren did whatever it took to manage her family home, which happened to be located immediately adjacent to Plymouth Rock, where her great-great-grandfather had disembarked from the *Mayflower* 140 years past.

Unlike most of her female contemporaries, Warren might also have been reading from the classics or writing a few lines of poetry in whatever spare time she could salvage. Although constrained by traditional gender expectations, this devoted daughter of Puritan New England cast her restless mind beyond her hearth and her church, for she was also an avid student of the European Enlightenment.

Warren's father, James Otis Sr., a prominent merchant-turned-lawyer/politician, had done everything in his power to prepare his two sons to acquire political prominence. Growing up in the Cape Cod town of Barnstable, the Otis boys had spent long hours around the kitchen table learning from their father, who believed his own career had been circumscribed by the fact that he had never attended Harvard. Wanting something better for James Jr. and Joseph, James the elder trained his sons as far as he could, then sent them to their uncle, the Reverend Jonathan Russell. Packing their books across the road to the parish house, the boys continued their studies with the very explicit goal of getting into college.

Neither James nor Joseph proved an eager student, but their younger sister, Mercy, did. Crashing the course, first at the kitchen table and then in the parish house, she learned classical languages, world history, English literature, and Enlightenment philosophy. She devoured everything that came her way, filtering it all through a Puritanical lens to heighten its moral tone and didactic purpose. Her Puritan sensibilities came not only from her teacher, a minister, but also from her mother, Mary Allyne Otis, who was there at her side with a religious homily to suit every circumstance. In the words of Jean Fritz, Warren's insightful biographer, Mary was "well acquainted with the meaning of *duty*, that abrasive word, that insatiable task master at the core of a New England woman's life." But since the duties that anchored a woman's world did not include going to college, Mercy, the star pupil, was left alone with her books and her tasks while James marched off to Harvard, having completed the bare minimum to gain admission, and Joseph went into the family business.[14]

As for Mercy, there was no place for her to go with her intellectual zeal, at least not yet.

The Oblong, New York. On November 21, 1760, Dr. Thomas Young was making his rounds somewhere in "the Oblong," a long, narrow strip of disputed land on the far eastern edge of New York. Wealthy land barons, English investors, two different Indian nations, the New York attorney general, successive waves of Yankee squatters, and at least three different political jurisdictions (New York, Massachusetts, and Connecticut) laid competing claims to real estate within the Oblong. This remote but turbulent place was a fitting first stop for a restless political activist who would soon be spreading revolutionary fervor in New York, Connecticut, Massachusetts, Rhode Island, Vermont, North Carolina, and finally Pennsylvania, where he would challenge Robert Morris for control of a government-in-the-making.

Dr. Young's first recorded run-in with established authority had come on August 8, 1756, when he was indicted in the Crum Elbow precinct, Dutchess County, for speaking and publishing "these wicked and false blasphemious words concerning the said Christian Religion (to wit) Jesus Christ was a knave and a fool." Whether or not he phrased his critique of traditional Christianity in quite these terms, Young's incipient Deism, which he would later refine and preach, was certainly out of step with mainstream beliefs. Not many of his neighbors would have agreed with his notion that a "beneficent Creator" had imprinted a "revelation of his eternal wisdom, unlimited power, and unspeakable goodness, upon every atom of the universe," and that "God" was no more than all those atoms, collectively called Nature.[15]

While George Washington, Henry Laurens, and Robert Morris had little reason and no inclination to challenge the status quo at the close of the French and Indian War, and Mercy Otis Warren, a woman and a Puritan, had been imbued with a spirit of submission and resignation, Dr. Thomas Young did not hesitate to challenge the existing order, nor would he readily submit. A grand fight for liberty and independence would suit him well.

Worcester, Massachusetts. On November 21, 1760, Timothy Bigelow had just turned twenty-one. His great-grandfather, an early emigrant from England, had held various town offices in Watertown, just outside of Boston. His grandfather had fought in King Philip's War, and his father, a cordwainer, had been active in the town affairs of Worcester, in the heartland of New England, where Timothy was born. Now, Timothy was ready to take his turn.[16]

Like his great-grandfather, Timothy decided to become a blacksmith, a trade that placed him in contact with every farmer in the township. He courted the daughter of one of them, Anna Rankin; less than two years later, on July 7, 1762, he would marry her and move into the house she inherited from her recently deceased father. Bigelow's new home, like his trade, would place him at the center of Worcester's known world, immediately across Main Street from the courthouse. There he would set up shop, fashioning tools and fitting horseshoes for his neighbors.

Having reached his majority, Timothy Bigelow assumed two public duties of an adult male. First, he trained with the militia. New England society had always been militarized, from the time that Anglos first displaced Native Americans to the recent war with the French, when militiamen from Worcester County rushed to the defense of a Fort William Henry, just across the New York border. So in 1760, when Timothy Bigelow drilled with his townsfolk on the monthly training days, he did so in earnest, thinking that someday he, too, might be expected to fight.

Beyond that, he participated in town meetings, for New England had always been politicized, as well, at least on the local level. The affairs of church and school, taxation and the division of land, the construction and repair of roads, issues of health and public mores—these were decided by the community as a whole, all property-owning males as well as a handful of property-owning widows, who gathered in the Congregational Meeting House at the south end of town. Like those who had come before him, Timothy Bigelow was ready to assume such offices as hogreave, fence viewer, and tything man.

While these duties might seem to pale by comparison with the civic and military service expected of George Washington and Henry Laurens, New Englanders like the Bigelows, accustomed to protecting and governing themselves, treated their military and civic tasks as serious responsibilities, and anybody who shirked either one was subject to a fine.

There was little glamour but lots of power in this tradition of self-governance and military self-sufficiency. Unlike Dr. Thomas Young, a future revolutionary cohort, Timothy Bigelow had no pressing desire to stir things up, but if people from beyond his tidy world challenged his way of life, he would be well prepared to respond.

Becket, Massachusetts. On November 21, 1760, at a small settlement nestled in the Berkshire Hills of western New England, twenty-two-year-old Susanna Plumb gave birth to her first and only child, Joseph Plumb Martin. Joseph's father, recently ordained, had just received an appointment to become the community's first minister for its Congregational church, to be paid primarily in produce.

Fifteen and a half years later, Joseph Plumb Martin would place his life on the line to defend a nation that had not even been imagined at the moment of his birth. By that time, the world Joseph inhabited would have changed dramatically, and Joseph himself, once he became a private in General Washington's army, would help change it even more.

Third Week in February 1761: Council Chambers of the Old Town House in Boston

According to John Adams, our nation's most communicative founder, the changes began one cold winter day in 1761, when attorney James Otis appeared before the Superior Court of Massachusetts to challenge the infamous Writs of Assistance, blanket search warrants used to detect smuggled goods. "Then and there was the first scene of the first act of opposition to the arbitrary claims of Great Britain," Adams wrote in retrospect. "Then and there the child Independence was born."[17]

Mercy Otis Warren thought so too, and in her *History of the Rise, Progress and Termination of the American Revolution*, written many years later, she was more than a bit pleased to report that the hero of the moment had been none other than her own brother, "James Otis, Esq. of Boston, . . . the first champion of American freedom." Otis argued before the court that since the Writs were not based on probable cause and did not specify time and place, Parliament must discontinue their use. Parliament itself was subject to natural law, he proclaimed. Because James Otis brought the British Parliament to bay on that fateful day in court, at least in his arguments, his sister boasted he "may justly claim the honor of laying the foundation of a revolution, which has been productive of the happiest effects to the civil and political interests of mankind."[18]

Had Warren seen fit to start her narrative further back in time, she would have had to admit that her brother took a rather circuitous route on his way to becoming a hero. In their studies at Barnstable, James had not kept pace with his own younger sister, and even at Harvard he proved a slow starter. He also displayed signs of a moody temperament that would someday grow from an idiosyncratic neurosis to a confirmed psychosis. Once, while entertaining a college party with his violin, he suddenly tossed his instrument aside and raced out the door, crying, "So Orpheus fiddled, and so danced the brutes!"[19]

But then one day James Otis Jr. heard the great evangelist George Whitefield preach at Harvard, and suddenly his life acquired meaning. From that moment on, James applied himself to his studies with purpose and passion. He passed the bar and eventually became a preacher in his own right, not in church but in the courtroom and Assembly, where he expounded on law and politics during the early days of resistance to British policies. "In his public speeches," his sister pronounced in her *History*, "the fire of eloquence, the acumen of argument, and the lively sallies of wit, at once warmed the bosom of the stoic and commanded the admiration of his enemies."[20]

Because the Council chamber in 1761 was no place for a woman, Mercy Otis Warren did not personally witness her brother's grandest moment. In fact, Mercy would never have thought to attend a session of the Superior Court, any more than she would have sought admission to Harvard. Her friend John Adams, on the other hand, held a ringside seat for the critical event, and more than half a century later, at a time when poets and artists were working overtime to lionize heroes of the American Revolution, he cast about frantically for an artist who could memorialize the scene and its hero. Adams never did find a willing painter, but his verbal depiction, cast in the form of instructions to the artist, shaped the way Americans ever since have viewed the onset of revolutionary activity. This is how Adams began:

That council chamber was as respectable an apartment as the House of Commons or the House of Lords in Great Britain, in proportion, or that in the State House in Philadelphia, in which the declaration of independence was signed, in 1776. In this chamber, round a great fire, were seated five judges, with Lieutenant-Governor Hutchinson at their head, as Chief Justice, all arrayed in their new, fresh, rich robes of scarlet English broadcloth; in their large cambric bands, and immense judicial wigs. In this chamber were seated at a long table all the barristers at law of Boston, and of the neighboring county of Middlesex, in gowns, bands, and tie wigs. They were not seated on ivory chairs, but their dress was more solemn and more pompous than that of the Roman Senate, when the Gauls broke in upon them.[21]

Facing off against the officious judges in their ceremonial garb, in full view of the pompous barristers, was a spirited, fiery lawyer, James Otis Jr., the star of the show. Observing the drama from close up was a youthful barrister, Adams himself, who, he told his would-be artist, "should be painted like a short thick archbishop of Canterbury, seated at the table with a pen in his hand, lost in admiration."

During the trial, Adams did not record his observations in great detail, but he did capture the gist of Otis's argument with a few notes:

As to acts of Parliament. An act against the Constitution is void: an act against natural equity is void: and if an act of Parliament should be made, in the very words of this petition, it would be void. The executive courts must pass such acts into disuse.[22]

With time, the event grew ever larger in John Adams's mind, and by 1817, in his instructions to the artist, his memory had imbued Otis with almost superhuman powers:

Otis was a flame of fire!—with a promptitude of classical allusions, a depth of research, a rapid summary of historical events and dates, a profusion of legal authorities, a prophetic glance of his eye into the futurity, and torrent of impetuous eloquence, he hurried away every thing before him.[23]

At least one other participant/observer was deeply impressed by James Otis's presentation before the court that day: Thomas Hutchinson, the chief justice and sworn enemy of the entire Otis family. What astounded Hutchinson about the high-sounding verbiage was its insincerity. It was all a cover, he maintained, because Otis's real motivation was revenge. James Otis Jr. had wanted his father, James Otis Sr., to become a judge on the very court over which Hutchinson now presided, but the royal governor had appointed Hutchinson instead. Otis was so incensed that ever afterward, he could be found "at the head of every measure in opposition" to the governor, the Crown, and Parliament. This personal affront, according to Hutchinson, was the immediate cause of the entire American Revolution. "From so small a spark a great fire seems to have been kindled," he wrote.[24]

Family, friends, and enemies all seemed to agree: revolutionary unrest, which led in the end to independence, started with James Otis Jr. and his dramatic appearance before the Superior Court in 1761. But before we proclaim Otis the prime instigator of all colonial resistance, perhaps we should take one more look at the instructions John Adams gave to the artist.

Adams's portrayal of the scene is vivid—he even describes two gilded portraits of British kings that were hanging on the walls, down to color, subject, style, and framing—but his picture is far from complete. Sixty-three merchants had submitted the petition against the Writs of Assistance. These men had hired Otis to plead their case; without them, there would have been no issue. Having gambled heavily on the outcome, many were in court that day, yet strangely, although central to the drama, such key figures make no appearance in Adams's account.[25]

Nor does Adams credit historical precedents that led to the courtroom confrontation. By 1759 the war started at Jumonville Glen was seriously depleting the British treasury. To generate income, the imperial ministry began clamping down on smugglers, who had been avoiding import duties for decades. Boston's merchants fought back. For two years prior to their appearance before the Superior Court, they had been suing for damages and signing petitions and persuading their own trade organization, the Boston Society for Encouraging Trade and Commerce, to take an active role in resisting the crackdown. Their Writs of Assistance petition continued in this vein, but it was hardly "the first scene of the first act of opposition."[26]

There was a movement brewing in Boston, and that saga needs to be presented on a broader canvas. The protagonists of this initial resistance, the early patriots who voiced grievances and acted on them, were unlikely heroes—smugglers in fact. To protect their interests, these men both avoided and challenged the taxes that restricted their trade.

Anyone in court that day in February could look out the windows at the end of the Council chamber and gaze down King Street to the Long Wharf, where the merchants' sloops and schooners and brigantines anchored to load and unload their goods, and beyond that, out to the open seas and straight toward the mother country that regulated colonial trade. That's where the merchants were supposed to focus their gaze, but Boston's men of trade, in pursuit of pecuniary gain, were also casting their restless eyes toward Holland, southern Europe, the West Indies, and Africa. To trade with these diverse places along the Atlantic rim, many were willing to break the law.

All this—the people, the politics, the self-interest—is lost in Adams's heroic "painting." Nor do smugglers make an appearance in Mercy Otis Warren's patriotic narrative. Even so, Warren and Adams were not entirely off base by highlighting this scene. For three-quarters of a century, the notion that citizens had a right to challenge the authority of government had been a centerpiece of the British Enlightenment, clearly elucidated by John Locke back in the time of the Glorious Revolution of 1688. Now, in 1761, James Otis and others were applying this notion to the politics-at-hand in colonial Boston. Smuggling buttressed by political philosophy—this would prove a potent combination. By framing their self-interest in a broader context, Otis helped people feel righteous, and righteousness was always at a premium in colonial New England. James Otis, and later his sister Mercy, pointed the way to the moral high ground, a promontory that American colonists would seize, occupy, and fortify with great fervor.

September 15, 1761: Ashley River Ferry, South Carolina

Eighteenth-century British colonists perched between two continents—Europe, which gave them their heritage, culture, and government, and America, which happened to be where they lived. Some, like Boston's merchant-smugglers, looked eastward across the Atlantic to acquire their fortunes; most looked westward, to the vast landmass that stretched to the horizon and beyond. From this last group emerged our second batch of incipient patriots: Indian haters, who did not like a government in faraway London putting brakes on their westward expansion.

Charles Town (as it was known at the time) was not the place to be in the late summer of 1761. Typically hot, humid, and dirty during that season, the

South's largest metropolis was experiencing a virulent epidemic, which people at the time labeled yellow fever and which modern medical experts believe was typhus. That is why Henry Laurens sent his wife and children away from the city, and that is also why people from three continents—the most powerful Euro-Americans in South Carolina, eight Cherokee Indians, and "TWO CARGOES of fine healthy *GUINEY* NEGROES"—all headed toward Ashley Ferry, a small settlement just a few miles away, instead of to Charles Town itself.[27]

Henry Laurens, one of South Carolina's most prominent merchants, had his hand in all three camps. The slaves, approximately two hundred per "cargo," were offered for sale by the firm of Austin, Laurens, and Appleby, which handled four of the nine shiploads coming from the "Rice Coast" of West Africa into South Carolina that year. The Indians, including the noted statesman Attakullakulla (known to white colonials as Little Carpenter)—who, like Laurens, had once traveled to London—were under his personal guard. Laurens himself had been one of the lead officers for 2,800 fighting men—South Carolina Provincials, British Royal Highlanders, and an assortment of Mohawk, Stockbridge, Chickasaw, and Catawba Indians, supported by a mile-long pack train of horses and several hundred head of cattle, managed in part by eighty slaves—who had just ventured deep into Cherokee country to destroy every village and field they could find.[28]

Now that the fighting was over, Colonel Laurens was ushering the Cherokee diplomats to conclude a peace settlement with the governor and his council. Proceedings opened on Tuesday morning, September 15, when Attakullakulla "called for fire to light his pipe, which being brought he smoked, then delivered the pipe to the Lieut. Governor and the Council, who smoked also." The pipe then passed to "all the Gentlemen present," including Laurens, whom Attakullakulla acknowledged had "brought me thither." The men on both sides were committed to ending the bloody Anglo-Cherokee War, so they followed the most honorable protocols. The meeting was cordial, albeit formal.[29]

Until Henry Laurens's best friend, Christopher Gadsden, crashed the party. Gadsden did not want peace. The scorched-earth campaign should have continued till each and every Indian village was destroyed, he maintained. He authored an official protest of the treaty negotiations on behalf of the Commons House of Assembly—"The only way to fight a Cherokee War is to destroy as many of these people as we can & when an opportunity offers to miss it by no means"—and he now tried to disrupt the proceedings.[30]

Laurens was outraged. He had traded with Cherokees for years, and he did not relish the task of destroying their towns and crops: "This work tho necessary often made my heart bleed," he wrote. Not only did he disagree with Gadsden over how to treat Indians, he also took offense with Gadsden's unsettling style. The two former buddies squared off, and the quarrel necessitated the intervention of two neutral parties, who kept the combatants from fighting a duel. Afterward, Laurens and Gadsden continued to tussle with their words, lots of words, over thirty thousand in a single piece penned by Laurens, the first of many lengthy invectives he would spew forth when he felt his honor or propriety was challenged.[31]

So ended the long and intimate friendship between two of South Carolina's favored sons, which had started virtually at birth. Henry and Christopher were born into prominent Charleston families within eight days of each other, in 1724 (I revert now to the modern spelling, Charleston). Close neighbors, they spent their childhood years together, and after that their lives followed similar trajectories. They each studied in Europe, married, and had numerous children, although Laurens buried at least eight of his. They established homes literally across the street from each other in Charleston's fashionable northeast end. They each inherited significant fortunes, which they extended through opportune business dealings. In 1757, they simultaneously launched their political careers in the Commons House of Assembly. Technically, they had to be elected; in truth, because of their standing in the community, membership in the Assembly was theirs for the taking.

As South Carolina began to mobilize for the French and Indian War, Laurens and Gadsden assumed their military responsibilities, and here is where their paths diverged. Laurens took the normal route, becoming an officer in the local militia, while Gadsden decided on a more novel approach that bypassed the traditional chain of command. Gathering recruits at Elisha Poinsett's tavern, he and some other men of import organized a Volunteer Artillery Company, with Gadsden as captain. Sanctioned by the Commons House of Assembly, Gadsden and his men, dressed in "blue coatees turn'd up with crimson, crimson jackets & gold laced hats, with white stockings," excelled in military exercise, a competitive sport at the time. All went well until the Crown-appointed governor of South Carolina refused to recognize the upstart company and invalidated Gadsden's election to the House, leading Gadsden to unleash a campaign against all "unexperienced governors . . . dizzied with a little power." If colonists presented a unified front, he said, the governors "would perhaps be a little more cautious, how they first causelessly trampled on the people's liberties." This, in a nutshell, was the genesis of the patriot movement in South Carolina, initiated by Indian-haters who wished to control their colony's military establishment.[32]

With his political maneuverings and strident tone, Gadsden got under Laurens's skin: "One poor rash headlong gentleman who has been too long a ring leader of people engaged in popular quarrels . . . is not a fit person to judge of public affairs," he wrote. People like Gadsden used "a cloak of patriotism merely to hide self-love & ambitious views."[33]

If Gadsden was becoming a patriot, Laurens remained a government man to his very core. Like a true conservative, he deplored "this unhappy time when all respect for the authority of government . . . seems to be at an end." Never would a man of honor and principle stoop so low as to challenge the legitimacy of the British Crown, Henry Laurens believed at the time.[34]

Two A.M., February 6, 1764: The Streets of Philadelphia

The watchman cried "Fire," and soon bells rang out—school bells, clock bells, house bells, carriage bells, and a true English set of eight calibrated bells on top of Christ Church—and drums reverberated and people dressed themselves hastily and placed candles in their windows (as they had been told to do) and flocked into the streets. "The alarm was terrible," the Reverend Henry Melchior Muhlenberg, a founder of the German Lutheran Church in America, wrote in his journal. "At dawn the alarm bells finally ceased."[35]

It wasn't a fire, and everybody knew it. "The Pextang Boys are coming," neighbor told neighbor.[36]

The Paxton Boys, as we call them today, or Hickory Boys, as they called themselves, were marching from the region around present-day Harrisburg with the avowed aim of killing Indian refugees, who were being housed in army barracks on the outskirts of town. At the close of the French and Indian War, in response to British general Jeffrey Amherst's prohibition of all trade along the frontier, Indians destroyed nine British forts and killed hundreds of white farmers, women and children as well as men. Outraged white residents of western Pennsylvania vowed to strike back, and by the fall of 1763, vigilantes were killing all the Native Americans they could find, including those living peacefully in Moravian missions. To protect these Indians from mob violence and prevent them from aiding those who were still hostile, Pennsylvania officials moved 127 Christianized Native Americans to Philadelphia. These were the objects of the Paxton Boys' wrath.

Providing a haven for Indians was not the only issue. The Paxton Boys were also furious that the Pennsylvania Assembly, dominated by representatives from the East, had failed to provide adequate military protection for frontier settlers. As Reverend Muhlenberg wrote in his journal, the westerners were planning "to come to the city in droves and destroy everything in *revenge*."[37]

When the alarm sounded at two o'clock Monday morning, February 6, the Paxton Boys had arrived at Germantown, only five miles distant. A few days earlier, one thousand men, vowing to protect their city, had formed themselves into six companies of foot soldiers, two of horsemen, and one of artillerymen; now their moment had arrived. Many carried their muskets and swords—and even battle flags left over from the French and Indian War—to Market Square, the hub of the city at the junction of Second Street and High (now called Market Street), an open swath of cobblestone bordered by the Court House, the Greater Meeting House, and long rows of covered market stalls. There, in the middle of the night, any man without a musket received one, and all prepared to defend their city against an invasion of seven hundred or fifteen hundred "frontiers men," reported to be in three bodies in three places, or one body "close at hand," or perhaps still "far off" but closing in fast from the east, or maybe from the west— rumors masquerading as news traveled quickly but inaccurately in the dead of night.[38]

Come dawn, after the nighttime alarm, various Philadelphians ventured to the Paxton Boys' encampment at Germantown for a firsthand look. The ruffians, they reported, wore blanket coats and moccasins, carried rifles, pistols, and tomahawks, and "uttered hideous outcries in imitation of the war whoop, knocked down peaceable citizens, and pretended to scalp them." This was street theater, but it worked, for it gave fright to the smug burghers who had come to gawk.[39]

On Tuesday, Thomas Willing, the mayor of Philadelphia, and Benjamin Franklin, the internationally renowned printer and scientist, and a handful of other important figures went to Germantown to try to talk sense into the Paxton Boys. The blue-ribbon peace mission was successful. The Paxton Boys agreed to send two of their own into Philadelphia to present their grievances ("Remonstrance of the Distressed and Bleeding Frontier Inhabitants of the Province") to the proper authorities, while the rest of the men went home, having already made their point. They had brought frontier-style violence into the lives of people who tried to ignore it.

Philadelphians were not accustomed to such events. During the war that had just devastated the interior regions of their colony, these burghers had

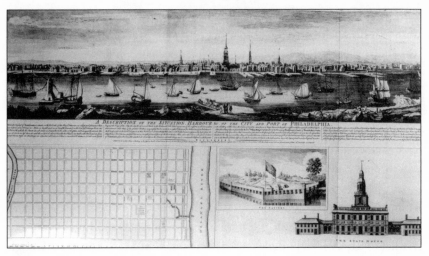

Figure 2. Robert Morris's Philadelphia in the 1760s, the commercial hub of British North America.

remained within an insulating urban cocoon, out of harm's way—indentured servants and others recruited to fight were notable exceptions. Radiant with man-made and sophisticated improvements, Philadelphia had recently surpassed Boston as North America's largest city. Streets were paved with stone and met each other at proper right angles. (The streets in Boston, by contrast, had evolved from cow trails.) Wagons, drays, coaches, chariots, and chaises carried freight and passengers over the cobbles, while pedestrians strolled on flat brick sidewalks. Since 1752, their city had even been lit at night. Three-story houses butted against each other, crowding out untamed nature and creating the ambience of a walled city. All this should have generated a sense of security, yet no man, woman, or child felt very safe or secure on that cold winter night in 1764, with hundreds or thousands of armed ruffians headed their way.

Robert Morris, even more than most Philadelphians, had been shielded from the horrors of frontier violence. Because of his increasing fortunes, Morris was also immunized against the wartime shortages of food and fuel experienced by city dwellers of lesser means. Born in Liverpool in 1735, Morris had come to the colonies at the age of twelve and apprenticed with Charles Willing, one of Philadelphia's leading merchants. At age fifteen he had become a clerk, and when he turned twenty-two, Charles's son Thomas had taken him on as a partner. By the time of the Paxton Boys scare, twenty-eight-year-old Robert Morris was a major player in the world of Philadelphia business. His partner, Thomas Willing, had meanwhile worked his way up through a series of political offices: commissioner for regulating trade with the Indians, justice of the City Court, justice of the Court of Common Pleas, alderman, city councilman, and finally mayor of Philadelphia, the office he held when he set off to Germantown to make peace with the Paxton Boys.[40]

By instilling fear and threatening the established order, the Paxton Boys foreshadowed the Revolutionary protest movements of the following decades. In 1763, as during the latter campaigns against British imperial policies, ordinary people propelled the movement forward. Common farmers challenged established authority in a violent manner, using street theater to dramatize their concerns; they triggered a massive outpouring of political pamphlets and cartoons; they mustered in a military manner, causing their opponents to muster and bear arms as well. All this presaged the civil unrest that would accompany, and to some extent drive, the American Revolution.[41]

There is another significant parallel between the march of the Paxton Boys and the American Revolution: control of the American interior was at issue in both instances. Native Americans of various nations, Europeans of various nations, and Euro-Americans of various ethnicities, religions, regions, classes, and for-profit companies were competing for the same space. The Paxton Boys demonstrated how easily this competition could escalate.

After the War: The Oblong, New York

The French and Indian War was over, land was at issue, and Dr. Thomas Young wanted his share, for doctoring in those days did not make a fellow rich.

Thomas was born in upstate New York (Ulster County) in 1731, the eldest son of recent Scots-Irish immigrants. At the age of seventeen, after minimal schooling but much reading, he apprenticed to a doctor in Albany, and within two years, a shorter apprenticeship than for most trades at the time, he was practicing medicine on his own. In 1753 he moved to a rural region of Dutchess County, New York, within the disputed Oblong, where he treated patients in their homes. Riding a circuit from across the Connecticut line on the east to the Hudson River on the west, he came into contact with salt-of-the-earth farmers struggling to make it on land they did not legally possess.

Although he respected the farmers for their hard labor, his own passions were political and intellectual. In 1761, combining patriotism with his love of words, the self-educated scholar published a lengthy elegy commemorating the recent Battle of Quebec, *A Poem to the Memory of James Wolfe . . . Who was slain upon the Plains of Abraham*, which included such memorable couplets as:

> Harpean *ululations, ursine growls,*
> And screaming *terrors of predicting owls.*[42]

Years later, residents in one section of the Oblong chose a new name for their township—Amenia, from the Latin *amoena*, or pleasant place—which according to local tradition was first suggested by their own published poet, Dr. Thomas Young.[43]

Sometime during the 1750s, Thomas Young married Mary Winegar, daughter of his landlord. To support his growing family, which eventually included two sons and four daughters, Young decided to augment his modest income by investing in land.

Since the 1720s, an unscrupulous trader from Albany named John Henry Lydius, making liberal use of rum, had been purchasing land from Indians, in violation first of French and then British authority. In 1760 Young acquired a small share in one of Lydius's speculative ventures in northeastern New York, but his investment would prove worthless if Lydius's claims did not receive governmental recognition. The problem, according to Young, was that New York's colonial government was then in the hands of "great land-jobbers" who charged their tenant farmers exorbitant rents, and these men did not want upstarts like Lydius to get a piece of their action. In 1761 New York officials denied Lydius's claims and warned all potential investors to shun him.[44]

Left with worthless paper, Thomas Young took his case to the public, setting quill to paper and publishing his second work, a long populist tract in which he argued that Lydius's project would "furnish many poor people with the means of very comfortable living, who must otherwise groan in poverty." Writing in prose this time, he displayed a promising rhetorical flair:

> Liberty and Prosperity (the *Household Gods* of Englishmen) have called loudly for our *blood* and *treasure*; We, the common people, have freely lavish'd both; we are impoverish'd in war, and now want land to exercise the arts of peace upon. . . . All we ask, request, and implore, is, that we may enjoy our undoubted rights, and not have them so cruelly rent out of our hands to give to people, at least no more celebrated for their loyalty or love to their country than we are.[45]

Sometime during his stay in the Oblong region, Thomas Young made the acquaintance of another political radical and blasphemous Deist, Ethan Allen, a tough from Salisbury, Connecticut, just across the border from the Oblong. Allen was full of piss and vinegar. Once, when hauled into court for the second time in less than two months for assaulting the same man, he ripped off his shirt (according to the court record) and exposed "his naked body and in a threatening manner with his fist lifted up repeated these malicious words three times: 'You lie you dog,' and also did with a loud voice say that he would spill the blood of any that opposed him."[46]

Drawn together by mutual interests and common beliefs, Thomas Young and Ethan Allen became fast friends, fellow students, and co-conspirators. They both liked to challenge authority, whether civil or religious. One Sunday in 1764, in front of the Salisbury meetinghouse, Dr. Young inoculated Allen with smallpox vaccine, in clear violation of Connecticut law. While most churchgoing New Englanders were opposed to inoculation for religious reasons, Young and Allen favored it on scientific grounds, and they wished to make a public display of their position. Afterward, while celebrating their civil disobedience in a tavern, the miscreants were confronted by local officials, who threatened to take Allen into custody. Allen then proclaimed in a boisterous manner that he would "have satisfaction" with his accusers, and if somehow he should fail, "By Jesus Christ, I wish I may be bound down in Hell with old Belzabub a thousand years in the lowest pitt in Hell and that every little insippid Devil should come along by and ask the reason of Allens lying there." Allen was not charged with violating the inoculation prohibition, but like Young at an earlier date he was hauled into court for blasphemy.[47]

Bravado and blasphemy aside, Thomas Young and Ethan Allen had serious business together. Young, six years Allen's senior and certainly better read, played the role of mentor, but Allen, an eager student, must have contributed his share to the discussion. As they worked out the fine details of their Deistic worldview, they decided to record their thoughts. Combining Young's untutored slant on the Enlightenment with Allen's knowledge of the Bible, they wrote a book, or at least the better part of one, in which they tore apart any literal reading of Christianity and substituted in its place a new credo, Reason. When Young moved away late in 1764, he took their unfinished manuscript with him, first to Albany, then Boston, Newport, and Philadelphia. Wherever he traveled, he protected, nurtured, and amended the book that would someday be known as Ethan Allen's Bible.[48]

As they talked philosophy and politics, Young gave Allen some very practical advice: invest in land, he told the younger fellow. Six years later, Ethan Allen purchased questionable deeds in northeastern New York, just as his mentor had once done. Applying the bullying tactics he had practiced in Salisbury, and working in conjunction with others who were willing to force the issue, the famous Green Mountain Boys, Allen would eventually make his claim stick, a goal that eluded his mentor. The land that Ethan Allen and the Green Mountain Boys wrested from New York would form the nucleus of a new state, and Thomas Young, though owning none of it, would supply the name: Vermont.

After the War: Belleview and Mount Vernon, Virginia

George Washington, like Thomas Young, wanted land, and he, too, felt he was entitled to it because he had offered his "*blood* and *treasure*" (to use Young's terminology) during the French and Indian War. To get what he thought should be his, Washington did not barter with Indians, as Lydius had done, but worked instead within the established channels of the British legal system. This meant that George Washington, now over thirty years old, had to ask King George III to grant him the land he wanted. In order to face west, he first had to face east.

Acquiring and developing tracts of land in the trans-Appalachian West was too large a task for any single individual, no matter how wealthy or well connected. Capital was needed to conduct surveys, build roads, and get people to live there, either as owners, renters, indentured servants, or slaves. Knowing this, and knowing that they had to present a good case to the Crown, George Washington, several members of the prominent Lee family, and various other Virginia gentry—some of the same people who had been trying to acquire land through the Ohio Company—formed themselves into the Mississippi Company. On September 9, 1763, gathering at the house of Thomas Ludwell Lee in Belleview, downriver from Mount Vernon, they wrote a letter "To the Kings most Excellent Majesty." Their audience was very different from Thomas Young's, although their ends were the same: to obtain legal title to land they had never seen. With a tone more obsequious than confrontational, they tried to show the king what he stood to gain by their project:

The increase of people, the extension of trade and the enlargement of the revenue are with certainty to be expected, where the fertility of the soil, and mildness of the climate invite emigrants (provided they can obtain lands on easy terms) to settle and cultivate those commodities most wanted by Great Britain . . . such as hemp, flax, silk, wine, potash, cochineal, indigo, iron &c. by which means the Mother Country will be supplied with many necessary materials, that are now purchased of foreigners at a very great expense—especially naval stores so essential to the very being of a commercial state . . . whilst the inhabitants of the infant settlement, finding their labour most profitably bestowed upon agriculture will not think of interfering with the Mother Country in manufactures but afford a never failing demand for them.[49]

The letter went on to outline the company's intentions: upon receiving rights to 2,500,000 acres on the east shore of the upper Mississippi, it promised to settle at least two hundred families within twelve years, "if not interrupted by savages or any foreign enemy."

So far, the king must have been pleased. These people understood their proper economic role within the empire: produce raw materials for the mother country, then buy its finished products. But there was a catch. The company's letter continued:

The memorialists most humbly submit it to Your Majesties great wisdom whether the remote situation of this country from the colonies already settled, may not render it expedient to protect the infant settlement from the insults of the savages. which protection might effectually be obtained, if Your Majesty were graciously pleased to order a small fort to be garrisoned at the confluence of Cherokee River with Ohio.

This killed the deal. A fort would cost money, as would the continual garrisoning of soldiers—not to mention the war that might break out if soldiers or settlers happened to get into another fight with Indians. The Crown was already in debt from the war started by Washington and his fellow Virginians the last time they marched off to the west.

Far from granting the Mississippi Company's request, the king and his government moved in the opposite direction. On October 7, 1763, the Crown issued a proclamation that forbade all new settlement past the Appalachian divide. It even required any British subjects "who have either willfully or inadvertently seated themselves" in the West "forthwith to remove themselves from such settlements." The westward thrust of the colonists was suddenly thwarted. Before, imperial authorities had entertained the possibility of establishing a whole new colony on the Ohio; now, all speculative schemes had to be suspended, at least "for the present"—a phrase repeated twice in the Crown's pronouncement.[50]

The Proclamation of 1763, as it was later called, came at the worst possible time for George Washington, who should have been prospering but wasn't. The spending spree he indulged in since marrying Martha had taken its toll. Although he invested as well as consumed, the end result was the same: by 1763 he was broke. He confided to a close friend, Robert Stewart:

> Besides some purchases of lands and Negroes I was necessitated to make adjoining me—(in order to support the expences of a large family)—I had provision's of all kinds to buy for the first two or three years, and my plantations to stock—in short with every thing—buildings to make, and other matters, which swallowed up before I well knew where I was, all the money I got by marriage nay more, brought me in debt.[51]

Tobacco and the slaves who produced it—the mainstays of Virginia's economy—were not enough to get George Washington out of debt. In fact, tobacco had helped plunge him into it, for his yield had been poor for three years running, and the market was even worse. Because of his focus on a single cash crop, Washington's economic well-being was determined by two things beyond his control: the market price for tobacco and the savvy of his British factor, Robert Cary. Repeatedly, Washington protested that Cary was selling his tobacco at too low a price, while charging too much for the wide variety of goods he was shipping to Mount Vernon. Washington's indebtedness had every appearance of going on forever, unless or until he either changed his spending habits or found a better way to make a living.[52]

Developing land in the West was his preferred way out, but the Proclamation of 1763 put a damper on his endeavors with both the Mississippi Company and the Ohio Company of Virginia. It also kept him from collecting his share of two hundred thousand acres near the Ohio River, which Governor Dinwiddie and his council had promised to Washington and his ragtag array of militiamen when they first headed west. According to the original order, the bounty land was to be divided "in a proportion due to their respective merit," and that meant that Washington, the commander, was due a handsome piece. Instead he got nothing, for the moment at least.[53]

After the War: Mepkin Plantation and Ninety Six, South Carolina

South Carolina's Henry Laurens, like Thomas Young and George Washington and countless other colonial Americans, went hunting for land after the French and Indian War. When his mercantile partnership dissolved in 1762, he decided he would rather be a planter than a merchant, and he shopped around for real estate. He started by purchasing a three-thousand-acre rice plantation in Mepkin, about forty miles from Charleston, to serve as a refuge from the disease-infested city during the hot summer months. Perched atop a forty-foot bluff overlooking the Cooper River, the Mepkin mansion offered a commanding view of the rich green rice fields, and the slaves who worked them, on the river plain below.[54]

Mepkin became Laurens's "home" plantation and would remain so for the rest of his life, but he still needed a place in town. In 1764, on a four-acre lot at the northern edge of Charleston, at the corner of present-day East Bay and Laurens streets, masons and carpenters constructed a large brick house for the Laurens family, while slaves from Mepkin built a great brick wall to surround a twenty-thousand-square-yard garden, which showcased (according to his son-in-law) "olives, capers, limes, ginger, guinea grass, the alpine strawberry, bearing nine months in the year, red rasberrys, blue grapes . . . from remote parts of the world; and also directly from the south of France, apples, pears, and plums of fine kinds, and vines which bore abundantly of the choice white eating grape, called Chasselates blancs."[55]

Fortified in Mepkin and Charleston, Laurens started looking farther about, not only in the South Carolina low country, where he would eventually operate four different plantations, but in the backcountry as well, just east of the line set by the Proclamation of 1763. "There is a large almost wholly unoccupied tract of about one hundred thousand acres of fine land at the place commonly called *Ninety Six*," he wrote to a business partner, "which at present is a *nuisance*, as it lies vacant & hinders the establishment of a great many useful settlers." To get rid of the "nuisance," he applied to the Provincial Council for grants of five thousand and eight thousand acres, promising to settle the land with immigrants from Hanover, Germany. (When these failed to materialize, he had slaves work the land instead.) Hoping to stretch his budding empire, he looked to neighboring colonies as well: "We shall in all probability have a large field open'd to the southward of this province . . . a considerable part of Louisiana with St. Augustine & all Florida," he wrote excitedly upon hearing of the initial peace terms in 1763. "I am told the lands are very good & that good indulgences will be granted to the first adventurers."[56]

After the War: British North America

Some American colonists, like Laurens, got the land they wanted, while others—both small-time operators like Thomas Young and large-scale investors like George Washington—did not. Many of the discontented were in fact rich and powerful men who competed with each other for the favors of the Crown. In Virginia, the Loyal Land Company, which included Thomas Jefferson's father, Peter, vied with the Ohio Company and the Mississippi Company for western land grants. These Virginia companies faced stiff competition from a powerful group of merchants and Indian traders from Pennsylvania. Calling themselves "Suffering Traders" who had lost business during the war, associates of this cartel formed themselves into a series of land companies—the Indiana Company, Illinois Company, and Grand Ohio Company (also known as the Walpole Company or Vandalia Company)—which involved both British investors and such prominent Americans as Benjamin Franklin and his son William, Samuel and Thomas Wharton, William Trent, George Morgan, Joseph Galloway, George Croghan, and Sir William Johnson, the last two with strong personal ties to the Iroquois Indians in western New York. With the approach of the Revolution, Robert Morris would acquire a stake in the interests of this group. Other Pennsylvania merchants applied for land as the Wabash Company and later the Illinois-Wabash Company (Morris would later acquire a share in this as well), while a group in Connecticut, noting that their colony's charter permitted expansion to the west, formed themselves into the Susquehannah Company and claimed lands in the Wyoming Valley, on the Susquehanna River one hundred miles northwest of Philadelphia, prompting stiff opposition from the Penn family, proprietors of Pennsylvania. The large field of competitors also included a group calling themselves "The Company of Military Adventurers," veterans of the Havana Campaign against Spain in 1762, who tried to collect bounty lands in the West.[57]

Company competed against company, colony against colony, for the spoils of war, while individual farmers, in direct defiance of the Proclamation of 1763, drifted across the mountains to squat, and diverse nations of Native

Americans jockeyed with each other as well as with Euro-Americans for control of land. Meanwhile, in faraway London, both royal officials and British-based companies tried to figure out how they could control and profit from the vast interior of the North American continent. It was a volatile mix. The quest for land, in aggregate, had a centrifugal effect on American society, as rival individuals, economic organizations, and political jurisdictions contended for the same resource. At this point, in the aftermath of the French and Indian War, the various British colonies along the Atlantic coast appeared more likely to war with each other than to war with their mother country.

But in fact, white American colonists with ambitions in the West had more in common than most cared to admit at the time: they were all being cramped by British law and British policies, which impeded their expansionist schemes. If they didn't have to face east in order to face west, if they didn't have to apply to the Crown for grants, they could more readily and expeditiously lay claim to trans-Appalachian lands. To be sure, they would still have to displace the Indians who were already there, but white colonists outnumbered Indians many times over, and if they worked together, they would probably prevail. British Redcoats were not essential, and neither was the king's approval.

Nobody entertained such treasonous notions at the close of the French and Indian War. Most colonists shared an allegiance to their Crown, a willing adherence to British law, and an affinity for a tradition that in their minds guaranteed more liberty and promised more opportunity than any on earth. Whether Pennsylvanians or Virginians, they were all British subjects, and they were not ready to throw all this away.

Not just yet, at any rate. But what if colonists were to find other reasons to oppose British authority, justifications with a greater moral force than hungering for land?

2

Liberty and Property—and No Stamps!

August 14 and 26, 1765: The Streets of Boston

In order to pay for the expenses of British troops stationed in America, Parliament passed a law "for raising a further revenue within your Majesty's dominions in America." Starting on November 1, 1765, colonists would be required to purchase government-issued stamps for "every skin or piece of vellum or parchment, or sheet or piece of paper" used for court documents, contracts, licenses, newspapers, almanacs, and even playing cards. It is difficult to imagine a bill better suited to arousing hostility. The first waves of patriotic dissidence had been limited to isolated pockets of smugglers and Indian-fighters. Then, when the Revenue Act of 1764 tightened restrictions on trade and levied duties on goods that had never been taxed before, much of the merchant community joined in. But with the passage of the Stamp Act in 1765, opposition spread to the citizenry at large, for the new tax affected virtually every British subject in America.[1]

As a broader section of the population became involved, the character of the dispute changed dramatically. Instead of petitioning and pleading their case in court, people took to the streets, and as they did, opposition turned to resistance. The incipient "revolution" began to look like one.

At dawn on Wednesday, August 14, there was a hanging in Boston. Suspended from a limb of a majestic tree known as the Great Elm, outside the home of Deacon Elliot on the corner of Essex and Orange (now Washington) streets, was a straw man and a boot. The dummy identified himself by the initials "A. O.," standing for Andrew Oliver, the man who had just been appointed distributor of stamps. Attached to his breast was a short poem: "A goodlier sight who e'er did see? / A Stamp-Man hanging on a tree!" The boot represented the Earl of Bute, nicknamed "Jack Boot," who had decreed in the name of the young King George III that ten thousand British Regulars would be stationed in America, to be supported by the colonists themselves. Out of this boot peeped the devil, holding a copy of the Stamp Act. The sole of the boot was painted green, an oblique reference to British Prime Minister George Grenville, author of the Stamp Act.[2]

The location was strategic. All farmers bearing produce to market had to cross "The Neck," a thin stretch of land connecting the Boston peninsula with the mainland, and when they did, they passed right by Andrew Oliver hanging from a tree. There, each in turn submitted to a mock stamping of his goods. Continuing into town, these farmers spread the news, and soon all of Boston was abuzz. By afternoon several thousand people had gathered at the spot, not just to look, but to participate. "So much were they affected with a sense of liberty, that scarce any could attend to the task of day-labour, but all seemed on the wing of freedom," the *Boston Post-Boy* reported. The South Writing School called off classes for the day so boys could take part.[3]

Government officials did not approve. Chief Justice Thomas Hutchinson dispatched Sheriff Stephen Greenleaf and a posse to disband the demonstrators, but when Greenleaf returned, he reported they "could not do it without imminent danger of their lives."[4]

With the approach of evening, while Governor Francis Bernard and his Council were discussing the day's theatrics in their chamber at the Town House—the same room that had housed the Writs of Assistance trial—the performance came to them. Several thousand people came parading up Orange Street, bearing the effigies and chanting, "Liberty and Property! No stamps!" According to contemporary accounts, Mr. Oliver and the boot actually traveled "through the Town House" (probably downstairs, where the Merchants' Exchange convened). Outside, the crowd "gave three huzzas by way of defiance," the governor reported.[5]

That was only the beginning of the evening's events. Governor Bernard explained what happened next:

From thence they went to a new building, lately erected by Mr. Oliver to let out for shops, and not quite finished: this they called the Stamp Office, and pulled it down to the ground in five minutes. From thence they

Figure 3. In Paul Revere's contemporary engraving, which he titled "A View of the Year 1765," Boston leads other colonies to battle the Stamp Act dragon, which is about to crumple the Magna Carta. To the right, an effigy hangs from the Liberty Tree, already enshrined and labeled with the date August 14, 1765, the day protesters first rose up as a body to oppose the measure.

went to Mr. Oliver's house; before which they beheaded the effigy; and broke all the windows next the street; then they carried the effigy to Fort Hill near Mr. Oliver's House, where they burnt the effigy in a bonfire they made of the timber they had pulled down from the building.

The crowd then stormed the house, using wood from the garden fence to beat down the doors, but Oliver of course had fled.[6]

This demonstration produced results. Governor Bernard retreated to Castle William, an island in Boston harbor, where the crowd couldn't reach him. The next evening, as another crowd was erecting a pyramid of tar barrels—in preparation, perhaps, to giving Andrew Oliver "a new suit of clothes," as the saying went—Oliver sent a letter stating that he intended to resign his commission as distributor of stamps.

News of the protest in Boston spread quickly, and in the weeks and months to follow, opponents of the Stamp Act from New Hampshire to South Carolina staged similar events, which produced similar results. Fearful stamp dis-

tributors in thirteen colonies, including Virginia's George Mercer, friend of
George Washington and a partner in the Ohio Company, either abandoned
office or agreed to resign.

For years to come, Boston's patriots celebrated the anniversary of August 14, 1765, the day they made a mockery of the Stamp Act. On the Great
Elm tree, where it all started, they commemorated the place and the event
with a copper plaque bearing the golden letters TREE OF LIBERTY.[7] Patriots in
a least a dozen other towns soon christened their own "Liberty Trees," while
"Liberty Poles"—giant flagstaffs, often trees stripped of their limbs—hosted
public meetings and demonstrations in at least fifty-five colonial towns.[8]

No single person can be credited with initiating the August 14 event. James
Otis Jr., for all the influence of his rhetoric, seems to have had little to do with
it. Contemporary sources attribute the planning to a group that met in William Speakman's distillery and called themselves the Loyal Nine. These patriots, midlevel merchants and craftsmen, are little known today and were not
particularly prominent at the time. The most influential associate was Benjamin Edes, one of the editors of the *Boston Gazette.*

Men from further down the social hierarchy also helped stage the dramatic
protest. Every year on November 5—Pope's Day, known in England as Guy
Fawkes Day, the anniversary of a thwarted Catholic conspiracy to blow up
Parliament—competing street gangs composed of Boston's artisans and laborers, one from the North End and one from the South End, marched
through town bearing elaborate effigies of the pope and the devil. Toward
dark, the gangs would brawl with stones and barrel staves, fighting for the
honor of torching the various effigies in a giant bonfire. Generally, this combative ritual vilified Catholicism, but on August 14, 1765, Northenders and
Southenders, working together, used their talents and their organizations to
vilify the Stamp Act instead. Within chamber doors, in courts or legislative
bodies, educated men might argue the finer points of law, but out of doors
these artisans and laborers and sailors and apprentices, many of whom could
not even vote, essentially nullified an act of Parliament.

On August 26, twelve days after the initial demonstration, Boston's "rabble" or "mob" (as conservatives liked to call their lower-class adversaries) was
at it again, and the tone this time was more spiteful yet. After rioting at the
homes of lower government officials, the crowd converged on the luxurious
mansion of Lieutenant Governor Thomas Hutchinson, on Garden Court
Street in the North End. "The hellish crew fell upon my house with the rage
of devils and in a moment with axes split down the doors and entered,"
Hutchinson wrote. As he himself fled "thro yards and gardens," pursued by

some of the rioters, the main body settled into the hard work of demolition: they tore down the interior walls and the cupola, splintered the furniture, and cut open feather mattresses. They threw the feathers out the window as mischievous boys might do, but these were not childish antics: they also scattered or destroyed various public documents, Hutchinson's research papers, and part of the manuscript for a history of Massachusetts he was in the process of writing. Looters pillaged 900 pounds sterling and a wide variety of portable valuables: silk shoes, laced gowns and petticoats, jewelry, watches, swords, knives, dinnerware, and anything gilded or laced with gold or silver, including a cane head with the lieutenant governor's crest and "a gauze handkerchief & sattin apron, both flowered with gold." Outside, the mob had its way with the formal gardens, leveling the fence and cutting down the trees and shrubbery. Down in the cellar, they consumed or emptied a dozen barrels of wine. "Gentleman of the army, who have seen towns sacked by the enemy, declare they never before saw an instance of such fury," wrote the contemporary historian William Gordon.[9]

Why such wrath?

Rioters leave few written traces to explain their actions. We know them by their deeds, and in August of 1765, deeds spoke louder than words. As resistance to British policies broadened and deepened, people of the lower orders insisted on having their say, and their manner of expression deviated from that of their so-called leaders. "Seamen, servants, negroes, and other persons of mean and vile condition," as Andrew Oliver once labeled the Boston "mob," did not behave like merchants or lawyers, but in their own crude manner, they were evolving into a potent political force. Their enemies reviled them, and their allies often disavowed them, but one way or another, they had to be reckoned with.[10]

October 5 and 7, 1765: Philadelphia

On Saturday, October 5, the royal ship *Charlotte* arrived in Philadelphia's harbor bearing both the official stamps and a commission for John Hughes, a close friend of Benjamin Franklin, who had been charged with the job of distributing them throughout Pennsylvania. By that time, of course, everybody knew about the dramatic resistance to the Stamp Act in Boston. People also knew that on August 27 in Newport, demonstrators had paraded through town bearing giant effigies of three notorious Stamp Act supporters, and that in the days following, they had replicated Boston's riot of August 26 by ransacking and pillaging the houses of several Stamp Act supporters. Now it was Philadelphia's turn.

Upon hearing that stamps had arrived, dedicated patriots sounded bells with muted tongues and dispatched Negroes to beat drums in muffled tones as if for a funeral, for the "Loss of Liberty" had to be mourned. By three in the afternoon, a large crowd had started to congregate in the State House Yard, and by four, several thousand citizens were debating what actions should be taken. But this crowd, unlike those in Boston or Newport, faced complicating circumstances. Three weeks earlier, many of the people now gathered before the State House had threatened to level Benjamin Franklin's house because they considered him a "warm advocate" of the Stamp Act. Although Franklin himself was in London at the time, seven or eight hundred artisans known as the White Oaks, Franklin's political "base," had gathered quickly to defend his home. If the current crowd marched on Hughes, they faced the possibility of opposition by an alternate crowd, and that could turn ugly indeed.[11]

Enter Robert Morris, making his political debut. Previously, Morris had tended to business while his partner, Thomas Willing, took care of politics. But Willing had just prevailed in a citywide election, running as a moderate (Old Square Toes, people called him affectionately) who garnered support from all sides of the political spectrum. Willing had to avoid taking sides, so his junior partner stepped up. But the task at hand was difficult indeed: to contest the restrictions of trade and unilateral taxation imposed by the Grenville ministry, while not sanctioning the destruction of personal property or any other disruption of civil society. There should be no repeat of the Boston riots.

The solution lay in negotiating a settlement between Hughes and the crowd, and because the crowd was not likely to cede much ground, Hughes must be encouraged to resign before, not after, his house was pulled down. To this end, coolheaded speakers at the State House Yard persuaded the assembled throng to send forth a seven-man diplomatic team that included Robert Morris.

Acting under authority of the crowd (an authority that made Morris a bit uneasy), the emissaries took a short walk to John Hughes's home. To obtain a personal interview, they had to mount the stairs and meet the Stamp Collector in his chamber, where he lay seriously ill. But when Morris and company asked Hughes to resign his commission rather than face the wrath of the thousands gathered outside, the ailing official held his own. He could not resign without forfeiting the £500 bond that two friends had put up for him in London, he told them, and then he ventured a gambit: he would indeed forsake his office if Morris and the other gentlemen present (all of whom were quite well off) agreed to pay his friends the value of the bond. To this, Morris responded with an alternative resolution: rather than "resign," Hughes could simply not accept the appointment.

After an hour of back-and-forth hairsplitting, Hughes finally promised not to implement the Stamp Act "until the said Act shall be put into execution generally in the neighboring colonies." This satisfied the delegates, but it angered the crowd. The *Pennsylvania Gazette* reported:

> On the gentlemen's return to the State-House, and reporting this answer, the company were instantly transported with resentment, and it is impossible to say what lengths their rage might have carried them, had not the gentlemen who waited on Mr. Hughes represented him in the light he appeared to them, at the point of death.

Their compassion aroused, the crowd softened. "Instead of the multitude repairing instantly to his house for a positive answer," they gave Hughes until Monday to prepare and sign a formal statement.[12]

On Monday, October 7, the same group of envoys visited Hughes to receive his final declaration. The Stamp Distributor had written his statement, but it included a troubling preamble: He was acting "under the demand of James Tilghmen, Esqr. Attorney at law, Messrs. Robert Morris, Charles Thomson, Archibald McCall, John Cox, and William Richards, merchants, and Mr. William Bradford, printer." Hughes was toying with these pillars of the community, who were guilty in his eyes of intimidation. He suspected that Morris and the others would not want their names committed to paper in this light, and he was correct: they insisted the passage be removed. For Robert Morris, the whole affair was distasteful enough already.[13]

John Hughes recovered his health, but his appointment to the office of Stamp Distributor had ruined his political career.

Robert Morris, on the other hand, was just embarking on his. It did not take him long to settle on methods of political protest more appropriate for a wealthy merchant than crowd intimidation. On October 25, Morris met with a group of fellow merchants at Davenport's Tavern, where they pledged unanimously to suspend trade with Great Britain until the Stamp Act was repealed. Their hope, they said, was "that their brethren the merchants and manufacturers of Great Britain will find their own Interest so intimately connected with ours, that they will be spurr'd on to befriend us from that motive, if no other shou'd take place." Thomas Willing chaired the meeting (this he could do, now that a direct confrontation had been averted), and he also headed an eleven-man committee that would "wait on the traders of this city to get this present agreement universally subscrib'd." By November 7, Willing and his committee had obtained over four hundred signatures for the document.[14]

Far better to challenge imperial policies this way, Morris and Willing reasoned, obliquely rather than directly. They bridged the gap between legitimate and illegitimate protest, but the path they tread was thin, and if tensions continued to mount, it would become more difficult yet to remain on a safe and comfortable course.

October 23, 1765: Residence of Henry Laurens, Charleston

Henry Laurens, Robert Morris's trading partner in Charleston, would have preferred to ignore the Stamp Act entirely. In three hundred extant letters dating from the spring of 1764, when news of an impending Stamp Act first spread to the colonies, to mid-October 1765, when the actual stamps arrived off the coast of South Carolina, Laurens mentioned the act not once. Although he continued to increase his landholdings during this time, he chose to pull back from all other worldly affairs. "I am at this middle state of life retreating by gradual steps from that bustle & hurry that my attention to commerce had unavoidably led me into," he wrote on May 30, 1764. His eight-year-old daughter, Eleanor, had just died on April 18, the fifth of his children to perish, and his wife, Eleanor, had taken to her chamber, as she did every time a child either entered or passed from the world—"as usual once in a round of a twelvemonth," Laurens explained. It was "a year of affliction—a dead eldest daughter, a sick summer, a sick & dying wife," he wrote in November. Struggling in his personal life, and still smarting from his public quarrel with Christopher Gadsden, he was in no mood for politics; he even declined an appointment to the prestigious Council.[15]

But in October of 1765, the Stamp Act caught up with Henry Laurens. News of the riots in Boston and Newport had been published in the *South Carolina Gazette* on September 28, and on October 11, in a letter to a local justice of the peace, Laurens finally took note of the tumultuous happenings that were sweeping the colonies:

> I hope you as a magistrate, as a good subject, as a prudent man, will do all in your power to discourage all the little apings & mockery in your town of those infamous inglorious feats, of riot & dissipation which have been performed to the northward of us & which may still (tho I hope not) be feebly imitated by some turbulent spirits in this metropolis.[16]

Laurens's forewarning was apt, for on October 19, the day after the official stamps and stamped paper arrived in Charleston harbor on board the *Planter's Adventure*, a crowd estimated at two thousand people mimicked the August 14 street theater in Boston set for set and deed for deed: the effigy of the stamp distributor, the boot, the devil, the parade through town, the bonfire, and the visit to the house of George Saxton, the stamp distributor. There were a few small changes. In place of the cute little ditty the Bostonians had attached to the stamp man, the Charleston version substituted a blunt warning: "Whoever shall dare attempt to pull down these effigies, had better been born with a mill stone about his neck, and cast into the sea." Thoroughly intimidated, George Saxton promptly resigned; thoroughly disgusted, Henry Laurens decried "the nonsensical fashion of burning boots & straw devils."[17]

Laurens's public disdain for the October 19 rioters made him personally suspect, and four nights later a crowd of sixty to eighty men—half itinerant sailors and half local townsmen—paid a visit to his new and stately residence in the prestigious Ansonboro district of Charleston. The intruders thought Laurens might be harboring the hated stamps in his house, they said; what they found instead was a woman eight months pregnant and her indignant husband. Laurens described the scene in vivid detail:

> At midnight . . . I heard a most violent thumping & confused noise at my western door & chamber window, & soon distinguished the sounds of *liberty, liberty & stamp'd paper, open your doors* & let us search your house & cellars. I open'd the window & saw a croud of men chiefly in disguise & heard the voices & thumpings of many more on the other side, assured them that I had no stamp'd paper nor any connexion with stamps, when I found that no fair words would pacify them, I accused them with cruelty to a poor sick woman far gone with child & produced Mrs. Laurens shrieking & wringing her hands adding that if there was

any one man amongst them who owed me a spite & took this base method to avenge himself, & would turn out, I had a brace of pistols at his service & would settle the dispute immediately, but that it was base in such a multitude to attack a single man. . . .

Mrs. Laurens's condition, having fallen into strong hysterics, prompted me to open the door, which in two minutes more they would have beat through. A brace of cutlasses across my breast was the salutation, & lights, lights, & search was the cry. I presently knew several of them under the thickest disguise of soot, sailors habits, crape masks, slough hate, &ca., & to their great surprise called no less than nine of them by name.[18]

Called upon to swear under oath that he had no knowledge of the stamps, Laurens replied that "I had voluntarily given my word & honour but would not suffer even that to pass from my lips by compulsion."

Despite his self-assured bravado, Laurens was deeply affected by his midnight visitors. One month and three days later, on November 26, Eleanor Laurens gave birth to a son named James. After the birth, Henry confessed to a friend that the intrusion into his home "both affected my mind & diverted me from all business in the counting house for some days, & indeed until Mrs. Laurens's fate was determined by giving LIBERTY to a very fine boy, who seems as if he had not been half so much frighted by smutty faces, turned coats, cutlasses, & bludgeons as his mother was." Nine years later, when poor James died, his father again dredged up the memory of his family's traumatic ordeal. The boy had been "mark'd by misfortune before his birth," he wrote. Henry Laurens would not forgive and forget, even though by that time he himself had become an active revolutionary.[19]

Christmas Season, 1765: Charleston

Unrest in Charleston continued after the first wave of resistance in October. In mid-November, Christopher Gadsden returned from an intercolonial Stamp Act Congress in New York, where he had failed to gain approval for a radical disavowal of Parliament's authority. (Instead, twenty-seven delegates from nine colonies could do no more than affirm their right to petition Parliament with "humble applications," and even that was too much for the group's president, Timothy Ruggles, who refused to sign the document.)

Back home, Gadsden continued to agitate, organizing meetings and writing polemics for the *South Carolina Gazette* under the banner "Aut Mors Aut Libertas," meaning "Either Liberty or Death." On one occasion, he wrote boldly that "none but the most infamous and abandoned cowards or place-men" would "hesitate a single moment" to defy the Stamp Act.[20]

This caused Henry Laurens to remark that Gadsden had become "ten times mad[d]er than he ever was. I'm sure he thinks himself nothing less at this time than Brutus or Cassius." While Gadsden advocated opening the Port of Charleston illegally—that is, without stamps—Laurens felt that operating outside the law could only further the reckless disrespect for proper authority.[21]

Laurens had good cause to worry, for civil authority in Charleston was being challenged not only by Stamp Act protesters but also by 1,400 seamen, beached in town because of the port closure. Some of these sailors apparently decided to do some rioting for personal profit rather than political advantage: "A parcel of sailors," wrote Lieutenant Governor William Bull, "having a mind to make the most of this suspension of law, formed a mob, to collect money of the people in the streets."[22]

In fact, neither angry patriots nor raucous sailors constituted the greatest threat to Charleston's security. That honor belonged to African Americans— four-fifths of the city's population. This black majority had a far greater stake in the notion of liberty than self-styled Sons of Liberty like Christopher Gadsden. White merchants, planters, and artisans, on the other hand, had a vested interest in keeping blacks suppressed. If slaves ever rose up and challenged their masters, the minor "mobbing" that so upset Henry Laurens on the night of October 23 would appear by contrast like an afternoon tea party.[23]

This awful prospect set white residents on edge. In mid-October, two days before the arrival of the official stamps, a grand jury warned "that slaves in Charles-Town are not under good regulation, and that they at all times in the night go about streets rioting. . . . It is not in the power of the small number of watchmen to suppress them, which hereafter may, without precaution, prove of the utmost ill consequences to this province." Jurors did not specify exactly what they meant by the term "rioting," but they did express some specific concerns. The law for "keeping a proper number of white men on plantations" was not being observed, they declared. On the Sabbath, when going to church, men tended to leave guns at home or even in the hands of attending slaves. Better precautions were necessary, the grand jury concluded, and a tax should be passed to support a standing slave patrol.[24]

In mid-December, in this climate of fear, a merchant named Isaac Huger told Lieutenant Governor Bull that his wife, while standing on her balcony, had overheard two slaves talking on the street below about an insurrection being planned for Christmas Eve. Bull immediately called an emergency session of his Council to report this piece of intelligence; acting swiftly and decisively, the Council called up a guard to patrol the streets and canceled Christmas for all black residents of Charleston. Traditionally, the city's slaves engaged in their own outdoor festivities over the holidays, but in 1765 they were instructed to stay inside.

On Christmas day, Bull reconvened his Council once again to report that ship captains had offered to provide a police force. While most other Christians celebrated the birth of Jesus, the lieutenant governor of South Carolina requested the Council to grant the captains "a hundred stand of arms to be distributed amongst the discretist of their people." He also received approval to hire Catawba Indians to search for runaway slaves in the countryside, for "Indians strike terrour into the Negroes, and the Indian manner of hunting render them more sagacious . . . in finding out the hidden recesses where the runaways conceal themselves from the usual searches of the English."[25]

Through the holiday season, white residents of Charleston remained in a state of alarm. "This place has been in an uproar for twelve days past, in consequence of a report which prevailed, that the Negroes had agreed to begin a general insurrection throughout the province," a resident reported in a dispatch to other colonial newspapers on December 29. "Every company in town mount guard day and night, and the severest orders given which has prevented it hitherto."[26]

The feared insurrection never did take place, perhaps because all the precautions had prevented it, or perhaps because the rumors had been exaggerated. Henry Laurens thought the latter. One month after the big scare, he wrote to his partner in Ninety Six, John Lewis Gervais:

> That disturbance that you heard of among our Negroes gave vast trouble throughout the province. Patrols were riding day & night for 10 or 14 days in most bitter weather & here in town all were soldiers in arms for more than a week, but there was little or no cause for all that bustle, some Negroes had mimick'd their betters in crying out "Liberty" . . . The whole seems to have terminated in the banishment of one fellow, not because he was guilty or instigator of insurrection, but because some of his judges said that in the general course of life he had been a sad dog, & perhaps that it was necessary to save appearances.[27]

In truth, slaves were not merely mimicking "their betters." They were mindful, more than whites, of what the loss of liberty entailed, and they resisted white oppression whenever and wherever they could. One of Laurens's own slaves already called himself by the name of Liberty, and two others ran away shortly before the Stamp Act protests began. Routinely, slaves engaged in subtle but effective forms of protest. In June of 1764, Henry Laurens jotted down a list of "good qualities" and "bad ones" for a slave named Abram, whom he was selling. He noted that Abram was skilled as a boatman, sawyer, carpenter, cooper, plasterer, and horseman, while also reporting that Abram "will deceive you as often as he can, . . . will pilfer trifles but always keeps out of greater scrapes, . . . will feign himself sick when he is not so." Abram was "ungrateful & disobedient to any man that uses him well and does not keep him close to work," Laurens warned. Only a small percentage of slaves ran away, and fewer yet dared plan or participate in armed insurrections, yet many, perhaps most, engaged daily in low-key personal recalcitrance such as Abram's.[28]

Henry Laurens, like most masters, could not appreciate the significance of Abram's cunning, for he did not bother to look at the world through Abram's eyes. Laurens held fast to the principle that buttressed the institution of human bondage in South Carolina: slaves were first and foremost to be considered as property, to be bought and sold and worked for profit.

Henry's son John, who as an adult would question the moral legitimacy of slavery, might have perceived things differently during that time. Although Henry hoped to educate John in England some day, the boy was receiving quite an education right in Charleston during the fall and winter of 1765–1766. John celebrated his eleventh birthday five days after his house was "mobbed" and two months before the panic of the holiday season. Continually he heard the cry of "liberty," and perhaps he noted its incongruous usage. Although such things are hard to trace, boys and girls of that age tend to see things literally, and the basic contradiction between the words and deeds of slaveholders during the Revolutionary era, dimly and reluctantly perceived by adults, might have been starkly obvious to the open mind of a child.

Early January 1766: Thomas Williams's Inn, Albany, New York

In October 1764, to avoid the "very extensive and fatiguing" demands on a country doctor (in the words of his brother Joseph), Dr. Thomas Young left the Oblong and moved to Albany. There, he also pursued his dubious land claims with John Henry Lydius, but that was not the half of it. It was in Albany, during the Stamp Act protests, that Thomas Young evolved from an idiosyncratic crank into an effective political activist.[29]

Because the larger port cities were so successful in intercepting the stamps and forcing Crown-appointed distributors to resign, there was little left to do in hinterland towns like Albany. Even so, several of Albany's patriots, hoping to assume some role in the struggle, conjured up their own local crisis. Just after New Year's, 1766, a group of young men from prominent families, who had been carousing at Thomas Williams's Inn over the holidays, decided to force a renunciation from all likely applicants for the office of local deputy to the stamp distributor. After settling on seven likely suspects, they hauled each one into their tavern courtroom to swear, under oath, that he never would seek the position. Six of the seven complied, but Henry Van Schaack did not. "I had no notion that a mob or any druncken set of men had a right to make me swear in that illegal way, for which reason I left them and went home," Van Schaack later wrote in a deposition, and he proceeded to list the names of his tormentors. One of the men he mentioned was "Dr. Young."[30]

The following evening Van Schaack was summoned again to appear at the same place, even though it was the Sabbath. This time his antagonists told him "that they would assemble to distroy me and my property" if he did not comply. Van Schaak applied to local magistrates for protection, but some of the officials were themselves part of the tavern crew, while others were closely related. Most of Van Schaack's accusers were local firemen. These people drank together, fought fires together, and liked to believe they were fighting tyranny together as well.

For two more days, the men from Williams's Inn escalated their threats, causing Van Schaack to seek refuge at the British garrison. A crowd of four hundred then invaded his empty house, destroyed much of his furniture, and posted on the door of the Dutch Church a picture of a man hanging from a gallows, accompanied by a caption: "Henry Van Schaack, the just fate of a traytor."

Van Schaack had had enough. Around midday on Tuesday, January 7, Dr. Thomas Young, a newcomer in town, personally ushered Henry Van Schaack, a prominent merchant and the Albany postmaster, to Thomas Williams's Inn, where he agreed at last "to take an oath in itself illegal, arbitrary and oppressive, extracted from me by a set of men who stile themselves Sons of Liberty."

This scenario replicated in miniature the larger crowd actions in Boston and elsewhere, but it was actually more representative of behavior in prerevolutionary America. The overwhelming preponderance of the population still lived in the countryside and small towns, where most of the people did most of their political talking and acting in small groups gathering in taverns. Within these venues, people communicated face-to-face. Whether they argued or agreed, they knew each other and even each other's families—Van Schaack, for instance, recognized all the men who tried to intimidate him. In closed societies within tavern walls, social norms could generally be enforced by the mere suggestion of ostracism, but if intimidation was needed, it was easily applied.

Ironically, these tavern venues helped subvert local hierarchies as well as enforce social norms. Drinking in groups, men were able to reinforce any incipient spirit of rebellion they might harbor. Lubricated, and seeing their friends lubricated as well, they shed traditional constraints and patterns of deference. Haughty behavior in this context was not tolerated, and this made it difficult for anyone to pull rank, as supporters of imperial policies were prone to do. It mattered little to the firemen-turned-patriots gathered in Thomas Williams's tavern if Henry Van Schaack ranked higher or lower in society than they did; what mattered was that he refused to cede to their collective will.

Flush with their successes, Thomas Young and the Albany "Sons of liberty" decided to embody themselves as an actual organization. To do so, they drafted a constitution, in which they pledged "to persevere to the last in the vindication of our dear bought rights and privileges." Any citizen refusing to concur with their principles, they vowed, "shall be considered by us as cold friends of liberty, and treated accordingly." Thomas Young was the first of ninety-four men to sign this constitution, and we might infer that he was also one of its authors, for he did have a penchant for writing, and the document's insistent tone was certainly consistent with his.[31]

Although Thomas Young had been in Albany barely a year, he was already playing a lead role in the local resistance movement—and even beyond. When the fledgling organization he had helped create assigned Young and three others to correspond with Sons of Liberty in other areas, the country doctor from the Oblong came into contact with John Lamb, Isaac Sears, and other popular leaders of the opposition in New York City. These men, calling themselves the Vox Populi (voice of the people), competed with land barons such as Robert R. Livingston, whom Thomas Young vilified, for control of New York's patriot movement. By aligning himself firmly on the side of these radicals, Young challenged both British imperial authority and New York's "great land-jobbers" simultaneously. His incipient populism, as yet poorly defined, started to mature and deepen, pegged to the cause of "liberty" that had cap-tured the imagination of British North America.[32]

May 19, 1766: The Boston Common, Liberty Tree, and "All Around the Town"

On March 18, 1766, Parliament officially repealed the Stamp Act. Faced with mounting opposition at home, and recognizing that the measure could never be enforced, the MPs concluded: "Continuance of the said act would be attended with many inconveniences, and may be productive of consequences greatly detrimental to the commercial interests of these kingdoms."[33]

Moderates and radicals alike could boast responsibility for the victory.

The American merchants' suspension of trade, which started in response to the Revenue Act in 1764 and gained momentum during the Stamp Act con-troversy, had caused a group of London merchants to complain to the House of Commons that commerce with North America was approaching "utter ruin." Meanwhile, weavers and glove makers from industrial cities in En-gland, having lost their jobs, marched on the Royal Palace and Parliament by the tens of thousands, demanding a resumption of trade.[34]

Popular protest in America also played a pivotal role. Because of crowd intimidation, nobody could even begin to administer the Stamp Act. Ten days before Parliament relented, Massachusetts Lieutenant Governor Thomas Hutchinson confessed that the crowd had usurped political power and en-sured the Stamp Act's demise: "Every where, it is the universal voice of all people, that if the stamp act must take place we are absolute slaves. . . . The authority is in the populace, no law can be carried into execution against their mind."[35]

But on the same day it repealed the Stamp Act, Parliament passed another measure, known as the Declaratory Act. "The said colonies and plantations in America have been, are, and of right ought to be, subordinate unto, and de-pendent upon the imperial crown and parliament of Great Britain," it said. King and Parliament thereby possessed "full power and authority to make laws and statutes of sufficient force and validity to bind colonies and people in America, subjects of the crown of Great Britain, in all cases whatsoever."[36]

Under different circumstances, the stern wording of the Declaratory Act would have engendered a furious response, but instead, most Americans chose to rejoice in their hard-earned victory, the repeal of the Stamp Act.

In Boston on Friday, May 16, merchant John Rowe wrote in his diary:

"Capt't Shubael Coffin arr'd from London abo' 11 of clock & bro't the glorious news of the total repeal of the Stamp Act which was signed by his Majesty King George the 3'd of Ever Glorious Memory, which God long preserve & his Illustrious House."[37] The following Monday, May 19, by decree of the town's selectmen, would be the official "Day of General Rejoicings."

And that it was:

> The ardor of the people was so great, that immediately after the clock strook one in the morning, the bell on the Reverend Doctor Byles's Church (as being the nearest to Liberty Tree) was set a ringing; which was soon answered by the bells on Christ-Church, at the other end of Town; and in a short time all the other bells of the Town strook in. Before two o'clock musick was heard in the streets, the drums beat, and guns fired. As soon as it grew light enough to see, the steeple of the Meeting House next the Tree of Liberty was hung with banners.—The tree decorated with flags and streamers, and all around the Town, on the tops of houses, were displayed colours and pendants.—About noon, the guns at Castle William were fired, which were soon returned by those of the South, North, and Charlestown Batteries, the train of artillery in this Town, and ships in the harbour.
>
> In the evening the town was universally illuminated, and shone like day: Fire-works of all kinds were every where play'd off, especially on the Common, where were exhibited the finest that were ever seen in New-England. Here also was erected an obelisk, covered with various hieroglyphics, and poetical lines, and illuminated within.[38]

The wealthy merchant John Hancock, whose brig *Harrison* had carried the good news from London, "gave a grand and elegant entertainment to the genteel part of the town, and treated the populace with a pipe of madeira wine." Bursting with goodwill, other merchants took up a subscription "for liberating all the poor prisoners in gaol for debt." Even conservatives took part in the festivities, for the British system of government, which itself had been taxed, survived. Governor Bernard, more than a bit pleased that the crisis was over, hosted the Council at the Province House, "where His Majesty's health, and many other loyal toasts were drank."

In Charleston, Christopher Gadsden commemorated the repeal of the Stamp Act by joining hands with twenty-five artisans—"defenders and supporters of

American Liberty," they called their association—around a large oak, which they christened Liberty Tree. The Commons House of Assembly told Gadsden and his two fellow delegates to the Stamp Act Congress that they should "set for their pictures at the publick expence."[39]

Henry Laurens, on the other hand, just grumbled. He summed up the entire commotion over the Stamp Act in a single sentence: "Nothing (with all submission I say it) could be more foolish than the whole conduct of [Parliament] in passing the Stamp Act but ours in the manner we have chosen to oppose it."[40]

Robert Morris, in his usual practical manner, celebrated the repeal by accepting an appointment from Governor John Penn as a member of the Board of Port Wardens. This was Morris's first public office, a reward for his part in averting violence.[41]

In Thomas Young's former stomping grounds, the Oblong, poor farmers who had been dispossessed of their lands celebrated repeal of the Stamp Act by marching en masse to New York City, where they "expected to be assisted by the poor people there." In the unsympathetic words of New York's governor Henry Moore, "The disorders which began at first in the towns have by degrees spread themselves into the country, and inflicted the people with notions that at this time every thing which had the appearance of resisting government might be undertaken with impunity." The farmers' celebration turned sour, however, when New York City's Sons of Liberty failed to come to their aid.[42]

To the north of the Oblong, on the Livingston Manor in the fertile Hudson River Valley, tenant farmers celebrated the Stamp Act's repeal by rising up against their landlords, "the assuming family of Livingston," as Thomas Young called them. The tenants freed prisoners from jailhouses and engaged in pitched battles with law enforcement officials, but in the end, their rebellion was squashed by three detachments of British Regulars. Thomas Young, who sympathized with the tenants, commented wryly: "The Earth is the Lord's and the fullness thereof—but N. York gentlemen have for about a century pretty strongly disputed his title & seem resolved that neither he nor his creatures shall have any share in the premises unless on the terms of being their servants forever."[43]

Dr. Thomas Young himself celebrated the repeal of the Stamp Act by leaving Albany and moving to Boston, the free-spirited Athens of America, where popular protest was most extreme and most effective. The suppression of the farmers' uprising offered final proof that the power of the New York landlords was too overbearing. As long as he remained in New York, Young's crusade on behalf of equal rights and opportunities was doomed to defeat— so why not relocate to a place where his radical political agenda would receive a warmer welcome?

George Washington did not exactly celebrate, for he had not participated directly in the Stamp Act remonstrations. But he had told his agent in London that he considered the measure "ill judged" because it hurt trade in both England and America, and after the act was repealed, two of his trading partners wrote to him: "We congratulate thee & all our friends in America upon the repeal of the Stamp Act. We . . . spar'd no endeavours to demonstrate the necessity of repealing it & are happy that we have in some degree been instrumental in accomplishing it."[44]

Washington's neighbor and close friend George Mason, a dour but very astute fellow, was one of the few Americans who looked ahead to the broader implications of the Stamp Act fiasco. Upon receiving news that the Declaratory Act had taken the place of the Stamp Act, Mason sat down and penned a lengthy letter to the Committee of London Merchants. With insight and foresight, he outlined the historical trajectory of the Revolutionary era:

> There is a passion natural to the mind of man, especially a free man, which renders him impatient of restraint. Do you, does any sensible man think that three or four millions of people, not naturally defective in genius, or in courage, who have tasted the sweets of Liberty, in a country that doubles its inhabitants every twenty years, in a country abounding in such variety of soil & climate, capable of producing, not only the necessarys, but the conveniencys & delicacys of life, will long submit to oppression; if unhappily for yourselves oppression shou'd be offered them? Such another experiment as the Stamp-Act wou'd produce a general revolt in America.[45]

Then, almost threateningly, and with even greater prescience, Mason added a rhetorical question: "Do you think that all your rival powers in Europe wou'd sit still & see you crush your once flourishing & thriving colonys, unconcerned spectators of such a quarrel?"

3

A Perfect Sense of Their Rights

1766: Plymouth, Massachusetts

Mercy Otis Warren's great-great-grandfather, Edward Dotey, had sailed to America on the *Mayflower*, but he was not a model Pilgrim. An indentured servant, he threatened mutiny while on board ship, quarreled with his neighbors, and later made history by taking part in the first known duel in Massachusetts. Dotey's rambunctious streak had been passed down to James Otis Jr., and perhaps to Mrs. Warren as well, but as an eighteenth-century woman from the heart of New England, she was not supposed to challenge or rebel against any sort of authority.

She was supposed to submit, and indeed she tried to, not just to men, but to God's will. One of her earliest poems, written before political protest entered into her life, was titled "Lines written after a very severe tempest which cleared up extremely pleasant":

> When rolling thunders shake the skies
> And lightnings fly from pole to pole,
> When threatening whirlwinds rend the air,
> What terrors seize th'affrighted soul!
>
> Happy the calm and tranquil breast,
> That with a steady equal mind
> Can view those flying shafts of death
> With heart and will at once resigned![1]

Figures 4 and 5. In 1763, when Boston's John Singleton Copley painted their portraits, Mercy Otis Warren was rearing small children and writing pastoral poetry, while her husband, James Warren, a gentleman farmer, planned to devote his life to advancing the science of agriculture. A few years later, both Mercy and James would become embroiled in the politics of resistance. *(Photographs © 2009 Museum of Fine Arts, Boston)*

Warren's focus on resignation was typical of the times. Women in particular traveled this road, for they had to bend so often to the unfathomable acts of God, who seized infants, children, and women in childbirth for no apparent reason. The need to surrender, a constant refrain in women's letters and diaries, contrasts starkly with political protest, which defined the life of Mercy's brother and an increasing number of her male acquaintances.

In 1765, while Boston erupted, Mrs. Warren was caring for four children: one-year-old Henry, three-year-old Charles, six-year-old Winslow, and seven-year-old James Jr. Nine years earlier, Mercy Otis had married James Warren, whose own great-great-grandfather had by chance sailed on the *Mayflower* along with hers. Mercy and James Warren lived in the heart of Plymouth, on the major thoroughfare between Boston and Cape Cod and only three hundred yards from the famous rock that had welcomed their ancestors a century and a half past. Shaded by giant elms, their house rose two and a half stories to a gabled roof and two chimneys. Inside, it boasted a formal entrance leading to a stately colonial staircase, paneled walls, broad window seats, and a grand salon, which Abigail Adams once compared to the one she stayed at in France during her husband's diplomatic mission. Within this dwelling, the Warrens raised their family and entertained a host of politically active patriots through the 1760s and 1770s.[2]

Household management for an extended family in colonial New England was a time-consuming affair, with tasks ranging from domestic industries, such as spinning and weaving, to managing the daily finances to disciplining the younger generation and imbuing them with religious reverence and a sense of duty. But tending to house and family (which she did with the help of her housekeeper, Ann) was not enough to satisfy the restless mind of Mercy Otis Warren. She had always stretched beyond traditional female roles, dating back to her childhood in Barnstable, when she picked up any book her brothers had tossed aside. Unlike most women of her day, she had been well educated, not only in domestic sciences, but in classical studies and current philosophy. So she was really the product of two traditions: Puritan New England, with its stern, Calvinistic interpretation of the Christian faith, and the transatlantic Enlightenment, with its focus on reason and science and the expansive opportunities open to humankind. To reconcile these, and to keep herself alert and alive, she developed and practiced the art of the written word.

She also paid attention to the world of politics, which both attracted and repelled her. The Stamp Act protests presented a particular challenge: on the one hand, Warren's gender, religion, and social standing led her to scorn any sort of rebellious behavior; on the other hand, her own brother "Jemmy" was instrumental in creating all the fuss. Because of Otis's flamboyant personality, he himself became a political issue. Friends of the Crown, unable to gain credibility by supporting the Stamp Act, settled for attacking its best-known opponent and calling him names: the Grand Incendiary, James Bluster, Esq., or simply, and most often, Bluster. On the eve of the 1765 election for Boston's representative to the Assembly, a minor customs official publicly ridiculed Otis, one of the candidates:

> As Jemmy is an envious dog, and Jemmy is ambitious,
> And rage, and slander, spite and dirt to Jemmy are delicious . . .
>
> And Jemmy is a silly dog, and Jemmy is a tool,
> And Jemmy is a stupid curr, and Jemmy is a fool,
> And Jemmy is a madman, and Jemmy is an ass,
> And Jemmy has a leaden head, & forehead spread with brass.[3]

This treatment rankled Otis's Puritanical sister, who looked at the political arena with suspicion bordering on contempt.

To observe her brother so embroiled in politics was bad enough, but the

Stamp Act chaos threatened to entangle her husband as well. In October of 1765, James Warren, on behalf of the Plymouth town meeting, drafted a strong indictment of the Stamp Act, and the following spring, with Mercy carrying their fifth and last child, James became a representative to the Provincial Assembly, a job that would require him to spend more time away from home. In response, Mercy consulted her muse and came up with a sweeping condemnation of all political behavior:

To J. Warren, Esqr.
An Invitation to retirement.

Come leave the noisy smoky town
Where vice and folly reign,
The vain pursuits of busy men
We wisely will disdain.

True happiness and lasting peace
We ne'er in Courts can find
Ambitious views and sordid hopes,
By turns distract the mind.

But in the peaceful calm retreat
Amidst the beauteous plains,
Where innocence with cheerful health
With love and virtue reign;

There free from envy, free from pride,
And all the dismal train
Of warring passions, endless strife,
The blackest source of pain.[4]

That's what the Stamp Act turmoil meant to Mercy Otis Warren at the time—it lured her husband away from the "peaceful calm" of their pastoral lives, where virtue reigned.

It would not be long, however, before she, too, joined the "dismal train," succumbing to the warring passions and contributing liberally to the strife that was enveloping British North America.

September 1, 1767: Charleston, South Carolina

Henry Laurens surprised even himself. He was not the sort of man, he thought, to tweak another fellow's nose. Nor was he the sort to offer a straightforward apology, even though he knew he had violated his own moral code:

> I am sorry that it fell to my lot to have such transactions with him. I know they are out of character & the very retrospect chagrins me, but who, just so circumstanced as I was could have done less? He is one of the most haughty, insolent, ignorant men take the three together, that ever was disguised in the habit of a gentleman, & I hope my friends will at least forbear to censure me that is all that I can hope for.[5]

The trouble started on March 20, 1767, the day a sixty-five-year-old "place-man" named Daniel Moore arrived in Charleston to assume his new post as customs inspector. Laurens at that time wanted to believe his political quarreling was over. "All those folks who through party heat in 1761 & 1765 affected to be very angry are now upon good terms with me," he wrote. "I go to church & come home again, to the House of Assembly and return to my habitation, avoiding all disputes about tenets, refn'd politics & party." But when Moore demanded favors and exacted exorbitant fees from Charleston's merchants to acquire personal wealth, and when he seized their ships if they failed to comply, Laurens could not forbear entering the fray.[6]

In May, when Henry Laurens and six others complained to Moore about his fees and his first ship seizure, the new customs officer threatened to "sweat them at law with their own money . . . before the summer was over." Come July, Moore made good on his pledge by seizing two of Laurens's schooners, which were bearing only shingles and ballast from his own plantations to Charleston. Moore offered to release the vessels if Laurens begged him with sufficient deference, but this of course Laurens refused to do. When the cases were tried in the Vice Admiralty Court on September 1, Judge Egerton Leigh upheld the confiscation of one of the vessels while releasing the other, although even in the second case he required Laurens to pay two-thirds of the court costs.[7]

Upon leaving the courtroom, Laurens and Moore continued to argue. A number of people gathered around them, and Laurens placed his left arm around Moore's back and onto his left shoulder, ostensibly to usher him through the crowd. Whatever Moore said at that moment set Laurens off, for suddenly, while securing his elderly victim with his left arm, he reached around with his right hand to grab and twist the nose of His Majesty's chief inspector of customs for the port of Charleston. From that moment, there was no turning back. Henry Laurens, the man who did not believe in opposing authority, had cast himself in the role of a resister.[8]

To avoid a duel and lasting disgrace, Daniel Moore departed Charleston, never to return. But Laurens continued to quarrel with Egerton Leigh, who, in addition to his Vice Admiralty judgeship, also held appointments as councilman, surveyor general, and attorney general, while on the side serving as an attorney in a new case against Laurens. Fuming at Leigh's abuse of his multiple office holdings, Laurens penned another series of venomous tracts, one totaling almost fifty thousand words. "As a soldier," he wrote, "the pompous Mr. Leigh" was "the veriest fribble [trifler] that ever was buckled to a bloodless blade." Laurens circulated his pamphlets not only in Charleston, but also in Philadelphia, Boston, and London, hoping to convince himself and others that his interests were more than just personal. Greater issues were at stake: the abuse of concentrated power by corrupt British officials and a corresponding trampling of American rights. "I tell you the enormous created powers vested in a sole judge of an American Court of Vice Admiralty threaten future generations in America with a curse tenfold worse than the Stamp Act," he wrote.[9]

Because of his publicized quarrels with Moore and Leigh, the once conservative Henry Laurens became known within patriot circles as something of a rebel. In Boston he was viewed in the same light as John Hancock, another wealthy merchant who had a vessel seized by British officials, and because Hancock was already a confirmed patriot, people assumed that Laurens must be one too. There was a kernel of truth in this, for his rancor, which he had formerly applied to the likes of Christopher Gadsden and the Sons of Liberty, now found a new focus. "Such men as that one in office," he wrote, referring to Moore in this case, "are the greatest enemies to Britain of any man in America, & as one vile priest does more injury to the cause of religion than two rakes, so does one such officer or man in power more prejudice to the interest of Britain in America than twenty mouthing Liberty Boys."[10]

In the eyes of American patriots, the personal abuses of power that so rankled Henry Laurens reflected systematic oppression by imperial authority. The brief interlude of harmonious feelings following repeal of the Stamp Act came to an abrupt end in 1767 when Charles Townshend, chancellor of the

Exchequer, persuaded Parliament to find new ways of clamping down on Americans and making them pay the expenses of an expanding empire.[11]

Townshend's policies seemed uniquely engineered to arouse resentment in America. To save money, he proposed stationing British troops in coastal cities rather than on the frontier, and when the New York Assembly refused to quarter the troops, he suggested that Parliament strip it of all its powers. Simultaneously, at Townshend's bidding, Parliament streamlined the customs department, allowing officials to extract money more easily from people like Henry Laurens. Finally, and most disastrously, Parliament instituted new import duties on glass, lead, paint, paper, and tea—the Townshend duties, they would be called. These new taxes presented American patriots with a concrete target, upon which they could focus their opposition to imperial authority. Whereas the Stamp Tax, which lasted only a matter of months, was viewed by many as no more than a temporary aberration from benign British rule, the fight over the Townshend duties would drag on for three years, allowing patriotic resistance to become deeply ingrained in the political culture of British North America.

Fall 1766–Spring 1768: Boston

Early in the fall of 1766, Dr. Thomas Young marched into Boston and proceeded directly to the hub of political activity: the Assembly chamber on the second story of the Town House, immediately adjacent to the Council chamber, where James Otis had appeared before the Superior Court to argue the Writs of Assistance case. Whereas each room felt spacious, with a lofty ceiling and tall windows, the Council chamber rarely housed more than two to three dozen men, comfortably seated, while in the Assembly chamber more than one hundred men had to cram tightly together as they hawked their political wares. Despite the geographic proximity of the two rooms, the atmosphere in the Council chamber was calm and deliberative, while that in the Assembly was hectic and often confrontational. Temperamentally as well as politically, Thomas Young was better suited to the lower chamber, which was just as well, because he would certainly not be welcomed in the upper one.

Young's timing was impeccable, for just as he arrived the Assembly had voted to fit its chamber with an upstairs gallery, from which the public could keep track of the actions of their representatives, and perhaps, by their very presence, influence those actions as well. Coming from New York, where people were repressed rather than empowered by the political process, Young thought this was a marvelous idea but, characteristically, he wanted to take it further than did anybody else. Like a true revolutionary, he favored "the dissolution of the present Town House on condition we might (at very considerable expence) have a structure equal to the most finished playhouse for the conveniency of all that chose to attend the debates of the house." Writing to a friend, he gushed forth: "No man can conceive the advantages that must arise to a Country from so noble a school of political learning. How many wou'd catch the fire!"[12]

Young did not get his playhouse, but he did get a gallery in the Assembly chamber, and we can be certain he made ample use of it. He had come to Boston to immerse himself in politics, and that is exactly what he did. Early in 1767, he wrote to Abigail Dwight, a former patient in Great Barrington, Massachusetts, "Your government contains many human beings with several of whom I have already had much satisfaction." Thrilled by the process of democratic self-government, and beginning to rub shoulders with those who were making it possible, Young expressed great delight: "I am quietly settled in your dear country . . . and think myself as happy as I can reasonably desire."[13]

But the word "quietly" did not truthfully describe Young's situation, and, given his disposition, it never would. Shortly after his arrival in Boston, Young confessed that because his passionate "ardor" to "serve my country is so much the desire of my whole soul," he had engaged in frequent and heated political debates, which scared off potential patients.[14]

Young's disputes were not limited to the realm of politics. Shortly after penning his letter to Dwight, a doctor named Miles Whitworth accused him of killing a patient they shared by bleeding her. Labeling the country doctor a "stroller," Whitworth chastised him in the *Boston Gazette*: "I believe no pretender to medicine in this country ever did in so short a time lead so many people prematurely to their graves as he has since his arrival here."[15] Young responded by calling Whitworth an "imposter" and "blockhead" and challenging him to a doctors' face-off, in which each man would submit answers to "questions in all the arts, sciences and languages preparatory to a just and rational knowledge of medicine, the science of medicine itself, or any other science that becomes the gentleman, the scholar, or the physician."[16] Whitworth's sixteen-year-old son promptly answered the challenge by giving Young a beating when they met on the street.[17] When Dr. Joseph Warren, a leading patriot and physician, joined the fray and publicly challenged Young's credentials, Young escalated the argument by threatening to sue Warren for loss of reputation, and Warren responded that Young would first have to establish that he had a reputation to lose. "Of late a new-coin'd word is come greatly into vogue," Warren wrote in the *Gazette*. "If in the public papers, inaccuracy, malevolence, bad grammar and nonsense, are to be found, they are immediately pronounced Youngisms.—Self-conceit, vain-boasting, and invincible impudence are frequently expressed by the word Youngism."[18]

After all this, did Young still love Boston?

Absolutely. A little cantankerous bickering was safely within the margins of his comfort zone, and even a dispute with such a prominent patriot as Joseph Warren could not distract him from his main mission: fighting for the rights of Americans to enjoy British liberties.

Although it took Boston's Whig activists a little time to become accustomed to Young's dissonant style, soon they did. Not long after their quarrel in the press, Warren called upon Young to "signify" his "high satisfaction" with his character. "I now assure you Sir," he told Young (according to Young's own rendering), "that whatever may heretofore have happened I have now a real esteem of you and hearty friendship for you."[19]

As soon as they would have him, Young joined forces with Boston's Sons of Liberty, whom he impressed by his ability to express patriotic sentiments with great flourish. In the spring of 1768, this group, meeting at John Marston's Whig Tavern, charged Thomas Young, Joseph Warren, John Adams, and two others with the important task of drafting a letter to John Wilkes, the radical English Whig who had become the hero of liberty-minded citizens on both sides of the Atlantic.

Wilkes, an MP, had been arrested and almost killed because he publicly criticized not only the prime minister but the king himself. Having escaped to France, Wilkes had just returned to England, where he was elected once again to Parliament. Offering their support to Wilkes and the cause he espoused, which they regarded as their own, Young and his "assistants" (as he described the other members of the committee) held forth boldly: "That the British Constitution still exists is our glory; feeble and infirm as it is, we cannot, we will not despond of it." The colonies were "on the point of bursting into flames," they wrote, and Boston was leading the resistance.[20]

By the time Wilkes received this letter, he had been placed in the King's Bench Prison. From there, he wrote back to his supporters in Boston. "I am extremely honoured by your letter," he said graciously. "Nothing cou'd give me more satisfaction than to find the true spirit of Liberty so generally diffus'd thro' the most remote parts of the British Monarchy."[21] We can easily imagine the joy this reply gave to Thomas Young, the country doctor from the Oblong, who was now communicating with one of the great men of his times. Readily embracing the notion that he and Wilkes were on a letter-writing basis, he penned at least four more letters on his own. "Flattering myself that little articles of intelligence will be received at least without disgust," he wrote, "I proceed to say, that my large acquaintance with the present disposition of this and the two neighboring Colonies of Connecticut and New York, enables me to assure you that the great power of a spirit of freedom . . . was never more conspicuous than at this promising juncture."[22]

February 11 and June 30, 1768: Assembly Chamber of the Town House, Boston

In December of 1767, John Dickinson sent a pamphlet he had just composed to James Otis, his former colleague from the Stamp Act Congress. In clear, persuasive language, *Letters from a Farmer in Pennsylvania* (Dickinson was actually a wealthy Philadelphia lawyer) presented the case against Charles Townshend's policies, and its author hoped that Boston patriots would use it to "kindle the sacred flame, that on such occasions must warm and illuminate the continent."[23]

This they did, and the "Farmer's" letters, published in local papers, triggered a vigorous public dialogue about the Townshend Acts and what could be done to oppose them. James Otis and Samuel Adams then drafted a circular letter to the legislative bodies in other colonies, urging them to join the Massachusetts Assembly in resisting the new measures. But on January 21, when patriots asked the full Assembly for permission to send the letter out, they were turned down. Again on February 11 they tried, and this time the Assembly endorsed the letter by a narrow margin. The gallery in the Assembly chamber had by then been completed, and looking down from that great "school of political learning" touted by Thomas Young, members of the general public could witness the heated arguments on the floor beneath them and cheer their side on, as if in a sporting match.

Immediately upon its approval, before opponents could regroup and force another vote, Samuel Adams, the Assembly clerk, dispatched copies to the various colonies, and from there, *the* Circular Letter (as people called it) took on a life of its own. Other assemblies considered and debated it, while across the Atlantic the British ministry not only opposed the letter but devised a scheme for repressing it. Lord Hillsborough, a hard-liner who had just been appointed to the new office of secretary of state for America, wrote a circular letter of his own, in which he instructed the governors of other colonies to dissolve their assemblies if they even considered the Massachusetts letter, and he specifically ordered Governor Francis Bernard to dissolve the Massachusetts Assembly if it failed to disavow and rescind its own words.

The stage was set for a showdown. Hillsborough's order was presented to the Assembly on June 21, 1768, and for over a week representatives on both sides of the issue, playing to the cheers and jeers of people like Thomas Young in the gallery above, escalated their political harangues to the next level. Otis, who had been cautioning moderation during the entire affair, suddenly let loose with a rant of unparalleled proportions. Parliament, he bellowed, was no more than a "parcel of button-makers, pin-makers, horse jockeys, gamesters, pensioners, pimps, and whore masters." He then ordered Hillsborough to rescind his own letter.[24]

If Lord Hillsborough seriously expected the Massachusetts Assembly to bow sheepishly under pressure, he showed little understanding of the depth of the problem. In the words of Thomas Young, "Men born and educated in the perfect sense of their rights and privileges can never resign them quietly."[25]

On June 30, the Assembly cleared the gallery and locked its doors to prevent the governor from intervening. A committee of influential patriots that included Adams, Otis, and James Warren presented for the consideration of the whole body a summary rejection of Hillsborough's demand, and in a decisive vote, 92 representatives elected to endorse the committee's defiant response, while only 17 favored rescinding. For the duration of the Revolutionary era, patriots celebrated their overwhelming victory by imbuing the numerals 92 and 17 with almost mystical powers, much as they had done with the number 45, the issue of John Wilkes's paper, *The North Briton*, that led to his incarceration. A week later, Thomas Young and Boston's Sons of Liberty commemorated both numbers by shipping two turtles across the Atlantic Ocean to John Wilkes, one weighing precisely 45 pounds, the other 47 pounds, for a grand total of 92 pounds, which, as the letter explained, had just become "Massachusetts' patriotic number."[26]

When the Assembly opened its doors, its officers were immediately summoned to the Council chamber in the adjoining room, where Governor Bernard had been waiting, perhaps even eavesdropping on the proceedings next door. (We do not know the extent of soundproofing in the wall between the chambers.) Bernard began the meeting with a stern lecture, then promptly dissolved the Assembly, as previously threatened. This left opponents of the

Townshend Acts at an impasse, for without an Assembly they had no formal political recourse.[27]

Only by engaging in politics "out of chambers" could patriots hope to prevail, yet many merchants were not so sure they wished to resuscitate the raucous disruptions and nonimportation agreements of the Stamp Act crisis. The battle over the Townshend Acts looked as though it might continue for some time, and if nonimportation became a habit, how were merchants to make a living? Although they opposed the new taxes, most were hesitant to make any financial sacrifices, which might or might not lead to its repeal.

Influential patriots such as Samuel Adams, James Otis, Joseph Warren, and James Warren, understanding that nonimportation was the best weapon in their arsenal, tried to persuade the cautious merchants to join in. So did Thomas Young, who had taken to writing open letters to Parliament and publishing them in the newspapers under various pseudonyms. "As matters now stand, we suppose the balance of trade much against us in the barter of golden chains for iron ones," he wrote in the *Boston Evening-Post*, and he went on to pledge "a steady and determinate resistance to such lawless and boundless thirst of power . . . tho' ourselves, our friends, our all, should perish in the effort." Only a handful of patriots at this point expressed themselves with such hyperbole, and Young had established his position among them.[28]

Young's strident style did not appeal to moderate or conservative merchants. Two weeks later, a writer using the name Trader complained that "brawling boys" were being led astray by "intirely new and strange politicians . . . who have no property to lose, therefore subject to no danger on that account, and whose only hopes of living are founded in anarchy and confusion; . . . and therefore thro' the pretended medium of patriotism, endeavor to gain the esteem of the unguarded populace." Although the author of this piece mentioned no names, it would be hard to believe he was not referring to Thomas Young, the foremost "new and strange politician" in town.[29]

Whether because of Young's efforts or despite them, moderates eventually joined in. On August 1, 1768, facing pressure from below, sixty merchants signed a sweeping nonimportation agreement, while another forty agreed to abide by it, although they did not formally sign. Boston's patriots had escalated their assault against the Townshend Acts on two fronts: politically, with the Circular Letter and their refusal to rescind it, and economically, with another round of nonimportation.

Would Bostonians stand alone, or would other colonial Americans follow suit?

October 1, 1768: Liberty Tree in Charleston

In Charleston on the afternoon of October 1, Christopher Gadsden and his artisan allies held an outdoor convention at a place they called Liberty-Point to nominate candidates for the upcoming Assembly election. This election seemed particularly critical, for when the new Assembly members met in November, they would have to address the Massachusetts Circular Letter and their governor's demand to reject it. The name of Henry Laurens was put forward, for these patriots no longer considered him an adversary, but Laurens failed to garner their endorsement, for he was still not radical enough to suit their tastes. Gadsden was, and he topped a slate of candidates for the six seats in Charleston's two parishes. Their business done, these "mechanicks [artisans] and other inhabitants of Charles-Town . . . partook of a plain and hearty entertainment," which the *South Carolina Gazette* described in some detail:

> About 5 o'Clock they all removed to a most noble LIVE OAK tree, in Mr. Mazyck's pasture, which they formally dedicated to LIBERTY, where many loyal, patriotic, and constitutional toasts were drank, beginning with the glorious NINETY-TWO Anti-Rescinders of Massachusetts-Bay, and ending with unanimity among the members of our ensuing Assembly not to rescind from the said resolutions, each succeeded by three huzzas. . . . In the evening, the tree was decorated with 45 lights, and 45 sky-rockets were fired. . . . About 8 o'clock, the whole company, preceded by 45 of their number, marched in regular procession to town, down King-street and Broad-street, to Mr. Robert Dillon's tavern; where the 45 lights being placed upon the table, with 45 bowls of punch, 45 bottles of wine, and 92 glasses, they spent a few hours in a new round of toasts, among which, scarce a celebrated Patriot of Britain or America was omitted; and preserving the same good order and regularity as had been observed throughout the day, at 10 they retired.[30]

Only three of the mechanics' six candidates prevailed in the election, but as it turned out, that didn't matter. In mid-November, when the new Assembly convened, it appointed Christopher Gadsden, Henry Laurens (who had been elected without the endorsement of the "mechanicks'" convention), and seven other members to draft a formal statement. This committee, composed of moderates as well as radicals, endorsed without qualification both the Massachusetts letter and a similar correspondence from Virginia, which had already voiced support for the Massachusetts position. The full Assembly promptly approved the committee report by a vote of 26 to 0, and immediately afterward, as in Massachusetts, the governor dissolved the Assembly. The vote on the Circular Letter led to the consecration of yet another sacred numeral for the patriots of South Carolina to celebrate—subsequent rounds of patriotic toasts in Charleston (and there would be many) rarely neglected to include "the unanimous 26."

Henry Laurens, formerly a defender of the Crown, had joined in the growing resistance to imperial policies. Not only did he support the Massachusetts letter, but he also broke ranks with many of his class by advocating a policy of nonimportation. "This constitutional way of opposing unconstitutional taxes and impositions is more likely to prove effectual than those measures which I complain'd of in the year 1765," he wrote.[31]

Although Laurens's politics had come full circle, his style had not. Mass meetings, endless rounds of toasts, and general carousing still offended him. On October 1, as the mechanics engaged in their grandiose display of patriotism, Laurens wrote to an old colleague from the Cherokee War, a British officer:

> To day a grand barbacu is given by a very grand simpleton. . . . If you hear that I am no longer a Parliament man, let not Your Excellency wonder, for I walk on the old road, give no barbacu nor ask any man for votes.[32]

If Laurens was becoming a patriot, that didn't mean he could abide political activities that went beyond the limits of respectable behavior. If he was willing to work in common cause with Christopher Gadsden, that didn't mean he had abandoned previous antagonisms toward his childhood friend, whom he still referred to in the most derogatory terms.

November 1768–November 1769: The Coffee House and Christ Church, Philadelphia

The City of Brotherly Love was key to the success of nonimportation. No matter that Boston and twenty-four other towns in Massachusetts, Rhode Island's two major ports (Providence and Newport), several coastal communities in Connecticut, and New York City had already signed on. Nonimportation was sure to flounder unless the merchants of Philadelphia, the most active traders on the continent, agreed to play along.[33]

But the battle here would be rough. Although Philadelphians overwhelmingly voiced their support for the Massachusetts Circular Letter at a mass meeting in the State House Yard on June 30, 1768, they remained divided on whether to resume economic warfare with imperial rulers in London.

Merchants remained wary, fearful of losing their source of wealth and warning that too much "republicanism" could result in the breakdown of civil society. According to "Philadelphus," writing in the *Pennsylvania Gazette*, it was fine to petition Parliament with "modest firmness," but the colonists must manifest "a becoming constitutional subordination to the mother country, that we may be free without anarchy."[34]

Most artisans thought differently, but their views didn't matter unless they could convince or cajole the merchants, who actually did the importing. "A Freeborn American," also writing in the *Pennsylvania Gazette*, tried to do just that:

> To you, ye respectable merchants and Citizens of Philadelphia!—to you do we, at this critical conjuncture address ourselves. . . . Upon you are centered the expectations of all British America. Upon your concurrence, your *speedy* concurrence, depends the success of the measures entered into by the northern towns. . . . Consider the happiness or misery of your posterity depends upon you. By all that is dear, then, we urge you, we most ardently beseech you, join with New-York and Boston. Shame us not, we intreat you: Let it not be a scandal to be a Philadelphian—a Pennsylvanian. Scorn all thoughts of delay.[35]

If the merchants let the public down, the writer warned, "the curses of thousands await thee."

In this debate, Robert Morris found himself once again occupying a tenuous middle ground. Like Philadelphus, he feared anarchy and preferred moderation, but like Freeborn American, he knew that inaction would destroy the American cause. Finally, on November 1, 1768, pushed from outside and from below, Robert Morris and about two hundred other merchants penned an ultimatum to the merchants and manufacturers in England, urging them to engineer a repeal of the Townshend duties. If policies didn't change, they warned, "it is our serious and candid opinion, the commerce between G. Britain and her colonies must of necessary consequence, greatly diminish, and the general importation of goods generally cease."[36]

The merchants had planned to wait until March before making good on their thinly veiled threat, hoping that events on the other side of the Atlantic would render further action unnecessary. But on February 6, 1769, with a vessel waiting in port to receive their requisitions for the following fall, they decided at last to endorse a sweeping nonimportation agreement. Instead of placing the usual orders, they told their agents in Great Britain to hold off on all purchases save for a carefully selected list of exclusions vital to the health, welfare, and defense of the colonists: gunpowder, shot, lead, sailcloth, wool-shearing implements (to help colonials make their own cloth), medicines, salt, coal, and schoolbooks. If any other items found their way to the local marketplace, the merchants promised not to purchase them and to "dis-countinance such persons" who had imported them.[37]

Although the agreement of February 6 seemed forceful, it was still provisional, pending further news from London. Days passed, then weeks, without any additional word of Parliament's deliberations. While other Philadelphians waited, hoping that moderate voices in London would save moderate voices in Philadelphia the trouble of taking sides, Robert Morris made a decisive move on the personal front: he got married.

The well-to-do thirty-five-year-old bachelor, among the most eligible in town, chose for his bride twenty-year-old Mary White, "a most amiable and accomplished young lady" (according to the announcement in the *Pennsylvania Gazette*) and the daughter of Esther Newman and Thomas White, a prominent lawyer, surveyor, justice of the peace, and founding trustee of Benjamin Franklin's Academy and College of Philadelphia, later to become the University of Pennsylvania. Mary, known by her friends and family as Molly or Polly, was more firmly ensconced in Philadelphia society yet lower in fortune than her husband-to-be, so the match seemed mutually beneficial.[38]

Richard Peters, rector of Christ Church, married Robert and Mary in grand style. The first and largest Anglican Church in Pennsylvania provided a fitting venue. In marked contrast to Pennsylvania's simple Quaker meeting-houses or the stark Congregational structures of New England, this church, like Robert Morris and his bride, celebrated worldly extravagance. It showed no shame in lavish display, from the crimson velvet drapery of the organ gallery to the box pews fitted "with cushions, silk lace, crimson velvet, carpets, silver fringe, brass tack and hooks, green binding and tassels." Architecturally, it was the most ornate structure in the city, with numerous bays and arched windows, including the first known Palladian window in America. Its steeple dominated the Philadelphia skyline, and its eight tonal bells were the only ones in town that could play a tune, which they did on church days, market days, or whenever a visitor could wheedle a performance from the bell ringer.[39]

On March 2, 1769, those melodic bells rang for Philadelphia's fashionable new couple, Mr. and Mrs. Robert Morris. Exactly 292 days later, the statistically average time for human gestation, Mary gave birth to the Morrises' first child, Robert Jr.

But if Mary Morris hoped to live in the lap of luxury, she unfortunately would have to wait, for eight days into her marriage, on March 10, her husband and his fellow merchants finalized the critical nonimportation agreement of the Philadelphia merchants, long awaited by American patriots up and down the Atlantic coast. By the terms of the agreement, Morris had to abstain from purchasing fine imported goods for the new country mansion he and Mary hoped to build on the east bank of the Schuylkill River, three miles outside of town.

Further, as a member of the special Committee of Merchants, Morris was charged with determining who had violated the agreement, then dragging these miscreants to the Coffee House, where they would be asked to confess their sins and mend their ways. Should the offenders refuse, their names would be published in the local papers so patriotic Philadelphians might shun their business.

Morris and the Committee of Merchants also communicated with their London counterparts, who they hoped would apply pressure on Parliament. In April, they penned a letter with the usual complaint—Parliament was "depriving them of their property without their consent"—but by November, they were demanding not only an end to the Townshend duties, but a complete repeal of the 1766 Declaratory Act (which had asserted the supremacy of Parliament "in all cases whatever"), an end to abuses of multiple officeholders, and the termination of Admiralty Courts with no juries. By the time of the November letter, many moderates had resigned from the increasingly radical committee, but not Morris. Having affixed his name, he did not wish to weaken the impact of nonimportation through internal dissension.[40]

Morris had stretched to the outermost limits of his radicalism. If and when the Townshend Acts were repealed, he hoped to lay the matter to rest, resume normal trade, and enjoy the fruits of unencumbered prosperity. "Liberty" to this merchant prince was not some abstract ideal, but just another name for the good life, a worthy enough end in itself.

May 17–18, 1769: The Apollo Room, Raleigh Tavern, Williamsburg

By the spring of 1769, nonimportation agreements had been adopted in all major ports in the North as well as many lesser ports and inland towns—but the South had not yet signed on. Although Virginia and South Carolina had come out firmly in support of Boston's Circular Letter, they had not yet made the critical shift from resolutions and petitions to economic warfare, where the battle over the Townshend Acts was most likely to be won or lost. Developing a nonimportation plan would be particularly difficult in Virginia, where goods were imported not by centralized merchants in a handful of cities but by the planters themselves, at their own private docks spread up and down the inland waterways of the Chesapeake.

Enter George Washington, who cut his Revolutionary teeth by helping to organize a nonimportation agreement in the most populated British colony in North America. Having achieved renown as a military man, Washington now demonstrated he could work with others in common cause to achieve political goals.

As a representative in Virginia's lower legislative body, the House of Burgesses, Washington had been involved in politics for over a decade. In 1758, upon returning from duty in the French and Indian War, he ran for office, and treating his constituency to a grand election-day party (33 gallons of beer, 28½ gallons of wine, 40 gallons of "rum punch," and "1hhd [hogshead] & 1 barrell of punch, consisting of 26 gals. best Barbados rum [and] 12 lbs. s. refd. sugar"), he topped all candidates with 301 votes. Once elected, Washington was expected to represent his constituents' interests, dole out patronage, and help Virginia govern itself in all local matters; in return for his services, he would earn respect, deference, and some degree of power. Certainly, when he entered the political arena, Washington did not expect to engage in heated disputes with the British Parliament, and even during the Stamp Act controversy of 1765, when others stepped forward, he made no public pronouncements and engaged in no political acts.[41]

But by 1769, much had changed. Challenging Parliament had become a political routine throughout the colonies, and Washington suddenly jumped from the back of the line to the front. On April 5, having just received a copy of the Philadelphia merchants' nonimportation agreement, he forwarded it to his good friend and close neighbor George Mason, along with an accompanying note: "I think the scheme a good one, and that it ought to be tried here, . . . but how, & in what manner to begin the work, is a matter worthy of consideration." Because petitions had failed, Washington suggested, there remained but two options: first, nonimportation, and should that fail, a resort to military might:

> That no man shou'd scruple, or hesitate a moment to use a–ms in defence of so valuable a blessing, on which all the good and evil of life depends; is clearly my opinion; yet a–ms I wou'd beg leave to add, should be the last resource, the denier resort. Addresses to the throne, and remonstrances to Parliament, we have already, it is said, proved the inefficacy of; how far then their attention to our rights & privileges is to be awakened or alarmed by starving their trade and manufactures, remains to be tried.

There were "private as well as public advantages" to adopting a policy of nonimportation for Virginia, Washington continued. Many colonists were "considerably indebted to Great Britain," he admitted, and "a scheme of this sort will contribute more effectually than any other I can devise" to relieve that burden. Washington himself was no stranger to debt, having never recovered from his spending spree of the early 1760s, and speaking in the third person instead of the first, he elucidated the personal benefits that would accrue to people like himself:

> The extravagant & expensive man . . . is thereby furnished with a pretext to live within his bounds, and embraces it.—Prudence dictated economy to him before, but his resolution was too weak to put it in practice; for how can I, says he, who have lived in such a manner change my method? I am ashamed to do it: and besides, such an alteration in the system of my living, will create suspicions of a decay in my fortune, & such a thought the World must not harbour.[42]

A nonimportation agreement, in other words, would allow indebted planters, who otherwise would be viewed as parsimonious, to cut their expenses in the name of patriotism.

Prompted by these private advantages as well as the public good, George Washington and George Mason endeavored over the next few weeks to adapt the nonimportation plans of the northern colonies to the particular exigencies of Virginia: the institution of slavery and the decentralization of trade. The fifth measure in their draft for a nonimportation agreement stated: "That they will not import any slaves, or purchase any imported untill the said Acts of Parliament are repeal'd." This was spurred by practical rather than moral concerns, for if fewer slaves were imported, the slaves whom these men already possessed would be worth more money. Furthermore, importation of slaves into Virginia had the tendency to lower the price of tobacco, which of course the planters did not want. George Washington and George Mason were at this point protectionists, not abolitionists. They hoped to increase domestic production while decreasing dependence on imports, whether the items in question were wool, linen, or slaves. Their early "Buy American" program covered the gamut.[43]

To overcome the problem of decentralization, Washington and Mason hoped to present their plan to the House of Burgesses, a body that happened to include the colony's most influential planter-importers; if the Burgesses signed on, they reasoned, other planters would follow suit. So when Washington left Mount Vernon on April 30 to attend the regularly scheduled session of the House of Burgesses in Williamsburg, he carried with him a draft of a nonimportation agreement, based loosely on Philadelphia's model but with local adaptations.[44]

The House convened on May 8, and on May 16, having dispensed with matters of local concern, it decided "to consider the present state of the Colony." Everyone knew what this meant, and it took delegates little time to pass resolutions claiming that they alone had the right to tax their fellow Virginians and that no citizens could be transported out of the colony to stand trial. The following day at noon, Lord Botetourt, the royal governor, summoned the Burgesses to the Council chamber, just as Governor Bernard had done in Massachusetts, and with the same result: "Mr. Speaker, and gentlemen of the House of Burgesses," he said, "I have heard of your resolves, and augur ill of their effect. You have made it my duty to dissolve you; and you are dissolved accordingly."[45]

But the business of the burgesses had just begun. "Immediately, with the greatest order and decorum," they marched a few doors west on Duke of Gloucester Street to Anthony Hay's Raleigh Tavern, where they were welcomed by a wooden bust of the great pirate himself, Virginia's founder, who assured them, by his very presence, that the desire for wealth ran deep in their blood. Proceeding inside and to the rear of the building, they entered the Apollo Room, a spacious gathering place with large-paned windows on both sides, the finest Virginia pine wainscoting beneath whitewashed walls and ceiling, and a fireplace built for logs as big as a man. These Virginians were no strangers to the Raleigh Tavern, where they had dined and drunk and in some cases lodged whenever the House of Burgesses convened. For men who spent most of the year on isolated plantations, government time was also a social time, and in the Apollo Room, which hosted balls as well as meetings, they had come together on previous occasions to celebrate the joys and comforts of the good life.[46]

But now the chosen few of Virginia had serious business to transact. Although they no longer met as an officially sanctioned body, they elected a moderator, Peyton Randolph, who just happened to be speaker of the recently dissolved Assembly. After a general discussion of the merits of nonimportation, Randolph chose a committee to draw up an agreement, which would be presented to the whole body the following day. George Washington served on that committee, for he possessed the work in progress that he and George Mason and probably several others had already pieced together. Remaining at the Raleigh Tavern late into the evening on the night of May 17, 1769, the committee prepared the final draft. At ten o'clock the next morning, as planned, the draft was presented, discussed, amended, and in the end approved by the body of the whole. Historians have argued over the years about who was the real "author" of the Virginia Nonimportation Resolutions of 1769, but this argument misses the point. As with most political acts of the times, men discussed and wrote and revised their resolutions, then voted on them, often several times, until agreement was finally reached; in the end, the true authors were the aggregate of those who lent their names to the final document.[47]

July 22, 1769–December 13, 1770: Liberty Tree in Charleston

Henry Laurens and other proponents of nonimportation in South Carolina encountered a unique obstacle, the opposite of that faced by patriots in Virginia. Importation here was too centralized, not too diffuse, because most overseas trade was conducted by a handful of Scottish merchants or factors for London firms, who did not identify with the American cause. How could such men be induced to enter into a nonimportation agreement that interfered with their trade? Laurens, a novice at political organizing, had no idea of how to proceed, so he swallowed his pride and followed the leadership of that "very grand simpleton," Christopher Gadsden, who spearheaded the nonimportation movement in Charleston.

Born and bred like Laurens, but with a personality and political persuasion closer to that of Dr. Thomas Young, Christopher Gadsden pursued nonimportation with single-minded passion. After his wife, Mary, died in January 1769, he shocked Charleston society by appearing at the funeral in blue homespun rather than a traditional black mourning suit, which had to be imported from England. For the next several months, realizing that the merchants needed to be forced rather than persuaded into nonimportation, he garnered support for a nonconsumption agreement among mechanics and planters, who refused to do business with any merchants who imported British goods. This had the desired effect, and on July 7, the merchants themselves came out with their own version of a nonimportation agreement.

The two agreements did not totally mesh, however. Mechanics and planters, for instance, insisted on prohibiting the sale of mourning clothes, while the merchants, with large quantities already in stock, listed these as an exception. For two weeks the groups engaged in detailed negotiations, and finally, under the Liberty Tree on July 22, 1769, Gadsden read aloud the joint agreement, paragraph by paragraph. The people discussed and voted on each measure, and in the end, the joint agreement was approved and signed by 268 men, headed by members of the legislature. Then, in a unique move, the meeting appointed a committee to enforce the agreement, composed equally of 13 mechanics, 13 planters, and 13 merchants. The success of nonimportation, and later the Revolution itself, depended on alliances that transcended particular interests, but this was the first time such a notion was implemented on a formal basis.

In Charleston, an unincorporated city without any governmental structure of its own, the political assemblies under the Liberty Tree were beginning to serve a function similar to that of New England town meetings. In 1768, meeting announcements were addressed to "MECHANICS and many other inhabitants of this town." In September 1769, a newspaper announcement referred more broadly to a "General Meeting of INHABITANTS . . . at LIBERTY TREE," and at this meeting, citizens were expected not only to address nonimportation, but also "to consider of other Matters for the General Good." By 1770 those who attended the monthly Liberty Tree gatherings were referred to as "the body of the people," as in northern cities. Formerly, politics in Charleston had been considered the province of those with ample property, but now ordinary people who worked with their hands joined with their "betters." Equally important, politics moved outdoors, and, as it did, the nature of political authority changed. Now, when political leaders made decisions, they could not rely merely on their own best judgment; they required the support of the body of the people for both moral sanction and political heft. (Slaves, the majority of the population, were not included in the body of the people, nor were white women, although Christopher Gadsden tried to enlist female support. Because women had "the principle management" of household economies, he argued, the nonconsumption agreement could not succeed without them.)[48]

By 1769 Henry Laurens, despite his former misgivings, was participating in these Liberty Tree meetings, and by 1770, because of his prestige, he was actually chairing some of them. Just as he was warming to the spirit of collaborative political action in the public arena, however, an unexpected calamity occasioned a retreat into his own private sphere.

On April 26, 1770, Eleanor Laurens took to childbed, as she had done at least twelve times over the last twenty years, not always with happy results. (Four infants had died during or shortly after birth, two within a single year; another three of her offspring had died during early childhood.) After each delivery, Eleanor had been confined to her bed for long periods, sometimes mourning a lost infant, and always trying to mend her own body. This moment of birth again turned into a sad affair. On April 27, Henry wrote:

> Mrs. Laurens was delivered yesterday of a daughter—they say a child likely to live, but the doctor & the women about her report to me that there is a bare possibility of the mother's surviving seven days. This gloomy prospect distresses me beyond description & in such a manner as you cannot feel. I was waiting the happy issue of her late circumstance in order to go to England with Jack or at least as far as Philadelphia, pleasing myself with thoughts of leaving my other children under the care of a tender watchful mother to them, & a faithful friend in all respects to me. In an instant the scene is shifted; clouds rise thick before me & darken my path. In a few days I may be obliged to disperse my children & lodge them with strangers. What can be more mortifying to such a father![49]

In fact, Eleanor clung precariously to life for days and then weeks. Time and again during this period, writing to friends of the sad situation, Henry mentioned his thwarted plans to take fifteen-year-old John to England to continue his education. Henry was particularly enamored of John, the eldest son, smart and healthy, a companion, not merely a child. In him he vested his dreams and his family's future—more now than ever, it seemed.

Not that Henry didn't care for his wife as she hovered "on the brink of eternity." Two weeks after the birth, he wrote of his baby daughter, "I have been too deeply affected by the mother's great distress to take any notice of it." At one point, Laurens was "encouraged by the physicians to entertain strong hopes of her recovering her health again," but the hope did not last long, and his steady stream of letters revealed a continuing and deep concern for Eleanor's fate.[50]

On May 14, with Eleanor lying ill in her chamber, Laurens broke away from the sadness that surrounded his home to serve as chairman for the monthly assembly at the Liberty Tree. In the past, he had used every available excuse to withdraw from political turmoil, but now, although he had reason enough to keep to himself, he did not. Laurens knew that this would be a particularly important meeting, for word had just arrived that all the Townshend duties had been repealed except the tax on tea, and rumors were circulating that the northern cities were about to terminate their nonimportation agreements. Would South Carolina hold firm until every tax had been repealed, even the one on tea?

Henry Laurens felt strongly that it should, and his view prevailed. "I hope and believe," he wrote, that South Carolina's nonimportation agreement "will continue to subsist until the grievances which we justly complain of from the late Acts of Parliament for raising a revenue in America are *all* removed from us." For this man of principle, the notion that Parliament could levy *any* taxes on the Americans was the crux of the issue.[51]

Eleanor did not recover. When she died on May 22, Henry expressed his confused state of mind with touching sincerity:

> My anxiety is ripened into grief if I turn to the right hand or to the left hand. If I go here or there I find something or other to refresh my sorrow and feel that something which constituted my happiness is gone from me. A hearty submission to Gods will and even thankfulness for many undeserved past and present mercies are intermixed with my complaints. I look round upon my children. I lament their loss. I weep for my own. I bless God that I have such children and that I have bread for them & yet I weep. This is human, and it is a true picture of my heart.[52]

Through most of the summer, Henry did withdraw from public life, although he continued to keep up with his own business affairs. Then he started to rebound. On August 13, he wrote, "I am now but beginning to subdue the powers of grief which that melancholy event brought upon me & which had borne down like a mighty torrent." Nine days later, he again attended the monthly Liberty Tree meeting, and he was not a passive observer. In fact, he was appointed to a committee charged with visiting a conspicuous violator of the nonimportation agreement and informing him "how *odious* his conduct appeared to the inhabitants; and to *advise* and *admonish* him" to mend his ways. Like Robert Morris, Laurens had become an enforcer, and just as significantly, he had agreed to take orders from the body of the people, a notion he would have mocked a few years past.[53]

On August 25, Laurens wrote, "The people in this Province stand firm in their opposition to the ministerial plan for taxing America. I hope we shall have fortitude to continue so, for one year more at least." He continued to hold this view, even when many of his compatriots began to waver.[54]

On December 13, 1770, at an assembly under the Liberty Tree, Laurens was unanimously elected to serve as chairman. At the close of the proceedings, the people gave thanks to Colonel Henry Laurens for his "impartial and faithful conduct" as the group's leader. This was typical of such events, both in Charleston and elsewhere. The body of the people would choose a gentleman of high standing to chair their meeting, then offer him a token gesture of respect at the end. For Henry Laurens, this touch of deference no doubt helped smooth the transition from paternalistic to revolutionary politics.[55]

4

A Violent Turn

September 5, 1769: British Coffee House, Boston

By midsummer of 1769, patriots in every major port had entered into some form of nonimportation agreement. As during the Stamp Act resistance, all British-American colonies south of Quebec and north of recently acquired Florida had united in opposition to Parliamentary taxation.

Still, few Anglo-Americans at the time detected even a faint whiff of "independence" in the air, and if they did, it frightened them. The movement toward economic autonomy ran counter to the colonists' feelings of allegiance toward the Crown and all it represented. "Patriotism" in 1769 did not signify loyalty to America but loyalty to the British Empire and British liberties, along with an eagerness to ensure that those liberties extended to all British subjects, including those residing in North America. Neither John Wilkes, the outspoken MP from Middlesex, nor William Pitt, the great Whig politician, had ever set foot in the New World, but these two icons were the patriots most celebrated in the colonies.

How to challenge the authority of Parliament without appearing to rebel against Great Britain was no easy matter. James Otis Jr., America's home-grown patriotic celebrity, internalized this dilemma, and it tore him apart. Prone to manic episodes in any case, Otis became particularly agitated in the late summer of 1769, when newspapers published letters from the customs commissioners in Boston that accused him of making "threats against the Government" and speaking "disrespectfully and threateningly against the Governor." Otis took great personal affront because the commissioners, "without the least provocation or color, have represented me by name as inimical to the rights of the Crown, and disaffected to his Majesty, to whom I annually swear and am determined at all events to bear true and faithful allegiance."[1]

Otis's multiday rant started on Friday, September 1, when he stormed into the customs commissioners' office in the Concert Hall and insisted on a "free conversation" with each of them. At seven the following morning, in the British Coffee House on King Street, he "demanded satisfaction" of the two commissioners who met him there, and afterward, he sent one of them a note: "Mr. Birch, I have reason to think and take occasion to tell you that you are a poltroon and a scoundrel, J. Otis." The day after that, Sunday, John Adams noted of his mentor: "Otis talks all; he grows the most talkative man alive; no other gentleman in company can find a space to put in a word; as Dr. Swift expressed it, he leaves no elbow room. There is much sense, knowledge, spirit, and humor in his conversation; but he grows narrative, like an old man; abounds with stories." Then on Monday, in the *Boston Gazette*, Otis called the commissioners "superlative blockheads" and singled out John Robinson for particular abuse. "I have a natural right if I can get no other satisfaction to break his head," he declared.[2]

On Tuesday, September 5, Otis "strutted about the town, denouncing vengeance against the first commissioner" he might see. Having heard that Robinson had purchased a cane, he entered the same store and bought "the fellow of it." He then proceeded to the British Coffee House, where he sat down in the front room and waited to see if Robinson or any other commissioner might show up.[3]

Robinson arrived sometime between seven and eight P.M. Observing that Otis had no sword, he went to a back room and deposited his, which left the rivals armed only with swollen tempers and twin canes, recently purchased from the same store. As the quarreling men removed themselves to one of the private rooms to engage in their "free conversation," Robinson upped the ante according to the custom of his times: he tweaked Otis's nose, just as Henry Laurens had done to Daniel Moore, the South Carolina customs collector. Later, Robinson justified his nose tweaking in an open letter to Otis: "Your insult was public, and I determined to give you a public chastisement; but I did not attack you abruptly:—We had a parley together, and I attempted to take you by the nose, which, one would think, was a sufficient warning of what was to follow. What ensued served to balance our accompts."[4]

What *did* ensue?

That was hotly debated in the press for the next several weeks. Otis claimed that several of Robinson's friends ganged up on him, but according to Robinson, "No man besides myself struck Mr. Otis, nor even offered him the least unfair play." In any case, Otis was seriously battered, suffering a large gash in his forehead that bled profusely.[5]

Patriots wasted no time in capitalizing on the incident. Dr. Thomas Young, after he treated Otis's wounds, wrote immediately to his hero, John Wilkes:

> At present our chairman, the Hon. James Otis, Esq., lyes wounded and much bruised in a rencounter with the infamous, base and cowardly John Robinson, Comr., etc., who insulted and fell upon him last evening at the British Coffee house, and with the assistance of half a dozen or more such scoundrels as himself, nearly murdered him before he escaped their hands.[6]

Otis himself quickly labeled the event an attempted "assassination," and the *Boston Gazette* followed his lead. "Working the political engine," to use John Adams's phrase, editors Benjamin Edes and John Gill harped on the "assassination" theme for weeks. Samuel Adams, writing disingenuously as "An Impartialist," contended that the so-called assassination had been "a preconcerted plan" and that Otis's cut in the forehead had been administered by "an edged weapon," presumably a sword. Although James Otis's increasing mental instability had rendered him of marginal use to the patriots, he could now serve their cause as a martyr.[7]

Mercy Otis Warren was frightened by the initial report of her brother's ordeal, which had been somewhat exaggerated by the time it reached Plymouth. "I saw you fallen," she wrote him, "I saw your wife a widow, your children orphans . . . your country in tears." Then, after learning his life was in no grave danger, she scolded him. He should never again "give or receive a challenge" and never allow anyone to "ruffle or discompose him." Dueling was against "the law of reason and the laws of God as well as man," she said. Recognizing that Jemmy might be reluctant to heed the advice of his younger sister, she concluded: "You will excuse the freedom of my pen, when you consider it is held by one who has your welfare more at heart, after a very few exceptions, than that of any other person in the world."[8]

Jemmy, rebounding from his manic state, soon regretted not only the Robinson encounter, but the entire course of his political career. "I have done more mischief to my country than can be repaired," he wrote two months later. "I meant well but am convinced I was mistaken." Then, two months after that, he was off on another rant. On January 16, 1770, John Adams noted in his diary that Otis had just disrupted his political club once again with his compulsive "trash, obsceneness, profaneness, nonsense, and distraction." Adams felt pity, not anger: "Otis is in confusion yet; he loses himself; he rambles and wanders like a ship without a helm. . . . I fear he is not in his perfect mind. . . . I fear, I tremble, I mourn, for the man and for his country; many others mourn over him, with tears in their eyes."[9]

And it got even worse. On February 26, Adams wrote: "He has been, this afternoon, raving mad; raving against father, wife, brother, sister, friend, &c." On March 16, John Rowe recorded in his diary: "Mr. Otis got into a mad freak to night & broke a great many windows in the Town House." And on April 22, Rowe noted: "This afternoon Mr. Otis behaved very madly, firing guns out of his window that caused a large number of people to assemble about him."[10]

Her brother's insanity, now transparent, troubled Mercy Otis Warren on several levels. Like Adams, she felt pity, but she also mourned the loss of rationality itself. For this fervent student of the Enlightenment, "reason" was both the defining principle of the universe and God's special gift to mankind. The fact that her brother had gone mad inspired Warren to celebrate the rational mind in verse:

**A Thought on the inestimable Blessing of Reason,
occasioned by its privation to a friend of very superior talents and virtues.**

> *What is it moves within my soul,*
> *And as the needle to the pole*
> *Directs me to the final cause*
> *The central point of nature's laws?*
> *'Tis reason, Lord, which thou has given*
> *A ray divine, let down from Heaven,*
> *A spark struck from effulgent light,*
> *Transcendant, clear,—divinely bright,*
> *Thou hast bestow'd lest man should grope*
> *In endless darkness, void of hope.*[11]

Shortly after James lost his political effectiveness, Mercy gained hers. For all her misgivings about "warring passions" and "endless strife," she would soon join the cause, trying, like her brother James, to keep to the high moral ground, but also, like him, plunging to the plains below more often than she would care to admit.

January 17–19, 1770: Faneuil Hall and
Thomas Hutchinson's House, Boston

Thomas Young was not haunted by the hesitations that plagued James Otis.
Now that resistance to the Townshend Acts had expanded from Massachusetts to the other colonies, Young urged his fellow patriots to seize the moment and force the issue. On June 30, 1769, with the nonimportation
movement at its zenith, Young wrote to Hugh Hughes, a fellow activist from
the New York Sons of Liberty: "This is the critical moment to play off the
whole force of America in every shape it can safely be exerted, to shew a despicable ministry how little they have to expect from a continuance of their
absurd and villainous measures."[12]

Young and his fellow activists in Boston were taking the notion of the body
of the people to a new level. In 1768, patriots had transformed the original merchants' organization, the Boston Society for Encouraging Trade and Commerce,
into the Merchants and Traders of Boston, which opened its membership to
small traders and even artisans who had been excluded by the BSETC. Then, in
January of 1770, the group broadened its base still wider, welcoming virtually
every citizen in town. The *Boston Gazette* explained why the merchants' trade
organization could become so inclusive: since "the Town itself subsists by
trade, . . . every inhabitant may be considered as connected with it." In its
new incarnation, the group became known as the Body of the Trade, or often
simply the Body. Gathering en masse in the large meeting room that Peter
Faneuil had constructed above his marketplace back in 1742 (the building
was gutted by a fire in 1761 but quickly resurrected), the Body—the voice
of the people—imbued the nonimportation movement with both heft and
legitimacy.[13]

Thomas Young savored these mass meetings at Faneuil Hall, in which
people like him, with little property but lots to say, freely participated. This
"school of political learning" was even better than the gallery in the Assembly
chamber, which he had praised so highly upon his arrival in Boston, for at
Faneuil Hall, ordinary people not only listened but talked. Writing to Hughes
in New York, he said:

> Often have I wished the deliberations of the people in your City could
> be conducted in the manner ours are in this. What a noble school is our
> spacious hall where the meanest [poorest] citizen ratable at £20 beside

the poll, may deliver his sentiments and give his suffrage in very important matters, as freely as the greatest Lord in the Land!¹⁴

Here's how the Body worked:

At Faneuil Hall on January 17, it decided to send a delegation of five men,
headed by William Molineux (a petty merchant turned political activist) and
accompanied by everyone else present—more than one thousand people—to
have a few words with William Jackson, one of the most obstinate nonsub-
scribers to a newly revised nonimportation agreement.

The next day, the Body reconvened to consider the case of merchants
Thomas and Elisha Hutchinson, Thomas Hutchinson's sons, who wanted to
sell tea, now that the old agreement had expired. Samuel Adams thought the
Body should visit the Hutchinson brothers all together, as they had done with
Jackson, and the town clerk, William Cooper, added that Boston must act
decisively to preserve its reputation with patriots elsewhere. But a young lawyer named Josiah Quincy Jr. noted that Thomas and Elisha lived with their
father, who had been serving as His Majesty's governor since Francis Bernard
had been recalled to London the previous summer, and that marching as the
Body to the governor's home might be considered high treason. James Otis was
asked for his legal opinion on the matter, but his response was incoherent.

Then the firebrands stepped in—William Molineux and Thomas Young.
Molineux said he was willing to risk being branded a traitor, for marching as
the Body was the only means to exert sufficient influence. Finally the country
doctor from the Oblong, addressing a packed house of politically astute Bostonians, delivered the most treasonous argument of the day. As paraphrased
by an observer, Young believed that "it was high time for people to take the
Govermt into their own hands to whom it properly belonged."¹⁵

And Young went one step further: "Such people as counteracted the general measures should be depriv'd of existence," he reportedly said. This was
not just a hotheaded outburst delivered in the heat of the moment. Four
months earlier, Young had quoted John Locke approvingly on the front page
of the *Boston Gazette*: whoever "takes away my liberty," Locke and Young
both reasoned, "has put himself into a state of war with me, . . . and therefore
it is lawful for me to . . . kill him if I can."¹⁶

We have no way of ascertaining how many agreed with Young's extreme
position, but we do know that action prevailed over caution. With Molineux
and his committee at the head, the Body filed out of Faneuil Hall and walked
to Garden Court Street in the North End, where a more unruly crowd had

ransacked Thomas Hutchinson's mansion a few years earlier. Thomas Young wrote a detailed, firsthand account of the encounter:

> They [the committee] proceeded first to the house of his honor the Lt. Gov. the residence of Messrs. T. & E. Hutchinson, followed by a body of 12 or 14 hundred men who marched in the most decent order, and ranged themselves before the gate, while the committee went in and knocked at the door. On this a sash was thrown up and his honor with his sons and his family promiscuously looked out. The committee posted themselves in order near the window, and his honor with an affected surprise says, Gentlemen, what means all this?
>
> Mr. Molineau answered, we have business with your two sons, and if your honor will please to admit us into your house I will communicate it.
>
> With a solemn shake of the head his honor replied, by no means!
>
> Mr. Molineau said he was sorry they were not that worthy to enter his door.
>
> His honor replied they cou'd not wonder he was backward to open his door when they considered what he had suffered 5 years ago from such an appearance.[17]

Arguments and negotiations commenced, with Hutchinson defending the actions of his sons from the window, the committee responding from below, and the Body lurking by the gate. After considerable back-and-forth, Hutchinson tried to pull rank. Young's account continues:

> He then putting himself into an important attitude said, Gentlemen, I am by the office I sustain, obliged to tell you, I highly disapprove of your conduct. When I was attacked before I was a private person, I am now the representative of the greatest monarch upon earth, whose majesty you affront in thus treating my person. . . . You are very near upon committing the highest crime in the state, and it is from a regard to you and this my native country that I enjoin you to separate and disperse.

Ignoring Hutchinson's ultimatum, the committee addressed his sons directly but could not get them to relent.

On January 19 at 10:00 A.M., for the third day in a row, the Body convened at Faneuil Hall to consider its next step in the Hutchinson affair. No further action was required, however, for the moderator announced at the outset that

Acting Governor Thomas Hutchinson, out of "great concern for the uneasiness of the people," had decided to ask his sons to deliver up the tea they had intended to sell. Years later, in his *History of Massachusetts-Bay*, Hutchinson said he had "reason to repent" his "concession," for he had been "triumphed over." He felt "more trouble and distress of mind from this error," he confessed, than "from the loss and damage to his private fortune" when his house and property had been destroyed by the mob of August 26, 1765.[18]

To triumph over their long-standing adversary, who now represented the Crown's authority in Massachusetts, was a great victory for the patriots, but for Thomas Young personally, the *process* was as significant as the *result*. Ordinary citizens, working in common cause, were taking public affairs into their own hands, as they should. Although their enemies tried to dismiss patriot leaders as self-serving demagogues and their followers as mindless sheep, Young painted a very different picture of political processes within Boston's resistance movement. All worked together for the general good, he wrote, with self-interest universally eschewed:

> No man among us esteems himself of consequence enough to trouble the public for any length of time with any thing barely relative to himself. The real subject matter, and that of public concernment, must engage the tongues and pens of our public declaimers, otherwise we shall soon be called to order, and with a good degree of becoming severity.

Best of all, plain people like himself were not only participating but driving the political agenda. "Many common tradesmen in this town display the wisdom and eloquence of Athenian Senators," he wrote. This was the sort of political leveling that would lead in the end to modern democracies, and Thomas Young, with a heightened and perhaps exaggerated sense of historical purpose, felt very proud to be a part of it all.[19]

January 17, 1770: Liberty Pole and Golden Hill, New York City; March 5–6, 1770: King Street and the Town House, Boston

In January 1770, while Boston's Body met at Faneuil Hall and marched to the homes and shops of recalcitrant merchants, patriots in New York engaged in a different sort of battle. Although they, too, leaned on obstinate merchants, their chief antagonists were British soldiers, who had been billeted in the city at public expense since the time of the French and Indian War. Not only did the Redcoats signify a repression of liberty, but in their off hours, off-duty soldiers engaged in two activities that enraged New York patriots: they competed with local sailors for work along the waterfront, and they hatched schemes to cut down the Liberty Pole.

New York patriots had erected their first Liberty Pole on the Commons in 1766 to celebrate the repeal of the Stamp Act, but soldiers in the nearby barracks quickly cut it down, causing patriots to erect a new one, which of course the soldiers then destroyed, and so on. Following this tradition, at eight o'clock on Saturday evening, January 13, 1770, a group of soldiers placed some powder in the fourth incarnation of New York's Liberty Pole. After the fuse to the powder fizzled, frustrated soldiers raided a nearby den of taunting patriots, Montagne's Tavern, breaking lamps and bowls and eighty-four panes of glass windows.

This triggered a weeklong series of violent if somewhat farcical confrontations between soldiers and patriots. Subsequent assaults on the Liberty Pole also failed, but at one o'clock Wednesday morning, after the patriots had relaxed their guard, soldiers cut down the icon once again, sawed it to pieces, and spread the remains at the doorway to Montagne's Tavern.[20]

The next day at the site of the ravaged pole, an estimated three thousand people gathered to seek revenge. They captured two soldiers, and when other Redcoats attempted to release the prisoners, the crowd turned on them as well, chasing them along the waterfront and up a gentle rise known as Golden Hill, named for the rich grain that once had grown there. When a new group of Redcoats came to rescue those who were being pursued, the crowd tried to hold them off with fists, rocks, clubs, and wooden staves grabbed from nearby sleighs, while the troops, still vastly outnumbered, wielded cutlasses and bayonets. Patriotic New Yorkers later dubbed this melee the Battle of Golden Hill and called it the first battle of the American Revolution.

Politically, patriots prevailed in the Battle of Golden Hill. The image of armed Redcoats battling ordinary citizens was easily exploited in news accounts that circulated throughout the colonies. In addition, patriots finally discovered an answer to the Liberty Pole dilemma: they encased their next pole in an iron cage so soldiers could not cut it down.

In Boston, two regiments of British troops, approximately one thousand strong, had occupied the town since September 1768, with the ill-concealed mission of keeping the patriots in check—"to quell their seditious spirits," as Thomas Young complained in the *Boston Gazette*. When the *Gazette* published a lengthy firsthand account of New York's Battle of Golden Hill on February 19, 1770, many Bostonians, not to be outdone by New Yorkers, stepped up their individual and collective taunting of the soldiers.[21]

The mood of the times was already confrontational. On successive Thursdays in February, the 8th, 15th, and 22nd, patriots staged demonstrations outside the shops of several merchants whom they claimed were violating the agreement. Giant wooden hands, painted with the word IMPORTER, pointed accusatively at the recalcitrants. Thursdays were marketing days, with farmers streaming into town, people milling about, and boys let out of school, so these public displays assumed a raucous, undisciplined tone.

On the 22nd, a former customs official and informer named Ebenezer Richardson tried to remove the giant hand in front of the shop of his neighbor Theophilus Lillie. When a youthful and rowdy crowd chased Richardson into his home, he opened his window and fired a shot into the swarm of assailants to scare them off, but the shot did more than intimidate: it killed an eleven-year-old boy named Christopher Seider, son of German immigrants. Richardson himself was then mobbed and might have been hanged on the spot had not William Molineux and other influential patriots prevailed upon the crowd to jail him and do things legally instead.

The following Monday, February 26, young Christopher Seider received the sort of funeral generally reserved for deceased individuals of higher standing: two thousand to three thousand mourners in grand procession, led by five hundred boys marching in pairs. "My eyes never beheld such a funeral," John Adams commented in his diary. "The procession extended further than can be well imagined. This shows there are many more lives to spend, if wanted, in the service of their country. It shows, too, . . . that the ardor of the people is not to be quelled by the slaughter of one child."[22]

Schoolboys and apprentices, unwilling to settle back into their daily lives after the funeral, instead lashed out at the most visible symbols of oppression: British Redcoats. Soldiers could not be seen in public without being jeered. Skirmishes continued through the week, and on Friday and Saturday, fights broke out between rope makers and soldiers who competed for their jobs.

On Monday evening, March 5, a sentry outside the Customs House on King Street, opposite the Town House, hit a boy who had been hurling abuses at him, which caused other boys nearby to join against the soldier, which caused the soldier to call for help from a half dozen other Redcoats who were on guard that night, which of course caused the crowd to grow and become even more animated. Around eight o'clock, somebody sounded the fire bell.

A good portion of Boston's population flocked into the streets, listened to rumors and spread them, and trod this way and that through snow and ice, by the light of a quarter moon, trying to figure out what was happening.

Dr. Thomas Young stationed himself on Royal Exchange Lane, at the edge of the King Street crowd, apparently as confused as everyone else. Signaling mixed messages, he sported a sword in his hand while telling others "it was best for us to go home," since the soldiers, who had "made a rumpus," were now "gone to their barracks"—this according to a firsthand witness, James Brewer, himself an ardent Son of Liberty. Young himself stayed close to the heart of the action, while the plaza on King Street between the Customs House and the Town House filled with people.[23]

Soldiers stationed in Boston were accustomed to receiving taunts like "damned rascally scoundrel lobster son of a bitch," and they were under strict orders not to respond with firearms. But on this particular occasion, shortly after nine, as frozen snowballs and slabs of ice pummeled them, and the crowd kept growing and pushing, and haughty boys dared the troops to fire, one finally did.[24]

After a short pause, other soldiers followed with shots of their own.

When smoke from the muskets had cleared, five men had been killed or mortally wounded (James Caldwell, a mariner; Samuel Grey, one of the rope makers who had quarreled with British soldiers a few days earlier; Crispus Attucks, part Indian and perhaps part African, a six-foot-two sailor and waterfront laborer; Patrick Carr, an Irish leather worker; and Samuel Maverick, a seventeen-year-old apprentice to an ivory turner), while another six had received serious wounds.

The following day, several thousand people gathered at an emergency town meeting in Faneuil Hall to issue an ultimatum to Acting Governor Thomas Hutchinson: the two British regiments that had been occupying Boston must leave. A committee of fifteen, chosen to deliver this message, marched over to the Town House, past the fieldpiece that guarded the entrance, and up to the Council Chamber, where Hutchinson was meeting with his Council. By the time the committee arrived, Hutchinson and the Council had already been warned by Boston's selectmen that "the minds of the inhabitants are considerably disturbed" and that "unless the troops should be removed, the most terrible consequences were to be expected." Even the justices of the peace from the neighboring towns, a more conservative group, had cautioned Hutchinson and the Council "that it would not be possible to keep the people under restraint, if the troops remained in town."[25]

Rather than concede, Hutchinson passed off the decision to the military officer in charge of the troops, Lieutenant Colonel William Dalrymple, who agreed to remove one of the units immediately and wait for orders from his superiors concerning the other. The committee took this compromise back to the town meeting, which by then had moved to Old South Meeting House, the largest church in town, to accommodate more people. There, the body of the people wasted little time in rejecting Dalrymple's proposal by a vote of four thousand to one. When a smaller committee of seven returned to the Council Chamber that afternoon and presented the people's ultimatum a second time, the Council unanimously advised Hutchinson to advise Dalrymple to comply, which he did.[26]

In his *History*, Hutchinson reported that Samuel Adams, chairman of the committee, said to Dalrymple "that if he could remove the 29th regiment, he could remove the 14th also, and it was at his peril to refuse it." Although this incident is often cited to demonstrate the immense personal power of Samuel Adams, it was not Adams himself who caused Hutchinson, his Council, and Dalrymple to relent, but the message he carried from the body of the people, and their fears of what the crowd might do next. The day before, rioters had gathered outside the Council Chamber window, just a few feet away, when the soldiers opened fire. Now, should their ultimatum be ignored, they would undoubtedly be there again, in far greater numbers, with nothing but mischief on their minds.[27]

Previously, royal governors had issued proclamations and decrees from the balcony in the Council Chamber—a single ruler, standing above, telling his people, standing below, how to behave. But that relationship had changed over the previous decade: the people below were now telling the men above what to do.

March 6, 1770–March 5, 1771: Manufactory House and the Streets of Boston

Mercy Otis Warren did not approve of the March 5 riot. "These sudden popular commotions are seldom to be justified, and their consequences are ever to be dreaded," she later wrote in her *History*. Only by the intervention of "a number of influential gentlemen"—men of her own class—was "the populace" prevented from perpetrating further violence.[28]

John Adams, the defense attorney for Captain Thomas Preston, the British officer in charge of the soldiers who fired, called the crowd "a motley rabble

Figure 6. Henry Pelham's depiction of the Boston Massacre. Pelham's drawing served as the model for Paul Revere's famous and influential engraving of the same scene.

of saucy boys, negroes and molattoes, Irish teagues and outlandish jack tars," and he singled out for particular abuse Crispus Attucks, "a stout molatto fellow, whose very looks was enough to terrify any person," and "whose mad behaviour, in all probability, the dreadful carnage of that night, is chiefly to be ascribed."[29]

Even so, the fact that British Redcoats had gunned down some apprentices, sailors, and mulattoes afforded great potential for propaganda. The victims, however lowly, suddenly became martyred heroes. On Thursday, three days after the killings, Boston's shops closed down while the "unfortunate sufferers" were carried to their graves in a funeral even larger than that for Christopher Seider. The *Boston Gazette* carefully noted that the procession was anchored by "a long train of carriages belonging to the principal gentry of the Town."[30]

The moral of the affair, the *Gazette* continued, was simple: "The Town of Boston affords a recent and melancholy demonstration of the destructive consequences of quartering troops among citizens in a time of peace, under a pretence of supporting the laws and aiding civil authority." Taking this message to the world, patriots gathered depositions from witnesses who laid all blame clearly on the soldiers, published these statements in a pamphlet they titled *A Short Narrative of the Horrid Massacre in Boston*, then dispatched it throughout the colonies and across the Atlantic to London.

The multitalented and enterprising patriot Paul Revere, sensing that a picture would be worth a thousand words, engraved, printed, and sold large quantities of a colorful, graphic image depicting "The BLOODY MASSACRE perpetrated on King Street, BOSTON, on March 5th, 1770, by a party of the 29th Regt." (He based his engraving on a drawing by Henry Pelham, who complained to Revere that he had been wronged "as truly as if you had plundered me on the public highway.") Taking considerable liberty with the facts, Revere portrayed the crowd as respectable burghers, with nary a sailor or a mulatto among them. While John Adams blamed the whole affair on Crispus Attucks, Revere thought it best to leave him out.[31]

The timing of the Boston Massacre, a tragedy but also a boon for the patriots, proved fortuitous, for on the same day that Redcoats spilled blood, Parliament passed a bill that threatened to destroy the resistance movement in America: it repealed most but not all of the Townshend duties. Although the repeal appeared as a major triumph for the nonimportation movement, Parliament had insisted on maintaining the tax on tea, more for principle than for revenue: "I am clear that there must always be one tax to keep up the right," King George III wrote to his new Prime Minister, Lord North, "and as such I approve of the tea duty."[32]

Half a year before the repeal, Thomas Young had pronounced that the "whole force of America" could be brought to bear against "a despicable ministry," but partial repeal of the Townshend duties drove a wedge between those who wanted to continue with nonimportation until the final tax had been removed (radicals, philosophical purists, and most artisans) and those who wished to use the limited victory as an occasion to end the disruptions in trade (moderates, pragmatists, and most merchants).[33]

In Boston, the latter group broke from the Body to form its own organization of "real merchants," and this caused Young and the radicals to rely more exclusively on intimidation by crowds to achieve their goals. In June, "attended by hundreds of men and boys," Thomas Young visited the store of the McMaster brothers and commanded them "in a magisterial tone" to shut their business and leave town within three days. In July, "one of our most bawling demagogues . . . a crazy doctor" (as one of his enemies once called him) led a parade through town in support of the plan to send all imported goods back to England. As Young himself described it, the procession

> was proceeded by the cryer and a french horn, and immediately followed by two drums, the most respectable North End sons, being principal tradesmen, &c: to these succeeded two pair of colors & two more drums, and thus proceeded the whole length of the town, the cryer proclaiming at every corner, *The voice of the Trade and the People will be attended to this afternoon at three oClock—Now is the Crisis—Will you be enslaved by a handful of importers, yea or nay?* [34]

By August of 1770, Young had established for himself a coveted place on Thomas Hutchinson's short list of unwanted rabble-rousers, side by side with Hutchinson's nemesis and Young's mentor, Samuel Adams. "The infamous Molineux and Young, with [William] Cooper [the Town Clerk], Adams, and two or three more, still influence the mob, who threaten all who import," Hutchinson wrote to former governor Francis Bernard. The "infamous" Young wore his notoriety as a badge of honor. Thinking that he might someday become the object of harsh reprisals, he allowed his imagination to run rampant:

> To send for Adams, Cushing, Brattle, Molineau, Young, Hancock, Cooper &c to throw them all into the black hole together, to bring them out gagged, & hang them in a row at Tyburn, would only raise a thousand heads in place of each, who like young Hannibal, would swear by all the Gods never to rest satisfied while the shadow of a tyrant profaned any corner of that Empire.[35]

But for all their bravado, Thomas Young and his fellow radicals were losing the battle to continue nonimportation. In New York City, as in Boston, patriots had split into opposing organizations upon hearing the news of partial repeal. At noon on Saturday, July 7, radicals met at City Hall and proceeded in the usual manner to march through town, hooting and hissing at the doors of their opponents. This time, however, a different crowd formed to confront

them, and when the two groups met at Wall Street, the war of words escalated into a war of canes and clubs, and the radicals, who had habitually
thrived on force, lost. Two days later, New York's merchants voted to end
nonimportation, except on tea.[36]

In Philadelphia, Robert Morris, Thomas Willing, and other moderates
managed at last to wrest control of the Committee of Merchants from the
radicals, and they ended nonimportation for all items except tea. The defection of both New York and Philadelphia dealt the terminal blow to nonimportation in Boston, and by the fall of 1770, when the Body stopped meeting
at Faneuil Hall, patriot activists like Thomas Young no longer drove the political agenda.

Although in retreat, these diehards continued to use theater and oratory to
remind the public that "liberty" had by no means been secured. On March 5,
1771, the first anniversary of the Boston Massacre, dedicated patriots transformed Paul Revere's house in the North End into "a very striking exhibition"
to commemorate the tragic affair. Contemporary newspapers described the
display in vivid detail:

> At one of the chamber-windows was the appearance of the ghost of the
> unfortunate young Seider, with one of his fingers in the wound, endeav-
> oring to stop the blood issuing therefrom: Near him his friends weeping:
> And at a small distance a monumental obelisk, with his bust in front:—
> On the Front of the pedestal, were the names of those killed on the 5th
> of March: Underneath the following lines: "Seider's pale ghost fresh-
> bleeding stands, / And vengeance for his death demands." In the next
> window were represented the soldiers drawn up, firing at the people as-
> sembled before them—the dead on the ground, and the wounded fall-
> ing, with the blood running in streams from their wounds—over which
> was wrote, FOUL PLAY. In the third window, was the figure of a
> woman, representing AMERICA, sitting on the stump of a tree, with a
> staff in her hand, and the cap of Liberty on the top thereof,—one foot
> on the head of a grenadier lying prostrate grasping a serpent,—her finger
> pointing to the tragedy.[37]

For the evening's climax, at the Manufactory House for the poor—a building
that patriots had once defended against British soldiers who sought to turn
the place into barracks—Dr. Thomas Young delivered a patriotic oration.
Young's speech set a powerful precedent: for the following decade, until superceded by Fourth of July celebrations, patriots commemorated the anniver-

sary of the Boston Massacre like no other day in the year, replacing the festivals of both August 14, the anniversary of the first Stamp Act demonstration, and March 18, the anniversary of the Stamp Act's repeal, and surpassing in vigor the annual Pope's Day events of November 5. Each Massacre celebration was highlighted by an official oration, delivered in subsequent years by such prominent patriots as John Hancock and Joseph Warren. Today, it is difficult for us to grasp the importance of these speeches, but at a time when public orations were perceived as politics, art, and sport rolled into one, the Massacre Oration was quite the event.

Although future Massacre Orations were put into print and sold throughout America, the first one, delivered by Young, was not. From accounts at the time, however, we know that he held forth in much the usual manner, recounting the massacre and discoursing on the nature of treason. But Thomas Young went one step beyond the habitual harangue and issued a dire warning that many in the audience might have dismissed as characteristic excess, a "Youngism": he warned that the British ministry was on the verge of revoking the Massachusetts Charter.

This was no excess, for Lord North's ministry was in fact contemplating just such a move. Three years later, it did annul the charter, and that's what triggered the people of Massachusetts, unified as never before, to throw off British rule in its entirety.

Fall 1770: Ohio Country

If Parliament bowed to economic pressure in repealing most of the Townshend duties, that pressure did not come from Virginia, where imports from England and Scotland actually increased in 1769 and rose to record levels in 1770. No matter how rigorously George Washington, George Mason, and other public-spirited planters adhered to Virginia's nonimportation agreement, the decentralization of commerce in the Chesapeake region prohibited the application of coercive measures used in port cities.[38]

For Washington personally, nonimportation had produced some positive effects. It disciplined his excessive spending habits, but beyond that, it linked his private life with the public good and introduced him to the language and dynamics of collective political protest. But nonimportation did not address Washington's main issues, both financial and political. What mattered most to Washington was his investment in western lands, placed beyond his reach by the Proclamation of 1763.

That impediment was not necessarily permanent, however. A single pronouncement emanating from the far side of the Atlantic would not suffice to keep Anglo-Americans out of the West, and Washington knew it. In September 1767, hearing that negotiations were already under way with Iroquois Indians to open up sections of the West for white settlement, he initiated a correspondence with William Crawford, a former officer in his regiment during the French and Indian War who had moved illegally with his family across the Appalachian divide. "I can never look upon that Proclamation in any other light (but this I say between ourselves) than as a temporary expedient to quiet the minds of the Indians & must fall of course in a few years," he wrote. "Any person therefore who neglects the present opportunity of hunting ou[t] good lands & in some measure marking & distinguishing them for their own (in order to keep others from settling them) will never regain it."

Hoping to position himself at the front of the line, he made Crawford a proposition:

> If therefore you will be at the trouble of seeking out the lands I will take upon me the part of securing them so soon as there is a possibility of doing it & will moreover be at all the cost & charges of surveying patenting &ca after which you shall have a reasonable proportion of the whole as we may fix upon at our first meeting. . . .
>
> A tract to please me must be rich (of which no person can be a better judge than yourself) & if possible be go[od] level; Coud such a piece of land as this be found you woud do me a singular favour in falling upon some method to secure it immediately from the attempts of any other as nothing is more certain than that the lands cannot remain long ungranted when once it is known that righ[ts] are to be had for them. . . .
>
> I would recommend it to you to keep this whole matter a profound secret, or trust it only with those in whom you can confide & can assist you in bringing it to bear by their discoveries of land and this advice proceeds from several very good reasons, and in the first place because I might be censurd for the opinion I have given in respect to the Kings Proclamation & then if the scheme I am now proposing to you was known it might give alarm to others & by putting them upon a plan of the same nature (before we coud lay a proper foundation for success ourselves) set different interests a clashing and very probably overturn the whole.

Washington's letter, replete with additional details and requests, specified the exact manner in which Crawford might keep the matter under "silent management": he should travel "under the pretence of hunting other game which you may I presume effectually do at the same time you are in pursuit of land."[39]

Crawford accepted: "I shall heartly imbrass your offer upon the terms you proposed," he wrote back, for he had already entertained "the same sceem in my head." In fact, he had already been approached by others with similar offers, but he did not know "in home [whom] I cold confide, and one hos intrust cold answear my ends and there own." Crawford did trust his former commander. Their minds traveled the same trails, down to the level of the "hunting sceem, which I intend befor you wrote me."[40]

The following spring, Crawford visited Mount Vernon to share the results of his search and collect some money, and that fall, at Fort Stanwix (now Rome, New York), Iroquois Indians ceded lands west of the Appalachians and south of the Ohio River, covering most of present-day West Virginia and parts of Kentucky and southwestern Pennsylvania. From the standpoint of most Indians residing within and proximate to the region, the Iroquois, who lived primarily to the North, had no right to make such a treaty, but even so, from the British point of view, the lands that interested George Washington could now be opened to sale and settlement.[41]

These lands interested others as well. In 1769, Daniel Boone made his first trek through the Cumberland Gap, in the southern part of the region. Thousands of others flocked west that year, and even Catharine Macaulay, the British historian so popular in America, announced she would like to end her days on the banks of the Ohio. Meanwhile, some of the most prominent men in England joined with Benjamin Franklin and other investors from America to seek 2,400,000 acres of the ceded territory.[42]

Responding to the competition quickly, Washington filed for the parcels that Crawford had located and pursued the bounty land from his service in the French and Indian War. He petitioned the Virginia Council to deed the two hundred thousand acres promised to himself and his soldiers, and when their petition was approved, the veterans gathered in Fredericksburg and asked their former commander to venture into the Ohio Valley and find the best available tracts, which they would then distribute among them. Once again, the former surveyor for the Ohio Company would be heading west to delineate and acquire land, this time without any resistance from the French.

On October 5, 1770, Washington embarked on his journey, traveling up the Potomac, across the divide near its northern fork, and then to Crawford's place, where his host showed him the land he had staked out on Washington's behalf. From there, Washington and Crawford proceeded to Fort Pitt (formerly Fort Duquesne), outfitted their party of eight, hired some Indian guides, and started down the Ohio River in a large canoe.[43]

After only two days on the river, Washington noted in his journal: "We received the disagreeable news of two traders being killed at a Town call'd the Grape Vine Town, 38 miles below this; which caus'd us to hesitate whether we shoud proceed or not, and wait for further intelligence." The following day this report was amended—only one person had been killed—and two days after that, they learned "the trader was not kill'd, but drownd in attempting to ford the Ohio." These sorts of rumors were commonplace in the borderlands: any tragedy was magnified in the telling, and blame was generally laid on Indians.[44]

On October 28, the group ran into an Indian hunting party led by a Seneca named Kiashuta (or Kiasutha or Guyasuta), who had accompanied Washington during his excursion in the Ohio in 1753. "Here we were under a necessity of paying our compliments," Washington jotted in his journal. This slowed the trip down, causing Washington to complain about the delay. "After much councelling the overnight, they all came to my fire the next morning, with great formality. . . . The tedious ceremony which the Indians observe in their councellings and speeches, detain us til 9 Oclock," he wrote. Like other Anglo-Americans who coveted the Ohio countryside, Washington viewed Indians as "tedious" impediments to his plans, even when they offered no armed resistance.[45]

Yet Indian presence in the Ohio could not be ignored. As the party made its way back upriver, more slowly of course than the trip downstream, Washington summarized the attitude of Native American peoples he had encountered along the way:

> The Indians who live upon the Ohio (the upper parts of it at least) are composed of Shawnas, Delawares, and some of the Mingos, who getting but little part of the consideration that was given for the lands eastward of the Ohio, view the settlement of the people upon this river with an uneasy and jealous eye, . . . notwithstanding the cessation of the Six Nation's [Iroquois] thereto.[46]

Washington returned safely to Mount Vernon on December 1, his mission accomplished. Eventually he would gain title to about 40,000 acres for his military service—28,000 in his own right, and another 12,000 by buying out other veterans—so in the end, the French and Indian War produced some personal dividends.[47]

But his land came at a price. If in 1770 Indians of the Upper Ohio flashed a "jealous eye" at a handful of white intruders, how might they react once many more thousands had encroached upon their domain? A dozen years later, after being pursued by various parties of vigilantes and soldiers, some authorized by Washington himself, would they not wish to exact a gruesome revenge?

William Crawford did not want to know the answer to this last question.

May 16, 1771: Alamance Creek, North Carolina; July 1772: The Catamount Tavern, Vermont

The first decade of resistance to imperial policies had been marked by various applications of intimidation and symbolic violence, but outright violence had been limited to personal beatings and an occasional tarring and feathering. When colonists in North America protested or even rioted, they were operating within a long and well-established British tradition: the lower orders could vent their anger, so long as they stopped short of armed insurrection or the taking of human life. In this vein, colonists hanged or burned only effigies, not real people. No matter how serious their political disagreements, Euro-Americans in those times did not often kill, scalp, or mutilate members of their own race; that sort of behavior was reserved for people whom they objectified and dehumanized—Indians and slaves. Only on the physical, cultural, and racial borderlines were traditional constraints abandoned.

The Boston Massacre was a notable exception, and that's what gave the event such emotive power. Soon there would be another, far more deadly.

In the summer and fall of 1768, as patriots in major cities and towns revved up their opposition to the Townshend Acts, farmers from the North Carolina backcountry embarked on a wave of protest tailored to their own concerns. Incensed by local officials who extorted illegal fees and by a regressive poll tax levied to finance a mansion for Governor William Tryon, the farmers vowed to withhold their taxes and threatened to close the Orange County Court in Hillsborough. Calling themselves Regulators—a term used in England for over a century, denoting people who tried to regulate the abuses of government—they advocated sweeping economic reforms: each person should be taxed "in proportion to the profits arising from his estate"; taxes should be paid in "the produce of the country"; the Church of England should not be supported with public monies. Politically, they wanted democratic elections, open assembly meetings with roll-call votes, and an end to representation by lawyers and clerks who were "intent on making their own fortunes . . . at the expense of the poor industrious peasant."[48]

To achieve these ends, Regulators tried entering the electoral process. They succeeded in placing two of their number in the Assembly, but just then Governor Tryon dissolved the Assembly because it supported the Virginia Resolves against the Townshend Acts.

In September 1770, North Carolina Regulators, who had been restrained in deeds if not in words, finally resorted to rioting. Not only did they close the court in Hillsborough, but they also beat up a few officials and intimidated several others. They hanged an effigy of a local official named Edmund Fanning, who had once said that all Regulators should "be shot, hang'd, &c., as mad dogs."[49]

The North Carolina Assembly responded to the riot by expelling one of the Regulator Assemblymen, Herman Husband, and passing an ex post facto Riot Act, applicable to the Hillsborough affair. Governor Tryon arrested Husband and mobilized a substantial military expedition to end the Regulation once and for all.

Boston's Dr. Thomas Young responded by rushing to North Carolina to help the Regulators—at least that's what Thomas Hutchinson reported in mid-January 1771. Hutchinson boasted to a friend in England that since nonimportation had ended in October, patriot rabble-rousers like Young were left with nothing to do:

> We have not been so quiet these five years. Our incendiaries of the lower order have quite disappeared. A Doctor Young, whose name has often appeared in the newspapers, has taken passage for North Carolina. He may have a chance among the "Regulators" there.[50]

Although there is no independent corroboration for Hutchinson's assertion that Young traveled to North Carolina, it does seem plausible. In early January, he published a letter giving medical advice in the *Massachusetts Spy*, and he was back in Boston by March 5 to deliver the first Massacre Oration, but between those times he left no sign of his presence. News of the Hillsborough Riot had appeared in the Boston papers in mid-November, and on December 20 the *Spy* reported that Regulators were preparing to march on New

Bern, the colonial capital, while Governor Tryon was raising the militia to oppose them. In Boston, on the other hand, nothing was happening, much to Thomas Hutchinson's delight and Thomas Young's chagrin. On other occasions, before and after, Young stated explicitly that he wished to place himself at the center of the struggle for liberty in America, wherever that might be—and in January 1771, with Boston and other major centers of resistance "quiet" (to use Hutchinson's term), the restless doctor and committed political activist was certainly tempted to venture to North Carolina, and possibly did.[51]

If Young did go, however, he left before the climactic moment of the Regulators' resistance.

On May 16, 1771, in the fields above Great Alamance Creek, about half-way between Hillsborough and Herman Husband's farm, upwards of one thousand provincial soldiers and armed militiamen under Governor William Tryon faced off against a body of Regulators at least twice that large, but poorly armed and organized. By eleven thirty in the morning, Governor Tryon had positioned his troops only thirty paces from the Regulators, close enough for lots of shouting and even a few outbreaks of fisticuffs. Then, just before noon, he ordered his artillery to fire a cannon and his soldiers to discharge their muskets. The Regulators broke ranks after the first volley but continued to fight from cover for about two hours. At one point, a small group managed to break through and capture the enemy's artillery, but since nobody knew how to operate the guns, they were quickly forced to withdraw.

When the fighting was over, Tryon's army held the field, having lost nine dead and sixty-one wounded. Estimates of Regulator deaths ranged from a low of nine to a high of three hundred, the latter figure something of a boast by one of the victors; the most reliable contemporary estimates of fatalities were in the fifteen-to-twenty range, plus about one hundred wounded and twenty taken prisoner. Unlike the Boston Massacre, this was not a fluke encounter but a pitched battle. Constraints on violence had been shattered.[52]

The following day, Governor Tryon ordered the hanging of James Few, a twenty-five-year-old carpenter and recent father of twins. Tryon probably meant only to scare his prisoner into recanting, but when Few remained defiant, proclaiming he "had been sent from heaven to relieve the world from oppression," he was killed. Twelve other Regulators were sentenced to be hanged; half were pardoned and the others executed. Tryon's army spent the next several weeks scouring the countryside for Regulators, offering both a carrot and a stick: he promised to pardon any who agreed to take an oath of allegiance, surrender their arms, and pay their taxes, but he would punish all who turned him down. Their movement crushed, over six thousand Regulators gave up and signed the oath.[53]

Back in Boston, Thomas Young finally found a way he could help. During the summer of 1771, after the arrival of news from Alamance, Young and his comrades flooded the press with a steady stream of letters sympathetic to the Regulators and highly critical of Tryon's suppression. Although the Regulators themselves had been defeated, their cause might live on, for according to Young and other Boston radicals, the farmers' fight for liberty and justice paralleled that of all American patriots. Indeed, the Regulators' rebellion foreshadowed a greater Revolution to come: ordinary citizens, declaiming against unfair taxation and abuses of power, stood tall against the armed might of a repressive regime.[54]

Far to the north, a different group of rural radicals fared much better.

During the late 1760s, Thomas Young's old friend and partner in crime from Connecticut, Ethan Allen, had been hunting and trading in the remote region of northeastern New York, which at that time extended to the Connecticut River. Land-hungry New Englanders, including several of Allen's friends, were purchasing cheap claims there, but their deeds were questionable, perhaps fraudulent. Although the Crown had granted the region to New York, Governor Benning Wentworth of New Hampshire declared on his own authority that the area came under his jurisdiction. Breaking the land into affordable units, Wentworth sold deeds to the sons of Yankee yeomen who hoped to start farms with little capital.

But New York speculators also held title to those lands, and late in 1769 two New Yorkers tried to evict settlers who possessed Wentworth grants. Sensing the dangerous precedent this might set, several owners of Wentworth papers decided to fight the evictions in court, and they hired a thirty-one-year-old outspoken trader, Ethan Allen, to find a lawyer and prepare a defense before the New York Supreme Court. Allen himself had purchased claims in the disputed area, just as his mentor Thomas Young had advised him to do, and much as Young had done a decade earlier.

From the beginning, the deck was stacked against Ethan Allen and the defendants: two of the presiding judges, the attorney general, and the plaintiff's lawyer all held New York deeds in the contested district. The outcome was a foregone conclusion, but after the trial Allen spoke provocatively to the victorious attorney and the attorney general: "The gods of the hills are not the gods of the valley." When his opponents asked what he meant by this cryptic remark, he replied: "If you will accompany me to the hills of Bennington, the sense will be made clear." The New York attorneys chose to remain in Albany.[55]

Upon returning to Bennington, Allen met with other holders of Wentworth deeds in Stephen Fay's tavern, a two-and-a-half-story unpainted structure guarded by a large but shabby stuffed catamount, or mountain lion, perched on top of a twenty-foot pole. It was here at the Catamount Tavern that Allen, his brothers, brothers-in-law, cousins, and other defenders of the New Hampshire deeds formed themselves into the Green Mountain Boys, an unauthorized militia with the single goal of intimidating anyone holding or enforcing New York titles. Over the next several years, Ethan Allen and the Green Mountain Boys burned houses and haystacks, demolished fences, and threatened the personal safety of their opponents, taking special care to blacken their own faces with soot or dress as Indians to add that special touch of terror. "They assemble themselves together in the night time," wrote a scared New York official near Bennington, "and throw down all the Yorker fences, etc., and drive the cattle into the fields and meadows and destroy both grass and corn, and do every mischief they can think of." Ann Grant, another Yorker, complained that the region had become "a refuge for the vagabonds and banditti of the continent."[56]

According to biographer Michael Bellesiles, Allen carefully cultivated his image as a mad savage, turning his "frontier swagger into an art form." Making ample use of political theater, he became master of the braggart's bluff; violence, he discovered, worked just as well if only implied. Once he seized two New York sheriffs and locked them in separate rooms. During the night he and his friends dangled life-size effigies outside each of their windows; in the morning each prisoner saw that the other had been hanged. He then arranged for them to "escape," one at a time. Each prisoner, retreating quickly to the safety of Albany, spread tales of Allen's barbarity, and the eventual discovery of the trick only added to his unsavory reputation.[57]

Humiliation offered more possibilities for creative staging than crude physical abuse. Charles Jellison, another biographer, describes what happened to Dr. Samuel Adams of Arlington:

Adams was set upon and taken by surprise by a small band of Green Mountain Boys, who carted him away to Stephen Fay's tavern. There in the long room, with Ethan presiding, his case was heard by the Bennington Committee of Safety, which wasted little time in finding him guilty of being a public nuisance. His punishment, at Ethan's suggestion, was to be public humiliation. Tied securely to an armchair, the doctor was hoisted by ropes to the top of the tavern signpost. There, twenty feet off the ground and on eye-level with Fay's stuffed catamount, he dangled in his armchair for two hours while the assembled inhabitants of Bennington looked on with wonder and amusement. At the end of his sentence, the doctor, noticeably chastened, was lowered, warned to mend his ways, and dismissed by the committee. "This mild and exemplary disgrace," according to Ira [Allen], "had a salutary effect upon the Doctor, and many others."[58]

In trials such as this, the Green Mountain Boys did not argue the finer points of law. The rights of the accused were limited to an opportunity to apologize and repent. Hearings were conducted in taverns; juries adjourned to barns; prisoners were detained in outhouses. These trials were not about justice but politics: they mobilized support, they humiliated those who resisted, and they intimidated the undecided with blatant displays of power.

Although the Green Mountain Boys used terror as a tool, their goal was not to kill or inflict pain but to convert. As they gained in strength, they actually minimized the likelihood of bloodshed, for nobody dared oppose them. The more violent the image, the less violent the reality. Ironically, intimidation served to limit armed confrontation; once, when a pitched battle seemed imminent, Ethan Allen caused the enemy to flee simply by hurling invectives. During the height of the controversy in the five years preceding the Revolutionary War, not a single person was killed in the disputed area on the west side of the Green Mountains.[59]

Several years earlier, Ethan Allen and Thomas Young had parted ways, but they proceeded to travel along parallel paths. Never too shy to resist established authority, each utilized implied violence to become a master in the art of crowd intimidation. The people rule, each said through deeds as well as words. Whether in Boston or Vermont, this type of popular politics could not easily be countered by men who claimed authority but lacked real contact with the people they tried to govern.

5

Politics and Tea

1772: The Warren Household, Plymouth

The patriots' struggle to enjoy basic British liberties did not proceed along a linear trajectory, gaining momentum steadily and culminating in a grand crescendo. Reading history backward, we are tempted to view it that way, but the fight had its ebbs and flows, and few people at the time expected it to culminate in actual warfare.

For almost two years following the collapse of nonimportation in the fall of 1770, no new issues arose to motivate and mobilize the patriots' base. This is not to say that all conflict ceased, but when clashes occurred, as they did in North Carolina and Vermont, they remained only local affairs. Angry patriots mobbed customs vessels in Philadelphia (November 1771) and Providence (June 1772), but these sparks failed to ignite any wider conflagration.

Robert Morris certainly welcomed the calm. His young bride, Mary, delivered two sons, Robert and Thomas, in quick succession. In 1770 Morris purchased an eighty-acre farm three miles from town, in the gentle hills by the Schuylkill River. There he paid for the construction of a solid stone mansion, which would serve the family as a retreat during the turbulent years ahead. There too he developed an elaborate estate, complete with hothouses for tropical fruits and his own personal icehouse, one the earliest in America devoted to private use. Political concerns receded to the very back of his mind, where, in his view, they belonged.[1]

George Washington did not mind the lull either. At home in Mount Vernon, he expanded the house and gardens yet again. Finding his dining room "lonesome" unless filled, he entertained some two thousand guests in the seven years preceding the Revolutionary War. During a single year, he went to church on only fifteen days but hunted foxes on forty-nine. He attended balls, plays, horse races, cockfights, and puppet shows; once, he paid a showman nine shillings for leading an elk to his home. He gambled, and of course he pursued more land in the West, which he admitted was itself a sort of lottery. He backed off from politics, not even bothering to attend the House of Burgesses unless some item of local concern was at stake. Joseph Ellis, a recent biographer, dismisses Washington's political activities during the period after nonimportation in a single sentence: "There was then, in the strange way that history happens, a five-year hiatus."[2]

Henry Laurens, oddly enough, remained a tad more politically active than Morris or Washington. Left with the care of his five children, Henry decided to bring the three boys to Europe to further their education. (Before Eleanor died, he had been planning to take John, the eldest; now, the others would come as well.) While his sons were in school, and between family field trips to places of cultural interest, Laurens educated himself by studying the latest in European technologies (a rice-pounding mill, a wind-powered sawmill, an innovative fire engine) and advanced agricultural methods for crops he could grow back home (silk, grapes, indigo). But he also represented South Carolina's patriots in an ongoing dispute with the British government. Before he had left home, his colonial Assembly had granted a £1,500 gift to the Wilkes Fund, demonstrating solidarity with the struggle for liberty in England; in response, the ministry decreed that the royal governor would not assent to any money matters until the Assembly recanted its mistake. Now, Laurens tried to get the North administration to back down by speaking with people in high places, including Lord Hillsborough, secretary of state for America. Temperamentally, he felt more comfortable with this sort of insider politicking than with public demonstrations.

While in England, Laurens observed a curious drama of apparent interest to himself and his peers back home: the famous Somerset case, in which a slave from Virginia sued for his freedom when his master took him to England. Although the case would seem to have enormous implications for slave owners like Laurens, he called it "comical" and paid it little heed. At least by Henry's telling, his own personal attendant, a slave named Robert Scipio Laurens, said that "the Negroes that want to be free here, are fools." That's what Robert's master wanted to hear, and all he needed to know. Slaves were better off staying with good masters than running to an uncertain freedom.[3]

While Morris and Washington withdrew from politics and Laurens participated only minimally, Mercy Otis Warren, who had once eschewed the entire political arena while declaring it sinful, suddenly entered the field with a vengeance.

Why now?

Personally and politically, Warren's brother James Otis was in a state of decline. His intermittent madness rendered him less effective than he had been, although he could and did still function between manic bouts. Worse yet, the movement he had helped to foster was floundering. The passion for liberty seemed in abeyance, and virtue was on the wane. Austere lifestyles, made necessary by nonimportation, were giving way to a new wave of decadence and ostentatious display. This sort of backsliding ran afoul of both the Puritan and the Republican in Mercy Otis Warren, and to top it all off, Governor Thomas Hutchinson, no friend to the Otis family, was enjoying an unexpected resurgence of popularity. With her father too old and her brother periodically too far gone to do much about all this, Mrs. Warren herself picked up the pen and went on the attack.

As much as any man or woman of the day, Mercy Otis Warren was prepared for the task. She had already written many a poem and kept up a lively correspondence with various wives of prominent Massachusetts Whigs (most frequently her close childhood friend Hannah Winthrop), and she had even written occasionally to the gents themselves (most notably John Adams). She had also read classical literature, which provided her setting, and Shakespeare, who modeled her style. Finally, because her brother had been so intimately involved, she had paid close attention to the politics of the day.

Warren chose as her genre dramatic satire.

For a publisher, she chose Isaiah Thomas, whose *Massachusetts Spy* was billed as a voice for the "Glorious Cause of LIBERTY" intended for "both sexes." The issues of March 26 and April 23, 1772, featured short excerpts from Warren's first play, *The Adulateur*, which she advertised to be a complete three-act drama.

For an arch villain (an ordinary villain would hardly suffice) she selected Governor Thomas Hutchinson, thinly disguised as Rapatio, the rapacious "Bashaw" of "Upper Servia." (A *bashaw* [*pasha*], technically a high-ranking official of the Turkish Empire, connoted any imperious or self-important person.) According to Warren, the native-born Hutchinson, who had risen higher than any other colonist, now repressed and plundered his own countrymen.

As secondary villains, she cast Peter Oliver (Hazlerod), who had succeeded

Hutchinson as chief justice of the Superior Court and was related to him through marriage, and his brother Andrew Oliver (Limpet), the former Stamp Act distributor who now served as the Massachusetts secretary of state. In Warren's play, Hazlerod and Limpet join such characters as Dupe, Gripeall, and Meagre to form Hutchinson's court, his adulators.

For a hero, she borrowed the time-honored name and tradition of Cassius, probably thinking, in a wishful way, of her own brother.

The play was a crude morality tale, with little shading between black and white. From Rapatio's opening soliloquy, Warren made it clear that her villain would be marked by evil thoughts as well as evil deeds:

> *O Fortunate!*
> *Could I have tho't my stars would be so kind*
> *As thus to bring my deep laid schemes to bear!*
> *Tho' from my youth ambition's path I trod,*
> *Suck'd the contagion from my mother's breast;*
> *The early taint has rankl'd in my veins,*
> *And lust for pow'r is still my darling lust;*
> *Despotic rule my first, my sov'reign wish;*
> *Yet to succeed beyond my sanguine hope,*
> *To quench the gen'rous flame, the ardent love*
> *Of liberty in SERVIA'S freeborn sons,*
> *Destroy their boasted rights, and mark them slaves,*
> *To ride triumphant o'er my native land,*
> *And revel on its spoils.*[4]

There was no hint of generosity or even nuance in Warren's vindictive attack—and this from the woman who six years earlier had condemned the "warring passions" raised by politics. Her rancor seemed to bother her, not so much because of her religious proclamations about the need to submit, but from a concern that she might have overstepped the "narrow bounds" that circumscribed a woman's life.

Mrs. Warren was no modern feminist, and at least on one level she actually believed in the traditional boundaries she was violating. In the words of biographer Jean Fritz, "She admired the old-fashioned, retiring virtues in a woman (even if she confessed to being deficient in them)." And deficient she was, for by every indication her adherence to the "retiring virtues"—the "gentleness, charity, and piety that adorned the female of earlier times," as she said—

was intermittent at best. When her husband, James, discoursed with other Whigs in the parlor of their Plymouth home, Mercy did not retire to the other room, as was the custom for women of her class, but stayed and listened and talked. And when she talked, men listened, impressed by her learning and her facility with verbal expression. They took her seriously, and with each additional visit, and each subsequent letter or publication, they would take her more seriously yet.[5]

November 1772: Faneuil Hall, Boston

According to William Gordon, the contemporary author of a Revolutionary-era history that preceded even Mercy Otis Warren's, it was in the Warrens' own parlor that the idea to revise and extend the Committees of Correspondence originated. Sometime during the summer or early fall of 1772, Samuel Adams was visiting the Warrens when James suggested to him that patriotic committees should be established not only in the major cities, as had been done in the 1760s, but also "in the several towns of the colony, in order to learn the strength of the friends to the rights of the continent, and to unite and increase their force." Adams, "pleased with the proposal," then took it back to his friends in Boston, who decided to implement the idea.[6]

This was a historic moment, if Gordon's account is correct, for in the years to come, the Committees of Correspondence that he claimed germinated in the Warren household would provide the "political engine" (Gordon's words) for the American Revolution. And Mercy Otis Warren, despite her gender, was part of the conversation that made it happen.

In truth, the origins of this revolutionary "engine" extended beyond the tidy venue Gordon assigned to it. Although the idea for the revamped Committees of Correspondence was no doubt discussed in the Warrens' parlor, it is not altogether clear that it *emanated* from there, as Gordon reported. Ideas such as this do not usually have a unique starting point but evolve from repeated discussions, which overlap and eventually congeal into a definitive program.

Three years earlier, Dr. Thomas Young had cheered his friends in New York when they tried to form similar committees in every local community in that colony. (The pressing issue for the New Yorkers at that time was to resist the appointment of an Anglican bishop in America, whom they feared would try to squash religious dissenters.) The New York attempt failed, however, because it was cumbersome. In a predominantly rural society, people in their separate communities did not have the time to attend numerous meetings over a single issue. That might work for a handful of urban activists like Thomas Young and his comrades, but not for ordinary farmers and artisans in the hinterlands.

Now, the idea being discussed by James Otis, Mercy Otis Warren, Samuel Adams, Thomas Young, and no doubt several others offered a way around this problem: the Committees of Correspondence could piggyback on the existing infrastructure for local government. Because the folks in every community already gathered periodically at their town meetings to elect officers and discuss issues of common concern, they could at these times discuss the larger issues of British policies as well, and beyond that, they could appoint standing Committees of Correspondence, empowered by their constituents to write other communities and coordinate resistance, if necessary. This would grant official standing to prominent patriots in each town, who would presumably be appointed to the committees, while it would simultaneously help to educate the populace at large and alert them to the threats of imperial overreach.

The scheme greatly excited Thomas Young, who, admittedly, was easy to excite. "We are brewing something here which will make some people's heads reel," he wrote to his compatriot in New York, Hugh Hughes.[7]

For the idea to work, however, it needed to be approved first by the Boston town meeting, which would initiate the communications, then by the various town meetings throughout the colony, and hopefully, at some point, by communities in other colonies as well.

At first glance, the timing seemed off. With patriotic sentiment on the wane, why would townsmen choose to confer on a group of patriot activists this public stamp of approval?

Fortuitously, right at this moment Lord North's administration in London handed the patriots a new cause to rally behind. Five years earlier, Charles Townshend (now deceased) had suggested that colonial governors, judges, and perhaps the entire "civil list" of governmental employees be paid directly by the Crown, using money collected from America through Parliamentary taxation. The policy wasn't implemented at the time, but North decreed it would be now.

Politically astute Americans were furious, and with good reason. Previously, their public officials were paid by the elected colonial legislatures and were therefore beholden to the people they ruled; now, without the power of the purse, citizens would be less able to hold corrupt officials accountable. Thomas Young noted with both anger and glee that the policy would finally prove to everyone that British rulers had "a design to enslave us."[8]

On November 2, after Governor Hutchinson refused to summon the Assembly to deal with the new crisis, the Boston town meeting convened at Faneuil Hall and established a standing Committee of Correspondence, empowered to communicate "the sense of this Town . . . to the several Towns of the Province and to the World." Among the twenty-one committee members were Thomas Young, Samuel Adams, James Otis, Joseph Warren, and William Molineux.

The next day, at the committee's first meeting, Adams, Otis, and the young lawyer Josiah Quincy were appointed to draft a summary of "the Rights of the Colonists," while Young, Warren, and the printer Joseph Greenleaf were charged with preparing a list of "infringements and violations" of those rights. Five years earlier, Joseph Warren had accused Young of "inaccuracy, malevolence, bad grammar and nonsense, . . . self-conceit, vain-boasting, and invincible impudence"; now, the two worked side by side for fifteen days as they hammered out an exhaustive catalog of everything that the king's ministers and Parliament had done to violate the colonists' liberties. Much of the language was excessive and inflammatory, suggesting Young's input: "Thus our houses and even our bed chambers, are exposed to be ransacked, our boxes, trunks & chests broke open, ravaged and plundered by wretches." Some of the most flamboyant terms, like "depravity of mankind," echoed Young's private correspondence.[9]

When the town met on November 20 to consider the committee's draft, a petty merchant named Aaron Davis announced to the assembled citizens of Boston that he "did not chuse to have anything to do with measures, wherein I must follow the lead of such men as Dr. Young." Davis objected to Young in part because of his outspoken demeanor (Young, he said, could not keep "that unruly member, the tongue, in due subjection") but mostly because of his religion. In a subsequent letter to the *Boston News-Letter*, Davis asked Young directly: "Do you believe the scriptures of the Old and New Testament . . . to be truly a revelation from God;—or that Jesus of Nazareth was the Son of God, and the appointed Saviour of the world? Do you believe that Jesus is risen from the dead, or that he is the appointed judge of the world?" Expecting Young's true answer to be no, Davis concluded: "There is nothing in your creed to distinguish you from the most thorough paced infidels, and virulent opposers of our holy religion."[10]

Davis's attempt to discredit Dr. Young, and thereby the Committees of Correspondence, failed. Not only did the town endorse the committee's work, but Samuel Adams, whose religion was beyond reproach, jumped to Young's defense while chastising Davis. He wrote in the *Boston Gazette*: "Doctor Young (I dare you to contradict me) has ever been an unwearied assertor of the rights of his countrymen: he has taken the post of hazard, and acted vigorously in the cause of American freedom. Such endeavours and exertions, have justly entitled him to the notice, to the confidence of the people."[11]

By November 30, six hundred copies of the "Boston Pamphlet" were available for distribution to the towns, and Young and his colleagues faced the daunting task of sending these out one by one, with a personalized letter to each recipient. "I have now finished eight long letters, a draught of resolves and inscribed inclosed and directed half a dozen pamphlets since Saturday evening, therefore fatigued to death," he wrote on Monday, December 21.[12]

The work was taxing but personally and politically rewarding. After six years in Boston, Young had earned a place in the inner circle of patriot activists, toiling alongside his mentor, whom he referred to privately as "the worthy Mr. Samuel Adams" and "the great Mr. Adams." Many generations later, historians would misrepresent Adams's talents, claiming he was the unique creator of the Committees of Correspondence and the prime mover of all mass protest in Boston, but Thomas Young knew differently. Adams's supreme talent was to welcome people like Young, or anyone else who might help, into the movement. Adams could politic in official bodies like the Assembly or the Boston town meeting; work in committees and small groups; or write resolutions, pamphlets, public letters to the press, and private letters to colleagues. He knew how to communicate effectively.[13]

Increasingly, Dr. Thomas Young did too. That's what it took to build and sustain a popular movement, and that's why the Committees of Correspondence would prove so important. In years to come, these groups would serve as an infrastructure for the Revolution, pushing radical politics forward at the local level while coordinating activities between communities. Without the collective endeavors of people such as Young and Adams, and their counterparts in other communities throughout the American colonies, there could be no successful movement for change.

In the fall of 1772, the immediate job at hand was to reach out and open the lines of communication. Once awakened, Young believed, the colonists might come to act as one in defense of their rights as British subjects. "We need not spill the blood even of mistaken enemies, if we can otherwise reduce them to reason, and make them our friends," he wrote to Hughes. But did Thomas Young truly believe that reason alone would suffice? Already, he was entertaining a Plan B should the appeal to reason fail, and the Committees of Correspondence, by extending popular support, would play an important role in that scenario as well: "If we must come to blows at last we can lose nothing by deferring the combat till our forces are well disciplined and all mankind possessed with the justice of our cause."[14]

March 1 and May 18, 1773: Worcester Meetinghouse

How would residents of the rural hinterlands, presumably less advanced in their thinking, respond to the Boston Pamphlet? Ninety-five percent of the people in Massachusetts lived outside of Boston, some in competing seaport towns, but the majority in the interior regions, where they either farmed or served the needs of the farmers. It was far from certain that these country folk would take up the torch raised by politicized city dwellers in the provincial capital.

But the returns flooded in: at least 119 early in 1773 and another 25 by the end of the summer. More towns responded than sent representatives to the General Court, and with just a handful of exceptions the replies were favorable, even effusive. In their own words and their own style, the country folk matched or surpassed the passion of the Boston pamphleteers. According to historian Richard Bushman, "In the smallest town there was at least one individual who could discourse on the British Constitution even if he could not spell."[15]

In Worcester, the seeds planted by Boston fell on fertile ground, for a revolution of sorts was already in the works. Ever since Worcester became the shire town of the newly formed Worcester County in 1731, three generations of John Chandlers and their close relations had dominated the local political scene by holding several offices apiece. In one year alone, the list of public positions occupied by three Chandlers and Timothy Paine, who married into the family, included Massachusetts councilman, town representative to the Assembly, chief justice of the Court of Common Pleas, clerk for that court, probate judge, register of probate, register of deeds, assessor, county sheriff, county treasurer, town treasurer, town clerk, moderator of the town meeting, town selectman, and colonel of the county militia. This concentration of power did not sit well with certain local citizens, who were coalescing into a significant countervailing force.[16]

As early as 1758, when John Adams was first practicing law under the tutelage of Worcester lawyer James Putnam (who had also married a Chandler), he reported in his diary that two self-taught Deists—Nathan Baldwin, a saddler, and Ephraim Doolittle, a hatter—tried to convince him to run for local office, since "the Chandler family had engrossed almost all the public offices and employment in the town and country." Adams declined, but seven years later, empowered by the Stamp Act crisis, these two "great sticklers for equality" (as Adams called them) were able to break through. When Timothy Paine and the youngest John Chandler were elevated to the Council, the town chose Ephraim Doolittle to serve as its representative to the Assembly, a spot traditionally reserved for a member of the Chandler clan. One month later, the town meeting instructed Doolittle to oppose the Stamp Act, and the following year, with Doolittle still the town's representative, Nathan Baldwin and two others drew up a radical set of instructions geared to curtail the power of the Chandlers and their ilk: end plural officeholding, limit official fees, outlaw bribery during elections, allow citizens to observe Assembly and Council meetings, and stop public financing of the elite Latin schools.[17]

For the next seven years, during an uneasy truce, neither faction moved aggressively to subdue the other. The Chandler clan retained most court positions, the dissidents determined the town representative and wrote his instructions, while each side contributed evenly to the town's cast of selectmen. That's where matters stood when the Boston Pamphlet arrived, upsetting the delicate balance.[18]

When the citizens of Worcester assembled for their regularly scheduled meeting on Monday, March 1, 1773, forty-one of their number submitted a petition to present the Boston Pamphlet for consideration. According to the official town records, "After some debate thereon," the motion to read the tract aloud "passed in ye affirmative." Then, once everyone had heard what Samuel Adams, Thomas Young, and the Boston Committee of Correspondence had to say, the town chose five men to draft a response. On this committee were three former selectmen associated with the Doolittle/Baldwin wing, a prominent merchant who was John Chandler's chief economic competitor, and a relative newcomer to politics, the blacksmith Timothy Bigelow.[19]

Bigelow, at age thirty-three, was hardly new to officeholding, having served previously as hogreave (1763), tything man (1766), surveyor of highways and collector of highway taxes (1769), and fence viewer (1771). None of these posts, however, would seem to prepare him for a lead role in the debate over imperial policies. Most likely, his cousin Joshua Bigelow, thirty-seven years his senior, played a role in Timothy's selection. Joshua had emerged as a leader of the dissidents, serving frequently since 1767 as town selectman and representative to the General Court, where he took an active role in the resistance to the Townshend duties, but he had just turned seventy-one, and it was certainly time for new blood.[20]

Although inexperienced in the larger political arena, Timothy Bigelow was well positioned to learn. For the past decade, since he married Anna Andrews and moved into her family home on Main Street, he had focused primarily on his family: Anna had borne four children, the youngest only eight months old, while Timothy was developing their land and adding bits and pieces, a half acre at a time, primarily to gain access to Mill Brook. But his work as a blacksmith placed him in relationship with nearly everybody in town, a valuable political asset, and it also placed him at odds with British imperial policies, which insisted that iron be sent across the Atlantic to be fashioned into tools there, rather than on American forges such as his. When local conversations addressed imperial policies, Bigelow listened, and now he too was eager to "discourse on the British Constitution," even though he possessed no more than a district school (elementary) education.[21]

Bigelow and his committee needed to draft a reply that was strong enough to reflect the patriotic sentiments of the town's radicals, yet not so shrill as to alienate its conservatives. The document they created was therefore heavy on Whig philosophy but light in particulars:

> It is our opinion that mankind are by nature free, and the end and designe of forming social compacts, and entering into civil society, was that each member of that society, might enjoy his liberty and property, and live in the free exercise of his rights, both civil and religious, which God and nature gave; except such as are *expresly* given up by compact. This we apprehend to be the scope of that noble system of government, the English Constitution, the great wisdom in giving so just a ballance of power, through all its parts, very justly excites admiration: and when we apprehend a designe to overthrow the same in one part by any person or persons, (by distroying dependance of one of the community, on the other, and substituting, in its room, a crafty, or political dependance, the former being as much superior to the crafty designes of wicked corrupt plunderers of mankind) it is our duty, to exert ourselves against it to the utmost of our power for by nature, and the Charter of this Province, we are intitled to all the rights, and privelages, of the above Constitutions, as though we were born within the realm of England: and it is . . .[22]

So it continued in a similar vein, almost two thousand words in scarcely a dozen sentences.

On May 18, at the next town meeting, the committee's draft was approved with no record of debate. Worcester's old guard seemed to have held their tongues, outvoted but not overly distressed by the proceedings. Patriots had been mouthing at British policies for years, and right at that moment, there was no reason to suppose that the letter to Boston would result in any significant harm. But the response to the Boston Pamphlet was only the beginning. To stay abreast of the growing crisis, the town meeting appointed Timothy Bigelow, William Young, and John Smith to serve as a standing Committee of Correspondence, charged with transmitting "the earliest intelligence to the inhabitants of this Town, of any designs that they shall discover at any time against our natural and constitutional rights."[23]

The sanctioning of a committee to communicate with radicals in other areas did upset the Chandler faction—and there were many of them, albeit not enough to constitute a majority: John Chandler IV and his fifteen adult offspring; John's younger brother Gardiner, the sheriff, with his six offspring; the Chandlers' brother-in-law Timothy Paine, with his ten offspring; the attorney James Putnam, and others. Although Chandler and company did not yet fight back in public, they grumbled among themselves. Dr. William Paine, one of Timothy's sons, confided to a friend that the radicals in Worcester were "devils" and a "sett of cussed venal worthless raskalls."[24]

Rascals indeed, if upsetting the established order can be considered a rascally affair. And Timothy Bigelow, a new spokesman for the upstarts and founding delegate to the highly partisan Committee of Correspondence, had suddenly become one of the lead offenders.

May–July 1773: The Warren Household, Plymouth

In Plymouth, the colony's original town, patriots did not wait for the Boston Pamphlet to create a Committee of Correspondence. On November 4, 1772, two days after Boston formed its committee, Samuel Adams wrote to James Warren: "I wish our Mother Plymouth would see her way clear to have a meeting and second Boston by appointing a Committee of Communication and Correspondence. The sooner this is done, I think, the better." Less than three weeks later, James Warren himself was appointed by the Plymouth town meeting to head its Committee of Correspondence.[25]

Mercy Otis Warren, of course, did not sit on that committee, for as a woman she was not part of the town meeting. But with her multifaceted literary talents, Mrs. Warren created a communication web of her own, writing countless letters and several plays that promoted the patriots' cause. She certainly had the interest, and increasingly she had the time: her "five fine boys," as John Adams called them, were growing up, with James, the eldest, off to college, and George, the youngest, old enough to be out from under his mother's constant gaze.[26]

Topping the list of her many correspondents was the historian Catharine Macaulay, England's "Celebrated Mrs. Macaulay," so popular with Whigs on both sides of the Atlantic. Although Macaulay had written to James Otis years before, giving James's sister an access point of sorts, Mercy still had to muster a good deal of nerve to introduce herself to the woman she regarded first as an idol, then a mentor, and finally, years later, a friend and colleague. The long list of American patriots who corresponded with Macaulay included John Adams, John Dickinson (the famous "Farmer" from Pennsylvania), the Reverend Ezra Stiles (future president of Yale), and Richard Henry Lee (who would one day introduce the motion for independence in the Continental Congress), but while male patriots appeared to seek some sort of historical recognition for their deeds, Macaulay's new female correspondent had a different motive: she sought the acquaintance, and ultimately the approval, of a very successful woman who shared her political and philosophical perspectives. Much as Dr. Thomas Young wrote unsolicited letters to the British political icon John Wilkes, Mercy Otis Warren hoped to initiate a transatlantic relationship with perhaps the most famous female intellectual in the British Empire.

Warren was smitten with Macaulay for many reasons: her politics, her influence, her style, and the fact that she was a woman. Combining patriotic fervor with stylistic flourish, she opened their correspondence:

Has the genius of liberty which once pervaded the bosom of each British hero animating them to the worthiest deeds forsaken that devoted Island; or, has she only concealed her lovely form untill some more happy period shall bid her lift her avenging hand to the terror of every arbitrary despot? . . . What fatal infatuation has seized the parent state that she is thus making illegal encroachments on her loyal subjects, and by every despotic measure urging these populous, brave, and extensive colonies to a vigorous union in defence of their invaded rights?[27]

And in her second letter to Catharine Macaulay, she raised the issue of gender and celebrated the new role of women in politics:

> You see madam I disregard the opinion that women make but indifferent politicians. It may be true in general, but the present age has given one example at least to the contrary. . . . When the observations are just and honorary to the heart and character, I think it very immaterial whether they flow from a female lip in the soft whispers of private friendship or whether thundered in the Senate in the bolder language of the other sex.[28]

Warren reached out to other women as well, most notably Abigail Adams, who looked up to her as she looked up to Catharine Macaulay. Flattered, even awed, that such an accomplished writer sought her literary companionship, Mrs. Adams penned her opening epistle to Mrs. Warren. Sandwiched between stylized apologies for her lack of writing talent, Abigail sought advice from Mercy, sixteen years her senior, on child rearing, "in which you have so happily succeeded." Within months, these two wives of prominent patriots were holding forth on the politics of the day, just as their husbands did, but with a greater nod to the dictates of Virtue than their menfolk evidenced. [29]

Mrs. Warren did not neglect Abigail's husband, who was becoming her biggest fan. For his personal perusal, she penned sixty-four lines of verse, which she called simply "To Mr. Adams." In thirty-two rhyming couplets, marked by no shortage of abstract nouns (Reason, Truth, Virtue, and so on, all capitalized), she entertained her audience of one and cajoled him to keep up the patriotic fight.[30]

In addition to her letters, Warren authored a sequel to *The Adulateur*, and this time, fulfilling her ardent real-life wish, she sent Thomas Hutchinson to his political grave in a play she called *The Defeat*.

In the excerpts published by the *Boston Gazette*, Rapatio opens by flaunting his arch villainy once again:

> *The trump of malice by my minions blown*
> *Shall blast the laurels of the fairest name,*
> *And stab the bosom of that patriot's fame,*
> *Who dare oppose my arbitrary sway,*
> *Or scorns to tremble at a despot's frown.*

But this time a group of patriots, like Rome's valiant senators, rise up and cast off the tyrant. Vanquished, Rapatio concludes with a less-than-tragic soliloquy, as he possesses no saving graces whatsoever:

> *Oh the reverie, the sad reverie of fortune!*
> *Stript of my plumes, my plunder and my peace.*
> *Peace did I say! that gentle heavenly guest,*
> *Has not resided in my canker'd breast,*
> *E'er since my native land, I basely sold,*
> *For flattering titles, and more sordid gold.*
> *The dreadful curses of the slaughter'd dead,*
> *Full vengeance pour on my devoted head.*
> *I fall unpitied, not one weeping eye,*
> *Shall wail my fate, or heave a tender sigh.*[31]

At least in the artist's imagination, that was the end of Thomas Hutchinson—or so it might appear, but the vitriolic pen of Mercy Otis Warren was on a roll, and two months later, again in the *Boston Gazette*, the satirist propped her villain on his feet once again for another beating. Shortly after the publication of the first installment of *The Defeat*, Massachusetts patriots disclosed the contents of Hutchinson's private correspondence, which had been obtained surreptitiously by Benjamin Franklin, who was serving as the colony's agent in London. In one of his letters Hutchinson had stated frankly, "There must be an abridgment of what are called English Liberties" in the American colonies. For Warren and her fellow patriots, this proved what they had long alleged: their governor, although born and raised in Massachusetts, did not have the interests of his homeland at heart. Warren could not resist driving the point home, and in her sequel to her sequel, Rapatio is forced to bemoan his defeat yet one more time:

> *Is the game up? Can I deceive no more?*
> *Could not my art, my sophistry and guile,*
> *All my precaution to conceal my plan*
> *Prevent the busy quick ey'd patriot's search?*
> *Have they the broad Atlantic travel'd o'er*
> *From Albion's bosom! fetched the guilty proofs*
> *Of our perfidious, bold, and black designs?*[32]

This was rough stuff, beating up on the fellow like that. Although Mrs. Warren, being a woman, never took her contentious politics to the taverns, where she might rub shoulders with those not of her standing (she preferred "a little company of the right stamp sociable learned virtuous & polite"), she conversed in her way with all who shared the conviction that British liberties in America were under siege by British authorities in London and "placemen" in the colonies who did their bidding. When tradesmen and apprentices picked up the *Boston Gazette* or *Massachusetts Spy* to read Warren's biting satire (not knowing the author was a woman, of course), they might not get all the classical allusions, but they certainly got the gist of her critique: colonial Boston was in the throes of an epic battle between the virtuous and the wicked, and this fight had larger repercussions, with the moral tone of the British Empire hanging in the balance.[33]

November 29 and December 16, 1773:
Old South Meeting House and Griffin's Wharf, Boston

Before dawn on Monday, November 29, 1773, Boston's Committee of Correspondence posted a handbill "in all Parts of the Town":

Friends! Brethren! Countrymen!

That worst of Plagues the detested TEA shipped for this Port by the East-India Company, is now arrived in this Harbour; the Hour of Destruction or manly Opposition to the Machinations of Tyranny stares you in the Face; every Friend to his Country, to himself and Posterity, is now called upon to meet at Faneuil-Hall, at NINE o'Clock,

THIS DAY,

(at which Time the Bells will ring) to make a united and successful Resistance to this last, worst and most destructive Measure of Administration.[34]

One might think this "most destructive Measure" was another round of taxation, but it was not. In fact, one tax on tea had just been repealed—but it wasn't the hated threepence per pound on American imports, the last of the Townshend duties, which remained unchanged. Instead, Lord North's administration in London, with Parliament's concurrence, had removed a separate tax on tea that passed through Britain on its way to America. The idea was to lower costs for the giant East India Company, the megacorporation that literally possessed its own colonies in South Asia. The company was overextended, but if its tax load were lessened, it could dump some of its enormous accumulated surplus—18 million pounds of tea—on the American market at a price competitive with smuggled imports from Holland. North reasoned that colonists had no reason to take offense: they could purchase tea at a lower price, while paying no new taxes.

Neither Lord North nor the members of Parliament understood the powerful union that had developed in America between commercial self-interest and ideology. The Tea Act angered both American smugglers, who resented competition from an oversize, government-backed corporation, and American patriots, who still smarted at the notion of taxation without representation. Since 1770, when all Townshend duties except that on tea were repealed, tea had become synonymous with taxation in the American mind. Now, dedicated patriots like Thomas Young could focus on that symbol to help resuscitate their political movement. "Tea is really a slow poison, and has the corrosive effect upon those who handle it," Dr. Young wrote in the *Boston Evening-Post*. "I have left it off since it became political poison, and have since gained in firmness of constitution. My substitute is camomile flowers."[35]

At nine in the morning, as the Committee of Correspondence had requested, several thousand merchants, artisans, apprentices, farmers, sailors, dockworkers, and so forth, from Boston and neighboring towns, showed up at Faneuil Hall to determine what would become of the eighty chests of strong, black Bohea tea (the preferred leaf in America) and thirty-four chests of other varieties (Singlo, Hyson, Souchong, Congou) that had arrived in port the previous day aboard a ship called the *Dartmouth*. Estimates for the size of the crowd varied from 2,500 to 6,000, but in any case, there were far too many people to fit inside the large hall on the second story used for town meetings. Immediately, the Body (as the people once again called themselves) adjourned to the more spacious Old South Meeting House, a few hundred yards away.

In this particular crisis, unlike previous ones, patriots faced a precise deadline. After twenty days in port, if a vessel remained unloaded, port officials had the right to seize its cargo, which they naturally would do under full military guard, and once the tea was seized and unloaded it would find its way to local markets, where demand outstripped supply. That would be an ignominious defeat for the patriots, to be avoided at all costs. Because the *Dartmouth* had entered port on November 28, the Body had only until December 17 to deal with "that worst of Plagues" tucked in its hold.

In Old South, before an aroused population that overfilled the pews and balconies, speakers proposed various solutions. Most agreed that the "consignees" (merchants who were slated to receive the East India Company's tea and place it on the market) should be persuaded to refuse the cargo. Most also agreed that if persuasion should fail, a little coercion would be in order. Samuel Adams went one step further: the tea should be sent back to London "in the same bottom" without being unloaded, thereby avoiding any payment of the hated Townshend duty. Dr. Thomas Young went further yet: patriots should raid the vessel and throw the tea overboard. Young was the first to suggest such a radical course in a public speech.[36]

Outright destruction of the tea was an idea before its time, for the Body still had nineteen days to seek a more peaceable resolution. The meeting sided instead with Samuel Adams, but his plan to ship the tea back faced a critical problem: the Body, however numerous, lacked the means to implement its will. Legally, no export from England could be reentered as an import; furthermore, no vessel could be dispatched from the harbor without clearance by port officials or the governor, and Thomas Hutchinson had no reason to satisfy the requests or even demands of his political foes. In fact, when Hutchinson heard of the meeting, he sent an official dispatch to Old South Meeting House: "I warn exhort and require you and each of you thus unlawfully assembled forthwith to disperse and to surcease all further unlawful proceedings at your utmost peril." When this message was read aloud, the Body responded with "a long and very general hiss" and continued with the business at hand. Samuel Adams took the podium to declare that the people always "had a right to meet together to consult for their own safety," but Thomas Young once again offered a more revolutionary retort to Hutchinson's ultimatum: because "the people assembled" had no "redress in any grievance," they found themselves in a "state of nature" beyond the reach of governmental authority.[37]

Days later, two more vessels arrived in Boston laden with East India Company tea: the *Eleanor* on December 2 and the *Beaver* on December 7. (A fourth vessel, the *William*, beached on the ocean side of Cape Cod.) Meanwhile, patriots continued to assemble and issue demands, but intimidation tactics that had worked in the past were rendered ineffective once the consignees and the port officials had retreated to Castle William, an island garrison under the protection of British troops. Although key players were beyond their reach, patriots placed a twenty-four-hour armed guard around the three vessels docked at Griffin's Wharf to make sure nobody unloaded the cargo. A handbill signed "THE PEOPLE" proclaimed that anyone attempting such a dastardly deed would be treated "as wretches unworthy to live and will be made the first victims of our just resentment."[38]

Was there any peaceable resolution?

Abigail Adams hoped there was, but she feared what might happen if not. One week after the *Dartmouth* appeared in port, she wrote to Mercy Otis Warren:

> The tea that bainfull weed is arrived. Great and I hope effectual opposition has been made to the landing of it. . . . The flame is kindled and like lightning it catches from soul to soul. Great will be the devastation if not timely quenched or allayed by some more lenient measures.
>
> Altho the mind is shocked at the thought of sheding humane blood, more especially the blood of our countrymen, and a civil war is of all wars, the most dreadfull such is the present spirit that prevails, that if once they are made desperate many, very many of our heroes will spend their lives in the cause, with the speech of Cato in their mouths, "What a pitty it is, that we can dye but once to save our Country."[39]

Civil war? Might it come to that? Many thought it might. John Andrews, a Boston merchant, wrote in his diary: "Twould puzzle any person to purchase a pair of p[isto]ls in town, as they are all bought up, with a full determination to repell force by force."[40]

As the deadline approached, Thomas Young's wild idea of dumping all the tea into the harbor did not seem so implausible after all. The patriots would soon have to make a move—and what other move could they make? Seize the vessels and pilot them out of the harbor? The giant cannons stationed at Castle William, capable of firing thirty-two-pound balls, made such an attempt unfeasible, as did the warships that Hutchinson had ordered to guard all the shipping channels.

The only other alternatives were to talk tough and beg, both of which the patriots continued to do.

On December 16, the day before port officials could legally seize the tea, more patriots than ever—perhaps as many as 7,000—poured into and milled around the venerable Old South Meeting House. Braving a cold and drenching rain, some came from as far as twenty miles away. This time the Body focused its attention on twenty-three-year-old Francis Rotch, beleaguered owner of the *Dartmouth*, whom it sent to see Governor Hutchinson. One last time, Rotch was instructed to ask the governor for permission to clear port with the *Dartmouth* and its load of tea.

Through the day the patriots lingered, awaiting a reply. (Rotch had to visit Hutchinson at his country home in Milton, seven miles away, where the governor had retreated to stay clear of the "mob.") At 3:00 P.M., they resumed their meeting to hear how Hutchinson responded, but Rotch failed to appear. Samuel Adams, Thomas Young, and others passed the time by delivering speeches. At 4:00, no sign of Rotch. Come 5:00, with Rotch still absent, some urged the meeting to adjourn, but they were outvoted. Finally, as daylight waned, Francis Rotch returned to a candlelit hall to announce what everybody expected: Hutchinson had refused the final request for clearance. The tea could not be shipped back.

What happened next has been misrepresented for a century and a half. Samuel Adams supposedly climbed on top of a bench (or so the story goes) and announced to the crowd: "This meeting can do nothing more to save the country." Everybody knew what he meant: that was the "signal" for the Tea Party to begin. "Instant pandemonium broke out amid cheers, yells, and war whoops," one recent narrative declares. "The crowd poured out of the Old South Meeting and headed for Griffin's Wharf." This story, now included in virtually every narrative of the Boston Tea Party, was fabricated ninety-two years later to promote the image of an all-powerful Sam Adams, in firm control of the Boston crowd.[41]

But according to numerous eyewitness accounts, Adams's statement "that he could think of nothing further to be done" could not have been some signal to start the Tea Party, for the timing was way off. Not until much later did Indian yells trigger a mass exodus from the meeting, and even then, Adams and Thomas Young tried to stem the tide, quiet the crowd, and continue the meeting. One observer wrote:

> About 10 or 15 minutes later [after Adams's statement], I heard a hideous yelling in the street at the S. West corner of the Meeting House and in the porch, as of an hundred people, some imitating the Powaws of Indians and others the whistle of a boatswain, which was answered by some few in the house; on which numbers hastened out as fast as possible while Mr. Adams Mr. Hancock Dr. Young with several others called out to the People to stay, for they said they had not quite done. . . . Immediately on the subsiding of the tumult within, Mr. Adams addressed the Moderator in these words, "Mr. Moderator, I move that Dr. Young make (or be desired to make) a speech"—which being approved of, Dr. Young made one accordingly of about 15 or 20 minutes length. The substance of which was (as near as I could collect, the People often shouting and clapping him) the ill effects of tea on the constitution—the

confidence he reposed in the virtue of his countrymen in refraining from the use of it, and also in standing by each other in case any should be called to an account for their proceeding. He affected to be very merry and when he had done, the audience paid him the usual tribute of bursts of applause, clapping, etc. and immediately Mr. Savage (the Moderator) dissolved the meeting.[42]

After Thomas Young's closing speech, many of the meeting's participants headed toward Griffin's Wharf.

By necessity, the conspiratorial destruction of tea was clothed in secrecy. Since anybody who participated in the illegal act would be subject to prosecution, and since the charges against him might include treason, all identities had to be concealed. Years later, however, when their actions could be regarded as heroic rather than treasonous, several of those who had taken part offered their own accounts of what transpired. Joshua Wyeth, a fifteen-year-old blacksmith's apprentice at the time, recalled:

To prevent discovery, we agreed to wear ragged clothes and disfigure ourselves, dressing to resemble Indians as much as possible, smearing our faces with grease and lamp black or soot, and should not have known each other except by our voices. Our most intimate friends among the spectators had not the least knowledge of us. We surely resembled devils from the bottomless pit rather than men.

At the appointed time we met in an old building at the head of the wharf, and fell in one after another, as if by accident, so as not to excite suspicion. We placed a sentry at the head of the wharf, another in the middle, and one on the bow of each ship as we took possession. We boarded the ship moored by the wharf, and our leader, in a very stern and resolute manner, ordered the captain and crew to open the hatchways, and hand us the hoisting tackle and ropes, assuring them that no harm was intended them. The captain asked what we intended to do. Our leader told him that we were going to unload the tea, and ordered him and the crew below. They instantly obeyed. Some of our men then jumped into the hold, and passed the chests to the tackle. As they were hauled on deck others knocked them open with axes, and others raised them to the railing and discharged their contents overboard. . . .

We were merry, in an undertone, at the idea of making so large a cup of tea for the fishes, but were as still as the nature of the case would admit, using no more words than were absolutely necessary. We stirred

Americans throwing the Cargoes of the Tea Ships into the River at Bofton

Figure 7. Thomas Young was the first to suggest in public that patriots dump tea into the Boston Harbor. This is the first extant American image of the Boston Tea Party, published in 1793. *(The Granger Collection, New York)*

briskly in the business from the moment we left our dressing room. I never worked harder in my life.[43]

Despite their disguises, the men who threw tea into Boston Harbor were no strangers to each other. More than half a century later, a writer named Benjamin Bussey Thatcher, while interviewing a participant, shoemaker George R.T. Hewes, jotted down the names of fifty-eight people supposed at the time, "on traditionary or other evidence, to have been more or less actively engaged in or present at the destruction of the Tea." A "Dr. Young" appears on Thatcher's list. There is no way to verify Thatcher's names, and at first glance, Thomas Young's participation would appear unlikely: he was the last to give a speech at Old South; he would have had to disguise himself and rush to Griffin's Wharf in record time; most other well-known patriots, fearing recognition, chose not to endanger themselves. On the other hand, Young would have been acting out of character had he stayed away from Griffin's Wharf on the night of December 16, while scores of others implemented his bold scheme and approximately one thousand supporters looked on.[44]

The evidence is inconclusive, but in one way or another, Thomas Young played his role. Possibly, by discoursing about the harmful effects of drinking tea in the waning moments of the meeting at Old South, he provided cover for the perpetrators and an alibi for himself and other prominent speakers; or perhaps, once the meeting was over, he hurried to the harbor to be with the rest—carpenters, housewrights, coopers, masons, merchants, farmers, shoe-makers, and various apprentices, as well as a leather dresser, distiller, book-seller, halter, coachmaker, painter, upholsterer, fisherman, shipwright, rope maker, cordwainer, barber, engraver, printer, bricklayer, and blacksmith—all working in silence, hoisting and chopping and heaving as quickly and efficiently as they could, within easy range of cannons at Castle William, artillery-laden warships, and several regiments of British Regulars who might interfere at any moment. We call it a "Tea Party" now, but then, for Thomas Young and Joshua Wyeth and all those who planned or executed the event, it was an act of rebellion, serious business indeed. Although they saw them-selves as patriots, they might be tried and convicted as traitors.

The following morning, John Adams penned a letter to his close friend James Warren:

The dye is cast: The people have passed the river and cutt away the bridge: last night three cargoes of tea, were emptied into the harbour. This is the grandest event, which has ever yet happened since the con-troversy, with Britain, opened.

The sublimity of it charms me![45]

But this "grandest event"—the purposeful destruction of 342 chests of tea, weighing over ninety thousand pounds and worth an estimated £9,000 to the East India Company—was likely to have repercussions. All American patri-ots suspected as much, and John Adams, writing in his diary the day after-ward, expressed their concerns:

What measures will the Ministry take, in consequence of this?—Will they resent it? will they dare to resent it? will they punish us? How? by quarter-ing troops upon us?—by annulling our Charter?—by laying on more du-ties? By restraining our trade? By sacrifice of individuals, or how?[46]

King George III, Lord North, and the majority of the British Parliament would soon answer these questions. Bent on punishment, and unable to fathom the depth of resistance, they would confirm the worst fears of American moder-ates and, perhaps, the highest hopes of American radicals. In the words of Dr. Thomas Young, their harsh reprisals would precipitate "the perfect crisis."[47]

Act II

Revolution

6

The First American Revolution

After December 16, 1773: New York, Philadelphia, Charleston, Plymouth, and Mount Vernon

The day after patriots brewed tea in the Boston Harbor, Paul Revere rode express to New York and Philadelphia to spread the news. Time was of the essence. The East India Company had sent shipments of tea to those destinations as well, and also to Charleston, South Carolina. For the events in Boston to influence events elsewhere, news had to arrive before the tea. If patriots in other cities learned of Boston's dramatic response, they could brew their own pots of tea. Or perhaps they wouldn't have to: by threatening to imitate Boston, they could induce the shipowners, consignees, and port officials to send the shipments back to London, unloaded.

Headed toward New York was the hefty ship *Nancy* bearing 211,778 pounds of tea—over twice the total amount on all four vessels sent to Boston. New York patriots had known for over two months that tea was headed their way, and like their counterparts in Boston, they had been mobilizing the resistance ever since. By early December, they had induced the consignees to give up their interest in the cargo, but New York's governor William Tryon, the man who had suppressed the Regulators while ruling North Carolina two years earlier, placed the man-of-war *Swan* at the entrance to the harbor and vowed to take charge of the tea.

On December 17, the day Paul Revere embarked from Boston, John Lamb, Thomas Young's compatriot and frequent correspondent, presided over a mass meeting that renounced Tryon's plan to guard the controversial cargo. The governor and the patriots stood at an impasse—until the evening of December 21, when Revere arrived in town with news of Boston's bold action.

This tipped the balance. According to British General Frederick Haldimand, the news "created such a ferment" that Tryon backed off. Fearing "dangerous extremities," the governor announced he would allow the tea-laden ship to return to London with its cargo untouched, just as the patriots demanded. Ironically, during all this hoopla, the *Nancy* was sailing away to the south, having encountered a fierce storm. To repair its damage, it pulled into Antigua instead of New York, and when it finally arrived at its destination the following spring, four months late, it turned right around and sailed back to London, much to the chagrin of its crew, many of whom tried to jump ship.[1]

Headed toward Philadelphia was the ship *Polly*, also loaded with over twice the amount of tea sent to Boston. There, as in New York, patriots had already cajoled the consignees to give up their interest in the cargo. Through the month of December, day by day, they waited for the *Polly* to arrive, but before it did, on Christmas Eve, the people of Philadelphia received Revere's dramatic dispatch from Boston, which was greeted "with the ringing of bells, and every sign of joy and universal approbation." The very next evening, on Christmas, the *Polly* was sighted twenty miles down the Delaware River at Chester, and the day after that, patriots escorted the ship's captain, Samuel Ayres, into Philadelphia and showed him broadsides posted about town from the "Committee of Tarring and Feathering," warning Ayres of "the pitch and feathers that are prepared for you." The captain certainly got the message, and in case he didn't, some eight thousand people gathered outside the State House the next day and promised to replicate the event in Boston unless Ayres piloted his ship from the harbor immediately. Less than two days after his arrival, Captain Ayres, his crew, and the *Polly* were on their way back to London.[2]

In Charleston, tea arrived over a month before the news from Boston. On December 2, the *London* sailed into harbor bearing 70,000 pounds of tea subject to the Townshend duty. Although local patriots were able to convince the consignees to reject the tea, they could not agree on what further action to take. After twenty days, with the duty still unpaid, the local customs collector ordered the tea to be unloaded under full military guard and stored in the basement of the recently completed Exchange Building, two stories below the Great Hall, where patriots had been holding their mass meetings.

Stories differ as to the fate of this tea: some say it rotted in its damp subterranean storehouse, others say that after the onset of armed conflict, patriots sold it to finance their war effort. In any case, when the next shipment of taxable tea arrived in Charleston almost a year later, it quickly found a wet resting place in the harbor.

In Plymouth, six days after the "glorious event" of December 16, Mercy Otis Warren received a personal request from John Adams for "a certain poetical pen, which has no equal that I know of in this Country . . . to describe a late frolic among the sea nymphs and goddesses." Flattered, Warren responded with over one hundred lines of verse commemorating the Tea Party, filled with forced rhymes and obscure classical references. A sample stanza:

> *The heroes of the Tuskurarine Race*
> *(Who neither hold, nor even wish for place [political office],*
> *While faction reigns, and tyranny presides,*
> *And base oppression o'er the virtues rides,*
> *While venal measures dance in silken sails,*
> *And avarice o'er earth and sea prevails) . . .*
> *Pour'd a profusion of delicious teas,*
> *Which waft'd by a soft Favonian breeze,*
> *Supplied the wat'ry Deities in spight,*
> *Of all the rage, of jealous Amphitrite.*[3]

At home in Mount Vernon, George Washington sat out the tea crisis, much as he had sat out the clamor over the Stamp Act. In over fifty extant letters penned from November 1, 1773, to the end of April 1774, during the heat of the events and afterward, he mentioned the turmoil over tea and taxes not a single time. Virtually all of these letters concerned the surveying, buying, selling, mortgaging, and settling of land. (He schemed to import droves of indentured servants from Palatine to settle his lands in the West, for instance, and Robert Morris, who purchased and peddled servants, advised him there were plenty of indentures for sale in Philadelphia.) Washington had played a prominent role in the previous war, and he would play an even more prominent role in the war to come and in the founding of a new nation—but at the time, although he continued to think any form of taxation without representation was a bad idea, he did not foresee that a confrontation over tea could have any significant impact on the fate of America, and he certainly did not suspect that it would affect his personal life. Until 1774, except for his brief involvement in the opposition to the Townshend duties, the future Father of our Country tended his own affairs and left the protests and political wrangling to others.[4]

December 27, 1773–June 20, 1774: Worcester

In the aftermath of what would one day be known as the Boston Tea Party, the patriots who pushed the movement to the next level came not from the urban centers of trade, politics, and culture, nor from the prominent plantations of Virginia, but from the rural hinterlands of the most rebellious colony— places like Worcester, Massachusetts. These unheralded rebels would be the first to seize political and military control from the mother country.

The patriots of Worcester celebrated the Tea Party with gusto. Less than a week after the event, John Adams wrote to James Warren:

> The spirit of Liberty is very high in the Country and universal. Worcester is aroused. Last week, a monument to Liberty was erected there in the heart of the Town within a few yards of Coll Chandlers door. A gentn. of a good sense and character as any in that County told me this day, that nothing, which has been ever done is more universally approved, applauded and admired than these last efforts. He says, that whole towns in the County were on tiptoe to come down.[5]

Taverns were abuzz, and talk soon evolved into action. On December 27, Timothy Bigelow, his cousin Joshua Bigelow, his fellow members of the Committee of Correspondence, and more than two dozen others met at the home of Asa Ward to found the American Political Society. Patriots in Boston had been meeting in political clubs for years, getting candidates elected to key positions and determining much of the agenda for the city's political activity. Why couldn't this sort of caucusing work in a small, self-contained community such as Worcester? As a private political club, the APS would not have to measure its words to meet the approval of prominent conservatives like John Chandler at the town meeting. It would be free to organize, inflame, and even prepare for war.

Joshua Bigelow, the town's representative to the Assembly for the past seven years, was elected chairman, while his younger cousin Timothy was given his second writing assignment: with veteran dissident Nathan Baldwin and rookie writer Samuel Curtis, the town blacksmith was asked to draft a set of "good and wholesome rules and regulations." The following week, when the APS reconvened, Bigelow, Baldwin, and Curtis announced that the mission of the fledgling organization would be to oppose "the machinations of some designing persons in this province, who are grasping at power, and the property of their neighbors." Because the stakes were so high, the committee suggested "that in all and every of our monthly meetings, our expenses for liquor, &c., shall not exceed six pence per man upon an average, and in our quarterly meeting, it shall not exceed two shillings per man." These men might drink, but not to excess, for they had important business to attend to.[6]

Thirty-one local patriots agreed to the committee's rules, and that was only the beginning. In less than a year, membership would grow to seventy-one, almost one-third of the enfranchised citizens of the town. Because these men could be counted upon to show up at every town meeting, effectively ensuring a majority, the APS became in effect a shadow government, determining the town's agenda and choosing candidates for local offices, who were invariably elected.

Twice in February, the energized APS met at the home of Timothy Bigelow, directly across Main Street from the courthouse. There, members discussed how to push their agenda forward, and by the evening of the 25th, they had hatched a "plan of proceeding" for the annual town meeting. Consequently, when the town convened in the Meetinghouse on March 7, Timothy Bigelow and two other APS members presented the citizens of Worcester with a passionately worded position paper addressing the two pressing issues of the day: the tea tax and the Crown's payment of salaries. Anybody selling contraband tea "must be considered, and treated by us, as enimys and trators to their Country," the declaration stated. If judges decided to accept any money from the Crown, the resolution continued, "we are not in the least bound in duty to submit, to the ordering and determining of such officers."[7]

These defiant words proved too much for the town's conservatives, who, according to local folklore, became "pale with rage." James Putnam, John Chandler's brother-in-law and allegedly "the best lawyer in North America," carried their standard, with the untutored Timothy Bigelow pitted against him. Eighty-six years later, Charles Hersey, who had listened to the tales of aging Revolutionaries when he was a young man, offered a secondhand account of the incident, undoubtedly embellished:

Figure 8. This engraving from the early nineteenth century depicts a contentious eighteenth-century New England town meeting. In spirit, this could have been Worcester, where patriots squared off in vigorous debate against Tories during the spring and summer of 1774. According to nineteenth-century accounts, Timothy Bigelow led the charge for the patriots. *(The Granger Collection, New York)*

Timothy Bigelow at length arose, without learning, without practice in public speaking, without wealth,—the Tories of Worcester had, at that day, most of the wealth and learning,—but there he stood upon the floor of the Old South Church, met the Goliath of the day, and vanquished him.[8]

The following month, the APS again took the lead, instructing the town's two grand jurors, Joshua and Timothy Bigelow, not to serve on the upcoming session of the Superior Court in Worcester, if Chief Justice Peter Oliver presided. (The other four justices had refused "the bribe offered them by the Crown," to use the words of the Worcester Town Meeting, while Oliver had not.) As an operative of the Committee of Correspondence, Bigelow communicated with like-minded cohorts from towns throughout the county to ensure that other grand jurors followed suit. Whether by conviction or intimidation, all prospective grand jurors in Worcester County joined the Bigelows in their pledge not to serve, and without them, the court could not conduct most of its business. Knowing this, and sensing that his presence would ignite a firestorm, Oliver wisely stayed away. Worcester patriots had kept the chief justice for the Province of Massachusetts from showing up for work.[9]

The APS continued its offensive, assigning Timothy Bigelow once again to a committee that would draft instructions for the town's representative. Legally, of course, this was a matter for the town meeting, but when the town convened in May, Timothy Bigelow and the APS committee morphed into an official town committee, which then instructed Representative Joshua Bigelow: "Whatever measures Great Britain may take to distress us, you be not in the least intimidated . . . but to the utmost of your power resist the most distant approaches of slavery." Representative Bigelow was placed under "the streckest injunction" not to approve compensation for the tea dumped into the Boston harbor; he was urged to conclude the impeachment proceedings against Chief Justice Oliver; and he was told to use his "utmost endeavors" to convene "a general Congress" of the Committees of Correspondence from throughout the colonies. (This convention, four months later, would evolve into the First Continental Congress.)[10]

Led once again by James Putnam, the "Tories" (a pejorative label applied by patriots, since most Americans considered themselves Whigs) aggressively continued their opposition. When it came time to vote, however, Timothy Bigelow and the American Political Society again prevailed: the instructions were adopted without alteration.

But Putnam and others did not let the matter rest. Immediately following adjournment, the town's conservative old guard gathered forty-three signatures on a petition that called for a special town meeting to reassess the previous votes and to consider disbanding the Committee of Correspondence. By law, the selectmen were required to honor this petition and call a special town meeting, so on June 20, both sides mustered their forces for a third and final showdown.

Although Putnam and company had gathered every "friend of government" they could, there were simply not enough of them in Worcester. Once more, the radicals prevailed, but this time, although outvoted, fifty-two local Tories drafted a dissent, which they published in the Boston newspapers and recorded in the official town minutes. The Protestors, as they called themselves, accused uneducated militants like the Bigelows of "spending their time in discoursing of matters they do not understand," while "neglecting their own proper business and occupation, in which they ought to be employed for the support of their families." They called the APS agitators "enemies to our King and Country, violators of all law and civil liberty, the malevolent disturbers of the peace of society, subverters of the established constitution, and enemies of mankind."[11]

Worcester was more divided than ever. In the early summer of 1774, it seemed unlikely that conservatives like James Putnam and John Chandler would ever settle their differences with radicals like Timothy Bigelow, Joshua Bigelow, and the American Political Society. With compromise out of the question, the only resolution was for one side or the other to triumph.

May and June 1774: Boston, New York, and Williamsburg

On May 10, a vessel ironically called *Harmony* sailed into Boston, bearing news from London that Parliament had closed the port as punishment for the destruction of tea. Only if the tea were paid for, the act said, would Boston's port be reopened.

While many were shocked, Thomas Young reasoned that the repressive measure might provide the catalyst for a final resolution to the disputes of the previous decade. "At length, the perfect crisis of American politics seems arrived," he wrote three days later, "and a very few months must decide, whether we and our posterity shall be slaves or freemen."[12]

By traditional accounts, closing the port of Boston brought all patriotic Americans together in support of their oppressed brethren, but this oversimplifies the response. Although many did express sympathy with Boston and some offered material aid, the Boston Port Act also rekindled the internal disputes from the Townshend Act era. Radicals and moderates in all the major cities immediately went at each other once again: Should nonimportation be resumed? If so, what items would be listed as contraband? Should Americans refrain from exports as well as imports, cutting off all trade with Britain? Should the restrictions extend to the British West Indies? To these traditional debates a new one was added: Should Bostonians pay for the tea?

According to Thomas Young, the division broke down along class lines:

> Those worthy members of society, the tradesmen, we depend on, under God, to form the revolution of the other ranks of citizens. . . . The yeomanry of our country towns are another effectual support. A covenant is handing about among them, and signing by thousands, not to purchase any British manufactures, imported from that Island, after the 31st of August next. This will insure a non-importation in this province, whether messieurs les merchands, will be graciously pleased to come into it or not.[13]

While tradesmen and yeoman rallied to the cause, many "merchands," as Young hinted, shuddered at the prospect of a new round of trade sanc-

Figure 9. This British cartoon from 1774, labeled "The Bostonians paying the exciseman, or tarring and feathering," abounds with symbols that represent Thomas Young's confrontational and theatrical style of political action: the Liberty Tree, the noose, tea being dumped into the water, the bucket of tar, and of course the victim's body covered with feathers. Although Young is not known to have participated in tarring and feathering, he did stand at the head of several crowd actions, and he openly advocated the use of heavy-handed methods of intimidation.

tions. At a Boston town meeting they staged a counterattack, proposing that the Committee of Correspondence, which was writing letters to garner support for the suspension of all trade, be not only censured but "annihilated." Although the motion failed by a large majority, it caused the moderate merchant John Rowe to write in his diary: "This affair will cause much evil one against the other. I wish for peace in this town. I fear the consequences."[14]

In New York, as rival factions resumed their feuds, Gouverneur Morris (no relation to Robert, although the two would soon become fast friends and colleagues) observed a large meeting in front of Fraunces Tavern: "I stood on the balcony, and on my right hand were ranged all the people of property, with some few poor dependants, and on the other all the tradesmen . . . who thought it worth their while to leave daily labor for the good of the country." Identifying with the men of property (his manor, Morrisania, covered much of the modern-day Bronx), Morris expressed the fears of his class with alarming clarity:

These sheep, simple as they are, cannot be pulled as heretofore. In short, there is no ruling them; and now, to leave the metaphor, the heads of the mobility grow dangerous to the gentry; and how to keep them down is the question. . . . The mob begin to think and to reason. Poor reptiles: it is with them a vernal morning, they are struggling, they are struggling to cast off their winter's slough, they bask in the sunshine, and ere noon they will bite, depend on it. The gentry begin to fear this. . . . I see, and I see it with fear and trembling, that if the disputes with Britain continue, we shall be under the worst of all possible dominions; we shall be under the dominion of a riotous mob.[15]

Days later, New York's gentry gained the upper hand (temporarily) and kept the city from entering another round of nonimportation.

In Virginia, George Washington appeared to embrace both sides of the issue: "[T]he cause of Boston . . . is and ever will be considered as the cause of America (not that we approve of their cond[uc]t in destroyg tea)," he wrote to George William Fairfax, a close friend whose aristocratic family bestowed its name on Fairfax County. But his quarrel with British policy added a dimension rarely expressed in Boston or other eastern seaports: not only was the ministry usurping the rights of Americans, it was also failing to live up to its chief obligation, furnishing protection from Indians. His letter to Fairfax continues:

[W]e shall not suffer ourselves to be sacrificed by piecemeal though god only knows what is to become of us, threatened as we are with so many hoverg evils as hang over us at present; having a cruel & blood thirsty enemy upon our backs, the Indians, between whom & our frontier inhabitants many skirmishes have happened, & with who[m] a general war is inevitable whilst those from whom we have a right to seek protection are endeavoring by every piece of art & despotism to fix the shackle of slavry upon us.[16]

Worse yet, Secretary of State Lord Hillsborough, infamous in America since the Townshend era, had suddenly declared, on no authority other than his own, that when the Proclamation of 1763 promised land to veteran officers of the French and Indian War, it had meant to reward only British Regulars, not Americans. This threw Washington into a full-blown rage. Having failed during that war to gain a commission as a British officer, and having spent a great deal of energy over the past decade trying to gain title to land he thought he had been promised, Washington fumed obsessively about "his Lordships malignant disposition towards us poor Americans; founded equally in malice, absurdity, & error." Aside from the danger it presented to the patents Washington was hoping to obtain, Hillsborough's arbitrary decree insulted all Americans. Bombastically, Washington asked "why Americans (who have serv'd his Majesty in the late war with as much fidelity, & without presumption, with as much success, as his British troops) should be stigmatiz'd." [17]

The fortuitous coincidence of Hillsborough's ruling with the crackdown on Boston caused George Washington to emerge from his political hiatus and immerse himself in the patriotic struggle—this time, for the duration. While the tea crisis had failed to stir him, the repressions that came in its wake certainly did. Suddenly, he "connected the dots," as we say today, or to use terms more appropriate to Washington's time and vocation, he meted the line between terminal points. Past politics and resentments, however disparate, fell into a pattern: Parliament's continuing insistence on taxation without representation, the preferential treatment given to British land speculators, his financial dependence on Robert Cary, his indebtedness to other British merchants, and perhaps even his rejection by Lord Loudoun, the British commander who had passed over his request for a commission almost two decades past. From his new perspective, this was all of a piece, and the vindictive, mean-spirited punishment of Boston proved the point once and for all: there was a "regular, systematick plan" to curtail American rights. Again and again in his letters during the summer of 1774, he seethed about the deliberate designs of the British ministry, which was attempting to impose "the most despotick system of tyranny that ever was practiced in a free government."[18]

Since British officials had already made up their minds, there was no longer any point in petitioning them for their favors. The time for pleading had passed. "Shall we after this whine & cry for relief, when we have already tried it in vain?" he asked rhetorically. "Shall we supinely sit, and see one Provence after another fall a sacrifice to despotism?" Certainly not. "The crisis is arrivd when we must assert our rights, or submit to every imposition that can be heap'd upon us; till custom and use, will make us as tame, & abject slaves, as the Blacks we rule over with such arbitrary sway."[19]

Summer 1774: Worcester

The Boston Port Act was only the beginning. In June, word arrived in America that Parliament had passed another punitive act, a measure so repressive it drove the people of one colony to cast off British rule entirely.

The Massachusetts Government Act unilaterally revoked key provisions of the colony's constitution, the 1691 Charter. Town meetings, the basis of local self-government, were outlawed; they could convene only at the pleasure of the Crown-appointed governor, who had to approve all agenda items. Members of the powerful Council, formerly elected, would henceforth be appointed by the king. All local officials, such as sheriffs and judges, would no longer be subject to the approval of elected representatives, while jurors would be selected by Crown-appointed officials, not by the people themselves.

In Worcester, the new Government Act dramatically altered the political landscape. Before, Tories could present a reasoned (albeit controversial) argument for remaining true to imperial authority; afterward, the Tory stance was entirely discredited. There was no way to argue that citizens could benefit by having their Charter and their most basic rights yanked away. Outraged patriots vowed to shut down the reorganized government—by arms if necessary—and they quickly made good on that pledge.

On July 4, Worcester's American Political Society declared "that each, and every, member of our Society, be forth with provided, with two pounds of gun powder each 12 flints and led answerable thereunto," and thirty-five of the men in attendance promptly agreed to "take and pay for" at least two pounds of powder apiece. Timothy Bigelow was one of a dozen men to offer more than the quota, and he also served on a two-man committee "to equally divide and proportion" the donated powder among all members. Apparently, the run on powder exhausted local supplies, for on July 22, Worcester merchant Stephen Salisbury told his brother Samuel that although business was slow, he was completely out of gunpowder; the demand was so great, in fact, that he was thinking of building his own powderhouse.[20]

Through the summer of 1774, Timothy Bigelow devoted his life to politics. He attended APS membership meetings and worked on its committees. He drilled with the militia. He distributed gunpowder. Most likely, he fashioned lead into musket balls, and he undoubtedly discoursed about the heightened tensions in virtually every conversation he had, whether at his blacksmith shop or elsewhere. Perhaps most significantly, as a key member of the town's Committee of Correspondence, he reached out to other committees throughout the country to widen the resistance. This paid off: on August 9, three days after Governor Thomas Gage received official orders to implement the Government Act, fifty-two delegates from twenty-two towns traveled to the shiretown, where they gathered in the widow Mary Stearns's tavern to scheme. They would close the upcoming session of the county courts on September 6, they vowed. The Court of Common Pleas and the Court of General Sessions, which served administrative as well as judicial functions, constituted the furthest reach of imperial authority, and shutting them down would terminate British rule in Worcester County.[21]

But patriots from the town of Worcester, knowing they had the upper hand, refused to wait four weeks for a confrontation. The APS appointed both Bigelows, Nathan Baldwin, and four others to suggest "something that they shall think proper for the town to act upon at our next town meeting," and putting their heads together, the committee settled on a devilish plan: at the next town meeting, in full public view, they would force the fifty-two Protestors to strike their names from the cranky dissent they had entered in the town record. The APS had little difficulty implementing this; by now, they were electing the town moderator at APS meetings and even issuing instructions to the town's selectmen. So on Wednesday, August 24, in the Meetinghouse, one at a time, the Protestors did as demanded, and then Clark Chandler, the clerk, was forced (in the words of the official resolution) to "obliterate, erase or otherwise deface the said recorded protest . . . in the presence of the town," first by a scratch of the pen through each line, but then, since some words could still be deciphered, by a series of tightly looped spirals. Finally, for full humiliation, the clerk for the town of Worcester—John Chandler's son—was forced to dip his own fingers in a well of ink and drag them over the first page of the protest. The short, irregular changes of direction in the defacements on this document suggest that Clark Chandler's hand was forced.[22]

With local supremacy ensured, Worcester patriots decided to force a resignation from their townsman, Timothy Paine, who had just accepted an appointment from the king to serve on the new Council. Bigelow and the Committee of Correspondence dispatched riders throughout the county, and on Saturday morning, August 27, somewhere between 1,500 and 3,000 men (estimates vary) from Leicester, Spencer, Brookfield, Rutland, Westborough, Shrewsbury, Grafton, Sutton, Oxford, and points beyond gathered on the Worcester Common. Organized into their militia units, and proceeding peacefully but deliberately, the assemblage selected five men to visit Paine at his home at the north end of town.

Under duress, Paine drafted a resignation, but the committee deemed it unsatisfactory. They wanted a more suppliant tone, so in his second draft, which the committee accepted, he thanked "the people of the county, from whom I have received many favors."[23]

Paine thought he was done, but when the committee read his statement to the crowd, the people said it would not suffice: they wanted to have the object of their attention appear before them in public. So the high-flown lawyer who had graduated fifth in his class at Harvard (according to social rank), and who preferred riding in a "handsome green coach, trimmed with gilding and lined with satin," was made to walk the length of the town to the Commons, where he met the assembled patriots of Worcester County. There, he stood submissively while one of the representatives read the resignation, but this too was not enough to satisfy: the people insisted Paine say the words himself, which of course he did.[24]

Even then, the people wanted more. With so large a crowd, not everybody could hear Paine's words, so he was forced to read them again and again— with his hat off, to emphasize his submission.[25]

This was only the beginning. The rest of Worcester's Tories would have done well to take note, for their turn was close at hand.

August 26–September 2: Boston, Springfield, and Cambridge

In Boston, simultaneously with Timothy Paine's humiliation, both sides pre-pared for the impending confrontation on September 6. Local "friends of government" alerted Governor Thomas Gage that Worcester radicals in-tended to shut the courts, and Gage, who had failed to provide Chief Justice Oliver protection back in April, promised to do better this time. "In Worces-ter, they keep no terms, openly threaten resistance by arms, have been pur-chasing arms, preparing them, casting ball, and providing powder, and threaten to attack any troops who dare to oppose them," Gage wrote to Secre-tary of State Lord Dartmouth. "I apprehend that I shall soon be obliged to march a body of troops into that Township, and perhaps into others, as occa-sion happens, to preserve the peace."[26]

But when Timothy Bigelow and the Worcester Committee of Corres-pondence got word that Gage intended to hold firm this time around, they made moves of their own to mobilize support. Immediately, they wrote to the Boston Committee of Correspondence, urging a multicounty convention. If Worcester patriots stood alone against British Regulars, the committee feared, they might well be crushed, but if they gained the assistance of freedom fighters from elsewhere, they could keep the Regulars at bay. The Boston committee, following Worcester's lead, called for representatives from the province's most populous counties—Suffolk (which included Boston), Middlesex, Essex, and Worcester, to convene on August 26 at Faneuil Hall, hallowed meeting place for Boston's patriots over the previous decade.[27]

Representing Worcester at the multicounty meeting were Timothy Bigelow and Ephraim Doolittle, the town's former representative to the Assembly, who had moved to Petersham, still within the county. Representing Boston were a host of patriot heavyweights, including Joseph Warren, Benjamin Church, William Molineux, Joseph Greenleaf, and Dr. Thomas Young. Although the Worcester pair were clearly outranked, Timothy Bigelow, who had been instrumental in calling the meeting, was honored with a position on the five-man committee charged with drafting resolutions. Eighteen months earlier, Bigelow's highest political position had been that of fence viewer; now, he was not only hobnobbing with Boston's famous patriots, but preparing a document for their approval.

At the table with Bigelow, representing Boston, was Thomas Young, by now a veteran at resolution writing. Bigelow and Young had been communicating indirectly through their respective Committees of Correspondence, but finally they sat together, drafting a set of resolutions that would set the standard for a revolution in the making. Their job was not only to inspire but to coordinate, and they accomplished both tasks. First and foremost, the document they created, which was ratified by the full convention, asked each county to shut down its courts: "Every officer belonging to the courts" who acted under the authority of the Massachusetts Government Act was to be considered "a traitor cloaked with the pretext of law," and they "ought to be held in the highest detestations by the people, as common plunderers." Knowing the British would not sit idly by, the authors then asked all patriots to learn "the military art . . . as necessary means to secure their liberties against the designs of enemies whether foreign or domestick." Finally, they called for a special Provincial Congress, to meet the first week of October, to provide some sense of order for the massive resistance movement.[28]

As leaders met in Boston, the rebellion continued with a life of its own, firmly based in local communities. On August 30 in Springfield, shiretown for Hampshire County, over three thousand patriots marched "with staves and musick" to unseat the court officials. "Amidst the crowd in a sandy, sultry place, exposed to the sun," said one observer, judges were forced to renounce "in the most express terms any commission which should be given out to them under the new arrangement."[29]

By September 2, upon hearing news from both Springfield and Worcester, Governor Gage appeared to be having second thoughts about forcing a confrontation. He confessed to Lord Dartmouth that although he had recently resolved "to send a body of troops to Worcester, to protect the courts there, and if wanted to send parties to the houses of some of the Counsellors who dwell in that County," he now heard "from undoubted authorities, that the flames of sedition had spread universally throughout the country beyond conception, the Counsellors already drove away, and that no courts could proceed on business."[30]

Later that day, Gage's doubts were confirmed, and then some.

Responding to news that British Regulars had seized some powder from a magazine in Somerville (across the Charles River from Boston), farmers from the surrounding countryside gathered on the neighboring common in Cambridge. Dr. Thomas Young, Dr. Joseph Warren, and four other members of the Boston Committee traveled quickly to the scene of the action to provide some leadership, order, and direction, but they didn't have to, for the well-behaved farmers, acting on their own, were peaceably but forcefully inducing two more counselors to resign. As Young described the event: "When Dr. Warren and I arrived there Judge Danforth was addressing perhaps four thousand people in the open air; and such was the order of that great assembly that not a whisper interrupted the low voice of that feeble old man from being heard by the whole body." The demonstrators had to endure "the scorching sun of the hottest day we have had this summer," Young wrote, but when the Bostonians suggested that the crowd choose a committee "to confer about the situation" in the cool of Captain Stedman's inn, the crowd's leaders, who had already been elected that morning, chose to remain outside with the people.[31]

That afternoon, the crowd surrounded the home of Lieutenant Governor Thomas Oliver, the second highest ranking official in Massachusetts, and forced him to resign his seat on the Council. As the day advanced, the people had "worked up to a fury," Oliver later told Gage, but even so, this was not simply intimidation as usual. Oliver acknowledged that his antagonists this time were "not a Boston rabble but the freeholders and farmers of the country."[32]

Meanwhile, a rumor spread throughout the New England countryside that British Regulars had not only seized some powder, but also killed six patriots and set Boston ablaze. The "news" ran rampant, and in no time some 20,000–100,000 men (that is the range of contemporary estimates) from every village and hamlet for hundreds of miles headed toward Boston to confront the Redcoats. From Worcester County alone, 6,000 took to the road, bearing what arms they could. A traveler from Connecticut reported, "They scarcely left half a dozen men in a town, unless old and decrepid, and in one town the landlord told him that himself was the *only man left*." In Shrewsbury, adjacent to the town of Worcester, this observer described the frenzy of the moment:

All along were armed men rushing forward some on foot some on horseback, at every house women & children making cartridges, running bullets, making wallets, baking biscuit, crying & bemoaning & at the same time animating their husbands & sons to fight for their liberties, tho' not knowing whether they should ever see them again.[33]

But alas, it was a false alarm. "The people seemed really disappointed," one man told John Adams two months later, "when the news was contradicted."[34]

September 6: Worcester

On Friday and Saturday, September 2 and 3, as they flocked toward Cambridge and Boston, Worcester patriots had puffed their chests. The following Tuesday, September 6, they toppled the old regime.

In their taverns and meetinghouses, patriots from throughout the county had been prepping themselves for a month. Militia units had elected new commanders, and militia training days, primarily social events for the past decade, had taken on new meaning. Musket barrels were cleaned, flintlocks checked, powder and ball rolled into cartridges.

All this preparation, along with the unexpected dress rehearsal provided by the Powder Alarm, would soon be put to use. If General Gage kept to his word, war would break out. The lines were drawn, and the stakes were high.

But Thomas Gage, a reasonable man, decided in the end to back off. The Boston garrison of three thousand Regulars was in no position to face off, on hostile ground, against ten times their number or more. Without enough forces to ensure victory, and without express authorization from the Crown, the royal governor of Massachusetts was not about to engage in armed confrontation. The American Political Society, meeting at Mary Stearns's tavern on the eve of the much-awaited showdown, got wind of Gage's decision and voted "not to bring our fire-arms into town" the following day. The arms and ammunition they had been gathering all summer had worked so well as a deterrent that they would not have to be used.[35]

So the courts would be closed without bloodshed. But how should the momentous event be dramatized?

Before dawn, local patriots entered the courthouse and boarded up the doors. Directly across Main Street at Timothy Bigelow's house, where the APS often met, representatives from the various Committees of Correspondence convened to coordinate the events of the day. As day broke, 45 militiamen from Winchendon (on the New Hampshire line), 156 from Uxbridge (on the Connecticut line), 216 from Brookfield (to the west), 85 from Northboro (to the east), and many more—a total of 4,622 aroused patriots from thirty-seven townships in Worcester Country—formed into their separate companies. Meanwhile, the Crown-appointed court officials, unable to access the courthouse, huddled together at Daniel Heywood's tavern, midway between the courthouse on the north end of town and the common on the south end, where the militiamen assembled.[36]

The Convention of Committees of Correspondence at Bigelow's house asked each of the thirty-seven militia companies to select a representative "to wait on the judges" and demand their recantations. (These representatives served for one day only, the ultimate in term limits.) They then suggested that the assembled throng move to a meadow just north of Bigelow's house and catercorner to the courthouse, and they themselves moved their convention outside "to attend the body of the people." Here in the countryside, there would be no distinction between leaders and the people.[37]

Final decision making lay with the body of the people, and when the people's representatives took the first draft of the judges' recantations back to the militia companies for a vote, the body found it lacking. So the representatives trudged back to Heywood's Tavern to hammer out a more conclusive statement, which of course needed to be resubmitted. This cumbersome system, heavily weighted at the bottom, proceeded only slowly, and when some militiamen evidenced impatience, the convention appointed a three-man committee to inquire about the delay.

Finally, by midafternoon, the stage was set. One by one, the twenty-five court officials were released from Heywood's Tavern, and each one, hat in hand, then made his way through the gauntlet of militiamen who lined both sides of Main Street, in full company formation, for a quarter mile. As they marched meekly to the courthouse and back, the officials were made to repeat their renunciations of office over thirty times so every militiaman could hear. With this ritualistic act of submission, all British authority disappeared from Worcester County, never to return.[38]

Officially, that should have sufficed: the courts were closed. But the people wanted more. Although Gardiner Chandler, the high sheriff, had been humiliated (he required an extra bodyguard of four men to ensure against abuse by the militiamen), his brother John had not yet walked, for he was not at that time among the court officials. To rectify this, John Chandler and the rest of the town's prominent Tories were also shuttled through the gauntlet, forced to read aloud the recantations they had signed two weeks earlier, when they inked through their signatures on the Protest.

All this was highly dramatic, but it was also scary, for the people of Worcester County, having dismantled their governmental apparatus, were thereby reduced to a "state of nature." To fill the void and prevent anarchy, the County Convention of the Committees of Correspondence met the next day to determine the minimal governmental machinery that would suffice "till the rising of the Provincial Congress, proposed to sit at Concord, on the second tuesday of October next." It appointed interim justices of the peace. It "put the laws in execution respecting pedlars and chapmen." Most significantly, it instructed the militias to prepare for the defense of the revolution they had just made: train according to "the Norfolk exercise" and procure "one or more field pieces, mounted and fitted for use; and also a sufficient quantity of ammunition for the same; and that the officers appoint a suitable number of men, out of their respective companies, to manage said field pieces."[39]

Two weeks later, timed to coincide with a scheduled meeting of the Superior Court, the County Committees of Correspondence met once again in Worcester. Governor Gage, of course, was no longer under the illusion that he could convene a court in Worcester, and he did not even try this time. After perfunctorily (and unnecessarily) instructing the sheriff to "adjourn the superior court appointed by law to be held this day," the convention got down to the main business at hand: preparing for war.

That's when the Minutemen were born. Because everyone suspected the British would strike back with military force but nobody could know how or when the offensive might come, the convention suggested that each town enlist one-third of its men between sixteen and sixty "to be ready to act at a minute's warning." It also recommended that the militia for Worcester County be reorganized into seven regiments, that the company for each town choose its officers, and that these company officers come together to choose field officers to command the newly formed regiments. This was to be a thoroughly democratic army of citizens, from bottom to top.[40]

Significantly, the County Convention did not meet at Timothy Bigelow's house this time: it moved across the street to the courthouse. The County Convention had taken on the role of a de facto government.

The APS had also outgrown Bigelow's house. With each meeting attracting over fifty men, members decided that Mary Stearns's tavern would be a more suitable venue.

Although meetings moved from his home, Timothy Bigelow's life had become consumed by politics and the prospect of war. On September 8, two days after the courts closed and one day after the County Convention of the Committees of Correspondence had adjourned, Bigelow helped organize a convention for patriotic blacksmiths from around the county. But he himself had little time these days to fire up his own forge, for he was burdened by the twin demands of talking (the principle medium of exchange for the APS and the Committees of Correspondence) and yelling (as captain of the town's militia unit, he needed to drill his troops several times a week on the common). Bigelow had demonstrated excellent leadership on the political front, and because of his strength and stature (over six feet tall, rare for the times), as well as his can-do attitude and his facility for working with others, his peers figured he would be able to lead on the military field as well.

But to call Timothy Bigelow a "leader" could be misconstrued, for it masks his relationship with the people who asked him to represent their interests politically and to bring out the best in their military endeavors. Because his leadership emanated from the people, he followed as much as directed, and in 1774, that was the only sort of command the patriots of the Massachusetts countryside would acknowledge. This was *their* revolution, not to be usurped for the power, gain, or glory of any individual. The very reason they rebelled was to ensure popular sovereignty, so they were in no mood to relinquish their say.

September 12, 1774: Boston and Newport

Thomas Young's life also took a dramatic turn during the tumultuous outpouring of popular sentiment in the late summer of 1774: on September 13, despite his long-standing affinity for the "Athens of America," he left Boston for Newport in an instant and never came back, abandoning the house he had recently purchased in the heart of town, just a block from his beloved Faneuil Hall.

Many people wondered, as we must today: with his cause ascendant, his political career at its zenith, and the fate of his country on the line, why did he choose to flee?

Elizabeth Adams, in a questioning tone, reported the news (mistaking the place of destination) to her husband, Samuel, who was off in Philadelphia at the time: "Doct Young is gone to live at Providence and carried his family. I much wonder he should go just now."[41]

One week later, Young explained his actions to Elizabeth's husband:

> You know my dear friend that my situation in Boston was calamitous on account of the constant terrors in which Mrs. Young was invelloped. The beginning of the late fortification so dismayed her that she took bed and appeared as [inanimate?] as a corpse. Humanity therefore obliges to seek an asylum for her.[42]

To John Lamb he wrote, "Mrs. Young's concern was so great for me that it impaired her health . . . and began to affect her reason."[43]

As disingenuous as this might sound, Young's move needs to be placed in context. As patriots took undisputed control of the countryside, General Thomas Gage tightened the lid on Boston, the only place he exerted any authority. In response to the Powder Alarm and the rebellion in Worcester and other interior towns, he fortified the Boston Neck and allowed people to pass only after being checked by guards. In Young's mind, Boston was no longer the citadel of freedom but a "state prison," a garrison city under military command. "My own disposition revolted at the tho't of being pent up within gates of which my mortal enemy held the keys," Young wrote to Lamb.[44]

That was the background. The precipitating event seems to have been a letter that was circulating about town addressed "To the Officers and Soldiers of his Majesty's Troops in Boston." The anonymous writer identified eighteen key "authors" of the "rebellion breaking out in this province" and told the soldiers that they would soon be expected to "put the above persons immediately to the sword and destroy their houses and plunder their effects." Both Thomas Young and Samuel Adams were of course on this list.[45]

Still, Thomas Young fled while the other seventeen alleged targets remained, and to explain this would not be easy. In a public letter to the people of Boston, many of whom questioned his judgment or his courage or both, Young pleaded his case. He had "A LARGE FAMILY OF HELPLESS CHILDREN" but no relatives in town to help care for them should he be taken prisoner. More to the point, Mary Young could bear no more: "I HAVE A WIFE, whose anxiety for my safety, began with the first opposition to the Stamp Act in the City of Albany; MANY PERILOUS INCIDENTS have renewed and augmented the distress of her mind, on this account, till it at length became intolerable."[46] Those "MANY PERILOUS INCIDENTS" probably lay at the heart of the matter. Thomas Young, feisty and argumentative, had a knack for provoking personal confrontations, and he often arrived home bloody and bruised. In 1767 he had been beaten by Dr. Whitworth's son (see chapter 3), and again in 1773, a sailor had to rescue him from "Whitworth's mob" (to use Young's term). According to his brother Joseph,

> Two . . . officers attacked him one night in the street. They knocked him down and probably supposing they had killed him, ran off. He was carried home to his family all bloody. When he recovered he said he should certainly have been killed, but as he had seen the blow coming he had moved his head to one side; the weapon in consequence had brushed down his temple, and spent its chief force on his shoulder. But this atrocious attempt to assassinate him had alarmed his wife to such a degree, that when he went out at night she frequently cried until he returned.[47]

There had likely been other such times, with more to follow. In a garrison town, where soldiers ruled, the specter of a battered James Otis (whom he had treated) or the victims of the Boston Massacre must have haunted Thomas Young; more to the point, it haunted his wife, Mary, and probably his son, John, and daughters, Susannah, Catharine, Sarah, and Mary.

Young's defense of his sudden flight probably did not satisfy all the comrades he left behind, but many, including Samuel Adams, continued to communicate with him and count him as one of their own. Indeed, Adams and John Hancock, when they finally fled Boston seven months later, would be regarded as heroes rather than cowards.

Whatever his reasons, and whether he was justified or not, Thomas Young was off to promote revolution in other climes. From Newport he concluded his public letter: "I can in this place serve the common cause of America as effectually as I have done in any part of it."

And that he did. Without missing a beat, Young continued to propagate resistance in his new (albeit temporary) city of residence. Simon Pease, a prominent Newport merchant and slave dealer, told a friend in Boston about a crowd that paid an unwanted visit to his house:

> I have since learnt that your infamous Dr. Young was the mover of the whole and harangued them. . . . It's a pity that such a fellow should get footing anywhere, but he is playing here the same game he did at Boston, and I am fearful with the same success, as some of our popular gentlemen countenance him too much.[48]

Thomas Young remained as committed to the cause as ever, even though he was missing the exciting conclusion to the grand rebellion in Massachusetts that he himself had helped foment.

October 1774: Plymouth, Worcester, Concord, Cambridge

In Mercy Otis Warren's Plymouth on October 4, as in Worcester four weeks earlier, several thousand militiamen gathered to dismantle the local government. Afterward, the rebels were so excited that they "attempted to remove a rock (the one on which their fore-fathers first landed, when they came to this country), which lay buried in a wharfe five feet deep, up into the center of the town, near the court house. The way being up hill, they found it impracticable, as after they had dug it up, they found it to weigh ten tons at least."[49]

So it went across the province: courts closed and officials abandoned their offices. In direct violation of the new law, the people persisted with their town meetings, the staple of New England self-governance. When Governor Gage arrested seven men in the capital, Salem, for calling a town meeting without his approval, three thousand farmers immediately marched on the jail to set the prisoners free. Two companies of British soldiers, on duty to protect the governor, retreated rather than force a bloody confrontation. Having gained the upper hand, local patriots forced the issue, as noted by Boston merchant John Andrews:

> Notwithstanding all the parade the governor made at Salem on account of their meeting, they had another one directly under his nose at Danvers [the neighboring town], and continued it two or three howers longer than was necessary, to see if he would interrupt 'em. He was acquainted with it, but reply'd—"Damn 'em! I won't do any thing about it unless his Majesty sends me more troops."[50]

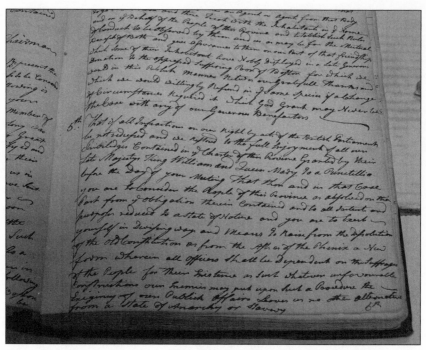

Figure 10. This instruction from the October 4, 1774, Worcester Town Meeting to Timothy Bigelow, its representative to the Provincial Congress, is the earliest known call by a public body to break from British authority and form a new government. This was twenty-one months before the Congressional Declaration of Independence.

By early October 1774, more than half a year before the "shot heard round the world" at Lexington, patriots in Massachusetts had seized all political and military authority outside of Boston. Ninety-five percent of the people in the province suddenly lived under the uncontested hegemony of the patriots; the remaining five percent lived within the city of Boston, which Governor Gage ruled only by military might. Throughout the preceding decade, patriots had written petitions, staged boycotts, and burned effigies—but this was something new. In the late summer and early fall of 1774, patriots did not simply *protest* government, they *overthrew* it. Then, after dismissing British authority, they boldly assumed political control through their town meetings and county conventions. One disgruntled Tory summed it all up in his diary: "Government has now devolved upon the people, and they seem to be for using it."[51]

One job was done, two remained: to create an alternative to the old government on the provincial level and to coordinate defense preparations, in anticipation of the expected counterattack by British Regulars. As Timothy

Bigelow and Thomas Young and the rest of the multicounty convention had suggested back on August 27, these tasks would be addressed by convening a Provincial Congress in early October.

On October 4, 1774, while patriots in Plymouth tried to move Plymouth Rock, their counterparts in Worcester issued instructions to Timothy Bigelow, whom they had chosen to represent them at the forthcoming Provincial Congress:

> You are to consider the people of this province absolved, on their part, from the obligation therein contained [the 1691 Massachusetts charter], and to all intents and purposes reduced to a state of nature; and you are to exert yourself in devising ways and means to raise from the dissolution of the old constitution, as from the ashes of the Phenix, a new form, wherein all officers shall be dependent on the suffrages of the people, whatever unfavorable constructions our enemies may put upon such procedure.[52]

Exactly twenty-one months before the Continental Congress would approve its own Declaration of Independence, the citizens of the town of Worcester had decided it was time to form a new and independent government, no matter what anybody else might say. This resolution, America's first recorded declaration of independence, was drafted the previous day at a meeting of the American Political Society. Had Timothy Bigelow not been the man to receive this momentous instruction, he most likely would have authored it.[53]

Placing his blacksmith work aside, and leaving Anna to care for five children under the age of ten (the youngest, Lucy, had been born during the heated debates with Tories the previous spring), Timothy Bigelow took his instructions and journeyed to Concord to meet with representatives from 209 of the 260 towns and districts in Massachusetts (a far greater participation than the old Assembly had ever inspired). Only the smallest and most distant communities failed to attend. The turnout was so large that the Congress moved to Cambridge, better equipped to accommodate all the delegates.

No sooner had Congress convened than the debates commenced. Not all delegates concurred that the old government should be thrown away, as per Worcester's instructions; many wanted merely to restore the 1691 Charter as it stood before the Massachusetts Government Act. But Bigelow and other delegates from the rural and western regions had had enough of sharing authority with an absent king and Parliament. Throw out the 1691 Charter altogether, they said, and go back to the more democratic Charter of 1621, under which citizens (not the Crown) had chosen the governor, while representatives in the Assembly and the Council (not Parliament) had exercised exclusive jurisdiction within the colony. This radical program scared the leaders from Boston and vicinity.

That wasn't the only difference. Western radicals advocated a standing army of fifteen thousand soldiers, and some even suggested that all patriots evacuate Boston so their newly formed army could attack the town and remove British Regulars from their bastion. We can easily imagine the fright this notion induced in the delegates from Boston, by now considered "by far the most moderate men."[54]

Although rural delegates from the West outnumbered their more urban counterparts, their views did not prevail. Historian L. Kinvin Wroth has calculated that more than two-thirds of the men who served on key committees or held multiple assignments in the first session of the Provincial Congress came from Boston or other trading towns of the East, even though these towns accounted for only twenty percent of the delegates. When political debates shifted from the taverns, commons, and meetinghouses of rural communities to the chambers of larger deliberative bodies, the established patriot leadership—more educated, more experienced, more renowned—was able to reassert control. Back in Worcester, Timothy Bigelow had become a major player in politics despite his lack of polish, but within chambers the tools of his trade, a hammer and anvil and bellows, were no match for the tools of his eastern colleagues: a solid education (often at Harvard), erudite rhetoric, and years of practice in political assemblies.[55]

Although he was unable to win approval for Worcester's radical agenda, Bigelow contributed his share to the success of the Provincial Congress. Known for his role in creating and training the Worcester Minutemen and reorganizing the Worcester County militias, he served on two committees: one to choose the best exercise for military training, the other to prepare a list of personnel in the various militias. Military preparations such as these drove the agenda of the Congress. On October 24, delegates appointed a committee to determine "the most proper time for this province to provide a stock of powder, ordnance, and ordnance stores"; later the same day, the committee issued its report—"*Now* was the proper time."[56]

Two days after that, the Congress announced a list of armaments it wished to procure:[57]

16 field pieces, 3 pounders, with carriages, irons, &c.;
   wheels for ditto, irons, sponges, ladles, &c., @ £30 .... £480 0 0
4 ditto, 6 pounders, with ditto, @ £38 .... £152 0 0
Carriages, irons, &c., for 12 battering cannon, @ £30 .... £360 0 0
4 mortars, and appurtenances, viz: 2 8-inch and
   2 13-inch, @ £20 .... £80 0 0
20 tons grape and round shot, from 3 to 24 lb., @ £15 .... £300 0 0
10 tons bomb-shells, @ £20 .... £200 0 0
5 tons lead balls, @ £33 .... £165 0 0
1,000 barrels of powder, @ £8 .... £8,000 0 0
5,000 arms and bayonets, @ £2 .... £10,000 0 0
And 75,000 flints £100 0 0
Contingent charges .... £ 1,000 0 0
In the whole £20,837 0 0

An arms race was under way.

7

Going Continental

September and October 1774: City Tavern and Carpenters' Hall, Philadelphia

Would other colonies support the rebellion, or would Massachusetts have to stand alone?

That decision fell into the hands of fifty-odd delegates (attendance varied) from twelve of the British colonies in North America. The intercolonial network of Committees of Correspondence and colonial assemblies that organized the Philadelphia convention sent invitations also to Quebec, Nova Scotia, St. John's Island, Georgia, East Florida, and West Florida, all of which declined. Still, the vast majority of British citizens on the continent had representatives in the most broadly based convention the Committees of Correspondence ever put together.

"All America," wrote Mercy Otis Warren in her *History*, "waited in anxious hope and expectation the decisions of a continental congress." One Connecticut politician wrote at the time: "Our whole dependence is in the wisdom, prudence and determination of the Congress, the highest and most respectable Council that ever was (and perhaps ever will be) in America." James Warren spoke of the group reverentially as the "Grand Council of America."[1]

More than simple deference contributed to the "anxious hope and expectation" the people placed in their representatives. Most Americans were sympathetic to Massachusetts, yet few wished to put themselves on a path that might lead to civil war unless they were assured of a united front. Unity was therefore paramount, and the only way to achieve it was for the fledgling

Continental Congress to come up with a coherent, cohesive plan that all could follow.

For all delegates, the pressure was on: "Great are our expectations, and great will be the expectations in Europe; and therefore great and difficult is the task assigned you," James Warren wrote to John Adams, who had been elected as a representative from Massachusetts. But for Adams and his three colleagues, the stakes doubled. Just as Timothy Bigelow and Ephraim Doolittle needed to broaden support for Worcester in their multicounty meeting of August 27, now John Adams, Samuel Adams, Thomas Cushing, and Robert Treat Paine had to garner backing for the rebellion that was happening right at that very moment throughout their own province. There was a difference, however: Adams and company were playing to a larger, broader, and tougher audience, including politically cautious delegates from the key colonies of New York and Pennsylvania.[2]

Before he embarked on his grand mission, John Adams asked James and Mercy Otis Warren for advice: "I must entreat the favour of your sentiments and Mrs. Warrens what is proper, praticable expedient, wise, just, good necessary to be done at Phyladelphia." James wrote back with his ideas for a continuing Congress and annual elections, but Mercy politely declined to contribute: "I shall not be so presumptuous as to offer anything but my fervant wishes that the enemies of America may hereafter tremble at the wisdom the firmness the prudence and justice of the delegates." A few weeks later, however, Mrs. Warren decided she had some important advice to offer after all. In a letter to Abigail Adams, she passed along some words to John: "Tell him I hope they will beware that no future annals may say they chose an ambitious Philip for their leader, who subverted the noble order of the American Amphyctiones [council of the ancient Greek league of Delphi] and built up a monarchy on the ruins of the happy institution." Mrs. Warren, ever suspicious of power and always vigilant against its corrupting influence, had no cause to worry that her good friend John Adams was unaware of the dangers, and yet, with hindsight, her warning seems almost prophetic, for Adams's alleged abuse of power lay at the heart of their later disagreements.[3]

Samuel Adams, like his cousin John, received advice from his friends before the convention commenced. Joseph Warren suggested that Adams get the Continental Congress to denounce the Massachusetts Government Act and endorse the efforts under way to resist it. To accomplish this, Warren proposed that he send Adams the resolutions from his forthcoming Suffolk County Convention, and that Adams find a delegate from some other colony to present them to Congress. Weeks later, this plan would be executed to perfection.[4]

Delegates began to arrive in Philadelphia about a week before the opening date, set for Monday, September 5. "We then rode into Town," John Adams wrote in his diary on August 29, "and dirty, dusty, and fatigued as we were, we could not resist the importunity, to go to the Tavern, the most genteel one in America." Genteel it was. Financed by Robert Morris and a group of Philadelphia investors who wished to socialize with each other in grand style, the recently completed City Tavern was built to emulate the grand drinking houses of London. The main floor was "fitted up" with "a genteel coffee room well attended and properly supplied with English and American papers and magazines"; above that, two stories of private meeting rooms and lodgings; below, in the basement, two large kitchens. It was here in the City Tavern that men representing the collected wisdom of America met, dined, drank, talked, and got to know one another, both before and concurrent with the formal proceedings.[5]

The venue for the official meetings proved controversial. Joseph Galloway, leader of the moderate Pennsylvania delegation, had arranged for Congress to meet in the Assembly room of the State House, home of the provincial government. But men with more radical ideas on their minds did not feel comfortable there: how could they freely oppose British authority while gathering at the seat of it? Instead, they proposed the downstairs meeting room of Carpenters' Hall, which, like the City Tavern, had just been completed. Built by and for the city's artisans, and housing Ben Franklin's Library Company upstairs, Carpenters' Hall was solid but not ornate, functional but not ostentatious. That is where the delegates chose to meet, literally and physically supported by ordinary men: each chair in the hall had been individually crafted by a Philadelphia artisan.

Before it could proceed with substantive matters, Congress had to devise its own rules of operation. Some were easy to agree on, as they were the custom of the times: "*Resolved*, That no person shall speak more than twice on the same point, without the leave of the Congress." Others were not in observance of contemporary norms: "*Resolved*, That the doors be kept shut during the time of business, and that the members consider themselves under the strongest obligation of honour, to keep the proceedings secret." If the proceedings became public, members feared, deliberations could quickly degenerate into political posturing and wrangling.

One item proved controversial: "*Resolved*, That in determining questions of this Congress, each Colony or Province shall have one vote." To populous states like Virginia, Pennsylvania, and Massachusetts, this seemed unfair, but there were more small colonies than large ones, and besides, nobody possessed the statistics necessary for weighted voting.[6]

Around two in the afternoon of September 6, as delegates were debating the voting procedures, they received alarming news that Boston had been bombarded by British artillery and six patriots killed. Two days later, they learned otherwise, but in the interim, delegates experienced in a dramatic manner the seriousness of the crisis. If the need for unity was evident before, it was even more so now.

Ten days after that, Paul Revere arrived in town with a fresh dispatch from Boston. This one carried a copy of the Suffolk Resolves, as previously arranged by Joseph Warren and Samuel Adams, along with a more accurate depiction of the rebellion that was enveloping Massachusetts. Warren himself had helped compose the Suffolk Resolves, and although they differed little in content from those of other Massachusetts counties, they were better crafted, and this undoubtedly impressed the learned delegates to Congress. On September 17, delegates endorsed the Suffolk Resolves unanimously: "This was one of the happiest days of my life," John Adams wrote in his diary. "In Congress we had generous, noble sentiments, and manly eloquence. This day convinced me that America will support the Massachusetts or perish with her."[7]

United support for the Suffolk Resolves masked deep divisions within Congress. On the conservative end, Joseph Galloway clung tenaciously to reconciliation, and he presented an ingenious scheme that he thought could bring it about. His plan would create a new legislative body in America, a "Grand Council" of representatives from the various colonies; both the Grand Council in America and the existing Parliament in Britain would have to agree on any law or tax applicable to Americans. Galloway's idea looked good on paper, but its time had passed, for the notion of shared authority no longer made any sense. Once Britain assumed arbitrary powers and the people of Massachusetts responded with outright rebellion, the Galloway Plan was doomed. Galloway himself was cornered into supporting the Suffolk Resolves, for to do otherwise was to risk being branded a traitor to the cause.

Leading the radical charge were Henry Laurens's antagonist, Christopher Gadsden, and Virginia's Richard Henry Lee and Patrick Henry. "Mr. Gadsden, leaves all N England Sons of Liberty, farr behind," Connecticut's Silas Deane wrote to his wife, "for he is for taking up his firelock, & marching direct to Boston, nay he affirmed this morning, that were his wife, and all his children in Boston, & they were there to perish, by the sword, it would not alter his sentiment or proceeding, for American Liberty, by which you may judge of the man." Pennsylvania's Joseph Reed wrote that compared to Virginians like Lee and Henry, "the Bostonians are mere milksops."[8]

While Galloway and a few other cautious souls favored compromise at all costs, and Gadsden, Lee, and Henry wanted to push resistance to the extreme, most delegates found themselves in a never-never land of cautious resistance, whatever that meant. How far should they go, they wondered.

That's certainly the question George Washington pondered. Just before embarking for Philadelphia as one of Virginia's seven delegates, he wrote: "For my own part, I shall not undertake to say where the line between Great Britain and the Colonies should be drawn, but I am clearly of opinion that one ought to be drawn; & our rights clearly ascertaind." The task faced by Washington and his colleagues, as they met behind closed doors for the better part of two months, was to draw that line somewhere.[9]

On the wrong side of the line was independence, with its treasonous connotations. When Washington heard from a fellow veteran of the French and Indian War that the "fixed aim" of Massachusetts patriots was "total independence," he rushed to "the Boston gentn. [gentlemen]" in Congress and asked them if this were true. John and Samuel Adams assured him the rumor was false (even though they knew otherwise), then instructed their friends back home to do everything in their power to slow down the revolution that was sweeping across the countryside. "Independency" and "the proposal of setting up a new form of government of our own" were ideas that "startle people here," John Adams told a friend in Massachusetts immediately after Washington's visit.[10]

Misled but duly satisfied, Washington responded to his informant: having heard "the real sentiments of the people" from their "leaders," he could now say "with a degree of confidence & boldness . . . that it is not the wish, or the interest of the government, or any other upon this continent, separately or collectively, to set up for independency. . . . No such thing is desired by any thinking man in all North America."[11]

The military option, unlike independence, was on the table—not formally, but in people's minds—and this naturally focused attention on the convention's most distinguished veteran, George Washington. In his diary, Adams jotted down a story that was circulating around town: "Coll. Washington made the most eloquent speech at the Virginia Convention that ever was made. Says he, 'I will raise 1000 men, subsist them at my own expence, and march my self at their head for the relief of Boston.'"[12]

Over and over the story was told, and although there is no firsthand documentation that Washington ever made such a speech, the rumor itself demonstrates that delegates were entertaining the possibility of armed conflict, and that as they contemplated the urgency of the crisis, they cast furtive glances Washington's way, thinking, daring to imagine, that just in case it came to that . . .

Back to the point at hand, they then told themselves. Before resorting to the military alternative, there was one more trick they must try: economic warfare, a continentwide nonimportation, nonconsumption, and nonexportation agreement that would cripple British trade and cause Parliament, King George III, and the North ministry to rescind their latest, most offensive measures.

It was the obvious next step, but it also created problems. One by one, individual colonies protested that if they were not allowed to export some key item, their economy would be ruined. Let us export tobacco, at least for the next year, Virginia pleaded. And rice, added South Carolina.

Although weakened by cessations to special interests, the Association (as people called it) was the most significant achievement of the First Continental Congress. Over the past ten years, patriots had gushed forth with thousands upon thousands of reasoned essays, imploring petitions, impassioned diatribes, and political harangues—words, all words. Now, at last, words had resulted in action on a united front. Americans of all regions and classes were drafted to fight an economic war that could be waged in every port, every store, and every hearth in America.

Although there had been many local associations in the past, joining them into a single package at this particular moment had profound implications. The Continental Association became the voice, and force, of Revolutionary America. The key lay in its implementation, outlined in section eleven:

That a committee be chosen in every county, city, and town, by those who are qualified to vote for representatives in the legislature, whose business it shall be attentively to observe the conduct of all personals touching this association; and when it shall be made to appear, to the satisfaction of a majority of any such committee, that any person . . . has violated this association, that such majority do forthwith cause the truth of the case to be published in the gazette; to the end, that all such foes to

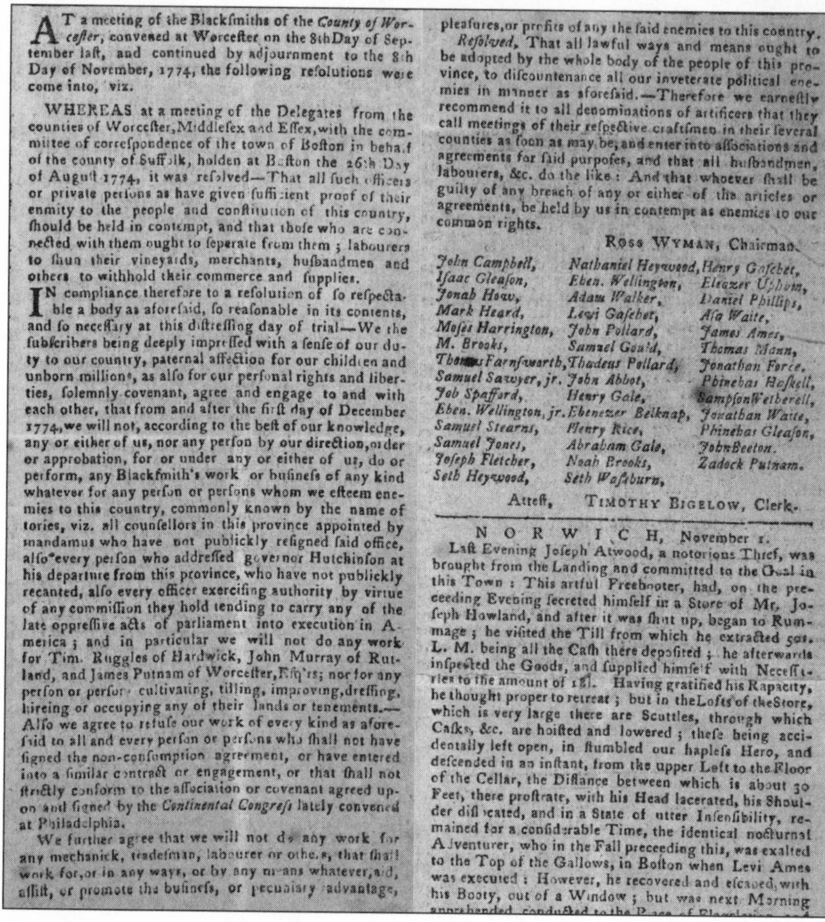

AT a meeting of the Blackſmiths of the *County of Worceſter,* convened at Worceſter on the 8th Day of September laſt, and continued by adjournment to the 8th Day of November, 1774, the following reſolutions were come into, viz.

WHEREAS at a meeting of the Delegates from the counties of Worceſter, Middleſex and Eſſex, with the committee of correſpondence of the town of Boſton in behalf of the county of Suffolk, holden at Boſton the 26th Day of Auguſt 1774, it was reſolved—That all ſuch officers or private perſons as have given ſufficient proof of their enmity to the people and conſtitution of this country, ſhould be held in contempt, and that thoſe who are connected with them ought to ſeparate from them ; labourers to ſhun their vineyards, merchants, huſbandmen and others to withhold their commerce and ſupplies.

IN compliance therefore to a reſolution ſo reſpectable a body as aforeſaid, ſo reaſonable in its contents, and ſo neceſſary at this diſtreſſing day of trial—We the ſubſcribers being deeply impreſſed with a ſenſe of our duty to our country, paternal affection for our children and unborn millions, as alſo for our perſonal rights and liberties, ſolemnly covenant, agree and engage to and with each other, that from and after the firſt day of December 1774, we will not, according to the beſt of our knowledge, any or either of us, nor any perſon by our direction, order or approbation, for or under any or either of us, do or perform, any Blackſmith's work or buſineſs of any kind whatever for any perſon or perſons whom we eſteem enemies to this country, commonly known by the name of tories, viz. all counſellors in this province appointed by mandamus who have not publickly reſigned ſaid office, alſo every perſon who addreſſed governor Hutchinſon at his departure from this province, who have not publickly recanted, alſo every officer exerciſing authority by virtue of any commiſſion they hold tending to carry any of the late oppreſſive acts of parliament into execution in America ; and in particular we will not do any work for Tim. Ruggles of Hardwick, John Murray of Rutland, and James Putnam of Worceſter, Eſq'rs; nor for any perſon or perſons cultivating, tilling, improving, dreſſing, hireing or occupying any of their lands or tenements.— Alſo we agree to refuſe our work of every kind as aforeſaid to all and every perſon or perſons who ſhall not have ſigned the non-conſumption agreement, or have entered into a ſimilar contract or engagement, or that ſhall not ſtrictly conform to the aſſociation or covenant agreed upon and ſigned by the *Continental Congreſs* lately convened at Philadelphia.

We further agree that we will not do any work for any mechanick, tradeſman, labourer or others, that ſhall work for, or in any ways, or by any means whatever, aid, aſſiſt, or promote the buſineſs, or pecuniary advantage,

pleaſures, or profits of any the ſaid enemies to this country.

Reſolved, That all lawful ways and means ought to be adopted by the whole body of the people of this province, to diſcountenance all our inveterate political enemies in manner as aforeſaid.—Therefore we earneſtly recommend it to all denominations of artificers that they call meetings of their reſpective craftſmen in their ſeveral counties as ſoon as may be, and enter into aſſociations and agreements for ſaid purpoſes, and that all huſbandmen, labourers, &c. do the like : And that whoever ſhall be guilty of any breach of any or either of this articles or agreements, be held by us in contempt as enemies to our common rights.

ROSS WYMAN, Chairman.

John Campbell,	Nathaniel Heywood,	Henry Goſebet,
Iſaac Gleaſon,	Eben. Wellington,	Eleazer Uſhorn,
Jonah How,	Adam Walker,	Daniel Phillips,
Mark Heard,	Levi Gaſchet,	Aſa Waite,
Moſes Harrington,	John Pollard,	James Ames,
M. Brooks,	Samuel Goald,	Thomas Mann,
Thomas Farnſworth,	Thadeus Pollard,	Jonathan Force,
Samuel Sawyer, jr.	John Abbot,	Phinehas Haſkell,
Job Spaffard,	Henry Gale,	Sampſon Wetherell,
Eben. Wellington, jr.	Ebenezer Belknap,	Jonathan Waite,
Samuel Stearns,	Henry Rice,	Phinehas Gleaſon,
Samuel Jones,	Abraham Gale,	John Beeton,
Joſeph Fletcher,	Noah Brooks,	Zadock Putnam.
Seth Heywood,	Seth Waſhburn,	

Atteſt, TIMOTHY BIGELOW, Clerk.

NORWICH, November 1.

Laſt Evening Joſeph Atwood, a notorious Thief, was brought from the Landing and committed to the Goal in this Town : This artful Freebooter, had, on the preceeding Evening ſecreted himſelf in a Store of Mr. Joſeph Howland, and after it was ſhut up, began to Rummage ; he viſited the Till from which he extracted 50s. L. M. being all the Caſh there depoſited ; he afterwards infeſted the Goods, and ſupplied himſelf with Neceſſaries to the amount of 18l. Having gratified his Rapacity, he thought proper to retreat ; but in the Lofts of the Store, which is very large there are Scuttles, through which Caſks, &c. are hoiſted and lowered ; theſe being accidentally left open, in ſtumbled our hapleſs Hero, and deſcended in an inſtant, from the upper Loft to the Floor of the Cellar, the Diſtance between which is about 30 Feet, there proſtrate, with his Head lacerated, his Shoulder diſlocated, and in a State of utter Inſenſibility, remained for a conſiderable Time, the identical nocturnal Adventurer, who in the Fall preceeding this, was exalted to the Top of the Gallows, in Boſton when Levi Ames was executed : However, he recovered and eſcaped, with his Booty, out of a Window ; but was next Morning apprehended conducted to the

Figure 11. Worcester County blacksmiths, organized by Timothy Bigelow during the overthrow of British authority in September of 1774, pledged to implement the new Continental Association two months later. Signing the pledge as the organization's secretary, Bigelow sent it to the *Boston Gazette,* where it appeared on November 28, 1774.

the rights of British-America may be publicly known, and universally contemned as the enemies of American liberty; and thenceforth we respectively will break off all dealings with him or her.[13]

With this provision, Congress created a new level of quasi-official authority. Each local enforcement committee, called a Committee of Safety or Committee of Inspection, quickly assumed both police and legislative powers in all matters pertaining to political conduct—and in those times, nearly everything *did* pertain to politics, not only what people said, but what they bought or sold, produced or consumed. Using the potent weapon of social and commercial ostracism, the "Committee" in every city, town, or village enforced standards of proper revolutionary behavior. The Association added a critical, on-the-ground component to the emerging revolutionary infrastructure, which until then had been embodied in the Committees of Correspondence and their various creations, the Provincial Congresses and the Continental Congress.

November 12, 1774–February 26, 1775: Philadelphia

On November 12, in a special citywide election, Robert Morris was selected for the Philadelphia committee charged with implementing the Association on the local level. Later, he would become the nation's supreme commander in all matters economic, but for the present, the man who would someday be called the Dictator was content to put in his time as a foot soldier.

On December 5, Morris received his specific assignment: as a member of Philadelphia's Committee of Observation and Inspection, district five (there were six districts altogether), he and nine coworkers would take turns patrolling the docks from Spruce Street to South Street, and then report their findings at 10:00 every morning at the London Coffee House. With his many connections on the waterfront and firsthand knowledge of the shipping industry, Morris was perfectly suited to the task.[14]

Over the next few months, the Committee of Observation and Inspection reported no significant violations of the Association. Particularly in Philadelphia, which had hosted the Continental Congress, radical and moderate patriots were willing to set aside their differences and focus on making the Association work. There was one problem, however: Although the Association had stipulated that "venders of goods or merchandise will not take advantage of the scarcity of goods," prices in Philadelphia did skyrocket during the winter of 1774–1775. While merchants like Morris scrupulously adhered to nonimportation, they were not particularly keen on charging less than the market would bear for their goods.[15]

Nor did Robert Morris wish to curtail his exports, which were not prohibited until September of 1775. (Hoping to sell off its surplus tobacco, Virginia had insisted on the delay.) In the interim, whatever freight he could ship eastward across the Atlantic was likely to fetch a high price, as British merchants and consumers anticipated future shortages. On February 26, with half a year remaining before the deadline, Morris wrote to a trading partner in southern Spain, James Duff:

Notwithstanding the disapointment of last year I have pushed freely and boldly this [year] having laden from 50 to 60 sail of stout ships since the 1st of November last. Some are gone up the Mediterranian some to Lisbon but mostly for England where I think is the best chance.[16]

We have no indication that Morris imported contraband British goods, but there are definite signs that he played the contorted market to his best advantage, capitalizing on rising prices on both sides of the Atlantic.

Again, Robert Morris trod a fine line, adhering to the letter of the Association but not necessarily the spirit. In his letter to Duff, he tiptoed across the deepening abyss, less certain than before that he would be able to pull off the feat:

> For my part I am a native of England but from principle an American in this dispute. The very extensive concerns in business which fall upon my management oblige me to decline any active part, otherways I should probably have had a large share in the publick transactions. However, I recommend constantly a steady, manly but decent & peaceable opposition as most likely to ensure success, and I pray God both for the sake of that country and this that such may be the issue.

But if his prayer was not answered? "God forbid the sword of civil war shoud e'er be drawn," he wrote, "but if it is, none can tell where or on what terms it will be sheathed again."

December 11, 1774–February 6, 1775: Charleston

At noon on Sunday, December 11, after thirty-nine months abroad and thirty-four days sailing across the Atlantic, Henry Laurens set foot on John Rose's wharf in Charleston. He hastened to his house in town, only a few blocks away, where he found a warm welcome from three slaves:

> I found no body here but three of our old domestics Stepny Exeter & big Hagar, these drew tears from me by their humble & affectionate salutes & congratulations my knees were clasped, my hands kissed my very feet embraced . . . they encircled me held my hands hung upon me I could scarcely get from them—Ah said the old man I never thought to see you again, now I am happy.[17]

Yes, it was good to be home, but Laurens would soon learn that much had changed while he was gone.

First (although he would realize it last), the institution of slavery was not as secure as it used to be. House domestics like Stepny, Exeter, and Hagar did not represent the sentiments of many field slaves, who were rapidly learning how to play the rift between the colonies and Britain to their own best advantage.

Second, although he had departed during a lull in the resistance movement, patriotic fervor was now at a fever pitch. "There is a spirit here which surpasses all expectation," he wrote to his eldest son, John, the day after he arrived.[18]

Next, John had grown up. Although not quite twenty-one, his favorite son was placed "second in command" and charged with looking after his two younger brothers, who remained abroad with him. John had also become Henry's best and most trusted friend, but there was a catch: he now had a mind of his own.[19]

Finally, there was a potent new political force in South Carolina politics: backcountry farmers, including people from the Ninety Six district, where Laurens had invested in land. This would certainly complicate Laurens's re-entry into the provincial world of political squabbles.

On January 11, precisely one month after his arrival, Laurens was elected to a convention that turned itself into South Carolina's First Provincial Congress. For the next eight days (the Sabbath included), from dawn to dusk, Laurens found himself immersed in the type of wrangling he so despised, dominated in his words by "a multitude of speechifying." At issue was the Association's exemption for rice, which the colony's delegation had managed to force from the Continental Congress. Why should rice planters receive such special treatment, others wanted to know. Henry described the situation to John, who had remained in England:

> Evil spirits had stirred up the jealousy of the indigo planter who complained that partiality had been shewn to the rice maker, the alarm spread through the several classes of tobacco planter lumber cutter, tar maker in short every planter and herdsman considered his constituent as injured in the supposed indulgence to rice.[20]

Most upset were backcountry farmers, whose resentments dated from the 1760s. Back then, styling themselves Regulators, they had taken the law into their own hands because South Carolina's powerful elite, dominated by eastern rice growers, had failed to provide any sort of governmental protection for the western districts. Now, their numbers having grown, these men challenged eastern hegemony with greater political force.

In the end, the Provincial Congress voted to confirm the rice exemption by a vote of 87 to 75. But much damage had been done, and regional jealousies would soon evolve into much more than heated debate.

Henry reported the discord to John, who countered with worse news yet. Before Parliament, with John looking on, King George III had affirmed his "firm and steadfast resolution to withstand every attempt to weaken or impair the supreme legislative authority of this legislature over all the dominions of my crown." John had also run into Thomas Hutchinson, the former governor of Massachusetts, who by chance was sharing his lodging house in Bath. When the discussion in the parlor turned to politics, "all agreed in our ruin, tho' they differ'd in the means of affecting it." Aside from some active dissent from people like Catharine Macaulay and John Wilkes, along with a small minority in Parliament, the debate in Britain centered on the proper means of enforcing submission.[21]

The deteriorating situation weighed heavily on John's father, who could easily imagine what might happen next:

> I feel for the distresses of my country, I weep for the horrid effects of civil discord which must soon be produced if we proceed in our contest with Great Britain, & tis impossible that we should forbear unless she will withdraw her oppressive hand.—Alas my country!, alas my children!, alas humanity!, you must be spoiled and massacred, you cannot reach the wished for land of liberty but through the wilderness & a sea of brothers blood.[22]

But John himself seemed more excited than depressed, and he did little to calm his father's apprehensions. In fact, he made them worse: "No person prays more heartily than I do for peace," he wrote, "but if through the pride and obstinacy of the Ministry, fighting becomes necessary, there is no man I hope would more gladly expose himself, or hold his life more cheap."[23]

To this courageous but brazen remark, John's father responded more as a loving and worried father than a proud and angry patriot:

> Your spirited declarations of readiness to bleed in your country's cause may sound well enough late at night in the Falcon [a coffee house in London]—

I entertain no doubt of your bravery & firmness, yet my dear son, I should be extremely deficient in my duty if I forbore to tell you freely, that talking & writing of the "cheapness" of ones life, bears no mark of either. . . . Reserve your life for your country's call, but wait the call.[24]

Yes, Henry should be concerned for the safety of his son. "Civil war," that dreaded term bandied about with increasing frequency, was no mere abstraction, and if in the end it came to that, *somebody's* son would certainly die.

January 1775: Plymouth

Mercy Otis Warren was a great fan of the Association, and for two good reasons.

First, it seemed the only possible alternative to war. With five sons and a husband who was willing to place his life on the line if need be, Mrs. Warren, like most other Americans, still prayed that British subjects would not be reduced to killing each other.

Second, the high moral tone of the Association suited her tastes perfectly. In addition to the nonimportation, nonconsumption, and nonexportation resolutions, Congress vowed to "encourage frugality, economy, and industry" and to "discountenance and discourage every species of extravagance and dissipation," including horse racing, gaming, cockfighting, and all other "expensive diversions and entertainments." It also stipulated that no "vendor of goods and merchandize" should take "undue advantage" of a "future scarcity of goods." This is exactly the sort of society Warren hoped to create: people acting frugally and industriously, with no interest in commercial profits or unseemly extravagance. It was a Puritan's dream come true.[25]

Years later, in her *History*, Warren marveled that "the recommendations of committees and conventions" were so diligently observed, even though they were "not enforced by penal sanctions." She would have preferred that Virtue alone had been the enforcing agent, but she knew it wasn't quite that way. Some folks had to be brought into line, and that required certain distasteful applications of social pressure:

Doubtless the fear of popular resentment operated on some, with a force equal to the rod of the magistrate: the singular punishments, inflicted in some instances by an inflamed rabble, on a few who endeavored to counteract the public measures, deterred others from openly violating the public resolves, and acting against the general consent of the people.

As a footnote to "singular punishments," she added: "Such as tarring and feathering &c."[26]

Because the actions of the "inflamed rabble," in the guise of patriotism, were an embarrassment to the upright Mrs. Warren, she tried to place them in historical perspective. The "irregularities" and "outrages" here were not so severe as with the "convulsions of Rome," the "confusions, the mobs, the cruelties in Britain" during their Civil War, or the "riots of London and Liverpool" over the previous decade, she noted. Still, they were too crude to suit her tastes. Consider, for instance, a contemporary newspaper account of a crowd in her hometown of Plymouth:

> Jesse Dunbar, of Halifax, in Plymouth County, bought some fat cattle of Mr. Thomas, the Counsellor, and drove them to Plymouth for sale; one of the oxen being skinned and hung up, the Committee came to him, and finding he bought it of Mr. Thomas, they put the ox into a cart, and fixed Dunbar in his belly, and carted him four miles, and then made him pay a dollar, after taking three more cattle and a horse from him; the Plymouth mob delivered him to the Kingston mob, which carted him four miles further, and forced from him another dollar, then delivered him to the Duxbury mob, who abused him by throwing the tripe in his face, and endeavoring to cover him with it, to the endangering his life, then threw dirt at him, and after other abuses, carried him to said Thomas's house, and made him pay another sum of money: and he not taking the beef, they flung it in the road and quitted him.[27]

This sort of public chastisement, hardly unusual, presented a moral dilemma for Mercy Otis Warren. Could a good Puritan woman like herself really condone such activities, even if done in the name of a higher cause? But without crowd coercion, how could transgressors be brought into line? The problem took on a personal dimension: might her own political lampoons offend her goddess Virtue? Although Mrs. Warren did not smear people with tripe, was it permissible to smear them with words, as she was wont to do?

Late in January of 1775, having just published yet another dramatic satire (*The Group*) that heaped abuse on the Crown-appointed Council members, she asked John Adams whether her "satiric propensity" should be "reined in":

Sarcastic reproaches have generally been decryed by the wise and the worthy. . . . How far, sir, do you think it justifiable for any individual to hold him up to the object of public derision? And is it consistent with the benevolent system of Christianity to vilify the delinquent, when we only wish to warn off the fatal consequences of his crime?

In particular, was it permissible for *women* to "vilify" individuals this way?

Though from the particular circumstances of our unhappy time, a little personal acrimony might be justifiable in your sex, must not the female character suffer . . . if she indulges her pen to paint in the darkest shades, even those whose vice and venality have rendered contemptible? [28]

Mrs. Warren's most ardent admirer responded with the assurances she wanted and needed to receive, and perhaps the answer she was fishing for:

If we look into human nature, . . . we shall find it is really a dread of satyr that restrains our species from exorbitances, more than laws, human, moral or divine, indeed the efficacy of civil punishments is derived chiefly from the same source. It is not the pain, the fire etc that is dreaded so much as the infamy and disgrace. So that really the civil magistrate may be said in a good sense to keep the world in order, by means of satyr, for gaols, stocks, whipping posts and gallows's are but different kinds of it. . . . The business of satyr is to expose vice and vicious men as such to this scorn and to enrobe Virtue in all the charms which fancy can paint.[29]

In the absence of legitimate governmental authority, Mercy Otis Warren, through her biting pen, was performing the socially useful and necessary function of a policeman. This was a role she could accept.

8

Blows Must Decide

January 17–April 18, 1775: Virginia

By initiating the Association, Congress had agreed to wage economic warfare against Britain. It did nothing, however, to prepare for or encourage real, physical warfare. That would be left to the individual colonies, should they decide to go that route, which was not in the least predetermined. Fortunately for Massachusetts, which was far along on the path to war, the next most belligerent colony proved to be Virginia, the largest and most influential in British North America.

Starting in the fall of 1774, in George Washington's Fairfax County as well as several other Virginia counties, patriots organized independent military companies of volunteers, separate and distinct from the militias, which were nominally still under the jurisdiction of the royal governor. At least five of these companies invited Washington to serve as their commander, and several asked him to procure military supplies while he was in Philadelphia attending the First Continental Congress. His own Fairfax Independent Company wanted him

> to make some enquiries with regard to the furnishing the company with a pair of colours, two drums, two fifes, and two halberts, if they are to be had in Philadelphia; which may be sent round by the first vessel for Alexandria. We leave it to you, sir, to determine whether it may be proper or necessary to vary from the usual colours that are carried by the Regulars or Militia.[1]

Not only was the Fairfax Company relying on Washington to do its shopping, but it was also calling on him to decide (at least symbolically) the fundamental question of the day: were the volunteer companies acting within the bounds of British or colonial law, or were they in fact setting off on a new and uncharted course, requiring new colors to represent new allegiances?

In Philadelphia, Washington shopped also for a treatise on military discipline and upgrades to his personal uniform: a new sash, epaulette, and gorget. His mind was moving in a military direction, and it continued to move that way when he returned to Mount Vernon. On January 17, he chaired a meeting of the Fairfax County Committee that called for immediate mobilization and asked each citizen to pay "three shillings per poll" to procure ammunition "for the common benefit, protection, and defence, of the inhabitants." Both George Washington and his neighbor George Mason offered their personal credit so the supplies could be purchased immediately, but when credit proved insufficient (demand in America for arms and ammunition so outstripped supply that merchants and gunsmiths adopted a cash-only policy), they visited their neighbors personally to collect the stipulated funds.[2]

Although Washington and Mason worked together on the mobilization, they almost fell out over a sensitive matter of policy. Mason was firmly committed to a fundamental notion of equality—"All men are by nature born equally free and independent," he wrote at the time, fifteen months before Thomas Jefferson enshrined a shorter statement of the same principle in the Declaration of Independence—and hoping to prevent the emergence of an elite class of officers, he insisted that the people themselves choose their own leaders (as they did in Massachusetts), that they do so annually, and even that they select different individuals each time. Washington, who considered himself a military professional, could hardly abide the wild notion of a democratic army with rotating leadership. But Mason then suggested a compromise: all officers would be limited to single-year terms, save for one particular individual: "The exception made in favor of the gentleman who by the unanimous voice of the company now commands it, is a very proper one, just due to his public merit and experience; it is peculiarly suited to our circumstances." This was the first known invocation of what historians have labeled the Washington Exception.[3]

Two days after the meeting of the Fairfax County Committee, Peyton Randolph, speaker of the House of Burgesses and president of the First Continental Congress, called for a colonywide convention of the Committees of Correspondence, to be held on March 20 at Richmond, a safe distance from the colonial capital of Williamsburg.

During the two-month buildup to the convention, as county committees gathered to select delegates, rumors ran rampant about the king and his ministry. "By a letter from Maryland yesterday," wrote George Mason on February 18, "I am inform'd that his Majesty has ordered his embassadors at the different courts in Europe to declare his American subjects in a state of rebellion." Back in November, King George III had written to Lord North, his prime minister: "The New England governments are in a state of rebellion. Blows must decide whether they are to be subject to this country or independent." Now, he was treating not only New England but all of America as sworn enemies.[4]

This was the backdrop for the weeklong Second Virginia Convention. (The First Virginia Convention had met the previous summer to select delegates to the Continental Congress.) The highlight of the gathering came on the fourth day, March 23, when Patrick Henry, Virginia's hawkish hard-liner, introduced a resolution declaring that "this colony be immediately put into a posture of defence," and that a committee be appointed "to prepare a plan for embodying, arming and disciplining such a number of men as may be sufficient for that purpose." The independent companies were to be molded into a single, coordinated army.[5]

Henry's resolution is known in history not so much for its content or its import, but for the speech he made in its defense. Although the words were never recorded, Henry's first biographer, William Wirt, composed a speech that American schoolboys for generations committed to heart and dramatized. The speech, which Wirt attributed to Henry forty-two years after the fact, closed with a classic call to arms:

> Why stand we here idle? What is it that gentlemen wish? What would they have? Is life so dear, or peace so sweet, as to be purchased at the price of chains and slavery? Forbid it, Almighty God!—I know not what course others may take; but as for me, give me liberty, or give me death![6]

The only firsthand record of the speech had a somewhat different ring:

> You never heard anything more infamously insolent than P. Henry's speech: he called the K——a tyrant, a fool, a puppet, and a tool to the ministry. Said there was no Englishmen, no Scots, no Britons, but a set of wretches sunk in luxury, that they had lost their native courage and (were) unable to look the brave Americans in the face. . . . This creature

is so infatuated, that he goes about I am told, praying and preaching amongst the common people.[7]

Most likely, the true spirit of the speech subsumed both these renditions. Patrick Henry, like others throughout history who have called for war, appealed to people's best and worst instincts—their belief in a just cause, their valor, their self-sacrifice, but also their hatred, their demonizing, their readiness to see the enemy as "wretches."

The resolution passed by a narrow margin, and Peyton Randolph appointed a twelve-man committee to work out the details of "embodying" a military force. Included in this group were Patrick Henry and Richard Henry Lee, who had made and seconded the resolution; several men who opposed it, to ensure a balance; and of course George Washington, the resident military expert. The committee report, passed unanimously by the convention two days later, "strongly recommended" that the Tidewater counties, where many of the richest planters lived, form "troops of horse," and that "every horseman be provided with a good horse, bridle, saddle with pistols and holsters, a carbine or other short firelock with a bucket, a cutting sword or tomahawk, one pound of gunpowder and four pounds of ball at the least." All other counties were to form companies of infantrymen "cloathed in a hunting shirt by way of uniform"—a peculiarly American adaptation of military attire that would define these soldiers as different from the European variety.[8]

Immediately after the Virginia Convention, upon his arrival home, George Washington received some unexpected bad news, seemingly off topic but in his mind very much to the point. Surveys for the two hundred thousand acres of bounty land, promised back in 1754 to soldiers who joined Washington's expedition into the Ohio country, had just been declared null and void. The problem, apparently, was that William Crawford, the surveyor, did not have the proper credentials. The previous year, Lord Hillsborough had tried to cheat Washington out of the lands he and other veteran officers had been promised in 1763—and now this! Initially, Washington treated the news as too "incredible" to believe; at worst, he thought, it was a trick of professional surveyors "to filtch a little more money from us." But when the rumors continued, he wrote an impassioned letter to the governor, John Murray, Earl of Dunmore, begging him to intervene. Five years earlier, after going through all the proper channels, Crawford had been assigned to survey the two hundred thousand acres "with all possible expedition," Washington explained. Since that time, he continued, many of Crawford's patents had been officially granted "under your Lordships signature & the seal of the colony." How could all this be reversed at so late a date, and *why*? "It appears in so uncommon a light to me, that I hardly know yet how to persuade myself into a belief of the reality of it," Washington concluded.[9]

To this letter, over one thousand words long, Lord Dunmore penned a perfunctory reply: the reason for declaring the surveys "null and void" was "a report that the surveyor who surveyed those lands did not qualify agreeable to the Act of Assembly directing the duty and qualification of surveyors." That's all he said. Dunmore's token response was penned on April 18, the day British soldiers set out from Boston toward Lexington and Concord.[10]

Such a piece of bureaucratic chicanery pushed George Washington even further over the edge. William Crawford was his good friend, business associate, and indispensable agent in the West. With many years of experience and unsurpassed knowledge of the lands he surveyed, Crawford was certainly better qualified than any quill-pushing official three thousand miles away, and besides, he had been preapproved. If fact, Crawford knew the land so well that countless others had asked him to survey it, and Lord Dunmore himself had just relied on him to lead a dangerous expedition into Indian country. The move was so blatantly illogical that only one explanation remained: British authorities would stoop to any level to keep Americans from receiving legitimate title to lands across the mountains. There was no way for Americans to own the West without addressing the arrogant abuses of governmental authority coming from the East.

January–April 16, 1775: Worcester, Salem, Boston, and Concord

Back in Massachusetts, it had been a long winter of waiting. In her *History*, Warren described the mood:

> The minds of the people at this period, though not dismayed, were generally solemnized, in expectation of events, decisive both to political and private happiness, and every brow appeared expressive of sober anxiety. The people trembled for their liberties, the merchant for his interest, the tories for their places, the whigs for their country, and the virtuous for the manners of society.[11]

This state of suspension placed a strain on the patriots. The decisive moves that radicals had pushed for the previous autumn—replacing the 1691 Charter with a new constitution and attacking British forces in Boston—were no longer on the table. Having learned that other colonies would not continue to support their rebellion if they went on the offensive, they had no choice but to wait, not the favorite pastime of an aroused populace. In March, Worcester County's Ephraim Doolittle, the man who had joined Timothy Bigelow in drumming up support in Boston the previous August, complained to the Provincial Congress: "We are continually breaking to peaces and a number of companys in my regiment are now in such circumstances and I fear if we are not soon called to action we shall be like a rope of sand and have no more strength." Timothy Bigelow, at home and training his militia company during a recess in Congress, learned that Colonel Thomas Wheeler, a true-blue patriot who had been a founding member and chairman of the American Political Society, "was determined not to have any further concern in the militia, he was now fully convinced he was wrong, &c."[12]

But through it all, men such as Bigelow, Doolittle, and James Warren (who, like Bigelow, was both a delegate to the Provincial Congress and an officer in the militia) made certain that patriots continued to arm and train. If British forces ever did initiate a confrontation—and sometime they must, for they were not about to let the Revolution of 1774 go unanswered— the rebels, instantly reenergized, would be ready to put up a formidable resistance.

Back in Boston, the British commander Thomas Gage waited as well. He could not initiate a major offensive unless he received additional forces, but he might go after the patriots' stockpiles of arms, if he could find out where they were, and if the patriots were not sufficiently prepared. So he sent out some spies, and at the end of February, he received their report:

> Committee of safety appointed by the Congress consisting of Hancock, Warren, Church, Heath and Gearey, these are to observe the motions of the Army, and if they attempt to penetrate into the country, imedietly to communicate the intelligence to Colo. Ward, Colo. Bigelow, and Colo. Henshaw, who live in or near the towns of Worcester, and Leicester. Colo. Warren of Plymouth and Colo. Lee of Marblehead, they are to send express's round the country to collect the Minute Men who are to oppose the troops. These Minute Men amount to about 15,000 and are the picked men of the whole body of militia, and all properly armed.
>
> There are in the country thirty-eight field pieces and nineteen companies of artillery most of which are at Worcester, a few at Concord, and a few at Watertown.

There whole magazine of powder consisting of between ninety and an hundred barrells is at Concord.

There are eight field pieces in an old store or barn, near the landing place at Salem, they are to be removed in a few days, the seizure of them would greatly disconcert their schemes.

Colo. Lee, Colo. Orne, Mr. Devons, Mr. Chever, Mr. Watson, and Moses Gill, are appointed a committee of supply, who are to purchase all military stores, to be deposited at Concord and Worcester.[13]

To disrupt the military buildup and seize some of the patriots' arms or powder, which target should Gage choose—Worcester, Concord, or Salem?

Worcester, where patriot forces were the strongest, was also the farthest away. That was definitely his worst bet.

Concord would also be risky. A military expedition there, or to any other inland location, would likely trigger a mass mobilization similar to the Powder Alarm, but better organized this time.

That left Salem, a coastal town within easy striking distance of Boston, so on Sunday, February 26, 1775, General Thomas Gage dispatched a contingent of 240 Regulars to seize the field pieces there. Under different circumstances, this might have been the spark to ignite a dreaded civil war, but it didn't turn out that way. The day being the Sabbath, men from throughout the township had gathered in church and were easily alerted. To defend against the Redcoats, these patriots simply lifted the drawbridge that lay between themselves and the advancing soldiers, and what might have been a bloodbath turned into no more than a shouting match, with angry patriots and British officers hurling invectives from opposite sides of the water. Patriots had plenty of time to whisk their arms away.

General Gage learned some lessons from the fiasco at Salem. The next time he ordered troops to march outside of Boston in search of arms, he would send greater numbers, instruct his soldiers to travel in the dead of night, avoid the Sabbath, and choose a route that did not have a drawbridge.

The February 11 issue of the *London Times* took seven weeks to make its way to Boston, but when it arrived on April 2, it set off a firestorm. Vowing to starve the errant colonists into submission, Lord North was closing the Newfoundland fisheries to Americans, cutting off all trade with anyone but the British, and mobilizing two thousand additional seamen and "a proper number of frigates" to enforce this embargo. "We are no longer at a loss what is intended us by our dear Mother," James Warren wrote to his wife Mercy. "We have ask'd for bread and she gives us a stone, and a serpent for a fish."[14]

There was more news yet: the king had dispatched four additional regiments from Ireland to Boston, the *Times* reported, and everybody in town knew immediately what this meant. Governor Thomas Gage, who was also commander in chief of the British forces in North America, had been ridiculed through the winter by his own soldiers—Old Woman, they called him—for sitting by and letting the patriots take charge of Massachusetts without fighting back. His excuse, he said, was that he did not have sufficient troops to take the offensive. Now, with reinforcements imminent, he would certainly make a move.[15]

The news broke the stalemate at the Provincial Congress. For months, radicals like Timothy Bigelow had been pushing to elevate the assemblage of militias into a full-fledged army, but moderates thought they should hold off, and their voices had prevailed by a narrow margin. But these voices were suddenly muted by Britain's warlike posture, and of the 103 delegates present (many had gone home, pending further developments), 96 voted in favor of a Massachusetts Army, and, further, they asked that Connecticut, Rhode Island, and New Hampshire "co-operate with us, by furnishing their respective quotas for general defence."[16]

General Gage was preparing as well. Again he asked his spies: could he possibly strike at Worcester, the very heart of resistance? There, according to a report written in French, patriots had accumulated fifteen tons of powder (hidden in places unknown), thirteen small cannon (proudly displayed but poorly mounted in front of the meetinghouse on Main Street), and various munitions (in the hands of a merchant named Salisbury and *"un grand chef"* named Bigelow). But the road there was rough, the journey arduous, and the patriots numerous, vigilant, and excessively hostile. Gage's soldiers would likely be ambushed and possibly annihilated.[17]

Concord offered better prospects, for it was much more accessible. Although the main road from the Boston Neck was thickly wooded and susceptible to ambush, the northern route via Lexington passed through open terrain. Unlike the forty-mile trek to Worcester, this twenty-mile jaunt could be accomplished in a single night, which allowed the possibility of a surprise attack. Furthermore, from loyalists residing in Concord, Gage learned the location of particular buildings that concealed stockpiles of military ordnance, and as a bonus, his troops might stop on the way at Lexington to seize Samuel Adams and John Hancock, who had sought refuge there.

The choice of a target became obvious: Concord was the place to go. But because there were no other viable options, patriots had little trouble predicting what Gage would do. On April 8, Dr. Joseph Warren dispatched Paul Revere from Boston to Concord with an urgent message: British Regulars would soon march to seize the patriots' cannons and other military stores, possibly the very next day. The message was not really necessary, however, because patriots in Concord, where the Provincial Congress was sitting (it had moved back from Cambridge, which was too close to Boston), had already figured it out themselves. Two days earlier, foreshadowing the events to come, James Warren had informed his wife: "This town [Concord] is full of cannon, ammunition, stores, etc., and the [British] Army long for them and they want nothing but strength to induce an attempt on them. The people are ready and determine to defend this country inch by inch."[18]

Back in Boston, meanwhile, residents were flocking from the city in droves, hoping to avoid the military rule that was sure to accompany outright conflict. Active patriots tried to remove valuable property before it was confiscated, while even people who had taken no special part in the conflict feared they might soon be subjected to the hazards of war, should Boston itself become a battlefield. On April 11, Boston merchant John Andrews noted "the streets and neck lin'd with waggons carrying off the effects of the inhabitants . . . imagining to themselves that they shall be liable to every evil that can be enumerated, if they tarry in town." Three days after that, the Provincial Congress recommended that donations intended for relief of the poor in Boston be used to help evacuate the city.[19]

On the morning of April 16, Paul Revere made a second ride westward, to Lexington this time, to confer with Samuel Adams and John Hancock about how to respond to Gage's imminent attack. On his way back, he met also with patriots in Cambridge and Charleston to fine-tune their warning systems. When the big moment arrived, the Minutemen, who had been training for months, needed to get the word.

That evening—Sunday, April 16, 1775—Timothy Bigelow and a handful of clandestine cohorts engaged in one of the era's most surreptitious feats of derring-do. Bigelow was just wrapping up his business at the Provincial Congress, where he had played a major role in the decision to create and organize a standing army. Now, he had to rush back to Worcester to ready his militia company for the call, which could come at any moment, and also to implement the resolutions of both the Provincial Congress and the Continental Congress, his new job as part of the five-man executive committee for

Worcester County. But on his way home, he had one more errand to run: he needed to stop off in Boston and pick up a printing press.[20]

Over the previous decade, patriots had utilized the printed word as an indispensable tool for political organizing, but most of the printing presses in the province were located in Boston, within the British garrison that was increasing its security measures daily. Soon, once military hostilities commenced, all remaining patriot activists would have to leave Boston or risk arrest, and whatever presses they left behind would of course be confiscated. Now was the time for patriots to grab a press and remove it from Boston, if they possibly could.

With apparent prescience, Bigelow had anticipated the problem back in December, when he asked Isaiah Thomas, publisher of the *Massachusetts Spy*, to establish a newspaper in Worcester. Thomas possessed impeccable credentials as a fervent patriot: while working in Halifax in 1765, he had defied the Stamp Act; he had secretly printed handbills for the Sons of Liberty; he had published the writings of the most prolific patriots (including Dr. Thomas Young and Mercy Otis Warren). He also had an impressive list of opponents: Thomas Hutchinson had sued him for libel, British troops had threatened to tar and feather him, and opponents of the Regulators had hanged his effigy in North Carolina. Understanding that Worcester was a secure haven for patriots, even though the town contained only one-tenth as many households as his current number of subscribers, Thomas followed through with the idea in February by issuing a prospectus for a newspaper to be called *The Worcester Gazette, or American Oracle of Liberty*.

A few months earlier, a move to Worcester seemed an intriguing idea, but now it was an urgent necessity. If Isaiah Thomas was to continue printing patriot rhetoric, he would have to move quickly, and Timothy Bigelow was the man to help him do it. The details of their endeavor were not recorded, but the broad outlines can be readily surmised. After printing the *Spy* for April 6, Thomas disassembled his press into separate components: carriage, plank, coffin, cheeks, cap, head and winter, and so on. (The entire press was too bulky and too heavy to manipulate within tight interior spaces.) Bigelow and some other strapping but unidentified patriots then piled these into a wagon, together with several cases of heavy lead type and a massive stone imposing table, used for laying out the type. The load in the wagon—large hunks of elm, white oak, and chestnut that constituted the press; lead type with boxes; and the imposing table, made of slate, marble, or soapstone— probably amounted to a couple of tons, but it was not immediately recognizable as a printing press and could therefore be carted to a landing on the Charles River without serious risk of discovery.

From there, after transferring their freight into a boat, Bigelow and company pushed off for the Charleston shore in the dead of night. Unfortunately, however, the night wasn't so dead as they wished it to be: the moon was full, while the HMS *Somerset* loomed on the river between Boston and Charleston to interfere with just such a movement as this. Risky business, indeed.

Somehow, the boat with pieces of press arrived on the opposite shore. There, the payload was hauled onto a wagon, which Timothy Bigelow guided home to Worcester—literally to his *home*, that is, where he and others deposited it in the cellar, alongside the cache of small arms reported by Gage's spy. The press arrived in Bigelow's house on April 18, followed two days later by its owner, who had remained briefly in Boston to gather up the rest of his effects.[21]

On this press, which Isaiah Thomas hastily reassembled, would soon be printed some of the most important propaganda ever disseminated by American patriots during their struggle against Great Britain. Just as the Bigelow family home had once served as headquarters for the American Political Society and the Worcester County Convention of Committees of Correspondence, it could now be used to broadcast information and ideas, distinctly partisan, to propel the revolution still further.

April 18 and 19, 1775: Boston, Lexington, and Concord

Around two o'clock on Tuesday afternoon, April 18, an unusually high number of British seamen descended from their ships to the Boston waterfront. In a stable nearby, a hostler overheard officers mumbling to each other, not able to conceal their excitement as they prepared their horses for riding. Later in the afternoon, a light infantryman was spotted "with his accoutrements on." By early evening, when civilians noted that the boats utilized for transporting troops were floating in the bay toward HMS *Boyne*, many came to realize that the time had come. The Regulars would march that night.[22]

Meanwhile, across the Charles River in Menotomy (now Arlington), the Provincial Committees of Safety and Supplies, charged with keeping an eye on army movements in Boston, had been meeting all day at Newell's Tavern. Two of the members, Richard Devens and Abraham Watson, rode off at sunset, but they hadn't gone far before noticing a "great number of British officers and their servants on horseback," riding westward toward Lexington. Devens and Watson returned hastily to Newell's, where they found Elbridge Gerry, Charles Lee, and Azor Orne still lingering. After a brief consultation, Gerry penned a short message alerting Samuel Adams and John Hancock that a contingent of officers was headed their way.[23]

By nine in the evening, militiamen in Lexington had received Gerry's warning and were gathering around Buckman's Tavern and the home of Jonas Clarke, where Adams and Hancock were staying.

Shortly thereafter, back in Boston, Dr. Joseph Warren summoned to his house Paul Revere and William Dawes, then dispatched these horsemen in different directions toward Lexington and Concord. Revere was to cross the Charles River, but before he did, he arranged that two lanterns be lit in the steeple of the Old North Church, a signal he had arranged with Devens and others from the opposite side of the river two days earlier. The Regulars were on their way, the signal announced, and they would cross the river in boats rather than march across the Boston Neck.

A watchman on the Cambridge shore saw the lanterns and alerted Devens, who dispatched another rider to Lexington with the latest news. Eighty-six years later, a poet named Henry Wadsworth Longfellow would publicize the signal lantern ploy, describing in great detail how Paul Revere and his horse waited fretfully to see how many lanterns would be lit. In fact, not Revere but another patriot had been waiting there, both that night and the night before, to receive the message.

When Revere reached the Cambridge shore around eleven o'clock, Richard Devens gave him a horse and warned him about the British officers, who had been dispatched for the very purpose of intercepting messengers. But the officers' mission had backfired. Because British horsemen had been spotted on the road, patriots in Lexington were alerted to the danger several hours before Revere even embarked on the ride that Longfellow would later extol.

While Paul Revere rode westward, other riders took off in different directions, northward to the New Hampshire line, eastward to Lynn and Chelsea and various coastal towns, and in a weblike manner across the countryside, to scores of nearby communities that had long been preparing for just such an event. As riders rode, church bells rang and gunshots sounded. Minutemen mustered in the dead of night at their local meetinghouses, village greens, or liberty poles.

As the message spread, over eight hundred Regulars marched. These were the handpicked elite of the Boston garrison: grenadiers, chosen for their size and strength and made to look even taller by their tasseled bearskin head-dresses, and light infantrymen, selected for their speed and dexterity and adorned with short red coats instead of the overblown variety, to allow greater agility on the battlefield. They gathered on a Back Bay beach at ten o'clock, crossed the Charles River to a swampy Cambridge shore by midnight, and spent the next two hours getting organized and trying (unsuccessfully) to dry off their fresh linen breeches and heavy square-toed boots, interchangeable from right to left, which would carry them on their forty-mile round-trip march. Properly aligned in their marching formations by two A.M., the Regulars trudged toward Lexington.

Around five in the morning, just as day was breaking, these sleepless British troops approached Lexington. They could hear bells and warning shots coming from every direction and they also found a company of local militiamen in formation on the village green.

What would these patriots do? They weren't so sure themselves, and in fact they had been discussing that very question as they waited through the night. Since the uprising of the previous summer, British Regulars and feisty patriots had faced off against each other on numerous occasions, puffing their chests and then withdrawing. Perhaps the militiamen who mustered on Lexington Green, vastly outnumbered, expected another standoff like that. Or perhaps not, but few probably thought the day would turn out as it did.

As the Regulars approached, they fanned out in two directions, not on purpose but through faulty communications. One group continued its march toward Concord, while the other took a right turn, past Buckman's Tavern and face-to-face with the militiamen on the green. The Regulars broke from marching formation into battle lines, and there the armies stood, separated by maybe sixty yards, nobody on either side knowing how to proceed. Then, whether by design or accident, somebody fired a shot, and this was followed by others, and soon the Regulars opened fire and offered a resounding volley.

Most of the militiamen fled. Of the eight patriots who died, two lay on the spot where they had originally stood. The rest were killed as they ran.

The Battle of Lexington was not really a battle but a slaughter. The victims were not professional soldiers who had agreed to pursue violence as a way of life, but plain village folks who thought they were defending their homes. There were eight pairs of fathers and sons on the Lexington Green that morning and, of these, only three pairs remained intact after the brief moments of horror that opened the Revolutionary War.

But the day was not over.

When the Regulars reached Concord, they found no militiamen standing in the way. Some had wanted to. As they mustered during the wee hours of the morning at Wright's Tavern, these farmers-turned-soldiers, like their counterparts in Lexington, debated with each other the prospect of defending their town. The younger, more impetuous Minutemen then sallied forth to the east, thinking they might face off against the Regulars there, but upon viewing the enemy's vast numbers, they wisely retreated. Again on Meetinghouse Hill, with a commanding view of Main Street, the Concord militiamen debated whether to stand and fight or stage a strategic retreat, and again they settled on the wiser course. They retreated from harm's way, waiting for their numbers to grow.

Unopposed as they marched down Main Street, the Regulars split their forces. Some continued in a northwesterly direction in search of four brass field pieces, smuggled out of Boston several months before, which were allegedly hidden on a farm across the North Bridge. Others remained in town to search buildings that had been identified by intelligence reports as harboring ordnance and powder. They didn't find much; most had already been squirreled away to more secret locations, some even buried beneath the furrows of recently plowed fields.[24]

Throughout the morning, Minutemen from neighboring townships arrived to bolster the patriots' numbers. By the time the contingent of Regulars seeking the brass cannon crossed back over the North Bridge empty-handed, approximately five hundred militiamen stood on the hill above them. Again the patriots debated what to do, and this time they decided to march down to the river and move into battle formation. As the armies stood on opposite banks of the narrow Concord River, neither with a clear plan for what might happen next, somebody fired "the shot heard round the world," as the poet Ralph Waldo Emerson would label it more than half a century later. The first pitched battle of the Revolutionary War, with each side a willing contestant, had begun.

The Americans enjoyed the advantage this time, for they fanned out along the west bank, while the Regulars found themselves trapped in a narrow roadway, unable to fire successive volleys without hitting each other. Pressed together, they made easier targets. After several of their number fell, the rest fled, their lines and discipline broken.

In town, the fleeing Redcoats regrouped with the balance of their forces. With nothing left to gain by the expedition, their commander, Lieutenant Colonel Francis Smith, ordered his troops to march toward Boston. At noon

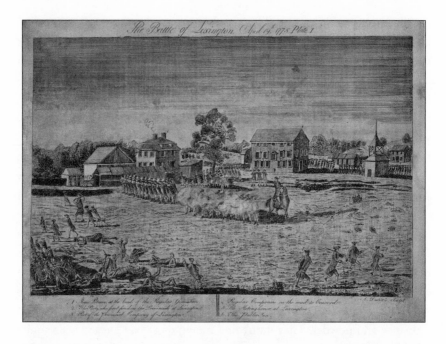

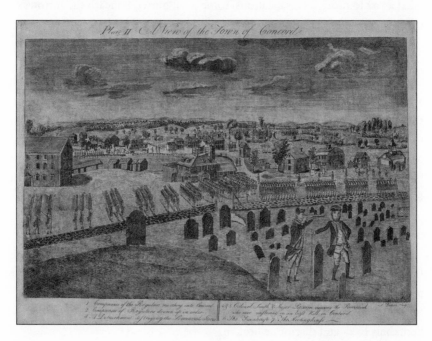

Figures 12–15. Amos Doolittle's contemporary engravings, based on the original paintings of Ralph Earl, depicted the dramatic events of April 19, 1775. *(Chicago History Museum)*

Plate III. The Engagement at the North Bridge in Concord.

1. The Detachment of the Regulars who fired first on the Provincials at the Bridge. 2. The Provincials headed by Colonel Robinson & Major Buttrick & the Bridge.

Plate IV. A View of the South Part of Lexington.

they started back, and for the first mile they encountered no resistance to their progress. But when they reached an intersection called Merriam's Corner, they began to receive serious fire from patriots, now grown in numbers to around one thousand, who leveled their sights and discharged their guns toward the fatigued British soldiers. A mile later, at Bloody Curve, the shooting intensified. The patriot force had by then swollen from a few dozen at dawn in Lexington, then a few hundred at midmorning in Concord, to a couple of thousand along the sides of Battle Road (as it came to be called), with more arriving hourly.

As the Regulars passed a second time through Lexington, they no longer thought about conquering the enemy. Mere survival would suffice. At two thirty in the afternoon, just east of Lexington, the fatigued and beleaguered Regulars received reinforcements: a brigade (three regiments) of British infantrymen, a battalion of Royal Marines, and some cannon manned by men from the Royal Artillery, all under the charge of Gage's second in command, Lord Hugh Percy. Although British soldiers found some security in numbers, patriots continued to attack them from the flanks. In the next town, Menotomy, militiamen fired from within houses, which in some cases caused the Regulars to break rank, charge the houses, and wreak revenge for the horrific day on any people they found within. It was an eighteenth-century foreshadowing of urban warfare.

The British soldiers finally arrived at the shores of the Charles River at seven o'clock, bloodied and battered after twenty-one hours of marching and fighting. Official reports listed 65 of their number killed, 180 wounded, and 27 missing. The wounded were ferried across the river for medical care in Boston; the rest lay down on the open ground at Bunker Hill to sleep. Later that night, it started to rain. The next morning, the drenched survivors on the north bank of the Charles River and the shaken British command in Boston found themselves literally besieged by thousands upon thousands of militiamen in Cambridge and other settlements surrounding Boston—and more patriots kept coming by the hour.

Because blood had finally flowed, not just in dribbles but in torrents, the events of April 19, 1775, assumed great symbolic significance. The memory of that special moment in our nation's history is indelibly inscribed and frequently celebrated in American lore. The "embattled farmers," we collectively recall, responded to Paul Revere's alarm, grabbed their hunting guns, rushed to the scene of the action, then ran through the hills, hiding behind trees and stone walls while firing away at the arrogant Redcoats, who marched foolishly on the road below.

This simple memory does not do justice to what these men did, for it pays no heed to the great collective effort that went into preparing for this momentous day, nor to the organized manner in which the patriots engaged their adversary. In truth, the patriots had been arming and training for months. When aroused from their sleep, not just by Paul Revere but by an intricate and very effective communications network, they mustered into their units, then marched together to the scene of the action. Once there, they continued to fight in as methodical a manner as the situation permitted. Historian David Hackett Fischer, the meticulous chronicler of the day's battles, concludes that from the confrontation on North Bridge to the time British reinforcements arrived, patriot militiamen "stood against the British force in large formations at least eight times. Six of these confrontations led to fighting, four at close quarters. Twice the British infantry was broken. . . . Altogether, it was an extraordinary display of courage, resolve, and discipline by citizen-soldiers against regular troops." Even during the final stages of the fighting, which appeared more random, militiamen traveled from one skirmish to the next in a reasonably coordinated pattern, communicating with each other and with their officers to ensure that their tactical engagements would achieve maximal results.[25]

Although they functioned in well-organized units, the method of their organization, by military standards, was not at all conventional. Officers were elected, not appointed, and they engaged in open dialogue with common soldiers. On-the-spot strategic decisions—whether to proceed to the left or the right, to fight or withdraw—were made not from the top down, but by deliberations and debates of the body of men in arms. Vocal disagreements with commanding officers, far from being punishable offenses, were the norm. By contrast, the British privates who were ordered to march through the night were never even told their purpose or destination.

This was a new kind of army, not very seasoned in fighting, but well versed in the arts of collective decision making, for the "embattled farmers" thought and acted as empowered citizens. The group processes of Massachusetts militiamen had been well rehearsed during the preceding decade of political protest, and beyond that, for more than a century, through their town meetings and community management of churches. Indeed, self-governance for these men had a deep religious foundation: the "covenant," an agreement among men to worship God together while acting collectively in their own behalf. The Minutemen who fought so effectively on April 19 had actually signed such a covenant, agreeing to forsake the security of their homes to secure the common good: "We whose names are hereunto subscribed, do

voluntarily inlist our selves, as Minute Men, to be ready for military operation, upon the shortest notice," they had promised each other.[26]

Covenants, town meetings, governance by the body of the people—these
had served the patriots well as they fought for liberty on the political battlefield, and also during the actual battles of April 19. But that day changed the
dynamics of the revolution these American patriots were making; henceforth,
the term *battlefield* would take on more than a metaphorical meaning. In a
full-fledged war, could a voluntary and democratic army even hope to prevail
over the largest and most efficient military organization in the world? If not,
would it change its character to become more competitive?

This suggests an even larger question, with no obvious answer at the time:
Would American patriots, faced with the social hardships and degradations
of an ugly and protracted war, compromise some of the values and principles
for which they were fighting?

9

Rage Militaire

After April 19, 1775: Northern Colonies

In Worcester, according to local lore, news of the invasion by Regulars arrived around noon of April 19:

> An express came to the town, shouting, as he passed through the street at full speed, "to arms! to arms! the war is begun!" His white horse, bloody with spurring, and dripping with sweat, fell exhausted by the church. . . . The bell rang out the alarm, cannon were fired, and messengers sent to every part of the town to collect the soldiery. As the news spread, the implements of husbandry were thrown by in the field, and the citizens left their homes with no longer delay than to seize their arms. In a short time the minute men were paraded on the green, under Capt. Timothy Bigelow: after fervent prayer by the Rev. Mr. Maccarty, they took up the line of march.[1]

Although we have no contemporary corroboration for the fallen horse, and the time of arrival seems implausible, the actual message that was delivered to Worcester still exists, and we know that Bigelow and his militiamen, upon receiving this missive, formed on the town common and traveled eastward sometime on April 19. They arrived too late to participate in the fighting but, finding themselves on the outskirts of Boston, many among their number remained to keep a watchful eye on the British Regulars. Together with upwards of ten thousand compatriots, these men formed the nucleus of an emergent Massachusetts Army, then, within days, a New England Army, and finally, two months later, the Continental Army.[2]

Fourteen-year-old Joseph Plumb Martin, who was living on his grandparents' farm in Milford, Connecticut, recalled the day he heard the news from Lexington and Concord:

> I was ploughing in the field about half a mile from home, about the twenty-first day of April, when all of a sudden the bells fell to ringing and three guns were repeatedly fired in succession down in the village. . . . I set off to see what the cause of the commotion was. I found most of the male kind of the people together; soldiers for Boston were in requisition. A dollar deposited upon the drumhead was taken up by someone as soon as placed there, and the holder's name taken, and he enrolled with orders to equip himself as quick as possible. . . . O, thought I, if I were but old enough to put myself forward, I would be the possessor of one dollar, the dangers of war to the contrary notwithstanding; but I durst not put myself up for a soldier for fear of being refused.[3]

Soon, recruits from the surrounding countryside billeted at Joseph's home on their way to war, duly impressing the budding youth: "Their company and conversation began to warm my courage to such a degree that I resolved at all events to 'go a sogering.'" But his "grandsire" would not let him enlist without his parents' consent. Because they lived far away and would probably not grant it in any case, young Joseph could do no more than watch enviously as other hometown boys marched boastfully off to confront the British Army at Boston:

> I accompanied them as far as the town line, and it was hard parting with them then. Many of my young associates were with them, my heart and soul went with them, but my mortal part must stay behind. By and by, they will come swaggering back, thought I, and tell me of their exploits, all their "hair-breadth 'scapes," and poor Huff will not have a single sentence to advance. O, that was too much to be borne with by me.[4]

James Warren, accompanied by his wife Mercy, was drumming up support for a New England Army in Providence, Rhode Island, when news arrived of "the bravery of the peasants of Lexington," to use Mrs. Warren's archaic and perhaps condescending phraseology. They had been in town but a few hours when the express rode through on the night of April 19. The Warrens hastily concluded their business, then rushed home to Plymouth "full of the most painful apprehensions" for the safety of their sons and the security of their home. Plymouth was a vulnerable target, they felt, because of its easy access by the sea. They contemplated moving to Taunton, well inland.[5]

Then James and Mercy parted ways, he to Watertown to attend the Provincial Congress, and she to stay home and prepare for a sudden evacuation, should the necessity arise.

And what of their sons? The eldest, James Jr., was a student at Harvard and thereby possessed the equivalent of a student deferment. But fifteen-year-old Winslow, Mercy's favorite, was approaching military age, and like Joseph Plumb Martin, he evidenced a fascination for the soldiering life. "Your son, Winslow, the bearer of this, has so great a desire to see the American Army that I thought proper to consent, as I supposed it would have no ill effect on his military disposition," she wrote to her husband, whose work at the Provincial Congress placed him in proximity to the American troops. But Winslow's mother wanted him merely to look, not touch: "Have him return as soon as possible," she insisted.[6]

Dr. Thomas Young responded to the news from Lexington and Concord by moving once again to the center of action—not northward toward Boston, where thousands upon thousands of ardent patriots were headed, but southward to Philadelphia, the site of the forthcoming Continental Congress, "where all my little influence shall be exerted in favor of the common good." After leaving Boston in such a hurry, Young could hardly retrace his steps—but he could hardly stay put either, not in this time of crisis, and not with his temperament.[7]

So he picked up in a flash, family and all. In Philadelphia, as in Boston, Dr. Young placed himself immediately in the public view by peddling his medical skills (he "is gitting into business fast," wrote a delegate from Rhode Island, who knew Young from there), then swiftly changed the subject to politics, his true calling. Only one year later, the itinerant doctor from the Oblong, Albany, Boston, and Newport would help write a new constitution for the state of Pennsylvania.[8]

According to tradition, although there is no contemporary documentation, Robert Morris was feasting with a large group of gentlemen at the City Tavern when he learned that the war had started. "The news was received by the company with the greatest surprise," wrote the nineteenth-century popular historian Charles Goodrich in his *Lives of the Signers of the Declaration of Independence*. "The tables, at which they were dining, were immediately deserted. A few only of the members, among whom was Mr. Morris, remained. To these, indeed to all, who had been present, it was evident that the die was cast."[9]

What was Mr. Morris thinking at that moment? Having walked the tight line between radical resistance and obsequious obedience for a decade, Morris had good cause to remain immobilized when he heard the line had been severed. Although he had certainly entertained the prospect of civil war, perhaps he never truly believed it would come. In fact, he had bet with his purse against it: at that very moment, his ships were carving through waves on the Atlantic, bearing the produce of America to England to beat the deadline for nonexportation.

But three months later, the truth finally set in: he could do "very little more business as a merchant until this affair is ended," he regretfully confessed.[10]

Back in Watertown, not far from Boston, James Warren and the Massachusetts Provincial Congress struggled with the difficult task of assembling a new army from diverse strands of local militias. They also did everything in their power to convince the other American colonies to join the military fight.

As its very first item of business after the military engagement, the Provincial Congress took depositions from firsthand witnesses to confirm the patriots' version of what had happened: brutal British Regulars had mowed down innocent farmers at Lexington, then despoiled the countryside and its people on their march back to Boston. They compiled several of these accounts, the ones that best conformed to their official story, into a pamphlet called *A Narrative of the Excursion and Ravages of the King's Troops*.

That pamphlet, which they distributed widely, was published by Congress's official printer, Isaiah Thomas, who had reassembled his press in the basement of Timothy Bigelow's house in Worcester while Bigelow himself helped organize the troops in Cambridge. Even before he published Congress's *Narrative*, Thomas had his press up and running and distributing propaganda that he himself composed. On May 3, exactly two weeks after the Regulars had marched, Thomas came out with the first issue of his revamped newspaper, the *Massachusetts Spy, or American Oracle of Liberty*. Under the banner "Americans!—Liberty or Death!—Join or Die!" Thomas wrote:

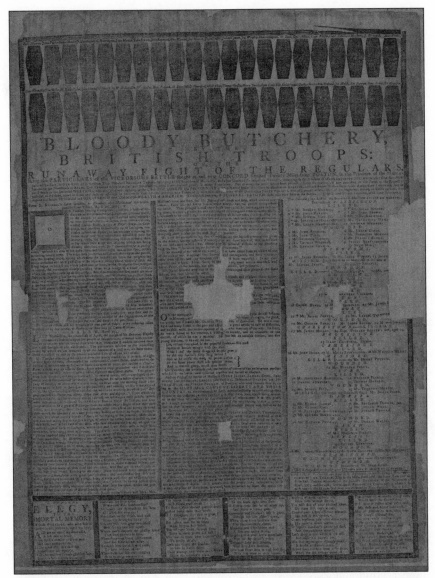

Figure 16. Ezekiel Russell's broadside, published by the *Salem Gazette* two days after the "Bloody Butchery" of April 19, was one of many propagandistic attempts to rally patriot resistance.

AMERICANS! forever bear in mind the BATTLE of LEXINGTON! where British Troops, unmolested and unprovoked, wantonly and in a most cruel manner fired upon and killed a number of our countrymen, then robbed them of their provisions, ransacked, plundered and burnt their houses! nor could the tears of defenceless women, some of whom were in the pains of childbirth, the cries of helpless babes, nor the prayers of old age, confined to beds of sickness, appease their thirst for blood!— or divert them from their DESIGN of MURDER and ROBBERY![11]

If such prose seems overly inflammatory, it served its purpose: to rally people for war. In the past, patriot propaganda had served political ends; now, it served a military end as well. Men were being asked to venture to the field of battle, and women to relinquish their sons, husbands, and brothers. For this, deep passions had to be aroused. People needed to feel abused, so they would then seek vengeance.

The message worked. Before, Americans had felt wronged; now, they could symbolize their victimization with a concrete, graphic event. In the wake of April 19, hungering for revenge, American patriots mobilized for war with a frenzy that historian Charles Royster has termed a *"rage militaire"* (somehow, the phrase sounds better in French). Patriots might have lost the misnamed Battle of Lexington, but they certainly won the war of words that followed. Because colonists were convinced they had been wronged, not only by taxes and laws but also by an invading army, tens of thousands joined together and willingly placed their very lives on the line.[12]

After April 19, 1775: Southern Colonies

The massive mobilization for war had a somewhat different trajectory in South Carolina and Virginia, where the patriots' drive for "liberty" was skewed by their dependence on chattel slavery.

The first military encounters in the South's two largest colonies occurred almost simultaneously with Lexington and Concord, at least a week before anybody in either place heard the news from Massachusetts. During the third week of April, patriots in South Carolina received the same alarming reports from London that had arrived in Boston on April 2. Sensing that war was imminent, Charleston patriots decided to strike first. On April 20, Charles Pinckney, president of the recessed Provincial Congress, appointed what was officially called the Secret Committee, charged with procuring arms "for the better defence and security of the people of these parts." The following night, this committee staged a three-pronged assault on public buildings and maga-

zines that housed the colony's military stores, including the State House itself. At eleven at night, with the tacit consent of the keeper of the State
House and the town watchmen, patriots bearing no disguises simply marched
to the top floor, broke open the door to the armory, and carried away "eight
hundred stands of arms, two hundred cutlasses, beside cartouches, flints, and
matches," in the words of William Henry Drayton, head of the Secret Committee. Meanwhile, others seized 1,600 pounds of gunpowder from two
nearby magazines.

According to Drayton, the State House raid was conducted under the ap-
proving eyes of Henry Laurens (at that moment chairman of the General
Committee), Thomas Lynch (a delegate to the Continental Congress), and
William Bull (a nephew of the acting governor, Lieutenant Governor William Bull, as was Drayton himself). This was not an action of the radical
fringe; preparing for war had become mainstream. The next day, when Lieutenant Governor Bull opened an official inquiry and offered a reward of
100 pounds sterling for any useful information, not a single person talked,
although every patriot in town knew the identities of the perpetrators.[13]

In early May, South Carolina patriots received two additional pieces of
news: first, a letter from Arthur Lee in London, addressed to Henry Laurens,
warned that Lord North's Ministry was planning to encourage slaves to rebel
against their patriot masters, and then, on May 8, word came that war had
just commenced in Massachusetts. Taken in tandem, and on top of everything else, these two items of information (even though one was only a rumor) convinced nearly everybody that war in South Carolina was not only
likely but inevitable.[14]

Nearly everybody, but not Henry Laurens. "God grant we may stop here—
that wisdom may interpose even now in this late hour," he wrote on May 22.
During the spring of 1775, Laurens engaged in some tricky mental and moral
gymnastics as he tried to reconcile opposing feelings: on the one hand, his
outrage against British arrogance and injustice, and on the other, his continuing belief that the basic organization of civil society should never be disrupted.
To alleviate the stress from such contradictory inclinations, he continued to
hope beyond hope for a peaceful settlement, even though all intelligence indicated otherwise. It was not the king himself who was to blame, he said, only
his evil-minded ministers. This old fiction, welcomed by many patriots in the
past, was no longer tenable, as proven by letters from his son John, who had
heard the king's harsh words in person.[15]

Henry Laurens felt trapped into fighting a revolution he did not really believe in. By temperament, he wanted to continue living in a "state of subordination" to the king and to the firm rules of civil society, but in fact, the very actions in which he was participating undermined people's "subordination" to civil authority. Indeed, at least for the moment, there was no civil authority at all, for government itself had been suspended. This bothered Henry Laurens deeply. Writing to his son James, who like John was still in Europe, he grumbled about living in "a Country in which the regular course of Government, is from necessity superceded by the arbitrary & inconsistent will of the people."[16]

Not all patriots were as troubled as Laurens by the demise of subordination and the breakdown of traditional authority. For Thomas Young and Timothy Bigelow, establishing a government according to the "Will of the people" was the object of the whole affair. Mercy Otis Warren, although suspicious of popular politics, was willing to go that route and even to live in a temporary "state of nature," without civil government, in order to achieve a greater goal: the establishment of a virtuous republic in America. Even Robert Morris and George Washington could view the temporary aberrations as useful if they served future goals: for Morris, unrestrained commerce, and for Washington, unfettered access to the American West. But for Laurens, the breakdown of authority struck at the very core of his beliefs; he sought no greater goal than returning to the ways of old.

And yet he went with the patriots' program. On June 1, Henry Laurens was chosen president of an emergency session of the extralegal South Carolina Provincial Congress. He opened the meeting by affirming the need to mobilize. "This colony cannot discharge her duty in defence of American freedom," he said, "unless we are put into a state of security against any immediate attacks by the British arms." He then supported his appeal to "the Lord of Hosts" by highlighting the news not only from Massachusetts but also from London: "There are just grounds, to apprehend an insurrection of the slaves, and hostilities from the Indians; instigated, by the tools of a wicked administration."[17]

On June 4, "after divine service had been performed before Congress," President Laurens was the first to sign his name to a military "Association." All the other members signed after him, pledging to resist "force by force" in defense of South Carolina's "freedom and safety," even at the risk of their "lives and fortunes."[18]

It was the most radical move a conservative man could take, and Henry Laurens did not sign without some reservations. In fact, before he set quill to paper to affix his name, he delivered a speech in which he issued two caveats, what today we might call signing statements. First, he wanted to make it perfectly clear that he had "repeatedly taken the Oath of Allegiance to King George the third" and that he continued to be "one of His Majesty's most dutiful & loyal subjects." Next, he took issue with a recent amendment to the Association, which stated that "we will hold all those persons inimical to the Liberty of the Colonies who shall refuse to subscribe." To apply this sort of pressure was "abhorrent & detestable," he felt. But even so, because he felt the Association would flounder without the president's approval, he went along. "And now under these necessary explanations of my duty & loyalty to my King & charity for my neighbours I will cheerfully subscribe this Association with my hand & upon proper occasion be ready to seal it with my blood," he concluded. Then, "without a shaking hand I signed," he informed John.[19]

It was a pivotal moment, and fraught with danger. To his younger son, James, he wrote:

> God knows my dear child if I shall ever again have the pleasure of em-
> bracing or even of writing to you—every day is big with perils & dangers
> & possibly if I do see you, our meeting may be more painful than absence
> & separation—I may be a prisoner, in chains & under sentence of
> death.[20]

But since Laurens personally and Americans generally had been wronged by the arbitrary abuse of power, a man of honor like himself was compelled to make his stand. *Honor*, that old-fashioned but irrationally compelling virtue, had led Henry Laurens to some strange places in the past, such as tweaking a man's nose, writing vindictive tomes, and coming to the verge of duels. Now, it placed him in absolute opposition to legitimate government, at the risk of his life if need be.

On April 21, the same day the Secret Committee of South Carolina seized the public supply of arms and powder in Charleston, Lord Dunmore, the royal governor of Virginia, jumped the gun on the patriots: between three and four in the morning, by the light of the waning moon, a detachment of fifteen marines crept through the streets of Williamsburg and removed the city's supply of gunpowder, fifteen half barrels, from the sixty-year-old octagonal magazine in the heart of town. Only as they loaded the cache aboard a vessel did a patriot see them and sound the alarm.

Aroused and infuriated, local patriots jumped from their beds and reached for their guns. By dawn a crowd of armed men was vowing "to repair to the palace, to demand from the Governor a restoration" of the city's powder. But the moderate leader Peyton Randolph was in town, and he counseled them to adopt a less hostile tone. That afternoon, the Municipal Common Hall (the city's governing body) sent a delegation to ask the governor to return the powder. This was no time to leave them without any means of defense, they argued: "We have too much reason to believe that some wicked and designing persons have instilled the most diabolical notions in the minds of our slaves, and that, therefore, the utmost attention to our internal security is become the more necessary."[21]

If patriots could play the "slave card," so could the governor: he had removed the powder "to a place of security . . . lest the Negroes might have seized upon it," he said, for he had heard of "an insurrection in a neighboring county." Two days later, upon learning that patriots from surrounding counties might march on Williamsburg, Dunmore suddenly decided to play a conflicting and much stronger slave card: if any harm should come from a patriot attack, he pronounced, he would "declare freedom to the slaves, and reduce the City of Williamsburg to ashes." This only fed the patriots' fears and added to their anger.[22]

The news from Lexington and Concord took a week to arrive in Virginia, but when it did, it further heightened the frenzy. During the last week of April, independent military companies from several counties gathered in Fredericksburg and vowed to march against the governor in Williamsburg. As they assembled, they asked for further instructions from the officer many had chosen to lead them in the field: George Washington. They hoped, and some assumed, that Washington was on his way to Fredericksburg to take command.

But Washington had no intention of leading an assault on Williamsburg. Responding politely to an invitation from the Albemarle Independent Company, he wrote: "I highly applaud the spirit you have manifested on this occasion," but there was "little occasion" to initiate a war in Virginia. Besides, he needed to fulfill his obligation to "the country at large" by attending a new session of the Continental Congress, slated to meet in less than two weeks.[23]

Williamsburg might well have been the wrong *place*, but it was not necessarily the wrong *time* to use military force. On May 4, when Washington left for Philadelphia, he carried his military uniform, recently refurbished, with him.

April 20–August 1775: Surrounding Boston

While George Washington was preparing to march off to war, over ten thousand other men from New England were already there, and they already had a commander: General Artemas Ward, whom the Massachusetts Provincial Congress had appointed the previous fall to lead the colony's militia. Ward was a wealthy merchant from Shrewsbury, adjacent to the town of Worcester, and he earned his position for two reasons: he had served as a colonel during the French and Indian War, and he was among the few members of the elite class in the western counties of the province to contest imperial abuse. As far back as 1767, Governor Francis Bernard had revoked Ward's military commission because of his outspoken opposition in the General Court, and on September 6, 1774, Ward had played a prominent role in ousting the court officials in Worcester—even though he himself had been one of the judges deposed.

During his first week on the job, Ward met with members of the Provincial Congress's Committee of Safety (which shared his headquarters at the Hastings House in Cambridge) to lay out a plan for changing the potpourri of militia companies from four New England colonies into a single army with a centralized chain of command. This was no easy task. Thousands of men who answered the call on April 19 had no intention of joining an army for more than a few weeks; it was planting season, and unless they returned home soon, their families would not have food come fall. Thousands more decided to stay but, to keep them on board, they had to be enlisted into a particular company—not their own militia company, but a unit within the newly formed army, commanded perhaps by a man they had never met. The structural problem of reorganization thereby turned immediately into a morale problem.

It was during this initial organization that Timothy Bigelow landed a big promotion: from captain of his town's militia to major, third in command in Artemas Ward's First Massachusetts Bay Provincial Regiment. (Because Ward also commanded the entire army, his attention to one particular regiment was minimal, and this left Bigelow essentially second in command.) Before, if Bigelow issued orders, only the local men who had elected him captain would have to listen; now, his orders were heard by six hundred soldiers within his regiment, some of whom already knew the blacksmith from Worcester, but most of whom did not.

Would Bigelow's new subordinates follow his orders? Why, indeed, would any of these feisty patriots, accustomed to thinking for themselves, submit their lives to the care of others? Back in December, the Provincial Congress acknowledged the unique character of its army by changing its drill book from a standard British text to one drawn up by Timothy Pickering, a lawyer from Salem. Patriot soldiers should be "clearly informed of the reason of every action and movement," Pickering's manual stipulated. This differed markedly from the European model, Pickering claimed: "'Tis the boast of some that their men are mere machines . . . but God forbid that my country-men should ever be thus regarded."[24]

Whether informed or not, and however much they were motivated, the farmers-turned-soldiers did not readily submit to military discipline. This bothered James Warren, who watched from nearby Watertown as the army in Cambridge struggled. Barely two weeks after Ward had assumed command, Warren wrote to John Adams:

> As to the Army, it is in such a shifting, fluctuating state as not to be ca-pable of a perfect regulation. They are continually coming and going. However, they seem to me to want a more experienced direction. I could for myself wish to see your friends Washington and L[ee] at the head of it, and yet dare not propose it, tho' I have it in contemplation.[25]

Organization and discipline were not the only problems faced by General Ward and other officials who tried to fashion an army from scratch. Within a matter of days, men with no particular training needed to build a complete infrastructure for upwards of ten thousand people, among the five largest concentrations of human beings in colonial America. (Soon, the Provincial Congress hoped, the number of soldiers would grow to thirty thousand.) How would all these folks be fed, clothed, armed, and housed? The problem of supplies was truly an emergency. On April 21, his second day in charge, Ward ordered "that the Commissary-General do supply the troops with pro-vision in the manner he can, without spending time for exactness."[26]

This concentration of soldiers, combined with their transience, created another significant problem: the spread of disease. Smallpox was already flourishing in New England, and crowded conditions threatened to trigger a full-fledged epidemic. Meanwhile, poor sanitation increased the incidence of communicative diseases such as diphtheria and typhus. On May 2, Ward did what little he could to lessen this danger by ordering "that vaults be immediately dug [and] that the parade and camp be cleaned away every day, and all the filth buried."[27]

Finally, General Ward and the Provincial Congress that hired him faced an obstacle they had little hope of overcoming: who would pay for all this? The Provincial Congress's own coffers were small, scarcely sufficient to cover the extra expense of supporting such a large army.

On May 16, less than one month after the instantaneous emergence of America's formidable homegrown army, the Provincial Congress concluded it didn't have the resources to support it. It asked the Continental Congress, which had convened in Philadelphia the previous week, to take over: "As the army, collecting from different colonies, is for the general defence of the rights of America, we would beg leave to suggest to your consideration, the propriety of your taking the regulation and general direction of it." At the same time, the Provincial Congress in Watertown asked the intercolonial assembly in Philadelphia for permission to function as a regular government. Delegates were tired of issuing "recommendations"; they would prefer to pass real laws.[28]

The Continental Congress responded in the affirmative to both requests. Yes, the Massachusetts Provincial Congress could consider itself a government according to the 1691 Charter, minus the Crown-appointed governor. (Many Massachusetts patriots had wanted more—"a more perfect" plan, in the words of James Warren—but they had to settle for this.) And yes, the Congress in Philadelphia would adopt the New England Army and turn it into a Continental Army, charged with protecting all thirteen colonies from any incursions by British soldiers.[29]

The Continental Congress demonstrated its commitment to the army surrounding Boston with three key measures.

First, to pay for the war it was about to fight, it issued $2 million in paper currency. These bills of credit were pegged to the Spanish dollar, not the British pound.

Second, it dispatched the most effective fighting units it could locate outside New England: twelve companies of riflemen from Pennsylvania, Maryland, and Virginia. ("They are the most accurate marksmen in the world; they kill with great exactness at 200 yards distance," John Adams promised James Warren.) Although the total amounted to just shy of one thousand men, the gesture was significant: New England would not be fighting alone.[30]

Finally, it appointed a new commander, a man not from New England. Some delegates to Congress had preferred to stay with General Ward, think-

Figure 17. George Washington, a military hero from the French and Indian War, was ready to serve if called. Charles Willson Peale painted this portrait in 1772 and called it "The Virginia Colonel."

ing that the Yankees, who still accounted for the bulk of the army, would prefer to take orders from one of their own. But most thought otherwise. To make the army truly "continental," and to attract support from the middle and southern colonies, they needed fresh blood, someone with a greater military reputation and a wider base of support than Artemas Ward.

Given these parameters, there were only two realistic candidates: George Washington and Charles Lee. Both men had served in the French and Indian War, but Washington had returned to civilian life while Lee went on to a distinguished military career, not only with the British Army but also as a soldier of fortune in eastern Europe. He had returned to America in 1773, settled in Virginia (with financial backing from Robert Morris), joined the resistance against Britain, and pushed for the formation of an army, which he himself hoped to lead. He was known to be bold, brave, and very bright, an excellent strategist. He was also quite eccentric, however. Although he had married (briefly) a Mohawk woman during his first stint in America, he paid more attention to his dogs and horses. He was crude in manners and obscene in discourse, and worse yet, he wanted to be paid handsomely for his services.

Congress settled instead on one of their own, a man they could trust and respect, so Lee had to settle for third in command, behind both Washington and Ward. (Because Ward was in perennial ill health, however, everyone knew that Lee was really second, not third.) Congress approved Washington's appointment on June 15, received his acceptance the next day, and drafted his commission the day after that. We do not know how much earlier he knew he would be called, but on June 3, Washington spent £30 for "cartooch boxes &c"; two days later he purchased a tomahawk and a new covering for his holsters; and on June 8, a week before his appointment, he bought "5 military books." Immediately after receiving his commission, he wrote to his wife, Martha: "I was apprehensive I could not avoid this appointment." Indeed, he had been actively "not avoiding" his appointment for several months.[31]

On June 17, the very day the Continental Congress approved Washington's commission, the army he was about to command proved it could fight valiantly without him. Having received intelligence that the British were preparing to cross the Charles River and stage a massive assault, patriot officers ordered the immediate fortification of Bunker Hill. The men charged with carrying out the task, however, decided nearby Breed's Hill would be easier to defend, and they worked through the night to build breastworks to shield them from the enemy's fire.

The British did in fact attack, first by firing cannon shots at the nearby town of Charleston and setting it ablaze, and then, around three in the afternoon, by sending an intimidating force of 1,500 Redcoats, muskets poised and bayonets shining, against the makeshift patriot stronghold. Several hundred patriots behind the breastworks held their fire until the advancing soldiers were about sixty yards away (not, as a popular myth suggests, until they saw "the whites of their eyes," which would have been only five or ten yards distant). Then the Americans leveled their own muskets and shot, killing and wounding so many Regular infantrymen that the rest decided to retreat. After regrouping, the Regulars charged again, and once more they were repulsed. Finally, after receiving a shelling by distant British artillery, the patriots relinquished their position in the face of a third assault. Technically, American soldiers lost the battle, but because they inflicted many more casualties (226 killed, 826 wounded) than they received (140 killed, 271 wounded), they claimed a victory of sorts. Among the patriots killed was Joseph Warren, who earned great accolades as the war's first martyr.

Six days after the Battle of Bunker Hill (as it was mistakenly called), George Washington, commander in chief of the Army of the United Colonies, embarked from Philadelphia to meet the men under his charge on the outskirts of Boston. He carried with him instructions to enforce strict discipline, take orders from Congress, and limit his forces to twice those of the opposing army. Congress had hired Washington to do a specific job, not to create a standing army that might grow and act on its own behalf.

Washington also carried a letter from John Adams, introducing him to James Warren and other prominent Massachusetts patriots. Unbeknownst to either Washington or Adams at this time, James Warren had just succeeded the deceased Joseph Warren as president of the Provincial Congress, and it was in this context that Warren was empowered to hand over the army to its new commander, along with an official warning that the troops might not live up to Washington's professional standards:

> The greatest part of them have not before seen service. And altho' naturally brave and of good understanding, . . . the youth in the Army are not possess'd of the absolute necessity of cleanliness in their dress, and lodging, continual exercise, and strict temperance to preserve them from diseases frequently prevailing in camps; especially among those who, from their childhood, have been us'd to a laborious life.[32]

These lads were to be Washington's soldiers, and they did not please him. Although the gentleman from Virginia was welcomed "with a grate deal of grandor" on the Cambridge Common on the morning of July 3 ("there is at this time one & twenty drummers & as many feffors a beting and playing round the prayde," wrote Lieutenant Joseph Hodgkins at 8:00 A.M.), and although Mercy Otis Warren reported from nearby Watertown two days later that "the people here are universally pleased" with Washington's appointment, and although from the day he assumed command Washington was addressed as His Excellency, the respect was not reciprocated. Educated patriot leaders, such as James Warren, Washington liked, but Yankee farmers and tradesmen playing at war he did not.[33]

Although Washington's public pronouncements on the character of his soldiers were polite and circumspect ("I need not make myself enemies among them," he confided), his private letters dripped with condescension and bristled with condemnation. Writing to Lund Washington, his cousin and manager of the Mount Vernon estate, he called Massachusetts soldiers "an exceedingly dirty & nasty people." This he expected of common privates, but here even the officers lacked breeding, polish, and education. To Richard Henry Lee, a fellow gentleman from Virginia who could understand such things, he complained that the officers were lax in "carrying orders into execution," preferring instead "to curry favor with the men (by whom they were chosen, & on whose smiles possibly they think they may again rely) seems to be one of the principal objects of their attention."[34]

This was no way to run an army, George Washington believed—but for soldiers from Massachusetts, it was the best possible way. A citizens' army (and that's the only kind of army they would tolerate) ought to reflect the will of the people who fought in it. Elsewhere, a blind obedience to military authority was beyond questioning, but in Revolutionary America, where people were exploring new ways to participate in public life, a secure relationship between civil and military society had yet to be established.[35]

Summer and Fall 1775: Throughout Virginia and Ninety Six, South Carolina

While George Washington was struggling with feisty Yankee soldiers, his peers back in Virginia tussled with the fighting force of their own colony. The situation in Massachusetts was understandable in light of the obvious discrepancy between the culture of deference, which shaped Washington's views, and the egalitarian thrust of revolutionary Massachusetts, but the robust opposition from common Virginians must have come as something of a surprise, even, and especially, to the gentry who tried to keep them in line.

Before the confrontations in Williamsburg and Lexington and Concord, the independent volunteer companies had "consisted entirely of gentlemen," in the words of George Mason, who had just taken over Washington's seat in the quasi-governmental Virginia Convention. When Mason had argued that officers should be elected, he assumed that the men chosen would be his peers, but many who answered the alarm during the last week of April 1775 were not of the same mold, and as the ranks of volunteers swelled, the composition and character of the companies changed. By June, the new members of the Albemarle Independent Company had only one-third the wealth (measured in land, slaves, horses, and cattle) as the original members. Indeed, one-third did not possess any slaves, which placed them in a class apart from the likes of Washington and Mason.[36]

This new class of volunteers did not always behave like "gentlemen." In Williamsburg, for instance, the independent company threatened to bring royal officials back to its own camp to face the wrath of citizen-soldiers. Such actions, characteristic of Dr. Thomas Young and the crowds in Boston, scared off political moderates, who still entertained the notion that reconciliation was possible. Other volunteers threatened to tar and feather those who refused to join, and they focused their attention particularly on the gentry who did not serve. As in Massachusetts, officers soon found it difficult to discipline the men who had elected them, and who might or might not vote for them in the future.

This was not the sort of military force that Mason, Washington, and others had hoped to form, and the Virginia gentry decided to do something about it. At the Third Virginia Convention, meeting in July and August, the delegates, gentlemen all (this was still Virginia, not Massachusetts), revamped the provincial military structure, eliminating the volunteer companies and placing in their stead a more organized and coordinated army of "minutemen," based on a very different set of rules. Officers were to be appointed, not elected, and they would be paid between twelve and one hundred times as much as privates. All recruits were expected to march and drill on a regular schedule, but overseers of slaves were exempt from service. Finally, and most significantly, recruits were to leave their homes and farms for eighty days the first year and sixty days in subsequent years, whether or not there was a war going on. The first twenty days of training would commence that fall—right in the middle of harvest season.[37]

These new rules were not exactly welcomed by the rank and file, who voiced their displeasure by refusing to sign up. Small farmers wanted simply to "go and fight the battle at once, and not be shilly shally, in this way, until all the poor people are ruined." As George Washington was trying to whip his Yankees into line, he began to receive troublesome news from home: "Virginia is in the greatest confusion, only one battalion of Minute Men compleat, and little prospect of the others being so," wrote one informant. "Our minute scheme does not equal the conventions expectation. The people do not come readily into it," said another.[38]

Problems of recruitment and discipline had crossed provincial boundaries. Cherishing their own freedom as much their country's, and imbued with a rambunctious spirit that undermined the deferential attitudes required for military service, healthy American males with other work to do thought twice before signing over their lives, however much they believed in the patriotic cause.

In the South Carolina backcountry, many freedom-loving people complicated the problem even more by defining their patriotism in quite different fashion: they decided the true enemies to the cause of liberty were the wealthy rice planters in the lowlands of their own colony, whom they perceived as threats to their own land tenures, and not the British Crown, which they felt protected them from both hostile Indians to their west and fervent patriots to their east.

Henry Laurens and the rest of the colony's ardent patriots found this out the hard way. On June 14, Laurens was appointed president of the newly created Council for Safety, imbued with the power "to direct and regulate the operations of the troops" and "to stamp, sign, and issue certificates, for the speedy raising such troops." This completed a Laurens sweep: he now headed the quasi-official legislative body of South Carolina (Provincial Congress), its executive arm (General Committee), and its department of defense (Council of Safety). When news started filtering in from the backcountry that people there would not play along, it fell upon Laurens, because of his powerful positions as well as his long-standing connections in the Ninety Six region (he owned two large plantations there), to convince these reluctant farmers to enlist in the Association.[39]

On July 14, Laurens wrote to Thomas Fletchall, an influential militia colonel in the Ninety Six district, who, rumor had it, was taking the side of the Crown: would he "choose to join the freinds of the glorious cause of freedom in defence of the liberties of the whole British Empire which must stand or fall with those of America," or would he "aid & abet the tools of despotism the only dangerous enemies of our misguided sovereign lord the King"? Laurens dispatched this letter along with two copies of the Association, one to sign and return immediately, the other to circulate within Fletchall's militia companies.[40]

Ten days later, Fletchall responded to Laurens's loaded question: "I must inform you Sir I am resolved and do utterly refuse to take up arms agt my King." He was not alone in this sentiment, Fletchall reported. He had presented the Association to every company in his regiment, just as Laurens had requested, but "I dont remember that one man offerd to Sign it." Instead, they drew up and signed their own resolution. Because the king had "not acted inconsistent with & subversive of the principles of the constitutions of the British Empire," they held, "we are determined not to take up arms against him." This did not mean the backcountry farmers were neglecting their duties to defend South Carolina, however. They were "ready & willing at all times to assist in defending the Province in order to oppose and suppress the incurtions of Indians, insurrections of Negroes, or any other enemy which may or shalle invade this Province."[41]

Not all backcountry residents were "disaffected" (as they said at the time) to the patriots' cause, but a great many were, perhaps even the majority. Historians today are still trying to fathom why some chose one side and some the other, and why these people hated each other so venomously. Allegiances crossed economic, religious, and geographic lines. The only discernible pattern is that farmers who arrived more recently tended to side with the British, while those with longer-standing claims, on average, preferred the patriots, but even this cannot be used as a clear predictor of loyalties.

In any case, polarized positions and isolated personal confrontations led stepwise to organized military conflict. Scuffles over gunpowder started in July, and by November 19, and continuing for three days, some 4,000 angry Americans, almost equally divided, were firing at each other around the courthouse in Ninety Six. Two men died (one from each side) and 64 more were wounded, the first bloodletting of the Revolutionary War in the Carolinas. One month later, at a place called the Great Cane Break, after many of their opponents had gone home for the winter, patriots won a lopsided battle, killing 5 and capturing 130.

But this was only the beginning, for the harder the patriots pushed, the more resistance they created. The early losses suffered by local loyalists engendered vengeful responses, thereby creating a new warrior class in the backcountry: hardened fighters whom the patriots called banditti and whom today we might term terrorists. Even in his moment of triumph, having ordered the clampdown on the local "insurrection," Henry Laurens was abetting what he most feared: the breakdown of civil society.

Summer and Fall 1775: Philadelphia

Many of the initial skirmishes of the American Revolution, from Concord to Ninety Six, were fought more for gunpowder than for territory. Robert Morris understood the direct correlation between access to powder and military viability, and he was fully prepared to do something about it.

Once fighting had commenced, it took but a short time for Morris to move beyond the initial shock and return to his comfort zone: commerce. Although business with Britain would be disrupted, why couldn't he trade elsewhere? During the French and Indian War, he had contributed simultaneously to the public good and his private purse by meeting the soldiers' needs. Now, he could do so again, and by becoming active, he generated in himself a positive outlook. "I think we cannot fail in succeeding in this most righteous cause," he wrote to his friend Charles Lee.[42]

On June 30, 1775, the Pennsylvania Assembly appointed Robert Morris, his partner Thomas Willing, Benjamin Franklin, John Dickinson, and twenty-one others to serve as a Committee of Safety, an executive body charged with outfitting soldiers and overseeing the war effort. This was an impressive group, dominated by wealthy men with important friends in far-away places. By putting their resources to use, Morris (who soon became the committee's vice president, second only to Franklin) and other members of the Committee of Safety were able to amass a stockpile of powder three times as large as that of any other colony.[43]

This took money, connections, and ingenuity. In July, for instance, Morris and Franklin engineered a scheme to seize powder stored in Bermuda. First, they had to convince Congress to allow an exemption to the nonexportation clause of the Association: in the British-controlled West Indies, Americans would be allowed to trade commodities for munitions. Then, meeting with a handful of Bermudans who had come to Philadelphia in search of foodstuffs (Bermuda had been seriously hurt by American nonexportation), Morris and Franklin arranged a secret rendezvous for the night of August 14, in distant waters. At the appointed time, the sloop the Committee of Safety had hired, the *Lady Catherine*, anchored off the coast of Bermuda, along with the schooner *Charles Town and Savannah Packet*, engaged by Henry Laurens and the South Carolina Committee of Safety for the same purpose. A raiding party from the two vessels went ashore, where their Bermuda cohorts guided them to the magazine that housed the powder. After a sailor gained entry through a vent in the roof and opened the doors, the Americans and Bermudans, working side by side, rolled barrel after barrel of gunpowder to the shoreline, loaded them onto local whaleboats, and rowed them out to the anchored vessels, which then sailed with their payloads back to the mainland.[44]

Whenever Robert Morris, Thomas Willing, and the Pennsylvania Committee of Safety ordered supplies, whether munitions or food or clothing or tents, they placed that order with one of Philadelphia's prominent mercantile houses; often, the designated firm would be that of Willing and Morris. In such cases, the two men would be parties to both ends of the contract. Willing also served as a delegate to the Continental Congress, where he likewise signed on to both ends of various contracts.

On November 3, 1775, Thomas Willing was joined in Congress by his junior partner. Six weeks after that, Robert Morris took a seat on the powerful

Secret Committee, charged with keeping the supply train flowing, and within months the committee's new workhorse became its chairman. John Adams, fond of assessing the character and utility of delegates to Congress, wrote of Morris: "I think he has a masterly understanding, and open temper and an honest heart.... He has vast designs in the mercantile way, and no doubt pursues mercantile ends, which are always gain; but he is an excellent member of our body."[45]

The private business of Robert Morris and Thomas Willing was becoming increasingly hard to separate from the public business of the Continental Congress. On December 2, Congress ordered "the Colonel of the Pennsylvania Battalion, now in the barracks at Philadelphia, to send a detachment of his regiment and keep a regular guard on the wharves of Messrs. Willing and Morris, and Mr. Cuthbert, to take care of the ships and stores belonging to the United Colonies."[46]

September 5–December 31: Cambridge, Newburyport, Kennebec River, and Quebec

Soldiers had enlisted and drilled. Officers had received their commissions. The army was taking on some semblance of organization. Equipment was being procured. But where was the war? For two months after George Washington assumed command, both sides did little more than stare each other down, neither willing to expose itself in a rematch of the bloodbath at Breed's Hill. All this waiting around did not suit Washington's temperament. "The state of inactivity, in which this Army has lain for some time, by no means corresponds with my wishes," he wrote to John Hancock, president of the Continental Congress, in September.[47]

To break the stalemate, Washington proposed to his officers a dramatic land-and-sea assault on the British garrison in Boston, winner take all. Unless they did *something*, he argued, the army might simply fall apart when enlistments expired that winter. Furthermore, he did not see how fifteen thousand soldiers could be housed and clothed through the winter.

"On the other hand," he admitted to his Council of War, which consisted of nine generals, including him, "the hazard, the loss of men in the attempt & the probable consequences of failure are to be considered." Wisely, in the face of "probable" defeat, the council voted against Washington's projected offensive.[48]

But there was another way to break the stalemate: make an end run around the concentration of British forces in Boston by invading the weakly guarded city of Quebec, gateway to the Saint Lawrence River and thereby to all of Canada.

To this end, Washington engineered a two-pronged maneuver: General Philip Schuyler, stationed in New York, would lead an army up the Lake Champlain corridor to the Saint Lawrence, take Montreal, then proceed downriver to the walled city of Quebec, while Colonel Benedict Arnold would head a separate contingent up the Kennebec River in Maine.

On the map, the plan looked good; on the ground, it was seriously flawed. Although the Lake Champlain corridor had been used frequently by invading armies, the Kennebec expedition was problematic: the Maine weather in fall bore no resemblance to the balmy autumns back in Virginia; the Kennebec, with its swift current flowing in the wrong direction, was quite unlike the navigable Potomac; and the pine-forested wilderness, with no source of supplies for the army, was less hospitable than any that even Washington had traversed. All this would soon become painfully evident.

Much to his credit, George Washington understood that the move was a gamble, and he hedged his bets by issuing an enlightened set of instructions to Benedict Arnold, cautious warnings that should perhaps be considered by modern American commanders before they march into foreign lands.

First, Arnold was "to discover the real sentiments of the Canadians towards our cause," for without their "favourable disposition," the expedition would inevitably flounder and fail. If "real" intelligence indicated the people were "averse" to an American presence, Arnold was "by no means to prosecute the attempt." He should also return if the weather became too severe or if any other "unforeseen difficulties should arise." In short, Washington gave Arnold free reign to cut and run should the circumstances turn sour.

Knowing that his troops (white and Protestant) did not share the values and customs of Canada's inhabitants (Indian and Catholic), Washington insisted that soldiers treat the locals charitably, never plunder or insult them, and above all, avoid "ridiculing" their religious ceremonies. ("As the contempt of the religion of a Country . . . has ever been deeply resented, you are to be particularly careful to restrain every officer & soldier from such imprudence & folly.") Any soldier who failed to treat the people and their religion respectfully, Washington said, should be given "such severe & exemplary punishment as the enormity of the crime may require. Should it extend to death itself, it will not be disproportionate to its guilt at such a time and in such a cause."

While clamping down on American miscreants, Washington insisted that all prisoners of war be treated "with as much humanity & kindness as may be consistent with your own safety & the publick interest." He told Arnold to restrain his troops "from all acts of cruelty & insult which will disgrace the American arms—and irritate our fellow subjects against us."

Finally, Washington instructed Arnold to spend his limited funds with "frugality & oeconomy, . . . keeping as exact an account as possible of your disbursements."[49]

Instructions in hand, Arnold was sent on his way. Under his command were 1,100 volunteers, all "active woodsmen" according to Washington's orders. Four of these rugged fellows were field officers, and one of those was Major Timothy Bigelow, second in command for one of the two battalions. About a dozen of the other volunteers came from Worcester, including Jonas Hubbard, who had taken over as captain of Worcester's company when Bigelow was promoted, and John Pierce, a surveyor who kept a detailed journal of the expedition.[50]

After a brief trip home to Worcester to tend to personal needs, Bigelow, Hubbard, Pierce, and the others headed to Newburyport, a port not far north of Boston. There, on Sunday, September 17, seeking both guidance and good luck, they attended divine service, military style. Marching with flags flying into the First Presbyterian Church, they formed two columns and presented their guns. The preacher, after walking through the lines to the rolling of drums, delivered his sermon: as Moses said to the Lord, "If thy spirit go not with us, carry us not up hence." The soldiers were moved. After the service, some convinced the sexton to open the tomb of George Whitefield, the famous revivalist of the Great Awakening, which lay within the church. Whitefield's body had decomposed in the five years since his death, but some of his clothes remained intact. The men cut his collar and wristbands into small pieces, which they used as relics to ensure success in conquering a land peopled by heathens, Catholics, and their British rulers.[51]

The following day, they departed by sea to the mouth of the Kennebec River, and thence upstream, against the current (an apt metaphor for their journey), toward the headwaters. Alternately rowing, dragging, and swimming their flat-bottomed boats, called bateaux, they schlepped their provisions and arms northward, and as they did so, the river steepened and narrowed and in the end disappeared. The weather turned cold and foul. Provisions began to run out.

Upon leaving the last white settlements, the caravan spread out: a small scouting party in the lead, exploring and establishing the way; a somewhat larger group in the middle, widening the trail when needed and building camps for the men to follow; the largest group in the rear, slowed down by hauling the bulk of the supplies.

By the middle of October, after carrying their boats away from the Kennebec River to a series of ponds almost a thousand feet higher, and from there on to the aptly named Dead River, the adventurers passed by the tallest mountain along the way, rising to over four thousand feet. Timothy Bigelow, while waiting for the party in the rear to catch up, climbed the peak—Mount Bigelow, as it has been called ever since—to reconnoiter the terrain ahead. Upon his descent, Arnold dispatched Bigelow on quite a different mission: backward toward the men in the rear, with instructions to bring up more supplies for the advance group, now short on food.[52]

The rear party did not give him much, for they had little to spare. The sad truth was that after a month on the road, only a few barrels of flour remained, and even fewer barrels of pork. If the men could shoot some bear or partridge, they would eat; if not, they had only a few more days before literally starving in the woods.

Then it rained, and rained some more, and snowed, and the river rose, and boats sank, and barrels of flour sprang leaks, ruining the contents within. Wet, cold, and hungry, the men pushed on through the "direful howling wilderness not describable," as one man wrote in his journal.[53]

On October 24, Colonel Arnold finally concluded he could not make it to Quebec with his full force. He called a council of his officers, and together they agreed to send back "all the sick and feeble." But these weren't the only ones to return. The following morning, despite the counsel of Timothy Bigelow and others, Colonel Roger Enos headed south with at least one-third of the original expedition. They were not even halfway to Quebec.[54]

For those who continued the outlook was bleak. Timothy Bigelow paused to pen what he believed might be his final words to his wife Anna, which he dispatched with the return party. This is one of Bigelow's few extant letters[55]:

On that part of the Kennybeck called the Dead river, 95 miles above Norridgewock

Dear Wife. I am at this time well, but in a dangerous situation, as is the whole detachment of the Continental Army with me. We are in a wilderness nearly one hundred miles from any inhabitants, either French or English, and but about five days provisions on an average for the whole. We are this day sending back the most feeble and some that are sick. If the French are our enemies it will go hard with us, for we have no retreat left. In that case there will be no alternative between the sword and famine. May God in his infinite mercy protect you, my more than ever dear wife, and my dear children, Adieu, and ever believe me to be your most affectionate husband,

Timo. Bigelow

Even with fewer mouths to feed, those who continued were on the brink of starvation by the end of the following week. They had to eat their candles. Some devoured the officers' dogs. By November 2, after days of this sort of fare, private Jeremiah Greenman jotted in his journal: "this morn when we arose many of us so weak that we could hardly stand we staggered about like drunken men." Later that day, and just in time, the famished soldiers came upon the first French Canadian settlement, and with it, some cattle. "Hear we killed a creatur and sum of ye men so hungrey before this creater was dressed thay had the skin and all entrels guts and every thing that could be eat on ye fires a boyling," Greenman wrote.[56]

Upon reaching the first settlement in Canada, Timothy Bigelow sent another letter home, quite different in tone from the first:

Dear Anna,

I very much regret my writing the last letter to you, the contents were so gloomy. It is true our provisions are short, . . . but we have this minute received news that the inhabitants of Canada are friendly, and very much rejoiced at our coming, and a very small number of troops in Quebec. We have had a very fatiguing march of it, but I hope it will soon be over.[57]

Receiving supplies from friendly inhabitants, the invading force proceeded, and on November 14 it arrived at Quebec. There, Arnold, Bigelow, and the rest of the officers mustered their soldiers on the Plains of Abraham, about three hundred yards to the west of the city's wall, where, according to surveyor Pierce, the patriots "Gave 3 huzzars and cheers and marched 2 times round in a circle in open view of the enemy." This display did nothing more than draw some sporadic cannon fire, but all the extant journals take note of the event. The men seemed pleased to behave in a military way after struggling so hard just to survive for the preceding two months.[58]

By this time, only about half the original force was fit for duty, hardly enough to storm a walled and fortified city. Rather than press the issue, Arnold and company awaited the arrival of the patriots coming via Lake Champlain, but that force, now under the direction of General Richard Montgomery, did not arrive until December 1, and it too had been weakened by the journey. With a significant number of men in both contingents breaking out with smallpox, Montgomery and Arnold decided to postpone the assault, pending the improved health of their soldiers, but as they waited, Governor Guy Carleton was able to reinforce the city's defenses and train a large force of sailors and militiamen to aid the British Regulars.

On December 26, with the terms of enlistment for most of their soldiers due to expire in five days, the American officers gathered in council to decide whether they had sufficient resources to stage the assault. Opinions differed, as reported by Pierce:

Last night we had a general review and to day they are taking their names to see how many will scale the walls and how many will not &c. amongst our men there is great searchings of heart with respect to scaleing of walls and what the event will be God only knows—Its not my opinion to scale nor the opinions of my Capt [Jonas Hubbard] nor Lt. that's well known and its not the opinion of Majr Bigelo neither.[59]

The men from Worcester, that hotbed of patriotism, were lining up on the side of caution—or perhaps cowardice, as some would say. Indeed, only two of Hubbard's company "signed to scale the walls of Quebeck." The others did not wish to risk their lives charging a city perched on cliffs and defended by a fighting force twice as large as their own. They preferred instead to heed George Washington's warning and call off the assault, with conditions having turned unfavorable.

Despite the opposition, eager voices prevailed, and Bigelow and Hubbard, against their better judgment, agreed to participate. The next day it stormed, right on cue, and the troops prepared for a nighttime attack. But then the weather cleared, causing another postponement.

Two days later, when Timothy Bigelow was seen dodging one of the random cannonballs fired into camp, he was "complained of for cowardice," although anybody would be a fool *not* to get out of the way if he could. Word had gotten out: Bigelow was less than enthusiastic, and for this he was punished in the military tribunal of public opinion. When men rev up for battle, caution is not what they wish to hear.[60]

But in this case at least caution was not uncalled for. The plan of attack, like the plan for Arnold's expedition, looked better on paper than on the ground. Montgomery and his men were to march from the southwest, drawing fire and diverting attention from Arnold and his men, who would creep around the city and approach from the northeast, scale the barricades into the lower town, then ascend the main road to the top of the cliffs and storm the main part of the city.

Fortuitously (or so it appeared at the time), snow fell again on the night of December 30. Well before dawn on the 31st, less than twenty-four hours before their terms of enlistment were due to expire, the soldiers mustered for their attack, hoping the storm would mask their maneuvers.

All did not proceed according to plan. Montgomery was killed at the very start, and his men were easily repulsed. That allowed the British defenses within the city to concentrate their attention on Arnold's troops, who were easily trapped along the narrow streets of the lower town, before they even had a chance to mount the cliffs. Arnold himself was wounded in the leg as he led the initial charge.

Over four hundred patriots were taken prisoner that day, including Timothy Bigelow. Jonas Hubbard, shot in the ankle, was imprisoned as well, and he would soon die of his wound. The leader of the artillery train, John Lamb (Dr. Thomas Young's cohort from New York City), had also been captured and injured, the left side of his face blown off by grapeshot, causing blindness in one eye. Later, Lamb would blame his sad fate and the patriots' loss on Worcester's hero Timothy Bigelow. Colonel Donald Campbell, on the other hand, singled out Bigelow and a handful of others for special praise in his official report on the battle.[61]

Had patriotism come to this? After trudging through inhospitable country at the onset of winter and nearly perishing from hunger, Timothy Bigelow was labeled a coward for his realism, reproached for losing a battle he had advised against, and held captive in a foreign land. More than a year before, he had celebrated the dramatic overthrow of British rule in his hometown, engineered in part from within his very own house. Then he had pushed for a new form of government, an early declaration of independence. That had all been so positive, progressive, and hopeful, but his experiences now were of a different order. Timothy Bigelow, now a military man, faced harsh realities and injustices peculiar to times of war.

Ironically, Bigelow's lot was not quite so miserable as it might have been. The very inequalities and biases he had long opposed, artificial distinctions of class and rank, suddenly worked in his favor. Once a common blacksmith, he was now a field officer, and as such, he was given preferential treatment by his British captors. While Private Jeremiah Greenman, also taken prisoner, complained he was confined to a "dismal hole," where "we live very uncomfertable for we have no room not a nuf to lay down to sleep," Bigelow and his peers lived rather comfortably in Le Petit Seminaire de Quebec, where they read, played cards, and exercised freely in the garden. While Greenman was fed "stinking salmond," Bigelow and his new peers were feted with "a good dinner, and a plenty of several sorts of wine" on the very day of their capture. It was the finest meal he had enjoyed in months.[62]

On January 1, 1776, his first full day of captivity, Timothy Bigelow was appointed major for the Continental Army's Twenty-first Infantry. He knew nothing of this, of course, and he was in no position at that moment to assume his post.

10

Liberty for All?

May–August 1775: Charleston

The military mobilization of 1775 pressured all inhabitants of British North America to take sides. As patriots and friends of the British ministry vied for support, each particular group and subgroup among the population, from backcountry farmers in South Carolina to French Canadians in Quebec, imagined how it might play the growing conflict to its best advantage.

The split among Euro-Americans propelled African Americans and Native Americans, long abused and generally overlooked by white statesmen, into the political spotlight. African Americans amounted to one-sixth of the population of the British colonies on the continent, and over half in many key districts in the South with access to the sea; Native Americans were the dominant population and most pervasive military force west of the Appalachian Mountains. These people, who battled for liberty on their own behalf, could hold the balance of power in their hands.

This made Henry Laurens shudder. Most other patriots in the South and West, perennially frightened by the prospect of slave insurrections and Indian raids, also took fright.

In early May, Laurens shared with the General Committee a report he had just received from London: a "black plan" was allegedly afoot to arm the slaves so they might rise against their patriot masters. Within days, a panic took hold of Charleston. The General Committee decreed that one hundred men should be added to the nightly patrol to "guard against any hostile attempts that might be made by our domesticks." As fear ran rampant, so did rumors. According to John Stuart, the British Indian commissioner, "Massacres and instigated insurrections, were words in the mouth of every child." On May 29, the *South Carolina Gazette* printed a new story from London: "There is gone down to Sheerness, seventy-eight thousand guns and bayonets, to be sent to America, to put into the hands of N*****s, the Roman Catholics, the Indians and Canadiens."[1]

Whether or not any of the rumors proved true, slaves certainly heard all the talk of "liberty." They also knew that whites were fighting each other, and they looked for wide enough cracks in the fissure to do them some good. They talked among themselves about all this, but if their words were overheard, or even if words were placed in their mouths, retribution was swift and harsh. From St. Bartholomew Parish, Laurens and the Council of Safety received a report that a slave referred to only as Prisoner George had been "preaching for two years last past to great crouds of Negroes," saying "That the young King . . . was about to alter the world, & set the Negroes free." Based on the testimony of a single slave, local patriots hanged Prisoner George.[2]

Henry Laurens, to his credit, was one of the few whites to think the alarms were exaggerated. "Upon the whole there appears very little foundation," he reported to John Laurens, for the "great fear & . . . amazing bustle" that gripped Charleston, "where the inhabitants are as suddenly blown up by apprehensions as gun powder is by fire." Even so, he thought that any proven transgression by slaves should receive the ultimate punishment: "Nothing less than death should be the sentence, & at this critical time no pardon or mitigation should be granted."[3]

On June 23, as Laurens penned these words, one man was bearing the burden of the patriots' fears: a free black named Jeremiah, whom Laurens preferred to call Jerry. An important figure in the Charleston harbor, Jeremiah was a fisherman, firefighter, and boat pilot who had guided men-of-war in and out of their moorings for years. He was relatively wealthy, worth 1,000 pounds sterling by one estimate, £700 by another, and he even owned some slaves. As a black man with significant resources and valuable skills, Jeremiah presented a threat to the patriots. He might pilot boats for the British, should they attempt to attack the city, and he might provide a critical link between British armed forces and the slaves of South Carolina.[4]

In early June, Jeremiah had been rounded up along with other slaves suspected of plotting an insurrection. Having no real proof for this, white patriots contented themselves with administering floggings to most of the suspects, more as a deterrent than punishment. But they did not wish to release Jeremiah, who could possibly do them significant harm in the future.

Despite his legal status as a freeman, Jeremiah was tried on August 11 under the Negro Act, which applied only to slaves. Based on the testimony of three slaves, two judges and five freeholders unanimously declared him "guilty of a design & attempt to encourage our Negroes to rebellion & joining the King's troops if any had been sent here." There was no physical evidence, and one of the witnesses had recanted his testimony. George Milligen, a loyalist, suspected that the slaves who testified against him did so "only to save themselves from a whipping, the only punishment they were told would be inflicted on Jerry."[5]

On August 18, Jeremiah was hanged and his body burned. He never admitted any guilt, even to a clergyman who hoped to extract a confession. As he was about to hang, according to Governor William Campbell, he "told his implacable and ungrateful persecutors God's judgment would one day overtake them for shedding his innocent blood."[6]

Was Jeremiah the boatman guilty as charged? A prosperous man with connections in the white community, and a slave owner himself, Jeremiah did not fit the profile of an insurgent or even an abolitionist. His "guilt," if we can call it that, was stated succinctly by Campbell: "He had often piloted in men-of-war, and it was strongly suspected (which I believe was his only crime) that he would have had no objection to have been employed again in the same service."[7]

Jeremiah's case was unique. White loyalists in those times were hounded, tarred and feathered, and perhaps sent into exile, but rarely, if ever, were they hanged on the mere suspicion of what they might do in the future. Something else was going on here, something with a distinctly racial twist. Jeremiah personified the worst fears of white patriots: what if black men, acting as their own agents, sided against them? Henry Laurens, while explaining his vote in favor of execution, offered a clue as to the true nature of Jeremiah's crime: "Jerry was a forward fellow, puffed up by prosperity, ruined by luxury & debauchery & grown to an amazing pitch of vanity & ambition & withal a very silly coxcomb."[8]

Jeremiah, in short, had forgotten his "place," and this turned out to be a capital offense. For Henry Laurens, subverting the social order, in this or any other manner, was the *ultimate* offense. That is why Laurens, starting in the summer of 1775, turned all his vile and rancor, some of which had been reserved for his fellow patriots, toward the British ministry, which he felt was undermining the social order by instigating "insurrections of our Negroes attended by the most horrible butcheries of innocent women & children." This one sin dwarfed all the excesses of the patriots: "When I consider these devilish machinations of a rash and wrongheaded cruel administration, I see an apology for every thing we have done."[9]

November 14–December 30, 1775: James River (Virginia) and Cambridge

Patriots had suspected it might come to this, and finally it did. On November 14, 1775, from HMS *Fowey*, docked in the James River, the royal governor of Virginia, Lord Dunmore, issued his famous/infamous proclamation:

> And I do hereby further declare all indented Servants, Negroes, or others, (appertaining to Rebels,) free, that are able and willing to bear Arms, they joining HIS MAJESTY'S Troops as soon as may be, for the more speedily reducing this Colony to a proper Sense of their Duty, to HIS MAJESTY'S Crown and Dignity.[10]

The impact was profound on both slaves and masters. Facing great risks and overwhelming odds, hundreds upon hundreds of African Americans, healthy men and women in their prime, left their plantations, crept through the woods to the water's edge, and swam or boated to British ships to cash in on Dunmore's offer of freedom. "Slaves flock to him in abundance," one bitter patriot wrote to another.[11]

From Mount Vernon, Lund Washington reported to his cousin George: "there is not a man of them, but would leave us, if they believ'd they coud make there escape." A few did, including a thirty-five-year-old "fine fellow" who later went by the name of Harry Washington. Harry had been born in Africa, taken as a slave, imported into Virginia by Thomson Mason (George Mason's brother), and purchased by George Washington in 1763 to drain the Great Dismal Swamp, one of his master's grand land schemes. Three years later, Harry was transferred to George's Mount Vernon plantation, and in 1771 he escaped, only to be captured shortly thereafter. Now, Harry Washington's prospects seemed much more promising; by hitching his star to the British military effort, in opposition to his former master, he could and would create a new life for himself.[12]

Less than three weeks after Dunmore made his dramatic offer, a dispatch from Williamsburg reported:

Since Lord Dunmore's proclamation made its appearance here, it is said he has recruited his army, in the counties of Princess Anne and Norfolk, to the amount of about 2000 men, including his black regiment, which is thought to be a considerable part, with this inscription on their breasts:—"Liberty to slaves."[13]

"Liberty to slaves"—such sweet words for the slaves themselves, and so bitter to their masters, who "were struck with horror," according to David Ramsay, Henry Laurens's future son-in-law. Instinctively, patriots translated their fear and trembling into anger. They dubbed Dunmore "King of the Blacks," an insult whose force we cannot even begin to fathom today. Congress accused him of "tearing up the foundations of civil authority and government." George Washington responded to Dunmore's "diabolical schemes" by calling him an "arch traitor to the rights of humanity." With great venom, he wrote to his fellow Virginian Richard Henry Lee:

If my Dear Sir that man is not crushed before spring, he will become the most formidable enemy America has—his strength will increase as a snow ball by rolling; and faster, if some expedient cannot be hit upon to convince the slaves and servants of the impotency of his designs. . . . Nothing less than depriving him of life or liberty will secure peace to Virginia.[14]

In the South, patriots used white anger and fear to heighten anti-British sentiment and bolster the waning military recruitment. Patrick Henry circulated a broadside of Dunmore's Proclamation in an effort to shore up enlistments. Newspapers abounded with derogatory references to slaves who had fled to Dunmore—terms such as "black banditti" and "speckled regiment." The strategy worked. A white teacher traveling in the Virginia backcountry noted in his journal that the impact of the proclamation was "to quicken all in Revolution." Richard Henry Lee wrote that "Lord Dunmore's unparalleled conduct in Virginia has, a few Scotch excepted, united every man in that large Colony." South Carolina's Edward Rutledge predicted that the proclamation would "more effectively . . . work an eternal separation between Great Britain and the Colonies,—than any other expedient, which could possibly be thought of."[15]

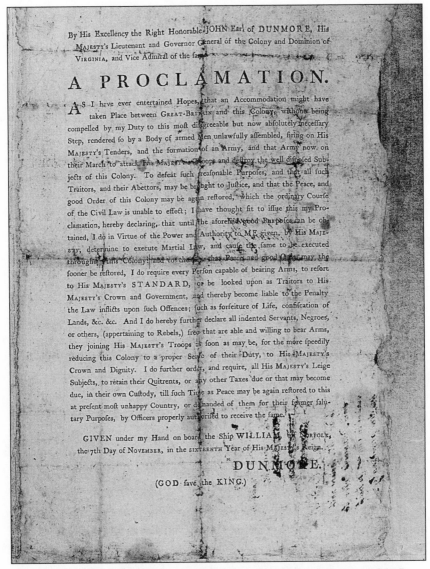

By His Excellency the Right Honorable JOHN Earl of DUNMORE, His Majesty's Lieutenant and Governor General of the Colony and Dominion of Virginia, and Vice Admiral of the same.

A PROCLAMATION.

AS I have ever entertained Hopes, that an Accommodation might have taken Place between Great-Britain and this Colony, without being compelled by my Duty to this most disagreeable but now absolutely necessary Step, rendered so by a Body of armed Men unlawfully assembled, firing on His Majesty's Tenders, and the formation of an Army, and that Army now on their March to attack His Majesty's Troops and destroy the well disposed Subjects of this Colony. To defeat such treasonable Purposes, and that all such Traitors, and their Abettors, may be brought to Justice, and that the Peace, and good Order of this Colony may be again restored, which the ordinary Course of the Civil Law is unable to effect; I have thought fit to issue this my Proclamation, hereby declaring, that until the aforesaid good Purposes can be obtained, I do in Virtue of the Power and Authority to ME given, by His Majesty, determine to execute Martial Law, and cause the same to be executed throughout this Colony; and to the end that Peace and good Order may the sooner be restored, I do require every Person capable of bearing Arms, to resort to His Majesty's STANDARD, or be looked upon as Traitors to His Majesty's Crown and Government, and thereby become liable to the Penalty the Law inflicts upon such Offences; such as forfeiture of Life, confiscation of Lands, &c. &c. And I do hereby further declare all indented Servants, Negroes, or others, (appertaining to Rebels,) free that are able and willing to bear Arms, they joining His Majesty's Troops as soon as may be, for the more speedily reducing this Colony to a proper Sense of their Duty, to His Majesty's Crown and Dignity. I do further order, and require, all His Majesty's Liege Subjects, to retain their Quitrents, or any other Taxes due or that may become due, in their own Custody, till such Time as Peace may be again restored to this at present most unhappy Country, or demanded of them for their former salutary Purposes, by Officers properly authorised to receive the same.

GIVEN under my Hand on board the Ship WILLIAM, off Norfolk, the 7th Day of November, in the sixteenth Year of His Majesty's Reign.

DUNMORE.

(GOD save the KING.)

Figure 18. Lord Dunmore's historic proclamation, which altered the parameters of the Revolutionary War in the South.

For the commander of the Continental Army, Dunmore's Proclamation created a very different problem. While Lord Dunmore welcomed African Americans into his army, George Washington rejected them, and that didn't make much sense, either militarily or morally.

On July 10, only one week after taking charge at Cambridge, Washington had instructed recruiting officers not to enlist "any stroller, negro, or vaga-

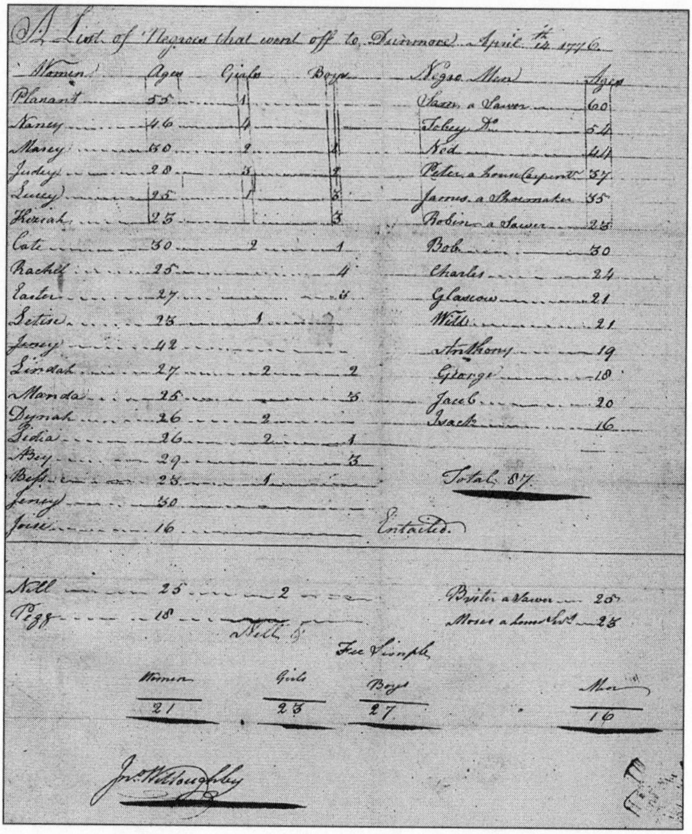

A List of Negroes that went off to Dunmore April 14th 1776

Women	Ages	Girls	Boys	Negro Men	Ages
Planant	55	1		Isaac a Sawer	60
Nancey	46	1		Tobey Do	54
Marcy	60	2	1	Ned	44
Judey	28	3	2	Peter a house Carpenter	37
Lucey	25	1	3	James a Shoemaker	35
Keziah	23		3	Robin a Sawer	23
Cate	30	2	1	Bob	30
Rachel	25		4	Charles	24
Easter	27		3	Glascow	21
Letise	23	1		Will	21
Jenny	42			Anthony	19
Lindah	27	2	2	George	18
Manda	25		3	Jacob	20
Dynah	26	2		Isack	16
Lidia	26	2	1		
Abey	29		3		
Bess	23	1			
Jenny	30				
Josse	16				

Total 87

Entailed.

Nell	25	2		Brister a Sawer	25
Pegg	18			Moses a ...	23

Nell 5

Fee Simple

Women	Girls	Boys	Men
21	23	27	16

Jno. Willoughby

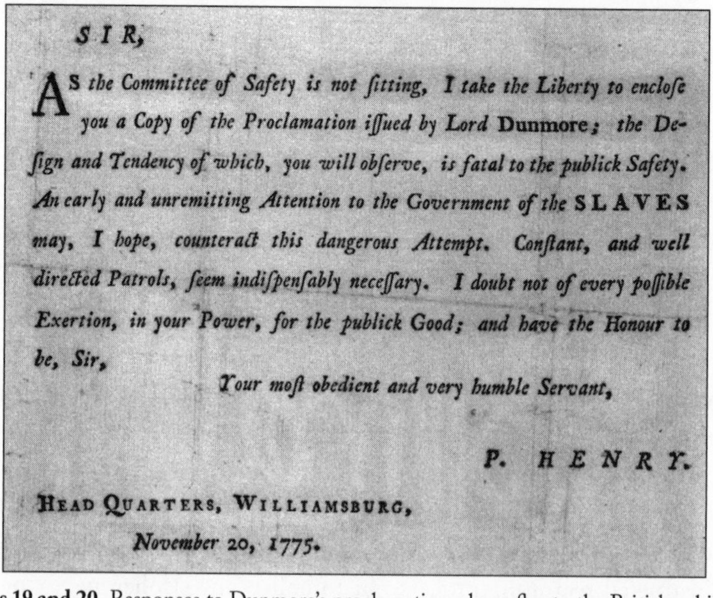

SIR,

AS the Committee of Safety is not sitting, I take the Liberty to enclose you a Copy of the Proclamation issued by Lord Dunmore; the Design and Tendency of which, you will observe, is fatal to the publick Safety. An early and unremitting Attention to the Government of the SLAVES may, I hope, counteract this dangerous Attempt. Constant, and well directed Patrols, seem indispensably necessary. I doubt not of every possible Exertion, in your Power, for the publick Good; and have the Honour to be, Sir,

Your most obedient and very humble Servant,

P. HENRY.

HEAD QUARTERS, WILLIAMSBURG,
November 20, 1775.

Figures 19 and 20. Responses to Dunmore's proclamation: slaves flee to the British, while patriot masters crack down.

bond." Although numerous African Americans had fought valiantly during the opening battles on April 19 and again on June 17 at Breed's Hill (one man, Salem Poor, was officially recognized by fourteen officers for his bravery), Washington considered the presence of enslaved soldiers within an army pledged to freedom an embarrassment, and in the racial language of the times, any black man, even if free, bore too close a resemblance to a slave. Yankee farmers were bad enough, but he drew the line at blacks. While he had inherited them in his army, he didn't want any more.[16]

Early that fall, on October 8, Washington convened his Council of War (all the generals, including himself, stationed at Cambridge) to consider what should happen to the army once current enlistments expired at the end of the year. The council studiously considered ten key issues Washington presented to them, starting with how large the fighting force should be (20,372, the generals decided), and moving on to such questions as how soldiers should be clothed and fed, how often they should be paid, and how long they should serve (one year at a time, no more). Here is the final question, with the generals' response:

10th. Whether it will be adviseable to re-inlist any Negroes in the new Army—or whether there be a distinction between such as are slaves & those who are free?

Agreed unanimously to reject all slaves, & by a great majority to reject Negroes altogether.[17]

After running this decision by Congress, Washington made it official in his general orders for November 12: "Neither Negroes, boys unable to bare arms, nor old men unfit to endure the fatigues of the campaign, are to be inlisted." By year's end, even heroes like Salem Poor were to be excluded from General Washington's whitewashed army.[18]

Two days later, Dunmore issued his proclamation. Even though Dunmore's offer of freedom applied only to slaves from Virginia, bonded African Americans everywhere got the message: they would be more welcomed in the king's army than in Washington's.

By the end of the year, with enlistments amounting to a mere fraction of the 20,372 he had requested, Washington suddenly realized he had made a mistake. Not only was he turning people away, but the black soldiers he had cast out "may seek employ in the ministrial Army." On December 30, two days before African American soldiers were to be sent packing, Washington reversed his previous orders:

As the General is informed, that numbers of free Negroes are desirous of inlisting, he gives leave to the recruiting officers, to entertain them, and promises to lay the matter before the Congress, who he doubts not will approve of it.[19]

Congress did approve, but with a caveat: "free negroes who have served faithfully in the army at Cambridge, may be re-inlisted therein, but no others."[20] It was not a heartfelt welcome.

While George Washington hesitated and Congress equivocated, white patriots from Timothy Bigelow's Worcester County were beginning to see a relationship between African American calls for freedom and their own. At a county convention on June 14, a month before Washington first banned African American recruits, the delegates resolved:

That we abhor the enslaving of any of the human race, and particularly of the negroes in this country, and that whenever there shall be a door opened, or opportunity present for anything to be done towards the emancipation of the negroes, we will use our influence and endeavor that such a thing may be brought about.[21]

Later, as the war deepened, Worcester representatives pushed for an abolition bill in the state Assembly, but the measure was tabled because of "an apprehension that our brethren in the other Colonies" might object. If thirteen states were to stay united in their opposition to British authority, they could not take up issues of great moral concern but divisive effect. The institution of slavery would remain intact, however much it compromised the principled stance of American patriots.[22]

December 18, 1775–March 25, 1776: Sullivan's Island, South Carolina, and Tybee Island, Georgia

Although Virginia's governor Dunmore was the only British official to promise emancipation, many slaves throughout the South assumed that if they offered their services to the British they would be set free. To some extent, this was true. The royal governor of Maryland, having retreated from dry land, granted asylum to slaves who managed to reach his ship. (By early 1776, all other governors in the South had likewise established floating capitals.)

When a British fleet appeared off the mouth of North Carolina's Cape Fear River, former slaves from as far as 150 miles inland presented themselves for service; British officers quickly organized these runaways into a company of "Black Pioneers" and put them to work as laborers, servants, and guides. From a vessel anchored in Charleston, a British captain admitted to angry patriots that he was harboring runaway slaves, and he boasted that he could have had five hundred more had he accepted all who sought asylum.

With limited space and supplies on their vessels, British captains did not accept every man, woman, or child who came their way. Even so, they did aid and encourage the runaways however they could. In the Charleston harbor, several hundred former slaves sought refuge on Sullivan's Island, protected by the guns of British ships anchored nearby. Sullivan's Island at that time was not exactly prime real estate—it housed the "pest house" for imported slaves who had come down with communicable diseases. In December 1775, it also housed an entire community of runaways, who occupied the pest house, built additional huts, and acted as if they intended to stay awhile.

By its very existence, this maroon community threatened local patriots, who feared that any haven for slaves would entice those back on the plantations to run away. It also presented an immediate threat. According to Henry Laurens, who headed the Council of Safety, Governor William Campbell was "protecting Negroes on Sullivans Island from whence those villians made nightly sallies and committed robberies & depredations" on coastal communities nearby. To "check" these "depredations," Laurens and the Council of Safety ordered a surprise attack, the first military offensive of the Revolutionary War in eastern South Carolina.

Before dawn on December 18, a patriot force of fifty-four infantrymen disguised as Indians landed stealthily on Sullivan's Island, set fire to the pest house, and sent its residents running. Some of the escaped slaves were killed on the spot or recaptured, while others, aided by landing boats from nearby British men-of-war, managed to escape. The next day, Laurens boasted that the raid would "serve to humble our Negroes in general & perhaps to mortify his Lordship not a little."[23]

But the matter did not end there. As British vessels left Charleston to avoid the patriots' blockade of their supply routes, they carried many of the fugitives with them, and this naturally angered patriots who regarded slaves as personal property. On January 20, Laurens sounded a warning to patriot commanders of nearby coastal communities: "Every one of them [British ships leaving the harbor] carried off some of our Negroes, in the whole amounting to no inconsiderable number—this will be sufficient to alarm every man in the Colony & put those on the sea coast & river sides more particularly on their guard." Because slaves working from British vessels might commit further "robberies & depredations," Laurens and the Council of Safety gave all patriots permission to start "firing upon any of the Men of War & their boats & men in attempting to land." A war for liberty was under way, with patriots lining up on the side of slavery.[24]

Later that winter, another maroon community of fugitive slaves congealed on Tybee Island, seventy-five miles south of Charleston in the Savannah harbor, and early in March, fearful patriot slave owners prepared to stage a repeat of the assault on Sullivan's Island. On March 14, Stephen Bull, a militia commander working with the Georgia Council of Safety, presented a sensitive issue to Henry Laurens and the South Carolina Council of Safety. The problem, Bull said, was that if the slaves on Tybee Island weren't killed, they might be "carried away, and converted into money [sold], which is the sinews of war." This would "only enable the enemy to fight us with our own money or property." But if the slaves *were* killed, who would reimburse their owners? Bull suggested that patriots should err on the side of caution and vote for death:

> It is far better for the public and the owners, if the deserted negroes . . . who are on Tybee Island, be shot, if they cannot be taken; . . . All who cannot be taken, had better be shot by the Creek Indians, as it, perhaps, may deter other negroes from deserting, and will establish a hatred or aversion between the Indians and negroes.[25]

Should principled American patriots really hire Indians to instill panic and kill slaves? Laurens had some hesitations. "It is an awful business," he wrote back, "notwithstanding it has the sanction of law to put even fugitive & rebellious slaves to death, the prospect is horrible." But practicality superseded morality in this case, so on behalf of the South Carolina Council of Safety, Henry Laurens and the South Carolina Council of Safety suggested that the patriots of Georgia proceed as Bull had suggested:

> We think the Council of Safety in Georgia ought to give that encouragement which is necessary to induce proper persons to seize & if nothing else will do to destroy all those rebellious Negroes upon Tybee Island or wherever they may be found. If Indians are best the most proper hands

let them be employed on this service, but we would advise that some discreet white men were incorporated with or joined to lead them.[26]

On March 25, forty white patriots disguised as Indians, along with thirty Creeks, staged their raid on Tybee Island. We have no firsthand accounts of the attack, but the royal governor of Florida, Patrick Tonyn, complained that the raiding party showed "signs of the most savage barbarity"—including brutal beatings and scalpings—and that "the white people exceeded the ferocity of the Indians."[27]

The very next day, March 26, 1776, the South Carolina Provincial Congress adopted a new constitution. In their preamble to this document, patriots claimed that Americans would be reduced "to a state of the most abject slavery" if they submitted to Parliamentary taxation. That was their main grievance, but there were others. Britain had "excited domestic insurrections—proclaimed freedom to servants and slaves—enticed or stolen them from, and armed against their masters—instigated and encouraged the Indian nations to war against the colonies." Logically and morally, these complaints made no sense. To oppose slavery, patriots defended it; to oppose the use of Indian warfare, patriots promoted it.[28]

On the same day the new constitution was passed, Henry Laurens was elected vice president of South Carolina and thereby chairman of a seven-member Privy Council. If slaves were to be murdered, if Indians were to be annihilated, or if Indians were to be hired to slaughter slaves, Henry Laurens and his Privy Council, along with President John Rutledge, were expected to authorize the deeds.

April 1776: Chota, Cherokee Country

In February 1776, Henry Laurens received a desperate letter from George Galphin, a white trader serving as an Indian commissioner for South Carolina patriots. Nonexportation, part of the Continental Association, had taken effect the previous fall, and it threatened to destroy relations with the Cherokees. "It is the trade with them that keeps them in our interest," Galphin reported. Without deerskins to export to England, "the merchants will not send in goods," thereby giving the Cherokees "great encouragement" to bring their skins to British traders in West Florida. Once a Cherokee-British alliance had been cemented by trade, "then we may expect an Indian War." Patriots had long feared that Britain was planning to incite Indians to fight against them, and now, by adhering to trade restrictions they had imposed upon themselves, they were driving Indians straight into the hands of their enemies. Henry Laurens and other South Carolina patriots had worked themselves into a corner.[29]

Galphin's reasoning was impeccable, and only a change in policy at the highest levels would prevent his prediction from coming true. "I must beg of you to write to the Congress," he implored Laurens. But Laurens never raised the matter with delegates to the Continental Congress, because he knew they would not listen. This was no time to weaken or amend the Association, now that armed hostilities had commenced. Patriots had to hold firm, and because they did, they lost all hope of keeping Cherokees out of the British camp.

The Cherokees faced political problems of their own. The previous year, after being pushed back by an aggressive force of Virginians, Attakullakulla and other Cherokee leaders had signed a peace accord at a place called Sycamore Shoals. Attakullakulla was no stranger to diplomacy; back in 1761, at Ashley Ferry near Charleston, he and Henry Laurens had helped bring an end to the Anglo-Cherokee War (see chapter 1). At Sycamore Shoals, however, he and other statesmen clearly received the worse end of the bargain: whether knowingly or not, they had relinquished rights to 27,000 square miles—the heart of Kentucky and some of Tennessee—to a group of land speculators who called themselves the Transylvania Company.

Dragging Canoe (Tsiyu-gunsini), one of Attakullakulla's warrior sons, wanted no part of this bargain. In fact, he had walked out during the second day of negotiations, and now, a year later, he refused to abide by the agreement. The Cherokees would not cede any more of their land, he stated boldly. He and his fellow young warriors would fight to the death to defend it, no matter what their elders said.

To fight, Dragging Canoe and company needed munitions, and fortuitously, early in 1776, these were headed their way. The British official John Stuart, Indian superintendent for the southern colonies, had just dispatched his brother Henry to Chickasaw and Cherokee country with "a full supply of ammunition and some presents to keep the Indians in good temper and to dispose them to pay attention to what we might find necessary to recommend to them."[30]

Hearing that Henry Stuart was on his way, Dragging Canoe ventured south to Mobile to greet him. There, according to Stuart's report of the expedition, Dragging Canoe inquired into the cause of the present quarrel and disorders in the colonies and the reason why their supplies of ammunition and goods (which were formerly brought from Georgia and Carolina) were stopped. He told me that their nation was under very great apprehensions and uneasiness, and complained much of the encroachments of the Virginians and inhabitants of North Carolina. He said that they were almost surrounded by the white people, that they had but a small spot of ground left for them to stand upon, and that it seemed to be the intention of the white people to destroy them from being a people.

Defensively, Stuart told Dragging Canoe that the king had commanded Americans to stay east of the mountains, but his orders had been disobeyed. Stuart also stated that the Cherokees themselves were partly at fault, for they had given away much of their land at Sycamore Shoals. Dragging Canoe immediately disclaimed all responsibility for the questionable treaty, blaming instead "some of their old men who he said were too old to hunt and who by their poverty had been induced to sell their land."[31]

After their meeting at Mobile, both Stuart and Dragging Canoe made their way to Chota, described by historian Colin Calloway as "the diplomatic, ceremonial, and political capital town of the Overhill [interior] Cherokees." There, Stuart heard a very different perspective from tribal elders, the people whom Dragging Canoe belittled as old men who could no longer hunt. The "principal Indians did not at all approve of the behaviour of the young fellows" who went out on raids, Stuart reported. They "hoped we would not pay any regard to what any of their idle young fellows said." The "old men" versus the "young fellows"—a major rift was in the making among the Cherokee.[32]

Shortly after Stuart's arrival in Chota, fourteen warriors from various nations to the north suddenly marched into town, their faces painted jet black. Having traveled for seventy days from their homes among the Shawnees, Delawares, Mohawks, Nanticokes, and Ottawas, they hoped to recruit the Cherokees to join them in a united front against white incursions. Their entreaty generated eager responses among youthful Cherokee warriors. "After this day," Stuart observed, "every young fellow's face in the Overhill Towns appeared blacked and nothing was now talked of but war."[33]

The combined presence of Henry Stuart and the emissaries from the north attracted representatives from numerous Cherokee settlements for a council in Chota's large, conical Town House. On the appointed day, a war standard was erected outside and the Town House posts painted black and red. Inside, seated on circular rows of thatched benches surrounding a large fire pit, hundreds of Cherokees listened to the visiting warriors' grand talks.

A Mohawk delegate spoke first. After urging people to fight, he "produced a belt of white and purple whampum"—a war belt, which he gave to Dragging Canoe. An Ottawa delegate then exhorted all Indians "to drop all their former quarrels and to join in one common cause." The most impressive presentation came from a Shawnee warrior, who produced "a war belt about 9 feet long and six inches wide, of purple whampum, strewed with vermilion," offered it to Dragging Canoe, and argued persuasively

> that the red people who were once masters of the whole country hardly possessed ground enough to stand on; that the lands where but lately they hunted close to their nations were thickly inhabited and covered with forts and armed men; that wherever a fort appeared in their neighborhood they might depend there would soon be towns and settlements; that it was plain there was an intention to extirpate them, and that he thought it better to die like men than to dwindle away by inches.[34]

How could any self-respecting youth resist a talk like this? Few did. After the presentations, "almost all the young warriors from the different parts of the nation" joined in singing a war song. Much as patriotic white youths preened their muskets and drilled with militias during the spring and summer of 1775, these young Indians sang war songs and prepared their "spears, clubs and scalping knives."

The elders, perhaps wiser and certainly more cautious, had lost control: "The principal chiefs who were averse to the measure and remembered the calamities brought on their nation by the last war, instead of opposing the rashness of the young people with spirit, sat down dejected and silent." Just as moderate whites like Henry Laurens could not contain or even slow down the radical patriots, judicious Cherokees like Attakullakulla had no answer to the militant frenzy that gripped young warriors.[35]

Two days later, Dragging Canoe, now painted black, proposed to Stuart and Cameron that they, too, take up the war belt. The British commissioners declined; in fact, they had opposed all along the warlike mood that was taking hold of the Cherokees at Chota. Yes, they wished to join forces with the Cherokees in the future, but the move was premature and doomed to failure, for the entire force of the colonists from Virginia and the Carolinas would be brought to bear against them. If, on the other hand, the Cherokees waited to coordinate their attacks with a British offensive from the east, they would stand a greater chance of success.

This strategic reasoning fell upon deaf ears. Why should warriors like Dragging Canoe heed the cautious counsel of white men, if they ignored their own elders? The warriors had made up their minds, and they were even willing to sacrifice the internal cohesion of their own communities to do what they thought best. These were rebellious times, in the Cherokee world as well as the British colonies. While both Attakullakulla and Henry Laurens might bemoan the loss of respect for traditional authority, too many people wanted to act on their own, without approval from above. The notion that these folks (whether whites or Indians) could seize control over their lives and their destinies had a riveting appeal, not easily tempered by voices of moderation.

March 31–April 16, 1776: Braintree, Plymouth, and Philadelphia

Traditional bonds of all sorts were loosening. Slaves fled their masters. Young warriors disregarded their elders. At least a few women, too, seized on the mood of the times to question time-honored hierarchies.

On March 31, Abigail Adams wrote her oft-quoted request for husband John to "remember the ladies":

> I long to hear that you have declared an independency. And, by the way, in the new code of laws which I suppose it will be necessary for you to make, I desire you would remember the ladies and be more generous and favorable to them than your ancestors. Do not put such unlimited power into the hands of their husbands. Remember, all men would be tyrants if they could. If particular care and attention is not paid to the ladies, we are determined to foment a rebellion, and will not hold ourselves bound by any laws in which we have no voice or representation.[36]

Readers have questioned whether this was an earnest appeal, the opening foray of American feminism, or simply a fanciful conceit, Abigail's private joke to her adoring spouse. But the next paragraph of her letter, generally omitted, suggests she was serious indeed, for she had a very specific agenda:

> That your sex are naturally tyrannical is a truth so thoroughly established as to admit of no dispute; but such of you as wish to be happy

willingly give up the harsh title of master for the more tender and en-
dearing one of friend. Why, then, not put it out of the power of the
vicious and the lawless to use us with cruelty and indignity with
impunity?

The argument was clear and indisputable. Although some men, John included, might treat women as friends rather than subjects, there was no structural reason for them to do so. Legally, women of the times had no defense
from what we today would call abuse, so the new code of laws, made by men
of goodwill, should certainly include real protections for women.

Did John take Abigail seriously?

As to your extraordinary code of laws, I cannot but laugh. We have been
told that our struggle has loosened the bonds of government everywhere;
that children and apprentices were disobedient; that schools and colleges
were grown turbulent; that Indians slighted their guardians, and negroes
grew insolent to their masters. But your letter was the first intimation
that another tribe, more numerous and powerful that all the rest, were
grown discontented. This is rather too coarse a compliment, but you are
so saucy, I won't blot it out.[37]

Whether or not Abigail was jesting, John certainly was. "We are obliged to go
fair and softly, and, in practice, you know we are the subjects," he continued.
"We have only the name of masters, and rather than give up this, which
would completely subject us to the despotism of the petticoat, I hope General
Washington and all our brave heroes would fight." Like a benevolent king or
a master who thinks he treats his slaves kindly, he did not even recognize the
institutional injustices that permit real cruelty. Confident that he himself was
not among the guilty, he felt free to tease.

But even through his teasing, John Adams revealed a deep disdain for the
revolution that was oozing well beyond the ordered universe of upper-class
Whig males. His reply concluded:

I begin to think the ministry as deep as they are wicked. After stirring
up Tories, land-jobbers, trimmers, bigots, Canadians, Indians, negroes,
Hanoverians, Hessians, Russians, Irish Roman Catholics, Scotch rene-
gadoes, at last they have stimulated the ——— [ladies] to demand new
privileges and threaten to rebel.

The peoples on Adams's far-reaching list had only one thing in common: they were all political outsiders, at least in the American colonies in 1776. Just as John did not or could not acknowledge Abigail's legitimate appeal on behalf of women, so did he dismiss categorically any complaints of such creatures as Indians, slaves, or Catholics. All these folks, insofar as they complained about anything, were no more than dupes of the British ministry.

This is not to say that John Adams thought lowly of women, or that he always dismissed them lightly. His relationship with both Abigail and Mercy Otis Warren demonstrates otherwise. Yet while professing his respect, and while showing it by writing to his female correspondents in such depth, Adams still marginalized women, as he did all other outsiders: they had no legitimate place in the tussle of political life, however clearly they could think and write. A few weeks after the exchange with Abigail, while arguing against extending the franchise, he contended that men "destitute of property" were too dependent upon other men to have a "will of their own," and if *they* gained the right to vote (God forbid), then *women* might follow, even though wives were forever dependent upon their husbands, and even though "Nature has made them fittest for domestic cares."[38]

Many of the outsiders had other ideas. People with no political standing, in ways determined by their particular circumstances, were doing everything they could to acquire one. While John Adams declined the invitation to "remember the ladies," and Henry Laurens attempted to squelch any rebellious notions among slaves, and George Washington regarded Indian notions of sovereignty as mere impediments to his own designs for land (see chapter 4), some among these populations developed agendas of their own, often in competition with people we know today as *the* American patriots, and sometimes in competition with each other as well.

The American Revolution was taking on a mind of its own, beyond the narrow definition its perpetrators intended. Such is the way of revolutions, this one included.

11

Independence

November 15, 1775: Watertown

Throughout the second half of 1775, all events pointed in the direction of a separation from Great Britain. In August, King George III declared that not only the people of Massachusetts, but "divers wicked and desperate persons" throughout "our colonies and plantations in North America" were in a state of rebellion. To suppress the uprising, he dispatched thousands of additional troops and dozens of ships. The rebellious colonials could not successfully resist such an onslaught without material aid from Europe, yet European nations refused to interfere with Britain's internal affairs. Only if the rebels formed a separate union could they expect to receive the assistance they needed.[1]

The logic was clear, and James Warren, among others, had little trouble figuring it out. On Wednesday, November 15, Warren wrote a letter to John Adams (still a delegate to the Continental Congress) from the master bedroom of the stately Fowle House on Mt. Auburn Street in Watertown, his temporary home and headquarters while he served as speaker of the Massachusetts Assembly and paymaster general of the Continental Army. Foreign powers were not willing to aid the patriots' cause, he noted, because Americans continued to acknowledge a "dependency" on the British Crown. To gain support, Congress needed to stop hesitating and take "capital and effectual strokes." What he meant, of course, was that Congress should declare independence from Britain, but he didn't say that. Even in the fall of 1775, over a year after the people of Worcester and other rebellious towns in Massachusetts had pushed for "independency," no recognized leader would dare step forth and embrace the *I* word.[2]

As James wrote, Mercy sat beside him. (She had come to visit for a few days, since her husband was never free to travel home.) They must have been discussing the subject at hand, as they often did during letter-writing time, for Mercy suddenly barged in. James was being too soft in his choice of language, she thought, and she proceeded to dictate more forceful words of her own, insisting that her husband write them down:

> She [Mercy] sits at the table with me, will have a paragraph of her own; says you [Congress] "should no longer *piddle* at the threshold. It is time to *leap* into the theatre, to unlock the bars, and open every gate that impedes the rise and growth of the American republic, and then let the giddy potentate send forth his puerile proclamations to France, to Spain and all the commercial world who may be united in building up an Empire which he can't prevent."

Then and there she composed some verse, *ex tempore*:

> *At leisure then may G[eor]ge his reign review,*
> *And bid to empire and to crown adieu.*
> *For lordly mandates and despotic kings*
> *Are obsolete like other quondam things.*[3]

Yes, Congress had indeed been piddling. The strategic logic of declaring independence, contrasted with the political need to disavow such a drastic measure, created a tension that colored every political move. Thomas Jefferson, who had taken George Washington's place in Congress, admitted on November 29 that only one thing stood in the way of taking the final plunge: "We want neither inducement nor power, to declare and assert a separation. It is will alone that is wanting."[4]

John Dickinson (once revered as the Farmer, who wrote so lucidly in opposition to British taxation, but now known in the Adams-Warren circle as the chief "piddler" in Congress) took advantage of that lack of political will. At his urging, the Pennsylvania Assembly issued binding instructions to their representatives in the Continental Congress: "We strictly enjoin you that you, in behalf of this colony, dissent from and utterly reject any propositions, should such be made, that may cause or lead to a separation from our mother country or a change of the form of this government."[5]

Delegates from New Jersey, Delaware, and Maryland also received instructions to oppose independence, while New York's contingent, conservative in bent, needed no prodding on that score. Early in January, James Wilson, a Pennsylvania delegate and political associate of both John Dickinson and Robert Morris, proposed that Congress itself take up the issue of independence, not to support it, but to come out once and for all against such a radical scheme. Wilson's motion was discussed and tabled, but his opponents, even as they argued against his measure, failed to declare their own support for independence. Precisely because their enemies called them traitors, patriots as rebellious as John and Samuel Adams had to demonstrate that they were not.

Robert Morris expressed the prevailing wisdom of the time: "For my part I abhor the name & idea of a rebel, I neither want nor wish a change of King or Constitution, & do not conceive myself to act against either when I join America in defence of constitutional liberty."[6]

But Mercy Otis Warren had seen enough of all this piddling. She was ready to take the big leap, and so were others, if only they could find the nerve. For these people to come forth, however, someone would have to speak first, proudly and publicly, on behalf of independence.

January–March 1776: Philadelphia

With politicians too cautious, the job of promoting independence fell quite by chance upon a newcomer to Philadelphia, a man of humble origins who had traveled about, with no fortune to show for it. He was a self-taught Deist and political radical, a talented and prolific writer. His name was Thomas . . .

Not Young, but Paine. Although Thomas Young fit the description in all other respects, and although he would no doubt have liked to be the man responsible for propelling the patriotic movement to the next level, he was not. Ironically, despite his transience and his alienating style, Young was still too much of an insider. Like his friend Samuel Adams and other radical patriots, he had disavowed any hankering for independence so often that the denials had become habitual. Although Adams and Young and the Warrens and many others had come by the close of 1775 to favor a separation, their prior insistence on allegiance to the British constitution had undermined the argument they now wished to make: Americans must cast off British rule, king and constitution included.

Thomas Paine was not so encumbered. A failed thirty-seven-year-old stay-maker, sailor, shopkeeper, teacher, and petty government official from England, Paine had arrived in Philadelphia on November 30, 1774, with little money. He did bear a note of recommendation from Benjamin Franklin, however, and that soon landed him a job as editor of the fledgling *Pennsylvania Magazine*. This work placed him in contact with many of the city's intelligentsia, including Dr. Benjamin Rush, an ardent patriot who practiced medicine among the working classes. Paine was a quick learner, and by talking with Rush and others he became versed in the controversy that subsumed all political life in his new home.

Like many other patriots in the fall of 1775, Dr. Rush had come to embrace independence privately but not publicly. He toyed with the idea of publishing his opinion, but decided better of it. "My profession and connections, which tied me to Philadelphia where a great majority of the citizens and some of my friends were hostile to a separation of our country from Great Britain, forbade me to come forward as a pioneer in that important controversy," Rush recalled years later. The itinerant Paine, on the other hand, "had nothing to fear from the popular odium to which such a publication might expose him, for he could live anywhere." That is why Rush encouraged Paine, who had also come to favor independence, to write a pamphlet on the matter. Rush himself (or so he said) provided the title: *Common Sense*.[7]

Although we have no independent verification for Rush's story, which was perhaps self-serving, the part about Paine having little to lose rings true. Indeed, Paine played his status as an outsider to its best advantage. Publishing the pamphlet anonymously, he assured readers that the author was "unconnected with any Party, and under no sort of influence public or private, but the influence of reason and principle." This was no incidental matter. While other patriot tracts were clouded by references to personal and political antagonisms (Thomas Young was particularly prone to this), Paine appeared to be writing on a blank slate.

Paine started his argument by addressing an issue that stood logically prior to that of independence: the merits of the British Constitution, revered at least in name by patriots and Tories alike. That reverence was misplaced, Paine argued. The Constitution was built upon "the remains of two ancient tyrannies: First.—The remains of monarchical tyranny in the person of the king. Secondly.—The remains of aristocratical tyranny in the person of the peers [House of Lords]." Only the House of Commons, representing the people, contributed in any way to the "freedom" so cherished by British colonists in North America. The other two pillars of the constitution only stood in the way.[8]

Here was an argument more radical than even Thomas Young had dared espouse. The problem was not bad ministers or even a bad king; it was the very *existence* of a king. In page after page, Paine laid bare the absurdities inherent in any monarchy.

He used logic: "The state of a king shuts him from the world, yet the business of a king requires him to know it thoroughly."[9]

He used derision: "One of the strongest *natural* proofs of the folly of hereditary right in kings, is, that nature disapproved it, otherwise she would not so frequently turn it into ridicule by giving mankind an *ass for a lion*."[10]

Mockingly, he pointed to the Norman invasion and the roots of British monarchy: "A French bastard landing with an armed banditti, and establishing himself king of England against the consent of the natives, is in plain terms a very paltry rascally original.—It certainly hath no divinity in it. . . . The plain truth is, that the antiquity of English monarchy will not bear looking into."[11]

Paine's central argument for independence followed logically from his drubbing of a constitutional monarchy. Americans had no business paying homage to a farcical system that contradicted the fundamental tenet of popular sovereignty: all governmental authority resides with the people themselves. Before, Americans had been wary of abandoning "King or Constitution," to use Robert Morris's words; now, Paine showed people they should be happy to cast off the whole British system.

Paine buttressed his case with some practical considerations. America need not depend on British trade, he stated. "Our corn will fetch its price in any market in Europe, and our imported goods must be paid for, buy them where we will. . . . As Europe is our market for trade, we ought to form no partial connection with any part of it." Even Robert Morris, still resistant to independence, could hardly dispute this part of the argument. Nor could he or anyone else dispute Paine's contention that governance from across the Atlantic Ocean presented needless difficulties. "To be always running three or four thousand miles with a tale or a petition, waiting four or five months for an answer, which when obtained required five or six more to explain it, will in a few years be looked upon as folly and childishness." America was just too large and far distant for this sort of nonsense. "There is something very absurd, in supposing a continent to be perpetually governed by an island," he stated flatly.[12]

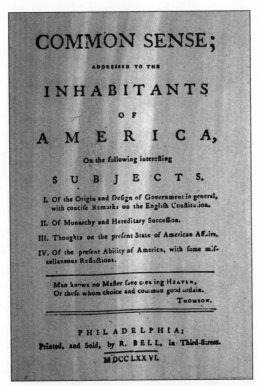

Figure 21. Title page of Thomas Paine's *Common Sense*. Paine wove his "remarks," "thoughts," and "reflections" into a powerful argument for independence that was difficult to refute. *(The Granger Collection, New York)*

Paine's style was as refreshing as his arguments. He wrote more plainly than was the fashion, more as people talk, so his words could be read aloud, as indeed they were. The pamphlet quickly made the rounds of the taverns in Philadelphia, and then in other cities, and across the countryside, in towns and villages and wayside inns across America. Those who did not know how to read heard Paine's arguments nonetheless. Within three months, approximately one hundred thousand copies of *Common Sense* had been sold (per capita, that would be ten million copies today). Probably the majority of citizens in the rebellious colonies either read or listened to Paine's words, and beyond that, they discussed his ideas. It was the most extensive book club in American history.

Thomas Young had once imagined that a large gallery in every provincial Assembly would provide common people with the best possible class in civic affairs: "No man can conceive the advantages that must arise to a Country from so noble a school of political learning," he had said in 1767. "How many wou'd catch the fire!" Now, Thomas Paine had provided an even better school for political learning: every tavern in the land, where any citizen could take an active role in a grand national debate on the most consequential issue of the day.[13]

Everybody reacted to Paine's ideas in one way or another, and most did "catch the fire."

Thomas Young embraced not only the pamphlet but Paine himself. Over the next several months, Young and Paine met with a handful of other radical patriots in Philadelphia, in taverns and at each other's houses, to plot the next steps for their revolution.

Mercy Otis Warren was so impressed by *Common Sense* that she circulated copies to people whom she thought needed it most. One recipient, James Bowdoin, responded: "Most of the author's observations are very just and I think will proselyte many to his doctrine. The more it is contemplated, the stronger is the conviction of the truth of it, at least this is the case with respect to myself."[14]

George Washington, already a closet proponent of independence, needed little convincing: "A few more of such flaming arguments as were exhibited at Falmouth and Norfolk [both devastated by conflagrations in the wake of skirmishes], added to the sound doctrine, and unanswerable reasoning con-taind in the pamphlet Common Sense, will not leave numbers at a loss to decide upon the propriety of separation," he wrote three weeks after the first copy hit the streets.[15]

Henry Laurens, on the other hand, denounced the "indecent expressions" in *Common Sense* to the South Carolina Assembly. On February 22 he wrote to John:

> I know not how the doctrines contained in it are relished in the North-ern Colonies, nothing less than repeated & continued persecution by Great Britain can make the people in this Country subscribe to them. . . . however, the author's reasoning, tho not all original, is strong & captivat-ing & will make many converts to Republican principles, if . . . the pres-ent scene of Kingly persecution is much longer continued.[16]

To Laurens's chagrin, the "Kingly persecution" did continue; in fact, during the final days of February, colonists learned that it had reached a new level. With its American Prohibitory Act, Parliament had banned all commerce in the rebellious colonies and declared that all American vessels were to be considered property of the Crown. Because the act applied to ships anchored in harbors as well as those on the open seas, British armed forces were granted full permission to raid American ports, seize anything they could, and take away all sailors. Rebellious American colonists were henceforth to be treated as "open enemies," beyond Britain's protection.[17]

The Prohibitory Act did as much to promote a final separation as Paine's *Common Sense*. Calling the new measure "the Act of Independency, " John Adams asserted boldly: "King, Lords and Commons have united in sundering this Country and that I think forever." American colonists had been booted out of the British Empire.[18]

Even so, those with a deeply conservative bent still balked, and indeed, their resistance hardened, for as independence became more likely, they feared all the more what it might entail: a radical restructuring of American society. Landon Carter, a wealthy slaveholder from Virginia, expressed his deepest concern to George Washington: "Independency," he said, was taking on a new interpretation among the common people: "by being independent of the rich men, every man would then be able to do as he pleased."[19]

There were other reasons for trepidation as well. With Britain out of the picture, shouldn't colonists be concerned about the designs of France or Spain in North America? And shouldn't they worry about each other? Virginia hoped to expand westward, as did Pennsylvania and New York and Connecticut and the Carolinas. Political, legal, and physical skirmishes were already being fought over who would gain title to which clumps of land. Would self-interest cause the United Colonies to disunite? And if they separated from each other, how vulnerable might they be? Even if they stayed together, could they realistically expect to prevail militarily over a nation with three times as many people and the most powerful army and navy in the world?

The political battle over independence was not yet over.

May 15, 1776: Williamsburg

Virginia caught independence fever in the spring of 1776. Not only did leaders like Richard Henry Lee and Thomas Jefferson embrace the idea, but common people did so too, with reasons of their own. Like other patriots, they resented the recent wave of British repressions, but beyond that, they hoped that a break from Britain would signal a new era in Virginia politics. The previous fall, common folk had balked when gentry assumed control of the militias (see chapter 9); now, they could act on their own behalf by helping to reshape their government. Those who dissented from the Anglican Church had a special reason to support a final break: disestablishment of the Church as Virginia's official religion. As Landon Carter and other gentry feared, "independence" had multiple meanings.

Throughout April, local communities voted for representatives to the Fifth Virginia Convention, scheduled to convene on May 6. In these elections, several long-standing leaders who resisted independence were replaced by candidates who favored a final break. The elections were revolutionary in style as well as content. Gone were the days when local gentry could assume victory, if only they threw a large enough party, as George Washington had done when he first entered the House of Burgesses back in 1758. Now, the people voted for candidates on the basis of political views rather than social standing, and they controlled the agenda by issuing specific instructions, as was the custom in New England. Citizens of Buckingham County, for instance, cautioned all patriots to "keep our primary object, and not lose ourselves in hankering after a reconciliation," and they instructed their representatives specifically "to cause a total and final separation from Great Britain to take place as soon as possible." The people had in their power the freedom "to choose what government we please for our civil and religious happiness," the voters said. And what kind of government did the folks from Buckingham suggest? "We ask for full representation; free and frequent elections; and that no standing armies whatever should be kept up in time of peace."[20]

The word "independence," once politically taboo, had turned into a rallying cry. On May 6, delegates convened in the capitol building at Williamsburg rather than in exile in Richmond. Outside, forty-five delegates who had also been members of the House of Burgesses ceremonially buried the old regime: that government would meet no more, they pronounced, because of actions taken by "the king, lords, and commons of Great Britain." The delegates then moved inside, where they debated not *whether* to support independence, but *how*. Some thought Virginia should simply declare independence on its own; others urged the convention to instruct its delegates to the Continental Congress to make a declaration there. After a week of deliberations, on May 15, the convention endorsed the latter alternative, but to underscore its intent it also decided to form a new and independent government. The most populous colony was the first "to *leap* into the theatre, to unlock the bars, and open every gate that impedes the rise and growth of the American republic," as Mercy Otis Warren had urged the previous fall. (Previously, New Hampshire and South Carolina had asked Congress for permission to form provisional governments, but Virginia did not even bother to ask, and it fully intended its new government to be permanent.)[21]

Virginians fully understood that this was a momentous occasion, and they celebrated as other Americans would soon celebrate their national holiday. A crowd gathered outside the capitol building in anticipation of the final vote, and when it came, some plucky fellows climbed the cupola to lower the British flag, then raised in its stead the Grand Union banner used by the Continental Army. Soldiers paraded and fired cannons, and festivities continued the following day with a grand display of patriotic inebriation, toasts, and fireworks.[22]

May 20, 1776: Philadelphia

In times such as these, Thomas Young flourished. In the spring of 1775, when he arrived in town, men of middling rank—the city's multifarious artisans, known at the time as *mechanics*—were beginning to mount a concerted challenge to local rulers, who traditionally had come from the "better sort" of society. In 1774, mechanics made up only 5 percent of Philadelphia's "Committee," the dominant body in city politics, but by February 1776 their share had risen to 40 percent. In 1774, only 6 percent of committeemen were assessed at less than £45; two years later, 63 percent fit into that category.[23]

Mechanics in Philadelphia had been flexing their muscles since the nonimportation movement in the 1760s, but this time they literally took charge, creating fertile ground for Young's populist politics. The immediate catalyst was the political mobilization of 1775. As in Virginia, the *rage militaire* had magnified class differences. Workingmen who answered the call to arms, called Associators, complained about the inequities of military service. Why did *they* serve, while those who could better afford the time did not? Why should they be forced to supply their own guns and uniform? Why was their recompense so minimal? Why were officers always chosen from the "better sort"? And a corollary: why were privates, most often workingmen, disciplined not by their peers, but by men of greater wealth and higher standing? "The laws of war are very arbitrary; and vest an absolute power in the hands of one class of men, over the lives of another who have no voice among them," wrote a man who called himself "A Freeman and Associator" in the summer of 1775. "An Association of freemen can and ought to be conducted on the principles of freedom."[24]

Although soldiers in other colonies expressed similar complaints, those in Philadelphia and proximate towns transformed their discontent into political action by organizing a Committee of Privates, with members elected by and from the rank and file in each company. Between September 1775 and October 1776, the Committee of Privates constituted a lobby powerful enough to redirect the course of provincial and even national history. For the first half year, the Privates jockeyed with the Pennsylvania Assembly over the terms and manner of military service. In the spring of 1776, however, such matters of personal and local concern suddenly merged with the political issue that dominated the political agenda at that moment: independence.

The foremost obstacle to a final break with Britain at this point was the recalcitrant Pennsylvania Assembly, which still insisted that its delegates to the Continental Congress oppose any such move. Because the neighboring delegations of Maryland, Delaware, and New Jersey tended to follow Pennsylvania's lead, the Assembly exercised a sort of veto power over independence. Knowing this, radicals put forth a slate of pro-independence candidates for the May 1 Assembly elections, but by razor-thin margins they failed to win enough new seats to take over the Assembly. This election did not reflect the true popularity of independence, however, for Pennsylvania law disenfranchised many man of the "lesser" and "middling sort," including the colony's large German population (about one-third of the total), who found it easier than others to disavow the British Crown. *All* men should be allowed to vote, the radicals maintained. As "Elector" (aka Thomas Young) wrote in the Philadelphia papers: "Every man in the country who manifests a disposition to venture his all for the defense of its liberty, should have a voice in its council."[25]

The radical notions of Thomas Young and Thomas Paine meshed well with the radical demands of the Privates. Working together, Philadelphia activists and the Committee of Privates responded to their electoral defeat with a bold scheme to *dismantle* the Pennsylvania Assembly. Allied with these political insurgents, at least for the moment, were pro-independence delegates to the Continental Congress, who also perceived that there would be no final separation from Britain until the power of the Pennsylvania Assembly was broken.

The timing for such a daring move was perfect.

On May 6, only five days after the election, word arrived in town that the

Crown was dispatching 45,000 troops to suppress the American rebellion, including a large contingent of mercenaries from German states such as Hesse.

Two days later, the British warships *Roebuck* and *Liverpool* sailed up the Delaware River toward Philadelphia, their giant cannons seemingly primed to pound the city into submission. Patriot forces quickly positioned their batteries and fired pot shots at the formidable vessels.

Emotionally, Philadelphians easily conflated these two nuggets of news. Foreigners might soon invade their city! In this charged atmosphere, arguments for moderation were easily negated by people's fears.

Right at this moment, on May 8, delegates to Congress started to debate the troubling issue of forming new governments back in the colonies. Those in favor argued it was time to emerge from the "state of nature," with no official rule; those opposed countered that forming new governments was equivalent to declaring independence, which was still off the table for several delegations. Over a two-day period, as delegates reasoned and quarreled, cannon shots echoed in the distance, heard dimly behind the closed doors of the downstairs chamber in the Pennsylvania State House. Then, on May 10, Congress passed a momentous resolution: assemblies or conventions within each colony should create new governments "where no government sufficient to the exigencies of their affairs" currently existed.[26]

Three days later, John Adams, Edward Rutledge, and Richard Henry Lee offered a preamble to the May 10 resolution: "It appears absolutely irreconcilable to reason and good conscience for the people of the colonies now to take the oaths and affirmations necessary for the support of any government under the crown of Great Britain." This was a direct attack on the Pennsylvania Assembly, which continued to administer such oaths as part of its formal proceedings. Henceforth, all such signs of allegiance should be proscribed: "It is necessary that the exercise of every kind of authority under the said crown should be totally suppressed." On the afternoon of May 15, after vigorous debate, the preamble passed by a vote of six colonies to four, with three abstaining.[27]

Adams and company had given the Philadelphia radicals and Committee of Privates the critical tool they needed to overthrow the recalcitrant Pennsylvania Assembly.

Over the next few days, Young, Paine, and several others met frequently to implement their rebellion within the rebellion. The group of organizers included Dr. Benjamin Rush (who had counseled Thomas Paine on the writing of *Common Sense*, and who had raised some hackles by his vigorous opposition to slavery), James Cannon (a mathematics teacher with a talent for writing political tracts), Timothy Matlack (a brewer and former Quaker, who had been expelled from the Friends because of debts, gambling, and the bad company he kept), Christopher Marshall (also a former Quaker, who kept a diary that chronicled the daily doings of this band), and several others— no large officeholders, but men who understood and practiced politics "out-of-doors." These activists first gained the sponsorship of the Philadelphia Committee, then plastered the city and surrounding areas with broadsides, in both English and German, that announced a mass meeting to be held at 9:00 on Monday morning, May 20, the day the Assembly was slated to reconvene.[28]

On the appointed day, despite a drenching rain, an estimated four thousand patriots showed up at the State House Yard to take down the government— not the British-controlled government in this case, but their own elected Assembly, which was headed by the famous "Farmer," John Dickinson, who had moved from the vanguard to the rear guard of the Revolution.

Unlike most mass meetings, this one was organized around the hard-driving logic of a formal syllogism. Colonel Daniel Roberdeau, a popular militia commander, opened by reading the Congressional Resolve of May 15, which called for the formation of new governments and the suppression of every vestige of British authority. (He read "with a loud stentorian voice that might be heard a quarter of a mile," John Adams wrote to James Warren later that day, and the people responded "with three cheers, hatts flying as usual," baring their heads to the rain.) Next came a formal reading of the hated Assembly instructions, which not only required delegates to oppose independence, but also ordered them to restore the "union and harmony between Great Britain and the Colonies" and oppose any "change of the form of this government." Thomas McKean then testified that the Philadelphia Committee had petitioned the Assembly to alter these instructions, but their plea was turned down.[29]

With the evidence laid bare, the conclusion was inescapable: since Congress wanted new governments free and clear of British authority, while the Pennsylvania Assembly refused to go that route, the Assembly was not "competent to the exigencies of our affairs." In a series of resolutions, passed either unanimously or with a lone dissenting vote, the gathering then stripped the Assembly of its authority and proposed in its stead a special Provincial Convention, empowered by the people to overhaul the entire governmental apparatus by calling a new Constitutional Convention.[30]

Could a meeting "out-of-doors" really do this, simply declare the old government null and void?

The Assembly thought not, and over the next few weeks it struggled for its life. Belatedly, it issued new instructions to its congressional delegation, which sidestepped the issue of independence and allowed the delegates to make up their own minds. This was too little and too late to satisfy the radicals. Strategically, the few radicals in the Assembly were able to cripple the entire body simply by refusing to show up, thereby denying a quorum and forcing it to dissolve.

Out of doors, meanwhile, Thomas Young and the radicals were on a roll. Writing again as Elector, Young unleashed a vitriolic attack on the existing constitution, which he called "mutilated," "wretched," "mangled," and "an imperfect thing." It destroyed "the right of election" by "giving advantage to the profligate and corrupt." Now was the time to change all that: "You have at length reached that inestimable period, when you may make the freest choice, and establish a form as perfect as the soundest wisdom ever conceived."[31]

Shortly after the mass meeting, Young set off to Lancaster and York, carrying with him the Congressional Resolve of May 15 and the call for a Provincial Convention from the May 20 mass meeting. Others fanned out in different directions, blanketing the interior regions with the appeal for a new government. Moderates tried to canvass the countryside as well, but with less success. One opponent, Edward Shippen Jr., warned his friend in Lancaster that "a certain New England man called Doctor Young of noisy fame" was headed their way, but by the time Young returned to Philadelphia on May 30, he and his compatriots could report that people across the province were mobilized and ready to send delegates to the forthcoming Convention.[32]

The most important endorsement for the Provincial Convention, and the death knell for the Assembly, came fittingly from the militias and their political arm, the Committee of Privates. On June 6, the Privates decided to poll each of the five militia battalions in Philadelphia, and four days later the battalion commanders heard directly from their men. Unanimously in two battalions, and overwhelmingly in two others, the men who had agreed to stake their lives for their country favored a new start for Pennsylvania's government, without Assembly interference. The commander of the remaining battalion refused to conduct the poll, for which he was hissed and publicly insulted.[33]

The date of the Provincial Convention was set for June 18. Nobody had any doubt that the Convention would endorse independence, instruct Pennsylvania's delegates in Congress to vote accordingly, and beyond that, build a new government from scratch.

Imagine Thomas Young's excitement. In Boston, he had first joined and then helped to lead the resistance; in Philadelphia, he was not merely resisting an old government but also creating a new one. He now had a shot at implementing his grand designs for a polity based exclusively on the will of the people.

But while Young, Paine, Cannon, Matlack, and the Committee of Privates entertained notions of creating new governmental forms along more democratic lines, others who had once allied themselves with these radicals began to shy away. Democracy? Was that what "independence" was all about? Not according to John Adams, one of the strongest proponents of independence in Congress. Adams wrote nervously to a friend on June 12: "The spirit of leveling, as well as that of innovation, is afloat." Adams's task was about to change: having helped unleash the genie, he now had to place it back in the bottle. To do so, he might have to join forces with some of the advocates of moderation he had just been actively opposing.[34]

As independence grew closer, the definition and ownership of that noble goal was up for grabs. New alliances would form around new struggles. Not often in human history is the world to be made over, and when that happens, some people take heart while others take fright. If this was to be a new nation, how new dare it be?

June 7–July 2, 1776: United Colonies of America

On Friday, June 7, Richard Henry Lee presented the Continental Congress with a three-part resolution:

> That these United Colonies are, and of right ought to be, free and independent States, that they are absolved from all allegiance to the British Crown, and that all political connection between them and the State of Great Britain is, and ought to be, totally dissolved.
>
> That it is expedient forthwith to take the most effectual measures for forming foreign alliances.
>
> That a plan of confederation be prepared and transmitted to the respective Colonies for their consideration and approbation.[35]

Although Lee had been one of the earliest advocates for independence, he was not acting merely on his own: on May 15, the Virginia Convention had called upon its congressional delegates to introduce just such a resolution.

By June 7, North Carolina and Rhode Island had also issued instructions for independence, and the delegations from Massachusetts, New Hampshire, Connecticut, and Georgia, although not under specific instructions, supported it. But what about New York, New Jersey, Pennsylvania, Delaware, Maryland, and South Carolina? Technically, with seven of the thirteen states in favor, Lee's resolution could have passed then and there, but politically that was out of the question. On a matter of so vital importance, a slim majority would hardly suffice; unanimity, or something close to it, was mandatory.

On June 8 and 10, the delegates engaged in heated debate. John Dickinson and James Wilson from Pennsylvania, Robert R. Livingston from New York, and Edward Rutledge from South Carolina argued that the time was not yet ripe, for there was still too much opposition in the middle colonies. They also warned that once all ties with Great Britain had been severed, France or Spain might try to conquer North America. Richard Henry Lee and George Wythe of Virginia, along with John Adams of Massachusetts, countered by observing that independence was already a point of fact, and that most Americans certainly realized this. Furthermore, France and Spain were far more likely to side against their traditional rival, Great Britain, which meant of course these nations would welcome the opportunity to aid the Americans—but only after a formal declaration of independence. Conversely, they would hesitate to send aid as long as the conflict remained a civil war within the British Empire.[36]

What could the delegates possibly do to break the impasse?

Fortunately, all could agree on one point: ultimately, the question should be decided by the people themselves. This simple truth seems so obvious to us today, but it was revolutionary for the time. A popular referendum on a vital matter of state!—this was not the normal way of conducting business in Europe. In America in 1776, on the other hand, people took the notion of popular sovereignty seriously, and they acted on it literally. Representatives were expected to do the bidding of their constituents, often set to paper in formal instructions. Now, at this critical juncture, both moderate delegates (who welcomed the delay) and more radical delegates (who were convinced the people were on their side) had little trouble postponing the decision for three weeks, during which time the various provincial conventions could ponder the matter and issue appropriate instructions.

The delay produced results, some instantaneously. On June 8, as the Continental Congress debated the matter in the main chamber of the Pennsylvania State House, the struggling Pennsylvania Assembly, meeting upstairs, withdrew its instructions to vote against independence. Although the new Assembly instructions neither approved nor disapproved of independence, the competing Pennsylvania Convention soon issued explicit instructions to support the Lee resolution.

Within a week, Connecticut, New Hampshire, and most importantly Delaware issued instructions to their representatives in Congress to declare independence. A week after that, New Jersey followed suit. The middle colonies were coming around.

But not Maryland, at least not yet. There, as late as May 21, the convention that served as a de facto government had unanimously reaffirmed its resistance to independence. Consequently, in response to Lee's resolution, Maryland's delegates walked out of the Continental Congress and headed back home, announcing they could not be party to a declaration of independence and they would not consider themselves bound by the decisions of Congress.

Did the people of Maryland really oppose independence so strongly? Apparently not, for when Samuel Chase and other pro-independence leaders asked the various counties to hold emergency conventions, these assemblies promptly repudiated the Provincial Convention's opposition to independence. The counties insisted that Maryland's delegates unite with the general will of the Continental Congress, and that "the sooner they declare themselves separate from, and independent of the Crown and Parliament of *Great Britain*, the sooner they will be able to make effectual opposition, and establish their liberties on a firm and permanent basis." Pushed by the county conventions, the Maryland Convention held an emergency session, and on Friday evening, June 28, it voted unanimously for independence. "See the glorious effects of county instructions," Samuel Chase wrote to John Adams that night. "Our people have fire if not smothered."[37]

Maryland was not alone. In other key colonies as well, numerous instructions from lower bodies to higher bodies played a prominent role in the final drive to independence. In Virginia, as we have seen, instructions from the counties spurred the critical vote on May 15; in Pennsylvania, the push came not only from county conventions but also from militia battalions. In Massachusetts on May 10, the Assembly had issued a call to the towns to express their ideas on independence and, within the next few weeks, fifty-seven towns issued calls for their representatives to support independence, while only one came out in opposition. Altogether, historian Pauline Maier has documented ninety distinct calls for independence from towns, counties, militia units, states, and, in New York, from the "General Committee of Mechanicks, in union," which urged its delegates to the Continental Congress to vote for independence. The New York mechanics, like many of the other groups, pledged to support independence "with our lives and fortunes."[38]

On the morning of July 1, just as Congress resumed debate on Richard Henry Lee's motion, Samuel Chase's letter of June 28 was delivered to John Adams, within chambers: Maryland, the staunchest opponent, suddenly supported independence! Even with Maryland's vote in tow, however, and even though the mood of the incipient nation was now clearly for independence, the proponents of Lee's resolution failed to garner unanimous support. Pennsylvania's congressmen voted against the resolution, four to three. The South Carolina delegation, without the radical Christopher Gadsden (he was back home leading the defense of Charleston, as discussed below), voted no as well. Delaware's delegates, despite their instructions, were deadlocked, one to one. These three delegations were empowered by their constituents to support Lee's resolution if they so desired, but they still held out; the representatives from New York, meanwhile, were expressly forbidden to vote for independence. The tally by the end of the day: only nine of thirteen delegations favored the resolution.[39]

By the following morning, much had changed. Delaware's Caesar Rodney had ridden hastily ("tho detained by thunder and rain," he wrote) to break his delegation's deadlock. South Carolina's delegates, perhaps concerned that their colony would be abandoned by other Americans at the very moment it was under assault by the British navy, decided to follow the lead of their colleagues and support the measure.[40]

All pressure was then on Pennsylvania. If it refused, moderates and conservatives at the forthcoming New York Convention might well prevail, and without these two large mid-Atlantic colonies, the union would be severed into halves and seriously jeopardized. If Pennsylvania went along with the rest, on the other hand, New York would be unlikely to hold out on its own.

Pennsylvania's delegates had two competing sets of instructions to govern their behavior. The Convention insisted they vote for independence, while the revised Assembly instructions said nothing on the matter, leaving each to make up his own mind. With three members supporting independence (Benjamin Franklin, John Morton, and James Wilson, who had changed his mind during the three weeks since June 10), any one of the four recalcitrants—Thomas Willing, Charles Humphreys, John Dickinson, and Robert Morris—could swing the tide.

It wouldn't be Willing, who had become increasingly resistant to the radical thrust of the Revolution, nor Humphreys, a Quaker who was still trying to prevent an all-out war. They held firm.

What about Dickinson? Could he possibly change his mind, like Wilson?

Not likely. The day before, he had led the opposition with a lengthy discourse, parsing words, conjuring a variety of complex arguments, and making dire predictions. The "piddler" or "tiptoe gentleman" (as Christopher Gadsden called him) was too invested in his own finely tuned positions to suddenly abandon them.[41]

That left Robert Morris. His vote either way would settle the matter.

Morris had every reason to oppose independence. He had spent the first twelve years of his life in England and the majority of his adult life trading with British merchants. His wife, Mary, who regarded the political upheaval in America as something of an intrusion into her social life, did not welcome the prospect of severing all trade with Britain, the source of so many material pleasures, and in this Robert certainly concurred. Morris's minister at Christ Church, the Reverend Jacob Duché, still offered prayers to the king during his service, even to the hisses of his congregation. Mary's brother William White, who would soon succeed Reverend Duché, preferred "submission" (his own word) to rebellion, at least at this stage. Robert Morris did not travel in revolutionary circles.[42]

Morris himself regarded independence as something of a wedge issue, which divided patriots and interfered with a united resistance to the abuses of Parliament. The question of independence, along with its corollary, the creation of new governments, had created a "great division amongst ourselves especially in this Province," he wrote. The ugly struggle between the Pennsylvania Assembly and the upstart Convention was a case in point. "The contest is who shall form them [new governments] & who upon such a change shall come in for the power." Only the harsh dictates of the king, which brought patriots back together, had prevented the internal dissension in Pennsylvania from mushrooming out of control.[43]

Opposed to independence because of birth, family, social and religious ties, business interests, political philosophy, and strategic reasoning, Morris by all rights should have voted against Lee's resolution. But if he did, he himself would be promoting the spirit of disunity he decried. Robert Morris was in a bind.

Unable to vote for independence, yet thinking better of voting against it, Morris abstained. So did John Dickinson. That permitted the Pennsylvania delegation to vote in favor, three to two. The final tally: twelve states (no longer colonies) for independence, none opposed.

The following day, July 3, John Adams wrote to his wife, Abigail:

The second day of July, 1776, will be the most memorable epocha in the history of America. I am apt to believe that it will be celebrated by succeeding generations as the great anniversary festival. It ought to be commemorated as the day of deliverance, by solemn acts of devotion to God Almighty. It ought to be solemnized with pomp and parade, with shows, games, sports, guns, bells, bonfires, and illumination, from one end of this continent to the other, from this time forward forevermore. [44]

Such a celebratory mood would have been considerably dampened had Robert Morris voted his true beliefs. How ironic that Robert Morris, a man of action, contributed so much by abstaining, or doing nothing.

Twenty-one months after the people of Worcester, Massachusetts, had instructed Timothy Bigelow to raise a new and independent government "from the ashes of the Phenix," and almost fifteen months after American patriots first fired shots at redcoated Regulars at Lexington and Concord, the ties with Great Britain had finally been severed. The *style* of the matter was in keeping with the *content*, and equally important. The grand national debate, conducted over the previous six months, had come to an end, and a workable (albeit not universal) consensus had been reached. Hundreds of thousands of citizens had participated in the process and affected the result. Again, John Adams to Abigail, on the day after the decisive vote:

Time has been given for the whole people maturely to consider the great question of independence, and to ripen their judgment, dissipate their fears, and allure their hopes, by discussing it in newspapers and pamphlets, by debating it in assemblies, conventions, committees of safety and inspection, in town and county meetings, as well as in private conversation, so that the whole people, in every colony of the thirteen, have now adopted it as their own act.[45]

Independence had been declared not merely by a single council, meeting behind closed doors in the Pennsylvania State House on July 2, 1776. This moment of national creation was made possible by the body of the people, that extralegal construct that emerged during the early days of unrest more than a decade before and drove the revolution forward since that time. The founding principle of the new nation, the very reason for its existence, was popular sovereignty, and the people had already proved, by their actions, that they could and would take the reins of government into their own hands.

July 4–August 14, 1776: United States of America

Having declared independence, Congress naturally wanted to *Declare Independence*. For years, American patriots had been resolving and declaring in grand fashion, and now that they had done something truly momentous, they wished to present what they had just decided in the best possible light.

Back on June 10, during the initial debate over Richard Henry Lee's motion, Congress had started the process of issuing a formal declaration, in case the motion would eventually pass. The following day, it appointed a five-man committee—Benjamin Franklin, John Adams, Thomas Jefferson, Robert R. Livingston, and Roger Sherman—to write the document. This committee then assigned the job of preparing the initial draft to Thomas Jefferson, who two years earlier had penned a powerful set of instructions, called *A Summary View of the Rights of British America*, for Virginia's delegation to the First Continental Congress. Jefferson's commission this time, as he saw it, was

> not to find out new principles, or new arguments . . . , which had never been said before; but to place before mankind the common sense of the subject, in terms so plain and firm as to command their assent, and to justify ourselves in the independent stand we were compelled to take. Neither aiming at originality of principle or sentiment, nor yet copied from any particular and previous writing, it was intended to be an expression of the American mind, and to give to that expression the proper tone and spirit called for by the occasion. All its authority rests on the harmonizing sentiments of the day.[46]

Jefferson succeeded in this task. His draft was amended first by members of the committee and then by Congress meeting as a whole, and on July 4, delegates accepted the final version, known ever since as the Declaration of Independence, the first of our nation's two founding scriptures. The *representation* of independence quickly overshadowed the *fact* of independence: broadsides of the Declaration placed "July 4" on their banners, and that date, rather than July 2, has been celebrated ever since as the nation's birthday.

In New York City, which George Washington and the Continental Army were preparing to defend against an anticipated British attack, news of the July 2 vote in Congress arrived on July 6. Immediately, according to Lieuten-

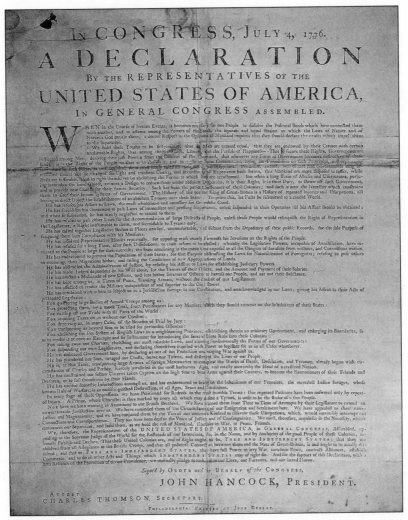

Figure 22. John Dunlap, a Philadelphia printer, set the type for this broadside on the night of July 4, 1776. Some two hundred copies were distributed through the colonies-turned-states, to be shared and read in public. Note that only two men signed the declaration on July 4, the president and secretary of Congress. Not until August 2 was an engrossed copy signed by other congressional delegates.

ant Isaac Bangs, "The whole choir of our officers . . . went to a public house to testify our joy." Copies of the Declaration arrived two days later, and on the morning of July 9 General Washington ordered that the complete text be read to the troops that evening "with an audible voice," so the soldiers would hear and understand "the grounds & reasons" for independence. "The General hopes this important event will serve as a fresh incentive to every officer, and soldier, to act with fidelity and courage, as knowing that now the peace and safety of his Country depends (under God) solely on the success of our arms," the order stated. (This was not the first item of the day's general orders, however. It appeared after sentencing two deserters to thirty-nine lashes, issuing passes to three city officials, moving a guard post "to the Market House near the Ferry-Stairs," and recruiting army chaplains—"The blessing and protection of Heaven are at all times necessary but especially so in times of public distress and danger.")[47]

After the formal readings on the various parade grounds, a crowd consisting of both soldiers and civilians gathered at Bowling Green and proceeded to yank down the giant gilded statue of King George III and his horse. Once on the ground, the people's former sovereign was sadistically mutilated, his head cleaved from his body, then his nose from his head, and the remnants of the skull placed on a spike. This part of the celebration was not according to general orders.[48]

When the Declaration reached Worcester on Saturday, July 14, Isaiah Thomas, who still published the *Massachusetts Spy* from Timothy Bigelow's basement, promptly read the full text to some townsfolk from the Meeting House steps. The next day, after service, the Declaration was read inside the Meeting House, and then on Monday evening, after word had spread to the surrounding towns, celebrations began in earnest. After listening to a third public reading on the common, a large crowd huzzahed and fired muskets and cannons and built bonfires and made as much of a commotion as had ever been heard in that staid New England town. Some marched up Main Street to the courthouse, where they tore down and burned the King's Arms. Some went to Mary Stearns's tavern and burned the sign that displayed the King's Arms there, then went inside and offered twenty-four toasts. Meticulously reported in Thomas's *Spy*, the rounds started with a prosaic "Prosperity and perpetuity to the United States of America," then became increasingly creative: "Perpetual itching without benefit of scratching, to the enemies of America" and "May the freedom and independency of America endure, till the sun grows dim with age, and this earth returns to chaos." To honor Timothy Bigelow and the local boys who had not yet returned from their captivity in Quebec, one man offered: "Speedy redemption to all the officers and soldiers who are now prisoners of war among our enemies."[49]

Robert Morris engaged in no revelry of any sort. All he did was get back to work. According to its official journal for July 4, Congress determined "that copies of the declaration be sent to the several assemblies, conventions and committees, or councils of safety, and to the several continental troops; that it be proclaimed in each of the United States, and at the head of the army." Then, without missing a beat, it went on: "Ordered: that Mr. Morris and Mr. Hewes determine the hire of Mr. Walker's vessel, which was employed by Commodore Hopkins in the service of the continent." This is the sort of task Morris had been performing for several months: hiring vessels, procuring arms and provisions, and otherwise servicing the army and fledgling navy. Through William Bingham, his agent in the West Indies, and Silas Deane, his agent in France (and also the congressional envoy there), Morris was able to develop a trade network that bypassed both British merchants and the British navy, which was bent on interfering with American commerce.[50]

Robert Morris did all this despite independence, not because of it. Three weeks after he had acceded to the majority in the critical vote of July 2, Morris explained why he continued to aid and abet the patriots' cause:

> It is the duty of every individual to act his part in whatever station his Country may call him to, in times of difficulty, danger & distress. . . . Altho the Councils of America have taken a different course from my judgements & wishes, I think an individual that declines the service of his Country because its Councils are not conformable to his ideas, makes but a bad subject; a good one will follow if he cannot lead.[51]

It was a noble sentiment, to be followed by noble actions. But there was something in it for himself as well. "It seems to me the present opportunity of improving our fortunes ought not to be lost especially as the very means of doing it will contribute to the service of our Country at the same time," Morris wrote to Silas Deane on August 11. Indeed, Morris was already leveraging his official position in Congress to increase profits for his private dealings. He and Benjamin Harrison, a business associate who had just become paymaster for the army in Virginia, entered into a scheme that played to their mutual advantage: Harrison would send business Morris's way, charging the Virginia government an extra 2 percent, while Morris would let out congressional contracts to Harrison, also at a 2 percent premium. Morris did not seem to find anything improper about this arrangement.[52]

Henry Laurens, like Robert Morris, did not celebrate independence. Because British ships interfered with maritime communications, the news took a full month to arrive in Charleston, but when it finally came, it triggered a spirited celebration similar to those in other cities and towns. (The Declaration was received by "loud acclamations of thousands who always huzza when a proclamation is read," Laurens commented caustically.) Wearing black because he still mourned his son James, who had died in an accident eleven months earlier, Laurens mourned an additional loss. He wrote to John, who was still in Europe:

> Even at this moment I feel a tear of affection for the good old Country & for the people in it whom in general I dearly love. . . . My heart is full of the lively sensations of a dutiful son, thrust by the hand of violence out of a father's house into the wide world. . . . I cannot rejoice in the downfall of an old friend of a parent from whose nurturing breasts I have drawn my support & strength.[53]

Henry's letter to John evidenced another strong feeling, also triggered by the revolutionary convulsions that had just reached their climax:

> You know my Dear Sir, I abhor slavery. I was born in a Country where slavery had been established by British Kings & Parliaments as well as by the laws of that Country ages before my existence. I found the Christian religion & slavery growing under the same authority & cultivation—I nevertheless disliked it. In former days there was no combating the prejudices of men supported by interest. The day I hope is approaching when . . . every man will strive to be foremost in shewing his readiness to comply with the Golden Rule. . . .
>
> I am not the man who enslaved them. They are indebted to English men for that favour. Nevertheless I am devising means for manumitting many of them & for cutting off the entail of slavery. Great powers oppose me, the laws & customs of my Country, my own and the avarice of my Country men. What will my children say if I deprive them of so much estate? These are difficulties but not insuperable. . . . I perceive the work before me is great. I shall appear to many as a promoter not only of strange but of dangerous doctrines.[54]

Had the Revolution really turned Henry Laurens into an abolitionist? Slavery was the ultimate test, for the nation as a whole and for Henry Laurens in particular. How far would the Revolution extend?

Laurens himself could not answer this question. In fact, the newness of all that was happening left him perplexed. "I am now by the will of God brought into a new world & God only knows what sort of a world it will be," he confided to John.[55]

While Robert Morris and Henry Laurens were conflicted over the implications of independence, Thomas Young saw the final separation from Britain as only the first step in a dramatic restructuring of the political order. On July 3, the day after the congressional vote, Christopher Marshall noted in his diary that his fellow activists James Cannon, Timothy Matlack, and Dr. Young had just "flourished away" at a meeting of the Committee of Privates, expounding on the qualities necessary for representatives to Pennsylvania's forthcoming Constitutional Convention, slated to meet on July 15. The delegates, said Young and the others, should not only evidence "zeal" in their "opposition to the tyranny of Great Britain," but they should also possess "great learning, knowledge in our history, law, mathematics, &c., and a perfect acquaintance with the laws, manners, trade, constitution and polity of all nations." They would be men of reason, new leaders for new times. At the convention, these forward-looking statesmen would point the way toward a new polity, based exclusively on the will of the people. Right at that moment in time, Thomas Young had every reason to suppose that this would happen. The historical trajectory in both Pennsylvania and the newly formed United States of America seemed pointed in that direction.[56]

Mercy Otis Warren also welcomed the opportunity to make the world anew. She dared to hope, she told John Adams, "that the American Republic will come as near the standard of perfection as the state of humanity will admit." Unlike Young, however, she could only *hope* for the best; she did not *predict* it would happen. "Man in general, as soon as he is a little elevated towards the pinnacle of power, . . . grows forgetful at once of primeval principles. . . . I am more and more convinced of the propensity in human nature to tyrannize over their fellow men." The military conflict enveloping the new nation only made matters worse: "A relaxation in virtue is usually the consequence of a state of war," she wrote. Still, although the Puritan pessimist in Mercy Otis Warren dampened the enthusiasm of the Enlightenment optimist, she mustered a prayer to relieve the gloom:

May the great Guardian of the universe who stoops to survey the rise of empire . . . inspire with vigour and unanimity the patriots of America.

May he make the decision of the present contest, the establishment of virtue, liberty, and truth, fixed on too firm a basis to be undermined by future despots![57]

While others pondered the fate of the infant nation, Timothy Bigelow was consumed by his personal circumstances: how to get back home, after his captivity in Quebec. The man who had been instructed by his constituents to initiate the first move toward independence was completely out of the loop when the final step was taken, almost two years later. Having experienced the hardships of a trek through the Maine wilderness and the bitter defeat under the walls of Quebec, Bigelow more than most knew that ideas and declarations would hardly suffice to make a new nation. Blood and tears were required as well.

George Washington knew this too. Independence, for him, was but a means to a greater end: prevailing in war. Without that, there was nothing.

And that's where fifteen-year-old Joseph Plumb Martin came in, for without him, and others like him, all that had been gained would soon be lost, and then some.

Act III

War

12

Battle Lines

July 6, 1776: Milford, Connecticut

On the evening of July 2, just hours after Congress voted for independence, Britain's North American fleet set anchor at Staten Island, in the New York harbor. In the weeks to follow, the brothers General William Howe and Admiral Richard Howe would muster a force of approximately 23,000 Regulars, 9,000 Hessian mercenaries, a few thousand seamen, and 427 seaworthy vessels, both transports and warships, armed with some 1,200 cannons ready to blast away at American targets. It would be the largest military force ever assembled by Great Britain for a single expedition until the twentieth century.[1]

Britain's object, simple in design and seemingly achievable, was to gain control of New York, cut the former colonies in two, and destroy the fledgling Continental Army.

George Washington, under orders from the Continental Congress, had to keep this from happening, but unlike the Howe brothers, he had no navy and just a bare skeleton of an army at his command. Who would help the General (as Washington was affectionately called) defend New York?

By the time recruiters for the state of Connecticut returned to Milford in the early summer of 1776, Joseph Plumb Martin had turned fifteen, not legally of age to become a soldier, but close enough to pass. A year earlier, he had looked enviously as older boys enlisted, but this time around Joseph was more determined to have his way. By threatening to run off and board a privateer, he managed to convince his grandparents that joining the army was a safer alternative. Now he too would be able to come "swaggering back" with tales of his "hairbreadth 'scapes."

> I one evening went off with a full determination to enlist at all hazards. When I arrived at the place of rendezvous I found a number of young men of my acquaintance there. The old bantering began. "Come, if you will enlist, I will," says one. "You have long been talking about it," says another. "Come, now is the time." Thinks I to myself, I will not be laughed into it or out of it. I will act my own pleasure after all. But what did I come here for tonight? Why, to enlist. Then enlist I will. So seating myself at the table, enlisting orders were immediately presented to me. I took up the pen, loaded it with the fatal charge, made several mimic imitations of writing my name, but took especial care not to touch the paper with the pen until an unlucky wight who was leaning over my shoulder gave my hand a stroke, which caused the pen to make a woeful scratch on the paper. "O, he has enlisted," said he. "He has made his mark; he is fast enough now." Well, thought I, I may as well go through with this business now as not. So I wrote my name fairly upon the indentures. And now I was a *soldier*, in name at least, if not in practice.[2]

Teenage boys like Joseph Plumb Martin, although not George Washington's first choice, were the ones most likely to sign up. Fearless in their innocence and incognizant of pain, they bargained with their lives, not fully understanding the waiver:

> I was told that the British army at that place was reinforced by fifteen thousand men, it made no alteration in my mind; I did not care if there had been fifteen times fifteen thousand, I should have gone just as soon as if there had been fifteen hundred. I never spent a thought about numbers; the Americans were invincible in my opinion.[3]

Invincible? It was not a mature assessment of the situation in New York.

September 15, 1776: Manhattan

Around noon on the Sabbath, as the heat of the day was building, General George Washington and Private Joseph Plumb Martin crossed paths in midtown Manhattan.

Martin was running helter-skelter from Kip's Bay, on the East River in what is now the mid-Thirties, to the Boston Post Road, and then northward, toward King's Bridge on the upper tip of the island. His aim was to place as much territory as possible between himself and the approaching Redcoats and Hessians, whose numbers would swell to thirteen thousand later in the afternoon.

The Connecticut farmboy-turned-soldier had spent the night in a ditch along the river, supposedly to guard against the imminent invasion. At dawn he watched the opposing force assemble and load onto boats, but he could do nothing about it. Late in the morning, around eleven, five warships floating in the East River started to pummel the shoreline, and they kept up a steady fire for fifty-nine minutes; the *Orpheus*, one of the vessels that propelled deadly missiles in Martin's direction, expended 5,376 pounds of powder during that time. The lad was shaken, both physically and emotionally. "There came such a peal of thunder from the British shipping that I thought my head would go with the sound," he recalled years later.[4]

Then came the first wave of enemy soldiers, about four thousand in number, and Private Martin, as green as soldiers come, had had enough. He fled, as did the other militiamen from Connecticut, who had been left on their own, although vastly outnumbered, to ward off the British advance. "Every man that I saw was endeavoring by all sober means to escape from death or captivity, which, at that period of the war was almost certain death," Martin wrote. "The demons of fear and disorder seemed to take full possession of all and every thing that day."[5]

George Washington experienced the moment very differently. From his outpost in upper Manhattan, several miles away, he heard the cannonade, jumped immediately on his horse, and galloped southward toward Kip's Bay. "To my great surprise and mortification I found the troops that had been posted in the lines retreating with the utmost precipitation," he wrote the next day. "I used every means in my power to rally and get them into some order but my attempt were fruitless and ineffectual."[6]

What exactly did Washington mean by "every means in my power"? We have several vivid descriptions, all of them secondhand. Seeking "death rather than life," the General placed himself "on the ground within eighty yards of the enemy, . . . drew his sword and snapped his pistols, . . . caned and whipped" the frightened Connecticut soldiers, and "struck several officers in their flight, three times dashed his hatt on the ground, and at last exclaimed, 'Good God have I got such troops as those!'" By another rendition, the wording was, "Are these the men with which I am to defend America?" While these accounts, possibly embellished, cannot be confirmed by direct witnesses, they certainly suggest that George Washington, known for his self-control, had lost it that day, and that his actions had attracted special notice. It is easy to see why the commander in chief was so on edge: the fate of his army, and with it the young nation, hung in the balance.[7]

Even prior to the British assault on Manhattan, a month before the Kip's Bay fiasco, Washington and his army had been placed on the run. By mid-August, there were so many British soldiers, Hessians, and seamen swarming around Staten Island and its harbor that it became, for an instant, the most populated city in North America. On August 22, the Howe brothers landed about 15,000 Regulars on Long Island, followed by 4,300 Hessians three days later. Washington answered by sending about 8,000 troops to Long Island, but on August 29 some 3,000 American soldiers stationed outside the Brooklyn Heights fortifications, directly across the narrow East River from New York City, were outflanked and overwhelmed by a much larger British force.

Joseph Plumb Martin watched the fighting that morning from a rooftop across the river in New York. "I distinctly saw the smoke of the field artillery," he wrote. "The horrors of battle then presented themselves to me in all their hideousness; I must come to it now, thought I." Sure enough, as he anticipated, the unseasoned lad was ordered to cross the river and join the fray. "Although this was not unexpected to me, yet it gave me a rather disagreeable feeling, as I was pretty well assured I should have to snuff a little gunpowder."

As soon as Martin arrived at the front later that day, he encountered some troops from Maryland who were trapped in a millpond, trying to swim to the other side as the enemy poured grapeshot upon them "like a shower of hail." These men did not appear invincible: "When they came out of the water and mud to us, looking like water rats, it was a truly pitiful sight. Many of them were killed in the pond, and more were drowned." This was real war, experienced firsthand.[8]

Seriously outnumbered despite their reinforcements, the Americans retreated to fortifications on Brooklyn Heights. Had Admiral Howe dispatched a portion of his navy into the East River to cut off their escape into New York, the struggling soldiers would have been trapped and easily subdued, but just then a violent storm kicked up and blew for the next two days. Although rain drenched the Americans and rendered their guns useless, the strong northeast wind kept the British fleet away, so on the night of August 29, in complete silence, George Washington, Joseph Plumb Martin, and the rest of the American soldiers were able to ferry across the river, unhindered by British vessels. Long Island and Brooklyn had been lost, but the army was still intact, at least for the moment.

Having lost Long Island so readily, Washington had to decide whether to abandon New York City without a fight. He did not ponder this alone, but consulted his Council of War, this time composed of more than a dozen other generals stationed with the main force of the army. These generals all agreed that in the face of superior numbers, training, and weaponry, and without a naval presence, the Americans were forced to wage a "war of posts," retreating to defensible positions rather than challenging the enemy head-on. But which posts were defensible? Was the city on the south tip of Manhattan Island one of them?

On September 7, the Council of War decided to divide their forces between New York City and posts to the north, primarily Fort Washington (on the highlands of upper Manhattan, overlooking the Hudson) and King's Bridge (the escape route to the mainland). But on September 12, by a vote of ten to three (Washington did not declare his position on these votes), the Council reversed itself: New York should be abandoned as soon as its extensive and critical stores (food, cloth, ammunition, and so on) could be removed. That's where matters stood when the British chased Joseph Plumb Martin from his ditch on the East River three days later—soldiers were busily carting from the city everything that might serve their needs.[9]

Because three to four thousand troops had not yet evacuated the city by September 15, the thirteen thousand Regulars and Hessians who landed in the middle of Manhattan were in a position to cut them off from the main American Army. If Private Martin and the Connecticut militiamen had put up enough resistance to slow down the British assault, troops from the city would have been able to march up the west side of the island to the (relative) safety of Fort Washington. But the militiamen didn't put up any resistance, and that meant the troops from the city, instead of retreating in an orderly maneuver, had to flee pell-mell. Hence the additional bedlam, and hence Washington's fit.

The commander in chief had never liked the idea of depending on green militiamen, and now his worst fears had been realized. Joseph Plumb Martin and the others, unseasoned and undisciplined, had refused to sacrifice themselves for the good of others. As it turned out, their sacrifice would have achieved no purpose, for the men from the city managed to escape nonetheless, but for Washington the horrific sight of his army disappearing before his eyes proved traumatic, to say the very least.

The following day, the Americans slowed down the British advance by holding on to Harlem Heights, below Fort Washington, and that bought Washington, still seething at the greenhorns, enough time to pen a cranky note to Congress:

> To place any dependence upon militia, is assuredly, resting upon a broken staff. Men just dragged from the tender scenes of domestick life—unaccustomed to the din of arms—totally unacquainted with every kind of military skill, which being followed by a want of confidence in themselves when opposed to troops regularly trained—disciplined, and appointed—superior in knowledge, & superior in arms, makes them timid, and ready to fly from their own shadows.... If I was called upon to declare upon oath, whether the militia have been most serviceable or hurtful upon the whole I should subscribe to the latter.[10]

Militias, by definition, were citizen armies, and therein lay the problem. Citizens, particularly of the American variety, cherished their freedom, while soldiers, of necessity, were expected to give theirs up. Republican ideology notwithstanding, citizens and soldiers simply didn't mesh: "Men accustomed to unbounded freedom, and no controul, cannot brooke the restraint which is indispensably necessary to the good order and government of an army; without which licentiousness, & every kind of disorder triumphantly reign."

To win the war, Washington reasoned, he would need a full-scale, full-time army. The men should be trained, disciplined (a mere thirty-nine lashes would hardly suffice), and committed to seeing the war through "for the duration," as the saying went. "To bring men to a proper degree of subordination is not the work of a day—a month—or even a year," the commander in chief warned. To recruit this professional crew, Congress (by way of the states, which would have to put up the money) needed to pay commissioned officers the going rate, closer to what they might earn fighting for the British, while offering attractive bounties to the enlisted men: money, new clothes and a blanket, and most of all land, 100 or 150 acres, taken of course from the vast tracts in the West, which would be America's for the taking upon war's end.

But was this possible? Even if Congress set aside its reservation about standing armies, would American men, "accustomed to unbounded freedom," agree to fight on the terms Washington demanded?

June–October 1776: Charleston and Cherokee Country

John Laurens was twenty-one years old at the time, the perfect age for military service, and he would have joined George Washington's army in an instant, for like his father he placed great stock in honor, and military honor above all else. Two years earlier, John had told Henry that if "fighting becomes necessary," he would "gladly expose himself" on behalf of the cause; now fighting *was* necessary, and John was chafing to do his share.[11]

But Laurens the younger was still in England, at his father's bidding.

Henry Laurens, on the other hand, was fifty-two years old and past his physical prime, weakened, according to his own reckoning, by personal grief and by the anguish of adjusting to the changing world around him. But even so, Laurens the elder insisted on doing his part, not just politically but in a military way. So when an armed British fleet appeared off the coast of South Carolina in the late spring of 1776, Laurens joined with his countrymen in preparing for the anticipated assault. This did the fading fellow wonders. With more than a little pride, he boasted to John:

> I, who you know had resolved never again to mount a horse, I who thought it impossible for me to gallop five miles in a day, was seen for a month & more every day on the back of a lively nag at ½ past 4 in the morning sometimes galloping 20 miles before breakfast & sometimes sitting the horse 14 hours in 18 & what you will say was more extraordinary I never got a tumble.[12]

Along with thousands of other patriots, Henry Laurens helped construct an elaborate system of trenches, barricades, redoubts, forts, and batteries in and about Charleston. On Sullivan's Island, which commanded the harbor, they heaped together piles of spongy palmetto logs, which could absorb British cannonballs. According to Laurens, the patriots were animated in their labor by "a love of Country & boldness arising from an assurance of being engaged in a just cause"; Laurens failed to note that African American slaves, who also helped dig the trenches and muscle the palmetto logs into place, were animated by orders and whips as well.

The defenses worked. When the British staged their assault on June 28, their cannonballs sank into the palmetto logs without doing any significant damage. Two of the invading vessels ran aground, a third was set ablaze by

American guns, and when three thousand British soldiers tried to wade across the shallow water that separated Long Island from Sullivan's Island, they found the tidal current too swift. British losses in the Charleston fiasco were over six times those of the Americans.

Meanwhile, on the western reaches of Euro-American habitation, Cherokee warriors such as Dragging Canoe, who had pledged to fight against encroaching white Americans during the council at Chota a few months earlier (see chapter 10), were engaged in "the glorious work of massacre & assassination," to use Laurens's words. Laurens and other patriots assumed the Cherokee raiders were instigated by British agents and acting "in a concerted plan with the ships and troops" on the coast, but in fact the young warriors were fighting very much on their own behalf, over and against the advice of British agents and even their own elders. By attacking isolated homesteads and killing the inhabitants, the warriors reasoned they could scare other whites away, but their timing could not have been worse. Local patriots, once they had repelled the attack on Charleston, faced no other threat in the region, and the Cherokee "ravages and murders" (again, Laurens's words) provided an excuse and an opportunity to continue fighting.[13]

Since the other southern states faced no immediate danger of invasion by British forces, patriots from around the region decided to gang up on the Cherokees. Griffith Rutherford, commander of the North Carolina Council of Safety, suggested that if "the frunters, of each of them provances" worked together, they could bring about the "finel destruction of the Cherroce nation." North Carolina's delegates to the Continental Congress announced that if their "duties as Christians" did not stand in the way, they ought "to extinguish the very race of them and scarce to leave enough of their existence to be a vestige in proof that a Cherokee nation once was." Thomas Jefferson, in a somewhat more subdued tone, hoped that "the Cherokees will now be driven beyond the Mississippi and that this in the future will be declared to the Indians as the invariable consequences of their beginning a war."[14]

And so it was that six thousand armed men from South Carolina, North Carolina, Virginia, and Georgia—having trained and mobilized for war, and with no other enemy to fight—marched against the Cherokee Indians during the late summer and early fall of 1776. William H. Drayton, a leading patriot in the South Carolina Assembly, instructed members of the expedition:

And now a word to the wise. It is expected you make smooth work as you go—that is, you cut up every Indian corn-field, and burn every Indian town—and that every Indian taken shall be the slave and property of the taker; that the nation be extirpated, and the lands become the property of the public.[15]

These directions were dutifully executed. On August 17, Henry Laurens wrote: "Col. Williamson [commander of the South Carolina forces] is pursuing the perfidous foolish Cherokees who have been instigated to murder & rapine on our Western frontier," and five days later Andrew Williamson reported back to Drayton: "I have now burnt down every town, and destroyed all the corn, from the Cherokee line to the middle settlements." (Williamson and Laurens were longtime friends; back in 1765, Andrew had sent Henry, as a present, a rattlesnake from the backcountry around Ninety Six.) By September 27, Henry Laurens could report to his brother James, who was residing in England: "I say we are tranquil in this State, because Col. Williamson's progress into the Cherokee Country has kept that troublesome people from our skirts. He is now in the middle settlements driving those perfidous wretches before him."[16]

The 1776 war against the Cherokees was a short and lopsided affair. For the Americans, the campaign had served as good practice, a warm-up for the fight against Britain. In the words of David Ramsay, a contemporary historian from South Carolina who would later marry Martha Laurens, Henry's daughter:

The expedition into the Cherokee settlements diffused military ideas, and a spirit of enterprize among the inhabitants. It taught them the necessary arts of providing for an army, and gave them experience in the business of war. . . . The peacable inhabitants of a whole state transformed from planters, merchants, and mechanics, into an active, disciplined military body.[17]

But from the Cherokee perspective, the 1776 raids by Dragging Canoe and other militants ended in disaster. The Cherokee people—old men, women, and children included—paid a heavy price because their young warriors were among the first Native Americans to wage war against the fledgling United States. Within three months, the vast majority of villages had been destroyed, and the people had been deprived of their autumn harvest. According to one

American soldier, the Cherokee "were reduced to a state of the most deplorable and wretched, being obliged to subsist on insects and reptiles of every kind."[18]

In two separate treaties the following year, the Cherokees agreed to give up the fight and cede large portions of their land. But once again, Dragging Canoe refused to sign the treaties negotiated by moderate leaders such as his father, Attakullakulla. Calling themselves *Ani*-Yunwiya, the Real People, Dragging Canoe and the other militants, the people who had actually waged the war, withdrew from the rest of the Cherokees. Led by young warriors rather the old chiefs, the inhabitants of four large towns that had been destroyed by the war decided to rebuild their settlements near Chickamauga Creek, to the south and west of their old homes, and start life anew. For the next seventeen years, these Chickamaugas, as they came to be called, would continue to resist the westward thrust of white settlers, while the remaining Cherokees struggled to find some place in the vanishing middle ground between the Americans to the east and their militant relatives to the west. Formerly one people, the Cherokee nation had split in two.[19]

Henry Laurens showed little understanding of the political divisions among his Indian opponents. He had placed his trust in the statesman Attakullakulla, who had agreed back in 1761 and again in 1775 to live in peace (see chapters 1 and 10). Assuming that Cherokees operated on a hierarchical power structure, and that Attakullakulla was among their top leaders, Laurens felt personally betrayed when Cherokees went on the warpath in 1776. "The Cherokees had amused us by the most flattering talks, full of assurances of friendship & promises to follow our advice," he explained to John. Then the "treacherous Devils" suddenly embarked on their murderous campaign, "without any pretence to provocation." The perceived duplicity counts in part for Laurens's venomous language.[20]

Laurens also felt betrayed by his former countrymen, the British, whom he believed were inciting both Indians and slaves to revolt. "Negro slaves & barbarous Indians have been taught to exclaim, 'down with the Americans & their estates will be all free plunder,'" he wrote to his daughter Martha. It was his job to stop such mischief: "Thus cruelly beset, howbeit my heart neither fails nor misgives me, I see it my duty to guard against every thing which may happen." This is what the Revolution meant to Henry Laurens, not a progressive restructuring of society, but quite the reverse, a buttress against unwanted change.[21]

July 15–September 28, 1776: Philadelphia

Thomas Young, among the most rambunctious of patriots, never showed an inclination to fight on the front lines, and he would have been a very bad candidate for the "subordination" Washington demanded of his soldiers. This is not to say he was above exposing himself to danger. In the summer of 1776, he served as a surgeon for the Philadelphia Rifle Battalion, and in December the Council of Safety appointed him "Senior Surgeon in the Continental Hospital" in Philadelphia, where he treated sick and wounded soldiers sent home from the front. There was certainly plenty of risk in that, for although Young had inoculated himself against smallpox years before, his work still exposed him to other communicable diseases that rampaged through the army.[22]

As always, however, Dr. Thomas Young focused more on political change than healing the sick or wounded. Along with his cadre of fellow radicals and the Committee of Privates, he promoted exactly the type of revolution that Henry Laurens feared and Robert Morris opposed: wresting control from the privileged classes and giving it to the body of the people, that amorphous group that had been pushing events from the bottom for more than a decade, up to and including the act of independence.

On July 15, Pennsylvania's Constitutional Convention gathered on the main floor of the State House, directly across the entry hall from the chamber occupied by the Continental Congress. Although their main object was to write a new constitution, the would-be solons first decided to replace the state's more conservative delegates to Congress, the ones who almost stymied the vote on independence. No longer would Thomas Willing, Charles Humphreys, or John Dickinson represent the people of Pennsylvania; only Robert Morris was spared the ax, for people were beginning to realize that he filled an indispensable role in supporting the war effort.

For almost two months, delegates to the convention discussed and argued about the new shape of government. Although neither Thomas Young nor Thomas Paine was elected to represent Philadelphia (both were still too new in town), some of their friends were, notably James Cannon and Timothy Matlack, and the ideas these delegates presented within chambers were those often discussed by Philadelphia radicals and the group that represented their political base, the Committee of Privates. Back in June, the Privates had advised that "great and over-grown rich men" and those "who were very backward in declaring you a free people" should not be sent to the convention. Now, they pushed to embody these views in a section of the declaration of rights intended to accompany the new constitution: "That an enormous proportion of property vested in a few individuals is dangerous to the rights, and destructive to the common happiness, of mankind; and therefore every free state hath a right by its laws to discourage the possession of such property."[23]

This measure engendered heated debate, and in the end it was rejected. Another controversial idea, however, became the centerpiece of the constitution: a unicameral legislature that represented people rather than property. Young, Paine, and company had been arguing all along that the will of the people should not be countered, diluted, or even checked by an upper chamber that represented wealth and privilege, and finally, riding the giant wave of popular participation in the political process, they got their way.

The document that was printed for public debate early in September included many other radical notions, all with an eye to ensuring popular control of the governmental process and limiting the possibilities for the accumulation and abuse of political power by individuals. The single legislative body was directly responsible to a widely expanded electorate, which included all adult, taxpaying males who had resided in the state for one year. Assemblymen, elected every year, could serve only four years in any seven-year period; members of the twelve-man executive council who served three consecutive years would have to sit out the next four; congressional delegates, elected annually, could not serve more than two terms in a row. County positions that used to be appointed became elected, and all officeholders had only to meet the minimum standards of the general franchise.

The state was required to print weekly reports on roll-call votes, while the chambers were to "remain open for the admission of all persons who behave decently." Most significantly, to give ordinary citizens an opportunity to participate in the governmental process, "all bills of public nature" had to be "printed for the consideration of the people" before coming to a vote, and no bill could be passed until the session after it was introduced.

This unique document, a blueprint for direct and democratic government, gave structure and form to the egalitarian sentiments of Thomas Young, his colleagues, and of course the Privates, who served as its primary advocates. It was particularly popular among those who had been traditionally left out or underrepresented, including the state's large German population and Scots-Irish Presbyterians, primarily from the western districts.[24]

The Pennsylvania constitution of 1776 was passed in its final form on September 28, after much revision during the period of public discussion. It was not universally acclaimed, however: of the convention's ninety-six delegates, twenty-three refused to sign the document. On October 17, opponents meeting at the Philosophical Society prepared a list of thirty-two changes they wished to make, and on October 21 and 22, about 1,500 people convened in the State House Yard to discuss the proposed alterations. Christopher Marshall, who bolted from his radical friends and now opposed the constitution, noted in his diary: "Chief speakers, against Convention, were Col. McKean and Col Dickinson; for the Convention, James Cannon, Timothy Matlack, Dr. Young and Col. Smith of York County." According to Marshall, "a large majority" of that particular assemblage voted in favor of revamping the new constitution before it could be implemented.[25]

Robert Morris, like Dickinson, feared that the people, if allowed to remain unchecked, might run rampant over men of property such as himself. He did not directly engage in the fight, however, for he was too busy keeping the Continental Army supplied and the Continental Congress in business, but upon his election to the newly created Assembly the following month, Morris promptly resigned his seat in protest.

We will never know whether the radical constitution of 1776 represented the views of the majority or minority of Pennsylvania citizens, for the matter was never put to a popular vote, but we do know that it was divisive. As Robert Morris had observed back in June, the issue of self-governance continued to create a "great division amongst ourselves especially in this Province." At issue was not only the constitution itself, but also the requirement that all citizens take an oath of loyalty to it. Radicals had hoped that the people, acting as a whole, would embrace their newfound power; in fact, the "people" in pluralistic Pennsylvania, with its mix of classes, regions, ethnicities, languages, and religions, did not operate as a whole, and many refused to pledge loyalty to a document with which they disagreed.[26]

In the late fall of 1776, just as the simmering divisions appeared to be approaching the boiling point once again, the matter was tabled, for Thomas Young, Robert Morris, and all other patriots in Philadelphia, no matter what their political orientation, were suddenly forced to deal with an even more compelling issue: the British Army was marching their way, heading south from New York.

The war was still on, and it was not going well.

September 30–December 19, 1776: New York and New Jersey

Two weeks after the helter-skelter "retreat" up Manhattan Island, George Washington groused to his cousin Lund Washington, manager of the Mount Vernon estate:

> Such is my situation that if I were to wish the bitterest curse to an enemy on this side of the grave, I should put him in my stead with my feelings; and yet I do not know what plan of conduct to pursue. I see the impossibility of serving with reputation, or doing any essential service to the cause by continuing in command, and yet I am told that if I quit the command inevitable ruin will follow from the distraction that will ensue. In confidence I tell you that I never was in such an unhappy, divided state since I was born.[27]

Focusing on what troubled him most, the commander in chief added once again that he did not have the "least chance of reputation" under the current circumstances.

Joseph Plumb Martin had different reasons to complain. Before he fled, he and his fellows had been ordered to place their packs in a pile, never to be seen again. Now, with the advent of autumn, Martin was paying the price:

> To have to lie as I did almost every night (for our duty required it) on the cold and often wet ground without a blanket and with nothing but thin summer clothing was tedious. I often while upon guard lain upon one side until the upper side smarted with cold, then turned that side down to the place warmed by my body and let the other take its turn at smarting . . . In the morning, the ground as white as snow with hoar frost. Or perhaps it would rain all night like a flood. All that could be done in that case was to lie down (if one could lie down), take our musket in our arms and place the lock between our thighs and "weather it out."[28]

How long could Washington and his struggling army, with little food or shelter, cling to the northern tip of Manhattan Island?

On October 12, the British landed a force on the eastern shore of the mainland at a place called Throg's Neck. From there, they were in position to march on King's Bridge from the north, thereby preventing Washington's further retreat and possibly capturing his army.

That's where matters stood two days later, when General Charles Lee, Washington's ambitious second in command, arrived back in camp. Lee at that moment possessed the "reputation" that Washington coveted, for he had just beaten the British at Charleston. In fact, he had done little more than assist the local resistance, and he had even recommended the abandonment of Sullivan's Island, but as commander he was entitled to receive full credit for the patriots' success. When people compared the two generals' performance records, as they inevitably would, Lee's victory provided a marked contrast to Washington's recent string of defeats.

Whether from deference, respect, or to satiate the known vanity of his potential rival, Washington immediately placed Lee in charge of his largest division and named the new fortification, on the west bank of the Hudson, Fort Lee. If British ships ever wanted to sail up the Hudson, they would have to run the gauntlet between the two forts named after generals, with dozens of cannons focused down at the river between them.

Lee responded to the commander in chief's hospitality with some quick and firm advice: get out of Manhattan, and do it immediately. Washington at this point agreed, as did most of the other generals, and on October 17, he issued orders to break camp at Harlem Heights and move northward, across King's Bridge to the mainland. Only Fort Washington, with its commanding presence over the Hudson, would be maintained.

Years later, Joseph Plumb Martin still recalled that march northward, one step ahead of the pursuing Redcoats. Weary and with no food to cook, he threw away his cast-iron pots by the side of the road. Pots and pans, known by the soldiers as "their iron bondage," were "at that time the most useless things in the army," Martin wrote.[29]

When Martin and his fellow soldiers reached White Plains, they were ordered to stand their ground and face the enemy. This they did. Although "we lost, in killed and wounded, a considerable number," and although the patriots gave ground in the end, Private Martin and the others fought without fleeing this time. But after the battle, having spent the night in a cold, wet ditch, Martin fell severely ill, and he was sent from the front lines to the "baggage" and left to fend for himself. "I had the canopy of heaven for my hospital, and the ground for my hammock," he wrote. For this fifteen-year-old private, the romance of soldiering was certainly wearing thin.[30]

For General Washington, too, matters continued to worsen. On November 16, the contingent he had left to guard his namesake fort gave way to an assault by British Regulars, Scottish Highlanders, and Hessian mercenaries. Over 50 Americans were killed, another 100 wounded, and more than 2,800

A Soldier's Life

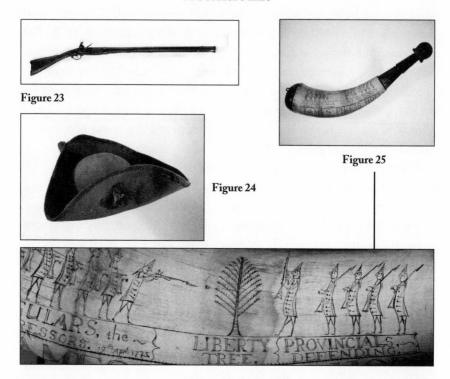

Figure 23

Figure 25

Figure 24

Figure 23. This .80-caliber "Committee of Safety" musket, of American manufacture but copied from a British model, was typical of those issued to militiamen such as Joseph Plumb Martin. **Figure 24.** This "tricorn" hat was worn by a Connecticut militiaman who served with Joseph Plumb Martin in New York and was killed in a skirmish on September 26, 1776. Often lacking full uniforms, militiamen took pride in their hats. **Figure 25.** Soldiers decorated their powder horns, which they fashioned from cattle horns, with a wide array of patriotic emblems. This one was owned by Massachusetts militiaman James Pike. *(Chicago History Museum)*

prisoners were forced to march out of the fort between two lines of enemy soldiers. Although it was a monstrous defeat, and at least in hindsight predictable, Washington did not assume primary responsibility, since he, like most of his other generals, had thought it wiser to withdraw than to hold on. A week earlier, he had written to General Nathanael Greene, whom he had placed in command of the fort: "I am therefore inclined to think it will not be prudent to hazard the men & stores at Mount Washington." He had entrusted Greene, who was "on the spot," to make the final decision. Greene, in turn, had left the fort in charge of Colonel Robert Magaw, who also resisted accountability, claiming he "could not get the men to man the lines otherwise he would not have given up the fort." With blame rapidly descending the chain of command, from Washington to Greene to Magaw to the soldiers on the ground, there was one lowly person at the very bottom whom everybody agreed was above reproach: Margaret Corbin, who "manned" the artillery of her fallen husband, and who would become the first female American to receive a soldier's pension for her service.[31]

While Generals Washington and Greene—both of whom visited the fort on the morning of the surrender, only to leave so they wouldn't be captured— passed the buck downward, General Charles Lee gingerly returned it upward, right to the commander in chief himself, the only man higher in rank than he was. If Fort Washington had been named Fort Lee, he protested, it would have been properly evacuated; by his own testimony, his last words to Washington were, "Draw off the garrison, or they will be lost." In confidence, Lee wrote to Horatio Gates, another general: "The ingenious manoeuvre of Fort Washington has unhinged the goodly fabrick we had been building. There never was so damned a stroke. *Entre nous*, a certain great man is most damnably deficient." Lee wrote to others as well, Benjamin Rush for instance, now a congressman, whom he knew would not keep a secret: "I must entreat that you will keep what I say to yourself, but I foresaw, predicted, all that has happened."[32]

Four days after the surrender at Fort Washington, the Americans ceded Fort Lee without putting up a fight. If it weren't for the season, British forces would probably have been able to chase down Washington's retreating army and defeat it, but European generals were not accustomed to staging offensives during the winter, when their soldiers would be exposed to the elements. So instead of continuing their pursuit, British officers decided to hole up. While their navy sought refuge in the secure harbor of Newport, Rhode Island, a contingent of the army raided the rich farmlands of New Jersey for produce to feed the troops.

General Washington could not afford to let down his guard, however. With British and Hessian forces in New Jersey moving slowly southward toward Philadelphia, Washington had no choice but to place himself between the advancing enemy and the nation's capital. If he gave up Philadelphia without a fight, his reputation would be forever damaged and he would likely be replaced as commander in chief.

Ironically, while General Washington's choices were circumscribed by the course of events, Private Joseph Plumb Martin enjoyed the freedom to shape his own destiny. His six-month tour was due to expire on December 25, and although he was pressured to reenlist, he was under no obligation to do so:

I had several *kind* invitations to enlist into the standing army, then about to be raised, especially a very pressing one to engage in a regiment of horse, but I concluded to try a short journey on foot first. Accordingly, I sat off for my old grandsire's. . . . I had learned something of a soldier's life, enough, I thought, to keep me at home for the future.[33]

Without Private Martin and many like him, Washington marched south toward Philadelphia with a threadbare and rapidly diminishing army, leaving the bulk of his soldiers to guard the Hudson Highlands and the Lake Champlain corridor (if these fell, the British could literally cut the colonies in two). He quickly realized, however, that his own force, fewer than four thousand men, would not be enough to make a stand at Philadelphia, so he ordered General Lee, who had been placed in command of twice that number, to come hastily with reinforcements. Lee wrote back saying he would come, but at his own pace. Washington wrote again, asking him to hurry, and Lee responded with excuses as to why he must dally. And so the two tussled, almost daily, for more than two weeks during the late fall of 1776. "I shou'd be glad to receive your instructions but I cou'd wish you wou'd bind me as little as possible," Lee wrote to the only man entitled to command him. "Detach'd Generals cannot have too great latitude."[34]

The tussling came to an abrupt halt on December 13, when British soldiers captured Lee and a dozen guards at White's Tavern in Basking Ridge, New Jersey. Washington offered the requisite remorse but no great sympathy. Lee's capture was "the effect of folly & imprudence . . . going three miles out of his own camp (for the sake of a little better lodging)," Washington wrote to his brother Samuel. In the same letter, the General issued a most pessimistic forecast: "If every nerve is not strained to recruit the new Army with all possible expedition I think the game is pretty near up—owing in great measure . . . to the accursed policy of short inlistments and depending too much on militia." The General was back to his old whipping boys, those citizen-soldiers whom he believed could not be entrusted with defending a young nation.[35]

Six days before Christmas, as more of Washington's men prepared to go home, a reporter embedded within the army—Thomas Paine—issued the first pamphlet of his *American Crisis* series. The opening words:

These are the times that try men's souls. The summer soldiers and the sunshine patriot will, in this crisis, shrink from the service of their country; but he that stands it now deserves the love and thanks of man and woman. Tyranny, like hell, is not easily conquered; yet we have this consolation with us, that the harder the conflict, the more glorious the triumph.[36]

It was a dynamic rallying cry, certainly necessary and perhaps effective. But the patriots needed more than words at this point. They needed men, arms, supplies, and, last but not least, some real-life success in the military way.

December 1776: Philadelphia

In his time of greatest need, George Washington turned to the person he knew could help him the most. Robert Morris, Congress's dependable workhorse and one of Philadelphia's best-connected merchants, was the man who could deliver the goods: arms and ammunition, food and clothing for the troops, and possibly even some hard dollars to convince wavering soldiers to stay in the army.

Morris readily obliged. Unlike many a patriot, from farmboys like Joseph Plumb Martin to patriarchs like Henry Laurens, Morris had absolutely no desire to assume a military role, not even a nominal one in the militia. When he was only fifteen, his father had been killed by a shot from a ceremonial cannon. At the age of twenty-one, while traveling to the West Indies on business, he had been captured by a French privateer and held prisoner in Cuba. After that, Robert Morris preferred to stay away from dangerous or exotic experiences, such as those that might accompany military service. He took risks with his money but not with his life. He would do his utmost to supply his compatriots with arms, but he himself did not care to bear them.

Yet it was Robert Morris who saved the Continental Army.

Although Morris had been in Congress scarcely a year, he had already made himself indispensable. Together with Benjamin Franklin, he served on both the Secret Committee of Commerce, charged with procuring supplies, and the Committee of Secret Correspondence, which communicated (sometimes using invisible ink) with foreign merchants and diplomats. Since Americans looked increasingly to European nations (France, Holland, and Spain) for the goods they needed to keep their army in the field, the business of these two committees overlapped. To facilitate trade, Morris offered the services of his agents abroad (including his high-living brother, Thomas, who had been carousing around Europe). Congress, meanwhile, dispatched a former delegate from Connecticut, Silas Deane, to seek gifts and arrange trade in France. Morris and Franklin, on behalf of the Secret Committee of Correspondence, gave Deane their shopping list: "If France means to befreind us or wishes us well, they shou'd send us succours in good muskets, blankets, cloaths, coating and proper stuff for tents, also in ammunition, but not like the Venetians wait untill we are beat and then send assistance."[37]

Morris served also on the Marine Committee, charged with creating an American navy and distributing the goods obtained by American privateers (privately owned vessels sanctioned to prey on British ships). Again, this committee dovetailed with the others, for they all had as their primary goal the procurement of necessary goods from abroad. Because of his multiple committee assignments, the entire matrix centered around Robert Morris. Back in October, when members of Congress wondered why they were not better informed about certain business of the Secret Committee of Correspondence, the Committee, in the persons of Franklin and Morris, replied: "We are . . . of opinion that it is *unnecessary* to inform Congress of this intelligence at present because Mr. Morris belongs to all the committees that can properly be employed in receiving & importing the expected supplys."[38]

As usual, Morris's public and private interests overlapped. Silas Deane, while serving as Congress's agent in France, performed double duty as Morris's own agent as well. And the infrastructure Morris established for privateers to sell the goods they had seized benefited him personally, for he, too, was entering that line of work.

Privateering was a touchy matter for Robert Morris. Although he had built up his fortune by seizing foreign vessels in the French and Indian War, he professed "scruples" about preying on British vessels, which might belong to his recent trading partners. In September, he told Silas Deane "this business . . . does not square with my principles," and yet he was not about to stand by and watch others "making large fortunes in a most rapid manner." On December 4, Robert Morris instructed his agent William Bingham to outfit the first of many cruisers that would profit him and support the government throughout the war:

I have procured a commission for Captain Ord to command a privateer. You may purchase, fit & man a suitable vessell for this purpose under his command. I propose that this privateer shou'd be a stout, good, & fast sailing vessell quite fit for the purpose, a ship, brigt, sloop or schooner just as you can best suit yourself. I think she shou'd have 12 to 16, six or four pounders & 100 to 150 men if to be got. . . . I think good business may be done amongst the outward bound West India men by cruizing to windward of Barbados where is also the track for Guinea men.[39]

This deep tangle of public and private affairs, everything from international diplomacy and trade to state-sponsored piracy, kept Robert Morris burning the midnight oil in Philadelphia in the first weeks of December 1776, as British forces advanced slowly but surely toward the city. News of the advance was updated daily, along with exaggerated estimates of the British strength, and their trajectory sent Philadelphians into something of a panic. People in fright took flight, much as their counterparts in Boston had done in early April 1775. On December 8, to restore some semblance of order, city officials declared martial law, and four days later, upon hearing that a British advance force had arrived in Burlington, less than twenty miles away, even Congress had had enough:

> Whereas the movements of the enemy have now rendered the neighbourhood of this city the seat of war, which will prevent that quiet and uninterrupted attention to the public business, which should ever prevail in the great continental council:
> Resolved, That this Congress be, for the present, adjourned to the town of Baltimore, in the State of Maryland.[40]

The problem was, much of Congress's most important business could be conducted only in Philadelphia, the hub of commerce and communications for the infant nation. To carry on its critical transactions, it left three members in town: George Clymer, George Walton, and Robert Morris. So while other delegates made their way to Baltimore, Morris stayed put to carry on the routine but necessary tasks of war: requisitioning supplies and paying bills, keeping the books, dispatching vessels, arranging deliveries, everything it took to keep an army in the field, ships afloat, and the nation financially solvent. It was difficult and lonely work. His family had evacuated to the home of Mary's stepsister in Maryland. Virtually all able-bodied adult males had mobilized into their militia units and left town. Five days before Christmas, Morris didn't even know if his colleagues Clymer and Walton were still around. The city "looks dismal & melancholy," he wrote. Only "Quakers &

their families," along with a few "sick soldiers" and a handful of "effective ones," the city's last defense, remained.[41]

Yet Morris pledged to stick it out to the end. To Silas Deane he wrote: "My own affairs necessarily detained me here after the departure of Congress and it is well I staid as I am obliged to set many things right that would otherways be in the greatest confusion. Indeed I find my presence so very necessary that I shall remain here untill the enemy drive me away." He kept wagons loaded with his valuable possessions, ready for an emergency escape in the event of a surprise attack.[42]

Morris's work did not go unappreciated by Congress, which on December 21 formally approved the "care of the public business as signified in Mr. Morris's letters." (On one day alone, Congress read on the floor twenty-three of his letters.) More significantly, it transformed the team of Morris, Clymer, and Walton into an emergency committee with the broad and unprecedented power "to execute such continental business as may be proper and necessary to be done at Philadelphia," and it gave this committee immediate access to $200,000, along with the authority to borrow as much "as the continental use there may demand." Since Clymer and Walton had to all intents and purposes disappeared from the public scene, one man, Robert Morris, now possessed the power to run the fledgling nation by himself. He could (and did) order salt to be removed into the country, purchase clothes for soldiers, rig boats with guns, commandeer wagons to evacuate the city, and make a myriad of on-the-ground decisions with no oversight, no check on his deeds.[43]

In more normal times, Congress had guarded its powers jealously, and for all the right reasons. It feared that an executive branch, with its inherent centralization of power, might start the new nation on the road to tyranny, much as it feared that a standing army might be used against the very people who had created it. But now, struggling for the life of the new nation, Congress relented by forming an ad hoc executive branch, empowered to take independent action. Like Robert Morris with his privateering, it abandoned its scruples. If the exigencies of war demanded a distinct executive as well as a professional army, so be it, republican principles be damned.

December 20, 1776–January 3, 1777: Delaware River

"This day & tomorrow the whole militia of this city & suburbs march to join Genl Washington. The country will follow the example of the city," Robert

Morris reported to William Bingham on December 4. Previously, the "spirit" of Philadelphia's fighting men "had gone to sleep," but in a mass meeting at the State House Yard two thousand new recruits had just signed on.[44]

"The Jerseys are in motion," Morris continued. There, harsh treatment at the hands of Hessian soldiers was triggering a spontaneous uprising of angry patriots. Militiamen from several New Jersey counties, as well as some from Pennsylvania, decided on their own authority to harass the British and Hessians, who had spread themselves thin to maximize the area they could plunder.[45]

One might think General Washington would take heart from this home-grown resistance movement, but he was in no mood to voice his appreciation for local militiamen. The Pennsylvania and New Jersey militias had turned out to fight only after "much reluctance and sloth," he complained. On December 20, with the enemy poised to take Philadelphia at any moment, Washington reiterated to Congress his disdain for militias and his request (now bordering on a demand) for a professional army:

> Short inlistments, and a mistaken dependance upon militia, have been the origin of all our misfortunes. . . . Can any thing . . . be more destructive to the recruiting service, than giving ten dollars bounty for six weeks service of the militia, who come in, you can not tell how—go, you cannot tell when—and act, you cannot tell where—consume your provisions—exhaust your stores, and leave you at last at a critical moment. These, sir, are the men I am to depend upon, ten days hence [when current enlistments were due to expire]. This is the basis on which your cause will and must for ever depend, till you get a large standing army, sufficient of itself to oppose the enemy.[46]

Then the General got down to specifics. By a "large standing army" he meant a minimum of 110 battalions, not just the 88 that Congress had established (on paper) back in September.

Washington did take heart from the arrival of General Lee's division, now under the command of General John Sullivan. Although reinforcements were "more than a month" late due to Lee's dawdling, at least they had come—and none too soon, for Washington was facing a deadline. In ten days' time his army might evaporate, just at the moment the Delaware River was likely to freeze solid, affording the British easy access to Philadelphia. Unless Washington acted soon, the young nation's capital was sure to fall, in his view.[47]

But what should he do? What *could* he do?

On Friday, December 22, General Washington received a letter from Colonel Joseph Reed, who had served as his secretary in Cambridge. Reed had attended college at nearby Princeton and knew the area well, and he also knew what was happening on the ground with the militia uprisings. A group of local militiamen, Reed reported, were rallying behind Samuel Griffin, a colonel from Virginia who headed a small force of artillerymen. Griffin and his men had somehow fallen through the cracks of the Continental organization, and Griffin had just decided, on his own authority, to stage an attack near Blackhorse, ten miles south of Trenton. Knowing this, Pennsylvania militiamen under Colonel John Cadwalader resolved to pester the enemy with their own strike nearby. "Will it not be possible my dear Genl for your troops or such part of them as can act with advantage to make a diversion or something more at or about Trenton?" Reed queried. "The greater the alarm the more likely the success will attend the attacks."[48]

As strange as it sounds, Joseph Reed was asking the commander in chief of the Continental Army to create a diversion for a militia attack. Stranger yet, the commander took the notion seriously. In Washington's despondent state, he was able to hear Reed's advice: fight the war with the army you have, not with the army you want but don't have.

Immediately on receiving Reed's letter, the General convened his Council of War. After quickly agreeing to strike at the 1,400 Hessians stationed at Trenton on the opposite shore of the Delaware River, the officers sketched out a plan. Local militiamen would line up a fleet of flat-bottomed freight and ferry boats, to be piloted across the river by John Glover and his Marblehead Mariners. (Four months earlier, these crusty seamen from Massachusetts had guided Washington's retreat across the East River in New York.) Washington himself would lead the main attacking force of 2,400 Continentals, crossing the Delaware ten miles above Trenton and then marching south; 800 militiamen from rural Pennsylvania, led by James Ewing, would cross near Trenton itself and cut off the Hessians' escape route; 1,200 Philadelphia Associators and 600 Continental troops from New England, under the command of John Cadwalader, would create a diversion twelve miles downriver at Burlington, to keep Hessian and Highlander forces there from aiding the Trenton outpost. The coordinated river crossings were to be staged under cover of darkness on Christmas night; the attack on Trenton was scheduled for dawn on December 26.[49]

The plan worked, although not exactly as imagined. The two southerly crossings were thwarted by large masses of ice floating in the river and on the opposite bank. But Washington's men made it across, and through a freezing rain and driving wind they continued to Trenton without being discovered. By the time they reached their destination, it was already light, but the same storm that made their approach so uncomfortable suddenly became their ally: the Hessian guards, cold and tired, had retreated indoors and were caught by surprise. The rest of the Hessian soldiers, alerted by gunfire, quickly arose and were able to put up some resistance, but Americans forced the issue with artillery fire, musketry, and bayonet charges. The battle was over within an hour. While some five hundred Hessians were able to escape, 22 had been killed and 896 taken prisoner.

Finally, after a year and a half in the field, George Washington had scored a clear victory in battle.

On December 27, the day after the Battle of Trenton, Congress granted the commander in chief permission to raise the twenty-two extra battalions he had requested a week earlier. It also gave him the personal authority to offer bounties for reenlistments, to set his own system for promotions, to appoint or displace officers up to the rank of brigadier general, "to arrest and confine persons who refuse to take the continental currency," and "to take, wherever he may be, whatever he may want for the use of the army, if the inhabitants will not sell it, allowing a reasonable price for the same." Despite its misgivings, Congress was now willing to accept and support a professional army under the leadership of one man, although it did add that all the new powers it had given Washington were to last for only six months or until "sooner determined by Congress."[50]

The following day, Robert Morris penned a letter to Washington on behalf of the Executive Committee: "Most sincerely do we rejoice in your Excellencys success at Trentown as we conceive it will have the most important publick consequences and because we think it will do justice in some degree to a character we admire & which we have long wished to appear in the world with that brilliancy that success always obtains & which members of Congress know you deserve." This was the praise Washington had been longing to hear, but Morris didn't stop there. Although he knew it was beyond his place, he couldn't help but offer some advice. "Such precious moments shou'd not be lost," he counseled. If Washington continued the pursuit, "those troops whose times of enlistment are now expiring will follow their successfull General although they would have left him whilst acting a defensive part."[51]

Washington and his Council of War were thinking along the same lines. Writing to Congress on December 29, he announced he was ready to "pursue the enemy in their retreat—try to beat up more of their quarters."[52]

There was only one problem: a large proportion of Washington's soldiers still hadn't reenlisted. Although His Excellency now possessed the authority to dole out bounties, he had no funds on hand to do so, and his troops were no longer willing to accept empty promises. Where could Washington get the money, on the instant?

He went to the source, as usual. "Tomorrow the Continental troops are all at liberty," Washington wrote to Morris on December 31. Only immediate cash could save the day. "If it be possible, sir, to give us assistance do it—borrow money where it can be done we are doing it upon our private credit—every man of interest & every lover of his country must strain his credit upon such an occasion."[53]

The General received Morris's money the next day, along with an accompanying letter:

> I was honoured with your favour of yesterday by Mr. Howell late last night, & ever solicitous to comply with your requisition. I am up very early this morning to dispatch a supply of fifty thousand dollars to your Excellency. You will receive that sum with this letter but it will not be got so early as I cou'd wish for none concerned in this movement except myself are up. I shall rouse them immediately. It gives me great pleasure that you have engaged the troops to continue, and if further occasional supplies of money are necessary you may depend on my exertions either in a publick or private capacity.[54]

The second crossing of the Delaware proved as difficult as the first, and shortly after arriving on the other side, the Americans learned that it would not be so easy to "beat up" on additional outposts in New Jersey. General Howe had dispatched General Charles Cornwallis and eight thousand Redcoats from winter headquarters in New York to oppose the rebel army, and by late afternoon on January 2 this force had arrived face-to-face with Washington's men in Trenton. Only the Assunpink Creek (a tributary to the Delaware) separated the two armies. Washington of course placed heavy guards at the single bridge and the most likely stream crossings, and these were able to keep the British away till dark. With his soldiers in a state of fatigue, Cornwallis decided not to stage a nighttime assault.

That evening, Washington called a unique war council, attended by a dozen commanding officers (including militia commanders) and even a few local civilians, who knew the lay of the land. Their options seemed limited. They could try to hold their ground against a larger and better-trained army, but should they be defeated, as was likely, that would be the end of the army, the end of the war, and the end of the independent United States of America. Or they could retreat, not across the Delaware (the boats had been drawn away) but southward on the east side of the river. Militarily, that was a viable option, but it would be a political disaster. It would nullify the effect of the patriots' one victory, dampen morale, and inhibit the recruitment of an army. "One thing I was sure of," Washington told Congress three days later, "was to avoid the appearance of a retreat."[55]

There was a third option, made available by local knowledge. A small road led off to the east, and thence northward toward Princeton, which had been Washington's next target. If Washington could manage to move some five thousand men along this road in the dead of night without attracting any notice, he could outflank Cornwallis's army, attack Princeton the next day, and then move on to Brunswick, the British storehouse for arms and supplies, before Cornwallis could catch up with him. The war council voted for this plan.

General Washington was no stranger to nighttime maneuvers. From his march on Jumonville Glen that opened the French and Indian War, to the fortification of Dorchester Heights that forced the British to abandon Boston, to his retreat across the East River in New York, to his crossing of the Delaware the preceding week, he had demonstrated that soldiers can move in the dark when they have to—quietly, and in large numbers. This time, he ordered a small force to stay behind, keep the bonfires burning, and hack at the ground with their picks and shovels so British guards across Assunpink Creek would think they were erecting fortifications.

At dawn on January 3, Cornwallis realized that the army he was about to attack had disappeared.

The Americans by then were approaching Princeton, which they overwhelmed. They also inflicted some damage on Cornwallis's rear guard, which they encountered along the main road just south of Princeton. Washington himself wanted to hasten to Brunswick, lured by the £70,000 British war chest he understood was there, but his officers counseled otherwise; the men were simply too weary to continue, they said. Washington listened and changed his plans. He would savor his victories and march toward Morristown, where he and his army could nestle down into winter quarters.

Reporting to Congress on January 5, the commander in chief had some uncharacteristically positive words for New Jersey and Pennsylvania militiamen. "They have undergone more fatigue and hardship than I expected militia (especially citizens) would have done at this inclement season," he admitted. "The militia are taking spirit and I am told, are coming in fast." Indeed, militiamen had contributed significantly to the recent successes, as had the various and sundry officers who participated in Washington's unorthodox war council.[56]

No small part of the army's survival was its commander's ability to heed counsel and adjust to the contingencies of the moment. Despite his prior notions and inclinations, George Washington had recognized the importance of assuming a more democratic style. To receive the respect he craved, he was adapting to the tone of the times. But as we credit the man for his ability to listen and adjust, we should also note that this was the only type of leadership freedom-loving patriots would accept and embrace.

December 29–31, 1776: Plymouth

Three days after Washington's first victory at Trenton, but before the news reached Massachusetts, Mercy Otis Warren received a very disturbing report. She wrote that night to James:

> The most deplorable accounts of the situation of our affairs have been confirmed this evening. "General Washington defeated—or what is worse forsaken by his army and on the point of quitting the service for want of support from his country. The Jerseys and its environs surrounded by the enemy, and the middle states in a temper only fit for slaves." It is a long time since I had any exalted opinion of the bulk of mankind, and history produces many instances of their forsaking their leaders on the approach of danger, but I have hoped for more virtue in Americans.

We might expect this report to throw a dedicated patriot like Mrs. Warren into a state of despair, but strangely, by her own account, the news triggered a very different response. Breaking into a hasty retreat, she first sought refuge in philosophy, then barricaded her feelings behind a wall of religious sentiment:

> Man is a strange being, and it has often been said that Woman is a still more unaccountable creature. I know not how it is, but notwithstanding

the present gloomy aspect of affairs, my spirits do not flag with regard to the great public pause. They rather rise on misfortune. I, somehow or other, feel as if all these things were for the best—as if good would come out of evil. We may be brought low, that our faith may not be in the wisdom of man but in the protecting Providence of God. . . . I suffer no desponding thoughts to dwell in my mind.

Two days later, on New Year's Eve, the earlier report was contradicted: far from being defeated, Washington had just triumphed at Trenton. This caused Warren's unpredictable emotions to take another strange turn: the news "has raised the sad countenances of our people as high as they were low on the late unfavorable accounts," she wrote to James, "but I own I rejoice with trembling." As always, Warren's Puritanical nature would not abide too much celebration.[57]

In truth, few American patriots dared to rejoice without some degree of trembling. Today, we celebrate "Washington's Crossing" without qualification, but at the time, there was no way of knowing whether a couple of victories in limited confrontations would have a lasting impact on the outcome of the war. All people could know for sure was that the Continental Army had not yet been defeated by the British or abandoned by Americans.

13

Home Rule—First Drafts

March–July 1777: Philadelphia and Vermont

The imminent threat of a British invasion in December of 1776 favored Thomas Young and the radicals in their continuing struggle with Robert Morris and the moderates for control of Pennsylvania. Now that they held the power, radicals could draw on a traditionally conservative argument: when "the drums beat to arms," people ought not "to blow up discord."[1]

In the aftermath of Washington's victories, however, moderates and conservatives resumed their attack on the new state constitution. Robert Morris, Pennsylvania's only moderate reelected to Congress in the February elections, found a few moments in his busy schedule to sign a petition favoring a special convention to overturn the radical constitution; Thomas Young, on the other hand, helped lead the constitution's defense. On March 18, with Charles Willson Peale (a budding portrait artist) in the chair and Thomas Young as secretary, a group calling itself the Whig Society opposed "a violent dissolution of the present bond of our society." Although threatened, the radical constitution prevailed.[2]

Even as he immersed himself in Pennsylvania's local struggle for power, Thomas Young, as always, looked outward to a wider arena. Since the Revolution was based on the notion of popular sovereignty, why couldn't other states, like Pennsylvania, adopt constitutions that placed the people themselves in direct control of their governments?

Young knew just the right place to extend his program of democratization.

Back in 1760, Young had filed for land in the northeastern corner of New York, but the New York monopolizers (as he called them) had invalidated his claim. Ten years later, his old buddy Ethan Allen had taken up land there as well, and this time, joining with others in similar circumstances, Allen was able to establish that possession is indeed nine points of the law (see chapter 4). Now, these folks from the New Hampshire Grants or New Connecticut, as it was variously called, were appealing to the Continental Congress for official recognition as a separate state. On April 7 and 8, Congress received their petition, along with entreaties from the New York Convention and the New York Council of Safety to deny the upstarts' request.

On April 11, Thomas Young weighed in on the matter with a remarkable broadside, which he addressed to "the Inhabitants of VERMONT, a Free and Independent State, bounding on the River Connecticut and Lake Champlain." This was the first known public use of the word "Vermont," which Young himself had just coined. By signifying the primary geographic feature of the area, the Green Mountains, Young captured the spirit of the place, and the name he conjured caught hold.[3]

Young opened his broadside with a large, bold heading: "IN CONGRESS, May 15, 1776," followed by the resolution of that date, passed almost a year earlier, that invited states to form new governments. Young was implying that the invitation applied to "Vermont" as well as to the thirteen original states, which of course it did not, and he proceeded to offer the most reassuring counsel:

I have taken the minds of several leading members in the honorable Continental Congress, and can assure you that you have nothing to do but . . . chuse members for a general convention, to meet at an early day, to chuse delegates for the General Congress, a Committee of Safety, and to form a Constitution for your state. . . . I will ensure your success at the risque of my reputation as a man of honor and common sense. Indeed they can by no means refuse you! You have as good a right to chuse how you will be governed, and by whom, as they had.

He then recommended that the people of Vermont model their new constitution upon that of Pennsylvania, "which, with a very little alteration, will, in my opinion, come as near perfection as any thing yet concerted by mankind."[4]

Young's broadside was well received by Ethan Allen and his allies, who followed his suggestions to a tee. At a convention on June 4 in the village of Windsor, Allen and company officially adopted the name Vermont for their state-to-be, and they called for a special constitutional convention a month later. There, they drafted a constitution based tightly on the Pennsylvania

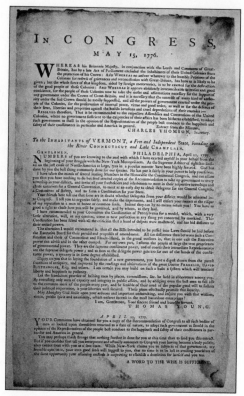

Figure 26. Thomas Young's audacious broadside was well received in "Vermont," but not in Congress. This would be Young's last political act.

model, and they went even farther down the radical path by abolishing slavery. (No other state had yet done so.) By opting for direct democracy, radicals in Vermont provided a clear contrast with the recently approved New York constitution, with its restricted franchise, an upper legislative body that represented property rather than people, a continuation of the landlords' estates, and a governor and council with power to veto legislation and even prorogue the legislature. Because the New York constitution promised to continue the power of the land barons, while that of Vermont empowered all citizens, local residents who had been sitting on the fence finally came to favor an independent state.

In the spring of 1777, Thomas Young was seeing the fulfillment of his life's work: independence declared, the new nation united in the war effort, a constitution in Pennsylvania that granted all power to the people, and a similar one in the works for the emerging state of Vermont. Working with his connections in Congress as well as his radical allies throughout the colonies, he believed he was pushing the Revolution upward to new heights.

Then, on June 24, 1777, while treating sick soldiers, Dr. Thomas Young suddenly died, a victim of one of the contagious diseases (we don't know which) running rampant through the army. In this he was not alone: many more American soldiers succumbed to disease during the American Revolution than died on the battlefield.

On June 25, the day after Young's death, Congress took up debate on the issue of Vermont's independence. Predictably, New York's delegates led the opposition: no way, they said, would they ever accede to Vermont's attempted secession. While the New England states, New York's traditional rivals, supported Vermont, they lacked New York's passion. For New York the matter was a deal breaker: if Vermont achieved official recognition, the last state to opt for independence might well become the first to abandon the new nation.

Congress bowed to New York's demands. As Samuel Adams reported to Richard Henry Lee on June 29, "Yesterday and the day before was wholly spent in passing resolutions to gratify N. Y . . . a matter which is not worth your while to have explained to you." Even though Adams, a personal friend, was no doubt one of "the leading members" of Congress referred to in Young's broadside, he was not willing to jeopardize national unity for the sake of Green Mountain secessionists.[5]

For New York's delegates to Congress, denying Vermont its independence would not suffice; they also sought a clear repudiation of Thomas Young and his infamous broadside. Only four days after Young's death, delegate James Duane reported to Robert R. Livingston (of "the assuming family of Livingston," in Young's words) that although some members wanted to let the matter rest out of "compassion" for the deceased's "distressed family," Duane and his fellow New Yorkers thought "it was of great consequence to us to have this wicked production censur'd and exposd, and this point was finally carried in our favour after a sharp conflict." The initial resolution read: "That the said printed paper, signed Thomas Young, is a false scandalous and malicious libel." Due to the efforts of Young's lukewarm friends in Congress, however, the final rebuke was just a bit less harsh:

That the contents of the said paragraphs [Young's broadside] are derogatory to the honour of Congress, and are a gross misrepresentation of the resolution of Congress therein referred to, and tend to deceive and mislead the people to whom they are addressed.[6]

The obituaries in the press were brief. One example: "Philadelphia, June 28. . . . Last Tuesday [June 24] died of a fever in the city, Doctor Thomas Young, one of the Senior Surgeons of the Military Hospital. He has left a sickly widow and six children wholly unprovided for." Not a word about Young's lifelong engagement in the Revolutionary struggle, always so controversial.[7]

Surely, Dr. Thomas Young deserved more notice than that. Despite a strident and abrasive style, Young had toiled endlessly to widen the scope of popular involvement in political affairs. As much as any other individual, he embodied the restless, raucous spirit of the body of the people. Working with both crowds and committees, he helped transform the Revolution from a dispute about taxes with Great Britain to a sweeping reevaluation of political relationships here in America.

But the current task at hand, the formation of viable institutions for self-governance, called for talents and sensitivities that Young seemed to lack: a civil tone, an ability to communicate with political opponents, and a taste for compromise and nuance, to name just a few. This is not to say that radicals had nothing to contribute: it was time for them to press for the institutionalization of true popular sovereignty within the new political order. But that job was not for Thomas Young. His former comrades, from Ethan Allen in Connecticut and Vermont to Samuel Adams in Boston to Thomas Paine, Timothy Matlack, and Charles Willson Peale in Philadelphia, along with other progressives who believed the revolution was as much about democracy as independence, would have to take up the torch.

1776–1780: The States

Like Pennsylvania, each of the other twelve states needed to develop a new constitution. None were starting from scratch. Under British rule, each colony had experienced at least partial self-rule, with citizens electing representatives to its lower house of the legislature, which held the power of the purse. But the lower houses had to contend with appointed governors, as well as with the governors' councils, which in most cases were selected and in all cases approved by the governor and/or the Crown. So colonial governments, reflecting Britain's House of Commons, House of Lords, and king or queen, contained democratic, aristocratic, and monarchical elements, functioning clumsily side by side. Now, with Britain out of the picture and monarchy discredited, Virginians and New Yorkers and citizens of all the other states, working separately, needed to settle on the proper balance of power within the new political orders.

As they prepared their new rules, all Americans who favored or at least accepted independence could agree on the basic concept of popular sovereignty: governmental authority stems from the people. But they disagreed on how broadly this principle should be interpreted and applied. Some, like Thomas Young, took the matter at face value: the exercise of power must always reflect the will of the body of the people. Others, generally men of means, believed the people themselves could become tyrants if not adequately checked. They wished their new governments to include various seats of authority, each one able to curb abuses by the others. "Property" (a polite abstraction signifying the owners of property) should be represented as well as the "people" in general.

In practical terms, this basic difference in philosophy played out in two ways.

First question: Should there be a single branch of government, directly beholden to the people, with the exclusive power to make laws and select officials to execute its policies? Or instead should there be two legislative branches, one representing people and the other property, as well as separate and distinct executive and judicial branches, each capable of exercising checks on the others?

Second question: Should the franchise extend to all citizens, regardless of personal wealth? Or instead should the right to vote be limited to those who possessed property, and if so, how much need a citizen own in order to grant him (not her) a stake in the government?

Thomas Young and the framers of the Pennsylvania constitution of 1776 favored the first options, as popularized in Thomas Paine's *Common Sense*. In reaction to Paine and the Pennsylvania radicals, John Adams published a pamphlet called *Thoughts on Government*, which argued for the latter alternatives. The first group advocated a thoroughly democratic government; the second, more of a republican form, with leaders drawn from the upper classes at the helm. The men who framed the various state governments were familiar with both ways of thinking, and the constitutions they created generally showed influences from each, with the second generally proving the dominant strain.

Witness the constitution of South Carolina, one of the most conservative. The temporary plan, approved in March of 1776, carried over the colonial restriction for the franchise (one hundred acres of land or its equivalent) and required assemblymen to own five hundred acres and ten slaves, or property worth £1,000. It also created an upper house of the legislature, to be selected by the lower house and thereby removed from the people, and a president, elected by the lower and upper houses and thereby even further removed from popular control. After independence, the legislature drafted a permanent constitution, which ensured that men like Henry Laurens would continue their hold on political power in South Carolina. The property requirement for assemblymen remained at £1,000, with even higher thresholds established for other officeholders: £2,000 for senators and a plantation worth £10,000 for the governor, extremely large amounts for the times. These wealthy individuals were empowered not only to make the laws, but also to appoint all other governmental officials. Even so, the new version included some democratic-leaning reforms: an end to the presidential veto power, direct elections for the upper house, cutting the property requirements for the franchise in half, and disestablishment of the Anglican Church.[8]

On the other hand, even the most radical constitution (Pennsylvania's) took care to check the power of a popular, unicameral legislature and the men it appointed to public office. A Council of Censors, elected every seven years, would investigate all possible violations of the constitution, then censure or even impeach any officeholders who had "assumed to themselves, or exercised other or greater powers than they are intitled to by the constitution." The censors could also call for a new convention to amend the constitution if it saw fit.[9]

The tension between democrats and republicans (as construed at the time) provided the political backdrop for all the new constitutions. Often, ideological differences were driven by class or regional conflicts. In Maryland, for instance, tenant farmers and small landholders from the western shore of the Chesapeake favored suffrage for all free males, annual elections for local officials and members of the legislature, and proportional taxation. Plantation owners on the eastern shore, worried that these people were trying to "introduce a leveling scheme," countered by proclaiming that "simple democracies" were "of all governments the worst." The propertied men who drafted the state's constitution suggested that senators be chosen by a special set of wealthy electors rather than by the people, and democrats could do no more than reduce the terms of senators from seven years to five.[10]

In Virginia, the first draft for the state constitution was prepared by George Mason, Washington's mentor in the field of political theory, who hoped to ensure that large plantation owners could resist any thrust from below. According to Mason, members of the lower house would have to possess estates worth at least £1,000 and those of the upper house £2,000 (as in South Carolina), while the latter would be selected by other wealthy "sub-electors" (as in Maryland). Upper-house members would stand for election every four years rather than annually, but this wasn't long enough for Thomas Jefferson, who thought at first they should serve for life, then modified his stance to nine years. When Mason's scheme came before the Virginia Convention, however, the full body of delegates removed his stringent property require-ments and his method of indirect selection for the upper house. But the con-vention did affirm his basic design for three independent branches of government, and the Virginia constitution, drafted and approved a few days before the Continental Congress declared independence, became a model for several other states.

George Mason voiced several themes common to the educated, propertied gentry who hoped to shape and control the new state governments. First, he affirmed that primary authority resided in the people, and this meant that all laws, particularly measures having to do with money, must originate in the lower house of the legislature. Next, he defined "the people" to exclude the underclasses (slaves and Indians) and the lower classes (freemen without property.) Women were also left out of the polity, as they were everywhere else but in New Jersey. Beyond that, he wanted wise rulers, taken from the ranks of the upper classes, to have sufficient power to check the will of the people, which he believed could be fickle, destabilizing, and destructive.

Finally, Mason insisted that the rights of citizens be protected against in-cursions by the government. In addition to the constitution itself, he prepared the first draft of Virginia's Declaration of Rights, and his list of protections still resonates today: freedom of the press, the free exercise of religion ("un-less, under colour of religion, any man disturb the peace, the happiness, or safety of society, or of individuals," Mason added), and a full list of protec-tions for the rights of the accused:

> That in all capital or criminal prosecutions, a man hath a right to de-mand the cause and nature of his accusation, to be confronted with the accusers or witnesses, to call for evidence in his favour, and to a speedy tryal by a jury of his [vicinity]; without whose unanimous consent, he can not be found guilty; nor can he be compelled to give evidence against himself.[11]

To these guarantees, the committee that reworked Mason's draft added an-other important protection: "That excessive bail ought not to be required, nor excessive fines imposed, nor cruel and unusual punishments inflicted."[12]

The full Virginia Convention accepted the work of Mason and the drafting committee, but it added one more sweeping check on governmental power:

> That a well-regulated militia, composed of the body of the people, trained to arms, is the proper, natural, and safe defence of a free state; that standing armies, in time of peace, should be avoided as dangerous to liberty; and that, in all cases, the military should be under strict subordination to, and governed by, the civil power.[13]

Mason himself did not think to include this, for he implicitly trusted the current commander in chief of the Continental Army, who happened to be his friend, neighbor, and collaborator. But others thought it best to place some safeguards in writing.

Virginia's Declaration of Rights had great historical impact. In June of 1776, Thomas Jefferson consulted Mason's draft of the Virginia Declaration as he penned his own first draft of the Declaration of Independence. Mason's "all men are born equally free and independent" became for Jefferson "all men are created equal," while Mason's cumbersome "enjoyment of life and liberty, with the means of acquiring and possessing property, and pursueing and obtaining happiness and safety" evolved into the more elegant "life, liberty, and the pursuit of happiness." (Both men, of course, were using the phrases of John Locke, repeated and refined by generations of European thinkers.) Shortly, four states placed passages from the preamble of the Virginia Declaration verbatim into their own constitutions, and finally, more than a decade later, Americans would use the Virginia Declaration of Rights as a model for their national Bill of Rights.

By March of 1778, all states had developed new codes of government except one: Massachusetts, the original hotbed of patriotism, which was still trying to get by with its rolled-over Charter of 1691, absent a royal governor. The problem there was that many radicals demanded that the new set of rules must stem from a special convention, with delegates elected by the people, rather from the existing legislature. Not until 1780 was a new state constitution, sanctioned by a constitutional convention, submitted to the towns for ratification.

The Massachusetts constitution of 1780 reflected the republican ideology of its primary author, John Adams. Power was neatly distributed among three separate branches rather than placed in the hands of a unicameral democratic legislature, as in Pennsylvania. Representation in the upper house of the legislature, the Senate, was apportioned according to property, not population. Officeholders would come from the middle and upper classes, with increasing property requirements for representative (£100), senator (£300), and governor (£1,000). Even requirements for the franchise were steeper than they had been before the Revolution. Ironically, with the passage of the new constitution, many of the soldiers hired to fight on behalf of the state lost the right to vote, while many more were rendered ineligible for public office.

Despite these restrictions, the Massachusetts constitution did promote certain democratic principles. All state officials were to be elected annually, while representatives to Congress, also elected annually, were subject to recall at any time. Further, at least on paper, citizens were granted final say in the ratification process: no provision would take effect without the approval of two-thirds of the people, as expressed in their town meetings. If a town objected to any part of the proposed constitution, it was encouraged to offer an amendment.

But there was a significant hitch to this progressive method of ratification. Short of calling for a second constitutional convention, which the first convention refused to do, there was no means for an amendment proposed by one town to be accepted or rejected by other towns or by the electorate as a whole. In effect, ratification turned into a take-it-or-leave-it affair. Although many towns objected to specific features and offered alternatives, and an exact tabulation of the returns on each item was never compiled, the convention declared the constitution ratified once two-thirds of the towns had voiced their general approval. Six years after they had first assumed political power, the people of Massachusetts started functioning under a government perceived to be of their own choosing.

July 21, 1775–November 15, 1777: The Nation's Capital

New state constitutions, although certainly necessary, would hardly suffice. Because the states could not stand alone, they had to stand together, and that meant they needed to provide form and substance to their hasty confederation. Here, they were more on their own, without precedents from their experiences within the British Empire. Unless they harked all the way back to ancient times, Euro-Americans in the mid-1770s could point to few actual examples of successful confederations among coequal states within their known world.[14]

So in their first stab at a national union, Americans were improvising. When members of Congress found themselves in the unenviable position of coordinating the wartime activities of thirteen disparate colonies, they had to act with no models to guide them. However much the learned delegates would have preferred to expound on philosophical principles, their agenda was determined instead by pressing necessities.

On July 21, 1775, Benjamin Franklin, who had tried unsuccessfully to fashion a confederation of colonies back in 1754, laid a scheme before Congress:

> That the power and duty of the Congress shall extend to the determining of war and peace, to sending and receiving ambassadors, and entering alliances, . . . the settling all disputes and differences between colony and colony about limits or other causes if such should arise; and the planting of new Colonies when proper. The Congress shall also make such general ordinances as tho' [thought] necessary to the general welfare . . . viz. those that may relate to our general commerce or general currency; to the establishment of posts; and the regulation of our common forces.[15]

But Congress immediately tabled the matter, for Franklin's plan for "a firm league of friendship" was much firmer than most colonists could yet handle. States with claims in the West were not about to cede them to Congress; southern states worried that a broad interpretation of "general welfare" might spell an end to slavery; small states could not accept representation according to population.

Early in 1776, as people started talking openly about independence, members of the Connecticut delegation came up with an alternate plan that denied Congress the power to settle the West, regulate commerce, or impose taxes on the states. This schema might create less resistance, but could it do the job? Would a weak confederation suffice?

Independence brought the issue of confederation to a head. On June 7, 1776, as part of his resolution to separate from Great Britain, Richard Henry Lee included two related proposals:

> That it is expedient forthwith to take the most effectual measures for forming alliances.
>
>   That a plan of confederation be prepared and transmitted to the respective colonies for their consideration and approbation.[16]

The time for definition had arrived, yet the process of arriving at that definition had just begun.

Five days later, Congress assigned one delegate from each colony (technically, the colonies would not turn into states for three more weeks) to a committee that would "prepare and digest the form of a confederation." That committee, in turn, assigned the task of preparing a first draft to Pennsylvania's John Dickinson, the famous Farmer, who had been dragging his feet on independence.[17]

Dickinson's draft, following Franklin's, favored a strong confederation with the power to determine western settlement and regulate commerce. It delineated a long list of Congress's "exclusive" powers in considerable detail, while suggesting some additional restraints on the states—most notably, an insistence that they not raise standing armies in times of peace. (The Connecticut plan, by contrast, had prohibited *Congress* from maintaining a standing army.) It even prohibited any state from seceding. But Dickinson did place one major constraint on Congress. Following the wishes of most of the local instructions favoring independence, he stipulated that Congress should never interfere with the "internal police" of any state.[18]

On July 22, the debates started, heated and even furious. Ironically, two of the major issues dealt with taxation and representation. Taxation *with* representation proved almost as problematic as taxation *without* representation.

Dickinson's draft, which had been slightly softened in committee, determined that the amount each state should contribute to the common treasury would be based on population, excluding Indians but including slaves. This infuriated the southern delegates, who maintained that slaves must legally be construed as property, not people; if slaves were subject to taxation, they argued, so should the oxen and horses that worked the land in the North. Six southern states voted to amend the Articles so that slaves would not be counted for purposes of taxation. (Eleven years later, in 1787, these same states would insist that slaves *should* be counted as people when determining representation in Congress.) But the seven northern states held firm, thereby defeating the amendment.

Meanwhile, delegates from the most populous states (Virginia, Pennsylvania, New York, and Massachusetts) complained just as loudly about Article XVII: "In determining questions in Congress, each colony shall have one vote." Wouldn't that give tiny Rhode Island or Delaware a disproportionate voice in determining the affairs of the nation? Was it really fair that the large states pay the bills, while the small states make the decisions?[19]

A third major item of contention: congressional control over westward expansion. States like Virginia, whose charters gave them access to land extending clear to the "South Sea" (Pacific Ocean), adamantly refused to cede their claims, and they managed to expunge the critical provisions that had given Congress the exclusive rights to purchase Indian lands, determine state boundaries (including western borders for states like Virginia), and dispose of all land outside those boundaries at its discretion. This infuriated states like Maryland, which had no claims in the West and was counting on Congress to open the land to everybody.

Passions ran high on these issues, too high for the comfort and security of the new nation. In the fall of 1776, after the military defeats in New York, and with British forces threatening the nation's capital, Congress decided to table the matter rather than risk alienating any portion of the still tenuous confederacy.

When Congress resumed its debates on the Articles of Confederation in May of 1777, the bickering states were just as obdurate as ever. Revolutionary fervor had come face-to-face with the understandable desire to protect particular interests, so once again Congress chose to avoid its most basic task: providing clear rules by which the new nation could govern itself.

But how long could Congress pretend to "govern" the United States of America based on sheer improvisation?

In the fall of 1777 two things happened to force the issue: France indicated that it was ready to form an alliance, and the continental currency had become almost worthless. France would ally itself only with a real nation, and the currency could not be salvaged without a real nation to back it.

Debates had to end. Controversial issues needed to be resolved, one way or the other. Everyone would not be pleased, but here's the final tally:

Each state, whether large or small, would receive only one vote.

Expenses would be proportioned according to the value of landed property, including improvements. This pleased the southern delegates, because slaves would not be taxed, and displeased the delegates from New England, where land was the most "improved." Although outvoted only five to four, with the other delegations split, the losers let it be.

The most enduring controversy centered on western lands. This was a deal breaker for Virginia, which wouldn't sign on if Congress usurped its claims. Disgruntled delegates from Maryland, defeated by Virginia's intransigence, finally allowed the Articles to be sent out for approval by the states, but that didn't mean their own state was ready to ratify them.

On November 15, 1777, Congress approved the Articles of Confederation,

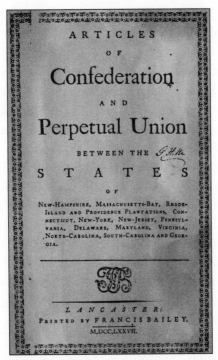

Figure 27. Title page of the first printed copy of the Articles of Confederation, 1777. The "perpetual union" would give way ten years later, when a convention in Philadelphia scrapped the original confederation. *(The Granger Collection, New York)*

subject of course to confirmation by the states. The final version had been weakened considerably from Dickinson's draft: no control of the West, no prohibition against secession, and, most significantly, a new article, placed at the very beginning, which alleviated fears that the states might be sacrificing too much: "Each state retains its sovereignty, freedom and independence, and every power, jurisdiction and right, which is not by this confederation expressly delegated to the United States, in Congress assembled." The states remained the basic sovereign units, and the Articles of Confederation would not take effect until ratified by all thirteen of them.[20]

That was a high threshold, particularly with some issues still so divisive. By the following summer, ten states had given their assent, but New Jersey, Delaware, and Maryland—all wanting Congress to take control of the West—still balked. In the meantime, the United States of America would remain under interim management.

1777: Philadelphia

George Washington stayed entirely clear of the divisive debates over the Articles of Confederation. Perhaps this was simply because he was too busy with military matters, or perhaps, as some biographers prefer to believe, this was due to his firm belief that "he who held the sword must not use its point as a pen." Most likely, he understood that Congress would take great offense if the head of the army became too free or forceful with his political opinions.[21]

Undoubtedly, Washington wanted the Continental Congress to possess enough power to keep its army in the field, but beyond that, we can only conjecture where his sympathies lay with respect to shaping the confederation. As a wealthy slave owner and land speculator from Virginia, he probably favored a restrictive franchise, taxation that excluded slaves, state ownership of the West, and representation according to population; these were certainly the positions advocated by Washington's friend, neighbor, and mentor in the field of political theory George Mason, as well as by Virginia's delegation in Congress. On the other hand, Washington, more than most, understood the value of centralized leadership.

Robert Morris knew very well where his sympathies lay, but like Washington he kept himself at arm's length from the debates in Congress, even though he himself was a member. This was clearly a matter of taste, not philosophy or even expediency. Morris simply preferred action over talk.

Much as Washington let George Mason defend their shared interests with the appropriate theories, Morris allowed his lawyer, James Wilson, to serve as his proxy in the political debates of the day. Wilson, who trained for the bar in Scotland, had lived through the recent turmoil in Pennsylvania; like Morris, he had resisted independence till July of 1776 and opposed the radical takeover of the state's government. Both Morris and Wilson realized that a strong central government could provide the best check on the democratic, egalitarian thrust of the Revolution.

Morris had a practical and compelling reason for favoring a strong government over a weak one: money.

The availability of currency had always presented a problem in colonial British America. With a negative balance of trade and no precious metals to mine, specie was in short supply. To make up for this, most trade was conducted simply on credit, with accounts settled only rarely, but even so, the colonies needed some currency, and all except Massachusetts figured out a way to issue paper money not pegged to specie. A colonial government would issue bills of credit, to be paid up with revenues from future taxes a few years later and then withdrawn from circulation. If more currency were then needed, new bills of credit would be issued.

When fighting broke out in the spring of 1775, the Continental Congress decided to follow the lead of colonial governments and issue its own currency to pay the expenses of war: $2 million in June, another million dollars in July, a total of $6 million by the end of 1775, and $25 million by the end of 1776. Rather than spend specie to feed, clothe, and arm the soldiers it kept in the field, Congress simply manufactured new money, which it used to pay off its private creditors. But how long could this continue without causing the new money to lose a hefty portion of its value?[22]

Not very long, Robert Morris thought. On December 20, 1776, six days before Washington's dramatic attack on Trenton, Morris wrote a lengthy letter to Silas Deane in France. After describing in vivid detail the sorry state of the army, Morris suddenly changed the subject: "I must add to this gloomy picture one circumstance more distressing than all the rest because it threatens instant and total ruin to the American cause unless some radical cure is aplied and that speedily. I mean the depreciation of the continental currency." Soon, he predicted, people would have so little faith in continental dollars that "force must be inevitably employed" to make people accept them as money. (In fact, at that very moment, with the British advancing toward Philadelphia, John Dickinson was advising his brother not to accept continental currency; this "defection," as Morris called it, caused the famous Farmer an immense loss of respect.)[23]

The surest way to avoid the imminent collapse of continental currency was to build faith in Congress, which had issued the bills of credit and would be expected to honor them. Strong Articles of Confederation were therefore a necessity, in Morris's view. A weak government that could not inspire absolute confidence would lose hold of its currency in short order.

Robert Morris had another good reason to favor a robust Congress. Like George Washington, he saw great commercial possibilities in the development of the American West, but unlike Washington, he did not happen to live in Virginia, which laid claim to a vast portion of the interior. Morris had several western schemes pending, including shares in various land companies (see chapter 1) and a controlling interest in a plantation on the Mississippi, on which he hoped to raise oranges with the labor of a hundred slaves. All of these projects required the approval of a government—but which one? If Congress controlled the West, Morris would be in a position to do as he pleased in the West. As with his business contracts, he might be able to play both ends of the game, granting land while simultaneously receiving it; even if he did not happen to serve on the committee that approved land grants, he was certain to have friends who did. But all this presupposed stronger Articles of Confederation than those finally approved by Congress.[24]

Finally, Morris had a simple personal interest in maximizing the authority of Congress. As a delegate, he worked alongside other prominent gentlemen, many with extensive business holdings that might serve his interests someday; in Pennsylvania politics, by contrast, he had to rub shoulders with upstart radicals of no social or economic standing. (In the wake of the new constitution, there was a 90 percent turnover in membership of the state Assembly.) If and when Congress returned to Philadelphia, Morris could dine at the City Tavern and drink Madeira wine (imported by his own firm, of course) with men he considered his equals. Simply as a matter of style, the choice was clear: he would rather that Congress govern, with the states clearly subordinate.

Congress did return to Philadelphia in March of 1777, so Robert Morris no longer had to run the show by himself. In April, resuming his private affairs, he started to invest freely, openly, and widely in privateering ("My scruples about privateering are all done away," he pronounced), and by June he was instructing one of his many agents to search for "good bargains" in "inland speculation which if well attended to will produce more certain and larger profits than any other branch." Robert Morris was back in business, and he found the return to his old lifestyle much to his liking—so much so, in fact, that in September he confided to a friend, "I now wish to be released from public business totally." Ideally, the Pennsylvania Assembly would terminate his appointment to Congress. That didn't happen, but Morris did ask for and receive a "leave of absence" from Congress.[25]

Just as Robert Morris was trying to wind down and bow out, Henry Laurens agreed to take a turn in Congress. Elected by the South Carolina Assembly on January 10, 1777, Laurens tried to "excuse" himself by saying he could not possibly attend till May at the earliest. But the Assembly said that would suffice, and Laurens acquiesced: "I call it therefore as I feel it, a command," he wrote to John. "I go."[26]

Laurens embarked for Philadelphia on June 7, took his seat on July 22, and two days later found himself embroiled in a debate. The Board of War had just suggested that American forces invade West Florida, an idea supported by Robert Morris, James Wilson, and probably a majority of the delegates. Laurens disapproved of the scheme. While others suggested that the expedition would be a cakewalk, Laurens knew that Indians in the area would make formidable enemies, particularly if allied with the British forces there. Bowing to Laurens's local wisdom, Congress scratched the plan. It also placed Laurens in charge of a special committee to oversee the defense of the lower South.[27]

In the next few months, Laurens would serve on more than a dozen other committees. Congress had found a new workhorse, much to the approval of many delegates. John Adams offered particular praise:

> They [South Carolina] have sent us a new delegate, whom I greatly admire, Mr. Lawrence, their Lt. Governor, a gentleman of great fortune, great abilities, modesty and integrity—and great experience too. If all the states would send us such men, it would be a pleasure to be here.[28]

But Laurens was less fond of Congress than it was of him. "Congress is not the respectable body which I expected to have found," he wrote on September 5. If Laurens had come to Philadelphia expecting calm deliberations among judicious and virtuous rulers, what he found instead was a boisterous clash of interests. Partisanship and provincialism were not limited to South Carolina politics.[29]

Could it be otherwise? Would better leadership make a difference?

In October, John Hancock resigned as president of Congress, a position he had held for almost two and a half years. Like his close friend Robert Morris, Hancock wanted to tend to his extensive interests in the private sector. According to Mary Morris, Robert's wife, her husband was offered the honor of becoming Hancock's successor. "Don't you feel quite important?" Mary wrote to her mother. "I assure you I do, and begin to be reconciled to independence." But Robert himself, however flattered, had little difficulty turning the position down, if in fact it had been truly offered to him, for he was trying to wind down his political activities, not crank them up.[30]

Henry Laurens, on the other hand, was still fresh, and his appointment to the highest civil office in the land was unanimous. John Adams, among others, thought an honorable Southerner who appeared to be above partisan politics was a wise choice. Laurens assumed the presidency of Congress on November 1, 1777, after only three months and a week as a delegate.

Two weeks later, President Laurens signed the final draft of the Articles of Confederation, which Congress hoped would shore up confidence in the struggling nation.

And the nation did need shoring. By the time Henry Laurens had ascended to the presidency, Congress was meeting in York, Pennsylvania, for Washington's army was again in retreat, and British forces under General William Howe had captured Philadelphia. The Pennsylvania State House, former home to Congress, was being used as a military hospital and a prison for American officers, while the State House Yard, at which the body of the people used to convene, was cluttered with camping Redcoats, three thousand miles from their homes across the Atlantic.[31]

The war continued, one campaign after the next, and the outcome remained in doubt. Only this much was clear: all the new rules, both state and federal, would come to naught if the Americans should lose.

14

In Victory and Defeat

February 8–October 17, 1777: Worcester, Bemis Heights, and Saratoga

When Timothy Bigelow returned to Worcester after six months of confinement in Quebec, his wife, Anna, was struggling to raise five children under the age of twelve. Unlike gentlemen soldiers, such as George Washington, Bigelow did not have a significant independent income, so he had been relying on his pay as an officer in the Continental Army to support his family. Now, if he wished to remain at home as a civilian, he would have to resume work as a blacksmith, winning back his customers from other men who had been fashioning metal for the people of Worcester in his absence. He would also have to accept defeat: he had gone off to war and lost.

This was not a viable option for a man recognized by his townsmen as their military leader. Timothy Bigelow had committed himself to the Revolution, for better or worse; unlike privates such as Joseph Plumb Martin, he was into it too deeply to simply walk away. So on February 8, 1777, when Bigelow was promoted to colonel and placed in charge of the Massachusetts Fifteenth Regiment of the Continental Army, he accepted his commission. To do otherwise, particularly after his courage had been questioned in Quebec, would have been unthinkable. The blacksmith had become a military man, and it was there he would make his mark.

As a colonel in charge of a regiment, Bigelow was expected to lead some six hundred American soldiers into battle—*if* he could find them. Many of the able young men from Worcester County had already seen military service during the siege of Boston in 1775 and the ill-fated defense of New York in 1776. They were tired, they had farms to tend at home, and like Joseph Plumb Martin, they had seen enough of "the soldier's life" to keep them "at home for the future."

This did not mean the men of Worcester had become unpatriotic. Having been on the vanguard of the Revolution from the outset, they, too, were committed to seeing the matter through, but not as professional soldiers. They preferred to hire others for that job, and although they already felt overtaxed by the war effort, both figuratively and literally, they agreed to offer a bounty of £20, over and above the state and Continental bounties, to any man willing to serve in the Continental Army under Worcester's banner. (By 1777, with the army shy of soldiers, Congress assigned quotas to the various states, and the states, in turn, allocated quotas to each town. Local citizens were then expected to come up with a specific number of soldiers, and also of blankets, shirts, and various provisions to support the troops.)[1]

Following the custom of the times, Timothy Bigelow had to oversee the recruitment and training of his regiment before leading them off to war. This took time. On April 8, the colonel ordered all recruiting officers to make their returns and send new soldiers to Worcester for training. Some came, but not enough, so recruiting continued through April, May, June, and July. Meanwhile, Bigelow resumed his participation in Worcester's political affairs. At four successive town meetings, from May 19 to July 21, he was elected to serve as moderator, an honor reserved for John Chandler in former times. At one of these, the town voted to pay Bigelow £11 5s "for his attendance on ye [Provincial] Congress in ye years of 1774 & 1775." A private in the army would now receive almost twice that amount, just for signing up.[2]

During the six months it took Colonel Bigelow to field his regiment, the British general John Burgoyne gained permission from London to launch a major assault from the north, down Lake Champlain to the Hudson River. Another British force, approaching from the west, would meet Burgoyne's army at Albany. If General Howe then marched his troops northward from New York City, the British would control the entire Lake Champlain–Hudson River corridor, severing New England from the rest of the colonies. This would bring the full force of the British Army within one hundred miles of Worcester.

Understanding the importance of the Champlain-Hudson corridor, Washington had stationed a significant portion of the Continental Army around the Hudson Highlands, Fort Ticonderoga, and Fort George. These would be outnumbered and probably overwhelmed, however, unless those weary patriots from the town of Worcester rose to arms once again, along with their neighbors from around Worcester County, from Hampshire and Berkshire Counties, and from eastern Massachusetts, too, as well as from New Hampshire, Connecticut, Rhode Island, upstate New York, and upstart Vermont. There were plenty of men capable of bearing arms, should they decide to do so. Even if these Yankees were hesitant to sign up for long stints in the Continental Army, they could still turn out as militiamen to defend their country on a case-by-case basis.

Burgoyne embarked from Canada on June 20 with a force of some five thousand Regulars, three thousand Hessian mercenaries, and one thousand female camp followers, who cooked, cleaned, hauled baggage, and serviced the sexual appetites of the soldiers. And these were not all. As he departed, Burgoyne issued a proclamation threatening to unleash thousands of Indians, who would spread their brand of terror across the land "under my direction." He hoped this would force submission; instead it aroused only anger, which could be easily transformed into resistance. Just as Lord Dunmore's promise to set slaves against their masters had made white Virginians more defiant than ever, so did the specter of Indian warfare heighten the resolve of Yankee patriots.[3]

Facing a threat that was proximate and immediate, Worcester patriots sprang to life once again. On July 21, with Timothy Bigelow presiding, the town meeting voted to procure "one hundred fire arms with bayonets for the use of the militia of this town." Six days later, a white woman named Jane McCrae was murdered and scalped, supposedly by Indians accompanying Burgoyne. News of the incident both heightened and hastened the mobilization of the militia companies across New England.[4]

Then on August 9, Horatio Gates assumed command of the Continental Army for the Northern Department. The previous commander, Philip Schuyler, was a Dutch patron from New York with little tolerance for the egalitarian bent of New England militiamen, but Gates, unlike both Schuyler and Gates's fellow Virginian George Washington, openly expressed admiration for the Yankee militias. The timing of Gates's appointment was perfect. If and when the militia units found their way to the battlefields, they would be welcomed and well utilized.

On August 16, at the edge of breakaway Vermont, the militias proved their worth. Burgoyne had dispatched several hundred Hessians and Tories eastward toward the Green Mountain area, in search of horses and cattle to transport and feed his tired army. There, near the village of Bennington, the raiding force encountered twice their number of New Hampshire militiamen under the command of renegade General John Stark, who had left the Continental Army after being passed over for a promotion. Stark's militiamen prevailed not once but twice, first over the original raiders, then, with the aid of additional militiamen from Vermont, over the reinforcements sent by Burgoyne. By the end of the day, Burgoyne's army had lost about nine hundred men, two hundred killed and seven hundred captured or missing.

When news arrived in Worcester of the British advance toward Bennington, 72 militiamen mustered and rushed forth, much as they had done on April 19, 1775, and September 2, 1774. Half of those who answered the call had been members of the American Political Society or had the same surnames as APS members. Worcester's original patriots were still on the job, but when they heard the battle was over, they returned home to await a further call. These men were not soldiers per se, marching about hither and yon in search of the enemy; they were farmers and artisans, willing to fight, but only when absolutely needed.[5]

Because of the increasingly militarized temper, Timothy Bigelow finally received enough recruits to fill his Continental regiment with full-time soldiers. He gathered and trained them in Worcester, intending to meet up with Gates as soon as possible. Before he did, however, Gates's army, which now included both Continentals and militiamen, faced off directly against Burgoyne's men, who had reached the upper Hudson River and were making their way toward Albany.

Heeding the advice of General Benedict Arnold, who had commanded Bigelow in the Quebec expedition, Gates decided to build fortifications on a bluff overlooking the Hudson called Bemis Heights, named after a man who operated a tavern along the road below. To continue southward, Burgoyne and his six thousand fighting men (the number had been reduced by the ardors of the journey and the defeat at Bennington) would have to make their way through the American forces, which had increased to about seven thousand men. On Friday, September 19, Burgoyne ordered troops to advance on Bemis Heights, but before they got there, American riflemen started sniping at them through the woods. One mile to the north of the fortifications, at a clearing on Freeman's Farm (Freeman was a Loyalist who had departed for Canada), the two armies faced off. By the end of the day, the British suffered almost six hundred casualties, the Americans about half that number, and nothing had changed. Americans retained their fortifications at Bemis Heights, while the British still controlled the area just to the north.

That's where the armies stood when Timothy Bigelow and the Massachusetts Fifteenth Regiment arrived on the scene two weeks later, on October 4. But the balance of power was tilting. While the British Army was getting smaller and wearier (General Howe never did dispatch his New York army to meet up with Burgoyne), the American forces increased daily. By October 7, they numbered about eleven thousand, twice the number of enemy soldiers fit to fight, and the usually somber mood of a military camp became rather festive. That morning Bigelow wrote to Stephen Salisbury, the leading merchant in Worcester, who lived across the street: "It is the happiest camp I ever was in." Bigelow's only complaint was that he was out of "brown sugar," which was apparently the occasion for his letter.[6]

Victory was in the air, and later that day it came. Burgoyne at that point had only two alternatives, neither very attractive. He could order a retreat to Canada, but because of the advancing season his soldiers might wind up freezing, starving, and eating their dogs. (This was the same time of year as Bigelow's disastrous Quebec expedition through the Maine woods.) Or he could push his soldiers on, although vastly outnumbered. He settled on the latter option, and it ended with predictable results: during the second Battle of Freeman's Farm, a hodgepodge American Army that included Timothy Bigelow's regiment of Continentals and thousands upon thousands of militiamen routed the British and Hessians handily.

On October 17, from nearby Saratoga, Bigelow reported to Salisbury: "We are now all around them and it is common to have thirty-five, or 50, deserters and prisoners come in for several days past. . . . Upon the whole I can hardly realize that the great Burgoyne is reduced to such a distressed situation as you may depend he is at present." All was well with the patriots, Bigelow wrote, except he still was awaiting his brown sugar.[7]

Burgoyne surrendered that same day, and over five thousand survivors of his expedition were taken prisoner. One Hessian officer offered a vivid description of the makeshift American Army, comprised mostly of militiamen, that had captured him: "Not a many of them was regularly equipped. Each one had on the clothes which he was accustomed to wear in the field, the tavern, the church, and in everyday life."[8]

When news of the victory reached Worcester, people there celebrated with thirteen discharges of the cannon stationed outside the meetinghouse, followed by the customary drinking and toasting. (By 1777 the number 13, signifying the states, had taken over from 45 and 92 as the "patriotic number" of choice.) Two weeks later, the huge train of fatigued prisoners straggled through Worcester on the way to the coast. When this motley parade reached Cambridge on November 7, Hannah Winthrop jotted down her impressions to Mercy Otis Warren:

> I never had the least idea that the Creation produced such a sordid set of creatures in human figure—poor, dirty, emaciated men, great numbers of women, who seemed to be the beasts of burthen, having a bushel basket on their back, by which they were bent double, the contents seemed to be pots and kettles, various sorts of furniture, children peeping thro' gridirons and other utensils, some very young infants who were born on the road, the women bare feet, cloathed in dirty rags, such effluvia filld the air while they were passing, had they not been smoking at the time, I should have been apprehensive of being contaminated by them.[9]

Any notions of British invincibility were forever shattered by the sight of Burgoyne's defeated army.

This was a victory of far greater proportions than Washington's raids on Hessian outposts in New Jersey the previous winter, and the consequences were truly international in scope. As soon as the news hit Europe, France agreed to form a commercial and military alliance with the United States. The same New England farmers who first overthrew British authority had now convinced one of the world's great powers that the American Revolution was a winnable affair.

August 9–November 15, 1777: Brandywine, Philadelphia, Germantown, and Fort Mifflin

On September 28, George Washington received a report that the Americans had prevailed at Freeman's Farm nine days earlier. This was not exactly the case, but even so, it gave cause for a great celebration: Washington ordered the ceremonial firing of thirteen cannons and gave a gill (four ounces) of rum to every soldier in his camp. Washington and his men, at that time, were in particular need of a morale booster. Two days earlier, General Charles Cornwallis had marched with a triumphant British Army through the streets of Philadelphia, cheered on by a crowd of loyalists and Quakers who thought peace and tranquillity had been restored in their city.[10]

Washington had not given up Philadelphia without a fight, and nobody in his army had fought more valiantly than a twenty-two-year-old newcomer from South Carolina, John Laurens.

A year earlier, upon reaching his majority, Henry Laurens's favorite son, without consulting his father, had decided to leave England, return to America, and join the Continental Army. He had two compelling reasons, either of which would have sufficed: he believed in the cause of liberty, and he believed that honor, particularly military honor, was a man's noblest ambition. In this he was not unlike his father, but John was young and impetuous, and that only raised the stakes.

There were complications, however. Before he left England, John Laurens happened to impregnate a young woman, the daughter of family friend. John of course behaved honorably by marrying the mother-to-be, but the circumstances of the marriage were perhaps not so honorable after all. The couple did it secretly, lest either father impose some sort of constraint on the matter. Then, with his wife, Martha, eight months along, John left England to become an American soldier, as previously planned. "Pity had obliged me to marry," he disclosed to his uncle James, but "the duty which I owe to my country" was of greater concern. One month later, baby Frances Eleanor was born. She would never meet her father.[11]

With a self-assurance passed on from his father, John Laurens became a soldier in a most unconventional style. Early in August of 1777, he traveled to George Washington's camp on the outskirts of Philadelphia and asked to be taken on as an aide to the commander in chief. Washington already had three excellent aides-de-camp, including the brilliant Alexander Hamilton, but he accepted young Laurens nonetheless, impressed perhaps by his personality, and most certainly by his fluency in French and his family ties. It would not hurt Washington's political standing to have the son of South Carolina's powerful representative in Congress at his side.

Henry Laurens, as a concerned father, was not too pleased with his son's career move. On August 9 he wrote to a friend:

> This morning Mr. John Laurens . . . joined Gen. Washington at head quarters near German Town as one of his family. . . . To tell you truly my sense of the matter—although I believe the young man will acquit himself well anywhere, yet I am persuaded he has made an indiscrete choice for his outset in life—His talents & his diligence would have enabled him to have been much more extensively & essentially useful to his country in a different line at the same time to have been the cement of mine & the builder of a new family.[12]

As much as Henry Laurens valued military honor, he preferred that the actual fighting, with all its perils, be left to other men's honorable sons. His precious and multitalented John, prone to rash and impulsive behavior, might wind up in trouble on the battlefield, Henry suspected. He had good cause for concern.

Four days after becoming a soldier, John reported back to his father from Washington's camp. All was well—the soldiers were exercising their military formations, eating well, and drinking, too—but this was not what he had come for. "We are all anxious to hear something that will give us employment of a different kind from that which we have at present," wrote the restless new recruit.[13]

John Laurens did not have to wait long to experience the thrill of battle. On August 25, General William Howe landed thirteen thousand British and Hessian troops from ships that had sailed up an inlet of the Chesapeake Bay, only fifty-five miles from Philadelphia. Washington determined to make his stand at Brandywine Creek, the halfway point to the nation's capital, and it was there, on September 11, that John Laurens not only tasted battle but devoured it. One private soldier described the fighting: "Cannons roaring muskets cracking drums beating bumbs flying all round. Men a dying woundeds horred grones which would greave the heardist of hearts to see such a dollful sight as this to see our fellow creators slain in such a manner." Through all this rode John Laurens, undeterred by the dangers. As the Marquis de Lafayette later reported to John's worried father: "It was not his fault that he was not killed or wounded. He did every thing that was necessary to procure one or t'other." John survived unscathed, but others were less fortunate: over one thousand American soldiers were either killed, wounded, or captured in the disastrous defeat that allowed the British to take Philadelphia.[14]

The next time, John Laurens was not so lucky. After marching into Philadelphia on September 26, British forces set up camp in nearby Germantown. Howe assumed Washington would not challenge him there, but he underestimated the audacity of his adversary. Spurred by the apparent success of the Northern Army, and perhaps envious of the accolades bestowed on its commanding officer, Horatio Gates, Washington decided to replicate the strategy that had worked the previous winter at Trenton: an all-night march and multipronged attack at daybreak. This time, however, both armies were much larger, and the impact of the surprise far less. Through the day on October 4, some twenty thousand men with guns fired away at each other, mostly but

Figure 28. George Washington's daring young aide-de-camp John Laurens, as portrayed by Charles Willson Peale, who copied his own 1780 drawing for this 1784 miniature. The Latin motto framing Laurens's image means, "It is a sweet and honorable thing to die for one's country."

not exclusively their enemies (confused by the fog and smoke of battle, General Adam Stephen ordered his men to attack the soldiers commanded by his colleague General Anthony Wayne), and when the day was done, once again, the Americans had been defeated, and more than a thousand soldiers killed, wounded, or captured. Among the wounded (not only once, but twice) was Henry Laurens's son.

As at Brandywine, John Laurens acted fearlessly in the Battle of Germantown. During the opening assault, a musket ball "went through the fleshy part of his right shoulder," according to a contemporary account. An hour later, his division came upon a large house, defended by over a hundred British soldiers. The injured Laurens and a comrade approached the house with the intent of setting it on fire. They failed and, as he withdrew, John received "a blow in his side from a spent ball."[15]

Henry's reactions were strong and mixed. When he first heard of the huge casualties, he feared of course that John was among them. Then he received a letter from John, who wanted to assure his father he was alive. Henry cried from joy when he saw the signature, but also from horror, for he knew his son would always be tempting fate this way. To John he expressed his relief and support:

> I congratulate with you my dear son, with my daughter with all our friends upon your happy escape. . . . If I were free . . . I would fly to assist as your nurse until you should be able to take the field once again. At this distance I can only help you with prayers & good wishes & thank you for the honour you have done me.

Even so, he could not help including a fatherly caveat: "Nor need I tell you that [it is] your duty to preserve your own health & strength [as much] as it is to destroy the enemy."[16]

To a friend, however, Henry articulated his feelings about John's bravado in a more forthright fashion:

> I still feel a resentment against him, although I judge it best to express it in the softest terms to himself, for the robberies he has committed. He has taken a husband & father from his young family, a guardian from his brother & sister, a son and friend from a dependent father—& I still look upon him as standing on the verge of eternity. Tomorrow I may again hear of his bravery sealed by his fall.[17]

*   *   *

Joseph Plumb Martin was a very different sort of soldier, and he came upon his service in a different way. In his hometown of Milford, as in Worcester, there were not enough volunteers to meet the quota, so the citizens devised an alternative mechanism for producing live bodies for the Continental Army. Martin described how this was done, and how he himself signed up for his second tour of duty, despite his earlier misgivings about "a soldier's life":

> The inhabitants of the town were about this time put into what were called squads. . . . Each of these squads were to furnish a man for the army, either by hiring or by sending one of their own number. . . . One of the above-mentioned squads, wanting to procure a man, . . . attacked me, front, rear and flank. I thought, as I must go, I might as well endeavor to get as much for my skin as I could.

Military manpower was placed on the open market, and Joseph Plumb Martin was in high demand. But to receive his onetime bounty, Martin had to sign up for "three years or during the war." (This ambiguous phrase would cause much consternation when the war extended beyond the time mentioned.) In retrospect, Martin felt the townsmen got the better end of the bargain: "They were now freed from any further trouble, at least for the present, and I had become the scapegoat for them."[18]

Joseph Plumb Martin was now a professional soldier, no longer just a part-time militiaman. This would be his life for the foreseeable future.

Once enlisted, Martin was inoculated for smallpox and assigned to the Hudson Highlands, where he helped guard the river corridor during the summer of 1777. That fall he was sent south to help George Washington defend Philadelphia. He arrived too late for the Battle of Brandywine and just missed Germantown, but had he been at either one, he likely would not have experienced the exhilaration felt by John Laurens. For Private Joseph Plumb Martin, war was more about survival than honor.

But Martin and other privates sent into harm's way did not possess much control over whether they survived or not. Witness Martin's experience at Fort Mifflin, which, along with Fort Mercer, guarded the Delaware River a few miles downstream from Philadelphia. Once the British had taken the city, these two forts assumed great strategic significance, for as long as they remained under American control, British ships could not sail up the river to supply the occupying army. Hoping to dislodge the Americans from their last bastions in the region, British artillerymen unleashed a continuous barrage of projectiles from the best warships in the world upon a sixteen-year-old lad from Connecticut and others who shared his assignment. Martin described the bombardment in graphic detail:

> During the whole night, at intervals of a quarter or half an hour, the enemy would let off all their pieces. . . . I was in this place a fortnight and can say in sincerity that I never lay down to sleep a minute in all that time. . . . The cannonade was severe, as well it might be, six sixty-four-gun ships, a thirty-six-gun frigate, a twenty-four-gun ship, a galley and a sloop of six guns, together with six batteries of six guns each and a bomb battery of three mortars, all playing at once upon our poor little fort, if fort it might be called.
>
> The enemy's shot cut us up. I saw five artillerists belonging to one gun cut down by a single shot, and I saw men who were stooping to be pro-

tected by the works, but not stooping low enough, split like fish to be broiled. . . . When the firing had in some measure subsided and I could look about me, I found the fort exhibited a picture of desolation. The whole area of the fort was as completely ploughed as a field. The buildings of every kind hanging in broken fragments, and the guns all dismounted, and how many of the garrison sent to the world of spirits, I knew not. If ever destruction was complete, it was here.[19]

Was there room for honor amid a scene such as this? Perhaps, but it was best not to display too much of it. Joseph Plumb Martin saw all too clearly what could have happened to him had he more resembled John Laurens:

In the height of the cannonade it was desirable to hoist a signal flag for some of our galleys that were lying above us to come down to our assistance. The officers inquired who would undertake it. As none appeared willing for some time, I was about to offer my services. . . . While I was still hesitating, a sergeant of the artillery offered himself. He accordingly ascended to the round top [and] pulled down the flag to affix the signal flag to the halyard. . . . The sergeant then came down and had not gone half a rod from the foot of the staff when he was cut in two by a cannon shot. This caused me some serious reflections at the time. He was killed! Had I been at the same business I might have been killed, but it might have been otherwise ordered by Divine Providence, we might have both lived. I am not predestinarian enough to determine it.[20]

After weathering two weeks of intermittent fire, followed by six days of round-the-clock bombardment, Private Martin and his commanding officers had had enough. On the night of November 15, they abandoned Fort Mifflin, but even that was fraught with peril. Martin and some others were left behind to set the remaining structures ablaze, and by the light of their flames British artillerymen were able to take some final deadly shots.

Joseph Plumb Martin survived, but he was shaken to the core. The defense of Fort Mifflin was "as hard and fatiguing job, for the time it lasted, as occurred during the Revolutionary War," he wrote in his narrative, "but there has been but little notice taken of it." Why? Martin had a simple answer, one that resonates today:

There was no Washington, Putnam, or Wayne there. Had there been, the affair would have been extolled to the skies. No, it was only a few

Figure 29. This contemporary image depicts the British reign of fire on Fort Mifflin and Private Joseph Plumb Martin. *(The Granger Collection, New York)*

officers and soldiers who accomplished it in some remote quarter of the army. Such circumstances and such troops generally get but little notice taken of them, do what they will. Great men get great praise; little men, nothing.[21]

Joseph Plumb Martin, a "little man" par excellence, received no special commendation for trying to defend the waterway to Philadelphia. Less than a week after he left Fort Mifflin, on November 21, he celebrated his seventeenth birthday by eating nothing and sleeping under the cold and drippy autumn sky. Four weeks later, because President Henry Laurens and the Continental Congress had declared December 18 to be a day of "general thanksgiving" for the "most signal success" of the army, Martin fared somewhat better: "*half* a *gill* of rice and a *table spoon full* of vinegar." After this thanksgiving feast, he was ordered to attend a sermon, where a preacher admonished the soldiers, "Do violence to no man." It is easy to see how Private Martin developed the ironic tone that infused his narrative of life in the Continental Army, and we can also imagine the deeper meaning of Martin's irony. More than mere entertainment, it served as a useful stratagem for personal survival, diffusing both his horror and his anger without negating either.[22]

December 19, 1777–June 19, 1778: Valley Forge

When Joseph Plumb Martin and the first wave of Continental soldiers hobbled into the army's winter quarters at Valley Forge the day after their thanksgiving feast, they were a sorry lot. "The army was now not only starved but naked," Martin recalled. "The greatest part were not only shirtless and barefoot, but destitute of all other clothing, especially blankets." Shoeless soldiers "might be tracked by their blood on the rough frozen ground," he added.[23]

The commander in chief had selected this site along the Schuylkill River, a mere twenty miles from Philadelphia, so he could keep a watchful eye on the British Army and harass it when appropriate. He did not have to wait long for an opportunity. Only three days after the army's arrival at Valley Forge, he received intelligence that a large party of British soldiers left Philadelphia on a foraging expedition. This party was vulnerable to attack, he reasoned, so he ordered his troops in readiness. But then: "When behold! to my great mortification, I was not only informed, but convinced, that the men were unable to stir on account of provision." This is how he reported the matter to Henry Laurens, president of Congress. Worse yet, the General was then told that "a dangerous mutiny" had broken out the previous evening among the hungry troops.[24]

Immediately, Washington queried his Commissary Department: how much food was on hand? "Not a single hoof of any kind to slaughter, and not more than 25 barrels of flour" for the entire army, came the response. And no more expected in the near future. Washington's new aide-de-camp, John Laurens, also reported the incident to the president of Congress: "I could weep tears of blood when I say it," he wrote to his father. "The want of provisions render'd it impossible for us to march."[25]

If the commissary supplied no food, if Congress supplied no food, if the states supplied no food, there was but one way the soldiers could be fed.

Joseph Plumb Martin reacted with "disgust" when called to duty on an empty stomach, having received no rations for days. But he showed up nonetheless, as required, and then learned that his assignment would not be so disagreeable after all. "We [eighteen privates and three officers] understood that our destiny was to go into the country on a foraging expedition, which was nothing more nor less than to procure provisions from the inhabitants for the men in the army ... at the point of the bayonet." General Washington had always insisted that his troops behave themselves around the civilian population, and never steal or plunder. But now, what else could he do? He not only authorized but commanded companies of soldiers, composed of men like Private Martin, to fan out across the nearby countryside and strip it clean. He called this "foraging," not "pillaging" or "plundering," but Martin, closer to the real operations, was not so polite. He insisted on the cruder term, "for I could not, while in the very act of taking their cattle, hay, corn and grain from them against their wills, consider it a whit better than plundering." Joseph Plumb Martin, unlike most privates, grew fatter, not thinner, during the winter at Valley Forge.[26]

Eventually, the soldiers did get some food, even if by devious means. But what would eleven thousand men do for shelter in the cold northeastern winter?

They had to build their own. Although weakened by hunger during their first few weeks at Valley Forge, the soldiers cut trees from nearby forests, grooved the logs (they had no nails), piled them on top of each other, suspended other logs on top of those, and filled in the cracks with mud and leaves. Inside, with branches from the trees, they constructed bunk beds, where weary men could sleep three high, and a hearth, where they might cook their scanty rations. In a short time a city was born, row upon row of these primitive cabins, each sheltering twelve men.

Clothes, shoes, and blankets proved more problematic, for these could neither be fashioned from local materials nor readily snatched from local residents. The Quartermaster's Department was in a shambles (there was no quartermaster general through most of the winter); the priority for the clothier general was uniforms for battle, not practical items to trap bodily heat; foreign orders for blankets never arrived. This left officers more or less on their own to come up with clothing for their men. Colonel Timothy Bigelow, for instance, had to write the folks back home and dispatch a messenger to Boston "for the purpose of procuring clothing for my regiment."[27]

Bigelow and his Massachusetts Fifteenth had journeyed south from Saratoga in late November, too late to join the battles around Philadelphia, but in time to wait out the winter with the rest of the main army. The chief business of the men in Bigelow's regiment, in the absence of a concerted campaign, was simply to survive, but rather than remain idle, they used the time to drill.

This is where Colonel Bigelow excelled; indeed, back in Massachusetts, he had been regarded as an expert in the matter. But the colonel was not in Massachusetts anymore, and beyond his own regiment, he exerted no further influence. George Washington wanted his whole army to train under the same drillmaster, and he chose not some blacksmith from Worcester but a seasoned European professional named Friedrich Wilhelm Augustus, Baron von Steuben. Historically, this Prussian veteran has received exclusive credit for whipping the Continentals into shape, even though Bigelow had been drilling his Fifteenth vigorously for half a year, and some of his men intermittently since the fall of 1774. Other officers had also drilled their men well, and, militarily speaking, the Continental soldiers at Valley Forge were not nearly so green as they have been portrayed. By the winter of 1777–78, most had been seasoned in battle, where they had performed well. (In their losses, they had been outnumbered or outmaneuvered, but not outfought.) True, they became more polished as soldiers at Valley Forge, but this was as much from a sense of group identification—they viewed themselves increasingly as professional military men, a class apart from civilians—as from repeated parading and mock firing.

John Laurens, as much as any other, came to see himself exclusively in a military role. While his new and close friend Alexander Hamilton immersed himself in the study of political economy, Laurens devoured every book on military matters he could find. (A French officer who served at Valley Forge informed Henry Laurens that he had sent away for "ten books for your mad and rash fellow John Laurens.") He also wanted to dress himself in the most stylish military attire, so "that I may not disgrace the relation in which I stand to the President of Congress, and the Commander in Chief of the armies of the United States, by an unworthy appearance." To his father, he issued a detailed shopping list for the items he would need to present himself well: "blue and buff cloth, linding, twist, yellow flat double gilt buttons sufficient to make me a uniform suit will be wanted, besides corded dimitty for waistcoats and breeches against the opening of a campaign, and I must beg the favor of you to write to some friend in South Carolina to procure me these articles—a pair of gold epaulettes and a saddle cloth may be added if not too expensive." Henry, of course, was expected not only to obtain these items, but to pay for them as well.[28]

John's fixation on military matters caused Henry to wonder how far his son was willing to take his passion. To which John responded: "You ask me, my dear father, what bounds I have set to my desire of serving my country in the military line—I answer glorious death, or the triumph of the cause in which I am engaged."[29]

Previously, such an audacious reply would have frightened Henry, but something had changed. Writing to a friend, he confessed that John "has forsaken father & wife & child, houses & beds & all for the sake of his country & the cause which possesses his whole heart," but although Henry himself was one of those forsaken, he went on to praise his son for his purity and passion, and to proclaim that more men like John Laurens "must come forth from every corner of our union to save us." Henry Laurens was now proud of his son. Perhaps he had simply given up on trying to alter John's reckless behavior, or perhaps, vicariously through his son, he was living out his own military dreams. Certainly, Henry was pleased that John was making something of himself. He addressed his son as colonel, until John reminded his proud father that officially he was only lieutenant colonel. Even so, not every man's son could become a trusted aide to the commander in chief, a member of his inner circle.[30]

George Washington, for his part, gained much by having John Laurens by his side during the winter of Valley Forge. Laurens penned many of Washington's letters and translated his correspondence, both written and oral, with French allies. (Many French officers, perhaps too many, were announcing themselves in camp, ready to serve the American cause.) Beyond that, Laurens was precisely the sort of officer that Washington coveted: well bred, highly literate, daring and honorable, and above all, supremely devoted, both to the cause and to Washington personally. And he just happened to be the son of the president of Congress.

John Laurens, with his loyalty and connections, had joined the Washington "family" (as the General himself referred to his top aides) at a critical moment. When people made the comparison between Washington's recent record on the battlefield and that of Horatio Gates, who presided over Burgoyne's surrender at Saratoga, the commander in chief did not come out on top. Was it time to replace him? Wouldn't new leadership, perhaps in the person of General Gates, freshen up the Continental Army?

Many wondered, and a few acted on this premise. On January 14, Henry Laurens sent to John a spurious letter that had been published in a Philadelphia newspaper, supposedly from George to Martha Washington, which cast doubts on Washington's commitment. Two weeks later, Laurens sent to Washington a provocative paper that had been dropped on the steps of Congress; the document listed forty-five (the original patriotic number) ways in which Washington was leading the army and the nation astray, culminating with: "That the people of America have been guilty of idolatry by making a man their god."[31]

Although discontent was widespread, one man in particular became identified with the drive to oust Washington: General Thomas Conway, an Irishman with twenty years of experience as an officer in the French Army. The previous spring, Conway had showed up in America with a letter of introduction from Silas Deane, who was still in France trying to obtain aid for the war effort. After distinguishing himself in battle at Germantown, Conway successfully lobbied Congress for an appointment as inspector general, and then proceeded to lobby against his commander in chief. In Congress, Conway's anti-Washington sentiments were espoused by Thomas Mifflin (the popular general from Pennsylvania, after whom Fort Mifflin was named) and several others who thought the increasing adulation of the commander in chief was not healthy for the emerging republic. Outside Congress, Horatio Gates himself was fueling the notion that Washington was not up to the job. Historically, the push to replace Washington has been labeled the Conway Cabal, although that suggests a level of coordination that perhaps was lacking, and Conway himself was certainly not the most influential member of the opposition.

Lines were drawn. Washington had the support of his devoted "family," including John Laurens, Alexander Hamilton, and Gilbert du Motier, Marquis de Lafayette, a charismatic French officer who had joined Washington's inner circle, as well as Nathanael Greene and most others in his branch of the army. Opposed (in varying degrees) were Mifflin and Gates, both of whom had been appointed by Congress to the Board of War to check Washington's power, and congressmen ranging from the conservative James Duane of New York to radicals like James Lovell of Massachusetts and Richard Henry Lee. Washington's most influential supporter in Congress was the president, John Laurens's father, who regarded the General as a "great & virtuous man."

Washington's first response to the discontent was to ignore it. This was no time for divisiveness, he felt, and he did not wish to fuel the discord with a strident defense. Then he changed his mind. He decided to confront Conway's accusation that he was a "weak general," and when Conway tried to back down, the clumsy retreat strengthened Washington's hand. By making public the challenge to his command, Washington caused his antagonists to disavow any intent to replace him. The opposition simply vanished, and Henry Laurens engineered a reconciliation between Washington and Gates.[32]

The commander in chief had weathered the storm. His leadership secure, he emerged from Valley Forge with renewed confidence. This was his war to win or lose.

Joseph Plumb Martin, Timothy Bigelow, and several thousand other men of the Continental Army weathered the storm as well. Their challenges were different from those of Washington and Laurens, but by spring most had fulfilled their mission at Valley Forge: to eat, stay warm, overcome disease, and think and act as soldiers.

When it broke camp on June 19, America's standing, professional army was healthy, intact, and ready to face off against the main force of the British Army in North America. But the Continentals were not as numerous as they might have been. During the winter, approximately two thousand had perished, mostly from disease, and over one thousand others had deserted. It was as deadly a time as any during the Revolutionary War, even though there were no major battles.[33]

June 28 and August 8–29, 1778: Monmouth and Newport

On June 18, the British occupying force, now led by General Henry Clinton, pulled out of Philadelphia and headed north toward the main army in New York. British strategists did not feel they had sufficient force to tackle the Pennsylvania interior, and they preferred to concentrate their resources.

Should the Americans try to head them off? Washington conferred with his officers, who expressed conflicting opinions. General Charles Lee, recently released from British captivity, was quick to offer advice, just as he had in New York, and once again, he struck a cautionary chord. Why risk an all-out confrontation, winner take all, between armies of approximately equal strength, he reasoned, when French support was on its way? John Laurens and a few others, on the other hand, wished to pursue and attack. Frustrated by the downtime at Valley Forge, the twenty-three-year-old lieutenant colonel was itching to fight. Americans should harass the British on their flanks, he argued, "and some opening may be given for such a stroke as would ruin Mr. Clinton's Army." Privately to his father, John admitted that his stance emanated from "a man of more zeal than judgment."[34]

After much discussion and repeated votes, Washington and his council opted to harass the British as they proceeded northward through New Jersey, with General Lee leading an advance force and General Washington and the main body bringing up the rear.

As Clinton's troops approached Monmouth, most of the way toward their safe haven in New York, Washington decided to make a concerted move. It was now or never, he felt. On the morning of June 28, after dispatching John Laurens and Baron von Steuben to reconnoiter, he ordered Lee, who was just east of Monmouth, to engage the rear guard of the British line, while he pulled up his own force to join the fray.

It was neither the place nor the time to attack.

Colonel Timothy Bigelow, who was in Lee's advance force, found that out the hard way. Attacking from the flanks, as he was ordered to do, Bigelow had to lead his men across several gullies while the British remained on the road. All the drilling on the parade grounds at Valley Forge was of no help as Bigelow's men scrambled across the broken terrain. The gullies hampered communications, and the American fighting units lost touch with each other. When Clinton turned around with his main force, he and his men had little difficulty repulsing the American advance. This is precisely what General Lee had hoped to avoid—a hasty, ill-conceived attack on unfamiliar ground, which placed the army at risk—yet here he was, in charge of just such an endeavor. Lee decided to retreat.

Joseph Plumb Martin was in the second wave of General Lee's forces, and just as he approached the action, he was told to retreat. "Grating as this order was to our feelings," he reported, "we were obliged to comply."[35]

As Washington pulled forward, the commander in chief encountered Lee's retreating men and broke into a rage, just as he had in midtown Manhattan during the battle of New York. Martin recalled Washington's response:

> In a few minutes the Commander in Chief and suite crossed the road just where we were sitting. I heard him ask our officers "by whose order the troops were retreating," and being answered, "by General Lee's," he said something, but as he was moving forward all the time this was passing, he was too far off for me to hear it distinctly. Those that were nearer to him said his words were "d—n him." Whether he did thus express himself or not I do not know. It was certainly very unlike him, but he seemed at the instant to be in a great passion; his looks if not his words seemed to indicate as much.[36]

As at New York, Washington ordered the retreating soldiers to turn around and stand their ground, and that was where the true battle began. Through the afternoon, privates like Martin fired away at their counterparts on the other side, while artillerymen from both sides launched missiles in the gen-

Figure 30. Commander in chief George Washington, seasoned by war. Compare this portrait, painted by Charles Willson Peale in 1779, with Peale's earlier depiction of Washington in 1772 (see page 200). *(The Granger Collection, New York)*

eral direction of their opponents. There were charges and countercharges, flanking moves and withdrawals. Through the mayhem, three things impressed upon Martin vivid images, which he recounted years later.

First, the blistering sun and overbearing heat. "It was almost impossible to breathe," he reported. "The mouth of a heated oven seemed to me but a trifle hotter" than the plowed fields the soldiers traversed on the outskirts of Monmouth. "None can realize it that did not feel it. Fighting is hot work in cool weather, how much more so in such weather as it was on the twenty-eighth of June, 1778."[37]

Next, the unique story of one particular woman, a so-called camp follower on the American side:

> A woman whose husband belonged to the Artillery, and who was then attached to a piece in the engagement, attended with her husband at the piece the whole time; while in the act of reaching a cartridge and having one of her feet as far before the other as she could step, a cannon shot from the enemy passed directly between her legs without doing any

other damage than carrying away all the lower part of her petticoat,—looking at it with apparent unconcern, she observed, that it was lucky it did not pass a little higher, for in that case it might have carried away something else, and ended her and her occupation.

This account, through the years, contributed to the creation of a mythic American heroine, Molly Pitcher.[38]

Finally, Martin recalled his own ambivalence about the very nature of his task:

When within about five rods (less than thirty yards) of the rear and retreating foe, . . . I singled out a man and took my aim directly between his shoulders. . . . He was a good mark, being a broad-shouldered fellow. What became of him I know not; the fire and smoke hid him from my sight. One thing I know, that is, I took as deliberate aim at him as ever I did at any game in my life. But after all, I hope I did not kill him, although I intended to at the time.[39]

For this seventeen-year-old farmboy-turned-soldier, killing had assumed a human face. He was far tougher than he had been when entering military service at fifteen; at Monmouth, for instance, he reported watching coolly as men's limbs were being amputated. But he was also beginning to comprehend the tragedy of war: young men die, some by his own gun. True, it was not until years later that he wished his aim had been bad, but the fact that the visual image played upon his mind reveals an emerging understanding of his ugly business.

At the end of the day, after furious fighting, nothing had changed. That night, Clinton and some ten thousand soldiers broke away quietly and continued toward New York. Washington and his surviving crew, only slightly more numerous, were in no shape to follow. American casualties were steep: 69 killed in battle, another 37 killed by the heat, 161 wounded, and 95 missing; British casualties were similar. Objectively, the Battle of Monmouth was a stalemate, but tactically the Americans lost, for they had tried and failed to trap and capture another large portion of the British Army in North America.

After the battle, John Laurens related the particulars to his father, along with his particular slant. "All this disgraceful retreating passed without the firing of a musket over ground which might have been disputed inch by inch," he complained, and he conjectured that if Lee had not fallen back, the day would have been theirs: "It is evident to me that Mr. Clinton's whole flying army would have fallen into our hands, but for a defect of abilities or good will in the commanding officer of our advanced corps. His precipitate retreat spread a baneful influence every where." This assessment is highly suspect: the armies were equally matched in terms of manpower, health, weaponry, and training, while neither side held a distinct advantage due to positioning or fortifications. Even so, John Laurens was not satisfied with a stalemate, and he found it expedient to blame the outcome on Charles Lee, his mentor's chief rival within the army. "Genl Lee I think must be tried for misconduct," he concluded.[40]

Two weeks after the Battle of Monmouth, George Washington dispatched a French-speaking member of his "family," John Laurens, to meet with Comte D'Estaing, who had just arrived off the coast of New Jersey with sixteen men-of-war under his command. With the help of the French navy, Washington could now challenge one or more of the British-held enclaves by the sea. His first choice was to go after New York City by both land and sea, but Laurens soon returned with a disappointing message from D'Estaing: the French ships of the line, laden with men and cannons, were too large to attack the British vessels anchored in harbor. So Washington and D'Estaing, with Laurens as the go-between, settled on attacking Newport, the haven held by the British for the previous two years. Because Washington had to remain with the main army around New York, he dispatched John Laurens to Rhode Island to handle the sensitive communications between D'Estaing and the commander of the American forces there, General John Sullivan.

It was a difficult task. Sullivan assumed he would be directing the entire affair, but D'Estaing refused to play a subservient role. D'Estaing wanted to attack as soon as he arrived on July 29, but Sullivan insisted he had to wait till he received more help from local militias and a contingent of the Continental Army, commanded by the Marquis de Lafayette. D'Estaing was forced to wait.

During the first two weeks of August, militiamen poured into Sullivan's camp daily, over five thousand, boosting the total American force to more than ten thousand. On board the French vessels, meanwhile, were another four thousand fighting men.

With Laurens's assistance, D'Estaing and Sullivan settled on August 10 as the day for a massive assault. But on August 9, after learning the British had withdrawn from his route of entry, Sullivan ordered his men to strike.

D'Estaing and his officers, as a point of national pride, objected furiously. "They conceived their troops injured by our landing first," John Laurens reported to his father, "and talked like women disputing precedence in a country dance, instead of men engaged in pursuing the common interest of two great nations."[41]

Just then, before D'Estaing could join the attack, a large British fleet under Admiral Lord Richard Howe sailed into view, and D'Estaing reacted by redirecting his course: he would have to take on the British navy first. The two fleets sailed out to sea to do battle, leaving Sullivan and his American forces on their own to tackle Newport.

To further complicate the matter, a drenching storm raced in the following night, making it impossible for soldiers to fire their arms. This same storm, as it turned out, battered both fleets at sea so badly that the anticipated showdown between rival naval powers never occurred.

On August 14, led by small contingent under John Laurens, the Americans forayed toward Newport, but they lacked the power to overwhelm the enemy. Instead, they started to lay siege.

On August 20, the French fleet reappeared, but D'Estaing announced he was leaving immediately for Boston to repair his ships before entering any battles. Sullivan dispatched Laurens to protest, but to no avail.

When the French fleet sailed off for the second time, the American militiamen began to drift away. Sullivan's force dwindled considerably; meanwhile, Washington sent word that British reinforcements were headed toward Newport, which meant that the Americans suddenly had to assume a defensive posture. Sullivan's army broke camp on August 28, and the next day British soldiers ventured out of Newport to give chase. John Laurens and a small detachment tried to slow up their advance, firing from behind trees at the lead contingent of Hessian soldiers, but they eventually had to cede the field. Later that day, the same Hessians charged twice with their bayonets at the right flank of the Americans, only to be repulsed by former slaves who had joined the black First Rhode Island Regiment of the Continental Line. John Laurens was impressed with the performance of the black soldiers, and General Nathanael Greene, whom Washington had dispatched to help Sullivan, was impressed with the fighting ability of John Laurens. "It's not in my power to do justice to Col. Laurens who acted both the general and the partizan," he reported to the commander in chief. "His command of regular troops was small but he did every thing possible to be done by their numbers."[42]

The east wing of the American defense was assigned to John Glover's brigade, which included Colonel Timothy Bigelow and the Massachusetts Fif-teenth. (In Bigelow's regiment, whites and blacks fought side by side.) Bigelow and his men also held firm, as did the rest of the American line. By the end of the day, the British had retreated to their stronghold in Newport.

As at Monmouth, the Battle of Rhode Island was technically a draw, for casualties were approximately even and no positions had changed. Strategi-cally, however, the Americans had suffered another setback: they had failed to dislodge or capture British forces they thought were vulnerable.

By the end of 1778, the broad parameters of the Revolutionary War had become clear to all. On the one hand, British forces were unlikely to conquer the American hinterlands, where tens of thousands of militiamen could mo-bilize on the instant to oppose them. On the other hand, American forces could not dislodge the British from their coastal enclaves, unless or until the French navy engaged the British navy in a serious way. Although militiamen were willing to defend their homes, they would not engage in serious, ex-tended campaigns. That left most of the fighting in the hands of the Conti-nental Army, which lacked the numerical strength to overwhelm its foe.

The war was a stalemate, with no end in sight.

In September, John Laurens rejoined George Washington and the main army, now stationed on the outskirts of New York to keep watch on the Brit-ish there. He could go back to writing the General's letters, but he hungered for something more. Where could he fight again?

Joseph Plumb Martin, meanwhile, was stationed in Connecticut, where he and his fellow soldiers prepared to spend the winter. As always, his hunger was literal, not figurative: the paucity of food and shelter caused him to obsess on the daily struggle for survival. "We got settled into our new winter quar-ters . . . and went on in our old Continental line of starving and freezing," he recalled. While officers talked of honor, Private Martin could think only of "filling my belly."[43]

Timothy Bigelow wintered in Providence, where he kept an eye on the British in Newport. Come spring, he was joined by Timothy Bigelow Jr., who celebrated his twelfth birthday in a military camp. Would this young lad, a second-generation revolutionary, someday fight by the side of his father? Could the war last that long, another three or four years?

There was no reason to suppose it wouldn't.

15

Falling Apart

March 7, 1778: Worcester

While Timothy Bigelow was off soldiering at Valley Forge, Monmouth, and Newport, his neighbors, friends, and family back in Worcester were facing hardships of their own. They paid higher prices for necessary items, and they taxed themselves through the roof to pay and clothe the men they sent to war. All that was bad enough, but it was salt that almost tore the community apart.

On March 7, 1778, a special committee appointed by the town meeting to investigate the financial doings of local officials issued a troubling report: "The selectmen engrossed to them selves the business of transporting said salt from Boston & have charged such sums per bush [bushel] as must amount to nearly 130 dollars above the original cost." Worse yet, "said salt was distributed to a part of the inhabitants of the town in very unequal and undue proportions." People living outside the town received more than their fair share, while "numbers of the inhabitants equally or more in need of salt, & equally entitled to a share, have received none."[1]

A small matter to us, but huge at the time. Salt was absolutely necessary for the preservation of food, and since the war had rendered it scarce, its distribution was strictly rationed according to state law. If the committee's allegations proved correct, it pointed to a supreme violation of the public trust.

Two days later, all seven selectmen and the treasurer were replaced.

The four-man committee that made the charges included Joshua Bigelow (Timothy's cousin) and three other members of the now-defunct American

Political Society; the selectmen they displaced were David Bigelow (Timothy's older brother and Joshua's cousin) and six previous members of the APS. New factions had emerged among old patriots. The Revolution in Worcester no longer proceeded with a unified front.[2]

October 5, 1778: Plymouth

The widespread breakdown of patriotic fervor disgusted Mercy Otis Warren. She had assumed, or at least hoped, that the Revolution would be a transformative experience: that the sacrifices required to overcome British rule would lead to a republic in which civic virtue prevailed over selfish interests. She had once believed, but by the fall of 1778, her dream had been dashed.

On October 5, Mrs. Warren published another poem in the *Boston Gazette*, not a dramatic piece this time, and certainly not a satire, but a simple lament, which she entitled, "The Genius of America weeping the absurd Follies of the Day." A sample portion:

> *The selfish passions, and the mad'ning rage*
> *For pleasure's soft debilitating charms,*
> *Running full riot in cold avarice' arms;*
> *Who grasps the dregs of base oppressive gains,*
> *While luxury in high profusion reigns.*
> *Our country bleeds, and bleeds at every pore,*
> *Yet gold's the deity whom all adore;*
> *Except a few, whose probity of soul*
> *No bribe could purchase, nor no fears control.*

Years later, when Warren republished the poem as part of a collection, she explained the context: "This piece was written when a most remarkable depravity of manners pervaded the cities of the United States, in consequence of a state of war; a relaxation of government; the sudden acquisition of fortune; a depreciating currency; and a new intercourse with foreign nations."[3]

Philosophy and morality aside, Mrs. Warren had a personal reason to feel estranged from the direction the country was taking: the previous May, for the first time in a dozen years, the town of Plymouth had failed to elect her husband as its representative to the state Assembly. Politically, James Warren appeared to be losing his influence.

Why?

His opponents claimed that he had failed to accept the responsibilities of political and military office, and they had a point. Warren had resigned from his post as paymaster general for the Continental Army, refused to accept an appointment to the Supreme Judicial Court of Massachusetts, and although a major general for the Massachusetts Militia, he had passed up several opportunities to accompany (much less lead) his men into battle. In James's and Mercy's view, he selflessly refused to acquire more power; in the view of others, he shirked his duties.

Perhaps, too, James Warren fell from grace because of his (and his wife's) disdain for the increasing democratization of political processes. In former times, James's family position had ensured he'd be treated as a leader; now, the "vulgar" classes (in Mercy's terminology) were taking a more active role. The war "has nearly destroyed the proper ideas of subordination, decency, and civility among the lower classes," she wrote. Meanwhile, new men were joining the ranks of the wealthy. "Fellows who would have cleaned my shoes five years ago, have amassed fortunes, and are riding in chariots," James grumbled. It was "a world turned topsy-turvy." His wife echoed this theme: "The world's turned upside down," she groused in her poem for the *Gazette*.[4]

Mr. and Mrs. Warren had their own explanation for James's loss of political position. Former Tories, allowed back into the fold against the better judgment of the Warrens, had teamed up with John Hancock, who had returned home from Philadelphia to cement his political power in Massachusetts. It was the machinations of Hancock, they felt, that led to James's displacement. Just as the Warrens had once blamed the British repression on the family's archrival, Thomas Hutchinson, now they leveled their sights on Hancock, who represented, in their eyes, the profligate, selfish turn in American society. Writing to Samuel Adams, who was still serving in Congress, an offended James Warren described the decadence in Boston in November of 1778:

> Most people are engaged in geting and some in spending money as fast as they can. Superb entertainments are very common. Genl. H [Hancock] gives a magnificent ball to the French officers, and to the gentlemen and ladies of the town next Thursday evening. Indeed all manner of extravagance prevails here in dress, furniture, equipage and living, amidst the distress of the public and multitudes of individuals.[5]

Adams, who had teamed up with Hancock in the early days of resistance, and who had fled with him through the hills when the British attacked Lexington, was as Puritanical as the Warrens, and he now shared their disdain for the man who once bankrolled the patriots of Boston and then served three terms as president of Congress.

In Plymouth and Boston, as in Worcester, former comrades were falling out.

December 1778–November 1779: Philadelphia

And in Philadelphia, too. There, factions in the nation's capital featured Henry Laurens on one side and Robert Morris on the other. In a nutshell, here's how it all came down.

Some members of Congress charged that Silas Deane, their former agent in France, had used his public position to further private interests, and Deane countered by vilifying Congress in public. Morris defended Deane, who had sent him much business from Europe, while Laurens sprang to Congress's defense, which led him to the brink of a duel with Deane. Morris, sick of it all, retired from Congress "to get back into my private station again," complaining as he left that "the time I have spent in it has been the severest tax on my life." Laurens, meanwhile, resigned his presidency in a huff, after being defeated in a series of parliamentary maneuvers.[6]

But Laurens stayed on as a congressman, and in his new capacity as chairman of the Commerce Committee (an evolution of the old Secret Committee of Commerce), he started to investigate the accounts of Robert Morris, the committee's previous chairman, whom he suspected had profited unfairly by issuing government contracts to himself. In the end, Morris was able to allay Laurens's suspicions, but the cantankerous Laurens then engaged in another round of "school-boy jarrings" (his own term) with John Penn from North Carolina, whom he mocked by singing a little ditty—"Poor little Penny, poor little Penny, sing tantara rara"—on the floor of Congress.[7]

Laurens continued to regress in his pettiness. He quarreled with his longtime colleague from South Carolina William Henry Drayton, then launched into a separate dispute with Charles Thomson, secretary of Congress, whom he criticized for poor note taking and for giving him only one (not two) copies of the latest official *Journal*. When Thomson descended from the platform at the head of the chamber to confront the former president, Laurens threatened he "had a good mind to kick him," whereupon Thomson "doubled his fist and said you dare not." And so it went, until Henry Laurens, the honorable gentleman from South Carolina, finally left Congress on November 9, 1779.[8]

Such were wartime politics, appearing to spiral ever downward. Robert Morris confessed to hating it all, and he did seem to avoid the wrangling whenever possible. Henry Laurens also claimed to hate politics, yet he played the game vigorously nonetheless. His feathers bristled whenever he felt his honor challenged, which was often. This had always been so, ever since his early confrontations with Christopher Gadsden and various British officials back in the 1760s. Now, however, the factionalism that Laurens decried, and yet practiced, was reaching epidemic proportions, and it threatened to tear the new nation apart.

1778–1779: The West

Personalities and petty politics aside, patriots squabbled over the elemental question: At war's end, who would be entitled to the spoils?

The ripest fruit, as George Washington understood from the beginning, was control over the West. Although Washington wisely stayed out of the political fray on this count, his good friend and neighbor George Mason looked after their mutual interests. Both men envisioned a westward-facing Virginia as the nation's leader in postwar expansion. To facilitate this, while Washington was trying to keep his army together at Valley Forge, Mason submitted a bill to the Virginia Assembly that would recognize the land claims of the Ohio Company (Washington and Mason were both major stakeholders), promote settlement in the West, and fund the war effort through sales of unappropriated lands. All this assumed that Virginia still extended westward to the "South Sea," as its colonial charter had stated.[9]

The bill didn't pass. It was contested by prominent planters from the Tidewater region, who realized that a population shift westward would eventually erode their power. Out-of-state speculators also opposed the measure, and they lobbied their business contacts within Virginia to defeat it.

Mason revamped his bill, and on June 22, 1779, a much-altered version passed the Assembly. Gone were the sections that promoted easy settlement by ordinary people and placed a limit on sales to any one person. (Robert Morris, not exactly a settler himself, would eventually procure some million and a half acres in Virginia's western reaches.) Gone too was the grandfathered recognition of the Ohio Company's claims, as well as those of other companies that preceded the war. Henceforth, the Virginia Land Office would issue all patents to land west of the mountains, save for the region north of the Ohio River, which the Assembly voluntarily ceded to Congress so that Continental soldiers might receive their bounties.[10]

The Virginia Land Office bill did not sit well with the prominent stockholders of the Indiana Company, the Vandalia Company, the Illinois-Wabash Company, and other out-of-state investors, who appealed to the Continental Congress. Control of the West should be a national issue, they argued.

In response to petitions by the Indiana and Vandalia companies, Mason correctly observed that the Articles of Confederation expressly prohibited Congress from determining western boundaries. There was a serious problem with his line of reasoning, however: the Articles had yet to be formally adopted, because Maryland, which claimed no colonial land in the West, refused to sign until its rival across the Chesapeake relinquished its claims. (It just so happened that Maryland's representatives in Congress held interests in the Illinois-Wabash Company, which Virginia refused to recognize.)[11]

To complicate matters, Spain, with an imperial presence from the Mississippi River westward, created even more dissension within the United States. In mid-1779, as usual, Congress was short on money, and what little money it had was losing value day by day. Spain suggested it might be of some assistance—but only if the United States grant it exclusive navigation rights to the Mississippi River and give up all ambitions to regions beyond. Landless states and some eastern merchants said fine; landed states and speculators with aspirations in the West adamantly refused.

Such were the confused and disheartening politics of westward expansion in the middle stages of the Revolutionary War. The military tale, by contrast, is easier to tell, but that story reveals that the young, struggling nation was hardly a paragon of virtue.

On the third day of 1778, George Mason, Thomas Jefferson, and George Wythe, on behalf of the Virginia House of Delegates, endorsed the mission of George Rogers Clark, who had proposed to lead his Kentucky militiamen on an expedition against Indians in the Illinois country. Mason and company promised that each of Clark's men would receive a share of the spoils: three hundred acres of land apiece.[12]

The full Virginia House of Delegates knew nothing of the expedition it had just endorsed. The matter had to be held secret, not only from the British and their Indian allies, but also from people like Robert Morris, who, as head of the Continental Congress's Committee of Commerce, had just dispatched James Willing, the brother of his old business partner Thomas Willing, to Pittsburg, and thence down the Ohio and Mississippi, with instructions to clear the rivers for American commerce and acquire gunpowder in New Orleans, in anticipation of a possible American assault on the British stronghold at Detroit. Virginia and the Continental Congress were planning alternate, and possibly competing, expeditions to conquer the West.[13]

Clark's men got there first, and for the next two years these frontier fighters swept through what is now southern Indiana and Illinois, alternately terrorizing and befriending Indian and French Canadian inhabitants and capturing the strategic British outposts at Kaskaskia (on the Mississippi, above the confluence with the Ohio) and Vincennes (along the Wabash River, tributary to the Ohio). Twenty-two months later, in November of 1779, Clark submitted a detailed account of his expedition to George Mason, one of his original sponsors. To convince both British soldiers and local inhabitants that his small force (never more than two hundred) was greater than it was, Clark wrote, he had employed clever stratagems, such as flying numerous regimental banners and firing shots from diverse positions. He had also resorted to sheer intimidation. On the outskirts of Vincennes, his men confronted a party of Indians who mistook them for British allies; showing no mercy, they killed most of the party, then scalped two and took six as prisoners. To impress other Indians living near Vincennes, Clark continued unabashedly, he had "ordered the prisoners to be tomahawked in the face of the garrison."[14]

While George Rogers Clark, on behalf of Virginia, asserted a military presence in the Ohio-Mississippi region, George Washington and the Continental Army focused on western New York and Pennsylvania. There, four of the six Iroquois nations—the Senecas, Mohawks, Cayugas, and Onondagas—had allied themselves with loyalists from upstate New York and British forces working from Canada. These allies, in various combinations, had fought with great effect at Oriskany (New York) in 1777 and the Wyoming Valley (Pennsylvania) in 1778. At Cherry Valley (New York) in 1778, loyalists and Mohawks overran a regiment of the Continental Army, while also killing and capturing many civilians.

The northern alliance was certainly impeding westward expansion, and no small group of frontiersmen could scare these people off. To conquer the Northwest would require resources of the Continental Army and the special attention of its commander in chief, who felt no great kinship with Native Americans. On May 31, 1779, General Washington issued specific instructions to General John Sullivan "to lay waste" to Indian towns "in the most effectual manner, that the country may be not merely overrun, but destroyed." Washington minced no words, and his orders evidenced a hateful tone:

The expedition you are appointed to command is to be directed against the hostile tribes of the Six Nations of Indians, with their associates and adherents. The immediate objects are the total destruction and devastation of their settlements, and the capture of as many prisoners of every age and sex as possible. It will be essential to ruin their crops now in the ground and prevent their planting more. . . .

You will not by any means listen to any overture of peace before the total ruinment of their settlements is effected. Our future security will be in their inability to injure us and in the terror . . . [and] severity of the chastisement they receive.[15]

To accomplish this task, General Washington placed 4,500 soldiers under Sullivan's command. It was by far the largest American military expedition of 1779, but its object was a bit unusual: it was a war not only against enemy soldiers or warriors, but also against women, children, livestock, fruits, and vegetables. On July 4, as the Continentals were preparing for their mission, they offered a patriotic toast: "Civilization or death to all American savages!" Then they systematically destroyed all vestiges of civilization they could find. The following winter, as Washington had hoped, many Iroquois people starved to death.[16]

The journals kept by several Continental officers boasted the "body count":

September 9: What corn, beans, peas, squashes, potatoes, inions, turnips, cabage, cowcumbers, watermilions, carrots, parsnips, &c. our men and horses cattle &c could not eat was distroyed this morning before we march . . . We totally distroyed the town and orchard.

September 15: At 6 o'clock the whole Army was turned out to destroy the corn . . . We were from 6 to 2 o'clock very bussy until we completed our work; it is thought we have destroyed 15,000 bushels of corn, besides beans, squashes, potatoes in abundance. . . . The method we took [was] to gather it into the houses putting wood and bark with it then set fire to the houses.[17]

According to a limited view of its mission, the Sullivan expedition was deemed a success. In a broader sense, however, it failed, for Iroquois warriors who survived only doubled their determination to disrupt white occupation of the borderlands. Furthermore, in native minds, George Washington had earned for himself a new name: Hanadaganeas—Town Destroyer.

October 4, 1779: "Fort Wilson," Philadelphia

Back East, the prolonged war intensified class divisions. Unprincipled merchants, and even farmers, hoarded scarce commodities in order to drive up prices; meanwhile, the depreciating currency drove prices higher yet. While most of the population suffered, the "forestallers," "engrossers," and "monopolizers" who tied up local markets prospered, as did speculators and "stock jobbers" (stock traders), who arranged to corner markets on a wider scale. The rich got richer, to the dismay of everyone else.

One of the merchants who grew conspicuously wealthy while others suffered was none other than Robert Morris, the man who had done so much for the Revolution during some of its most trying moments. For Morris, forestalling and monopolizing were standard business practices. At the age of fifteen, while his boss was traveling abroad, the young clerk had cornered the Philadelphia flour market, thereby inducing scarcity and raising prices. People were upset, but Charles Willing, after he returned, praised the entrepreneurial spirit of his eager clerk. In October of 1776, Morris had written to his associate, John Bradford: "What think you of buying up in your state all such prize goods (not perishable) as sell cheap and laying by awhile." Now, in the spring of 1779, prices of food and dry goods were skyrocketing, and Philadelphians suspected that Robert Morris had something to do with it. He had just purchased a large shipment of goods, which should have pulled down prices, but instead prices rose faster than ever. Was Morris forestalling, while the rest of the population either paid the price or went without?[18]

The common people of Philadelphia took matters into their own hands, much as they had done several times before. Christopher Marshall and Charles Willson Peale, who had worked closely with Thomas Young during the internal revolution of 1776, helped organize a mass town meeting for May 25. Young himself certainly would have been on the front lines for this struggle, but others now took his place.

In the run-up to the meeting, on the night of May 23, secret propagandists plastered a broadside around the city:

For our Country's Good!
    In the midst of money we are in poverty, and exposed to want in a land of plenty. You that have money, . . . down with your prices, or down with yourselves. For by the living and eternal God, we will bring every article

down to what it was last Christmas, or we will down with those who opposed.

We have turned out against the enemy and we will not be eaten up by monopolizers and forestallers.

Come on Cooly[19]

The ad hoc town meeting two days later, held as usual in the State House Yard, vowed to roll back prices on key items such as "rum, sugar, flour, coffee and tea" to "what they were on the first day of May," and it appointed a twenty-six-person committee to enforce this extralegal resolution. It also appointed a six-man committee, including Peale, Marshall, and Thomas Paine, "to enquire of Mr. Robert Morris, or others, what part he or they have acted" in the raising of prices.[20]

Morris defended himself with a rare statement to the press, in which he pleaded innocence: "I am really at a loss to conceive why my name should, without sufficient grounds, be so frequently mentioned in the public papers, and held in such an odious point of view." Since the time of the Stamp Act crisis, he boasted, he had exerted himself on behalf of "the general cause of America"; he had "imported thousands of good settlers into Pennsylvania;" he saw around him hundreds of "fellow citizens" who owed their "fortunes" to him. For all this, he should receive thanks, not blame.[21]

The investigating committee was not convinced: "However unwilling Mr. Morris may be to acknowledge the term engrossing or monopolizing, . . . we are at a loss to find any other name." And yet, the committee admitted, Morris' actions did not warrant "the rigorous sense generally applied to those words," and they let him off with nothing but a scolding. He should be more willing to surrender "individual ease & advantage" and keep his focus on the public good, they preached.[22]

The merchant prince had avoided punishment, but his troubles were not yet over. On July 27 at the State House Yard, in the face of "two or three hundred men of the lower orders of the people armed with large staves or bludgeons" who had positioned themselves near the stage, Morris and a handful of others tried to convince an enraged populace that price controls were not working and should be abandoned. After being shouted down, Morris and company moved to College Yard to organize their own resistance efforts. With Morris serving as chairman, this alternate group decided to put up its own slate of candidates, headed by Morris himself, for the enlarged 120-member price-control committee, to be chosen by a citywide election on August 2.[23]

The election received a record turnout, and the outcome was decisive: 2,115 for the radical ticket, only 281 for Morris and the opponents of price control.[24]

Robert Morris had more than his personal reputation at stake; his philosophy was under siege as well. Price controls violated his first rule of trade—"that commerce should be perfectly free, and property sacredly secure to the owner." On September 10, eighty "merchants and traders" published a polemic against price fixing in the *Pennsylvania Packet*: "The limitation of prices is in the principle unjust, because it invades the laws of property, by compelling a person to accept of less in exchange for his goods than he could otherwise obtain, and therefore acts as a tax upon part of the community only." Morris was one of the signers and likely one of the authors.[25]

Philosophy aside, price controls did not do the job. Rather than sell at lower prices, merchants simply held back their goods, thereby adding to the problem. They also tried to peddle their products elsewhere, and when some goods found their way back to Philadelphia, they fetched a higher price yet on the black market. This of course only added to the rage of poor folks and political radicals. On August 29, another broadside appeared: if "any person whatever, though puffed like a toad, with a sense of his own consequence, shall dare to violate the least resolves of our Committee, it were better for him, that a mill-stone was fastened to his neck, and he cast into the depth of the sea, or that he had never been born." The heavy-handed threat was signed this time by "COME ON WARMLY," a step up from "Cooly," who authored the May 23 broadside.[26]

Militiamen, many from the lower and middle classes, voiced yet another complaint: those who did not serve in the army were the very ones who were now getting rich. When they gathered to drink and toast, they offered a new round: "May only those Americans enjoy freedom who are ready to die for its defense." Robert Morris, by this line of reasoning, was not entitled to any sort of freedom, whether personal or commercial, for despite all his public service he had never raised a gun in his country's defense.[27]

But he *would* soon raise a gun, even if he didn't point it at enemy soldiers.

On the morning of October 4, 1779, "great numbers of the militia," organized by the Committee of Privates, gathered at Burn's Tavern, near the commons on Tenth Street. Food was becoming ever more scarce, prices had risen 50 percent in ten days, and militiamen decided the time for meetings and resolutions had passed. They asked the seasoned radical Charles Willson Peale, who was serving as a lieutenant in the city's militia, to lead a march to the homes of Tories and monopolizing merchants. Peale declined, but the militiamen, many of them German Americans, "disregarded every danger" and "only looked straight forward, regardless of the consequences." (Peale's words.) At noon they started on their rampage.[28]

The militiamen started by rounding up four men suspected of violating the price regulations and bringing them back to Burn's Tavern, beating the "Rogue's March" with fifes and drums. Then they headed east on Arch Street, and then south toward the City Tavern on Second and Walnut, where somewhere between twenty and forty of the city's most prominent "gentlemen" were "parading on the pavement," pledging to uphold law and order. Robert Morris and James Wilson, who had come to the defense of Morris and other accused merchants, were among the City Tavern group.

As the militiamen approached, fifes blowing and drums beating, the City Tavern men retreated. Earlier in the day, the city's "Silk Stocking" company of Light Horse had been on the scene to defend their fellow gentlemen, but they had gone home for their midday dinner. Wilson, Morris, and company, left on their own and greatly outnumbered, retreated along Walnut to Wilson's house, a stand-alone, three-story brick structure with a copper roof. It would make a good fortress, if needed.

The militiamen followed them there, then raised three cheers as the "better sort" huddled inside, doors barred and shutters shut. The taunts of the crowd were too much for a one-armed veteran named George Campbell, who threw open a shutter either to yell back or to shoot. Accounts of the incident varied, with each side claiming the other fired first, but in any case, the first shot was followed by many more, fired in both directions. This was no mere puffing of chests, but an all-out battle, with casualties on both sides. The men on the outside, with no cover, suffered the most: at least five were killed and fourteen wounded. Although we have no direct account, it seems likely that Robert Morris did not sit idly by while others acted, and quite possibly his fire hit somebody.

Some of the militiamen charged the building and forced their way inside, but when two were wounded as they tried to mount the stairs, they withdrew. The militiamen would stake the battle on the field piece that was just then being drawn into position. Once they had broken the brick fort, they would resume the charge.

Just then, Pennsylvania president Joseph Reed appeared at the head of a hastily assembled crew of horsemen, some "Silk Stocking" gentlemen as well as a few Continental cavalrymen stationed in town. Sabers drawn, Reed and those under his command rushed into the crowd. The militiamen wisely held their fire and soon dispersed—or at least they tried to, for Reed and company, representing the legitimate force of the state and the nation, rounded up all they could. The men from within Wilson's house emerged to join Reed's forces as they marched the prisoners away, but as the victors passed along the streets they were booed and hooted; they even had to dodge some "large stones and bricks."[29]

The "Battle of Fort Wilson" was over. Technically, the militiamen had been defeated, but they had certainly shaken things up. Henry Laurens, still a congressman residing in Philadelphia, reported immediately to John Adams: "We are at this moment on the brink of a precipice & what I have long dreaded & often intimated to my friends, seems to be breaking forth a convulsion among the people."[30]

Tensions continued in the aftermath of the battle. When militiamen in nearby Germantown gathered with the intent of freeing their comrades from the Philadelphia jail, President Reed ventured to Germantown in an attempt to change their minds. In Reed's absence, Timothy Matlack, another compatriot of Thomas Young's who now served as secretary to the Executive Council, decided it was best to free the prisoners on bail rather than risk another confrontation with the gathering crowd in Philadelphia and the militiamen from Germantown. Meanwhile, the haughty Benedict Arnold, who had tried to join the fight on behalf of the besieged gentlemen, was accosted by a "mob of lawless ruffians" (his words), causing him to apply to Congress for a twenty-man bodyguard. Through all this, Robert Morris huddled inside his town house, too scared to light a candle at night, while James Wilson sought refuge a little farther away, in Morris's country manor. (Wilson had replaced Morris as the militiamen's chief antagonist because the shots that killed five of their men had been fired from his house.) In a series of messages delivered by a black servant, Morris first instructed Wilson to hide in the attic; to pass the time, Wilson was to dispatch the servant to the basement for some high-quality wine. The following day, when tempers in town failed to cool, Morris advised Wilson to head for safety in New Jersey. Left unsaid: Morris's mansion would be safer if Wilson were not inside.

Joseph Reed, meanwhile, did what he could to appease the Philadelphia militiamen. He promised that their concerns would be addressed in the Assembly, and so they were. A new law was passed "more effectually preventing engrossing and forestalling," and one hundred barrels of flour were distributed to the needy, with a preference given to those signing up for the militia.

Furthermore, men who refused to serve in the militia would henceforth face steep fines, with the rich paying according to the value of their estates. Reed also asked the gentlemen who had fired from Fort Wilson to turn themselves in; many did, but not Robert Morris.[31]

An uneasy peace returned to the streets of Philadelphia. Five months later, all parties on both sides were pardoned and the matter set to rest.

Fort Wilson signified the end of the alliance between discontented militiamen of the "lower sort" and radical activists of the "middling sort" in the nation's capital city. Peale, who headed the radical Constitutional Society, had refused to join with the militiamen, and then Reed, known to champion the common people, had taken up the sword against them. These leaders and others like them, however sympathetic to the plight of the lower sort, did not wish to jeopardize the security of the state or the ongoing fight against Great Britain by encouraging a full-scale social revolution on the home front. Thomas Young's dream—that the lower and middling sorts would come together as the body of the people to create a new society on more egalitarian terms—suffered a severe blow at Fort Wilson; in the end, it was really the upper sort, people like Robert Morris, who benefited most.

January 3–May 25, 1780: Jockey Hollow, New Jersey

If food shortages and a collapsing economy could trigger an armed confrontation in the City of Brotherly Love, imagine the potential for violence in the camp of the Continental Army, where soldiers with guns and bayonets endured great hunger and received no pay for months on end the following winter.

In mid-December of 1779, Joseph Plumb Martin and most of the other soldiers in Washington's main army moved to the hills of New Jersey, about thirty miles due west of the British Army in New York City. While Washington set up his headquarters at Morristown, the soldiers started to build their crude winter cabins about five miles to the southwest, in a region locals called Jockey Hollow.

No sooner had they arrived than it started to snow, and once the first snow hit the ground it never melted for three months. On January 3, according to army surgeon James Thacher, "we experienced one of the most tremendous snowstorms ever remembered; no man could endure its violence many minutes without danger to his life." By the time the storm subsided, snow lay four to six feet deep on the ground. Soldiers huddled inside their tents and cabins, consuming what food they had on hand. Once that ran out, they simply did without, for the snow had cut off all supply lines.[32]

Joseph Plumb Martin remembered that time well:

> We were absolutely, literally starved. I do solemnly declare that I did not put a single morsel of victuals into my mouth for four days and as many nights, except a little black birch bark which I gnawed off a stick of wood, if that can be called victuals. I saw several of the men roast their old shoes and eat them, and I was afterwards informed by one of the officers' waiters, that some of the officers killed and ate a favorite little dog that belonged to one of them.[33]

Two years earlier at Valley Forge, soldiers had suffered from cold and hunger, but that winter was actually milder than the historic average, while the winter of 1779–1780—the Hard Winter, as it was called for generations after—was the coldest ever recorded, before or since, by Euro-Americans inhabiting the northeastern seaboard of the United States. The New York harbor froze solid, allowing cannons and cavalry and sleighs loaded with firewood to travel at ease between New Jersey, Manhattan, Long Island, and Staten Island. Sleighs traversed the Chesapeake Bay from Baltimore to Annapolis, and saltwater inlets froze as far south as North Carolina. (This was the winter the Iroquois Indians had to face after the Sullivan expedition had destroyed their houses and food supplies the previous summer.)

In the wake of the January storm, General Nathanael Greene worried: "The army is upon the eve of disbanding for want of provisions." One month later, Greene repeated his warning, and sure enough, approximately eight hundred soldiers deserted from the Jockey Hollow camp during the Hard Winter—but this was no more than the going rate of desertions over the duration of the war. Lads like Joseph Plumb Martin (now nineteen years old) were tough and seasoned by now, and despite all the privations they had to face, most remained true to their cause.[34]

Finally spring came, and with it the promise of better days ahead. The problem was, those better days never arrived. The soldiers could endure hardships when they knew nature was to blame, but they had less patience with the Continental Congress, which had failed to pay any wages for five months and had supplied so little meat that each soldier now received only a small fraction of his standard daily ration. (To be fair, the states were as much at fault as Congress,

for they did not all deliver their quotas, and various state laws impeded the sale
of scarce commodities to the army, for fear of driving up prices for civilians.)

On or about May 21, the supply line totally collapsed. Little meat turned
once again to no meat, and the Continental troops started to contemplate
what actions they might take. With poetic precision, Joseph Plumb Martin
elucidated the time-honored dilemma faced by suffering but patriotic soldiers:

> The men were now exasperated beyond endurance; they could not stand
> it any longer. They saw no alternative but to starve to death, or break up
> the army, give all up and go home. This was a hard matter for the soldiers
> to think upon. They were truly patriotic, they loved their country, and
> they had already suffered everything short of death in its cause; and now,
> after such extreme hardships to give up all was too much, but to starve to
> death was too much also. What was to be done? Here was the army
> starved and naked, and there their country sitting still and expecting the
> army to do notable things while fainting from sheer starvation.[35]

On May 25, the collective wondering evolved into collective (albeit un-
planned) action. Again, Martin's own words:

> We had borne as long as human nature could endure, and to bear longer
> we considered folly. Accordingly, one pleasant day, the men spent the
> most of their time upon the parade, growling like soreheaded dogs. At
> evening roll call they began to show their dissatisfaction by snapping at
> the officers and acting contrary to their orders.

The growling and snapping soon escalated. When an officer called one of the
soldiers "a mutinous rascal," the rebel defiantly pounded the ground with his
musket and called out, "Who will parade with me?" Martin reported the response: "The whole regiment immediately fell in and formed" with the dis-
senter, Martin included.

Martin and the others then marched to the neighboring camp, where another regiment joined them, and together the two regiments embarked to the
parade grounds of the other two Connecticut regiments. Purposely, they had
no leader to call out marching orders, "lest he be singled out for a court-
martial." They simply marched to the beat of the drums.

Officers of the other two regiments tried to outsmart the insurgents by
ordering their men to parade without arms. Some of these officers then

Figure 31. This 1777 cartoon, titled "The Soldiers in the Field doing duty," illustrates the plight of Joseph Plumb Martin and his comrades in the Continental Army. The men's words:
First soldier: "Keep up courage, my boys, we will soon bring those Villains to terms."
Second soldier: "These d___d Extortioners are the worst enemies to the country."
Third soldier: "I serve my country for sixteen pence per day, pinched and cold."

stalked the insurgents "like wolves on a sheep" and seized a private from the ranks, but immediately the officers found "bayonets of the men pointing at their breasts as thick as hatchel teeth." (A hatchel, or hackle, was a comb with rows of metal teeth for making hemp fiber ready for weaving.) This was serious business. How far would the incipient mutineers take this?

Not that far, they finally decided:

> After our officers had left us to our own option, we dispersed to our huts and laid by our arms of our own accord, but the worm of hunger gnawing so keen kept us from being entirely quiet. We therefore still kept upon the parade in groups, venting our spleen at our country and government, then at our officers, and then at ourselves for our imbecility in staying there and starving in detail for an ungrateful people who did not care what became of us.[36]

George Washington, in his headquarters only five miles distant, faced his own dilemma: should he crack down or give in? Although he was in most cases a strict disciplinarian, and although he proclaimed, as any commander would, that mutiny "cannot in any case be justified," the circumstances this time softened his response. The next day, he sent out a flurry of desperate requests for cattle, and beyond that, he actually took the side of the Connecticut rebels. Writing to Jonathan Trumbull, governor of their state, he explained the conditions that produced the brief rebellion in the most sympathetic terms:

> It is with infinite pain I inform you, that we are reduced to a situation of extremity for want of meat. On several days of late the troops have been entirely destitute of any, and for a considerable time past they have been at best, at a half, a quarter, and eighth allowance of this essential article of provision. The men have borne their distress with a firmness and patience never exceeded, . . . but there are certain bounds, beyond which it is impossible for human nature to go. We are arrived at these. The want of provision last night produced a mutiny in the army of a very alarming kind.[37]

Two days after Martin and company had so dramatically registered their complaints, a shipment of pork and thirty head of cattle arrived in camp. The immediate crisis was over, but without significant, structural changes in the methods used to supply the army, the future looked bleak. On May 28, a despondent commander in chief, as disillusioned with his countrymen as was Private Martin, complained to Pennsylvania's president Joseph Reed:

> I assure you, every idea you can form of our distresses, will fall short of the reality. There is such a combination of circumstances to exhaust the patience of the soldiery that it begins at length to be worn out and be seen in every line of the army, the most serious features of mutiny and sedition.
>
> We have every thing to dread. Indeed I have almost ceased to hope. The country in general is in such a state of insensibility and indifference to its interests, that I dare not flatter myself with any change for the better.[38]

Three days after penning these gloomy words, Washington received yet more disheartening news: Charleston, the South's only major port, had fallen to the British.

May 12, 1780: Charleston

Back in June of 1776 and again in June of 1779, British forces had tried but failed to take Charleston. In those attempts, the British command had treated South Carolina's capital city as just another target in the southern theater, something of an auxiliary to the main war, but by December of 1779 British policy makers had concluded that winning the South provided the key to breaking the deadlock in the North, and the gateway to the South was Charleston. This time, no matter the expense or the loss of human lives, they were not to be denied.

On the day after Christmas, Sir Henry Clinton set sail from New York with fourteen warships and ninety transports, loaded down with 8,500 soldiers and their weaponry. Due to winter storms, not all of these arrived safely in South Carolina, but reinforcements were quickly dispatched, and by early March 1780 Clinton had over 10,000 men and an imposing fleet of vessels equipped with guns that were ready to batter the city into submission.

To defend Charleston, patriots could muster little more than 5,000 fighting men, split evenly between local militiamen and Continental soldiers. John Laurens, who had left Washington's "family" to fight in the southern theater, was given command of some 250 Continentals, but if he had had his way he would be leading a much larger contingent of all-black soldiers. More than two years earlier, he had hatched his scheme: arm a significant number of "able bodied men slaves," who were well equipped to become "gallant soldiers" because they had "the habit of subordination almost indelibly impress'd on them." After fighting on behalf of patriots, these men would then receive their freedom.[39]

George Washington disapproved, for if Americans armed slaves, the British would follow suit, and "the upshot then would be, who can arm fastest?" Henry Laurens also thought it was a terrible idea: "The more I think of ... your scheme, the less I approve of it," he told John. But Henry, still president at the time, supported his son nonetheless when the matter came up for a vote, and Congress recommended that South Carolina and Georgia raise a force of three thousand slaves, recompensing their masters up to $1,000 apiece. The South Carolina House of Representatives, however, nixed the idea. David Ramsay, who would later marry John Laurens's sister, reported at the time: "The measure for embodying the negroes ... was received with horror by the planters, who figured to themselves terrible consequences."[40]

As the British approached Charleston in the early spring of 1780, white officials did acknowledge the merits of utilizing forced labor to their own advantage, and they placed about one thousand enslaved African Americans to work on fortifications for the city. When John Laurens suggested that these people should be rewarded with their freedom should the city survive due to their efforts, he was simply ignored.

With his slave scheme defeated, and knowing the patriots were seriously outnumbered, Laurens still saw one way of ensuring victory. He wrote to his mentor, George Washington: "Your Excellency in person might rescue us. All Virginia and No Carolina would follow you. The glory of foiling the enemy in his last great effort, and terminating the war, ought to be reserved for you." But the General, using sound military judgment, did not wish to engage in a winner-take-all confrontation at Charleston, where his forces would be trapped on the tip of a peninsula (Charleston lies between two rivers, the Ashley and the Cooper) while enemy warships controlled the harbor. Stuck at the time at Morristown, he replied politely, "If it were proposed by Congress I should not dislike the journey," but he was certain Congress would prefer that he patch up the main army, which appeared on the verge of unraveling.[41]

Washington's pessimistic assessment of the situation in Charleston proved well founded. On April 8, British warships moved past the fort on Sullivan's Island that had protected the harbor back in 1776. Meanwhile, Clinton moved his massive land forces down the peninsula to the edge of the city. John Laurens, disobeying orders, harassed the invading army with his small force, but to no avail. Soon, the Continentals and militiamen would be trapped on their peninsula, just as Washington feared.

To keep British ships from surrounding the city, patriots sank four of their own ships and connected the masts with an impenetrable web of ropes, thereby blocking the entrance to the Cooper River. They hoped this would allow them to escape across the Cooper, but British forces simply marched by land to control the opposite bank, where they could mow down any Americans who tried to flee. By mid-April, the city of Charleston, with over five thousand soldiers inside, was completely surrounded, and British artillery opened fire.

The bombardment continued day by day, and with supplies in the city growing scarce, General Benjamin Lincoln, the Continental commander, considered giving up. He was opposed, however, by John Laurens and the chief civil officer of Charleston, Christopher Gadsden. Ironically, Henry Laurens's son and his sworn enemy, equally hawkish, had become allies, at least for the moment. Laurens the younger was one of the few dissenters when sixty-three of his fellow officers voted at last for capitulation, while Gadsden, upon hearing that Lincoln had discussed terms of surrender without consulting him, flew into a rage.

But the military issue was settled, and on May 12, 1780, almost 5,500 patriots laid down their guns. It was the largest American surrender of the Revolutionary War and the third largest in our nation's history, surpassed in numbers only at Harpers Ferry in the Civil War and Bataan in World War II. When British and Hessian soldiers moved in to take over the city, they wasted little time in cutting down Charleston's Liberty Tree, which had played host to so many patriot gatherings in the years leading up to the Revolution.

September 3, 1780–February 1, 1781: The Atlantic Ocean and London

The fall of Charleston sent Henry Laurens into a funk, even though he was not there at the time. Laurens was rarely an upbeat fellow even in the best of times, but now he had new reasons to grumble.

First, his son was a prisoner of war. John was not dispatched to one of the infamous prison ships like the *Jersey* in New York harbor, where so many Americans succumbed to diseases brought on by tight quarters and poor sanitation, nor to the *Sandwich*, *Torbay*, or *Pack Horse* in Charleston harbor, to which many of the lower-ranking captives were sent. But he did have to take an oath of allegiance to the Crown and promise never to fight again on the side of the rebels, unless or until he was exchanged. That hurt Henry and almost destroyed John, who complained that it was "the greatest misfortune of my life to be deprived of my arms & activity at such a juncture as the present."[42]

Next, on the first day of British bombardment, Henry's house in Charleston's fashionable Ansonborough district had received a serious pounding. After the British took over, his personal secretary reported the damage:

A shel . . . entered through the roof of the passage & boarsted in the midst of it, threw the mahogany stairs in flinters. . . . The number of shots entered through the house, kitchen, counting house, smoke house, stable, garden wal, & fens, are so numberous not to be counted. . . . The stable and kitchen is entirely down, the house barely worths repairing, the garden entirely destroyed. The brick house has suffered least, & now a barack for Hessian soldiers.[43]

What probably hurt Henry the most was the destruction of the four-acre garden, the pride and joy of his deceased wife Eleanor.

Laurens's home plantation in Mepkin was worse for the wear as well, not from bombs but from plundering. British troops pillaged the place twice, making off with expensive pewter ware, teapots, coffee cups, and knives, not to mention Henry's horses (including a prize black stallion) and cattle, and of course all the cash they could find, as well as his complete supply of liquor.[44]

And at least twenty of his slaves, who appeared to have left of their own accord. One of these was Frederick, whom Henry reported had always been "a very good lad before the war." In Henry's eyes, the war had "contaminated" his slave; in Frederick's eyes, it created the opportunity to escape. These two fellows, a master and the man he purported to own, had not seen the last of their disagreements (see chapter 18).[45]

From his vantage point in Philadelphia, Laurens had no control over any of this, but he could still help his floundering nation, which in his own rendering was "sick indeed." His new job was as at least as crucial as any he had performed before: Congress wanted him to travel to Holland, the home of his ancestors, in search of desperately needed Dutch loans.[46]

On August 13, 1780, the former president of Congress, bearing a trunk full of personal and official papers, embarked from Philadelphia aboard a small but swift brigantine called the *Mercury*. The "little packet ship," as Laurens called it, did not make its way directly to the high seas, for it awaited a military convoy. When this failed to materialize, the *Mercury* entered the Atlantic and headed due east, accompanied by just a single armed vessel. Six days out to ocean, the escort ship turned back, unable to keep pace with the *Mercury*.

Only two days later, at dawn on September 3, a sail appeared on the horizon. If navigated properly, according to Laurens, the *Mercury* could have avoided contact with the mystery vessel, but its captain "put her before the wind" instead of keeping her sails "close," and by eleven o'clock, the twenty-eight-gun British frigate *Vestal* had come near enough to fire cannonballs between the masts of the *Mercury*. Laurens threw overboard his most secret documents, then, upon the urging of his secretary, he placed the rest of his papers in a large bag weighted with shot and threw that into the ocean as well. Before the bag could sink, however, British sailors hooked it and drew it to their deck. Included in this batch was a draft of a treaty that Laurens had intended to propose to Dutch officials.

About one in the afternoon, Henry Laurens was received "cordially" in the cabin of Captain George Keppel. He offered the British officer his sword and his purse, but Keppel declined: "Put up your money, sir, I never plunder," he told Laurens. Keppel would content himself with having captured the highest-ranking political prisoner of the American Revolution—indeed, the highest-ranking American civilian ever taken by an enemy in our nation's history.[47]

Before carrying his prize back to London, Keppel headed north to St. John's, Newfoundland. There, exchanging vessels, he took Laurens on board the sloop *Fairy* and headed toward England. Also aboard the *Fairy* were a handful of other Americans who had been captured by the cruiser *Proteus*, and one of these was Winslow Warren, the second son of James and Mercy Otis Warren.

Winslow's mother had not wanted him to go. What she wanted was for Winslow, who lived at the time in Boston, to make the short trip to Plymouth once in a while, but in this she was disappointed, for it seems that twenty-year-old Winslow preferred at that stage of his life to distance himself from a mother who could be a bit overbearing. So instead of going to Plymouth, he was off to Holland, and perhaps France soon after, to make his way in the world.

Unlike brother Charles, Winslow had chosen not to attend Harvard; unlike brother James Jr., he had resisted military service, and he even stayed clear of any political involvement in the tumultuous affairs of the Revolution that consumed the attention of his parents. He chose instead a career in commerce, and because Holland and France were the chief exporters of goods to America, a trip to the European continent seemed altogether logical.

It might also prove adventurous, perhaps even fun, and that is exactly what so bothered his mother. On March 25, 1780, the day after Winslow's twenty-first birthday, Mercy Otis Warren wrote him a long and excruciatingly ponderous letter, so filled with advice for his forthcoming journey that it would have made Polonius proud. In Europe Winslow would confront "the successful arts of intrigue and seduction . . . practiced by both sexes"; he would be lured by "the most elegant pleasures shining through the enchanting vizard of politeness." (Not that Boston was much better, she observed: "Both in Europe and America, the prostitution of moral sentiment is the fashion of the times.") Winslow was particularly vulnerable to these temptations because of his own "taste for elegant amusement," but he could "parry" them "by calling into action those philosophic maxims which are beautiful in theory, but in practice sublime." On and on it went, page after page. Mercy always knew she was too heavy with advice, and she tried to rein herself in, but she didn't stand much of a chance. Puritanical preaching was in her blood and possibly even her genes—but if so, that particular gene had not been passed on to Winslow, who had more charm and wit than philosophy. Perhaps that is why Mercy favored him so: he was her biggest challenge, and also her most amusing chum.[48]

In Newfoundland and on board the *Fairy*, Winslow Warren and Henry Laurens, fellow prisoners, discussed the circumstances of their respective captures. Laurens assured Warren that the papers his captors had retrieved from the bag were unimportant. At the time, Warren did not understand why Laurens was so insistent on telling him this.

When the *Fairy* docked at Dartmouth, England, on September 28, Henry Laurens was placed under heavy security and whisked off by coach to the Tower of London; there, on October 6, he began his solitary confinement in the very cell that John Wilkes once occupied. (Wilkes, now free, was busy railing against the British ministry for its "unjust" war in America.) He was watched over by two wardens and deprived of pen and ink. Beneath his window was a fixed bayonet, pointed upward, and just in case, the next day, a workman placed iron bars on his windows. Laurens was expected to pay rent for his close quarters and purchase his own "meat & drink, bedding coals candles &c." To his jailor, he commented sardonically: "Whenever I caught a bird in America I found a cage & victuals for it."[49]

Winslow Warren, by contrast, was allowed to roam through town. Among the many interesting Americans he befriended in London was the young painter John Trumbull, son of the Connecticut governor, who had crossed the Atlantic to study under the famous Benjamin West. On one occasion, Winslow visited the Tower of London, where he had a brief sighting of Henry Laurens: "He was walking on the platform attended by the Royal Guard," Winslow wrote his parents. "We bowed to each other, but it was out of my power to speak to him. This is a favour not permitted even to his son. He appeared very well." That was the extent of their "visit."[50]

On November 13, the status of both Laurens and Warren took a turn for the worse, for the London papers that day announced that a popular British officer, Major John André, had been hanged in America six weeks earlier. André had recruited General Benedict Arnold, formerly a great American hero, to pass along secret information that would have enabled the British to take West Point, and because the Americans could not get their hands on Arnold to punish him, they treated André as a spy rather than a normal prisoner of war.

This did not portend well for Henry Laurens. As pressure mounted in Britain to avenge André's execution, Laurens emerged as the most likely victim. It did not help that among his salvaged papers, which he had assured

Winslow Warren were unimportant, was a secret draft of a treaty he had hoped to negotiate with Dutch officials. This document, although in no way official, provided the pretext for Britain to declare war on Holland. Perhaps Henry Laurens was in over his head, ensnared by the intrigues of international affairs.

Warren was also affected by André's execution. Several of his friends, including Trumbull, were arrested as secret agents, casualties of the spy hysteria that gripped London in the aftermath of the Arnold/André affair. Three times Winslow himself was called in for questioning by Lord Hillsborough, the British official most vilified by Americans, who was currently serving as secretary of state for the Southern Department. Hillsborough had looked through the papers seized from Warren upon his capture, and although he discovered no valuable state secrets, he was impressed nonetheless; according to Winslow, his interrogator "lavished many praises on my mother's letters," and then added, "Mr. Warren, I hope you will profit by her instructions and advice." This was the first and only time Mercy Otis Warren and Lord Hillsborough teamed up, both urging an impressionable young American to resist the corrupting influence of Continental Europe.[51]

Hillsborough tried to convince Warren to return to America and "persuade my father and friends to submit to the best of Kings," but Winslow responded that his "business abroad was commercial, not political," which was the truth, although his mother might have wished he paid a bit more attention to the American cause. On February 1, 1781, Hillsborough released Winslow Warren on condition that he get out of England and proceed to Holland. His confinement was over, but his soul was still on trial: could he resist Europe's allegedly corrupting influence?

British officials were not about to release Henry Laurens, their prime hostage. They would have liked to exchange him for John Burgoyne and his captured army, but the Americans did not think that was such a good bargain. Laurens would stay put, indefinitely—unless the increasingly vindictive mood in Britain led to a more definitive resolution.

September 3–November 14, 1780: Liberty Tree, New Jersey, and Hartford, Connecticut

While Americans as diverse as Henry Laurens and Mercy Otis Warren, Joseph Plumb Martin and George Washington feared that the Revolution was becoming unhinged, some patriots of practical bent focused on what might possibly be done to turn things around. On September 3, 1780, Alexander Hamilton, Washington's aide-de-camp and John Laurens's intimate friend, detailed a prescription for healing the ailing nation: discard the Articles of Confederation (they had yet to be ratified in any case, because Maryland was still holding out) and start anew, creating a governmental structure with centralized authority. Give Congress the power of the purse. Through land taxes, poll taxes, and most of all the revenue from the disposal of all Western lands, Congress would be able to raise and support a decent army—not just for the moment, but after the war as well, a standing army. According to Hamilton, "Congress should have complete sovereignty in all that relates to war, peace, trade, finance" and so on, more than a score of crucial powers that should be granted to Congress. Not the least of these was the authority to create a national bank, which would give large private investors a financial stake in the government.[52]

Internally, Congress must be organized differently: "Congress is properly a deliberative corps and it forgets itself when it attempts to play the executive." Each department should have a single man at the helm, and Hamilton even suggested who those men might be: General Philip Schuyler (his soon-to-be father-in-law) as President of War and Robert Morris as Financier. Here were the outlines of a truly national government, with an emphasis on efficient management, but Hamilton stopped short of the ultimate centralization of power, a single man in charge of everything, a chief executive.

Was the Revolution, initiated in opposition to the centralization of power, turning against itself? Hamilton was not concerned about this: "We run much greater risk of having a weak and disunited federal government, than one which will be able to usurp upon the rights of the people." Power, not liberty, was the issue at hand; ironically, Hamilton penned his proposal from Washington's temporary headquarters at a place called Liberty Pole.

From the standpoint of the original Revolutionaries, whether populists like Thomas Young or idealists like Mercy Otis Warren or theoreticians like Warren's brother James Otis, the most worrisome part of Hamilton's proposal was the manner he suggested for its adoption: a special convention, to be held within the next two months, invested "with full authority to conclude finally upon a general confederation." No need to send the new arrangement back to the states or the people, Hamilton thought. This truly did violate the spirit of the Revolution, which had been propelled all along by the singular belief that all governmental authority resides with the people themselves. Never in Hamilton's scheme would the people as a body have a say in their new form of government.

Hamilton's was not the only remedy suggested, nor was it the most ex-treme. Also in early September, John Mathews, a delegate from South Caro-lina, introduced a motion in Congress that "fully authorized and empowered" General Washington, "in the most compleat & ample manner," using any measures he wished, to raise and equip an army of 25,000 soldiers. It did not stop there. Washington would also be empowered "to do all such matters & things as shall appear to him necessary to promote the wellfare of these United States." He could draw on the treasury as much as he wished, and there would be no oversight. Indeed, Congress would be required "in the most solemn manner . . . to support him and to ratify whatever shall be by him done."[53]

The "most scandalous motion" (as one delegate labeled it) to grant Wash-ington dictatorial powers never came to a vote. As desperate as the na-tion might be, the prevailing sentiment was not to give up on republican government.[54]

Hamilton's ideas were not adopted either, but they came a bit closer, and they would receive serious consideration later on. Starting on November 8 and continuing for a week, delegates from the four New England states and New York met in Hartford to address the breakdown of support for the army and consider measures to remedy it. One proposal: to streamline the workings of government, a "dictator" should be established in each state. That idea was rejected in favor of two other schemes: to give Congress the power of taxation and to grant Washington the authority to collect supplies from the states by whatever means he saw fit. This echoed the motion proposed by John Mathews, but with Washington's dictatorial powers limited to a specific realm.[55]

The Hartford Convention, although it had no legal authority, raised the hackles of committed republicans. James Warren, for one, complained to Samuel Adams:

> Surely history will not be credited when it shall record that a convention of delegates from the four New England states and from the next to them met at Hartford in the year 1780, and in the height of our contest for public liberty and security solemnly resolved to recommend it to their several states to vest the military with civil powers of an extraordinary kind.[56]

Those who supported the extreme measures argued that George Washing-ton, their chosen dictator, was a virtuous man and could therefore be trusted not to abuse his powers, but this argument did not work for Warren:

General Washington is a good and a great man. I love and reverence him. But he is only a man and therefore should not be vested with such powers, and besides we do not know that his successor will be either great or good. Much less can we tell what influence this precedent may have half a century hence.

Washington himself kept a safe distance from the controversy. Although he continued to push for greater control over the army, he evidenced no desire to extend his powers into the civilian domain. Was this simply from personal modesty? A lack of interest in exercising power? Not likely: George Washington might have been virtuous, but like most other men through history who have headed armies, he was not without ambition. A more likely explanation: the commander in chief understood the basic parameters of the American Revolution. Unlike Hamilton, who missed out on the decade of unrest prior to the outbreak of war, Washington was well acquainted with the political dialogue that led in the end to rebellion. Governmental authority resides in the end with the people governed. Standing armies, a threat to civilian society, are to be discouraged. These were cardinal principles. Every time he commanded his soldiers not to plunder, every time he ceded to the will of Congress, George Washington demonstrated his willingness to operate within those guidelines. This was not only virtuous but practical, for to do otherwise would have risked even more serious division. The army was already too much a class apart; if it usurped civilian powers, or if it was even perceived as *wanting* to usurp those powers, the fragile alliances among patriots might be shattered forever.

Better that Congress rule, for better or worse. Yes, Washington would continue to ask for more soldiers, more supplies, and greater authority over the conduct of the war—but that was it. Since military rule was poor policy as well as poor philosophy, the Continental Army had no choice but to beg and plead for the wherewithal to survive, much as it had been doing all along.

Winter 1780–1781: Worcester and Jockey Hollow

But how much longer could soldiers hold out? Joseph Plumb Martin, for one, was willing to stay on the job:

My conscience never did, and I trust never will, accuse me of any failure in my duty to my country, but, on the contrary, I always fulfilled my engagements to her, however she failed in fulfilling hers with me. The case was much like that of a loyal and faithful husband, and a light-heeled wanton of a wife. But I forgive her and hope she will do better in the future.[57]

But many others were not. In December 1780, the main army discharged 4,070 soldiers whose terms of enlistment had expired, while it signed up a mere 98 new recruits to take their place. Among those who left were 108 men from Timothy Bigelow's Massachusetts Fifteenth Regiment. With its ranks depleted, the regiment was disbanded on New Year's Day, 1781, and Colonel Timothy Bigelow was officially "deranged," meaning discharged from his regimental command.[58]

These were not the best of times for Timothy Bigelow. Years earlier, shortly after returning from the disaster at Quebec, John Lamb, Thomas Young's compatriot from New York, had issued a report accusing Bigelow of behavior unbecoming an officer during the assault on the walled city. Lamb had received grapeshot across the left side of his face and suffered the loss of his left eye, and for whatever reason (we do not have the details of his accusation), he appeared to blame both his wound and the failure of the mission on Bigelow, who had been less than enthusiastic about the attack (see chapter 9). When Lamb's accusation reached Washington, the commander in chief discussed the affair with Bigelow and "intimated that it might be necessary for him to clear it up." But nothing happened, and there the matter stood for over three years. Washington apparently put little credence in the charges, for he and Congress continued to entrust Colonel Bigelow with command of a regiment.[59]

But the controversy did not go away. In the summer of 1780, Lamb renewed his charges, and on February 5, 1781, Colonel Timothy Bigelow stood before a five-member court of inquiry, ordered by Major General William Heath, to defend his actions "in consequence of aspersions against his conduct on that day by Colonel Lamb." The final ruling:

The court after reading and considering the evidence produced in support of the charge, and those in favor of Colonel Bigelow with his own remarks in justification of his conduct are of opinion that Colonel Bigelow's conduct in the attack on Quebec the 31st of December 1775 is not reprehensible but that his behavior was consistent with the character of an officer.[60]

Bigelow was exonerated at last, but his enthusiasm for the military had dulled. The record on his whereabouts after his exoneration is sparse, but we can surmise he was in Worcester the following month, for Anna gave birth to the Bigelow's sixth child, daughter Clarissa, on December 29, 1781. (The Bigelows' other five children were born before Timothy went off to war.) We also know he was looking ahead to civilian life. He had organized a group of sixty men to create a town from unsettled lands in central Vermont, and on October 21, 1780, the General Assembly of that would-be state (it would not gain admission for another eleven years) resolved that 23,040 acres "be granted . . . unto Col. Timothy BIGELOW and Company," provided they come up with £480 "in hard money, or its equivalent in Continental currency." On August 14, 1781, the Vermont Assembly granted Bigelow and company their official charter, allowing them to settle the land so long as they reserved "all pine trees suitable for a navy."[61]

Timothy Bigelow, worn down by the war, was planning for his life ahead. So too were all his neighbors back in Worcester. The trouble was, the war was still in progress; there was no end in sight, yet few men were willing to join the army, not even those dedicated patriots who first declared themselves free from British rule back in 1774. In one forty-six-day period during the winter of 1780–1781, the citizens of Worcester squabbled in five successive town meetings over how to meet their quota for Continental soldiers. Votes were taken and retaken, resolves passed and then rescinded. In the end, the town divided its citizens into "classes," balanced according to wealth, and each class had to figure out some way of producing one soldier.[62]

The net result was that poor men were hired to do the fighting while all others, including the most vocal patriots, stayed home. Of the twenty-one men who enlisted in the army early in 1781 to fulfill the quota for the town of Worcester, not one had been a member of the American Political Society, nor had any answered the initial call to Lexington and Concord. These were not the men who started this war, but they were the ones who were being asked to finish it. Of ten recruits with known occupations, seven were farmers, two were shoemakers, and one a butcher. At least two were African American. They were either too poor to vote or they did not come from Worcester, for not a single one appears on the list of town voters for 1779.[63]

Meanwhile, in Jockey Hollow, Continental soldiers of the Pennsylvania Line prepared to settle in for another winter. That's what their commander in chief had ordered them to do, at any rate, but many had other notions. They had enlisted for "three years or the duration of the war," and since three years had passed, they were ready to pack up and go home. Their officers, however, interpreted the terms of enlistment differently; although three years had passed, they observed that the "duration of the war" had not, so they told the soldiers they would have to stay put.

About nine o'clock on the evening of January 1, 1781, many and perhaps most of the 2,400 troops from the Pennsylvania Line picked up where Joseph Plumb Martin and the Connecticut Line had left off the previous spring: they mutinied, and this time they were not so quick to draw back their claws.

On New Year's day, Washington had ordered that a gill of rum be distributed to all men remaining on duty. Whether this was intended as an incentive to stay or simply an act of goodwill, it backfired. The drinking triggered round after round of boisterous complaints, and with both the liquor and the complaints fostering a general spirit of camaraderie, the men finally got the nerve to act on their grievances. As with the Connecticut Line, this started with parading under arms, but then it moved on to seizing artillery, facing off against officers who tried to stop them (one officer was killed this time), and by midnight upwards of one thousand Continental soldiers were marching southward, vowing to take their complaints straight to the halls of Congress.

Washington certainly understood the mutineers' complaints. While new recruits received lucrative bounties, these veterans could not even collect their measly wages. Naturally, they were tempted to leave when their three years were up, then either head home for good or reenlist and collect a new bounty. Yet their actions had disastrous consequences for the Continental Army, which could hardly afford to lose any more men. And besides, ceding to *any* demands of mutineers ran counter to the core values of all self-respecting commanders in chief, and George Washington was no exception.

Faced with no good options, Washington adopted a shotgun approach to minimize the damage. He tried to keep the news from spreading to the encampment at West Point; he readied his troops there, should he decide to call on them to squash the mutiny; he ordered General Anthony Wayne, who commanded the Pennsylvania Line, to position himself between the mutineers and the British, who of course were trying at that very moment to seduce the rebellious Pennsylvanians with offers of better pay and food; he sent word to Congress not to flee as the soldiers approached. This last item was critical. For years, the commander in chief had been careful to avoid the illusion of military interference with civilian affairs, and all he (and the nation) had gained from his acquiescence would be lost in a moment if out-of-control Continental soldiers should invade Philadelphia and force Congress to run.

Days passed, each bringing news of the mutineers' advance toward the nation's capital. On January 6, Washington heard that Pennsylvania's civilian authorities had specifically requested that he *not* lead soldiers their way to head off the mutineers. Joseph Reed, president of Pennsylvania, told Washington he would negotiate with them himself, much as he had done with the insurgents at Fort Wilson. That settled the matter—but only for a few days. After hearing from John Laurens and the Marquis de Lafayette that the mutineers would not let up on any of their demands, which included at this point absolute amnesty, Washington set in motion a plan to head south after all.

But he never did. On the evening of January 15, exactly two weeks after the trouble began, Washington received word that President Reed and the civilian authorities had negotiated a settlement, or, to be more precise, had ceded to the mutineers' demands. All three-year men would be allowed to leave the army; they could go home if they wished, or should they decide to reenlist, they would receive the appropriate bounty. Worse yet, because records were unavailable for the dates and terms of each soldier's enlistment, anyone who simply gave his word that he had been in the army for three years would be granted his discharge.

The mutiny had been resolved at too great a cost, Washington suspected. What if the whole Pennsylvania Line decided to leave? (Most did, as he feared.) Beyond that, the settlement would have "a very pernicious influence on the whole Army," he predicted. Now, anytime soldiers had a grievance (and that would certainly be often, given the sacrifices they were being asked to make), they would try to replicate the success of the Pennsylvania Line.[64]

Sure enough, on January 20, two hundred men from the New Jersey Line rose up in defiance of their officers and vowed to march on Congress. This time, Washington knew exactly how he wanted to respond: "I prefer any extremity . . . to a compromise," he told Congress three days later. "Unless this dangerous spirit can be suppressed by force, there is an end to all subordination in the Army, and indeed to the Army itself." To implement his plan, he ordered General Robert Howe "to compel the mutineers to unconditional submission and execute on the spot a few of the principal incendiaries," leaving the exact manner of repression to Howe's discretion. Accordingly, in the dead of night on January 26–27, General Howe and a detachment of five hundred men surrounded the mutineers' cabins, trained their artillery on these targets, and gave the miscreants five minutes to come out and surrender, without conditions. From the men's officers, Howe learned the identities of three ringleaders and twelve others who had been particularly active in the uprising. The twelve were then turned into a firing squad and ordered to execute first one ringleader, and then a second. The lesson was over. "I hope this will completely extinguish the spirit of mutiny," General Washington wrote in a circular letter to the states.[65]

Yet harsh repression, Washington warned Congress, was not the final solution to the plight of the Continental Army. The underlying problem—lack of financial sustenance—needed to be addressed:

> More certain and permanent funds must be found for the support of the war, than have hitherto existed. Without them, our opposition must very soon cease. The events that have recently taken place are an alarming comment upon the insufficiency of past systems.

To his young confidant John Laurens, Washington expressed his alarm more succinctly yet: "It may be declared in a word, that we are at the end of our tether.... Now or never our deliverance must come."[66]

16

Endgame

Summer 1780–Spring 1781: The Carolinas

If the Americans were in such desperate straits, why weren't they easily subdued by the most powerful empire on earth?

Because that empire was experiencing problems of its own. In 1778 France
had declared war on Great Britain, and the following year Spain joined on
France's side. In the summer of 1779, a combined French-Spanish force of
sixty-six boats and ten thousand men prepared to invade southern England.
For several weeks, the allies cruised the English Channel, and only a breakdown in communications prevented an all-out assault. Meanwhile, France
and Spain laid siege to the British stronghold at Gibraltar and challenged the
British-held island of Minorca, also in the Mediterranean. Naval battles
heated up as the European rivals vied for control in the West Indies. Then in
December of 1780, thanks in part to the bungling of Henry Laurens and the
inadvertent capture of his papers, Holland allied itself with France and Spain.
Because the Dutch controlled the Cape of Good Hope, the critical outpost at
the southern tip of Africa, French ships sailing to India and the East Indies
could resupply while British ships could not, and this affected the battle for
hegemony in the Indian Ocean. In India itself, an anti-imperialist movement
that rivaled that in the United States threatened British control. Russia, too,
was threatening to enter the fray against Britain.

The British Empire, in short, was spread thin across the globe, and other
European powers, sensing its weakness, had seized the opportunity presented
by the American Revolution to break British dominance. Because the United

States was only one of many battlegrounds, Britain could expend no more than a limited portion of its resources in the American theater. To fight a global war required money and men, and the British citizenry was beginning to balk at the cost.

Here in America, the war was at a stalemate, and with the passage of time, the prospects for victory seemed to recede for both sides. Every time the Redcoats and their hired Hessians ventured into the interior, they met with considerable resistance. Conversely, the Americans proved unable to dislodge the British from their coastal enclaves. It seemed that neither side could win this war, but eventually one side must lose. The only question was: who would lose first?

This was the context in which the British high command decided to make one last surge in the southern states, which allegedly boasted a high proportion of loyalists. Once the forces under Clinton had secured Charleston, British intelligence predicted, loyalist partisans would combine with Regulars to take over the countryside.

The intelligence was partly correct, for in the South preexisting feuds had created a bifurcated society, and those who opposed local patriots wound up siding with the British, regardless of any predisposition toward the Crown. Many of these so-called loyalists, however, turned out to be discontented "banditti" (as patriots called them), who roved in bands, pillaged and terrorized local inhabitants, and justified their acts by claiming they were avenging past wrongs. Antagonisms quickly escalated in this environment, as patriots retaliated with similar outrages against their sworn enemies. Major William Pierce of Georgia described the fighting in the summer of 1781:

> Such scenes of desolation, bloodshed and deliberate murder I never was a witness to before! Wherever you turn the weeping widow and fatherless child pour out their melancholy tales to wound the feeling of humanity. The two opposite principles of whiggism and toryism have set the people of this country to cutting each other's throats, and scarce a day passes but some poor deluded tory is put to death at his door. For the want of civil government the bands of society are totally disunited, and the people, by copying the manners of the British, have become perfectly savage.[1]

The sudden presence of British troops served as a catalyst for the internecine warfare. At a place called Waxhaws, less than three weeks after the fall of

Charleston, the British lieutenant colonel Banastre Tarleton commanded a force of 40 British Regulars and 230 American Tories against a small force of Continentals led by Colonel Abraham Buford. Tarleton's men overwhelmed Buford's, and when the patriots tried to surrender, many were hacked to pieces by their Tory foes. On many occasions afterward, patriots who prevailed on the battlefield cried out "Tarleton's Quarter!" or "Remember Buford!" as they slashed away at opponents who were trying to surrender.

The battles in the South were particularly deadly. At Camden on August 16, 1780, some 250 patriot soldiers were killed and another 800 wounded in a rout. General Horatio Gates, who had gained such fame for the victory at Saratoga, fled from the battlefield in great haste, riding 170 miles in three days to safety.[2]

At King's Mountain on October 7, over 1,000 patriot militiamen, many from west of the Appalachian Divide, faced off against a similar number of Tory militiamen commanded by the British major Patrick Ferguson. This time the patriots prevailed, then gave Tarleton's Quarter to many of the Tories who were attempting to surrender. Some 150 Tories were killed, an equal number wounded, and the remaining 700 captured.

At the Cowpens on January 17, 1781, the American general Daniel Morgan figured out how to maximize the untrained militiamen under his command. He placed them on the front line and ordered them to fire exactly three times before retreating; when they turned and ran after firing, they lured the advancing enemy under Tarleton into the direct fire of the experienced Continentals. British losses this time were 120 killed, 200 wounded, and 527 captured.

At Guilford Court House on April 25, Continentals and militiamen under General Nathanael Greene, who had replaced Gates as commander of the Southern army, fought an extended battle against British forces under General Lord Cornwallis. Casualties were steep on both sides, with each losing close to one-third of its men (killed, wounded, captured, or missing). The British held ground at the end of the day and therefore claimed victory, but upon hearing the news, James Fox, a member of Parliament who was critical of the war, echoed Plutarch's famous words by proclaiming: "Another such victory would ruin the British Army!"[3]

At Eutaw Springs on September 8, in another indecisive bloodbath, 223 young men were killed, 726 wounded, and almost 300 never accounted for at the end of the day. The British allegedly "won" this confrontation, but it fulfilled no grand design and achieved minimal strategic results.

These were only the famous battles; there were countless others, many of which pitted Americans against Americans. In South Carolina alone, local men fought pitched battles against each other at least 103 times when nary a Brit was in sight. "The whole country is in danger of being laid waste by the Whigs and Tories who pursue each other with as much relentless fury as beasts of prey," wrote General Nathanael Greene shortly after he assumed command.[4]

Although Carolina's civil war generated no definitive victor, it did produce a significant change in the character, and therefore the meaning, of the American Revolution. After the unbridled butchery, any romantic notions that gentlemanly behavior governed the battlefield were no longer tenable.

April 1781: Mount Vernon

George Washington missed the war in the South. As commander in chief, he felt he had to remain with the main army on the outskirts of New York City to guard against a British takeover of the critical Hudson River corridor. His position there, although essentially defensive, also offered an intriguing offensive possibility. The French Comte de Rochambeau had arrived in Newport in July of 1780 with almost five thousand soldiers under his command; if French warships could ever neutralize the British navy, Washington hoped that his army would unite with Rochambeau's to trap and defeat the British in New York.

For month after month, the French navy remained cautious, Rochambeau remained in Newport, and Washington could muster no more than an occasional and incidental jab at his adversaries. Meanwhile, the British command dispatched its latest high-profile recruit, the traitor Benedict Arnold, and a force of 1,600 to the shores of Chesapeake Bay and the Potomac River, where the Redcoats raided plantations owned by high-profile patriot leaders such as George Washington. The invading soldiers took property at will, burned houses as they pleased, and encouraged slaves to abandon their liberty-loving masters.

On Thursday, April 12, the British sloop of war *Savage* set anchor by Mount Vernon, and, according to the ship's log, thirteen "black refugees" immediately appeared on the shore asking for asylum; three days later, just a bit upstream, five more enslaved African Americans clambered aboard the *Savage* in search of their freedom. George Washington had claimed most of these human beings as his property, while Lund Washington, George's dis-

tant cousin who managed the Mount Vernon plantation, professed ownership of the others. Later, Lund prepared a partial list of those who ran: "Peter,
an old man, . . . Gunner, a man about 45 years old, valuable, a brick maker, . . .
Sambo, a man about 20 years old, stout and healthy, . . . Daniel, a man about
19 years old, very likely, . . . Deborah, a woman about 16 years old," and so on,
seventeen names in all, each with an encapsulated description.[5]

The raid on Mount Vernon embarrassed George Washington. How could
the commander in chief protect the country when he couldn't even protect his
own home? And how could he be making such a fuss about freedom, while
his own slaves mocked his words by seeking freedom with his foes? Washington's world was crumbling around him. The fates of his family, his home, his
livelihood, and, yes, his slaves, were all in the hands of America's most notorious traitor while he himself was far away, helpless.

February 20, 1781–February 21, 1782: Philadelphia

The sorry state of Washington's personal circumstances echoed that of his
nation, and the largest problem, more significant in the long run that any
particular military defeat, was the total collapse of Continental currency. In
1779, the market rate of exchange was eight Continental dollars for one dollar in specie. The rate then climbed steadily higher, reaching about one hundred to one by the end of the year. On March 18, 1780, Congress tried to halt
the runaway depreciation by calling in all previous issues of Continental currency at a fixed rate of forty to one and issuing in their stead interest-bearing
notes backed by the states. The measure didn't work, for the value of the new
notes did not hold fast. The dollar continued to plummet, and its fall raised
fears that the nation would lose all its credit, both at home and abroad.

The collapse of the American monetary system needed to be addressed in
a hurry, for without public credit, the national government could not continue to function, let alone carry on a war. The time for complaining had
passed. Something had to be done.

On February 7, 1781, Congress resolved to create three "civil executive
departments" that would be headed, as Alexander Hamilton and others had
suggested, by individuals, not committees or boards. The first office listed
was Financier, followed by Secretary at War and Secretary of Marine. The
priority was clear: without a workable financial system nothing else was
possible.[6]

On February 20, Congress unanimously elected Robert Morris to serve as Financier. No other candidates received serious attention. But why would Morris, who was profiting greatly in the private sphere, consent to reenter public service, with all its attendant woes?

Not for any private gain, Morris assured Congress three weeks later, for "Providence" had treated him well, and he was looking forward to working less and enjoying the "relaxation and ease" made possible by his good fortune. "If therefore I accept this appointment, a sacrifice of that ease, of much social and domestick enjoyment and of very material interests, must be the inevitable consequence." His "sole motive," he explained, was "the *Public* Good" (his emphasis), since "the want of arrangement in our monied affairs" needed some fixing.[7]

But Morris would accept the job only under three conditions. First, he must be allowed to continue in private business, and Congress had to put this in writing, so that "no doubt may arise, or reflections be cast, on this score hereafter." Clearly, he still smarted over previous allegations that he had used his public office for private gain.

Second, Morris insisted that he, not Congress, appoint "all persons who are to act in my office."

Third, and most controversial: he must have "the absolute *Power* of dismissing from office or employment all persons whatever that are concerned in the official expenditures of public monies." (Again, his emphasis.) This caused many within Congress and without to balk. Congress hemmed and hawed, but in the end it consented to Morris's demands, for it really had no choice in the matter. Nobody else possessed the resources, the credit, the contacts, the experience, and the steely nerves necessary for the job.

In addition to the powers he demanded at the outset, Congress soon granted him others. It placed all money borrowed from foreign governments directly in his hands. It permitted him to import or export goods on the nation's tab. It allowed him to issue private contracts to supply the army, and it placed the entire Marine Department under his control. It granted him the authority to deal with foreign ministers, thereby allowing him to operate his own department of foreign affairs. Meanwhile, the state of Pennsylvania, the nation's most prominent commercial center, granted Morris the authority to run its official business more or less by himself.[8]

Morris accepted the job not only to exert unprecedented power, but also because he had a plan: to hitch public credit, which had failed, to private credit, which thrived. Despite the war—indeed, *because* of it—the private economy flourished in certain fields. Commodity farmers sold their produce at jacked-up wartime prices. Merchants reaped great profits, for demand outstripped supply. Privateering brought a tenuous prosperity to seaport towns. The distribution of wealth was certainly uneven, but many of the rich were getting richer, and these men had money to invest. Morris's idea was to create a national bank, capitalized by private investors, which would extend its credit to the government. In this manner, wealthy men would assume public debt, and once they did, they would make sure the government did not fail.

The bank would operate without restraints. There would be no limitations on the type of investments, no restrictions or regulations, no time limit for the charter. To keep operations secret from "national enemies," the books would have to be closed. One person alone would provide oversight: "the officer who is appointed to manage the monied interests of America," that is to say Financier Robert Morris. Although the very notion of such an institution flew in the face of republican ideology, the struggling nation was held hostage to Morris's scheme. Despite the scanty oversight and the absence of any provision within the Articles of Confederation for chartering such a bank, Congress took a mere nine days to approve the Bank of North America, for it really had no other options.[9]

Raising capital for the new bank, however, proved more troublesome than gaining the consent of Congress. Three months later, it was still not capitalized, for men with money hesitated before investing in any scheme pegged to the public sector, even indirectly. Then suddenly, late in the summer of 1781, John Laurens returned from France with $463,000 in specie. (After being released from his parole through a prisoner exchange, Laurens the younger had been sent abroad by Congress, with Washington's blessing, to borrow whatever funds he could.) Congress directed Laurens to turn his payload over to the Financier, who quickly dispatched a train of fourteen wagons and fifty-six oxen, accompanied by a large military escort, to carry the treasure from Boston, where Laurens had landed, to Philadelphia. Morris then used this new money to finish capitalizing his bank. The original idea for capitalization had been turned on its head: instead of private capital coming to the aid of public, the sudden infusion of public capital allowed the bank to commence operations, with private investors assuming control of public funds.

On November 1, investors in the Bank of North American gathered at the City Tavern and elected Morris's former partner, Thomas Willing—Old Square Toes—to serve as their first president, and by January the bank was up and running.

Financial Meltdown: Problems and Solutions

Figure 32

Figure 33

Figure 34

Figure 32. To stabilize the Continental currency, Congress called in all its notes, issuing in return state notes that promised one dollar in hard money for forty dollars of the old currency. Hence this Virginia banknote from 1781, not due until 1792. Even these devalued notes, however, failed to hold their value. *(The Granger Collection, New York)* **Figure 33.** Robert Morris (standing) and Gouverneur Morris: the Financier and Assistant Financier at work in 1783, as depicted by Charles Willson Peale. *(Courtesy of the Pennsylvania Academy of the Fine Arts, Philadelphia; bequest of Richard Ashhurst)* **Figure 34.** With this twenty-dollar "Morris note," a sight draft payable to the bearer by the cashier of the Office of Finance, Morris substituted his personal credit for that of the nation. His own signature was key: unlike other currency, Morris Notes held their value.

While the national bank helped the flow of credit, its notes were too large and issued too infrequently to function as the nation's only currency. That's why the Financier created "Morris notes," drafts of $20 to $100, redeemable in specie, signed by himself and watermarked "United States." Morris's own signature was key, for he vowed if the government couldn't make good on the notes, he would: "My personal credit, which thank Heaven I have preserved throughout all the tempests of the War, has been substituted for that which the country had lost." Starting in November of 1781, Morris notes superseded Continental currency in common business transactions. The bad news was that people placed more trust in the financial viability of a single individual than they did in the solvency of their government; the good news was that this particular individual, who had profited greatly from the war, was now willing to stake his fortune on behalf of a bankrupt nation.[10]

By early 1782, Morris's reign was well under way. No other appointed government official in United States history has had the term *reign* assigned to his tenure with such casual abandon. But then few others have had the term "Great One" or "Dictator" associated with their names either, and nobody else, before or since, has exerted as much power over Congress. Late in 1781, Joseph Reed commented wryly to Nathanael Greene:

> The business of that august body has been extremely simplified, Mr. Morris having relieved them from all business of deliberation or executive difficulty with which money is in any respect connected, and they are now very much at leisure to read dispatches, return thanks, pay and receive compliments, &c. For form's sake some things go thither to receive a sanction, but it is the general opinion that it is form only.[11]

Still, despite the Financier's clout, he lacked the one power he needed most: the ability to tax. Without a secure source of future revenues, the national government would have a difficult time convincing people to lend it money. In his plan for a National Bank, Morris explained that the government would extend credit "in anticipation of taxes," yet at the time, Congress did not possess the authority to levy a tax of any kind. Only the states held that power, because only the states were directly responsible to the people. Unless or until the states, and the people within them, granted Congress the power to raise money through taxes, even the Financier himself could provide no more than stopgap measures to shore up the bankrupt nation.[12]

October 17, 1781: Yorktown, Virginia

As the Financier endeavored to solve the nation's monetary problems, the commander in chief puzzled over how to crack the military stalemate. Here, the French held a trump card—but would they play it?

By May of 1781, Washington had spent the better part of a year trying to coordinate efforts with the French Army and navy stationed in Rhode Island, where they were accomplishing nothing more than guarding the Newport harbor. Washington had first proposed a combined attack on New York City, which the British had occupied since 1776; then he tried to interest his allies in an assault on British forces in Virginia; after that failed to materialize, he went back to advocating New York. The truth was: it was not his to decide. Technically, the French forces had been placed under his command; in reality, they would fight when and where they wanted.

All this came to a head when rumors suggested that a large French fleet under Admiral Comte de Grasse was headed toward the West Indies, with instructions to stop over on the North American continent to assist the effort there. If this fleet joined with French ships already in New England, the allies would be in a position, for the first time in the war, to challenge British control of the coast.

Washington had heard talk like this before, and he didn't place much faith in it until the last week in May, when he received a letter from John Laurens (still in Europe), sent two months earlier, that confirmed the rumor. By June 13, he was sure of the matter: de Grasse was on his way. But where would he alight ashore? New York, to challenge the main British force directly? The Chesapeake, to cut the chain of supplies to British troops there? Or perhaps even Charleston, to reestablish control over the Deep South?

Rochambeau preferred the Chesapeake, but Washington, who had been arguing for New York, suggested that de Grasse himself decide, based on intelligence of the whereabouts of the British fleet at the time of his arrival. The land forces under Washington and Rochambeau could then march speedily to meet up with de Grasse. After six years of fighting, George Washington understood that the circumstances of war constantly change, and that flexibility was the supreme military virtue.[13]

Whatever de Grasse's destination, Rochambeau and Washington needed to combine their forces and prepare to move on a moment's notice. Rochambeau and his army arrived on the outskirts of New York in early July, and there Washington waited for further word of de Grasse's whereabouts.

Waited and worried, that is. The states had not met their requisitions for more soldiers. As of July 15, the main army around New York had only 5,835 men available to fight, far short of the 10,250 Washington had promised Rochambeau two months earlier. Furthermore, there was no money to pay these soldiers, nor sufficient stores of food for their projected offensive.[14]

As he had done so often in the past, Washington appealed to the most powerful civilian in the nation to help him out: Robert Morris, the recently anointed Financier. And as usual, Morris did all in his power to garner resources. He scurried after money and flour. He reorganized the supply chain. (Instead of transporting the states' requisitions of supplies to the army, he ordered them to be sold in local markets, and he then used the money to purchase what the soldiers truly needed from nearby sources.) This helped, but it was not enough.

Early in August, Congress requested Morris and Richard Peters of the Board of War to visit Washington at his camp at Dobbs Ferry. The agenda: the future of the Continental Army. How could it be kept in the field?

Morris and Peters arrived on August 11 for the high-level confab. They talked for days, and as they did, on the afternoon of August 14, Washington received the news he had been waiting for: de Grasse was headed to the Chesapeake with twenty-five to twenty-nine warships and 3,200 fighting men on board. But there was one hitch: the French admiral intended to stay two months at the most, for he had a date to rendezvous with Spanish forces in the West Indies in mid-October.[15]

Immediately, Washington placed the wheels in motion. Rather than commit his scheme to writing, he sent Morris to Congress with news "of our situation, our prospects, and designs." Then on August 19, Washington led about half the men under his command southward; Rochambeau followed with his full force a few days later. As cover, Washington made visible movements suggesting an impending assault on Staten Island. How well this worked is debatable. From Philadelphia, where many loyalists still resided, Robert Morris reported to Washington on August 28: "Too many people have for some days past seemed to know Your Excellency's intended movements."[16]

While Washington and Rochambeau marched their troops, Morris worked at a feverish clip to line up the food, wagons, and boats the soldiers would need. He wasted no energy on faraway states; instead, he sent out urgent appeals to Maryland, Delaware, and New Jersey. He also mobilized the available resources of his own state, Pennsylvania, which he himself controlled.

Around one o'clock on the afternoon of August 30, Washington and Rochambeau arrived in Philadelphia with their respective armies. Morris and other prominent Philadelphians ventured to the edge of town and escorted the generals to the City Tavern for a public reception. Washington then made a brief appearance before Congress, and, from there, he and his entourage headed to Morris's house on the waterfront, where the Financier put out an "excellent repast" for the American and French dignitaries. "We had all the foreign wines possible with which to drink endless toasts," wrote Baron Ludwig von Closen, one of Rochambeau's aides. In his diary, Morris himself chronicled the toasting:

> The owners of several ships in the harbour ordered them out in the stream and fired salutes whilst we drank the United States, his most Christian Majesty [king of France], his Catholic Majesty [king of Spain], the United Provinces [Dutch Republic], the Allied Armys, Count De Grasse speedy arrival &ca.[17]

Although the toasts were truly international in scope, noticeably missing was the once-obligatory homage to the British monarch.

On September 5, having just headed southward from Philadelphia, Washington received news that de Grasse's fleet had arrived in Virginia, tangled briefly with some British ships, and held its position. Meanwhile, the French fleet that had been stationed in New England managed to slip into the Chesapeake, producing an overwhelming superiority. Uncharacteristically, the British navy was outclassed. The southern branch of the British Army, commanded by Lord Cornwallis, could now be entrapped.

Still, Washington fretted. Might General Clinton send reinforcements from New York? Could Cornwallis escape by land, or might he and his army surreptitiously cross the Chesapeake and head north?

Such schemes could be thwarted, but only if Washington's land force came through, and that was not a foregone conclusion. A familiar problem was reemerging: as Robert Morris recorded in his diary, "great symptoms of discontent had appeared" among the soldiers as they passed through Philadelphia. The mutinous spirit was alive and well amid the rank and file of the Continental Army. It would no longer suffice to tell the troops the moment was critical, for they had heard that too many times before. Now, men like Joseph Plumb Martin demanded to be paid—in hard cash, no less—before they ventured once again into battle. When Washington arrived at the northern shore of the Chesapeake, he found the troops even more restless than he had imagined, and on September 6, the day after receiving the good news about de Grasse, he penned an urgent message to the man who held the purse strings of the nation:

> Every day discovers to me the increasing necessity of some money for the troops. I hope by this time you are provided to give a month's pay. . . . I may leave in a few hours. I cannot do it, however, without intreating you in the warmest terms to send on a month's pay at least, with all the expedition possible. I wish it to come on the wings of speed.[18]

But Washington's entreaty was not necessary, for the Financier had already taken care of business. The evening before, he had begged a loan of "20,000 hard dollars" from the French minister Anne-César, Chevalier de la Luzerne, to be repaid by October 1. Morris guaranteed the repayment from his own funds if necessary but, ironically, his actual plan was to pay back the French loan with a different bucket of French money, the hard cash John Laurens had just obtained on his foreign mission.[19]

The soldiers were paid, and the expedition continued. "We each of us received a MONTH'S PAY, in specie," Joseph Plumb Martin recalled years later. "This was the first that could be called money, which we had received as wages since the year '76, or that we ever did receive till the close of the war, or indeed, ever after, as wages."[20]

Joseph Plumb Martin was one of over sixteen thousand men—Continentals, Virginia militiamen, and French soldiers—who converged on the Yorktown Peninsula, between the James and York Rivers, to lay siege to some seven thousand British and Hessians under the command of Lord Charles Cornwallis. For the previous three years, Martin had been stationed with Washington in the proximity of New York, where he engaged in various minor skirmishes with the enemy and numerous forays into the countryside to procure food, his never-ending obsession. In the summer of 1780, General Washington had ordered that one soldier from each regiment, "an able bodied man, intelligent, sober, and engaged for the War," be drafted into a "Corps of Sappers and Miners," which would specialize in the construction of trenches (saps) and fortifications. Martin was selected, and soon thereafter he was promoted to the rank of sergeant. The spirited young fellow was an excellent choice for the corps—able-bodied, intelligent, engaged for the duration of the war, and perhaps as sober as a self-respecting soldier could be. Now, Martin and his cadre of sappers and miners would assume center stage, leading the effort to construct the physical infrastructure for an all-out, eighteenth-century siege.[21]

On September 28, Martin and the rest of the besieging force marched from Williamsburg. Upon reaching the outskirts of Yorktown, the sappers and miners started their work:

> We now began to make preparations for laying close siege to the enemy. We had holed him and nothing remained but to dig him out. Accordingly, after taking every precaution to prevent his escape, we settled our guards, provided fascines and gabions [bundles of brush and cylindrical wickerwork, used in earthen fortifications], made platforms for the batteries, to be laid out when needed, brought on our battering pieces, ammunitions, &c.[22]

By October 6 all was in place to begin the bombardment, and by Martin's count "ninety-two cannon, mortars and howitzers" began pounding away at the British forces encamped within Yorktown.

The siege was under way, and Sergeant Joseph Plumb Martin began serving twenty-four-hour shifts in the trenches he had helped to build. When not on active duty, he scoured the nearby environs for food and drinkable water, much as he had been doing throughout the war. (Virginia had been suffering from a drought, so staples like flour or corn were scarce.) Save for the money in his pocket and the rarity of being on the offense rather than defense, it was everyday life as usual for the Continental Army.

The circumstances, however, were highly unusual. One unique feature caught Martin's attention:

> During the siege, we saw in the woods herds of Negroes which Lord Cornwallis (after he had inveighed them from their proprietors), in love and pity to them, had turned adrift, with no other recompense for their confidence in his humanity than the smallpox for their bounty and starvation and death for their wages. They might be seen scattered about in every direction, dead and dying, with pieces of ears of burnt Indian corn in the hands and mouths, even of those that were dead.

After the siege, the former owners of these enslaved African Americans offered rewards for their return. Martin helped one master get hold of a man he claimed to own, for which he received "twelve hundred (nominal) dollars," worth only one actual dollar, which he later spent on "one single quart of rum."[23]

On the night of October 14, Sergeant Martin participated in one of the most dangerous missions of the war. In preparation for a bayonet assault on a British redoubt (earthwork fortification), Lieutenant Colonel Alexander Hamilton, who had finally received command of a regiment, gave Martin and his corps a most difficult task: to lead the charge and cut through the dense thicket of abates (pointed sticks) British soldiers had erected for their defense. Just as Martin approached the spiked web, he received enemy fire. A man beside him fell, as did another friend, but the sappers did their job and the bayonet charge succeeded. Hamilton's regiment seized the redoubt, aided by a battalion commanded by John Laurens, who had rushed south from Boston to join the fray as soon as he returned from Europe. Meanwhile, French forces took the neighboring redoubt, and by the end of the evening the allies were digging trenches within 250 yards of enemy lines.

Two nights later, General Cornwallis tried to ferry soldiers across the York River to a small British outpost at Gloucester, from which they might have a better chance of bursting through the Allied lines, but a squall disrupted the maneuver, and the soldiers returned to their base at Yorktown. Cornwallis and his army were completely surrounded, with little hope of escape.

The following morning, shortly after nine o'clock on October 17, 1781—the fourth anniversary of Burgoyne's surrender at Saratoga—a British officer appeared in the field between the armies bearing a white handkerchief and a letter for General Washington:

> Sir, I propose a cessation of hostilities for twenty-four hours, and that two officers may be appointed by each side, to meet at Mr. Moore's house, to settle terms for the surrender of the posts at York and Gloucester.
>
> I have the honor to be, &c
Cornwallis[24]

The first ambassador Washington chose to "settle terms for the surrender" was John Laurens, his trusted friend and devoted aide. (Laurens was so devoted to his mentor that he had fought a duel with Charles Lee, Washington's longtime rival, for having "publicly abused General Washington in the grossest terms.") Laurens, although young, had gained some experience in the art of negotiation during his recent mission to France, and besides, his fluency in French would facilitate communication with Rochambeau's representative, Louis-Marie, Viscount de Noailles, brother-in-law to the Marquis de Lafayette.[25]

Washington himself dictated the broad outlines of the surrender: the captured British and German soldiers would not be allowed passage back to Europe; all "artillery, arms, accoutrements, military chest and public stores" would be delivered to the captors; the British would tend to their own sick and wounded. Laurens was to insist on these, while considering any ameliorating proposals the British envoys might suggest.[26]

Through the day on October 18, and almost till midnight, Laurens and de Noailles hammered out the fine points with their British counterparts. British officers, because they were gentlemen, would be permitted special treatment, but the entire army captured within Yorktown would have to submit to a humiliating ritual of surrender, much like the one Laurens himself was forced to endure after the surrender of Charleston.

The following day, Joseph Plumb Martin and thousands of others witnessed the formalities:

> After breakfast, on the nineteenth, we were marched onto the ground and paraded on the right-hand side of the road, and the French forces on the left. We waited two or three hours before the British made their appearance. They were not always so dilatory, but they were compelled at last, by necessity, to appear, all armed, with bayonets fixed, drums beating, and faces lengthening. . . . They marched to the place appointed and stacked their arms; they then returned to the town in the same manner they marched out, except divested of their arms.[27]

Another eyewitness, Aedanus Burke from South Carolina, wrote at the time:

> They marched through both armies in a slow pace, and to the sound of music, not military marches, but of certain airs, which had in them so peculiar a strain of melancholy, and which together with the appearance before me, excited sentiments far different from those I expected to enjoy.[28]

Half a century later, a patriotic text announced that the song being played was called "The World Turn'd Upside Down," and Americans ever since have embraced that notion, although there is no contemporary evidence to support this. If that were indeed the tune, it was an adaptation of a popular melody commonly known as "When the King Enjoys His Own Again," words the British soldiers were more likely to embrace. But in our national memory,

Yorktown enjoys a special place, and we, like the victorious army at the time, have chosen to celebrate it on our own terms.

June 23–December 31, 1781: Tower of London

John Laurens celebrated the victory at Yorktown by trying to get his father out of jail. The British commander he had helped to capture, Charles Cornwallis, was not only an earl and a general, but also the constable of the Tower of London. This meant that Henry Laurens's chief jailor was now a prisoner of the United States, and beyond that, John reasoned, Cornwallis might be an appropriate candidate for a prisoner exchange.

Through an intermediary, Laurens ran the idea by Cornwallis himself, who naturally approved. He then approached Washington, but although the commander in chief agreed in principle, he stated that such matters fell under the jurisdiction of Congress. Even so, Laurens passed word to Cornwallis, and through him to Sir Henry Clinton, commander of the British Army in North America, that Washington endorsed the proposal. Yet a major problem remained: how could Laurens, whom the British considered a prisoner of state, be exchanged for Cornwallis, who was clearly a prisoner of war?[29]

Henry Laurens's status had been an issue from the start. Just before he was sent to the Tower of London, Laurens had been quizzed before a panel of the British secretaries of state and other high-level officials. The following day, the London *Evening Post* reported on the "examination":

Did Laurens consider himself a subject of the British Crown?

No.

To what kingdom was he then subject?

"No kingdom whatever," he reportedly answered. He had "no other superior than the United States of America, collectively represented by Congress."

Had he ever considered himself a British subject?

Yes, he responded, but "when men found themselves aggrieved, and had no prospects of redress," they had the right to "withdraw their allegiance," which he had done.

After being told he would be committed to the Tower, Laurens went on the offensive. His examiners were "violating the law of nations to detain an ambassador," he insisted, and he "hoped every court in Europe would shew their detestation of such conduct."[30]

The British, in short, treated Laurens as a disloyal subject, a traitor, a prisoner of state. Laurens considered himself a legitimate ambassador, illegally detained, of an independent nation, and he would not bow to the authority of his captors.

But eight months later, after a damp and lonely winter, Laurens altered his tone. Confinement had taken its toll on his health and his finances, and he petitioned Parliament "to mitigate the rigor of his imprisonment" by granting him the access to pen and ink, the right to receive visits from his son John, and "such further indulgence . . . as to Your Lordships wisdom & goodness shall seem fitting." Gone was the defiant tone. To curry favor, Laurens detailed his long history of allegiance to the British king, dating back to his first public service in the 1750s. He was always considered a "King's man & Governors man," he wrote. He had opposed the Stamp Act rioters, and had even repulsed them from his home. During the turbulent two years prior to independence, he had "persisted in discountenancing all acts of compulsion & violence" directed at loyalists. He had decried the ideas of Thomas Paine, had opposed independence, and had wept openly when it came. Conveniently, the petitioner failed to chronicle his run-ins with the customs officials, his chairmanship of meetings under Charleston's Liberty Tree, his recruitment of Revolutionary soldiers, his presidency of both the South Carolina Provincial Congress and the Continental Congress, and his undeviating support for George Washington, who led Americans into battle against the British Army.

Although Parliament never did consider Laurens's petition, Edmund Burke, the influential, pro-American MP, tried to negotiate his release. Before Yorktown, both Burke and delegates to the Continental Congress talked of exchanging Laurens for John Burgoyne, but that ran into two obstacles: first, the dissimilarity between a prisoner of war and a prisoner of state, and, second, Burgoyne's unpopularity in England. Then on December 1, upon Burke's suggestion, Laurens submitted a second petition, much briefer this time, but still presenting himself as less than a revolutionary:

> That the representer for many years at the peril of his life & fortune ardently laboured to preserve & strengthen the ancient friendship between Great Britain & the Colonies; & that in no instance he ever excited on either side the dissentions which separated them,
> That the commencement of the present war was a subject of great grief to him, inasmuch as he foresaw, & foretold in letters now extant the distresses which both countries experience at this day.[31]

Figure 35. Henry Laurens in 1782, shortly after being released from the Tower of London. John Singleton Copley, the artist, chose to portray Laurens in his prime, dealing with matters of state while president of Congress in 1778. *(The Granger Collection, New York)*

The fortunes of war had changed considerably over the previous half year, and Laurens now dared to ask for more than lenient treatment: if he would be "enlarged from his present restraint," he would "strictly conform to such rules as shall be prescribed for his conduct, & that with all possible dispatch he will procure or obtain the release of such British officer, or other British subject or subjects, prisoner or prisoners, in America as shall be deemed an adequate equivalent in exchange." In other words, Laurens promised to negotiate his own prisoner exchange.

Still, the legal issues lingered, but on the last day of the year, rather than wait for a final solution, British officials set Henry Laurens free on bail, under the pretense that he could then tend to his poor health. It is doubtful anybody expected him to be imprisoned again, and sure enough, he wasn't. Four months later, Laurens was officially exchanged for Lord Cornwallis.

January–March 1782: Burlington, New Jersey

Joseph Plumb Martin celebrated the victory at Yorktown by spending the winter "snugly stowed away . . . in a large elegant house, which had formerly been the residence of the Governor, when the state was a British province." Warm and secure in his makeshift dormitory, far away from the enemy, his fortunes appeared to be on the rise. But it was here in "Green Bank," the plush estate of William Franklin, Benjamin's loyalist son and the last governor of colonial New Jersey, that the six-year veteran, having just turned twenty-one, faced his closest brush with death.[32]

The trouble started in January when two of his housemates came down with "a species of yellow fever." One recovered, the other did not. Soon others contracted the disease, and in February Martin himself fell ill: "It took hold of me in good earnest. I bled violently from the nose, and was so reduced in flesh and strength in a few days that I was as helpless as an infant." More than twenty of his housemates joined Martin in his misery, forcing the officers to transform one of the regal chambers into a hospital.

There, "among the sick and dying," Martin took his spot: "We lay on sacks filled with straw, our beds mostly upon the floor, in a rank on each side of the room, with an alley in between." The orderly arrangement, combined with idleness and delusions, set his mind to evil work. The man closest to the door on his side of the room died. Then the fourth patient in his row followed suit. Methodically, Death was seizing every fourth man, Martin concluded, and he quickly sized up his position: he was the fifth man after that, not the fourth, so he should be safe. But what if the Reaper made a minor miscalculation?

Fortunately for Martin, the Reaper remained on course, skipping the next three in the row and taking the fourth, his immediate neighbor. Martin expressed relief, not remorse: "After his death, I felt myself exempted," Martin admitted, and this "helped . . . toward my recovery." Years later, with perspective, the former patient mused philosophically: "When the body is feeble and the head weak, . . . such strange whims will often work great effects. . . . I know it by too frequent experience."

His conjurings aside, Joseph Plumb Martin was aided in his recovery by one of those random acts of love and kindness that mitigate human suffering during times of war, famine, or epidemic disease:

There was ... in the city a widow woman that rendered us the most essential service during our sickness. As we were unable to eat anything and had only our rations of beef and bread to subsist upon, this widow, this pitying angel, used almost every evening to send us a little brass kettle containing about a pailful of posset, consisting of wine, water, sugar, and crackers. O, it was delicious, even to our sick palates. I never knew who our kind benefactress was; all I ever knew concerning her was that she was a widow. The neighbors would not tell us who she was nor where she lived. All that I, or any others who had been sick, could learn from them was that she was a very fine, pious and charitable lady. Perhaps she did not wish to have a trumpet sounded before her alms and therefore kept concealed. I hope Heaven will bless her pious soul.[33]

As frequently as soldiers complained about the lack of civilian support, they certainly cherished such individual acts by very kind people. Martin's "pitying angel" was not alone in her efforts. Collectively and politically, civilians had been reluctant to support the army; individually, many offered generous assistance. If all veterans of the war had told their tales, few would omit, because few could forget, stories about their particular angels.

March 8 and June 11, 1782: Gnadenhütten Mission and Wyandot, Ohio

George Washington did not celebrate the victory at Yorktown with much fanfare. While others were proclaiming that the tide had turned and the war was nearing an end, the commander in chief redoubled his efforts to build up the Continental Army. Eight days after Cornwallis signed the terms of surrender, Washington warned Congress that a failure to pursue the war would "certainly expose us to the most disgracefull dangers." In the following weeks, he reiterated this message more than a dozen times. To Nathanael Greene he confided:

My greatest fear is that Congress, viewing this stroke in too important a point of light, may think our work too nearly closed, and will fall into a state of languor and relaxation; to prevent this error, I shall employ every means in my power, and if unhappily we sink into that fatal mistake, no part of the blame shall be mine.[34]

The war was far from over, and Washington understood this better than most. Just to the south, in the West Indies, British and French fleets continued to battle for control of the seas. In addition, British land forces were still formidable: 17,000 troops stationed in New York; 9,000 in Canada; 11,000 in South Carolina and Georgia; 10,000 in the West Indies—a total of 47,000 men, several times the size of the Continental Army. In this context, the capture of 7,000 fighting men at Yorktown was hardly a crippling blow. Both the British at Saratoga and the Americans at Charleston had suffered comparable defeats, and yet they had continued to fight. The question was not whether the British *could* continue the war, but whether they had the will to do so, and the answer to that was beyond the control of George Washington, the Continental Army, or the Continental Congress. The outcome was likely to be determined by Britain's concurrent struggle with France in the West Indies, with France and Spain in the Mediterranean, with the Netherlands in the North Sea, South Africa, and the East Indies, and with anticolonial insurgents in India.[35]

Closer to home, conflict continued without missing a beat on two distinct fronts: the Carolina backcountry, where homegrown patriots and loyalists still pursued each other with relentless fury, and the vast region west of the Appalachians, where Native Americans struggled against white vigilantes, state militiamen, and federal soldiers.

To the northwest, the Sullivan scorched-earth expedition of 1779, intended to suppress Iroquois resistance, had produced the opposite effect. The following year, some 830 warriors killed or captured 350 white Americans, seized and destroyed six forts and over seven hundreed houses and barns, and eradicated great quantities of food, avenging what Sullivan and company had done to them. In 1781, at least sixty-four small bands of warriors, traveling light but inflicting great carnage, continued their angry rampage.

To the southwest, Dragging Canoe and the Chickamauga branch of the Cherokees continued their fierce resistance to any white intrusions, regardless of what transpired between British and American armies on the Eastern Seaboard in the fall of 1781 (see chapter 12).

In the Ohio country, most of the once-friendly Delaware had turned hostile after a series of deceptions and murders by white militiamen and vigilantes. Some Delaware, attempting to avoid the hostilities, moved in with Moravian missionaries, but on March 8, 1782, volunteers from the Pennsylvania militia, smarting over the latest wave of raids by hostile warriors, vented their anger by systematically butchering ninety-six noncombatants—

twenty-eight men, twenty-nine women, and thirty-nine children—who were gathering food at the Gnadenhütten Mission. David Zeisberger, one of the missionaries, recounted the story of the massacre as it was told to him by one of two survivors, who had escaped into the bushes:

> Our Indians were mostly on the plantations and saw the militia come, but no one thought of fleeing, for they suspected no ill. The militia came to them and bade them come into the town, telling them no harm should befall them. . . . They made our Indians bring all their hidden goods out of the bush, and then they took them away; they had to tell them where in the bush the bees were, help get the honey out; other things also they had to do for them before they were killed. . . .
>
> They prayed and sang until the tomahawks struck into their heads. The boy who was scalped and got away, said the blood flowed in streams in the house. They burned the dead bodies, together with the houses, which they set on fire.[36]

The Gnadenhütten Massacre escalated the cycle of violence, if that was at all possible. As warriors from the Delaware, Shawnee, and other Western nations mustered their forces, some five hundred militiamen, mostly from Pennsylvania and a few from Virginia, gathered on the western bank of the Ohio for an attack on Indian towns along the Sandusky River. They elected as their leader Colonel William Crawford, the seasoned backwoodsmen, soldier, and surveyor whom George Washington had recruited as his land agent back in 1767.

Crawford and company anticipated a search-and-destroy mission against scattered bands, but they encountered instead a well-organized resistance. Finding themselves outmaneuvered and seemingly outnumbered, they attempted a retreat. Although the main body withdrew unharmed, small parties that broke off on their own were picked off. When Crawford himself peeled off to look for his missing son, son-in-law, and two nephews, he was surrounded and taken prisoner.

William Crawford's captors apparently knew who he was, for they accorded him special treatment. According to a fellow captive, who later escaped, he was stripped, beaten, and tied to a post by a fire. Warriors shot him repeatedly at close range, pummeling their prisoner not with bullets but with gunpowder, which lodged under his skin as it burned. Women poked him with burning sticks until his entire body, genitals included, was spotted with scalding

contusions. Crawford crumbled and weakened. To a cheering crowd, his captors then cut off his ears, scalped him, and watched him roast till he died.
Although his fellow prisoner might have embellished the story (torture tales
were a familiar frontier genre), it seems likely, under the circumstances, that
William Crawford did indeed pay a high price for atrocities committed by his
countrymen.[37]

In July, more than a month after the fact, George Washington received the
news that his friend and partner had been captured by Indians, then "burned
and tortured in every manner they could invent." Although his informant
spared the details, these simple words were temptation enough for Washington's imagination to run wild, if he allowed it to do so. We might expect that
the news would provoke anger and stimulate an impulsive urge for revenge,
but instead, this seasoned soldier was able to step back and look at the situation from the Indian point of view: "No other than the extremest tortures
which could be inflicted by savages could, I think, have been expected ...
under the present exasperation of their minds for the treatment given their
Moravian friends." Then, with cool, military composure, the general issued
orders appropriate to the circumstances: "For this reason, no person should at
this time, suffer himself to fall alive into the hands of Indians."[38]

Although George Washington was able to lay part of the blame for Crawford's suffering and death on his own bloodthirsty countrymen, he stopped
far short of acknowledging his own hand in the matter. Three years earlier, as
commander in chief, he had ordered 4,500 Continental soldiers to spread
"terror" among Indian populations, to seek the "total ruinment of their settlements," and to capture "as many prisoners of every age and sex as possible"
(see chapter 15). While carrying out these orders, some soldiers had given
their own creative interpretations to such words as "terror" and "ruinment";
one American officer, for instance, reported proudly that he and his buddy,
after killing some Indians, had "skinned two of them from their hips down for
boot legs." Mutilation, scalping, and torture were part and parcel of white-
Indian conflicts, and George Washington, with his military offenses in the
West, did his part to perpetuate the cycle of violence.[39]

Most Indians understood General Washington's role in the conflict, and
the warriors who captured William Crawford also knew of Washington's
relationship with their prisoner. With them at the time was Simon Girty,
the famed American backwoodsman who had served as a recruiter for the
Continental Army before switching over to the Indian-British alliance,
and Girty was certainly cognizant of the Washington-Crawford connection.

While Indians along the Sandusky River could not get directly at Town Destroyer, as they called Washington, they could and did take vengeance on his surrogate—friend, agent, and fellow warrior.

Through their deeds, the people who treated William Crawford so cruelly delivered a message that George Washington could not easily ignore. He had always wanted to push west, but he faced a series of obstacles: first French traders and adventurers, then the British imperial government, and always the Native Americans who lived there. He had fought a lengthy war against the French, which he himself instigated at Jumonville Glen more than a quarter century past. Now he was immersed in a lengthy war against the British, with the French by his side. But even if he and his countrymen emerged as victors against European nations, the longtime residents of the American West would continue to resist. These people were more than "tedious" impediments, as Washington had regarded them in his visit to the Ohio country back in 1770. They were freedom fighters, at least as committed as any American patriot to the complete sovereignty of their own nations, and like Washington himself, they were not above using terror to achieve their goal.

August 27, 1782: Combahee Ferry, South Carolina

While General Washington *warned* that fighting would continue after Yorktown, Lieutenant Colonel John Laurens *hoped* it would. Without a war, Laurens could not achieve his two overriding goals: "gaining fame" by his performance on the battlefield, and proving that slaves could be turned into soldiers.[40]

Early in November, as Washington journeyed north to rejoin the watch around New York, John Laurens, by his own request, headed back to his native South Carolina to serve under General Nathanael Greene. Once there, he was immediately elected to the House of Representatives, and in that body he reintroduced his scheme for arming slaves. The patriots needed to take back Charleston, he argued, before diplomats in some distant place negotiated a peace settlement that preserved the status quo—but they couldn't do it without tapping in to the state's most available pool of new recruits.

Through the first week of February 1782, the House debated Laurens's controversial proposal. During previous debates, opponents noted that owners would have to be recompensed for their loss of property, and because the state was perennially broke, it could never afford the buyout. This time, however, Laurens neutralized that argument: slaves would be recruited from the confiscated estates of rich loyalists, with no compensation needed.

On paper, the proposal looked sound, but it never stood a chance, for the thought of placing guns in the hands of blacks still evoked horror among most whites in the slave states. When a vote was finally taken, Laurens lost by a seven-to-one margin. Instead of arming slaves, the House decided to offer a special bounty—one African American slave—to any white man from South Carolina willing to sign up with the Continental Army.[41]

John Laurens also faced difficulties in his quest for military honor. Things started well: for his first assignment, General Greene gave the ambitious young officer license to plan and execute a surprise assault on a British post, and just before the attack, Laurens delivered an inspirational talk to his men. Here are his notes:

> The Col. entreats the troops to place their principal reliance on the bayonet, which is the weapon of the brave, and when they are ordered to charge, to rush forward with that decisive ardour which characterizes the defenders of liberty & the rights of mankind. In all circumstance, he depends upon their inflexible maintenance of order, and bids them remember that bravery alone extinguishes danger.[42]

But after demonstrating his prowess as a motivational speaker, Laurens was forced at the last moment to abandon the plan because of a breakdown in communications.

Despite this setback, Greene offered Laurens a prestigious position: permanent command of "Lee's Legion," an elite corps of light dragoons formerly led by the legendary "Lighthorse Harry" (Henry Lee III, father of Robert E. Lee of Civil War fame). Although Lee's Legion had earned renown by its performance at Camden, Guilford Court House, and Eutaw Springs, its previous successes, along with the popularity of its former commander, proved problematic for Laurens. The men now under his charge (including also a separate regiment of infantrymen from Delaware) regarded Laurens's appointment as an act of patronage: Greene, they said, was trying to curry favor with Washington by elevating the commander in chief's favorite young protégé. Troop discipline, tied closely to feelings of loyalty, waned. "I'm sorry to inform you that Col Laurens is by no means popular with the Legion," Greene wrote to Lee four months after Laurens assumed command.[43]

Militarily, the eager lieutenant colonel found little to do. The problem, according to Laurens, was that the British, secure in their Charleston stronghold, refused to come out and fight. Every once in a while, Laurens and his men could harass a foraging party, but there was little glory in that. "The present is an insipid idle time," Laurens complained to Greene after a month in his new position. While the enforced idleness grated at him, his chafing at the bit irritated his commander. Laurens "wishes to fight much more than I wish he should," General Greene confided to Lee.[44]

In May, news arrived in South Carolina that Parliament had suspended its military offensives in North America. (The immediate catalyst was the surrender of Minorca in the Mediterranean; after that, coming in the wake of Yorktown, even hawkish MPs were forced to admit that in order to preserve the empire, the British might have to retreat from North America.) If there was little to do before, there was even less now. Recognizing Laurens's craving for action, Greene gave him the most dangerous job available: gathering intelligence close to enemy lines.

On August 1, the British in Charleston received orders to evacuate as soon as they practically could. With the war winding down, it was time for patriots like Laurens, who had served their country as soldiers, to consider how they might best serve their country during times of peace. From Albany on August 15, Alexander Hamilton wrote to his best companion: "Quit your sword my friend, put on the *toga*, come to Congress. . . . We have fought side by side to make America free, let us hand in hand struggle to make her happy." Sound advice, but it came too late, for John Laurens was reacting very differently to the transition.[45]

On August 21, a detachment of British soldiers embarked from Charleston to gather food for their garrison from plantations along the Combahee River. This sort of thing wouldn't be going on for long, and John Laurens knew it. The British would soon be gone, and once they left, Laurens would have no more opportunities to acquire military honors. This was his last chance, and he vowed to make the most of it.

Shortly before dawn on August 27, John Laurens and 50 men under his charge, hoping to surprise the foraging party, found 150 British soldiers ready for battle. Laurens faced two options: he could wait for an additional party of 150 patriots to join him, or he could attack the enemy right away, although outnumbered three to one. According to one of the officers under him, Captain William McKennan, Laurens had little difficulty making up his mind. Appearing "anxious to attack," the impetuous Laurens "could not wait until the main body of the detachment would arrive, but wanted to do all himself, and have all the honor."[46]

The battle was brief. The Americans charged, the British fired one volley, and Laurens received at least one bullet, as did several other Americans. Those who could still move quickly withdrew. Reinforcements arrived in time to cover the retreat, but they made no counterattack. American casualties were extremely high for such a small encounter: 2 dead, 19 wounded, and 3 missing.

One of the dead was John Laurens.

Two centuries later, historian Howard Peckham, in his exhaustive compilation of American casualties during every battle of the Revolutionary War, accorded Laurens the military honor he craved. Here is Peckham's single-sentence description of the battle of Combahee Ferry, South Carolina: "When a large body of British troops tried to land from their ships, Col. John Laurens led a smashing attack of Continentals, but lost his life." That is certainly how the favorite son of Henry Laurens wished to be remembered.[47]

John Laurens died as he lived, passionately and impetuously. Somewhere along the line, he had confused the means of the Revolution (military struggle) with its professed ends (national sovereignty under a republican form of government). He had come to view war not as a necessary process along a path toward peace, but as a final destination. War itself was noble, for it provided him the opportunity to acquire military honor, the highest mark of a gentleman. This was a distinctly European attitude. By contrast, in America since the beginning of unrest, patriots had professed displeasure with a standing army and its attendant military culture, always a threat to the peace. A republican army, they insisted, must remain subservient to civilian needs.

The war, in short, had caused John Laurens to lose perspective. Wars have a way of doing that, even "good" wars, and especially long wars, like this one. There was no way that people's hope for a new America could not be affected by eight years of military travails. All the sacrifices, as well as a nagging reluctance to make those sacrifices, were bound to eat away at high-sounding ideals.

Now, with fighting coming to an end, Americans could take stock. The nation was free, but what remained of the Revolutionary vision?

Act IV

Nation

17

Settling Up

November 29–30, 1782: Paris

If peace were to come, as someday it must, who would arrange it?

On July 15, 1781, Congress appointed five men to negotiate an end to the war: Benjamin Franklin, ambassador to France; John Jay, ambassador to Spain; John Adams, ambassador to the Netherlands; Thomas Jefferson, governor of Virginia; and Henry Laurens, formerly commissioned as ambassador to the Netherlands but currently imprisoned in the Tower of London.

Laurens did not want the job. "Taking into consideration my present very infirm state of health," he wrote to Franklin, the senior member of the delegation, "I have resolved to decline the honor intended me by Congress." Prison life had taken its toll, and now he wanted to heal. Upon his release, Laurens repaired to the spas of Bath, and thence to southern France, where his brother James lay terminally ill. Also there were his daughters, Martha and Mary, whom he hoped to escort back to America.[1]

On May 30, 1782, Laurens gave formal notice to Congress that he did not intend to serve. But when the delegates received his letter in September, they resolved immediately: "his services . . . could not be dispensed with." Sixteen voted to make Laurens stay on board, while only three were willing to accept his resignation.[2]

It wasn't until November 12 that Laurens heard from John Adams that his presence was required in Paris. Also, in the same letter, Adams informed Henry Laurens that his son John had just perished in battle. The two pieces of news, working in tandem, brought the former president of Congress out of retirement. Not only did Congress command him to serve, but John Laurens did too. "Thank God I had a son who dared to die in defence of his country," he wrote back to Adams the same day. Henry had to live up to his son's example and return to public service. "My country enjoins," he wrote. "I must therefore, also at all hazards to myself, obey & comply. Diffident as I am of my own abilities, I shall as speedily as possible proceed & join my colleagues."[3]

Laurens's colleagues (excluding Jefferson) had already been hard at work. Franklin and Jay engaged informally with their counterparts from Britain, France, and Spain during the summer months, while Adams, after arranging for a critical loan in the Netherlands, joined for the more formal proceedings in October. First and foremost on the agenda was British recognition of American independence: King George III, his Council, and Parliament had a difficult time uttering the *I* word, yet until they did, the American commissioners insisted there could be no serious talks. Next came the distribution of land: Canada, the Great Lakes, the trans-Appalachian region, and West Florida were all in play, as were navigation rights to the Mississippi and fishing rights off Newfoundland and Nova Scotia. Britain, the United States, France, and Spain all had something to say about who was entitled to what, with barely a nod to the rights of the native peoples.

Britain's basic strategy was to treat separately with each party, thereby splitting apart the three nations aligned against them. Legally, the American commissioners were not supposed to go for this. Their instructions from Congress, issued four months before the Battle of Yorktown, reflected America's dependence on French goodwill at that time:

> You are to make the most candid and confidential communications upon all subjects to the ministers of our generous ally, the King of France; to undertake nothing in the negotiations for peace or truce without their knowledge and concurrence; and ultimately to govern yourselves by their advice and opinion, endeavouring in your whole conduct to make them sensible how much we rely on his Majesty's influence for effectual support in every thing that may be necessary to the present security, or future prosperity, of the United States of America.[4]

Nothing could be clearer, yet Franklin and Jay, with the concurrence of Adams later on, decided on their own that they could strike a better deal if they left out the French, who would bring in such extraneous issues as control of Gibraltar and Minorca. Strangely, the Count de Vergennes, the French foreign minister, went along with separate talks, for he did not wish to be bogged down with American demands. So despite Congress's injunction, the talks proceeded along parallel lines, with the proviso that no deal would become final until the various negotiations had been concluded.

Spain wanted to choke off American expansion by controlling all navigation along the Mississippi at the very least, and gaining full control of trans-Appalachian lands at the best. Britain wanted access to the Mississippi and posts at the northern and southern ends (Canada and West Florida), but it evinced little interest in hanging on to the Ohio country, which had already led to two protracted wars and unfathomable expenses. France would have liked to gain back some or all of what it had lost during the Seven Years' War, but it dared not ask for that, knowing it would destroy the American alliance; instead, it sought a balance of power in America. The United States wanted Canada and the entire American West, up to and including the Mississippi. Access to the West was among the chief issues that led to the war, and now that peace was at hand the victors hoped to collect the spoils.

By treating separately, Britain and the United States were each able to get most of what they wanted: they would share the Great Lakes, with Britain keeping all land to the north and the United States getting most everything else. Trade along the Mississippi would remain open to both nations, while Spain, the chief rival to each on the North American continent, was simply ignored. Although the Americans did give up their wild notion of annexing Canada, they were still the true winners. When Vergennes saw how his allies had made out, he exclaimed that British concessions "exceed all that I could have thought possible." Privately he grumbled, but he decided to play along rather than jeopardize the peace.[5]

The major issues seemed to have been settled by November 25, when the final round of British-American negotiations commenced at the lodgings of Richard Oswald, the lead British negotiator. But John Adams was not satisfied, nor were Oswald and his colleagues. For Adams, the issue was fishing rights in the North Atlantic; for British negotiators, the key item was compensation to loyalists whose estates had been confiscated.

For four more days the ministers of peace bickered over "Tories and King Cod," and then on Friday, November 29, Henry Laurens finally entered John Jay's suite at the Hôtel d'Orléans to participate in the very last scene of a long and drawn-out drama. Ironically, facing Laurens on the British side was his longtime business associate and friend Richard Oswald, the man who had posted bail for his release from the Tower of London.[6]

This was Laurens's one and only chance to make his presence felt. Long an advocate of American fishing rights, he threw his weight behind Adams and the New England fishermen. When Franklin noted that American patriots as

Figure 36. The American peace commissioners in Paris, left to right: John Jay, John Adams, Benjamin Franklin, Henry Laurens, and secretary William Temple Franklin. Benjamin West's painting is unfinished because the British commissioners refused to pose. Laurens's contributions were limited. After posing for the painting and arranging for slaves to be returned to their masters, he headed home, without signing the final treaty. *(The Granger Collection, New York)*

well as loyalists should be recompensed for their wartime losses, Laurens added that British soldiers had stolen many a slave from plantations in South Carolina, and the slaves' owners should certainly be paid. Once on this subject, Laurens did not let up. The following day, with negotiations over and the treaty draft presented for approval, he insisted on having the last word by interlining a clause in Section VII: British armed forces should evacuate their coastal enclaves without "carrying away any Negroes, or other property of the American inhabitants."[7]

That was the full extent of Henry Laurens's participation in the Paris peace talks of 1782. It was a strange legacy for his recently martyred son, who had been so obsessed with turning slaves into soldiers and eventually granting them freedom.

But Laurens's last-minute insertion was to be expected, as was Oswald's quick assent. Laurens was the only commissioner with credentials to represent America's slave-owning South, while Oswald, his trading partner, was one of the largest slave merchants operating on West Africa's "Rice Coast."

Both men believed in protecting the "property" rights of slave owners. Before the war, Laurens had served as Oswald's agent in South Carolina, selling slaves fresh off the ships to his fellow plantation owners. In 1783, after the two had agreed on the terms of peace, Laurens offered the use of his own plantations to resettle Oswald's slaves from Florida, which Britain was ceding to Spain.[8]

Not that either man felt particularly good about the "curse of slavery," as Laurens called it. Laurens hoped the "entail of slavery" would end someday, and Oswald wished to circumvent the harsh conditions slaves experienced under Spanish rule, yet despite their increasing sensitivities, they worked together to provide a smooth transition so the institution of slavery, which they had actively fostered before the war, would continue unfettered, even as their respective nations pulled apart.[9]

December 29, 1782–March 15, 1783: Philadelphia and Newburgh, New York

Through the fall of 1782 and into the winter, Americans heard rumors that peace was nearly at hand. Most welcomed an end to the war, but several constituencies had good reasons to fear the impending cessation of hostilities.

Slaves who had fled to the British in search of freedom worried that they might be returned to their masters. Indians who had sided with the British feared their allies would give away lands without consulting the native inhabitants. Loyalists suspected they would be hounded, deprived of their property, and perhaps even exiled in the wake of the British defeat.

The concerns of these three groups are readily apparent, and they all proved well founded. The preliminary treaty did indeed tromp on the interests of slaves and Indians, and while it appeared to give some protection to loyalists, it left matters up to the individual states, which often lagged in offering security. The worries of two additional factions are less apparent.

Continental soldiers feared that, after the fighting had ceased, they would all be sent home without receiving their accumulated back pay. Congress owed these veterans lots of money for services rendered, but once their services were no longer required, the men who had risked their lives for their country would lose political clout. If peace came before they were paid, they might never get paid at all.

Additionally, rich and powerful nationalists, many of whom were creditors to the bankrupt nation, sensed that "war is indeed a rude, rough nurse to infant states," in the words of Gouverneur Morris, Robert Morris's assistant superintendent of finance. Peace was "not much in the interest of America," he contended, for it made people less willing to tolerate a strong, central government that could place the nation on a firm financial footing.[10]

What would happen if these last two groups, representing arms and wealth, banded together? Might they be tempted to seize the reins of power, notwithstanding all the fuss over "liberty" and a republican form of government?

That seemed a distinct possibility.

Two days before the close of 1782, a contingent of officers from the Continental Army arrived in Philadelphia with a memorial for Congress:

> Our distresses are now brought to a point. We have borne all that men can bear—our property is expended—our private resources are at an end, and our friends are wearied out and disgusted with our incessant applications. We, therefore, most seriously and earnestly beg, that a supply of money may be forwarded to the army as soon as possible. The uneasiness of the soldiers, for want of pay, is great and dangerous; any further experiments on their patience may have fatal effects.[11]

Before submitting their plea to a general session of Congress, the army envoys paid a visit to the Financier himself, the only man in the nation who could find and release the funds.

Robert Morris understood the urgency, but just at that moment his major source of funds, the French government, dried up. There was not the "slightest hope" for a new loan, the French ambassador in Philadelphia informed him, and any overdraw on existing loans would seriously endanger "the credit and the honor of the United States." And Morris saw no other way of meeting the officers' demands.[12]

On January 24, 1783, six days after the French cut him off, the Financier stunned Congress with a surprise announcement:

> Circumstances have postponed the establishment of public credit in such a manner, that I fear it will never be made. To encrease our debts while the prospect of paying them diminishes, does not consist with my ideas of integrity. I must therefore quit a situation which becomes utterly insupportable.[13]

It remains unclear whether Morris's resignation stemmed from frustration or calculation; most likely, the two worked in tandem. Congress and the nation would have to step up, and perhaps, if he cut them off, just as France had just done to him, Americans would be shocked into generating reliable revenues. He certainly hoped they would, and he suggested he just might change his mind if they did. He would continue to serve till the end of May, but "if effectual measures are not taken . . . to make permanent provision for the public debts of every kind, Congress will be pleased to appoint some other man to be Superintendant of their Finances."

Congress took the bait. Over the following weeks and beyond, members debated feverishly the various suggestions for raising funds. Nationalists continued to argue for granting Congress the power to tax, even though Congress's earlier scheme for a national impost had been laid to rest when Virginia joined Rhode Island in opposition. Now, nationalists threw around ideas for a salt tax, poll tax, land tax, house tax, or whatever.

But all this came to naught, because the Articles of Confederation had not granted Congress the right to levy any tax at all. Antinationalists were of no mind to alter the law of the land, even if the war debt amounted to a whopping $34,115,290 owed to private creditors and soldiers and another $7,885,085 due to France and the Netherlands. They proposed instead to distribute the debt among the states and let people there figure out how to come up with their share, yet they stumbled over the thorny issue of how much each state should pay. Congress tried apportioning the debt according to the value of land, but because methods of appraisal varied, this seemed unfair. It then decided to switch to population as the key indicator, but delegates squabbled about whether to include slaves in their calculations. Southern states said no, because that would increase their burden; northern states said yes, because slave labor provided wealth. In what would become a grand tradition of irrational compromise, Congress agreed in the end that slaves would count as three-fifths of a person. Years later, when debating the issue of representation during the Constitutional Convention, each side would reverse its position, the South arguing to count slaves and the North resisting, yet ironically, the same magic fraction would be carted out once again to settle the matter.[14]

All this meant little to the soldiers who wanted to get paid. No matter what Congress concluded during the debate, which dragged on for months, states would take a long time to come up with their share. So while politicians talked, at least some soldiers figured it was time to act.

On March 10, at the army's headquarters in Newburgh, George Washington learned that a group of malcontents were calling for a meeting of all officers to discuss the army's "alternative," should Congress not meet their demands. And the plan under consideration was radical indeed: "You will retire to some unsettled country, smile in your turn, and 'mock them when fear cometh on.'"[15]

In response, Washington preempted the radicals' meeting with one of his own. At noon on Saturday, March 15, before all officers ranked from captain on up, the commander in chief of the Continental Army, contrary to the custom of the times, issued a personal appeal:

> Let me entreat you, gentleman, on your part, not to take any measures, which, viewed in the calm light of reason, will lessen the dignity, and sully the glory you have hitherto maintained. . . . And let me conjure you, in the name of our common country, as you value your own sacred honor, as you respect the rights of humanity, and as you regard the military and national character of America, to express your utmost horror and detestation of the man, who wishes, under any specious pretences, to overturn the liberties of our country; and who wickedly attempts to open the flood-gates of civil discord, and deluge our rising empire in blood.[16]

As soon as their commander left the gathering, the officers "resolved unanimously" to "reject with disdain the infamous propositions contained in a late anonymous address."

The so-called Newburgh Conspiracy had been thwarted, but not the indelible mark it left on the political landscape. Many wondered whether nationalist politicians, people like Alexander Hamilton, Gouverneur Morris, or even the Financier himself, were behind the officers' threats to raise arms and secede. Both Hamilton and Gouverneur Morris had suggested often that public creditors ally themselves with disgruntled officers, who in a sense were creditors too. Gouverneur Morris, fond of producing shock by overstatement, had even hinted that the army, "with swords in their hands," might further the nationalists' cause. "The only wise mode is for the Army to connect themselves with public creditors . . . and unremittingly to urge the grant of general permanent funds," the assistant financier proclaimed. "The Army can now influence the Legislatures and, if you will permit me a metaphor from your own profession, after you have carried the post the public creditors will garrison it for you."[17]

This kind of talk, even if only metaphorical, fed the fears of antinationalists, who suspected something of a coup might be in the works. They had long entertained concerns about the Financier and the extra powers he had forced Congress to grant him. (James Warren, for one, referred to Robert Morris as "Premier," "King," "more than a King," and "Grand Monarch of America.") By association and prejudice, the Financier and his outspoken assistant were implicated in the alleged conspiracy, even if they had no actual hand in the officers' thwarted protest.[18]

Discord and suspicion defined the times. Peace seemed within reach, but not its fruits.

May 6, 1783: Tappan, New York

News of the November 30 preliminary treaty took over three months to reach the United States. When it finally arrived, on the morning of March 12, 1783, it came aboard a ship named *Washington*, owned by Robert Morris, who, ironically, had been troubled by the prospect of peace.

No great celebrations ensued. Congress was out of cash and low on credit. Trouble was afoot with the army. Besides, the treaty had to clear several more hurdles before becoming official. France and Spain had to make their own separate agreements with Britain, and then Congress had to ratify the measure, as did the Crown and Parliament. Elaborate street celebrations, such as those following the Stamp Act repeal and independence, would have to wait, if they were to happen at all.

George Washington, for one, was not convinced by the preliminary treaty. As soon as he heard the word, he wrote to Congress: "The Articles of Treaty between America and Great Britain . . . are so very inconclusive . . . that we should hold ourselves in a hostile position, prepared for either alternative, war or peace."[19]

Congress, on its part, was pleased with the outcome of the negotiations, but several members expressed considerable displeasure over the process. Why hadn't the commissioners included France in the talks, as instructed? For days on end, delegates debated whether or not to censure the American peacemakers for violating congressional orders.

Then rumors started to circulate: France and Spain had successfully concluded their treaties with Britain. The rumors were soon confirmed by more definitive news, and finally by an official dispatch. All talk of censure stopped, and on April 15 Congress ratified the treaty. Then, without missing a beat, it instructed the commander in chief "to enter into the necessary preparatory arrangements relative to the 7th Article of the said Treaty."[20]

Article 7 as amended by Henry Laurens, that is. How could Washington or anyone else enforce that last-minute clause barring the British from "carrying away any Negroes"?

On the morning of May 6, 1783, the commander in chief of the Continental Army met with his British counterpart, Sir Guy Carleton, within a square-beamed parlor of a simple stone residence at Tappan, a small community on the west bank of the Hudson River, twenty-five miles north of New York City. We have various accounts of the high-level confab, some from each side, and they agree in almost every particular.[21]

Washington opened by placing three items on the agenda: the timetable for British evacuation, the treatment of prisoners, and the matter most on his mind: "The preservation of property from being carried off and especially the Negroes," as stipulated in Article 7.

Carleton addressed the first item by agreeing to withdraw his troops "with all possible dispatch," although he could not fix a precise date because of the fickle seas. To prove his sincerity, he announced "upwards of 6,000 persons," including "a number of Negroes," had already embarked.

That was the trigger. According to a British diarist, "Mr. Washington appeared to be startled—already embarked, says he." Another account, less dramatic in tone, confirms this: "General Washington thereupon expressed his surprize that after what appeared to him an express stipulation to the contrary in the treaty, Negroes, the property of the inhabitants of these states, should be sent off."

Carleton responded by offering his own interpretation of the treaty: "property" meant property at the time the treaty was signed. Negroes under his care had come to the British as free people, having already left their former masters.

To Washington, this was mere sophistry. Slaves were still property after they had run away, and the rest was hogwash. According to one British account, Washington pressed his demand for return of the slaves "with all the grossness and ferocity of a captain of banditti."[22]

Carleton then assumed the moral high ground: "Delivering up Negroes to their former masters . . . would be a dishonorable violation of the public faith pledged to the Negroes in the Proclamations." (Left unsaid: if Britain went back on its word now, it would never be able to enlist the help of slaves in the future, as in fact it would during the War of 1812.) The British government might be open to paying former masters for their losses, however. With this in mind, Carleton had already started a registry of Negroes who were embarking on British ships, so that the two governments, if they agreed on compensation at some future date, would have records of who had left.

In response, Washington accused Carleton of violating "the letter and the spirit of the Articles of Peace." Far from attaining the moral high ground, the British were simply breaking their word. And Carleton's proposed alternative—future compensation—was just not workable. The value of a slave consisted "in his industry and sobriety," Washington stated, and these could not be determined for some registry prepared by strangers. (Left unstated: the value of slaves also lay in their fertility, and this too was not easily ascertained.)

And so it went for several more rounds. The meeting ended without resolution, to be resumed the following day. Washington ordered a gala repast that evening for Carleton and company, but his illustrious guest claimed illness and failed to attend. Nor did he show the next day, pleading the same "indisposition." Washington, ever the realist, knew he was beaten. "I have discovered enough . . . in the course of the conversation," he reported to Harrison, "to convince me that the slaves which have absconded from their masters will never be restored to them."[23]

Washington's pessimistic outlook proved well founded. In fact, at least one of the people he himself claimed to own had already sailed for Nova Scotia a week before his fruitless meeting with Carleton: a woman named Deborah, married to Harry Squash. The *Book of Negroes*, a register of three thousand escaped slaves who left New York City aboard British vessels in 1783, described Harry and Deborah briefly:

Harry Squash, 22, stout middle sized, (Mr. Lynch). Property of Mr. Lynch, purchased from Captain Huddleston, Royal Artillery.

Deborah his wife, 20, stout wench, thick lips, pock marked, (Mr. Lynch). Formerly slave to General Washington, came away about 4 years ago.[24]

Although Washington had been informed of Deborah's escape from Mount Vernon (see chapter 16), he probably did not know she left the country for good on April 27. But he suspected she and others in her situation might try, and to ward them off he recruited the services of Daniel Parker, a New York merchant who had been supplying the army with provisions. Virginia's governor Benjamin Harrison had just sent Washington a list of slaves from his home state who had fled to the British and were presumably in New York, so

Washington asked Parker to find these people, and, while he was at it, to look for his own escaped slaves as well as those claimed by his cousin Lund. The General understood it would be a difficult task: "I am unable to give you descriptions; their names being so easily changed, will be fruitless to give you." But he listed the names nonetheless, just in case: "If by chance you should come at the knowledge of any of them, I will be much obliged by your securing them, so that I may obtain them again."[25]

We have no indication that Daniel Parker managed to find any of George Washington's former slaves, but we do know that, in addition to Deborah, at least two others made their way from New York to Nova Scotia:

> Aboard the *L'Abondance*, which sailed on July 31: "Harry Washington, 43,
>   fine fellow. Formerly the property of General Washington; left him
>   7 years ago." [26]
> Aboard the *Concord*, which sailed on November 30: "Daniel Payne,
>   22 years, ordinary fellow, (Maurice Salt). Formerly slave to Gen. Washington, Virginia; left him about 4 years ago." (Earlier, in his list of runaways, Lund Washington had included: "Daniel, a man about 19 years old, very likely.")[27]

Freedom had not come easily for Deborah Squash, Harry Washington, and Daniel Payne. Harry, who left Mount Vernon in response to Dunmore's Proclamation at the outset of the war, took great risks in order to do so. Deborah and Daniel probably had an easier time leaving, but all three had to assume, with no guarantee, that the British would both grant freedom and provide some avenue for employment. Then, once the British lost the war, they worried that they might be handed back to their former master. New York in 1783 provided no safe haven for the likes of Deborah, Harry, and Daniel. Flocking by droves to the city in search of lost "property," masters and/or their hired slave-catchers hunted the streets, alleys, and even buildings for people they still claimed to own. Sometimes, if they managed to make contact, masters or their agents tried to entice the escapees to return voluntarily; other times, they simply seized the people they claimed were theirs. In his memoir, an escaped slave named Boston King recalled those pivotal moments:

> We saw our old masters coming from Virginia, North-Carolina, and
> other parts, and seizing upon their slaves in the streets of New-York, or
> even dragging them out of their beds. Many of the slaves had very cruel

masters, so that the thoughts of returning home with them embittered life to us. For some days we lost our appetite for food, and sleep departed from our eyes.[28]

Few if any former slaves submitted willingly, and some, when threatened or captured, forcibly resisted. As Frank Griffin was being dragged away with a rope around his neck by a man claiming to be his owner, an escaped slave known as Colonel Cuff confronted the kidnapper at gunpoint and had him arrested by British authorities. Another group of blacks actually murdered a slave owner who was carrying off the wife of one of the rescuers.[29]

By fleeing to the British, thousands upon thousands of enslaved Americans had turned the turmoil of the Revolution to their own advantage. Disorder among the whites had provided an opportunity for these people; now, they refused to return to slavery because of Henry Laurens's addendum to a treaty among white men and the commander in chief's attempts to enforce it.

June–October 1783: Philadelphia and West Point

By the spring of 1783, Continental soldiers were ready to go home, but before they did, they wanted some recompense. This placed Congress in a quandary: it had no money with which to pay the troops because all available funds were being spent on basic provisions for those very same men. The only way to save money was to send the troops packing, with no more than a promise of payment in the future. But that would infuriate the veterans, who were likely to cause a ruckus when they arrived back home, which in turn would infuriate civilians, who would then be even less likely to make good on the soldiers' back pay.

This conundrum affected the lives of Robert Morris, George Washington, Joseph Plumb Martin, and Timothy Bigelow, each in a different way.

On May 1, the Financier told Congress he did not wish to leave office without addressing the issue of soldiers' pay, and two days later, he formally withdrew his resignation. He would not retire, he told his friend George Washington, until he could "procure some little relief to your Army," send them home content, and thereby allow Washington himself to "lay down the cares" of his "painful office." Working with Congress, Morris then came up with a temporary solution. (All solutions were temporary until Congress could generate its own funds.) He would print up certificates for three months' pay, to be redeemed by the states six months hence. With these in hand, soldiers might agree to disband, even without the one month's pay in hard cash Congress had promised them back in January.[30]

On June 2, following the Financier's plan, the commander in chief ordered furloughs for all soldiers who had enlisted for the duration of the war, with formal discharges to follow once the "definitive Treaty of Peace" had been signed. But there was a hitch: the six-month certificates were not yet ready to distribute, despite Morris's best efforts to have them printed in a hurry.

On June 12, a contingent from Maryland, on their way home from New-burgh, decided to stop off in Philadelphia to pick up their certificates in person. Because they evinced a "mutinous disposition," they received their certificates within a day of arrival, and this aroused the jealousies of troops stationed in the city, who sent word out to other Pennsylvania Continentals that raising a stink worked. On June 20, several hundred soldiers from Lancaster marched into town with fife and drum, bayonets fixed, to join their Philadelphia comrades-in-arms. The following day, when the combined contingent surrounded the State House to present their demands, delegates from Congress, unable to satisfy them, simply adjourned and walked out through the gun-waving troops. When Congress next convened, it did so in Princeton rather than Philadelphia.

The mutineers' multiple demands had a familiar ring: not simply one month's salary and the promise of three months' more, but full pay for all the time served; at least half the total to be paid at the time of discharge and the rest at specified dates, "with lawful interest"; compensation for uncollected rations; patents for the land the soldiers had been promised. Yet the simple reason for denial was familiar as well: insufficient funds. However deserving, the soldiers could not win. Upon hearing that Washington was dispatching troops to oppose them, they finally laid down their arms.[31]

Sergeant Joseph Plumb Martin, stationed at West Point, had been anticipating the moment all spring. Rumors of peace traveled about camp, but "we were afraid to be *too* sanguine, for fear of being disappointed." To judge whether the rumors were correct, Martin and his fellow soldiers kept a keen eye on "General Washington's watch chain," the great chain (each link weighed five hundred pounds) placed across the Hudson every spring when the ice broke to keep British ships from sailing up the river. If Washington ordered the chain to be set in place, the war was still on; if not, peace was around the corner.

The chain remained on land, and on June 11, nine days after Washington issued his orders, Martin's captain appeared with furloughs in hand for all the "war men," those who, like Martin, had signed on for the duration of the conflict. They were free to go home if they wished, the captain announced, or they could remain to pick up their certificates, which were still not ready. Martin chose to stay. "I had waited so long I was loathe to leave there without them," he recalled.

Then a fellow soldier, who had not received his furlough (he still had half a year to serve), offered Martin $16 in specie and some of his possessions to serve as a substitute for the next six months. Martin accepted, reasoning that if he took the trade, he could leave with both money and certificates in hand. He would then head for "the western parts of the state of New York, where there was a plenty of good land to be had as cheap as the Irishman's potatoes." There, Martin and a pal "would get us farms and live like heroes."

In mid-October, when news arrived that the final treaty had been signed, the army formally discharged Joseph Plumb Martin, with only one condition: before leaving, he had to cut two cords of firewood for the dwindling garrison at West Point. That was it, his final duty. Martin was free to go, and he did, but not exactly as planned. His friend, impatient, had departed earlier, and Joseph wound up selling some of his certificates to a speculator just to get decent clothes for the road.

The twenty-two-year-old veteran left with some regrets for, having first signed on at the age of fifteen, the army had become his life, and its community of men his family:

> I confess, after all, that my anticipation of the happiness I should experience upon such a day as this was not realized. . . . We had lived together as a family of brothers for several years, setting aside some little family squabbles, like most other families, had shared with each other the hardships, dangers, and sufferings incident to a soldier's life; had sympathized with each other in trouble and sickness; had assisted in bearing each other's burdens or strove to make them lighter by council and advice; had endeavored to conceal each other's faults or make them appear in as good a light as they would bear. In short, the soldiers, each in his particular circle of acquaintance, were as strict a band of brothers as Masons and, I believe, as faithful to each other. And now we were to be, the greater part of us, parted forever; as unconditionally separated as though the grave lay between us. . . . Ah! it was a serious time.[32]

The Revolutionary War had given this teenage farmboy not only an extended family, but also a sense of himself and a place in history. He had done his part, and he had to feel good about that. Even better, he had survived, and he certainly felt good about *that*. Financially, however, he had nothing to show for his efforts. Physically, he was probably the worse for wear. Vocationally, he had learned no trade. In practical terms, life in the army had done little to prepare Martin for civilian life.

He was now on his own, for better or worse.

By May 12, 1783, Timothy Bigelow was back in Worcester, for on that day the town meeting appointed the colonel to serve on a committee to investigate counterfeit currency. Also on that committee was Timothy Paine, the former "mandamus counselor," who had adjusted to the times and was once again a functioning member of the community. Ironically, the one-time Tory was now thriving, while Bigelow, the man who had helped overthrow British authority and Tory influence in Worcester, and had led his townsmen into battle, and had suffered extreme hardships and even imprisonment on his country's behalf, was struggling.[33]

During Bigelow's long absence, the former town blacksmith (and perhaps his shop) had turned rusty, and besides, his customers were content elsewhere. Over the previous eight years, other men had been fashioning the tools, nails, and horseshoes for Worcester's agrarian population. To support his family, which now included his wife, Anna, a toddler (Clarissa), two school-age children (Rufus and Lucy, ages eleven and nine), and three teenagers (Nancy, Timothy, and Andrew, ages nineteen, sixteen, and fourteen), Bigelow had been relying on his officer's pay, but he had been "deranged" for over two years, and he needed to come up with an alternate source of income.

That's certainly where the Montpelier scheme fit in. Although it seems unlikely that Timothy intended to move his family there, it appears more than likely that he hoped to make considerable money by selling shares or parcels in over 23,000 acres of New England real estate. Unfortunately, the Montpelier investment failed to live up to its promise, at least for Bigelow personally. The proprietors waited for three years to hold their first organizational meeting, and by that time Timothy Bigelow, their original organizer, was no longer involved. To make ends meet, he must have already sold his shares. The first white settler in Montpelier did not occupy the land until 1786.[34]

Bigelow did have one other hope: cashing in on his investment with the military. Back in 1780, by threatening to abandon their posts, Continental officers had extracted a pledge from Congress for lifetime pensions of half their wartime salaries. That would certainly help, if Congress or the states possessed the money and desire to make good on the promise, but Congress, of course, was broke, and back in the states, most civilians balked at the idea of supporting military men for the rest of their lives. Civilians felt they had already been forced to sacrifice too much, and now that the war was over, they argued that all payments to officers should cease. Aside from raw economics, the notion of supporting a permanent military organization, even if the officers were retired, ran afoul of republican ideology.

Such was the attitude of Timothy Bigelow's friends and neighbors in Worcester. In June of 1782, the town meeting instructed Samuel Curtis, its representative to the General Assembly, to oppose "half pay during life" for "deranged" officers who were "not in actual service." Almost a decade earlier, Bigelow and Curtis had teamed up to draft the initial rules for the fledgling American Political Society, but although they stood shoulder to shoulder at that critical juncture, they parted ways now. Together, Bigelow and Curtis and other politically active patriots had toppled British rule, but now, with nary a Brit in sight, and with no foreign rule of any sort, they viewed their world from differing and even competing perspectives. If the onset of a war tends to bring people together, as it did in 1774 and 1775, the close of this war found civilians and the men who had done the fighting farther apart than ever.[35]

That rift would continue, with no small effect on the postwar political climate of the emerging nation.

November 25–December 4, 1783: New York City

The United States commissioners (minus Henry Laurens, who had turned in his resignation and was preparing to return home) signed the final treaty of peace in Paris on September 3, 1783, and in mid-October Americans heard the news. The war was officially over.

Even so, a huge British Army remained in New York City, which had served as its central headquarters since 1776. Loading some twenty thousand soldiers and thirty thousand loyalists onto seaworthy vessels and sending them away presented Sir Guy Carleton with a great logistical challenge. He had been working at it all summer, but the last of the Redcoats did not abandon their posts and row out to their ships until one in the afternoon on Tuesday, November 25. On that crisp autumn day, with the wind blowing strong at their backs, George Washington, mounted on a stately gray, and New York's governor George Clinton, on a bay gelding, rode south from Harlem toward the city at the lower end of Manhattan Island, where they led a grand procession through cheering crowds. Although Washington was the celebrity, it was Clinton, on behalf of the civilian government, who formally took possession of the City and State of New York.[36]

At the end of the day, Governor Clinton, General Washington, and assorted dignitaries retreated to Fraunces Tavern, on the corner of Pearl and Broad, the site of many a patriot gathering before the war, and also the place where escaped slaves had recently sought certificates that allowed them to depart on British transports. The revelers that night offered thirteen toasts, starting with the basic "The United States of America," but finishing with five stirring tributes to the idealistic foundations of the free and independent nation:

9. May justice support what courage has gained.
10. The vindicators of the rights of mankind in every quarter of the globe.
11. May America be an asylum to the persecuted of the earth.
12. May a close union of the states guard the temple they have erected to liberty.
13. May the remembrance of this DAY be a lesson to princes.[37]

Festivities continued for a week. The following Tuesday evening, the Corps of Artillery put on a "splendid display of fireworks," as Washington described it. Over the course of an hour, a diverse array of nine hundred distinct explosions filled the sky over the "prodigious concourse of spectators" gathered at Bowling Green: "balloon and serpent," "moon and seven stars," "cascade of fire," "Chinese fountain," "illuminated pyramid, with Archimidian screws, a globe and vertical sun." Watching from the harbor were soldiers and sailors aboard the last of the British transports, waiting for the proper conditions to venture into the ocean. Washington would not depart until they did.[38]

On December 2, the day of the fireworks, a group of recent Irish immigrants delivered a congratulatory address to General Washington, who replied in the spirit of the eleventh toast from Fraunces Tavern:

The bosom of America is open to receive not only the opulent and respectable stranger, but the oppressed and persecuted of all nations and religions; whom we shall wellcome to a participation of all our rights and previleges, if by decency and propriety of conduct they appear to merit the enjoyment.[39]

Finally, on December 4, the last of the British vessels sailed away. As they did, Washington summoned the handful of senior officers still in town to meet him at Fraunces Tavern, and there, in the banquet room on the second floor, he bid them a brief farewell. He then headed home to Mount Vernon. In case there had ever been any doubt, the United States of America would remain under civilian rule, as it had been throughout the war.[40]

Washington's farewell at Fraunces Tavern was a ceremonial curtain call, for he had already delivered his real address. Back on November 2, in a lengthy piece he titled "Farewell Orders issued to the Armies of the United States of America," the commander in chief had thanked and congratulated his soldiers, then offered the comforting words they most wanted to hear. Rather than face "a national bankruptcy and a dissolution of the union," the states would certainly comply with "the requisitions of Congress" to pay the men their due.

But even these "Farewell Orders" were little more than an afterthought, for back on June 8, as soldiers were receiving their furloughs, he had issued a lengthy circular letter to the states, which he himself termed his "Legacy." (Although Washington did not pen all thirteen copies, it took his assistants two weeks to duplicate the twenty-three pages and send them out to each state governor.) Here was the real grit. Before leaving the public stage, Washington wished to capitalize on his tremendous influence. Soon, he would not be able to issue general orders and command others what to do, but now, as a winning general at the pinnacle of his career, people still listened. This was his chance to shape the future.

Washington opened his "Legacy" in an urgent tone:

> According to the system of policy the states shall adopt at this moment, they will stand or fall, and by their confirmation or lapse, it is yet to be decided, whether the Revolution must ultimately be considered as a blessing or a curse. With this conviction of the importance of the present crisis, silence in me would be a crime.

And then, pulling no punches, in language that was as emotive as it was persuasive, he presented his own "system of policy," a broad outline for a stronger national government:

1st. An indissoluble union of the states under one federal head.

2dly. A sacred regard to public justice.

3dly. The adoption of a proper peace establishment.

4thly. The prevalence of that pacific and friendly disposition among the people of the United States, which will induce them to forget their local prejudices and policies. To make those mutual concessions which are requisite to the general prosperity, and in some instances, to sacrifice their individual advantages to the interest of the community.

The last of these, Washington felt, was self-explanatory, but he expounded at length on the others.

On the first measure: "There should be lodged somewhere a supreme power to regulate and govern the general concerns of the confederated republic, without which the union cannot long endure." By "supreme power" he meant neither God nor an individual executive, but a national government, a "supreme authority" over and above the separate states.

Next, "public justice." Washington gave this a very precise definition: public creditors and unpaid soldiers must be given their "due." (No other constituencies were mentioned under the heading of "public justice.") For want of the power to execute this, Congress had passed the matter back to the states, and the General devoted more than half his letter to an appeal, or rather a lecture, on how important it was that each state come through. All debts must be paid for the nation to survive.

Finally, a "peace establishment." By this he meant an armed force to protect the nation, but he did not propose a standing army, anathema to most of his contemporaries. As much as Washington had complained about the militias during the war, he realized that a citizens' army was the only type of military force Americans would approve. Even so, he argued, "the formation and discipline of the militia of the continent should be absolutely uniform," and this led him back to his main theme: the nation could not survive without the "adequate authority" of a "supreme power." It was the absence of such a power, he concluded, that had led to all the problems during the war.[41]

Robert Morris, Gouverneur Morris, Alexander Hamilton, and their fellow nationalists were certainly pleased with the thrust of Washington's "Legacy." Yes, the General was retiring, but the man Americans most adored was firmly on their side. This could prove useful sometime.

18

Desires and Discontents

September 1–October 4, 1784: Ohio Country

One week and a day before the close of 1783, on his way from New York to Virginia, General Washington appeared before Congress to make it official:

> Having now finished the work assigned me, I retire from the great theatre of action; and bidding an affectionate farewell to this august body under whose orders I have so long acted, I here offer my commission, and take my leave of all the employments of public life.[1]

He then continued homeward, to embrace that elusive "private life" that so many public officials have claimed to crave, then and now. Waiting for him at Mount Vernon was his wife, Martha, who had accompanied her husband through much of the war and shared his lodgings at various headquarters with numerous members of the General's military "family." At home, things would be different, for Mount Vernon was *their* headquarters.

Washington had been preparing for his return to Mount Vernon for at least three months. In September he placed an order with Daniel Parker, whom he had asked to retrieve his escaped slaves, for a set of white table china ("Not less than 6 or 8 dozn. shallow and a proportionable number of deep and other plates, butter boats, dishes and tureens"), and for six dozen wineglasses and three dozen beer glasses just like those Samuel Fraunces (proprietor of Fraunces Tavern) had just showed him. Clearly, the master of Mount Vernon expected he might be receiving company upon his return, and in this he was not mistaken. Foreign dignitaries, retired army officers, fellow Virginians renewing their acquaintance, and a host of others, motivated by curiosity or self-interest, lined up for a chance to visit America's foremost citizen, and he, ever gracious, agreed to host them. On June 30, 1785, a year and a half after returning home, Washington jotted in his diary: "Dined with only Mrs. Washington which I believe is the first instance of it since my retirement from public life." So much for privacy in the "private life" of George and Martha Washington.[2]

All this cost money. When Washington entertained during the war, he did so at public expense, but now he was on his own. "My living under the best economy I can use must unavoidably be expensive," he complained to a nephew who was hoping to borrow money. Having accepted no remuneration during almost nine years of military service, he found himself in the same financial pinch as before the war: expensive habits coupled with an undependable income, determined by economic markets beyond his control.[3]

Before, during, and after the war, George Washington believed his financial future lay in the acquisition and development of western lands. "It has ever been my opinion," he wrote to his half brother John Augustine Washington while the war was in full swing, "to have my property as much as possible in lands. . . . A few years peace will inundate these states with emigrants and of course enhance the price of land far above the common interest of money." Washington's interest in real estate development had both a private and a public aspect, and the two were thoroughly intertwined. Privately, he hoped to capitalize on the lands he already had, either by developing them, renting them out, or selling them off at high rates, and then, with money in hand, he could increase his investments by acquiring additional real estate. Publicly, he pushed for an infrastructure (roads and waterways) that would increase the value of his properties, and simultaneously he advocated laws that would facilitate orderly and profitable settlement of the West.[4]

Now that he had the time, Washington decided to address all of this in person. On September 1, 1784, traveling with three servants, six horses, and a friend who had western lands of his own, he left Mount Vernon and headed toward the Ohio country, the first trip west since 1770. His mission was two-fold: check up on his private holdings and prospect for the best place to cut a canal through the Allegheny Mountains, thereby joining the Potomac with the Ohio and creating a water passage from the Atlantic Ocean to the great American interior.

On one of the tracts he visited on the far side of the mountains, 2,813 acres near the Monongahela River, Washington confronted a speculator's worst fear: squatters were living on his land. He had long feared that freeloaders, whom he called "banditti," would take liberties with the law by settling on land that wasn't theirs, but the people he found on his tract did not fit the stereotype. They were "*apparently* very religious," he observed (his emphasis), and more to the point, they had made significant improvements on the land, which he catalogued meticulously, squatter by squatter. (One example: "Duncan McGeechen. 2 acres of meadow. 20 do. [ditto] arable land. A good single barn, dwelling house spring house & several other houses. The plantation under good fencing.") These were solid, industrious farmers, the kind Washington believed should be populating the West—but they were living on *his* land, and he was not about to cede them his title.

Torn, Washington proposed a compromise:

> I told them I had no inclination to sell; however, after hearing a great deal of their hardships, their religious principles (which had brought them together as society of Ceceders [Presbyterians]), and unwillingness to separate or remove; I told them I would make them a last offer and this was—the whole tract at 25/. pr. acre, the money to be paid at 3 annual payments with interest; or to become tenants upon leases of 999 years, at the annual rent of ten pounds pr. ct. ann.[5]

This was an offer the farmers had to refuse. Where would these people, who lived close to the earth, come up with over £3,500 in hard cash? And what white farmer in the American West would consent to committing himself and his family, for more generations than he could imagine, to tenancy? The squatters "determined to stand suit for the land," Washington reported, meaning they would take their chances when Washington hauled them to court to evict them. But even with no other options, the farmers' choice was a bad one: no court within the new nation would deny George Washington the right to land he thought was lawfully his, and certainly not one in "Washington County," the appropriate jurisdiction.

The ghost of William Crawford hovered over Washington's expedition. One of the squatters inhabited a cabin that Crawford had built as he surveyed the tract on Washington's behalf. When Washington tried to locate Crawford's survey notes, which would have settled the matter of his ownership, they were nowhere to be found. Worse yet, when the squatters had their day in court, they argued that Washington's claim was invalid because Crawford

Figure 37. "A map of the United States of America agreeable to the peace of 1783," published in London in 1783. The new nation had more than doubled in size, and this meant that George Washington was finally free to pursue his dream: developing the American interior.

was not a licensed surveyor—the same bogus argument made by the British before the war (see chapter 8).

And of course there were the memories. Although he did not dwell on Crawford in his businesslike diary, Washington no doubt conjured images of his most frequent and trusted companion in the West, and when he did, he must have found it difficult to suppress visions of his friend's mutilated body. Certainly, Crawford's memory came to the fore when Washington met with Captain John Hardin, another crusty westerner who had been on that fateful expedition. It might also have come into play when Washington heard repeated warnings that Indians just to the west were gearing up for war and it would not be safe to travel onward.

This gave cause for real concern: George Washington might share William Crawford's fate, should he continue with his journey. No longer protected by an army of soldiers, the man Indians called Town Destroyer was vulnerable anywhere his presence became known along the borderlands between white and Indian lands. To the north, Senecas and Mohawks and other Iroquois Indians were outraged that their British allies had "ceded" lands they thought to be theirs. To the south, Dragging Canoe and his Chickamauga diehards were continuing to fight white intrusions, and there was talk of a sweeping pan-Indian alliance. And just to the west in the heart of the Ohio Valley,

Shawnees, Miami, and even many Delaware Indians, once allied with the United States, were gearing up for the next round.

Prudently, Washington decided to head back home rather than visit lands still farther to the west that he and Crawford had once coveted. It's a good thing he did. "Had you proceded on your tour down the river, " wrote Thomas Freeman, his new western agent, the following year, "I believe it would have been attended with the most dreadfull consequences. The Indians by what means I cannot say had intelligence of your journey and laid wait for you."[6]

By his own reckoning, Washington's trip was a success, for upon his return to Mount Vernon on October 4, he proudly concluded, "The more the navigation of Potomack is investigated, & duly considered, the greater the advantages arising from them appear." Although his visits to his personal lands had proved a bit disappointing, he had accomplished his larger mission, and he could now drum up financial and political support for a great waterway to the West that would pass within view of his porch at Mount Vernon. He had started this task before the war, only to see it postponed by more pressing matters; now, he was poised to realize his vision.[7]

Within a week, Washington was on task, garnering support for the chartering of a new Potomac Company in the state capitals of Virginia and Maryland, which shared access to the lower reaches of the river. He encountered no resistance, nor did he falter in raising the initial capital required to get the company started. "I would hazard all the money I could raise upon navigation of the river," he crowed to Robert Morris, although in fact he had little capital to spare.[8]

At their first meeting, the Potomac Company's subscribers determined that George Washington should be their president. Not only was he the driving force behind their scheme, but as the most revered man in America he could also exert the greatest influence on the company's behalf. This was a new role for the former commander in chief, who formerly would never admit to the pursuit of private interests under color of public business.

And the president of the Potomac Company did conflate his private interest with public policy. True, he was committed to opening the West, and that was for the good of the nation. An inland waterway would simultaneously open economic opportunities, enlarge the population, pay off the war debt, and counter Spanish control of the Mississippi and British influence on the Great Lakes and St. Lawrence. But that did not mean the best possible route passed by Mount Vernon. Many easterners, also on behalf of the nation, proposed alternate routes: Pennsylvanians eyed the Schuylkill as a possible link from the Atlantic; New Yorkers reasoned that the Hudson could easily be connected with Lake Erie; and some fellow Virginians thought that the James River, which happened to flow through their region of the state, offered greater prospects than the Potomac. Washington's preference for the Potomac, above all others, showed more than a pinch of self-interest. In arguing on its behalf, he urged his political allies and potential investors to act swiftly so they wouldn't fall behind the Potomac Company's competitors, who were already fast at work to promote their particular regions.

None of this was wrong, but it did point to a change of perspective. In his "Legacy" letter, General Washington had preached that citizens should "sacrifice their individual advantages to the interest of the community" and "forget their local prejudices and policies." Those were the words of a wise republican leader, an exemplar of public virtue. Now, however, George Washington was just a citizen, one among many. Yes, he could argue for his plan, but he could no longer pull rank, either militarily or ethically. He was not above the fray, but within it.

November 1, 1784: Philadelphia

With the war over and the daily business of a workaday world now supreme, perhaps the ideal of the selfless republican leader had become irrelevant. Robert Morris certainly thought so. The notion of "selflessness" had always been a bit of a stretch for this merchant prince—"The proper object of a reasonable man [is] the pursuit of riches," his partner, Thomas Willing, wrote in his diary—but the war had required him to lean toward high-mindedness despite himself; drastic times had called for drastic measures, and private interests needed to be tempered by public spirit. With the coming of peace, however, the pursuit of personal profit, the stimulus of all economic activity, could resume its proper place at the fore.[9]

This is not to say that government, the embodiment of the public good, had no place in Robert Morris's post-Revolutionary America. He was a practitioner, if not a theoretician, of classic liberalism at a time when liberal thought was just evolving into laissez-faire capitalism. Society worked best if the marketplace led the way, he believed, but government had to provide a modicum of security for that to happen. The nation was still mired in debt, threatening private credit as well as public. Only a strong national government could pay off old debts and free up new credit. While Congress continued to toy with the notion that the states could be cajoled into paying all debts, including the expenses that Congress itself had incurred to keep the Continental Army in the field, Morris suspected this would never happen. All public debt should be subsumed by a national government and paid off by national revenues, he insisted, and he suggested four ways in which Congress could acquire funds: import duties (he listed twenty-four items, ranging from 50¢ per pound for brown sugar or empty black glass bottles to $36 per pound for bottled wine), export duties (eight items, from 6¢ per pound for salted beef to $180 per head for horses), an excise tax ($6 per gallon for "all distilled liquors to be collected at the still"), and a sharply graduated tax on houses, based on the number of glazed windows (no tax for the first five, 50¢ for fewer than ten, and then increasing steadily, peaking at $100 for a seventy-window mansion). But the notion that Americans were ready to nationalize taxation was way off the mark. By listing his taxes in such detail, Morris ensured the plan's defeat.[10]

For all the powers Robert Morris had been handed by Congress, he still failed to carry the day. If he had battled uphill during the final years of the war, the slope grew steeper yet after the signing of the peace treaty, just as he and his assistant, Gouverneur Morris, had expected. In the waning days of his "reign," delegates in Congress who opposed centralization ascended to power. These included Arthur Lee of Virginia, Morris's sworn enemy since the beginning of the war; Arthur's brother Richard Henry Lee, who had drafted the congressional resolution calling for independence; and Elbridge Gerry from Marblehead, Massachusetts, a close friend and staunch political ally of James and Mercy Otis Warren. Gerry and the Warrens referred to Robert Morris and the nationalists as the Oligarchy, and in the postwar political climate, Gerry and his allies in Congress were able to push through an act abolishing the office of superintendent of finance, thereby terminating Morris's reign.[11]

On November 1, 1784, the nation's one and only financier turned in his commission. On a personal level, Morris seemed to welcome his fall from power. Throughout his last year in office, he had paid more attention to private matters than to public, and he seemed relieved to be doing so. Tending to his mercantile enterprises, he faced fewer demands and received greater rewards. Now, he would be his own master, not beholden to Congress or anyone else, save only his business associates.

Morris's postwar business ventures ran the gamut. As soon as the preliminary treaty had been signed, he resumed relationships with his British trading partners, and he also pursued a scheme he had hatched during the early stages of the war: develop and then monopolize the tobacco trade with France. Back then, he appeared to be offering a public service, for American tobacco growers needed a new market, since they could not trade with Britain; this time, however, there was no such pretense. By negotiating a contract with the French Farmers General that gave him a monopoly on tobacco exports to France, Morris was able to force down the price of tobacco here in America, much to the chagrin of planters in Virginia and Maryland. (Thomas Jefferson, a tobacco planter who happened to be serving as ambassador to France, lobbied in vain to get the contract annulled.) But the problems of others were no longer his own. He was free to play the market for what it was worth and let the "invisible hand" settle the rest.

Most dramatically, Robert Morris opened a lucrative trade with China. His *Empress of China*, a former privateering vessel, sailed from New York City on February 22, 1784, laden with ginseng, tar, turpentine, brandy, and wine, and it returned on May 10, 1785, bearing tea, silks, and chinaware. Morris followed this voyage with another by the *Empress of China*, and then several others with different vessels, and he soon extended his sphere to India as well.

Even more than before the war, Robert Morris was playing high-stakes games on a world stage, and because of the huge investments required for each venture, not all his associates were able to maintain their seats at the table. One partner, Washington's slave-catcher, Daniel Parker, was forced to flee the country, just a step ahead of his creditors, who included both Morris himself and the Continental Congress. Another, John Holker, dissolved his partnership with Morris when they wrangled over the settlement of accounts.

But this was business as usual for the retired Financier. While in office, he had played for higher stakes yet, where losses could affect an entire nation, not just an entrepreneur, partnership, or company, but now that he was a private citizen, he could play selfishly once again, just for fun and profit. No longer fettered by the weight of public credit affixed to his own, he was free to invest much and often, and he usually came out ahead.

Robert Morris's change of lifestyle certainly met with the approval of his wife. When she had married the well-to-do bachelor back in 1770, Mary White had thought she was getting a merchant prince, not an overworked public official with the weight of the nation on his shoulders. After November 1, 1784, she had her husband back, along with his generous parties. In 1785, the year following Robert's retirement from public office, Mary Morris even received a new house, a brick mansion in the heart of town that had been occupied in the recent past by Richard Penn, the British general Wil-

Figures 38 and 39. In 1782, at the height of his power, Robert Morris commissioned portraits of himself and his wife from Charles Willson Peale, a radical democrat who had once been a political foe. The subjects selected their own costumes and settings. Robert, the solid man of affairs, chose to project practicality rather than pomp, while Mary indulged freely in dazzling fashion. From her sculpted headdress to her classical surroundings, Mrs. Morris announced she was a true lady of the world, not to be constrained by any American tendency toward leveling.

liam Howe during the occupation, and Benedict Arnold, while still a patriot and serving as military commander of the city.

Not that the two had abandoned their high living through the war. Robert's portraits reveal that he had put on considerable weight even during the lean years, unlike the perpetually hungry Joseph Plumb Martin or the horseback-riding General Washington. The Morrises had continued to entertain throughout, and among their favorite guests were George and Martha Washington, whenever they passed through town. Toward the end of the war, a visiting French dignitary commented on Morris's abode and style of entertainment: "His house is handsome, resembling perfectly the houses in London. He lives without ostentation, but not without expense, for he spares nothing that can contribute to his happiness and that of Mrs. Morris, to whom he is much attached."[12]

But now that the fighting was over and there were no more calls for sacrifice, Robert and Mary Morris could ratchet up their lifestyle and show some ostentation if they pleased, with neither remorse nor repercussions. "Dinner time I generally have the pleasure of Mr. Morris's company and often two or three guest's strangers, who swarm in our city from all parts of Europe and are numbers of them recommended to Mr. Morris's particular attention, and which we find most agreeable this warm weather to see in a family way," Mrs. Morris wrote in July of 1783, just as her husband was beginning to divorce himself from public duties. These frequent visits by foreigners allowed Mary Morris the opportunity to display her learning and play the role of a cultured and worldly woman, which, as we can infer from the classical imagery that adorns her portrait, she fashioned herself to be. And now, when she wanted to throw a ball, the wife of America's foremost merchant could do so openly and patriotically. There were no longer any public expectations of sacrifice, and that suited her just fine.[13]

For Mary Morris, the interruptions of war and revolution seemed as though they might be over, but her husband knew better, for without "a just and vigorous government" to protect commercial interests, the whole edifice could easily collapse.

1781–1785: Milton Hill and Boston

Of all Robert Morris's numerous critics, few showed as much rancor as Mercy Otis Warren, who called him, in the waning days of his reign, "one of the most dangerous characters in the United States," and who accused him of trying to establish "an American monarchy and an hereditary nobility."[14]

Mrs. Warren had several beefs with the nation's most powerful civilian. First, Morris had failed to approve the appointment of her favorite son to an official post in Portugal. Winslow's mother had lobbied her many contacts within the government, but Robert Morris alone had the authority to grant the position. "Whatever appointments any young gentleman now in Europe may expect, must come thro the hand of the *Financier*, a new created officer among us, vested with such vested powers that no monies are paid, no places filled, but by his authority," Mercy explained to Winslow. But Morris would not bow to the pressures exerted by a concerned republican mother from Massachusetts.[15]

Beyond the personal affront, Warren regarded Morris's reign as poor political form: "Thus we may see sovereigns without a crown, republics without freedom, and several other many-headed monsters that the patriots of 1775 never dreamed of," she complained to Winslow. Power should never be so concentrated.

It was also a matter of style. Robert Morris epitomized and appeared to legitimate the crass commercial culture that was enveloping the nation. The "present ideas of elegance," she grumbled, had "universally taken hold" of a people who used to favor "economy." Further, Mrs. Warren was convinced that the desire to acquire "innumerable superfluities" from foreign markets drained the country of money, and that was driving the nation to ruin. It was a very different economic analysis than Robert Morris's.[16]

All this amounted to "a burlesque on government," a clear violation of "the first principle of the revolution." Morris and his ilk were steering the nation completely off course:

> We have set Great Britain at defiance, we have weathered the shocks of war—we have hazarded all, and waded through rivers of blood to estab-lish the independence of America, and maintain the freedom of the human mind. But alas! if we have any national character, what a hetero-geneous mixture—we have a republican form of government with the principles of monarchy, the freedom of democracy with the servility of despotism, the extravagance of nobility with the poverty of peasantry.[17]

Before the Revolution, Mercy Otis Warren had blamed the ills of imperial misrule on a single individual, Thomas Hutchinson; now, two men above all others shared culpability for America's social and political depravity—Robert Morris and his Massachusetts counterpart John Hancock, who had been elected as the state's first governor under the 1780 constitution, and who held on to power through lavish displays of wealth and a shameless dispensing of political patronage. Because Hancock, a political opponent of her husband, was closer to home, Mrs. Warren heaped even more abuse on him than she did on Morris. To her friend Elbridge Gerry, she compared the governor unfavorably with history's most famous dictator:

> Caesar had talents,—he had valour, intrepidity, activity, and magnanim-ity as well as ambition. . . . But modern times exhibit more wonderful phenomenons. We have seen a man without abilities idolized by the multitude, and fame on the wing crown the head of imbecility. We have seen a people trifling with the privilege of *election*, and throwing away the glorious opportunity of establishing liberty and independence on the everlasting basis of virtue. We have heard them trumpet the praises of their idol of straw, and sing of sacrifices he never had the courage to

make. . . . We have seen this state *baby* of the Massachusetts repeatedly chosen the first magistrate of this Commonwealth. We see him triumph in the zenith of popularity, though so debilitated, as literally to be borne about on the shoulders of sycophants.[18]

But while the Puritanical Mrs. Warren reproached Robert Morris and John Hancock for leading the nation astray, she failed to cast any blame on a certain family of prominent patriots from Massachusetts who also seemed to have wandered from the virtuous path: James and Mercy Otis Warren, formerly of Plymouth, now residing at Milton Hill, the formidable country estate created by Thomas Hutchinson, aka Rapatio, the reviled archvillain of Mrs. Warren's farcical dramas.

During the tumultuous pre-Revolutionary years, to escape from the Boston crowds, Hutchinson had commissioned a nine-room mansion on an imposing hill across the Neponset River, five miles south of the city—sufficiently removed to create a barrier, but still close enough to view the skyline of the provincial capital. He had furnished the house with elegant imports and planted the grounds with exotic trees, shrubs, and flowers. Here at the Monticello of Massachusetts (as the estate would be called by later generations), Hutchinson created for himself and his family a country haven, but he fled to England in 1774 and lost title during the Revolution, when patriots confiscated the estates of loyalists to finance the war effort.

In 1781, after spending £3,000 and going deeply into debt (contrary to their espoused philosophy), James and Mercy Otis Warren moved to their former enemy's estate. Their sudden departure from the family home at Plymouth raised some eyebrows: "This remove is thought by some an extraordinary step at our time of life, is applauded by some & thought by others to be wrong," James observed to Winslow, whom he asked to purchase some "handsome" London wallpaper to refurbish the new abode. In their conscious minds, as evidenced by extant letters, the ascetic Warrens conveniently missed the irony of their situation. Instead, they renamed Hutchinson's manor Tremont and called it their "little villa," insisting it was not so ostentatious after all, while continuing to lash out at the ostentation of others.[19]

Mercy Otis Warren's personal crusade against decadent lifestyles came to a head early in 1785, when she let loose a zero-tolerance rampage aimed at Boston's new Sans Souci Club. There, according to her description to son George, "the younger class of gay people in the town," men and women alike, could not only dance and be merry (which was not so bad), but also try their luck at "forty card tables" (very bad indeed, "a ridiculous institution for such a country as this"). True, all bets were limited to 25¢, but it was the *principle* of gambling that set Warren off, not the amount, for the first sin is always the worst:

> Experience teaches that there are no bounds to the encroachments of pleasure when anyone once steps over the line of propriety in the pursuit, and in my opinion the establishment for gaming, though the stipulations first may be for the most trivial sum, is replete with consequences of the most alarming nature. It is a vice which soon becomes a pleasurable habit followed by the dark and painful passion of avarice—a passion which has no place in the bosom of youth, . . . nor is there any way to escape the contagion of this fashionable amusement, but a determined resolution not to play at all.[20]

Warren's censure was joined by others. "If ever there was a period wherein reason was bewildered and stupefied by dissipation and extravagance, it is surely the present," wrote "Observer" (rumored to be Samuel Adams) in the *Massachusetts Centinel*. "We are prostituting all our glory as a people for new modes of pleasure, ruinous in their expenses, injurious to virtue, and totally detrimental to the well being of society."[21]

For Mercy Otis Warren, the cultural war over the Sans Souci Club took on a personal dimension when her own mentor, the famed British historian Catharine Macaulay, graced it with her presence. Warren had been excited to meet "the celebrated Mrs. Macaulay" on her first visit to America, but the woman she met in Boston in September of 1784 did not share all of Mrs. Warren's values. First of all, the former Mrs. Macaulay was accompanied by her new husband, William Graham, who was literally half her age (when they had married six years earlier, Macaulay was forty-seven, Graham only twenty-one). Macaulay also showed up with coiffed hair, painted face, and "plumpers in her cheeks to hide toothlessness." Although the uncoiffed, unpainted, and unplumpered Mrs. Warren hardly approved, she managed to overcome these differences, and she even defended Macaulay/Graham in the face of her many local critics—but when Macaulay appeared at the Sans Souci and then accused Warren of authoring a shoddy piece spoofing the club (a work that was below the literary standards of both), the mistress of Tremont had had enough. Warren confronted her mentor directly, extracted and accepted an apology, then offered her renewed friendship. But differences in outlook remained between the worldly Mrs. Macaulay and the provincial Mrs. Warren, who had hoped the American Revolution would restore traditional virtues rather than undermine them.[22]

While Mrs. Warren had not authored the controversial San Souci spoof, she did lash out at the rampant corruption of values with a new round of dramatic satires. In 1784 she completed a political drama titled *The Ladies of Castile*, which featured a group of virtuous, freedom-loving Spanish rebels who challenged royal authority back in the sixteenth century. Then she followed with *The Sack of Rome*, her most complex dramatic verse, in which she demonstrated how the same sort of moral decay that was besetting America had wreaked devastation on the world's greatest empire. Warren did not sport well-defined heroes and villains this time; instead, the entire cast, motivated by various forms of lust, greed, and hunger for power, became entangled in a web of intrigue and revenge that weakened a once-great society. In her graphic depiction of ancient corruption, based loosely on Edward Gibbon's *Decline and Fall of the Roman Empire* (three volumes had just been published, with three more yet to come), Mrs. Warren hoped to sound the alarm for her own time.

James Warren, like Mercy, abhorred the alleged moral depravity of the postwar years—so much, in fact, that he actually sought public office once again, the first time in many years. In the early stages of the war, James had served as a major general of the Massachusetts Militia, speaker of his state's House of Representatives, president of its Board of War, one of three members of the Navy Board for the Eastern Department, and paymaster general for the Continental Army. But he had long ago retired from all these positions, and when he was offered the powerful and prestigious post of Massachusetts lieutenant governor in 1780, he turned it down. Likewise, two years later, he declined to serve in the Continental Congress, just as he had turned down various offers for judicial appointments. Instead, James Warren had preferred to remain at Milton Hill, where he could farm according to the latest scientific methods and possibly contribute to man's knowledge of agriculture. "Nothing is more irksome to him than the idea of once more emerging from the quiet scenes of domestic bliss and the calm hours of contemplation, to engage in the arduous attempt of saving a young republic from the consequences of their own folly and ignorance," Mercy wrote to Winslow in the fall of 1784.[23]

But duty called, and opportunity suddenly appeared. In January of 1785, John Hancock, complaining of poor health, decided to take a reprieve as governor, and this opened the field for the first contested election since Hancock had assumed control five years earlier. (The Massachusetts governor, like nearly all elected officials in the young nation, had to stand for office annually.) Surprisingly, James Warren offered his name for consideration.

And so did several other notable figures, who had been waiting in the wings. When voting in the towns failed to produce a majority winner, the election was thrown into the Massachusetts House and Senate. On May 25, after evaluating the four top vote getters, including James Warren, the House chose two finalists, and the Senate then selected the winner. Warren failed to make the cut in the House, due in large measure to the concerted opposition of Hancock himself, who still held considerable sway. "He [Hancock] cares not who is Governor," Mrs. Warren wrote during the campaign, "provided it is neither Mr. [Samuel] Adams nor the man upon Milton Hill, to which last he and his party are making the most strenuous opposition."[24]

Losing was not new to the Warrens. In fact, they generally felt their world was on a downward turn, even when Americans won the war and even as their allies in the Continental Congress rose to power. Somehow, the public virtue they cherished always seemed to recede into the nostalgic past or the illusive future; quite possibly, viewing public affairs in this light interfered with the Warrens' ability to affect the present.

Still, the Warrens had good cause for concern. True, their nation had successfully defended its independence on the battlefield, but to what end? Could it yet stand by itself? Luxuries purchased by John Hancock, Robert Morris, and other wealthy individuals of the merchant class, many of them former loyalists, were creating a significant cash-flow problem, not only in Massachusetts but in other states as well, and with hard money pouring out to British merchants, little was left for struggling farmers. Ironically, Americans were once again beholden to the very people they had just defeated in war. Bad morals (as defined by the Warrens) thereby led directly to bad economics and bad politics, just as they had during the prewar nonimportation struggles. After all the sacrifices during the long, hard military struggle, the United States remained under economic siege.

January 7–September 15, 1785: Mepkin Plantation

Henry Laurens's long-awaited homecoming was not a joyous event.

Laurens sailed from Falmouth, England, on June 22, 1784, but rather than going straight home to South Carolina, he traveled via New York and then Trenton, New Jersey, where Congress was supposedly meeting, to obtain his "honorable discharge" and to answer any "enquiries respecting my conduct, in the missions I have been honored with"—that is, to stave off any criticisms that might be hurled in his direction on account of his questionable performance in the Tower of London. Finding Congress in recess, he waited around for three months till the appointed date for the new session, then handed in his resignation to the eight delegates who happened to have arrived on time. He could have just as easily done it all by mail. When Congress finally mustered a quorum several weeks later, the delegates never even bothered with an official reply. They had more pressing matters before them, including how to fill the gap left by the Financier, who resigned simultaneously with Laurens.[25]

When Laurens finally set foot on his Mepkin plantation on January 7, 1785, he found the place a mess, for the British occupation had taken its toll. "My shattered estates," he wrote, were in "deplorable stile." And his town abode in Charleston, which Laurens visited a week later, had fared even worse, not only during the occupation but, most tragically, upon the Americans' return:

> The British had battered my dwelling house in the course of their cannonade, but left a house capable of repair. The Americans have torn down & carried off all the sashes, doors, windows, chimney backs, wainscotting & even cutt up a great part of the flooring, and left the house totally irreparable.... The dangers which I have sustained from my country men are exceedingly great, both in town and country, & they are the most grievous. I had good ground for expecting friendly attention & protection from those in whose service I had expended large sums of money, hazarded my life, & suffered fifteen months cruel imprisonment.[26]

So it was time to rebuild, even if he had to start from scratch. Rather than worry over the remnants of his Charleston house, Laurens relegated the ruins to firewood and ordered a crew to construct a brand-new dwelling, "a Carolina Palace" with "twenty good rooms" and "ten fire places free from duty" (not to be used as kitchens). All this would take money, lots of it.

Laurens's situation was hardly unique. During the British occupation and the civil war that raged across the Carolinas for the last three years of the war, numerous plantations had been burned and ransacked. As masters like Laurens moved toward restoration, demand for building materials and household items soared, and because many of the items had to be imported, money poured out to foreign merchants, mostly British, while credit wore thin. To make matters worse, as patricians imported more slaves to compensate for those who had fled during the war, additional sums sailed overseas to British traders; in 1784 alone, South Carolinians spent almost a quarter million dollars importing 4,922 enslaved Africans. To pay for all this, planters should have exported rice and indigo but, as luck would have it, alternating droughts and floods for three successive years reduced both rice and indigo exports to less than half their prewar values.[27]

The South Carolina economy was as much in shambles as Henry Laurens's personal estates. The unfavorable balance of trade led to a shortage of circulating money, which meant that personal debts could not be paid. This affected not only debtors but also creditors like Henry Laurens, who had loaned the government much money during the war. Because money was so scarce, taxes collected during 1785 were less than one-tenth the amount of the previous year in several districts; that meant that South Carolina would be unable to meet its requisition from Congress for its fair share of the war debt and, on a more personal level, that Henry Laurens could not cash in on his war bonds. Nor could he collect from private debtors, who simply had nothing to give him. The best he could hope for was payment in kind: the legislature had authorized debtors to pay up with land instead of cash, but they relinquished only their worst tracts, their "pine barrens" that had no real worth.[28]

So Henry Laurens, one of the state's preeminent citizens and once among the wealthiest, was flat broke. On April 16, 1786, he informed a friend from Philadelphia: "Often within these 15 months, my stock of cash has been reduced below a dollar."[29]

He did still have his slaves, however, or at least most of them, those who had not run away during the war. Like other cash-poor but land-rich plantation owners, Laurens could count on the labor of enslaved men, women, and children, who tended to his fields and serviced his every need. As much as Henry Laurens complained of the institution of slavery, he absolutely depended upon it. Without this, he had nothing.

This is why he was so upset with those who had fled to the British (see chapter 15). Like George Washington, Laurens hoped to retrieve his former chattels; unlike Washington, he pursued them aggressively, perhaps more from principle than necessity, for the supreme right of a man to control his own property was at stake.

When Laurens heard that one man, Ishmael, had turned up in St. Augustine, he asked a friend there to reason with him, promising Ishmael in writing "that if he would return of his own accord I would pay his passage and every thing that was passed should be forgotten & forgiven." Perhaps, too, Laurens's friend might run into another former slave, Brutus. If so, the same offer of clemency should be extended to him. But to an objective ear, or to Ishmael and Brutus, who already felt like free men, Laurens's offer of mere clemency might not sound so reasonable after all.[30]

On April 6, 1785, Alexander Hamilton, writing from New York, informed his best friend's father that one of his former slaves, Frederick, had just turned up in the city jail. Frederick had a story to tell: during the siege of Charleston, he had helped dig trenches on behalf of the patriots, and John Laurens, who was there at the time, had granted him his freedom. This was "a tissue of lies," Henry maintained. His son never would have freed a slave not his own, and besides, according to evidence from the time, Frederick was among those who followed the British when they raided the Mepkin plantation a few months later. Worse yet, at a later date, Laurens had paid good money to retrieve Frederick in Georgetown, where he showed up as a prisoner aboard an American cruiser. But Frederick "had broke thro' and escaped and had not been heard of till now."[31]

Henry Laurens's first response was to convince Frederick to return on his own accord, all expenses paid and all past sins absolved. "It would grieve me to hear he was enslaved by any one, who has a shorter claim of property in him than I have," Laurens told Hamilton. "I wish to give him a chance of being rescued from slavery." Apparently, Frederick did not accept Laurens's weak offer.

New York officials soon released Frederick and placed him in the charge of the recently formed New York Manumission Society, whose founding members included Hamilton and John Jay, its first president. Apparently, although the letter has not survived, the society wrote Laurens requesting permission to free Frederick, for Laurens responded sternly: "You acknowledge I have property in Frederic, be pleased to leave me free to exercise my judgment." He addressed his letter to the special attention of John Jay, his former negotiating partner in Paris, and as per Laurens's demand, Jay and the Manumission Society opted for property rights over freedom and delivered up Frederick. To retrieve the man he claimed to own, Henry Laurens paid 13 pounds sterling for attorney fees and the passage back, as well as $40 for Frederick's upkeep in New York.[32]

Financially, it was not a good bargain. On September 15, shortly after Frederick's arrival, Laurens wrote Jacob Read, his attorney, to thank him for his efforts, but as the master of Mepkin gazed down from his house, with its commanding view of the fields below, he happened to notice Frederick: "There he goes, carrying a little dirt out of the garden, not earning his victuals." Laurens saw "no prospect of pecuniary gain" from a man who worked so slowly, and besides that, he was reluctant to turn this defiant man loose "among his old fellow servants who are now a happy orderly family." If Frederick's behavior continued a few more weeks, Laurens vowed, he would have to remove "the burthen upon me" and sell him. So much for providing Frederick with "a chance of being rescued from slavery."[33]

If Henry Laurens, through his actions, appears today as a stereotypical slave owner, that's certainly not how he chose to view himself. Boasting to Hamilton, he presented his credentials as a magnanimous master:

Some of my Negroes to whom I have offered freedom have declined the bounty. They will live with me. To some of them I already allow wages, to all of them every proper indulgence. I will venture to say the whole are in more comfortable circumstances than any equal number of peasantry in Europe. There is not a beggar among them, nor one unprovided with food, raiment & good lodging. They also enjoy property. The lash is forbidden. They all understand this declaration as a substitute: "If you deserve whipping I shall conclude you don't love me & will sell you." . . . Yet I believe no man gets more work from his Negroes than I do. At the same time they are my watchmen and my friends. Never was an absolute monarch more happy in his subjects than at the present time I am.[34]

These ethical gymnastics, however self-serving they appear to us, seem to have worked for Henry Laurens. "I am acting therefore agreeable to the dictates of my conscience," he informed Hamilton, whom he knew shared his son's views on slavery.

Frederick saw things differently. Never the contented slave of his master's imagination ("He was always a very good lad before the war," Laurens told Hamilton), Frederick had used the opening presented by the Revolution to escape. He tasted freedom briefly, but then he was captured. After another round of escape and capture, he was thrown in jail. With his fate placed in the hands of the New York Manumission Society, he had reason to expect he would be free at last, legally and therefore permanently, but his hopes were dashed by the machinations of his master. And so he trudged on, silently defiant, expressing his discontent in the only manner left open to him.

Henry Laurens would never allow himself to understand how Frederick felt. As the master, he believed that freedom was his to bestow, not Frederick's to demand. But in fact he would never bestow it because he could not afford to do so. The ability to command slave labor was all he had left.

August 17, 1786–May 18, 1787: Massachusetts

James Warren saw it coming. On April 30, 1786, he wrote to John Adams, who was serving as his nation's first ambassador to Great Britain:

> The constant drain of specie to make remittances for baubles imported from England is so great as to occasion an extream scarcity. Commerce is ruined and, what is worse, the husbandry and manufactures of the country cannot be supported. . . . No debts can be paid, or taxes collected. . . . Everything seems verging to confusion and anarchy.

Even allowing for the Warrens' habitual exaggerations, much was amiss, and something needed to be done. "Great wisdom and address are necessary," Warren wrote, yet the General Court "give no satisfaction to their constituents."[35]

A new revolt was in the offing. Indebted and disgruntled farmers turned out of doors, much as they had done twelve years earlier when they first overthrew British authority everywhere in Massachusetts outside of Boston (see chapter 6). Hoping to stage a repeat performance, they gathered in taverns, called for county conventions, and prepared for a forceful resistance. On August 17, forty-one of the fifty towns in Worcester County sent delegates to a convention in Leicester, and five days later, fifty of the sixty towns in Hampshire County sent delegates to a meeting in Hadley. Farmers-turned-activists in the counties of Middlesex, Berkshire, and Bristol also held conventions. The grievances listed at these meetings bore a striking resemblance to the earlier complaints against the Massachusetts Government Act in 1774: the courts were out of control, the upper body of the legislature was not representative, government officials should be paid directly by the people. But the objects of the complaints, the antagonists, were different this time around. While farmers and the inland regions were hurting, merchants in the seaboard towns prospered. Furthermore, the East enjoyed a lopsided share of political representation, while it paid a disproportionately small share of the taxes, which were based largely on land rather than the wealth generated by commerce. According to the disgruntled farmers, Massachusetts had become a two-tiered society, both politically and economically.[36]

Following a script that had worked so well before, common folk from the interior regions tried to close the courts so they could not be sued for debts. (Between 1784 and 1786, roughly one-third of the adult males in Worcester and Hampshire Counties were involved in suits for the collection of debts.) The Court of Common Pleas for Hampshire County was slated to meet in Northampton on August 29, one day shy of the anniversary of the court closure in 1774. Again, "a large concourse of people" marched under fife and drum to the courthouse, and again the judges retreated to a nearby tavern, tried to negotiate with the insurgents, and agreed in the end to adjourn the court without conducting any business.[37]

One week later, on September 5, 1786, the script was repeated in the town of Worcester. Back on September 6, 1774, thousands of insurgents had flooded into town, taken over the courthouse, and forced the judges to submit to their authority; this time, although they numbered only in the hundreds, the Regulators (as they called themselves) hoped to produce the same result. Wearing sprigs of evergreen, just as they had done during Revolutionary years, they occupied the courthouse, bayonets in hand, and waited for the judges to appear. "I am determined to stand with firmness and resolution," said their leader, Captain Adam Wheeler, a fifty-five-year-old veteran of both the French and Indian War and the Revolutionary War. "We have lately emerged from a bloody war, in which liberty was the glorious prize aimed at. I early stepped forth in the defence of this country, and cheerfully fought to gain this prize; and liberty is still the object I have in view."[38]

Undaunted, Justice Artemas Ward approached the courthouse and faced off against his adversaries. Ward had also been a judge in 1774, but back then he had supported the insurgents' demands and freely stepped down; this time, in a two-hour harangue, Ward tried to convince his neighbors that they were engaging in treasonous acts and ought to quit their rebellion. The Regulators would have none of it. Leveling bayonets at Ward's chest, they forced the judges to retreat.

Ward and company then tried to convene the court in the United States Arms Tavern, the same spot on Main Street where deposed judges had huddled twelve years earlier. But the insurgents insisted the court must adjourn, and the following day, surrounded by a hostile crowd of some four hundred men, many bearing arms, the judges acceded.[39]

But authority was only suspended this time, not dismantled. Over the course of the next four months, while Regulators closed county courts in Concord (Middlesex County), Taunton (Bristol County), and Great Barrington (Berkshire County), their opponents, including virtually all merchants and moneyed men of any sort, did everything within their power to muster a countervailing force.

First, they tried calling out the local militias, but too many militiamen, sympathetic with the Regulators, refused to line up against their neighbors.

Next, they asked the federal government to step in, and on October 21, Congress commissioned loans for half a million dollars for the support of an army that could suppress the "dangerous insurrection" in Massachusetts. But the plan faced a major problem: the loans were to be administered through the states, which were hopelessly behind with prior obligations to Congress. Only one state, Virginia, agreed to raise money for a federal army.[40]

That left Massachusetts on its own, but like Congress, the state government was flat broke. All it could do, other than deny the Regulators' various petitions, was pass a series of repressive laws, including a riot act that forbade twelve or more people from gathering with arms and a sedition act that made it illegal to spread "false reports to the prejudice of government." It also gave local sheriffs the power to shoot and kill protesters, and it promised to confiscate their land and subject them to "thirty-nine stripes on the naked back" should they resist. Leading the vindictive charge, of all people, was Samuel Adams. "Our old friend Mr. A[dams]," James Warren informed John Adams, "seems to have forsaken all his old principles and professions and to have become the most arbitrary and despotic man in the Commonwealth." Samuel Adams, for his part, saw no contradiction between his earlier and current behavior. Public protest, even armed revolt, was legitimate when directed against a regime over which the people had no control, but not permissible against an elected, constitutional government.[41]

Riot act or not, the Regulators persisted. Twice more they kept the court from transacting business in Worcester.

Not until the third showdown, at the end of November, did a Revolutionary War veteran named Daniel Shays join the local insurgents there. Shays had been recruited by Regulators to help direct the military aspect of their insurgency, and henceforth their opponents, whether through ignorance or design, steered public attention away from the collective and substantive demands of the insurgents by attributing "Shays' Rebellion" to the designs of a single individual. Ever since, writers and students of American history have taken the easy path by allowing one person's name to substitute for a complex social movement.

Finally, in January of 1787, merchants and professionals from Boston and other eastern cities decided to take matters into their own hands. With the personal sanction of Governor James Bowdoin, himself a wealthy wholesaler, 129 men with money ponied up the funds to raise a 4,400-man army for a month to go after the insurgents. Although the western counties, where the Regulators were strong, could not produce their full quotas, plenty of men from the East signed up. Some were veterans, many not. Even a few merchants who had never fought before stepped forward to support a cause that was truly their own. Among the recruits were two young men eager to get a brief taste of military life: Henry Warren, age twenty-two, son of James Warren, former general in the Massachusetts Militia, and Timothy Bigelow Jr., age nineteen, son of Colonel Timothy Bigelow from the Continental Army. Neither Henry nor Timothy, however, fought for quite the same reasons as their fathers. Henry had just moved to Boston, where he hoped to establish a commercial career, and Timothy had just graduated Harvard, where he rubbed shoulders with many of the state's elite. These men on the rise clearly identified with the haves, not the have-nots.

Toward the end of the third week in January, Major General Benjamin Lincoln (the major general in the Continental Army who had had the dubious distinction of surrendering Charleston, South Carolina, to the British, but the more honorable distinction of accepting Lord Cornwallis's surrender at Yorktown) led a private army of some three thousand makeshift soldiers toward Worcester, where the Regulators were expected to close the court yet a fourth time on January 23. In fact, the insurgents had other ideas. The harsh legislation and formation of a counterrevolutionary army had led them to one conclusion: the solution to their problems would have to be military as well as political. So while Lincoln's army awaited them in Worcester, they planned to seize the federal arsenal in Springfield, which Timothy Bigelow had guarded at the end of his military career a few years back. If the insurgents could "possess themselves of the arsenal at Springfield," Congress feared, they could "produce a state of anarchy and confusion" and "probably involve the United States in a civil war." That fear was warranted: the Springfield arsenal, in the heart of rebel country, might provide the Regulators with the means to stage a full-scale assault on Boston.[42]

The Regulators almost pulled it off with a three-pronged attack, but one of the messages was intercepted, and they were never able to marshal their full force at one time. Then, once the rebel assault was repulsed, Lincoln's army began to hunt them down. At Petersham on February 4, having marched through a driving snowstorm, the well-fed and well-equipped men from the

East surprised the hungry and ragtag farmers from the West. Although scattered resistance continued for several months, there would be no civil war. The Regulators had been squashed.

James and Mercy Otis Warren, despite their horror at the breakdown of civil society, and despite the participation of their son in Lincoln's army, favored neither side. They sympathized with the Regulators' demands but could not sanction armed resistance. Mercy Otis Warren conveyed her mixed reactions to John Adams: "There seems to be on the one side a boldness of spirit that sets at defiance all authority, government, and order, and on the other, not a secret wish only, but an open avowal of a necessity for drawing the reins of power much too tight for republicanism." While most of her class ganged up against those in defiance of authority, Warren thought the greatest, most lasting threat lay with those who drew the reins too tight, and who were even "crying loud for monarchy and a standing army to support it."[43]

Timothy Bigelow's hometown of Worcester was divided. Historian Kenneth J. Moynihan has calculated that the town meeting voted in favor of the county conventions during the Regulation by a slim but consistent majority of 54 to 46 percent. Intimidations and humiliations such as those used in 1774 can achieve results if supported by upwards of 90 percent of the people, but when the populace is more evenly divided, enforcing the will of a narrow majority leads to civil strife rather than social or political transformation. Further, in this case, unlike in 1774, the insurgents faced an enemy closer to home and therefore better able to mobilize against it. Colonel Bigelow himself sided against the rebels this time; struggling financially, he lent a grand total of 12 shillings for the support of Lincoln's army.[44]

Though the Massachusetts Regulation of 1786–87 failed, it certainly had an impact. The earlier, more successful court closures, upon which it was modeled, had initiated a stream of events that culminated in the formation of a new nation: the British counterattack at Lexington and Concord, the ensuing military conflict that made a peaceful settlement unlikely, and finally the declaring of independence. But the later, failed rebellion, which involved fewer direct participants, also influenced the course of events, although not in the manner intended. Much as 1774 closures prompted an aggressive reaction from the British, the 1786 version caused people on the top to tighten "the reins of power," as Mrs. Warren described it.

And not just in Massachusetts, but throughout the United States. In nearby Connecticut, New Hampshire, and Vermont, protesting farmers toyed with rebellion. In Rhode Island, debtors gained control of the legislature and forced the state to issue paper money. Governmental leaders in New York, North Carolina, and Georgia debated whether to circulate paper money in their own states in order to escape the wrath of indebted farmers. In York, Pennsylvania, two hundred men armed with guns and clubs took back cattle that had been seized by the government in lieu of taxes. Farmers closed courts in Virginia, Maryland, and New Jersey. After a court closure in Camden, South Carolina, Judge Aedanus Burke believed that not even "5,000 troops, the best in America or Europe, could enforce obedience to the Common Pleas."[45]

In this context, the protests in Massachusetts, because they evolved into armed rebellion, triggered a raw nerve. The entire nation appeared at risk. The day after Christmas, 1786, George Washington expressed his concern to Henry Knox, the man whom Washington had left in charge of the remnants of the Continental Army three years earlier:

> I feel, my dear General Knox, infinitely more than I can express to you, for the disorders, which have arisen in these states. Good God! Who, besides a Tory, could have foreseen, or a Briton predicted them? . . . Notwithstanding the boasted virtue of America, we are very little if anything behind them in dispositions to every thing that is bad.[46]

While Washington complained, confirmed nationalists like Robert Morris, Gouverneur Morris, Alexander Hamilton, and John Dickinson knew exactly where to take this crisis. For a full decade, they had been pushing for a stronger and more unified government, always losing out in the end to deep-seated fears of a central and thereby distant authority. Now, those fears were matched by others of equal power: economic collapse, social upheaval, and political disintegration. This was their political moment. If the nationalists played their cards right, they might yet wind up with the centralization they thought was necessary to give the United States a firm financial foundation and enduring governmental structure.

19

New Rules

May 20, 1785–May 14, 1787: The West, Annapolis, and Philadelphia

On October 21, 1786, when Congress wanted to raise money for a federal army to suppress the "dangerous insurrection" in Massachusetts, it was so deeply in debt that no responsible investor would even think of lending it more—unless, of course, it could put up an attractive collateral to back the dubious loan. What security could a bankrupt nation possibly offer? The answer was obvious: "The proceeds of the first half million acres of the western territory, which shall be sold in pursuance of the acts of Congress."[1]

The United States was cash-poor but land-rich. Opening the West offered the nation an exit route from insolvency. By the mid-1780s, states that once had laid claim to the West had ceded control to the federal government, and on May 20, 1785, Congress approved a very precise plan for how the West would be divvied up and sold. All land, no matter the terrain, was to be measured off into a giant rectangular grid, with north-south and east-west lines dividing the earth into "sections" of one square mile apiece. Some sections were reserved for local schools, some for veterans, and some for various uses of the federal government, but the bulk were to be sold off for not less than a dollar an acre, with all money accruing to the United States of America.

Aside from filling the national coffer, the West offered tremendous opportunities for individuals and families. As Americans struggled for their livelihoods east of the Appalachians, they could always look to the other side of the mountains, to land that appeared ripe for white settlement. Speculators understood this and lured people westward: "Here you may enjoy inviolate your rights and properties—be instrumental in founding a mighty empire—help make America the garden of the world—and rear a paradise on its surface."[2]

The new nation was certainly expanding, even though it had yet to figure out how to stabilize its money flow or solidify its government. Population jumped dramatically after the war, as did the range of Euro-American settlement, the amount of land under cultivation, and homegrown manufactures.

None of this portended well for native people between the Appalachians and the Mississippi River. While the United States believed it owned that vast territory by virtue of the Treaty of Paris, local Indians felt otherwise:

> As we were not partys [to the treaty], so we are determined to pay no attention to the manner in which the British negotiators has drawn out the lines of the lands in question ceded to the States of America. . . . His Brittannick Majesty was never possessed either by session, purchase, or by right of conquest of our territorys and which the said treaty gives away.[3]

These were the words of half-Creek Alexander McGillivray, who helped unite Creeks, Choctaws, Chickasaws, and Cherokees (along with the breakaway Chickamauga) to oppose the expansion of the United States.

This pan-Indian resistance, aided by Spanish arms, presented a clear and present danger to prospective white farmers, but the states, no longer in control of the territories, could not provide military protection, while Congress had no more than a handful of soldiers at its command to guard a few outposts and armories. There was no standing army because the people would not tolerate it, any more than they would tolerate standing taxes issued from a centralized authority. Although occupying the West would someday be a great boon for the national treasury, in the short run it would cost Congress both money and political capital, both of which it lacked.

Not all citizens of the United States staked the future of their nation on westward expansion. Eastern merchants feared that if western farmers developed an alternative trading route down the Mississippi, their own Atlantic trade would no longer monopolize American commerce. Many easterners also worried that a large western population would threaten their own influence on national politics. Consequently, New York's John Jay, the nation's secretary of foreign affairs, negotiated a treaty with Spain that sacrificed American claims to the Mississippi waterway for several decades in return for trading privileges that would benefit seaboard merchants. While northern states approved the measure, the five southern states, closer to the western lands, balked. Through the late summer of 1786, Congress debated the issue, and because nine states were required for ratification, Jay's treaty languished.

The net result of Jay's proposed treaty was to divide the union along strictly regional lines, not over slavery but trade. Simultaneously, individual states feuded with each other about trade issues. New York, for instance, decided on its own to tax New Jersey for goods shipped through the New York City harbor, to which New Jersey strongly objected.

Broke, without an army, and bogged down by both class and regional strife, Congress was left with little clout. One might think that in such problematic times, the nation's attention would be riveted upon the highest deliberative body to see what it might do, but if truth be told, few seemed to notice or care about the proceedings of Congress. Since the close of the war, delegates had found it difficult merely to convene a quorum, let alone lead the nation. Many of the most experienced statesmen, if elected to Congress, chose to stay at home to fight more immediate political battles.

Yet ironically, as weak as it was, Congress was under suspicion for power mongering. Such distrust was not new: from the very beginning, back in 1776, those who advocated a stronger role for the national government were accused of trying to heighten their own influence and authority, and, more recently, the "reign" of the mighty Financier had broadened and deepened the misgivings. Congress was caught in a bind, too feeble to act yet suspected of being too strong. Any attempt to exert or usurp greater powers would only heighten popular resentment.

Still, without some sort of concerted action to thwart the centrifugal tendency, the states might fly apart.

Early in 1786, the Virginia legislature called for a separate convention in Annapolis, Maryland, to consider "a uniform system" for the "commercial regulations" between the states. The New England states were suspicious, and though some selected delegates, none of these attended. Hampered but not defeated by the small turnout, the intimate gathering at Annapolis called for another convention to be held nine months later "to take into consideration the situation of the United States" and to suggest measures that would "render the constitution of the federal government adequate to the exigencies of the union."[4]

In Congress, the idea for a second gathering met with no more than a lukewarm reception, and the whole plan might well have languished were it not for the disturbances in Massachusetts and elsewhere the following winter, which created the air of a national emergency. In February of 1787, Congress sanctioned a new convention, to be held on May 14 in Philadelphia "for the sole and express purpose of revising the Articles of Confederation." A separate convention, it resolved, was "the most probable mean of establishing in these states a firm national government." Such wording would not have been approved a few months earlier.[5]

This time twelve of the thirteen states selected delegates, and most actually planned to attend. A few did not, notably Henry Laurens, who claimed he was simply too tired to deal with this sort of thing, and Patrick Henry and Richard Henry Lee of Virginia, confirmed opponents of the nationalists. Of those who did agree to attend, only a few expressed fears that a strong central government threatened the liberties gained by the Revolution. Among the most wary were Elbridge Gerry, the Warrens' close ally, and George Mason, neighbor and longtime friend of George Washington. These men did not automatically dismiss the idea of a central government, but they remained alert to its possible dangers.

The upcoming convention drew considerable notice within the state legislatures, which selected delegates and in some cases issued strict instructions (Delaware, for instance, insisted that each state must retain an equal voice in Congress), but it garnered only spotty interest in town and county political venues, where people were groping with more pressing local issues. For more than two decades, Americans had been staging conventions in every way, shape, and form, and to suit every purpose, and in the minds of many, this must have appeared like more of the same. If this gathering ever managed to come up with some significant suggestions (judging by past performances and current jealousies, the odds were stacked against such an outcome), the folks back home assumed they would have ample opportunity to affirm or deny the propositions, as required by the Articles of Confederation. Besides, it would take but a single state to stymie any evil scheme.

This sort of grassroots inattention provided fertile ground for men who wished to till the soil in a novel manner and plant some unexpected seeds.

May 25–September 17, 1787: State House, Philadelphia

By May 14, the appointed day, delegates from a grand total of two states were in Philadelphia. Most Pennsylvania delegates did not have to travel, while the other state, Virginia, still lacked two key members, Governor Edmund Randolph and George Mason, one of the most respected theoreticians in the state and nation. Such a pathetically weak turnout did not portend well. Was this convention, like that at Annapolis, slated for oblivion?

Slowly over the next eleven days, delegates arrived, and on Friday, May 25, the convention finally achieved a quorum of seven states. (Nobody had actually bothered to define what constituted a quorum, so the number seven was conveniently borrowed from the Continental Congress, which, at the time, was having difficulty fielding a quorum for its own meetings in New York.) On that day, twenty-nine men gathered in the East Room of the Pennsylvania State House and took their seats in Windsor chairs, each provided with a writing desk, arranged in a semicircle. Although many of the delegates to this convention had been in the room before, only two, Robert Morris and Connecticut's Roger Sherman, had signed both great documents that emanated from that location: the Declaration of Independence and the young nation's working constitution, the Articles of Confederation.

No dirt farmers could be found in that room, although there were plenty of gentleman planters. Also present were numerous lawyers and a healthy share of graduates from Princeton, Yale, and Harvard, the nation's preeminent colleges. Politically, these men could be classified as moderate to conservative. Most had actively opposed independence during the grand debate in the early months of 1776. (Only four had voted in favor of the congressional resolution on independence, and one of those, James Wilson, had spoken passionately against it just three weeks earlier, while another, Elbridge Gerry, would soon take issue with the results of this convention.) Now, many of these cautious patriots were the foremost advocates of a nationalist agenda, not only men like Hamilton and Dickinson, carryovers from Annapolis, but also the most powerful of all, Robert Morris, who had recently reentered the public arena to mount yet another challenge to the radical Pennsylvania constitution, and who now decided that this was the opportune time and the most auspicious setting to further the goals he had been unable to attain during his tenure as financier. Although Morris himself was neither a theorist nor a public speaker, he had by his side his brilliant lawyer, James Wilson, for whom he had risked his life back in 1779, and his assistant financier, Gouverneur Morris, the one-legged, high-living rhetorician from New York, whom he had recruited to serve as a member of the Pennsylvania delegation. G. Morris and Wilson would be the most frequent speakers in the upcoming days, followed by James Madison, Roger Sherman, George Mason, and Elbridge Gerry.

Madison, a thirty-six-year-old planter-scholar from Virginia, was relatively new to the nationalist camp, and he brought to it fresh energy and ideas. He also brought to the convention an impressive work ethic:

> I chose a seat in front of the presiding member, with the other members on my right & left hands. In this favorable position for hearing all that passed, I noted in terms legible & in abreviations & marks intelligible to myself what was read from the chair or spoken by the members, and losing not a moment unnecessarily between adjournment & reassembling of the Convention I was enabled to write out my daily notes during the session or within a few finishing days after its close. . . .
>
> I was not a little aided by practice & by a familiarity with the style and the train of observation & reasoning which characterized the principal speakers. It happened also that I was not absent a single day, nor more than a casual fraction of an hour in any day, so that I could not have lost a single speech, unless a very short one.[6]

It is largely due to the labors of this statesman–turned–court reporter, whose "notes" extend to over 225,000 words (about six hundred printed pages), that we know so much about the doings within the East Wing of the Pennsylvania State House throughout the summer of 1787. These notes, which gave ample space to the input of all speakers, but which featured his own remarks in somewhat greater detail, fed the later notion that James Madison was the primary author of the Constitution, which in truth was a thoroughly collaborative affair, with each word deeply pondered and many important provisions altered time and time again.[7]

One other delegate deserves special mention: George Washington. As with Robert Morris, Washington's impact on the convention cannot be measured by the number of times he expressed his personal views, which happens to be one. Washington's importance lay in his mere attendance, for he lent the gathering an air of authority and legitimacy it might otherwise have lacked. When it would come time for the convention to seek approval from the states and the people, Washington's endorsement would prove particularly crucial. Those who might try to thwart the will of the convention would have to oppose the nation's most revered individual, a considerable political risk. As much as George Washington, like Robert Morris, would have preferred to stay in retirement, he understood the significance of his attendance. With characteristic precision, the General had arrived in Philadelphia on the evening of May 13, one of only five out-of-state delegates to avoid being tardy.

There was no public fanfare on May 25, a rainy day in Philadelphia, to mark the commencement, although the delegates did muster a bit of flourish inside. Things did not go exactly as planned, however. The host Pennsylvania delegation had resolved to nominate George Washington to serve as president, and its illustrious elder statesman, Benjamin Franklin, was supposed to perform the honors. But Franklin was too weak to go out in the rain, so Robert Morris took his place. Morris was a natural choice, not so much because he had been the most powerful civilian in the nation's history, but because of his close personal connection. Washington was lodging with the Morris family at the time, as he often did when passing through town. Over the next several months, when the workday was over and James Madison retreated to write up his notes and other delegates socialized in various configurations, Morris and Washington relaxed in each other's company, whether dining in formal parties or simply in "a family way," with hostess Mary Morris.[8]

Washington's nomination was seconded by John Rutledge of South Carolina, thereby affirming solidarity across regional lines, and of course he was approved by unanimous consent. After Morris and Rutledge accompanied the president to his new chair at the front, Washington offered some characteristically modest words, in conformity with custom. With only a mere quorum present, the delegates selected a committee to prepare some rules and then adjourned.

On Monday, May 28, the rules committee reported back. Two measures, both common to the times, suggest the curious mix of democratic and deferential forms that marked the convention. First, no member would be permitted to speak a second time "upon the same question" before every other member had been given a chance, and he could not speak yet again without "special leave" from the house. Second, upon adjournment, "every member shall stand in his place, until the President pass him."[9]

On Tuesday the delegates agreed to abide by an additional restriction: "That nothing spoken in the house be printed, or otherwise published, or communicated, without leave." Enforced secrecy, unlike the other rules, rubbed against the prevailing ethic of the times. Throughout the Revolutionary era, Americans had been insisting on transparency in their deliberative bodies, but these men did not wish to be beholden in any way to outsiders, even if that meant they would have to shut all windows and doors throughout the muggy Philadelphia summer, so no passersby could hear. They wanted to be left alone, free to decide what they would, and so they pledged their honor, gentleman to gentleman, that they would keep all deliberations to themselves.[10]

Then, with forty delegates from eleven states present, the meeting began to address substantive matters. Edmund Randolph, governor of Virginia, the largest state in the confederation, announced that because Virginia had been the first to call for a separate convention, it fell upon her to lay matters on the table for proper consideration. While waiting in Philadelphia for others to show up, delegates had been meeting "two or three hours, every day" to come up with a preliminary plan, which Randolph now presented to the body.[11]

The Articles of Confederation were not performing the task expected of them, Randolph opened. That document had been drafted during different times, "when the inefficiency of requisitions was unknown—no commercial discord had arisen among any states—no rebellion had appeared as in Massachusetts—foreign debts had not become urgent—the havoc of paper money had not been foreseen." To "remedy" these various ills, the Articles of Confederation needed to be "corrected and enlarged."[12]

Having laid out the need, Randolph presented a fifteen-point proposal, commonly called the Virginia plan, which bore very little resemblance to the current confederated government but a great deal to many of the existing state governments. There would be two branches of a "national legislature," the first elected by the people, the second elected by the first. Any legislation would need the approval of both. There would also be a "national executive" to be chosen by the legislature, a "national judiciary," and a "council of revision," taken from the executive and judicial arms, which could "negative" a law. The legislature, however, could override the negative by "_____ of the members of each branch." This was one of several blanks left in the plan, which also avoided getting into other details, such as length of terms.

This basic formula for a separation of powers, although lacking in the Articles of Confederation, was neither new nor controversial, but other measures were. Apportionment should no longer be on the one state, one vote basis, but determined instead by population or "quotas of contribution." Furthermore, state governments would be "bound by oath to support the articles of union," thereby becoming inferior to a more central authority. Finally, ratification of these alterations would be by special conventions "to be expressly chosen by the people," thereby sidestepping entrenched powers within state legislatures that might object to relinquishing authority. These provisions were sure to raise some hackles.

The following day, May 30, the gathering took up the Virginia plan, starting with its weakly worded preamble. Gouverneur Morris immediately objected: Why doesn't the convention come right out and state its true intention? Following Morris's lead, Randolph substituted much stronger language: "A *national* government ought to be established consisting of a *supreme* legisla-

tive, executive & judiciary" (emphases in Madison's notes). This addressed
the heart of the matter, and there followed a short but spirited discussion "on
the force and extent of the particular terms *national* & *supreme*." Elbridge
Gerry and Charles Pinckney quickly sounded the alarm: because the existing Articles of Confederation contained no such language and had no such
intent, and the new plan bore so little resemblance to the old, delegates
were clearly overstepping their bounds. Gerry and Pinckney "expressed a
doubt whether the act of Congress recommending the convention, or the
commissions of deputies to it, could authorise a discussion of a system
founded on different principles from the federal constitution [the Articles of
Confederation]."

But Gouverneur Morris, unfazed, bullied on: a "federal" government was
no more than "a mere compact resting on the good faith of the parties," while
a "national, supreme" government implied "a compleat and compulsive operation." Since "federal" had proved too weak, it was time to try the tougher
brand. "In all communities, there must be one supreme power, and one only,"
he said boldly. Morris and the nationalists carried the day. Of the eight states
that voted, six approved the revolutionary and unconstitutional move to create a single national government with supreme authority. To all intents and
purposes, the Articles of Confederation—a contract among sovereign states,
each "supreme"—had been scrapped. Henceforth, should the proceedings of
the convention be ratified, there would be one sovereign nation, not thirteen
sovereign states.[13]

No wonder the delegates had agreed so readily to work in secret. Imagine
the uproar back in the states, had people known that their existing constitution was being cast away, with only a brief debate and token resistance. Had
each American citizen been asked at that very moment whether he would like
to submit to the supreme authority of a distant national government vested
with sweeping powers that superseded those of his own state, the nays would
have dwarfed the ayes.

James Warren, had he attended the convention, would likely have flown
into a rage, but he was occupied as speaker of the House in Massachusetts,
trying to piece together the mess in his own state. For all his pessimism,
which sometimes bordered on paranoia, Warren had not seen the danger
coming. Others did. Richard Henry Lee, for one, had just warned George
Mason, who was headed to the convention, against "the danger attending
upon the states parting with their legislative authority." The delegates should
not "rush from one extreme to another" and grant Congress too much power

simply because it currently had too little, Lee advised. "Every free nation, that hath ever existed, has lost its liberty by the same rash impatience and want of necessary caution."[14]

The legislature of Rhode Island had also been suspicious, and that's why it declined to send any delegates. Under the Articles of Confederation, all amendments required unanimity, and that gave even the tiniest of states veto power over vital issues such as taxation. The majority of Rhode Island legislators wished to keep it that way. They worried that the convention in Philadelphia "might be the means of dissolving the Congress of the Union and having a Congress without a Confederation," and their fear was confirmed with the passing of Gouverneur Morris's proposal. In their minds, Americans should stick with "the wisdom of men" who had framed the original Articles ten years past. These founding fathers had been "instrumental in preserving the religious and civil rights of a multitude of people," and should their good work be undone "we must all be lost in common ruin."[15]

But these voices were not heard within chambers at the State House in Philadelphia on Wednesday, May 30, 1787, when a handful of men from six states determined that the United States of America should start over from scratch. From that point on, the question was: what form should the new government take?

There was one broad field of agreement: to prevent the excessive concentration of power in the hands of one man or a few, the government must feature multiple branches, each possessing distinct responsibilities. Together, these various centers would create an interdependent web, with each component empowered to check abuses by the others.

Yet as they tried to fashion the proper mechanisms, delegates wound up expressing many of the same antagonisms, based on self-interest, that had led to the convention in the first place. Some of the major points of contention are well known, starting with the very first item of the Virginia plan: dispensing with the "one state, one vote" rule of the Articles of Confederation in favor of voting according to population. The Delaware delegation announced at the outset that if they lost their equal say, they might have to "retire from the convention." Immediately, the Virginia delegation backed off and agreed to table the matter. When the convention addressed the issue again a month later, tempers rose to such a fever pitch that delegates referred the matter to a special committee, composed of one representative from each state. Despite the heated emotions, it took this committee only a single session to arrive at a workable compromise: apportionment in the lower house would be determined by population, while in the upper house, each state, whether large or small, would have an equal voice. This did not take any special genius, but it did require a spirit of conciliation.[16]

Also well known is the compromise over slavery: apportionment in the lower house of Congress would be according to "the whole number of free persons" plus "three-fifths of all other persons." (The word *slave* never appeared in the official document, although delegates used it freely in the debates.) Clearly, this was a solution based on convenience alone, without even a pretense of ideological justification, yet the exact fraction, which appears so arbitrary, had an interesting historical precedent. In the later days of the Revolutionary War, when Congress was apportioning the tax burden among the states, Northerners insisted that slaves, who produced wealth, must be counted so Southern states would pay their full share; Southerners countered that slaves should be left off the register, because legally slaves were not citizens but property. Now, each region reversed its stance: Southerners suddenly decided that slaves were people, not property, while Northerners wanted them left off the books, to deprive the South of additional representation in Congress. To resolve the earlier debate, Congress had decided to include three-fifths of all slaves when assessing taxes; now, although positions were transposed, the convention based its compromise on the exact same fraction.

No issue received more attention than the role of the executive, for which there were no acceptable precedents. In colonial times, the national executive had been in the hands of a hereditary monarch, while the executive power for each of the colonies had been vested in an appointed governor. For a nation based on popular sovereignty, none of this could serve as a model. Not only were the delegates starting from scratch, but they had to avoid even the appearance of regressing back toward a monarchy.

The problems were various but interrelated. Should the executive role be entrusted to one man or several? How long should he/they serve, and could he/they repeat in office? Who would select the executive(s)? Who would pay him/them? Should he/they simply carry out the will of the legislature, or should he/they serve as a check on the legislative branch? If the latter, should the executive have exclusive power to "negative" a bill, or should some members of the judiciary or a separate council also have a part? Would its negative be absolute, or could it be overturned? Finally, should the executive be subject to impeachment and, if so, by whom?

Initially, delegates found no consensus on any of these matters. Edmund Randolph argued vigorously against a single executive, calling it "the foetus of monarchy," and the New Jersey plan, an alternative to the Virginia plan, also favored a "plurality." But practicality prevailed, and the idea of a multiple executive was voted down.[17]

The proposed terms of office ran the gamut: eight, ten, eleven, twelve, fifteen, or twenty years ("the medium life of princes," Rufus King explained), or even forever "during good behavior" (Gouverneur Morris's preference). But the longer terms, however popular within this chamber, would never be approved by the people at large. Because a fifteen- or twenty-year presidency might turn people against the entire plan, the only serious contenders were four years or seven, with delegates opting for the shorter term so long as the executive could be reelected.[18]

The issue of selection proved most problematic. On June 1, according to Madison's notes, James Wilson declared "at least in theory" that he favored "an election by the people," but few delegates wanted to follow this theory to its logical conclusion. The following day, Wilson himself backtracked, having devised an alternative: the people, divided into three large districts, could vote for "electors," who would then gather to choose the executive. Even this was too much for Elbridge Gerry, who figured "that the people ought not to act directly even in the choice of electors, being too little informed of personal characters in large districts, and liable to deceptions." Gerry prevailed, and Wilson's proposal failed, two states to eight. Instead, the convention gave the power to choose the chief executive to the national legislature. Delegates preferred to weaken the separation of powers rather than vest the power to elect a president with the people themselves.[19]

More than six weeks later, delegates reaffirmed that the national legislature should choose the executive, but Gouverneur Morris mounted a furious drive to overturn the decision, arguing that it would subject the executive to party politics and destroy his ability to check the legislature. Morris's view prevailed, and two days later, the convention decided that the executive should be chosen by a group of electors. Five days after that, it concluded that the elector scheme was simply too cumbersome and returned to the original plan, but Morris repeated his arguments time and time again until finally, in early September, he got his way: the president would be selected by special electors, apportioned among the states according to the total number of members in Congress. To this day, Americans are prohibited from voting directly for their president.

Distrust of the people ran so deep that many delegates didn't want citizens to vote directly for *anyone*, even their representatives in Congress. Better to delegate all authority to wise, virtuous, and disinterested leaders, they said. On May 31, Roger Sherman, sounding more like a prewar Tory than a Revolutionary, set the tone for a lengthy and very illustrative debate on the proper role between the people and their government: "The people he said immediately should have as little to do as may be about the government. They want information and are constantly liable to be misled."

Elbridge Gerry, who had once sided with popular resistance, seconded Sherman's stance: "The evils we experience flow from the excess of democracy." Gerry admitted outright that he had been "too republican heretofore: he was still however republican, but had been taught by experience the danger of the levelling spirit."

But then George Mason, from aristocratic Virginia, suggested that these once-republican Yankees were retreating too vigorously from the founding principle of the nation. At least the "larger branch" of the national legislature should be elected by the people, since "it was to be the grand depository of the democratic principle of the government." While he agreed with Gerry that things had gone too far in favor of the people, he warned against a backlash: "He admitted that we had been too democratic but was afraid we should incautiously run into the opposite extreme."

It fell to James Wilson to come to the people's defense. Wilson was hardly a populist—back in 1779, with Robert Morris, he had faced off against "the people" at "Fort Wilson" (see chapter 15)—but he was willing to follow the train of a rational argument, wherever it might lead. And in this case, if one started with the premise that government depended on the will of the people, the conclusion seemed obvious:

> Mr. Wilson contended strenuously for drawing the most numerous branch of the legislature immediately from the people. He was for raising the federal pyramid to a considerable altitude, and for that reason wished to give it as broad a base as possible. No government could long subsist without the confidence of the people. In a republican government this confidence was peculiarly essential.

James Madison then elaborated on this theme. In several states, he noted, the first branch of the legislature appointed the second, which in turn appointed a governor or council, and these made still further appointments. Implicitly, Madison expected some such arrangement in the new national government. But if even members of the lowest branch were not directly elected, "the people would be lost sight of altogether, and the necessary sympathy between them and their rulers and officers too little felt." Referring to himself in the third person, Madison summarized his position: "He was an advocate for the policy of refining the popular appointments by successive filtrations, but thought it might be pushed too far."[20]

Wilson and Madison expressed the overriding aim of the convention perfectly: to create a "federal pyramid" with "successive filtrations" between the people, who formed the nation's true foundation, and their leaders, whom the people should entrust to run their government. The job of the delegates was to construct just the right pyramid, along with rules for how those filtrations should work.

But could there be too many levels of filtration? That's what worried George Mason. During a debate over the powers of the executive, Mason alerted his colleagues to a crude reality they might be missing as they spent day after day, week after week, and eventually month after month talking to each other and nobody else: if the people outside their chamber felt left out of the new system, they would refuse to approve it. "Notwithstanding the oppressions & injustice experienced among us from democracy," he said, "the genius of the people is in favor of it, and the genius of the people must be consulted." So as the delegates proceeded, this was their challenge: to fashion an edifice in which the people were distanced from the normal workings of government, but not so far removed as to offend "the genius of the people."[21]

By September 8, after multiple drafts, endless debates, and countless decisions and reconsiderations, most delegates concluded they had had enough. The document wasn't perfect, they all knew, but most felt they could live with it, and they were by and large satisfied with their work. So they turned it over to a five-man committee that included three nationalist heavyweights: Hamilton, Madison, and Gouverneur Morris. This committee charged Morris with adding the final polish, and four days later Morris presented his work. Tortuous sentences were now readable, and one in particular stands out. Initially, the opening words of the preamble read: "We the people of the states of New Hampshire, Massachusetts . . ." and so on, listing all thirteen, proceeding from north to south. Morris turned this into the form we all know and love: "We, the people of the United States." The shift was at once a stylistic improvement, a political expedient (should any of the states fail to ratify the new constitution, it would not have to be altered), and a confirmation of the document's nationalist slant.

For a few more days, delegates pecked away at this detail and that, but they had reached the point of diminishing returns. Finally, on September 17, the venerable Benjamin Franklin, his eyes too weak to read his own writing, asked James Wilson to read a carefully crafted summation he had prepared, simultaneously modest and self-congratulatory, and it was his statement that sealed the deal:

> I confess that there are several parts of this constitution which I do not at present approve, but I am not sure I shall never approve them. . . . I agree to this constitution with all its faults, if they are such, because I think a general government necessary for us. . . . I doubt too whether any other convention we can obtain may be able to make a better constitution. . . . Thus I consent, Sir, to this constitution because I expect no better, and because I am not sure it is not the best.[22]

The final document—what we know today as the United States Constitution—met the needs of its authors. By superseding the old Articles of Confederation and affirming national supremacy, it granted Robert Morris and his fellow nationalists the one thing they had most craved: the ability of a central government to levy taxes. Like gold, national taxation was a simple treasure with strength and beauty, the foundation upon which the credit and future of the United States depended. Although Americans in the future would never tire of celebrating both the document and the men who created it, rarely have they acknowledged its key component, the opening to Article 1, Section 8: "The Congress shall have the power to lay and collect taxes, duties, imposts and excises, to pay the debts and provide for the common defence and general welfare of the Unites States, . . . [and] to borrow money on the credit on the United States." Without this, there would be no point to all the rest. To taxes we owe our Constitution, however much we might complain.

Robert Morris and many others in the room had another cause for satisfaction, deeply buried in Article 1, Section 10, and well concealed within several clauses of a rambling sentence: "No state shall . . . make any thing but gold and silver coin a tender in payment of debts, [nor] pass any law . . . impairing the obligation of contracts." So much for paper money and related schemes back in the states. Henceforth, the central government would take charge of the economy. Creditor relief, not debtor relief, would be the law of the land.

George Washington also had cause to celebrate. Like Morris, he had favored national taxation, but his interests were more broadly conceived. A central government favored a strong nation, more able to expand. A national army, no longer prohibited, could protect United States interests in the West.

Beyond that, through his direct involvement in the Revolution, Washington had become increasingly committed to republican government. The core component of the prevailing Revolutionary ideology—all government must be rooted in the will of the people—had worn off on the General, and as much as any other statesman participating in the Philadelphia convention, he was pleased by the elaborate structure of checks and balances in the final document, intended to stymie the power grabbing of would-be dictators or oligarchs. Having been so careful for so long not to abuse the power he had, he perhaps had the most to gain by ensuring that no others would abuse power in his stead.

And yet this man of aristocratic breeding (at least by American standards) did not have to worry that the new government would be subjected to the whims of a fickle populace. Only one-half of one-third of the "federal pyramid" was subject to direct control by the people, just enough to ensure its philosophical foundation, but not so much as to prevent domination by men of his own class and standing, better versed in the arts of government.

Yet for Washington, and for at least a few others, as well, there remained a nagging doubt: had the delegates gone too far in their attempts to keep the people at a safe distance from their government? The people's only direct link were their representatives in the lower house, and according to the new rules, there could be no more than one of these for every forty thousand people, as recorded in a periodic census. Previously, in their colonial and state governments, many and perhaps most citizens *personally* knew the men who represented them; now, few would. This bothered Nathaniel Gorham (a conservative from Massachusetts) so much that on the final day, following Franklin's moving plea, he proposed a last-minute revision: change forty thousand to thirty thousand, not so much to suit his own beliefs as "for the purpose of lessening objections." Under normal conditions, the other delegates would have resented Gorham's last-minute intrusion, but the idea resonated with President Washington, who chose this bizarre moment to issue his only substantive contribution of the convention.

Madison noted the incident in some detail: "When the President rose, for the purpose of putting the question, he said that although his situation had hitherto restrained him from offering his sentiments . . . and it might be thought, ought now to impose silence on him, yet he could not forebear expressing his wish." Washington then announced that he supported the proposed reduction, not only to prevent "objections," as Gorham had argued, but because the disproportionate ratio between citizens and their representatives was "an insufficient security for the rights & interests of the people." Of course, the change in numbers would not significantly alter that arrangement, but at least it was a step in the right direction, and in light of the unorthodox timing, it demonstrated Washington's serious concern that in their secret dealings with each other "the rights & interests of the people" had already been rendered insecure.[23]

With Washington's unexpected endorsement, Gorham's motion passed without opposition.

George Mason, Washington's friend and neighbor and a man of equal social standing, did not only *suspect* the delegates had gone too far in shutting the people out, he *knew* it. "The dangerous power and structure of the government," he proclaimed, "would end either in monarchy or a tyrannical aristocracy; which he was in doubt, but one or the other, he was sure." Mason stated the basic problem succinctly: "This constitution has been formed without the knowledge or idea of the people." Then he offered a solution, which to him appeared obvious: "A second convention will know more of the sense of the people, and be able to provide a system more consonant to it. It [is] improper to say to the people, take this or nothing." Mincing no words, Mason pronounced "that he would sooner chop off his right hand than put it to the constitution as it now stands."[24]

Edmund Randolph, the man who commenced the proceedings, also refused to accept the conclusions. He refused to sign because he feared the people would reject it, and that would lead to "anarchy and civil convulsions." Like Mason, he favored a second convention; then, once the people had been allowed the chance to offer their input, they would more readily assent.[25]

Elbridge Gerry, playing the role of curmudgeon, offered numerous reasons for his refusal to sign the final document. One was practical: like Randolph, he predicted it would only add to the disorder, and he was particularly concerned about its impact in Massachusetts, where democracy, "the worst of all political evils," had run amok. Others were picky, like "the power of Congress over the places of election." But he also voiced two sweeping criticisms that were sure to resonate with the public: the power of the legislature to "make what laws they may please to call necessary and proper" and to "raise armies and money without limit." These would be difficult measures to sell.[26]

But the other thirty-nine delegates who lasted till the end, despite reservations about this section or that, agreed with Gouverneur Morris: "The moment this plan goes forth all other considerations will be laid aside, and the great question will be, shall there be a national government or not?" The whole was greater than the sum of its parts, and so they signed on.[27]

Before adjourning to a farewell dinner at the City Tavern, delegates addressed one last matter of housekeeping: what should they do with the official journal? Rufus King noted, and nobody dared dispute him, that "if suffered to be made public, a bad use would be made of them by those who would wish to prevent the adoption of the constitution." One option was to destroy them, but delegates balked at that; they might need to prove themselves someday against false allegations. Instead, they placed the journals under the care of the most trustworthy man in the house, their president, who would keep them secret until Congress—the new one, that is—ordered otherwise.[28]

September 17, 1787–June 29, 1788: Delaware, Pennsylvania, New Jersey, Georgia, Connecticut, Massachusetts, Maryland, South Carolina, New Hampshire, Virginia, New York, North Carolina, Rhode Island

The delegates did well to keep their proceedings private. Imagine the reactions had the public learned that men indoors had connived to give the people "as little to do as may be about the government." Over the previous two decades, American patriots had insisted that the people must have their say, and no amount of backsliding could erase that notion.

In theory, the convention delegates acknowledged that the people would need to vote on the matter in some form, and in practice, they knew their plan would not work unless the people accepted it as their own. Delegates had struggled with how to do this. Mere language would be a start, so they introduced their new constitution with the enticing and memorable phrase, "We, the people." But that alone would not ensure ownership by the public. They knew that many (and perhaps even most) Americans would be reluctant to scrap the old system in favors of theirs, so they needed to alter the rules of the game, which under the current Confederation would have required the unanimous approval of the states. Although they possessed no authority to do so, they determined that the new constitution would go into effect as soon as it was ratified by special conventions in at least nine states. (James Madison suggested a bare majority of seven, but other delegates thought this an invitation to further disunion.)

Although this method of ratification was in clear violation of existing law under the Articles of Confederation, it held sway. The convention sent the proposed constitution to Congress, which was still sitting in New York, and on September 28, Congress passed it along to the state legislatures, who were instructed to convene separate conventions. Already, by accepting the ratifying process suggested by the men in Philadelphia, Americans were granting the new constitution an elevated status.

Supporters wasted no time in both implementing the ratification process and arguing on behalf of the new constitution. By working quickly, they hoped to approve the new plan before a strong opposition could coalesce. In Philadelphia on September 17, the very day the convention adjourned, Pennsylvania's delegation sent word to the state's Assembly, meeting one floor above in the State House, that they wished to present the document, and the following morning, at eleven o'clock, they did so. Immediately, the Assembly discussed arrangements for a statewide constitutional convention, and a week later it decided to publish three thousand copies (one thousand in German) of "the Constitution agreed to in Convention, for the government of the United States," even though the document had already appeared "in all the gazettes, as well as in handbills."

But the opposition mobilized too, and it was significant, just as some of the convention delegates had feared. A handful of dissenters who had left the convention early, including New York's Robert Yates and John Lansing and Maryland's Luther Martin and John Mercer, were bent on stirring up resistance in their home states. In Virginia, nonsigners George Mason and Edmund Randolph were joined by some of the state's most respected leaders, including Patrick Henry and Richard Henry Lee, who believed the convention had sacrificed the people's liberties. In Massachusetts, the cantankerous Elbridge Gerry was sure to have allies. The republican spirit was still strong there, personified by such men as Samuel Adams, president of the Senate, and James Warren, speaker of the House. And with the state still reeling from the Regulators' insurrection and the crackdown against it, nobody could safely predict what might happen.

Approval in other states would also be difficult. Would South Carolina agree to a constitution that permitted Congress to interfere with slavery, even though twenty years hence? Would Connecticut, which had opposed the very existence of the earlier Annapolis convention, suddenly approve the results of this one? And what about Rhode Island, which had refused to attend, fearing (correctly, as it turned out) that the gathering would forsake a federal structure in favor of a national one?

And so the battle was on.

Supporters of the convention drew first blood in a subtle but compelling manner: they chose the best possible name (federalist) for themselves while ascribing the worst (antifederalist) to their opponents. Throughout the Confederation period, *federalist* connoted a friend of effectual government, which at the time was seen as not merely desirable but necessary. *Antifederalist*, on the other hand, was a term of derision, hurled at those accused of obstructing the legitimate workings of government by impeding its ability to collect money. Fortuitously, when a convention was called in 1787 to revise and upgrade the Confederation, it was dubbed the *federal* convention, and by association, if not by logic, supporters of the convention's proceedings could thereby be labeled federalists. Seizing the opportunity, these partisans grabbed the term as their own, which meant of course that those who opposed them became antifederalists—negative obstructionists at best.

The great irony here is that the so-called antifederalists actually favored a federal system based on shared sovereignty, while their opponents, the nationalists, wanted something more. "A union of the states merely federal" was not enough, Gouverneur Morris had maintained at the start of the convention, for it was no more than "a mere compact, resting on the good faith of the parties." The federal model, he said, should be supplanted by a "national, supreme government." This was the main point of the whole affair, but in a remarkable display of early Orwellian doublespeak, those who opposed mere federalism commandeered its good name. It was perhaps the most successful, enduring, and significant spin control in American history.[29]

Names and labels aside, there was much of substance to debate, and debate there would be, in pamphlets and newspapers and countless conversations. Many of the extant printed arguments are being collected by the State Historical Society of Wisconsin, which over the past three decades has reproduced them in twenty hefty volumes and a multitude of microform supplements entitled *The Documentary History of the Ratification of the Constitution*. (The project is not finished; with six of the thirteen states left undone, editors project at least seven more volumes on ratification and an undisclosed number focusing on the Bill of Rights.) All the oral discussions and altercations, meanwhile, remain unrecorded, although we know by firsthand descriptions that they could get rather heated. We also know there was no shortage of physical confrontations, reminiscent of the most passionate days of the Revolution. In those earlier times, however, people styling themselves "friends of government" tended to be on the receiving end of riots, while this time around, ironically, many if not most illegal intimidations were staged by people in favor of creating a stronger government.

Despite the zealous commotion, some of the debate was conducted on a high intellectual plane, with proponents and opponents of the new constitution reaching deep into their storehouses of political philosophy to support their respective positions. Essays abounded with references to classical history, the legal writings of William Blackstone, the political theories of French philosopher Montesquieu, and so on; today, discourse on this level is to be found nowhere outside the narrow confines of academia. We would be hard pressed to find another time in human history when such a large percentage of the citizenry immersed themselves so deeply in the subtleties of political philosophy and the minute details of governmental forms.

Although in its scope and consequence the debate over ratification resembled the earlier debate over independence, structurally the two were very different. The first time around, discussions at the grassroots level worked their way upward, starting in taverns and local newspapers, proceeding to town and county meetings, then to state conventions, and finally to the climactic congressional declaration. This time, the discussion commenced from a small focal point at the top, the Federal Convention, and worked its way downward, first to the state legislatures, who made arrangements for elections and ratifying conventions, and then down to the local level, where the delegates were selected and where every citizen could take part. At that point the direction shifted and the debate became more centralized again, but never totally so. Instead of one grand climax, the nation had thirteen mini-climaxes, the final votes of the separate state conventions.

The first great confrontation on the statewide level occurred in Pennsylvania, which for Federalists (we resort to common usage now, complete with capitalization) was a must-win state. The odds there seemed in the Federalists' favor, for the new constitution was clearly partial toward commerce, and Philadelphia remained the commercial capital of the nation. Should the favorites fail to carry the day in the very state that had hosted the Federal Convention, the momentum would swing against ratification nationwide.

The outcome in Pennsylvania was not a foregone conclusion. Resistance was strong in the interior regions, where farmers harbored resentments parallel to those of the Massachusetts Regulators. These people already felt removed from the seats of power, and the new government promised to be even less responsive to their needs than the old one. Pennsylvania's regional jealousies, always severe, were thus renewed during the ratification debate.

So, too, was another local source of contention: the continuing tussle over the 1776 state constitution (see chapter 12). For a decade, "Constitutionalists" (the radicals of old) had withstood pressures from "Republicans" (moderates like Robert Morris) to overturn the measure. With Constitutionalists turning into Antifederalists and Republicans into Federalists, familiar foes went at each other again on a slightly altered terrain.

In the Assembly chamber on September 28, the same day Congress sent the proposed plan of government to the rest of the states, the skirmishing commenced. During the morning session, assemblymen argued over the projected ratifying convention: those supporting the new constitution (the majority) wished to stage the convention quickly and on their home turf in Philadelphia, while those opposed (the minority) wanted more time to organize against it and a venue closer to the center of resistance. The Assembly broke for lunch, but when it reconvened it had no quorum, for the minority members failed to show up. Without them, the majority could conduct no business, and the convention would certainly be delayed.

When the Assembly tried to meet the following morning, it was still two members shy of a quorum. The speaker dispatched the sergeant at arms to hunt them down, and soon he returned with his prey, James M'Calmont and Jacob Miley. M'Calmont immediately protested that "he had been forcibly brought into the Assembly room contrary to his wishes," and "he begged he might be dismissed." But of course he was made to stay, and now that the Assembly was legally constituted, it went about its business of scheduling elections for November 6 and a convention on November 20.[30]

By circumstantial but highly suggestive evidence, it appears the kidnapping was engineered by Assemblyman Robert Morris, who had come out of political retirement to mount yet another assault on the radically democratic Pennsylvania constitution of 1776. Four days after the affair, M'Calmont brought suit against Captain John Barry, the only man he recognized in the mob that had captured him. Barry, a ship captain in the employ of Robert Morris, had no particular reason to involve himself with the internal workings of the Pennsylvania Assembly, unless he was asked or hired to do so. Most likely, Robert Morris assigned Barry and his sailors the task of strongarming the recalcitrant politicians to achieve a quorum.[31]

Morris and the Federalist assemblymen had their way, but they were made to pay a price. The Seceding Assemblymen, as they called themselves, published a broadside that outlined their side of the story, from the beginning. The Pennsylvania delegates to the Federal Convention had been instructed only to recommend "further provisions" to the existing Articles of Confederation, and they "had no authority whatever from the legislature to annihilate the present Confederation and form a constitution entirely new." There was also the small matter of a governmentally sanctioned riot. When M'Calmont and Miley were seized, the dissenters complained, "their lodgings were violently broken open, their clothes torn, and after much abuse and insult, they were forcibly dragged through the streets of Philadelphia to the State House, and there detained by force, in the presence of the majority." Over the next five weeks, this broadside was reprinted twelve times within Pennsylvania (including once in German) and sixteen times in six other states plus Vermont. The word was out: Federalists were too quick to violate the law, on both a grand and petty scale.[32]

George Mason, although not a resident, contributed to the opposition in Pennsylvania. Before leaving Philadelphia, he had met with Antifederalist members of the Assembly, who arranged for the publication of his "Objections to the Constitution formed by the Convention." Mason was particularly concerned about the absence of a declaration of rights, such as the one he had written for the Virginia constitution of 1776; the small size of the House, which could not adequately represent the people; the excessive authorities granted to the Senate; and the power of a simple majority to legislate trade issues. The essay was reprinted in twenty-five newspapers from Maine to South Carolina, and on October 7, Mason sent a copy to George Washington, who disagreed with its contents and took offense at his friend's effort to mobilize resistance. "He [Mason] rendered himself obnoxious in Philadelphia by the pains he took to disseminate his objections amongst some leaders of the seceding members of the legislature of that state," Washington wrote to James Madison, who was more in line with his own persuasion. The mounting differences between these close neighbors and former political allies had clearly placed a strain on their friendship.[33]

On Saturday, October 6, Philadelphia Federalists fought back with a mass meeting in the State House Yard. Organized by city Republicans to nominate candidates for the upcoming Assembly elections, the gathering morphed into a rally for the new constitution. To the casual onlooker, it would appear the Revolution had returned: thousands of local citizens were meeting in the open air to address the pressing political issue of the day, giving shouts of "huzzah" as public speakers said what the people wanted to hear. But the lead members of the cast had changed. This time, instead of radicals like Thomas Young, it was men of moderate and conservative persuasion who stood up on the stage to "harangue" the crowd (to use the parlance of the times).

The keynote speaker turned out to be James Wilson, Robert Morris's lawyer. Eight years earlier, Wilson had been forced to defend his home from an angry crowd (see chapter 15), but circumstances had changed, and here he was, not only participating but taking a lead in outdoor politics. Item by item, Wilson countered the critics. The new constitution did not contain a declaration of rights because it didn't need to, he said. All powers not granted still resided with the people, and any enumeration of these rights would imply that others, not listed, now belonged to the government. A standing army was not only appropriate but necessary to protect the needs of the nation, and in fact one already existed in the "cantonments along the banks of the Ohio." State governments, far from being annihilated, still maintained power over the selection of senators and the president. The powers of the Senate, accused of being aristocratic, were strictly circumscribed by those of the House and the president. National taxation would allow Congress to assume the states' war debts, which had proved so burdensome to the people.

Wilson's speech at the State House Yard provided talking points to Federalists everywhere, and it became an instant classic. By the end of the year, it had been reprinted in thirty-four newspapers in twenty-seven towns across the country, a far wider contemporary circulation than the *Federalist Papers*, which would achieve so much renown in later years. George Washington sent a copy to Virginia for use by Federalists there, explaining that Wilson was "as able, candid, & honest a member as any in the Convention," and hoping that his speech would "place the most of Colo. Mason's objections in their true point of light."[34]

The November 6 elections sent a majority of Federalists to the November 20 Pennsylvania convention. With virtually all delegates committed at the outset to one position or the other, the three-week gathering was more of a debating society than a deliberative body. Opponents tried to include fifteen amendments that bore a point-by-point resemblance to Mason's writings, but to no avail. On December 12, the delegates voted 46–23 in favor of ratification. The following day, Mary Morris wrote excitedly to her absent husband:

As you know that I am something of a politician, I therefore could not forbear informing you that the federal government is agreed to by our convention. They finished last evening; great demonstrations of joy were expressed by the populace. They did not forget you. We had three cheers.[35]

The result came as no surprise to Robert Morris. On November 12, assured by the elections that Federalists would prevail in Pennsylvania, he and Gouverneur Morris had departed for an extended tour in Virginia, nominally "to aid the Federalists," but also to collect debts and lean on their tobacco suppliers, for the French Farmers General had started to complain about late deliveries.

Grassroots resistance in Pennsylvania actually heightened after the official vote of the ratification convention. In the interior town of Carlisle, Antifederalists broke up a Federalist victory celebration, and in the ensuing riot the insurgents prevailed. The following day, the two sides staged back-to-back demonstrations, with Antifederalists burning James Wilson and Thomas McKean, the state chief justice, in effigy. Four weeks later, twenty-one of the Antifederalist rioters were jailed, and when seven of these refused to post bail, several hundred local militiamen marched on the jail to free them.[36]

More peaceably, over six thousand citizens signed a petition requesting that the Assembly censure its delegates to the Federal Convention for violating the Articles of Confederation and revoke the decision of the state ratifying convention. Although the move stalled when the Assembly adjourned, the petitioners, as well as the rioters, delivered a potent message: a Federalist victory did not guarantee compliance, and without the assent of the body of the people, no new constitution would be secure.[37]

Massachusetts was up for grabs. On September 22, just before news arrived from Philadelphia with results from the Federal Convention, Mercy Otis Warren reported to Abigail Adams, in London at the time, on the political climate back home:

> A dead calm reigns among us that I fear will be succeeded by contrary appearances when the doings of the Convention are divulged. . . . Many are disposed to adopt the results of their deliberations be they what they may; others are perversely bent on opposition though even a well digested Federal plan may appear; a third class will as obstinately oppose what appears to them wrong as they will decidedly support whatever they think right, as that lends to the general welfare.[38]

Warren should probably be included in the second group—a month earlier, in a letter to Catharine Macaulay, she had complained that the delegates in Philadelphia were "busy genius's now plodding over untrodden ground, and who are more engaged in the fabrication of a strong government than attentive to the ease, freedom and equal rights of man"—but she preferred to see herself as one of the wait-and-see crowd, for she understood the immensity of the task as well as its potential risks:

> Our situation is truly delicate & critical. On the one hand we stand in need of a strong Federal Government founded on principles that will support the prosperity & union of the colonies. On the other we have struggled for liberty & made costly sacrifices at her shrine, and there are still many among us who revere her name too much to relinquish (beyond a certain medium) the rights of man for the dignity of government.[39]

Local Federalists would find it difficult to persuade Mercy Otis Warren and the old stalwarts of revolutionary ideology in Massachusetts that the proposed constitution had not crossed that "certain medium."

The ratification process started in the General Court, where Samuel Adams presided over the Senate and James Warren over the House. Neither Adams nor Warren publicly opposed the new constitution at the outset, but privately and anonymously they expressed their concerns. Adams summed up his discontent pithily: "I confess, as I enter the building I stumble at the threshold. I meet with a national government instead of a federal union of sovereign states." Warren, writing as "The Republican Federalist," took particular objection to the federal convention's "take this or have none" ratification process: "This may be language adopted to slaves, but not to freemen." But in their official capacities, neither Adams nor Warren saw fit to enter the fray just yet. On October 25, the Massachusetts Senate and House set the date for a January convention and directed the selectmen of each town to hold a special meeting to choose delegates.[40]

Citizens took these local elections seriously. In Worcester on November 8, Isaiah Thomas's *Worcester Magazine* published both James Wilson's State House Yard speech and Elbridge Gerry's explanation of his opposition to the Massachusetts General Court. "We wish not to prejudice our readers one way or the other," Thomas explained. But many residents of Worcester were already prejudiced, reflecting the fault lines drawn during the Regulators' uprising the previous winter. In a hotly contested election, Samuel Curtis, one of the founding members of Worcester's homegrown American Political Society, gained one seat, while the second spot fell to David Bigelow, Timothy's brother, who edged out Timothy Paine, one of the Crown-appointed mandamus counselors whom Curtis and the Bigelows and thousands of others had deposed in the Revolution of 1774 (see chapter 4). Paine had worked his way back into the political arena, representing the anti-Regulator faction the previous winter (his two sons were major local creditors, even though one was still in exile) and now the Federalist faction. On the third and decisive ballot, Bigelow had 88 votes to Paine's 87. The tight race in Worcester presaged a close contest statewide.[41]

Throughout the Revolutionary era, Massachusetts town meetings had issued instructions to their delegates on controversial matters such as this. This time, although a handful instructed in favor of approval and a larger percentage instructed their delegates to reject the new constitution, most refrained from instructions. The issues were too complex to resolve without further consideration. Almost everyone favored changes to the Articles of Confederation, yet few approved every section of the proposed document. Better to elect like-minded delegates and let them figure out how to deal with the situation, most reasoned. Some of the towns that issued instructions actually reflected this ambivalence. Witness a committee report from Southborough, only a few miles from Worcester:

It is our opinion that the Federal Constitution, as it now stands ought not to be ratifyed, but under certain limitations and amendments it may be a salutary form of government, which limitations & amendments we think best to submit to the wise deliberation of the Convention.

The town meeting accepted this report, and then added "that the constitution by no means be set up as it now stands, without amendments." The Federalist notion of "take this or nothing" ran aground in the hinterlands of Massachusetts, where people were used to deciding things for themselves.[42]

In January, over 360 delegates braved the harsh New England winter to show up in Boston for the convention. Although the number of eligible delegates was pegged to the number in the General Court, this was the largest turnout ever. In part this was due to the magnitude of the issue, but there was another factor in play: Antifederalists had pushed the state to pick up all expenses, thereby making it possible for representatives from small, less affluent, and more distant towns to attend.

In fact, there were so many delegates they couldn't all fit in even the largest chamber at the State House. To accommodate the numbers, the convention moved to the Congregational Church on Brattle Street, but the acoustics there were so bad that nobody could follow the proceedings. So it was back to the State House, where men who considered themselves of some importance packed tightly against each other, with no place to sit. Finally the Long Lane Congregational Church offered its venue, complete with a stove (not all churches had one) and a gallery, which could hold up to eight hundred spectators.[43]

For the next three weeks, from January 17 to February 6, that gallery was nearly always full. People came not only to listen but to participate, for during the evenings and recesses, many of those who watched corralled delegates to lobby for their positions. Here at last, on the physical plane, was Thomas Young's political dream house, his "structure equal to the most finished playhouse for the conveniency of all that chose to attend the debates." Young himself, were he alive and in Massachusetts, would probably have been there, politicking as an Antifederalist who jealously guarded the people's liberties. Even if for some reason he had changed his orientation, this is still where he would want to be. For a political zealot like Dr. Young, a show like this was not to be missed.[44]

At the outset of the convention, Antifederalists were in the majority, but their opposition in many cases was "soft." If delegates proposed some amendments, as the town of Westborough demanded, some Antifederalists might agree to ratification. So on January 31, Governor John Hancock, recently emerged from retirement, proposed a compromise: Massachusetts should ratify the new constitution, but it should also "recommend" nine amendments for future consideration. To the surprise of many, Samuel Adams came out in support of Hancock, his sworn political enemy for the past decade. Hancock's amendments, Adams said, would "conciliate the minds" of opponents, particularly "the people without doors."[45]

It was a remarkably small sop to offer Antifederalists. Except for the first one—"all powers not expressly delegated to Congress are reserved to the several states"—the amendments only poked at the edges of the elaborate framework devised at the Federal Convention, leaving the deep structural framework intact. They included neither severe constraints on the national government nor sweeping guarantees of individual rights. Furthermore, Hancock's proposal did not address the question of how these amendments might be introduced, promoted, and adopted.[46]

Weeks earlier, James Warren had seen the amendment ploy coming. "The state convention will in all probability be warmly urged to accept the system, and at the same time to propose amendments," he wrote under the pseudonym of "Republican Federalist." This might fool "the *weak* and *unwary*, but not persons of discernment," he contended. Mere recommendations were worthless because Federalists, once their constitution had been approved, would use the cumbersome amendment process to sabotage any new provisions. "If therefore it is the intention of the convention of this state to preserve republican principles in the federal government, they must accomplish it *before*, for they never can expect to effect it *after* a ratification of the new system."[47]

But weak as they were, the amendments did the trick. Although most Antifederalists remained firm, enough of them bent. Starting at four o'clock in the afternoon on February 6 and proceeding for a full hour, the delegates voted, one member at a time. The gallery above was packed but hushed. There was "profound silence, all attention," according to one observer. "You might have heard a copper fall on the gallery floor," wrote another. The final tally: 187 (mostly from the East) for ratification with recommended amendments, 168 (mostly from the West) opposed. A shift of ten delegates would have changed the outcome, and possibly the course of future ratification debates in other key states.[48]

David Bigelow voted nay. Worcester's other delegate, Samuel Curtis, was one of only nine men absent on that day. Seth Newton, the single delegate from Southborough, voted yea. James Warren, though speaker of the House, had not been sent to the convention by his town of Milton and therefore could not cast a vote. Statewide, the vote reflected regional divisions, with the three western counties opposing ratification 91–33 (in Worcester County, it was 43–7), while Suffolk and Essex Counties, home to Boston and other port towns, supported the new constitution 72–11.[49]

The Antifederalist defeat energized one old republican warrior, Mercy Otis Warren. Writing as "A Columbian Patriot," Mrs. Warren gushed forth a lengthy diatribe that not only elucidated eighteen major objections to the new constitution, but also vilified its writers and sponsors. "From the first shutting up the doors at the federal convention," to taking "so bold a step as the annihilation of the independence and sovereignty of the thirteen distinct states," to the "attempt to force it [the new constitution] upon them [the people] before it could be thoroughly understood," to "the trivial proposition of *recommending* a few amendments . . . into the convention in Massachusetts," she saw a concerted attempt to fool the people and foil republican government. Should this conspiracy succeed, the people would lose crucial political liberties they had gained by the Revolution: annual elections, rotation of elected officials, direct access to representatives, absence of aristocratic

Figure 40. Federalist engraver Amos Doolittle published this cartoon in the midst of Connecticut's ratification debate, calling it "The Looking Glass for 1787. A house divided against itself cannot stand." The wagon in the center, weighted down with debts and paper money, symbolizes Connecticut, which is pulled in opposite directions by Federalists on the left, saying "Comply with Congress" and "I abhor the antifederal Faction," and Antifederalists on the right, who cry out "Tax Luxury," "the People are oprest," and "Success to Shays." A complete key to the cartoon can be found on the Web at http://biblioteca.universia.net/html_bura/ficha/params/id/7807675.html.

rule, freedom of the press, prohibition of warrantless searches and seizures, civil trials by jury, freedom from military oppression, local control of taxation and indeed of all decision making. It was a formidable list. Antifederalists had a new standard-bearer for the final rounds, although they had no clue the author was a woman.[50]

Although Massachusetts was the sixth state to ratify the proposed constitution, and none had yet rejected it, the jury was still out, as the Columbian Patriot reminded her readers. True, Delaware, New Jersey, Georgia, and Connecticut had already approved, but these were smaller states of less consequence, and they had placed their various self-interests ahead of the national good. Virginia had not yet weighed in, for the people there "have wisely taken time to consider before they introduce innovations of a most dangerous nature." Rejection in Virginia seemed likely, Warren predicted—"her inhabitants are brave, her burgesses are free, and they have a Governor [Patrick Henry, an Antifederalist] who dares to think for himself"—while it was almost certain in Maryland and New York. Then there were South Carolina, North Carolina, New Hampshire, and Rhode Island, and the latter two at least would probably come out in opposition, Warren prophesized. Even in Pennsylvania, resistance remained so strong that the results of its hurried convention might be overturned.

With hindsight, Mercy Otis Warren seems to have been overly optimistic, but at the time she was not far off base. The outcome was truly in doubt. Even if Federalists managed to clear the low threshold that they themselves had created—nine states instead of thirteen—they would not have much of a nation if certain key states rejected the new plan, or if too many people remained reluctant, suspicious, and perhaps even defiant.

One week after the Massachusetts decision, New Hampshire delegates convened in Exeter. With all state leaders and newspapers on their side, Federalists assumed they would prevail—but they didn't. Antifederalist activists combed the rural regions, and many remote towns issued strict instructions opposing ratification in any form. Federalists countered with ten days of pontification at the convention, but they failed to muster a majority. They did manage to stave off a straightforward rejection, however, and with members split down the middle, the convention adjourned till June, allowing plenty of time for the folks back home to ponder and debate the matter more thoroughly.

In Rhode Island, even the Federalists had to admit they faced an uphill battle. The agrarian party that swept into office in 1786 had instituted sweeping reforms that favored debtors, including the creation of paper money, while Article 1, Section 10 of the proposed constitution, if adopted, would reverse all their gains by prohibiting states from issuing money or passing laws for debt relief. Federalists could only hope that their superior rhetoric might persuade delegates at the convention to go against the will of their constituents, but the Antifederalist legislature foiled this measure by voting 43–15 not to hold a convention at all. Instead, in March, by a similar margin, legislators decided to put the issue to the people themselves in a statewide referendum. Knowing they would lose, Federalist merchants in the large towns boycotted the elections, so on March 24, when citizens gathered in town meetings to express their wishes, they rejected the constitution by an overwhelming margin, 2,711–239. Although the numbers were exaggerated by the merchants' boycott, the Rhode Island election does give cause to wonder: how would the proposed constitution have fared in other states had the people themselves decided the matter, rather than delegates at conventions?

But the tide soon turned back. On April 26, the Maryland state convention supported the new constitution 63–11, and on May 23, South Carolina followed suit, 149–73 (with Henry Laurens voting in the affirmative). In Maryland, Federalists relied on two arguments with local appeal: a strong central government would promote westward expansion (conveniently, Maryland had bought into Washington's notion that the key to the West was the development of a Potomac waterway), and the new plan of government guaranteed that small states would dominate the Senate and have a large say in selecting the president. In South Carolina, Federalists pointed to the constitutional support for the institution of slavery: the three-fifths clause, protection of the slave trade for twenty years, and the fugitive-slave provision, which guaranteed that other states respect the slaveholding rights of white South Carolinians. Federalists faced significant opposition in the interior regions, just as they did in many other states, but representation at the convention was heavily weighted in favor of the low country. The final blow to resistance in South Carolina came midway in the convention, when news arrived that Maryland had voted for ratification, the seventh state to do so. After South Carolina's ratification, only one more state was needed for the proposed constitution to pass its own nine-state threshold.

In June, delegates convened in both New Hampshire and Virginia. From a Federalist perspective, New Hampshire would be nice to have onboard, but Virginia was absolutely essential. Should the nation's largest and most populous state bow out, the "United States" might become seriously disunited. North Carolina, still undeclared, would probably follow its neighbor's lead, and with those two gone, South Carolina and Georgia might reconsider, preferring instead to join a new confederacy of slave states. For convenience, Virginia's northern neighbor along the Potomac, Maryland, might shift allegiance as well, and because all these states were proximate to the western territories, a Southern confederacy could challenge the Eastern states (as the North was often called at the time) for title to the West. The South might even claim to be the "legitimate" United States of America, should it agree to abide by the original Articles of Confederation.

The Virginia convention met first, gathering at the State House in Richmond on June 2. Five of the state's seven delegates to the Federal Convention were there, including James Madison, one of the driving forces behind the new plan, and George Mason, one of the leading opponents. Noticeably absent was George Washington, who chose to stay home. It's not that he didn't care. Throughout the preceding winter, Washington had sent out numerous letters drumming up support for the new constitution, and now, as the Vir-

ginia convention was about to open, he wrote: "A few short weeks will determine the political fate of America for the present generation and probably
produce no small influence on the happiness of society through a long succession of ages to come." But the former commander in chief had already lent his
prestige to the Federal Convention, and his presence in Richmond, which
might be deemed inappropriate, could fuel the opposition. Washington and
everybody else knew he stood to become the first president under the new
constitution, and rather than appear power hungry, he preferred to stand back
and let others take the lead during debates that were likely to become quite
contentious. So on June 2, while other statesmen were convening in Richmond, George Washington was at the Falls of Shenandoah, meeting with the
board of directors of the Potomac Company to inspect work on a major canal,
part of the great waterway that would connect the Atlantic with the Ohio
River and the American interior.[51]

Also absent from Richmond was former governor Thomas Jefferson, who
had so aptly summed up the "American mind" in his draft of the Congressional Declaration of Independence twelve years earlier. Jefferson was serving
as ambassador to France at the time, and perhaps because of his distance, he
viewed the events back home with remarkable clarity. He approved "the general idea of framing a government which should go on of itself peaceably,
without needing continual recurrence to the state legislatures," and he com-
mended the Federal Convention for brokering the "compromise of the opposite claims of the great & little states" and for constructing a workable
edifice based on checks and balances among three distinct branches. That
said, many people remained hesitant to embrace the new form, and for good
reason: "A bill of rights is what the people are entitled to against every government on earth, general or particular, & what no just government should
refuse, or rest on inference." And there was one other matter that would have
been easy enough to adjust, but which would not have interfered with the
new powers of a central government: "rotation in office," or what we call
today term limits. If people knew that governmental officials could not
keep themselves in power indefinitely, they would be much less suspicious.
But Jefferson's voice of moderation, responsive to both sides of the great debate, was not heard, either during the Federal Convention, where his ideas, if
adopted, might have preempted much of the later criticism, or at the ratifying
convention in Richmond, where he would have been uniquely positioned to
conciliate the warring factions.[52]

Although such prominent Virginians as Washington and Jefferson were
absent, two well-known out-of-state Federalists made surprise appearances

as spectators: Robert Morris and Gouverneur Morris. This was no accident. Tobacco shipments to Europe had become the backbone of Robert Morris's financial empire, and his trade might be severely hampered should Virginia choose to go its own route. Personally as well as politically, the former Financier and assistant had much at stake in the outcome.

All eyes were on Richmond. The parameters of debate had changed since the time of the Pennsylvania convention half a year earlier, when pro and con factions would barely speak to each other. With results in from ten other states (news from South Carolina arrived on June 4, just as formalities concluded and debate began), three political truths had emerged: some sort of sweeping alternative to the Articles of Confederation would eventually be approved; that change was likely to be based in large measure on the plan developed at the Federal Convention; the fears of the plan's opponents would not be assuaged without the passage of amendments. With these realities in mind, delegates narrowed their focus to the only two available options: the constitution could either be approved first and amended later, or vice versa.

According to contemporary observers, Federalists and Antifederalists were almost evenly divided at the outset, although Federalists might have held a slight edge. A week later, on June 12, Robert Morris tried to ascertain who was in the lead: "Day by day the debates are supported with ability & pursued with ardour on both sides, and knowing ones pronounce that the event [result] is doubtful. Each side tend to count a majority in their own favor." Then Morris himself, an ardent Federalist, weighed in: "Following the example, I am inclined to think that the Constitution will be adopted by Virginia." Despite the oratory of some of America's greatest statesmen, no minds seemed to have been changed either way.[53]

On June 24, having completed their line-by-line analysis, leading proponents of each side offered their closing arguments. Patrick Henry opened the session, and he finally addressed a topic of particular interest to Virginia's leading gentry: under the sweeping "general welfare" clause of the proposed constitution, Congress could "pronounce all slaves free." Since the majority of congressional representatives would come from the eight northern states, they would have little knowledge of slavery and "at some future period" would try to abolish it. This was not merely idle speculation, Henry warned: "They have the power in clear unequivocal terms, and will clearly and certainly exercise it." Indeed, during "this last war," Congress had already meddled in the matter, recruiting blacks for the army with a promise to set them free. (Ironically, the chief architect of that scheme was actually a southern slave owner, John Laurens.)[54]

Virginia Federalists played the slave card as well, not just to counter Henry's assault, but also to invoke new fears. Should Virginia not join the new union, it would be left vulnerable to Indian attacks, slave insurrections, and foreign invasions. The state was unable to defend itself, as the last war evidenced. White masters had stayed home to keep their slaves in line, while small farmers resisted the call to arms issued by officials of the planter class. British ships had met with no naval resistance as they stormed up the navigable waterways, at least until the French showed up. That's the way it would always be, unless Virginians received help from the outside. A state that relied on slave labor could not rely on slaves for defense. However productive and prosperous, Virginia was in no position to make a go of it on its own.

But the fearmongering, which went both ways, had no more effect than the more lofty debates. On June 25, Antifederalists introduced a resolution "that previous to the ratification of the new constitution of government recommended by the late Federal Convention, a declaration of rights, ... together with amendments to the most exceptionable parts of the said constitution, ought to be referred by this convention to the other states in the American confederacy for their consideration." The measure failed, 80–88. Immediately thereafter, delegates voted to ratify the new constitution, 89–79.

Delegates did attach forty recommended amendments, however. Half of these, which the convention characterized as a "Declaration or Bill of Rights," guaranteed various rights to individuals; the other half altered the constitution itself by checking the powers granted to specific branches of government. Although these amendments were mere proposals, advocates of a declaration of rights managed to sneak into the formal ratification what we would today call a signing statement:

In the name and in behalf of the people of Virginia [we] declare and make known ... that every power not granted thereby remains with them and at their will: that therefore no right of any denomination can be cancelled abridged restrained or modified by the Congress by the Senate or House of Representatives acting in any capacity by the President of any department or officer of the United States except in those instances in which power is given by the Constitution for those purposes: & that among other essential rights the liberty of conscience and of the press cannot be cancelled abridged restrained or modified by any authority of the United States.[55]

With Virginia's ratification, the nine-state hurdle had been cleared. At this historic moment, "the new constitution of government recommended by the late Federal Convention" officially became *the* Constitution, with a capital C. The confederacy that called itself the United States of America had transformed itself into a single nation.

On June 25, the day the convention in Richmond ratified the Constitution, George Washington, at home in Mount Vernon, wrote in his diary:

> Thermometer at 56 in the morning—62 at noon and 60 at night. Morning clear & cool with the wind fresh from no. wt. at which point it continued all day.
>
> Rid to the Ferry, French's and Dogue run plantations.
>
> At the Ferry—the plows, hoes and harrows were preparing for, and putting in Irish potatoes. Began cutting the rye at this place not so much because it was ripe, as because it was of little worth, and because the grain would get nothing by remaining and the straw would grow worse. To what cause, unless to its being sown too early, or too thick, to ascribe the meanness of this rye, I know not; in the autumn it looked the most promising of any I had.
>
> At French's— Began to plant potatoes. . . .[56]

And he finished recounting his rounds, just as he had done daily since the first of the year, with no mention of the people who powered those plows and hoes.

Three days later, Washington learned that the second New Hampshire convention had voted for ratification on June 21, which meant that Virginia had actually been the tenth state to ratify, not the ninth. This gave extra cause to celebrate, and on that very day, Washington rode to Alexandria to join in the "public rejoicings." He stopped off at his plantations along the way, and once the last toast had been offered and all the huzzahs had ceased, he came straight home. That evening, he expressed his pleasure in a characteristically reserved tone: "I think we may rationally indulge the pleasing hope that the Union will now be established upon a durable basis."[57]

The day after that, the master of Mount Vernon noted in his diary: "Towards evening the appearances of rain encreased but none fell." And so he continued in his pastoral ways till the end of the year and into the next, knowing full well that his own life, like that of the nation, had dramatically changed.

July 4, 1788–December 15, 1791: United States of America

Finally, at least for Federalists, the celebrations could begin.

Francis Hopkinson, the judge, poet, and ardent Federalist who organized the "Grand Federal Procession" in Philadelphia, worked on short notice. News of the Virginia and New Hampshire ratifications arrived only a week before the Fourth of July, already something of a holiday in the youthful United States and the perfect date for a patriotic parade. To meet the deadline, Hopkinson and the "Committee of Arrangement" mobilized the city's numerous artisans, who had been politicized by a generation of revolutionary activity. Organized according to their separate trades, each of forty-four different groups—cordwainers, bricklayers, coopers, brewers, engravers, whip manufacturers, and so on—tried to outdo the others by constructing creative, gargantuan floats.

With active involvement by the populace, the great tradition of street theater that had flourished during the days of Revolutionary protest staged a sudden and dramatic comeback. Butchers marched two oxen side by side down the street, one labeled ANARCHY and the other CONFUSION. The banner strung between their horns read, "The Death of ANARCHY and CONFUSION Shall Feed the Poor and Hungry," and at the conclusion of the parade, the men who led the oxen made good on their word by practicing their trade. On another float, blacksmiths heated swords in a working forge and then pounded them into plowshares. It was truly a people's event, with some five thousand participants strung out for a mile and a half along the three-mile route. In the words of Philadelphia physician Benjamin Rush, "Every tradesman's boy in the procession seemed to consider himself as a principal in the business. Rank for a while forgot all its claims."

Even floats marshaled by dignitaries paid homage to the rank and file. Pennsylvania Chief Justice Thomas McKean rode atop a carriage with a giant, framed copy of the Constitution, below which was inscribed in gold letters, "The PEOPLE."

The featured display in this rambling parade was the "GRAND FEDERAL EDIFICE," a large dome supported by thirteen Corinthian columns (one per state, of course) and adorned with a frieze showing thirteen stars. Carried on a carriage and drawn by ten horses, the edifice rose to a height of thirty-six feet above street level. The previous evening, workers had climbed and limbed trees along the course to accommodate the magnificent structure.

At the conclusion of the parade, James Wilson delivered the featured oration. Or at least he tried to, for as he started to speak, ships in the harbor let loose with a string of gun salutes that stole the show and wouldn't let up. This was a celebration, after all. The time for talking had passed.

But the Grand Federal Procession was more than a party, unless by "party" we mean a political party. Organized and executed by Philadelphia Federalists who wished to bury the opposition, the event contained several not-so-hidden messages. Of the thirteen columns supporting the Grand Federal Edifice, only ten were finished. The other three represented New York, North Carolina, and Rhode Island, yet to ratify the Constitution. Similarly, a flag on the float created by "Gold-smiths, Silver-smiths, and Jewellers" showed ten bright stars, three with considerably less shine, and a hint of a fourteenth. In Hopkinson's own words, this last star was "of equal luster with the first ten (which had already ratified), just emerging from the horizon, near one half seen, for the rising state of Kentucky."[58]

The parade played well in Philadelphia, but it would not have done so everywhere. In Providence, Rhode Island, where the mood was very different, a group of Federalists (outnumbered in the state, but still numerous in the city) tried to rejoice on July 4, only to be confronted that morning by a thousand Antifederalists. The dissidents insisted in the most forceful manner that the revelers only celebrate independence, not the still-controversial Constitution. After forcing this concession, Antifederalists staged their own party, and in their toasts, with each new round of drinking, they demonstrated their unwillingness to concede defeat:

1. Confusion to all usurpers and tyrants throughout the thirteen states.
2. The old Confederation, with proper amendments.
3. May the sons of freedom in America never submit to a despotic government.
4. May each state retain their sovereignty in the full extent of republican covenants. . . .[59]

In New York, meanwhile, delegates to the state ratifying convention were still locked in a heated battle, and the debate continued to rage among the populace, as well. In Albany, on the day of the Grand Federal Procession, Federalists and Antifederalists engaged in street battle. Without New York, the new nation would be considerably weakened, and the outcome there remained very much in doubt.

Resistance to the plan of the Federal Convention had always been strong in New York, and as in Virginia, local interests lay at the heart of the matter. To finance its war debts, New York had relied on two measures that would be threatened by a strong central government: an impost (much to the chagrin of the state's neighbors, who imported goods through New York City) and land sales (western tracts and the confiscated property of loyalists). At the start of the ratification debate, opponents in the state legislature outnumbered proponents by more than two to one.

To counter the prevailing public opinion in New York, two of the state's prominent Federalists, Alexander Hamilton and John Jay, wrote feverishly in defense of the proposed constitution. Looking for out-of-state support, they tried to enlist Gouverneur Morris, and when he declined, they turned to James Madison, who accepted. These three writers quickly penned a significant body of work, which in March of 1788 they collected into the first volume of essays they called *The Federalist*. The tenth essay, written by James Madison, presented to the public an intriguing argument he had expounded at the convention in Philadelphia: a large republic, which most people had assumed would be unstable, would in fact prove more stable than a small one, because no local faction could muster enough support nationwide to challenge the existing order. "A rage for paper money, for an abolition of debts, for an equal division of property, or for any other improper or wicked project, will be less apt to pervade the whole body of the Union, than a particular member of it," Madison wrote.[60]

The 500 printed copies of *The Federalist* no doubt had some impact on the debate in New York, although not so much as to warrant the book's reputation in subsequent times as "third only to the Declaration of Independence and the Constitution itself among the sacred writings of American political history." (Compare the numbers: 500 for *The Federalist*; 100,000 for *Common Sense*.) To counteract the influence of such prominent Federalist writers, Antifederalists distributed 1,700 copies of Mercy Otis Warren's *Columbian Patriot*, not knowing, of course, that it had been written by a woman. Warren's work, however, played only to mixed reviews even among those on her own side. Antifederalists in New York came largely from the middle ranks of society, not the educated elite, and at least one group, the Albany Antifederal Committee, thought the writing was "in a stile too sublime and florid for us common people in this part of the country."[61]

The New York convention met in Poughkeepsie starting June 17, concurrent with both the New Hampshire and the Virginia conventions. Although the elections had returned forty-six Antifederalists and only nineteen Federalists, the fact that eight states had already voted to ratify earned the Federalists a place at the table. When delegates learned at the end of a week that New Hampshire had voted for ratification and the new covenant would go into effect with or without New York, Federalists acquired a strategic advantage to offset their small numbers. Some of the Antifederalists weakened, fearing that if the convention voted against ratification, pro-Federalist districts might try to join the union of other states; civil strife, already fused and ready to ignite, might ensue. Antifederalists offered to ratify with conditional amendments, but Federalists would have none of it. Finally, on July 26, the convention voted 30–27 for ratification. Yet Antifederalists managed to attach a preamble that amounted to a full-scale Bill of Rights, far more detailed than that of Virginia, and they also won approval for a circular letter, addressed to the other state legislatures, recommending a second federal convention to consider amendments.[62]

One week later, on August 2, North Carolina became the first state to take a firmer stance: ratification would be contingent on calling a second constitutional convention to consider amendments. Unless and until that happened, delegates refused to give their assent. In November, Virginia added its voice to that of New York and North Carolina and called for a second constitutional convention.

Consider, then, the state of the nation: eleven states were in, one was out, and one had placed itself in waiting. That might seem good enough, but it wasn't. Margins of victory in the key states of Massachusetts, Virginia, and New York had been embarrassingly small, and three states had formally issued a call for a new national convention to consider changes. Dissidents in Pennsylvania, although their state had been among the first to approve, continued to growl. Worse yet, throughout the nation, farmers who had hoped for reform remained hesitant, defiant, and potentially even rebellious. Even if statesmen within chambers managed some sort of solution, great numbers of people on the grassroots level remained too fearful of a powerful central government to grant it moral authority. Not a good start for a nation that styled itself a republic.

Many months earlier, Thomas Jefferson, writing from abroad, had offered his optimal scenario for a resolution to the grand debate:

> I wish with all my soul that the nine first conventions may accept the new Constitution, because this will secure to us the good it contains, which I think is great & important. But I equally wish that the four lat-

est conventions, whichever they may be, may refuse to accede to it till a declaration of rights be annexed. This would probably command the offer of such a declaration, & thus give to the whole fabric, perhaps as much perfection as any one of that kind ever had.[63]

The first part had come to pass, and the second step was not far off the mark. True, only one state had absolutely insisted on changes, but the "American mind" (to use the term Jefferson had applied to the debate over independence) seemed to think that the process should remain open. Substance aside, it was a matter of form. "Take this or nothing," having accomplished its mission, had now run its course. The people, or at least a very significant chunk of them, were making it clear they still wanted their say.

Meanwhile, with a blueprint in place, the existing federal Congress sitting in New York, acting solely as an interim agent, established procedures to create the new government. On September 13, 1788, Congress set a schedule for the selection and meeting of presidential electors, as well as a precise date for the new Congress to convene: "the first Wednesday in March next." From there on out, the new rules would apply.[64]

On January 7, 1789, a "raw & chilly" day in northern Virginia, George Washington rode to the Fairfax County Courthouse to cast his vote for his district's presidential elector.

One month later, when Virginia's electors gathered to vote for president, they agreed unanimously on George Washington. So too, on that same day, did the electors of the ten other states that had ratified the Constitution. The outcome was never in doubt; indeed, no other person was seriously considered, unless prefaced by "if Washington should decline . . ."

Washington's decision to accept the office was also predetermined, although he exerted his greatest mental powers to convince himself it was not. His first line of defense was to hope that he would not be offered the job. This had its problems, however, for the only realistic scenario that would lead to that outcome would be an Antifederalist majority in the Electoral College, resulting in an Antifederalist president intent on subverting the Constitution from within. He dared not hope for that. His next line of defense was simply to wait and see if he were chosen, but this was a weak fortification at best, for by nature it could not last. He *would* be chosen, and sooner or later he would have to decide.

Personally, Washington had two strong incentives to say no: first, his "invincible attachment to domestic life," and second, his previous pronouncement of the same. Having already retired and, more to the point, having done so with such force of conviction, he was vulnerable to accusations of hypocrisy, and, worse yet, of craving the great powers of the presidency he had helped create at the Federal Convention.

These reasons could be overcome, Washington admitted to friends, if "the good of my country" demanded he accept. The only valid excuses would be public and political, not private. If he believed that "some other person . . . could execute all the duties full as satisfactorily as myself," that would suffice, or if he thought "some very disagreeable consequences" might result from his refusal. However much he wished to remain at Mount Vernon, he had become so committed to the public sphere that if he shirked his duty now, he risked losing not only the respect of others, but his self-respect as well.[65]

When Charles Thomson, secretary of Congress, arrived at Mount Vernon with the formal job offer on April 14, Washington handed him a preprepared acceptance letter. Two days later, he headed for New York, and there, on April 30, 1789, the former commander in chief of the Continental Army took the oath that made him president. Ironically, with that oath, he resumed his military command, but this time as a civilian.

Ten men before George Washington had served as "President of the United States in Congress Assembled" under the Articles of Confederation, and three men before that (including Henry Laurens) had held the title of "President of the Continental Congress of the United States of America," but Washington was the first to take office under the greatly expanded presidential powers of the new Constitution. His title would be simply "President of the United States." A majority in the Senate wanted to add "His Highness," exactly the sort of high-handedness that Antifederalists had feared from that body, but with an early application of the Constitution's checks and balances, the House wisely refused to play along, and the new government was spared a momentous political blunder.

In his acceptance speech, the new president acknowledged that Congress, to address "the objections that have been urged against the system" and relieve the "inquietude which has given birth to them," might want to initiate the amendment process. This would be fine, he said, so long as "a reverence for the characteristic rights of freedom and a regard for the public harmony" did not lead members to make any alteration that "might endanger the benefits of an united and effective government." (In private correspondence, he spelled out his bottom line, the one item that must be preserved at all costs: Congress's power of direct taxation.) Already, in his very first moments in office, Washington assumed the role of a mediator. Federalists should be willing to bend, he implied—but not too far. He left unstated the strategic reasoning: by starting the amendment process, Congress might control its extent; if it failed to act, states would push for a new constitutional convention, far more difficult to keep in check.[66]

Less than six weeks later, on June 8, James Madison presented a set of amendments to the Congress. Many Federalist representatives and senators still opposed all amendments on principle, and Robert Morris, elected to the Senate from Pennsylvania, attacked Madison personally for bowing to Anti-federalist pressure. Madison had "got frightened in Virginia," Morris mocked, referring to Madison's difficult campaign for a Senate seat (he lost) and then for a place in the House (he won, but only narrowly). Congress debated the desirability of initiating amendments, sent the matter to committee, and on September 25, after considerable refinement but little change in substance, passed Madison's proposals along to the state legislatures in the form of twelve amendments. According to the Constitution, these would become the law of the land if three-quarters of the states approved.[67]

Far from being "frightened," Madison was responding positively to the mood of the nation. The final resolutions of seven states (Massachusetts, Maryland, South Carolina, New Hampshire, Virginia, New York, and North Carolina), as well as the minority report in Pennsylvania, had proposed scores of distinct amendments. Many proposals appeared on several lists, a few on virtually all. One amendment proposed in all these states would have altered the fundamental premise of the new Constitution: Congress would not have the power to tax unless the separate states had already turned down federal requisitions for funds. Virginia broke its list into two categories, some pre-serving individual rights, others affecting the working of the new govern-ment; New York alone offered thirty-one in this latter category, including such prodemocracy measures as a larger House of Representatives, prohibi-tion of government-sanctioned monopolies, term limits for senators and the president, restrictions on a standing army, a method for recalling senators, more specific procedures for impeachment, open meetings of Congress, the frequent publication of congressional proceedings, and returning authority over debtor relief to the states. Of this vast array of procedural changes, only two made Madison's final cut: the increased size of the House, and a stipula-tion that any raise in congressional salaries, which according to the Constitu-tion were to be set by Congress itself, would not take effect until after the subsequent election. The message was clear: Federalists, in control of both the House and the Senate, would finally tolerate a Bill of Rights, which would have no real impact on the functioning of government, but they refused to allow much tinkering with the document developed by the Federal Convention.[68]

Back in the states, in the face of Antifederalist agitation, enough Federalists relented to permit passage of ten amendments, first in New Jersey, then in Maryland, and so on, until on December 15, 1791, Virginia's endorsement fulfilled the three-quarters requirement for ratification. But the two structural amendments failed. Neither of these presented any serious threat to the overall plan, but too many Federalists opposed the measures nonetheless, simply to keep the original system pure.

The ten that passed, on the other hand, have been heralded ever since as America's Bill of Rights: freedom of speech, press, and religion; the right to bear arms; protection against unwarranted searches and seizures; rights of the accused to confront the accuser and to a speedy trial by an impartial jury; prohibitions against forced confessions, double jeopardy, confinement without due process of law, excessive bail, and cruel and unusual punishment. (Only one of the amendments, barring the forced quartering of soldiers, has not played a significant role in the nation's subsequent history.) The final two items answered once and for all the Federalist argument against a listing of rights, which they contended would imply that others, not listed, were not granted: "The enumeration in the Constitution, of certain rights, shall not be construed to deny or disparage others retained by the people," and "The powers not delegated to the United States by the Constitution, nor prohibited by it to the States, are reserved to the States respectively, or to the people."

Previously, Federalists had built their case against a bill of rights on this basic premise: any enumeration of rights was unnecessary, because all powers not specifically granted to the central government, by implication, remained with the states or the people. With historical hindsight, we can safely pronounce this defense naive. Rights that were merely implied rather than specified would not have enjoyed the same force of law, nor could they have presented such a clear-cut claim to the high moral ground. Without precise stipulations, subsequent generations would have had a more difficult time defending the freedoms they had earned, particularly in times of stress, when personal liberties are most seriously threatened.

With the ratification of the Bill of Rights, the Constitution was complete, although certainly not impervious to orderly change. Both Federalists and Antifederalists had finally had their say. In time, in the public consciousness of the nation, the original draft and the first ten amendments would merge into one; today, if you ask ordinary citizens to state specific provisions in the

Constitution that seem special or relevant to their lives, you will receive a list heavily represented by provisions that were not drafted at the Federal Convention of 1787.

Ironically, the second most divisive moment in our nation's history, the great ratification debate, culminated in a document that has served ever since to unite rather than divide. (Top honors in the divisive moment department belong of course to the Civil War.) Legally, the Constitution serves as a stable reference, susceptible to evolving interpretations, but always there in its original form to ensure that changes are approached gradually and peaceably. Politically, it provides a common language with which opposing viewpoints can present their case. Symbolically, it unites a diverse people, who come in many cases from foreign and distinct traditions, with a firm and common definition of the American polity. It is "our" Constitution, the supreme law of the land.

1761–1791: British American Colonies and the United States of America

Perhaps the greatest irony is this: one of the features of the Constitution that was most divisive at the time, the seclusion and secrecy of the Federal Convention, has evolved into a symbol of national unity. Back in 1787 and 1788, many Americans resented the great presumptions of a small group of men— "oligarchs" they were called—who took it upon themselves to scrap the existing government and create a new one, without any input from the people outside. Today, on the other hand, Americans of all political persuasions point proudly to their wise "Founding Fathers," those dedicated and patriotic geniuses who sweated together through the hot summer days in Philadelphia, sheltered from the world outside, to create such a marvelous document. The work of these men has withstood the test of time and made America great, people say.

If this view of our nation's founding has brought us together, it has done so at a price. In our reverence, we sacrifice both historical accuracy and a meaningful national treasure, the collective work of the Revolutionary Generation.

Our nation was not "founded" in Philadelphia in 1787, and its "founders" included a cast much broader than the gentlemen present at the Federal Convention. The nation's founding was an extended process, marked by several key events but including as well the times in between. Back in the 1760s, two decades earlier, activists like Thomas Young joined with large numbers of common people, many of whom were acting on the political stage for the first time, to force changes in British imperial policies. Adding their voices to the popular protests, idealists like Mercy Otis Warren, with visions of a creating a virtuous republic, denounced all measures that interfered with the people's basic right to govern themselves. Land developers like George Washington resented British restrictions on westward expansion. Merchants, who thrived through transatlantic commerce, pushed for unrestricted trade to further their own self-interest, but when the anti-imperial movement shifted to the streets, and when trade boycotts threatened their own livelihoods, many had second thoughts. Caught in the middle, men of means like Robert Morris and Henry Laurens tried to walk a fine line that permitted effective resistance but stopped short of social upheaval. Despite the factional differences between moderates and radicals, these constituencies perceived American interests in ways that could not be easily reconciled to the British imperial system. Although they still viewed themselves as British citizens, they were thinking and acting independently—as Americans.

In 1774, all this came to a head when British repressive policies led the people of one colony, Massachusetts, into outright rebellion. Inspired by both a long tradition of self-rule and the political activism that had swept through the cities during the previous decade, a new breed of country and small-town activists, farmers and tradesmen like Worcester's Timothy Bigelow, staged not merely a protest but a revolution, effectively terminating British rule. That led to a British counterinsurgency the following year, and once the political struggles had regressed into military conflict, most Americans arrived at a political stance that was almost unthinkable a few years past: they should shape their futures apart from Great Britain. Although moderates hesitated, they were pushed from below to take the risky next step. On July 2, 1776, following six months of public debate in meetinghouses and taverns across the land, and pursuant to instructions from their constituents, delegates to the Continental Congress declared independence.

Britain would not give up her colonies without a fight, and fight she did. The protracted war to preserve independence created a new set of patriotic heroes: officers like Commander in Chief George Washington, who forsook a much easier life back on his plantation in Virginia, and privates like young Joseph Plumb Martin, who placed himself in harm's way before he could fully appreciate either the political intricacies that put him there or the full extent of the dangers. Of those who had initiated the resistance, some, like Timothy

Bigelow, transformed themselves into full-time soldiers, but most retreated back to private life, except for occasional stints in the militia.

This is where the notion of "founding heroes" gets murky. Wartime scarcities called for sacrifices most Americans were not eager to make. People turned on each other, with civilians resenting soldiers and vice versa. The economy crumbled, and one rich man, his fortunes augmented by the same conditions that deprived so many others, came to the rescue by placing his own personal credit in the service of the nation. But the nation paid a political price, granting powers to the Financier that idealists thought unbecoming to a republic.

The quest for founding heroes gets murkier yet when we shift our attention to African Americans. Some fought for the Americans, many more sided with the British in their quest for freedom, and most tried to navigate the troubled waters in such as way as to gain more control over their own lives. Native Americans, as well, acted first and foremost in ways that would favor their own right to self-determination, not only as individuals but also as nations in their own right. When we look at the fundamental principle that drove the American Revolution, the right of people to govern themselves, these groups, in their various ways, acted as patriotically and heroically as any others, but from our limited, nationalistic perspective, we find this difficult to acknowledge or define.

In the decade following independence, despite all the troubles, Americans fashioned new governmental structures both on the state and confederate levels. To some extent these worked as well as might be expected, yet the confederate government contained one fatal flaw: it lacked the power to raise money on its own. To rectify this would require the approval of all thirteen states, and when this proved unfeasible, people who had been advocating a stronger central government since the outset organized a convention to amend the existing rules. Instead of making amendments, however, this gathering decided to abandon the old rules entirely and start fresh, imposing a new structure on the eleven-year-old nation. Although they chose to do so without interference from the people out of doors, who would undoubtedly have made their task more difficult, they needed in the end to submit their ideas to the people for validation. To do less than that, to decide matters on their own and then impose them on all other Americans, would have been a direct violation of the right of self-government, the very principle responsible for the founding of the nation—and, most likely, the body of the people would not have tolerated such a usurpation of authority.

In the debate that followed, Americans weighed the pluses and minuses of the new plan, and also the propriety of its formation. Should people "take this"—the total plan—or should they take "nothing" and start the process over? Was it even appropriate for them to be presented with these limited options?

Because one side prevailed and the Constitution has endured, Americans ever since have looked back at those times from a distinctly Federalist perspective: our "Founding Fathers" laid down an excellent set of rules for us to live by, and we are grateful. The most popular narrative goes one step further: the Constitution, their creation, has worked not only well, but better than any alternative. This special group of very wise men made all the perfect choices.

It is true, the framers did many things right. First and foremost, the Constitution achieved its major objective: giving the central government of the United States sufficient power to stand on its own feet. Immediately, this meant the ability to tax, thereby enabling the United States to discharge war debts, restore its credit, provide stability for its currency, and gain a place among nations. Furthermore, simultaneous with the granting of new powers, the Constitution created an elaborate array of checks and balances to guard against the concentration and abuse of governmental authority by any individual or factional group. Last but not least, it allowed for change. New states could join the union in an orderly fashion, and new rules or limitations on government could be instituted through a viable amendment process.

But if the framers of the Constitution had taken the "genius of the people" more seriously, they might have done better yet. During the ratification debates, citizens who were not at the Federal Convention suggested dozens of intriguing ways the Constitution might be amended and improved, yet these ideas were dismissed out of hand by Federalists who refused to entertain any alterations.

One cluster of failed and forgotten amendments focused on limiting the military presence within the new nation: capping the time of military service, requiring a two-thirds vote (one state wanted three-fourths) to create a standing army, circumscribing the power of the central government to draft militias for national service, and, most significantly, demanding a two-thirds vote of both houses of Congress for any declaration of war. The last measure would have corrected a serious flaw in our Constitution, which permits a simple majority to send the nation to war, while requiring a two-thirds vote to end it.

Another cluster addressed the terms of officeholders. At the Federal Convention, ideas for how long the president should serve ranged from three years to twenty, and in the end, delegates allowed him to exercise his powers for life, pending reelections. These parameters would have differed dramatically if the population at large had been consulted, and through various amendments, Antifederalists proposed to set limits on the number of times an individual could be elected to the same office. Mercy Otis Warren, for one, predicted that without legal restrictions, the powers of incumbency would often result in "the perpetuity of office in the same hands for life." But this warning remained unheeded, the Constitution remained as it was, and the enduring effect of incumbency has contributed to the lasting and destructive American assumption: the government is "them," not "us."[69]

Although the structural amendments proposed by Antifederalists were shunned, the amendment process proved viable, first with the Bill of Rights, and then, through the years, with a successive whittling away at the framers' restrictive handiwork: emancipation of slaves, direct election of senators, term limits for the president, and extension of the franchise to women, nonwhites, and people old enough to die for their country. We have both Federalists and Antifederalists to thank for this, the former for providing within the Constitution the mechanisms for its alteration, and the latter for pushing the issue. Although most of their amendment proposals failed, Antifederalists could and did claim credit for ten successful ones, which demonstrated that change was indeed possible. The system was not immutable. The nation would grow and evolve, despite and because of all the contentious debates.

20

Lives and Legacies

Back in the mid-1770s, during the peak of Revolutionary fervor, Mercy Otis Warren started chronicling the history of those momentous times. She kept copies of letters she sent to others, which she could use for notes and mine for her history. She consulted the British *Annual Register*, fortuitously written by pro-American Whigs, which presented a detailed account of the ongoing struggle for independence in America. Intermittently over the next decade and a half, Mrs. Warren set quill to paper, and once the new government was set in place, she decided it was time to compile her writings into a comprehensive book. She would be America's Catharine Macaulay, taming the past to further republican ideals.

Mrs. Warren suffered one disadvantage: being a woman, she didn't have the opportunity to rub shoulders with many of the people she would be writing about. Even her husband, James, had limited expertise in this matter, having declined several opportunities to play politics on a wider stage. So she wrote to her friend in Congress Elbridge Gerry:

> I should like to know a little more of the real character of some who have arisen and figured in our times than I have yet had an oppertunity that will justify a sketch from my pen, perticulary the *great* Financier Mr. R. Morris, James Wilson, &c. Is Patrick Henry a good or a bad man? What is become of Mr. Laurens, Gadsden, and many others of the best patriots of '75?[1]

Some of her questions could be answered easily. Laurens had removed himself from the political scene. After Gadsden was taken prisoner at the fall of

Charleston, he defied British authorities and was thrown into solitary confinement in an old Spanish prison. Upon his release ten months later, he resumed his political activities and personal vendettas in South Carolina, but he never again figured in national politics. James Wilson was rewarded for his talents and his efforts on behalf of the new Constitution with a judgeship on the first United States Supreme Court.

Questions of character admitted no simple answers. Was her fellow Antifederalist Patrick Henry a true champion of liberty or a rabble-rousing, slave-owning demagogue? Was the "*great* Financier" (Warren's pen dripped with sarcasm) really the archvillain the Warrens had made him out to be? If he were the devil incarnate, how could George Washington, whom Mrs. Warren esteemed, cavort with him and treat him with such respect?

This touched on a larger, more sweeping issue. In her book, Warren hoped "to make a few strictures on the origin, the nature, and the probable consequences of the new government," but what stance should she take? She had recently opposed the new Constitution with great fervor, yet that document was now the law of the land, and if she continued to rail against it, she might be considered unpatriotic. This was the dilemma faced by all Antifederalists during the early days of Washington's avowedly Federalist administration, which now governed the United States according to rules that the Federalists had fashioned for the nation.[2]

Mrs. Warren encountered this conundrum not only intellectually but practically. However tightly she clung to her idealism, this devoted mother had her sons' careers to consider. Henry had set his mind on a government post, and the closest to home was collector of the Port of Plymouth. (Unable to afford their mansion on Milton Hill, the Warrens had moved back to Plymouth early in 1787.) To procure Henry's appointment, she solicited the aid of old friends who had come into power, men like John Adams, now vice president, and Henry Knox, the secretary of war. She even sent a copy of her new book of poems and plays to Alexander Hamilton, secretary of the treasury, the longtime arch-nationalist closely allied with Robert Morris. She informed Adams boldly that it was his duty to support "the interest of the children of your friend." She seemed to assume that the new government, like European courts, would be fueled by patronage, but Knox and Adams informed her otherwise: "The president is decided to make his nominations on the highest principles of impartiality," Knox instructed. Adams's reply was beyond brusque: "In the first place, I have no patronage; in the next, neither your children nor my own would be sure of it if I had it." Henry did not get the job, and the Federalist fellow who did,

Figure 41. Winslow Warren, Mercy's and James's prodigal son, as painted by John Singleton Copley in 1785. *(Photograph © 2009 Museum of Fine Arts, Boston)*

according to Henry's mother, was "the most contemptible character in the district."[3]

Mercy's favorite son also needed her help. Unable to secure an appointment abroad, Winslow had returned home deeply in debt, and once here he fell deeper yet. Early in 1786, while traveling through Connecticut, he received a court order to answer the claims of his creditors, and six days later, on the floor of the Boston Exchange, on the ground floor of the State House, he assaulted the man he thought responsible. According to Henry Knox, who witnessed the "caning match," Warren attacked his unarmed antagonist "without giving him the least precious notice." Any resemblance to the famous caning match involving Winslow's uncle James seventeen years earlier (see chapter 4) was purely coincidental.[4]

At his day in court, Winslow lost. He went to jail, broke loose, and fled the state. That's when he vowed to join the army, as so many young men in trouble have done through the years, and his mother consented to help him out. The war was over, she reasoned, there was little danger, and a stint in the military would do Winslow some good. So she solicited her friend Henry Knox, and surprisingly, despite his firsthand knowledge of Winslow's hot temper, Knox secured for Winslow an appointment as lieutenant in the Second Infantry.

Just then the law caught up with the escaped convict. Because his case involved two states (Connecticut and Massachusetts), Winslow was tried by the newly organized United States Circuit Court. This time, upon his conviction for nonpayment of debts, Warren was placed with common felons, without the privilege of exercise or access to the yard. (State courts commonly distinguished between debtors and felons, but the federal court did not.) Winslow Warren's imprisonment caused a minor sensation among devout Antifederalists: was this the way of "justice" under the new national government, debtors cast into prison under inhumane conditions?

Winslow's release in the spring of 1791 caused his mother even greater consternation, for without so much as a farewell visit home, he set off for war, not to oppose an oppressive imperial power, but to fight against Indians who were offering stiff resistance to white incursions on land they considered their own. That's why the federal army suddenly doubled in size; that's why Winslow Warren gained an appointment, despite his lack of a military background; and that's why Mrs. Warren fretted. Suddenly, fear for her son's safety merged with her long-standing opposition to "the high handed designs of Federalism." Although she herself had lobbied for Winslow's appointment, she now resumed her own habitual war chant: the very existence of a standing army violates republican principles. The war of expansion her son was expected to fight was simply not necessary. "There is territory sufficient within the thirteen United States, for the conveniency of many generations to come," she wrote.[5]

On November 4, 1791, along the Wabash River in the Ohio country, the United States Army suffered its worst-ever defeat at the hands of Native Americans. Of 920 soldiers who reported for duty the day before, 632 were killed and 264 wounded. Winslow Warren was among those slain.

"Good God, what a stroke for Aunt Warren," exclaimed her Federalist nephew Harrison Gray Otis, the first in the family to hear. "It will kill her I fear."[6]

Almost. Winslow's aggrieved mother turned first to God, vowing "to be silent and not open my mouth because the Lord has done this." As with so many women of the times, she acceded to "the Providence of an infinitely wise, just, and beneficent being, who has the right to resume the choicest of his gifts on his own time and manner." But trusting to Providence did not suffice and, characteristically, Mercy Otis Warren soon picked up her pen in anger. In a scathing essay, she denounced the "expansive war" and "the impolicy that has plunged a young country into bloodshed disgrace and misery to procure a wild and distant country while the Atlantic states are not half inhabited." She even insinuated that the ill-fated expedition had been staged to "urge a pretense for the necessity of an augmented standing army." But she never published that essay.[7]

For the next several years, Mercy Otis Warren withdrew from the political life of the young nation, which continued on a trajectory not to her liking. By the time her former friend John Adams succeeded George Washington as president in 1797, his political views had strayed so far from her own that the two could find little common ground. In 1798, the Adams administration sponsored four Alien and Sedition Acts, granting unprecedented authorities to governmental officials and outlawing the publication of opposing viewpoints. To Mrs. Warren, President Adams had betrayed the Warren-Adams family friendship, the years of common cause and common struggle, and the most deep-seated ideals of the Revolution.

Then things changed. The election of 1800 resulted in a resounding repudiation for the Federalists and the ascendancy, at last, of her own Antifederalists, who had renamed themselves Republicans and found the perfect presidential candidate in Thomas Jefferson. In a strange and unholy alliance, Jefferson had brought together small farmers, who constituted the majority of the population and whom he viewed as the future of the nation, and slave-owning patriarchs of the South, of whom he was one. Together, these constituencies outpolled the once-powerful Federalists, who represented to both Warren and Jefferson the unwholesome values of crass commercialism. Years earlier, Mercy Otis Warren had warned that in Federalism lay the seeds of tyranny, and although the Adams administration appeared in her mind to have proven her correct, it had also alienated enough voters to ensure its defeat.

What Warren had failed to predict was the orderly (albeit not overly friendly) change of administration. With Jefferson's election and assumption of the presidency, the nation had proved itself capable of peaceful change and transition. This loomed large in her mind. So, too, did the fact that her side was now on top, and, last but not least, that her son Henry finally got the governmental post denied him more than a dozen years past.

It was the perfect time for Mercy Otis Warren to present *History of the Rise, Progress and Termination of the American Revolution*, in the making for three decades and finally published in 1805. Now, when she told how the Revolution had been a great and heroic struggle for republican values—"the natural equality of man, their right of adopting their own modes of government, the dignity of the people"—she could do so unabashedly and unapologetically, for the majority of the nation was beginning to see things her way.

Warren's three-volume *History* was weak on facts but strong on "Biograph-

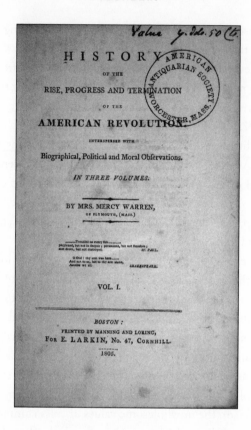

HISTORY
OF THE
RISE, PROGRESS AND TERMINATION
OF THE
AMERICAN REVOLUTION.
INTERSPERSED WITH
Biographical, Political and Moral Obfervations.

IN THREE VOLUMES.

BY MRS. MERCY WARREN,
OF PLYMOUTH, (MASS.)

VOL. I.

BOSTON:
PRINTED BY MANNING AND LORING,
FOR E. LARKIN, No. 47, CORNHILL.
1805.

Figure 42. Title page of Mercy Otis Warren's magnum opus. Once an ardent Antifederalist, Warren could finally heap praise on the United States Constitution—after the addition of the Bill of Rights, and after Thomas Jefferson, who shared her republican principles, had ascended to power.

ical, Political and Moral Observations"—her appendage to the title. As with all revolutions, she contended, the American version had started strong but then slowly regressed, culminating in John Adams's betrayal once he assumed the presidency. (Adams understandably objected to this negative press, and in a series of heated interchanges, the two aging patriots resumed their tussle for the soul of the nation.) Still, the American Revolution fared better than most. Although threatened repeatedly by factionalism, intrigue, personal ambition, acquisitiveness, monarchical impulses, and a seemingly endless war, the core principles managed to survive.

Although the bulk of her *History* focused on resistance, revolution, and war, Warren needed in the end to deal with the Constitution, now firmly ensconced at the heart of the nation's body politic. This was difficult, but with something of a sleight of hand she pulled it off. First, she rushed through the Federal Convention in a single sentence, plus a footnote and a paragraph complaining about its secrecy. She then gave full voice to the Antifederalist response and the resultant Bill of Rights, which she viewed as the salvation of Revolutionary ideals.

This somehow allowed her to tout the Constitution, which she had once contested, as the final embodiment of the Revolution's ideals. It was a bit of a stretch, but in her exuberance for Jeffersonian republicanism, she allowed herself to make the switch:

> Perhaps genius has never devised a system more congenial to their wishes, or better adapted to the condition of man, than the American constitution. . . . On the principles of republicanism was this constitution founded; on these it must stand. . . . The present representative government may stand for ages a luminous monument of republican wisdom, virtue, and integrity.[8]

The new order was so grand, in fact, that it permitted (and even demanded) westward expansion, which Warren once had accused of killing her son. Although military conquest was not republican, moral conquest was:

> The wisdom and justice of the American governments, and the virtue of the inhabitants, may . . . render the United States an enviable example to all the world, of peace, liberty, righteousness, and truth. The western wilds, which for ages have been little known, may arrive to that stage of improvement and perfection, beyond which the limits of human genius cannot reach, and this last civilized quarter of the globe may exhibit those striking traits of grandeur and magnificence, which the Divine Economist may have reserved to crown the closing scene, when the angel of his presence will stand upon the sea and upon the earth, lift up his hand to heaven, and swear by Him that liveth for ever and ever, that there shall be time no longer.[9]

With those jubilant words Mercy Otis Warren ended her account. Having spent most of her adult life ridiculing, resisting, and scolding, the sharp-penned muse of the Revolution concluded her magnum opus with a grandiose millennial vision, reasonably satisfied with both her life and her nation, and perhaps a bit surprised.

•   •   •

Robert Morris, on the other end of the political spectrum, had every reason to feel contented in 1789, when the new Constitution took effect. Since
he first entered Congress in 1775, and through his "reign" as Financier in
the early 1780s, he had been pushing for a stronger central government that
could provide the nation with a firm financial foundation, and now at last,
after years of tussling over the direction of the new nation, his views had
prevailed.

Immediately following ratification of the Constitution, Pennsylvania chose
Morris to serve as one of its first two senators. Then, upon assuming office as
president, George Washington asked his good friend, frequent host, and financial patron to serve as the first secretary of the Treasury. Morris of course
was the natural choice; after all he had done to save the nation from bankruptcy, to pass him by would have been an extreme insult. But Morris declined. Executive responsibility would get in the way of his private ventures,
and particularly now, when the nation could stand on its own, he was unwilling to sacrifice the private for the public.

Washington then gave the Treasury post to Alexander Hamilton, allowing
Morris to rest easy. Hamilton's economic and monetary policies were identical to those he had been championing all along, highlighted by national taxation and an assumption of state debts. Morris was perfectly content with a
modest role out of the limelight, pushing the program through the Senate.
Within that body he worked tirelessly, as he had done through the early days
of the war in the Continental Congress; during the first six years of the United
States Senate, he served on more committees than any of his colleagues. Unlike an office within the executive branch, however, his position as a senator
allowed him to pursue his own business ventures.

In Pennsylvania, Morris and his party finally prevailed in another political
battle. Ratification of the federal Constitution triggered a new assault on the
state's radical constitution of 1776, with its unicameral legislature and strict
adherence to democratic principles. Conservatives like Robert Morris and
James Wilson had been hammering away for years, and now at last they possessed both control of the state Assembly and a new, convincing argument:
the state constitution should be brought into line with the federal one. Wilson and a cadre of like-minded political operatives pressed the Assembly to
call for a new constitutional convention, while Morris urged them on. Pennsylvania was "ripe for change," he wrote, so it was time to "push on boldly."
Radical defenders of the old constitution, outnumbered, decided to settle for

a compromise. They agreed to overhaul the old form, so long as there were no further restrictions of the franchise and the people themselves could elect state senators. Wilson, Morris, and company could make these concessions, for the rest of Pennsylvania's new constitution, passed in 1790, mirrored the national one, with its checks on popular control.[10]

Now that the new governments on the state and national levels were finally empowered to perform their primary functions—guaranteeing stability and protecting property—Robert Morris could indulge his entrepreneurial appetite to its fullest. Turning his attention from the tobacco trade, which had gone stale, he cast his sights on America's greatest resource: land. Like Washington, Franklin, Henry, and almost every other industrious man of the world of those times, whether involved politically or not, Morris believed that buying and selling hunks of the North American landmass offered unparalleled opportunities for investment. As European settlers flocked to the young nation in search of a better life, land prices were sure to rise, and for those with foresight and capital, profits must rise as well.

Although Morris had dabbled in land speculation before the war, he waited till the nation's finances were sound to throw all his resources that way. In August of 1790, he purchased a huge tract of 1 million acres in New York, then sold it less than two years later for almost three times the original price. A good start, but only that. Why stop at a mere million acres?

In 1795 Morris pooled his resources with two other major investors, John Nicholson and John Greenleaf, to form the giant North American Land Company. Relying on credit, the company purchased 6 million acres in seven states: New York, Pennsylvania, Virginia, Kentucky, North Carolina, South Carolina, and Georgia. Before realizing any profits, however, Morris and company first had to meet their obligations, and this meant they needed to attract additional investors.

To pay their bills, the company offered for sale 1,800 shares at $100 each. Tapping in to his extensive network of moneyed men, Morris presented a most attractive proposal:

> This is one of the best plans that ever was formed in America. It will be useful to the new country by bringing large tracts of land in several states forward to cultivation much sooner than would otherwise have happen'd, thereby adding strength & wealth to the states respectively where the lands are. It will prove convenient & profitable to the projectors, who will continue to hold a large interest in it, and it will be exceedingly prof-

itable to all who shall buy the shares, for beside the annual dividend of six p/cent, I have not the smallest doubt that in the course of the fifteen years proposed as the term for the duration of the plan, they will also receive dividends to the accounts of at least <u>four</u>, but I believe <u>ten</u> times the capital they invested. As a proof that I think so, I am determined to retain as many of my shares as convenience will admit. . . . The increasing value of these estates is beyond the comprehension of mankind.[11]

It was a speculator's millennial vision, profits beyond imagination.

As Morris searched for investors both in America and abroad, he soon found there were too many schemes such as his, and they could not all be capitalized. Besides, the commerce-friendly government had no defense against the free market's cyclical enemies—contraction and the tightening of credit—and it was the wrong time within the rhythmic business cycle to drum up large sums. The North American Land Company failed to achieve its capitalization, which left Robert Morris, for the first time in his life, unable to meet his outstanding obligations.

Still, Morris bullied on. With borrowed money, he staged a treaty council with Iroquois leaders, cajoling them to deed him lands in return for cash. (The money, of course, was to be provided by other investors.) He continued to finance work on a colossal house of marble in the heart of Philadelphia, intended upon its completion to become the grandest palace in America. In 1795, although the marble walls stood bare and without a roof, he placed orders for mirrors worth $25,000 and some of the fanciest furniture in Paris. In former times, when his credit had been good, such behavior would have presented no problem, but now, with credit tight everywhere, his ran out. Word spread that Robert Morris could not make good on his debts, and nobody would lend him a dollar.

By the fall of 1797, the former Financier found himself "besieged with creditors," not just figuratively, but literally. Secluding himself within his country estate at "The Hills," nicknamed Castle Defiance, he braced himself for their charge. Some tried to enter by subterfuge. Others gathered and made a fuss at the gate. From within, desperately, he tried to liquidate his holdings and mortgage his properties, first his investments, then his marble palace, then his lots and houses in town. In a last-ditch attempt to pay off debts, he sold his dinnerware and furniture and borrowed against the trees and shrubs in his garden. This was far too little and far too late. On February 14, 1798, an angry creditor refused to settle, and a local sheriff took Robert Morris to the Walnut Street Gaol.

For more than three years, Robert Morris languished in jail, confined (except for privileges of the yard) to a room with double-grated bars across the windows. Years earlier, when the nation was bankrupt, he had stepped forward to bail it out; now, nobody reciprocated. Friends like George Washington might have helped if they could, but his debts were just too vast: $2,948,711.11, by final tally. He had fallen from the richest man in America to the poorest (unless some other debtor could match that impressive total).[12]

Morris's associate James Wilson, also a big-time speculator, fared no better. While serving on the Supreme Court, he, too, became caught in the credit crunch. To escape his creditors, rather than hide behind barricades, Wilson fled. When one of his creditors (Pierce Butler, a fellow delegate to the Federal Convention) initiated legal proceedings against him, Wilson was riding the Southern Circuit of the court, and faced with the prospect of a court appearance on the other side of the bench, he decided to lie low in Edenton, North Carolina. There, half a year after the Financier had taken up residence on Walnut Street in Philadelphia, Associate Justice of the Supreme Court James Wilson—co-author, promoter, and interpreter of the United States Constitution—fell ill and perished, a delinquent in the eyes of the law.

Today, it is difficult to imagine the shame. For men of business at the time, credit was the ultimate measure of status and self-worth. While landed gentry like Henry Laurens cherished their honor and would do anything to defend it, merchants like Robert Morris pointed to their credit as proof positive that other men trusted and respected them. Now, when a person goes bankrupt, he or she has a chance to start over, and respect is not lost forever; then, when a man of means went broke, he rarely recovered. In the eyes of the world and his own eyes as well, he was viewed as either tragic or pathetic. Those were the only options.

Ironically, Robert Morris's last contribution to public affairs was not merely inadvertent, but directly counter to the thrust of his life's work. Before he went to jail, the federal government, although empowered to pass legislation regulating bankruptcy, had done nothing about it. To men in power, the term *debtor* had previously connoted poor farmers, but if the Financier himself could go to jail, who among them was really safe? In 1800, Federalist congressmen pushed through a bill that allowed a debtor to be set free upon the approval of two-thirds of his creditors, and under that law Robert Morris was finally released from prison.

In 1789, George Washington ascended to the presidency, assuming once again the job of commander in chief. Five years later, in the middle of his second term, he exercised the power granted him under the Constitution to lead the armed forces into combat.

Opposing Washington in the field were neither British Redcoats nor Hessian mercenaries nor any other foreign soldiers. Instead, the first president of the United States rode westward across Pennsylvania to combat an insurrection of thousands upon thousands of American citizens who had been defying the new federal government.

The trouble started in 1791, when Treasury Secretary Alexander Hamilton made use of Congress's newfound power of taxation to push through a controversial excise tax on all whiskey, even that of domestic origin. The new toll reached deep into the pocketbooks of wheat farmers in the upper Ohio Valley, who had been turning their crops into whiskey, an easier product to transport to distant markets. These farmers took issue with the new tax not only because it targeted them and endangered their livelihoods, but also because the revenues were being used to pay off wartime speculators in government bonds. Rich men who had purchased notes at discount prices stood to make huge profits at the farmers' expense—*if* the farmers paid their taxes, which they refused to do.

In 1765, crowds had intimidated Stamp Act tax collectors and forced them to resign; now, western farmers resorted to many of the same techniques. They threatened the tax collectors with humiliation and bodily harm should they refuse to resign, and then, if these warnings went unheeded, men with blackened faces administered a variety of abusive punishments that included tarring and feathering, carting, branding, and the destruction of personal property. None of this was new. Crowds of revolutionary patriots had used these bullying tactics years ago to keep British officials at bay.

Resistance grew. The tax-resisting rebels, once again calling themselves Regulators (because they "regulated" the abuses of government), tried to play back the Revolution, step by step. Farmers erected Liberty Poles to protest unfair taxation, not only in Pennsylvania's western counties, but across the state. Fiercely democratic, the crowds voted at every turn, just as earlier crowds had done during the Massachusetts Revolution of 1774. They formed into local "patriotic societies," which communicated with each other through "committees of correspondence." This revolutionary infrastructure enabled them to gather in great numbers, and on August 1, 1794, marching under a flag bearing six stripes (one for each of four rebellious counties in Pennsylvania and two in northwestern Virginia), somewhere between six thousand and nine thousand men marched to Braddock's Field, where they threatened to seize stockpiles of arms and ammunition. Insurgents from six counties initiated plans to secede from the Union rather than submit to unfair taxation.[13]

Alexander Hamilton, whose partisan policies had triggered this resurgence of revolutionary fervor, labeled the movement the Whiskey Rebellion and urged President Washington to squash it with military force before it spread to Kentucky, Maryland, Virginia, the Carolinas, and Georgia, where other backcountry farmers were also expressing their discontent. Washington hesitated, hoping to avoid the unsightly scene of an American Army marching on its own citizens, but in the end, he asked Supreme Court Justice James Wilson to certify that all legal avenues had been exhausted so he might call out the militia, and he pleaded with Pennsylvania authorities to lend their support. Because the rebellion struck "at the root of all law & order," he told them, "the most spirited & firm measures were necessary, for if such proceedings were tolerated there was an end to our Constitution & laws."[14]

So on September 30, the president himself headed west from Philadelphia, once again the nation's capital, toward the same region in the Upper Ohio Valley that he had tried to wrest from the French forty years earlier. (The heart of resistance, ironically, was in Washington County.) This time, instead of the ragged party of Virginia volunteers who surprised a handful of French scouts at Jumonville Glen, the commander in chief of the United States mustered an armed force of 12,950 militiamen from Pennsylvania, New Jersey, Maryland, and Virginia. The mere presence of this massive army, larger than the Continental forces during much of the Revolution, forced the insurgents to back down, and Washington himself turned back toward Philadelphia before even arriving in rebel territory. By clamping down with force, Washington had delivered a powerful message: the American Revolution was over. There would be no repeat performances, for this government, embodied under authority of the people themselves, would enforce its laws.

For George Washington, the Regulators' resistance to the whiskey tax proved once and for all the perils of factional politics, taken to their logical conclusion. This above all else threatened the young nation, he felt. In 1796, while announcing that he no longer wished to serve as president, the sixty-four-year-old Washington warned the nation of the dangers it might face without him. One stood out above the rest, "the spirit of party":

It serves always to distract the public councils and enfeeble the public administration. It agitates the community with ill-founded jealousies

Figure 43. In 1795, when Gilbert Stuart painted this portrait, George Washington was nearing the end of his second term as president. In Stuart's rendition, Washington has completed his transition from a military to a civilian leader. Compare with earlier portraits of Washington in 1772 and 1779 (see Figures 17 and 30, pages 200 and 331).

and false alarms, kindles the animosity of one part against another, foments occasionally riot and insurrection. It opens the door to foreign influence and corruption, which finds a facilitated access to the government itself through the channels of party passions.[15]

Washington had always tried to remain above this insidious spirit of party, and by his own reckoning that was his greatest legacy. If Americans followed his example and managed to transcend factionalism, their nation would remain united and strong.

But the "spirit of party" had already reached even deeper than Washington feared, for the president himself, despite his better judgment, had succumbed to it. Since 1787, when the nation split over the proposed constitution, Washington had identified himself exclusively with one side, the Federalists. Like others of his persuasion, he never fully appreciated the plausible viewpoints of his opposition, as a truly disinterested leader must do. According to Washington, for instance, the Regulators of 1794 were stirred to act not by their own reasonable grievances, but by the "Democratic Societies" of his political opponents, "the same set of men endeavoring to destroy all confidence in the Administration." These people, radical Antifederalists, hoped "to disquiet the public mind" and "draw a line between the people and the government," and that's why they convinced gullible western farmers "that their liberties were assailed." In explaining his repression of the insurgency to Congress, he closed by "imploring the Supreme Ruler of nations . . . to turn the machinations of the wicked to the confirming of our Constitution." An official appeal to God to change the minds of political foes is hardly the mark of nonpartisanship.[16]

If George Washington, during his final political acts, fell short of his own professed ideal, this reveals more about the nation than about his own character. Insofar as citizens from diverse perspectives were taking active roles in the political process, the notion that virtuous, disinterested leaders who transcended the "spirit of party" could govern an unwieldy populace became less and less viable. The competing parties in the New Republic represented real people with legitimate differences on important issues, and by countering their opponents they could further their own programs. The citizenry, in short, was engaging in the same sort of spirited political behavior that propelled the nation to its independence.

Although he did not wind up governing a virtuous republic, immune from the divisive effects of partisanship, George Washington served the nation well, even within a factionalized world. As president, he exerted his forceful leadership *through* politics, not above them. He would have his way, but because he refused to place himself too far in advance of public opinion, his authority bore more weight.

During the Pennsylvania Regulators' insurgency, for instance, Alexander Hamilton hammered at Washington repeatedly to use military force against the western insurgents, regardless of the outrage such an action might engender among the Antifederalists. "I have long since learned to hold popular opinion of no value," Hamilton admitted. But Washington, because he at least aspired to nonpartisanship, took a different approach. "To array citizen against citizen," he wrote, was a step "too delicate, too closely interwoven with many affecting circumstances, to be lightly adopted." To the end, he remained politic in his politics.[17]

At least in appearances, George Washington insisted that he must act as a president, not a Federalist, for in a government meant to serve the people, appearances counted. Courting public approval was not weak, but necessary. Ironically, in his old-fashioned way, the well-heeled general from Virginia who had always craved respect was giving the nod to an evolving American democracy, where the people's will mattered above all else.

Henry Laurens supported the new Constitution, even though he had turned down the chance to help write it. Having once served as president of Congress, and by nature a fan of government from above, Laurens would have preferred to bestow more powers upon the presidency, but he would not quarrel now with the results of the Federal Convention, and in fact, he didn't really seem to care that much: "Little harm or little good can the system do to me as an individual," he wrote late in 1787. "I am hastening out of its reach."

Despite his apparent indifference, Laurens consented to serve as a delegate to the ratifying convention, and there, in the upstairs hall of the Exchange Building that he had helped erect two decades earlier, he cast his vote in favor of ratification. It was a fine moment for a retired statesman, and afterward, in the victory procession, Laurens enjoyed a place of honor as first of the "Gentleman Planters." According to one newspaper account, "That venerable, steady patriot, Col. Laurens, graced the planters with his company, in a characteristic style of dress, and the day was happily terminated in social festivity."[18]

According to his 1915 biographer, David Duncan Wallace, Henry Laurens "spent his remaining years as a kindly, progressive planter" at Mepkin, "this delightful bluff amid a beautiful park overlooking the river." That's how Laurens himself preferred to view his final days.[19]

But what about his slaves, who toiled in the rice fields below the "park"? Back in 1776, Laurens had viewed slavery as the curse of America; now, he contented himself with the pleasing notion that slavery would end on its own some years down the line, and in the meantime, he would do his part by acting as a beneficent master. That would have to suffice. We have no further indication of Henry Laurens's passionate concern for the fate of his many slaves. Upon his death, he freed only one, a loyal carpenter named George. The rest were divvied up among his three surviving children and John's daughter, Fanny, as were the twenty thousand acres of land these enslaved men and women were expected to work.[20]

Henry Laurens could resume a comfortable life supported by the labor of others because crucial hierarchies remained in place. In the early days of the Revolution, Laurens felt the social structure was in the process of breaking down; immediately after the war, when he returned home, it looked as though society had in fact been shattered; but in the end, he felt reassured that the old ways had endured, modestly altered but not entirely destroyed.

Alexander Hamilton, John Laurens's best friend, handed Henry Laurens concrete proof that order had returned. Like many other wealthy patriots, Laurens had invested in the war effort by purchasing government bonds. Some had done so early on, for all the best reasons; others had done so just to find a good deal, buying bonds later at huge discounts. Now, Hamilton's Funding Act rewarded all investors by stipulating that prior loans would be redeemed at full value. This is what struggling farmers like the Pennsylvania Regulators so resented, but this is what allowed Henry Laurens to enjoy his last days without financial worries, for he was the proud owner of $56,854.20 in government notes.[21]

We do not know the cause of Henry Laurens's death late in 1792, but we do know he had been complaining of ill health for the last decade of his life, ever since emerging from the Tower of London. We also know he didn't want to be buried, fearing he might smother underground while still alive. Daughter Martha, while still an infant, was being prepped for her funeral when someone noticed a faint movement, or so the family story went, so Henry, to avoid any chance of a premature burial, insisted he be cremated. A strange tale, and a strange fear, at life's end, but Henry Laurens had always fretted that life would not proceed as it should, and even in death he didn't want to take any chances.

When George Washington assumed the office of president of the United States under the new Constitution, a dozen years had passed since the death of Thomas Young. Much had changed over that time. When he died, in June of 1777, the trajectory of Young's cause—shaping a polity based exclusively on the will of the people—seemed to be on the rise: within the previous year, Congress had responded to popular pressure by declaring independence, Pennsylvania had enacted a constitution that placed all power in the direct hands of the people, and Young had every hope that the internal revolution there would spread to other states. But in retrospect, we see that the trajectory had just reached its zenith and would be headed downward. Conservatives over the next several years were able to reclaim some of the ground they had lost. A war-weary people and a war-torn economy might have furthered popular discontent, but not popular power. The notion of democracy had been in ascent, but by the 1780s, after the war, people whom it threatened were able to revive its negative connotations. An "excess of democracy" was the cause of the young nation's troubles, said Elbridge Gerry at the Federal Convention, as he and others changed the rules to limit its further expansion.

Even so, although radical democrats no longer prevailed, several of Thomas Young's former cohorts, as well as many other politically active citizens, clung tenaciously to the credo that the people themselves should run everything, unchecked from above. Regulators in Massachusetts in 1786 and Pennsylvania in 1794, as well as a host of other farmers who struggled to have their say, followed a tradition personified by the peripatetic revolutionary from Amenia, New York.

On one occasion after he died, Thomas Young himself received some personal notice for his progressive activities. In October of 1786, during the height of the Massachusetts Regulation, his old partner in crime Ethan Allen, along with two others, presented a memorial to the Vermont legislature on behalf of Young's widow and children, who had been left destitute by his demise nine years earlier:

We beg leave to represent our former worthy friend Doctor Thomas Young, deceased, . . . [for] the decided part which he took in our favour in the most critical moments as respected the existence of this state, having pointed out the system to be pursued to establish government by a separate jurisdiction & to whom we stand indebted for the name of Vermont.[22]

A fitting tribute, but the legislature took no action on the request to grant Young's family a tract of undeveloped land.

A few years later, Thomas Young's work on behalf of the New York secessionists from the Green Mountains came to fruition, even if he was not specifically acknowledged. In 1791 Vermont was admitted to the union as the fourteenth state, and its official constitution, approved two years later, maintained several of the democratic features of the 1777 constitution Young had recommended: annual elections for both representatives and the governor; a single-house legislature with open sessions and published roll-call votes; no upper house representing propertied interests; term limits for representatives to the United States Congress; abolishment of debtors' prisons; a "counsel of censors" to evaluate the workings of the government every seven years and propose amendments to the constitution; and a detailed and extensive declaration of rights, including a revolutionary guarantee left out of the national version: "The community hath an indubitable, unalienable, and indefeasible right, to reform or alter government, in such manner as shall be, by that community, judged most conducive to the public weal." While the Pennsylvania constitution of 1776 (upon which this one was based) had been repealed in 1790, prodemocracy forces in Vermont were able to sustain these special features of popular control over governmental process.[23]

Looking ahead in time, beyond the 1790s, we see that Thomas Young's principles of popular government gained mainstream acceptance, even if he himself gets no acclaim. Democracy was still a controversial notion in the early years of the nation, but that certainly changed. Although few people today would approve the heavy-handed tactics of intimidation practiced by Young and his compatriots, his commitment to participation by common citizens in political life cannot be matched by the prominent "Founding Fathers." Whereas they hoped to create a republic, with citizens electing virtuous leaders to make all the decisions, he favored democracy, in which people do more than just vote. Only sixty years later, when Alexis de Tocqueville journeyed through the country, it was Young's nation he saw: he called his book *Democracy in America* (although he did not approve of all he observed). The Revolutionary body of the people, Dr. Young included, had pointed the nation that way.

Colonel Timothy Bigelow, among the first of America's Revolutionaries, had to wait till the Civil War to become a hero.

After returning to civilian life in Worcester, Bigelow found it difficult to make ends meet. His blacksmith trade never revived. His investment scheme in Montpelier, Vermont, failed to pay off. He sold and mortgaged small parcels of local real estate he had acquired over the years, but mortgages increased his debts, and by February of 1790 he was facing financial ruin. He saw two options: sell the family house and farm in central Worcester to pay all his debts, or go to jail. He chose the latter. To save his property, he conveyed title to his son-in-law and checked into debtors' prison. The record book for the Worcester County jail reads:

> *Timothy Bigelow, Worcester, Esquire.*
> *Time of commitment, February 15, 1790, by Execution.*
> *By authority of Levi Lincoln, Esq.*
> *Description: Six Feet, Dark Complexion.*
> *Discharged April 1, 1790, by Death.*[24]

On April 7, 1790, on the same piece of machinery that Bigelow smuggled from British-controlled Boston fifteen years earlier, the patriot printer Isaiah Thomas published the briefest possible obituary in his *Massachusetts Spy*: "Died. In this town Col. Timothy Bigelow, aged 50." That's all Thomas had to say about the man who helped him escape and allowed him to set up shop in his basement during the early days of the Revolutionary War. Curiously, in the same issue, Thomas reported that Timothy Paine, the former Tory, and Artemas Ward, first commander in chief of the Continental Army, had polled an equal number of votes for state senator in the town of Worcester. The political beat went on, but Timothy Bigelow was done.

Meanwhile, the colonel's son Timothy Jr. was embarking on a career in law and politics. Due to his father's standing and connections during the war, the son had been able to attend Harvard, where he gained connections of his own. He joined the bar, ran for public office as a Federalist, and eventually became speaker of the Massachusetts House of Representatives. The Bigelow story was not unusual: sons of Revolutionaries became political figures in their own right, without any revolutionary designs.

Isaiah Thomas went on to establish a vertically linked chain of business enterprises, from printing presses to bookstores. Devoted to preserving the history that he himself witnessed, he founded the American Antiquarian Society in Worcester, which remains to this day one of the nation's foremost institutions for historical research. This, too, was not atypical: in the wake of the American Revolution, future generations looked backward to their roots, finding meaning and purpose for their nation by studying and touting its beginnings.

In 1861, the same year Henry Wadsworth Longfellow catapulted Paul Revere to stardom with his famous poem, patriots from Worcester, looking back to the Revolution for heroes of their own, rediscovered Colonel Timothy Bigelow. The man they found, however, was not the blacksmith–turned–political organizer who joined with his fellow townsmen to overthrow British rule in 1774, but the military leader who marched off to war eight months later, then rose in the ranks of the Continental Army. Like so many other communities in the second half of the nineteenth century, Worcester wished to affirm its patriotic past by pointing to its Revolutionary soldiers (officers preferred), so they erected a monument on the town commons, eight Roman columns supporting a gabled roof, and a turret above that, topped by a conical cap. The inscription on one face reads:

In memory of
The Colonel of the 15th Massachusetts Regiment
of the Continental Army
in the War of Independence
This monument is erected by his grandson
Timothy Bigelow Lawrence
Anno Domino 1861

Other faces list the battles in which Bigelow fought and his birth and death dates, while buried within are a lock of his hair, a lead ball supposedly cast in Bigelow's forge, and some gunpowder.

A generation later, when women from Worcester who could trace their ancestry back to Revolutionary days formed a local chapter of the Daughters of the American Revolution, they assumed the name of the town's highest-ranking soldier, and since that time, subsequent generations of the Colonel Timothy Bigelow Chapter of the Daughters of the American Revolution have kept his memory alive by maintaining and preserving his monument.

One other historical plaque in Worcester relates indirectly to Bigelow's legacy, a small, simple tablet across from the exit to the Pearl-Elm Municipal Garage, tucked back from the sidewalk and readable only by the most astute pedestrian:

On his way to take command of
the Continental Army at Cambridge
GENERAL GEORGE WASHINGTON
was entertained in this spot then
occupied by Stearns' tavern
July 1st 1775
Erected by the Worcester Continentals
April 19, 1915

Herein lies the quintessential transformation of America's Revolutionary memory. The tribute gives no nod to Worcester's patriots of '74, Timothy Bigelow included, who first upended British rule. Lost and forgotten is the rich story of the American Political Society, its battle with local Tories, and the ultimate victory over British and Tories in 1774, so much of which transpired within the walls of Mary Stearns's tavern (see chapter 6). Instead, we learn that one famous man ate here, even though nothing in particular happened on the night he blessed the town with his presence. A strange omission, indeed, and a consequential one, not just because Bigelow and others have not received due credit, but because the soul of the Revolution is lost, the story of how ordinary people worked together to seize control of their lives, their town, their county, and their country.

Such rousing tales of our lesser-known founders might not be lost forever, and Joseph Plumb Martin, the Revolution's Everyman, can take part of the credit for that.

Martin's experiences after the war, like those during it, were typical. He settled along the coast of Maine (then still part of Massachusetts) and homesteaded land he thought to be free. But he was mistaken, for Henry Knox, one of George Washington's favorite generals and his first secretary of war, claimed that Martin's hundred-acre farm was his, along with approximately six hundred thousand other acres of Maine real estate called the Waldo Patent. Martin protested that he had a right to the land he worked, and he continued with his life. In 1794, at the age of thirty-three, he married the eighteen-year-old daughter of a neighbor.

In 1797, after Knox's claim had been legally upheld, Martin agreed to pay $170 for the farm he himself had created. But with a growing family and meager resources, the farmer could not come up with the money, and four years later he was forced to prostrate himself before the major general: "I throw myself and family wholly at the feet of your Honor's mercy, earnestly hoping that your Honour will think of some way, in your wisdom, that may be beneficial to your honor and save a poor family from distress," he wrote. The feisty private could not have enjoyed groveling, and in a style foreshadowing his later narrative, he suggested the intensity of his feelings: "I have nothing more to add, for fear of offence, though Sir my heart is full enough."

Apparently this plea did not suffice, for by 1811 Martin's farm had shrunk to half its size, and seven years after that, he owned no real estate at all. We know this because Joseph Plumb Martin, like tens of thousands of other Revolutionary War veterans, appeared before a court in 1818 to testify first that he had fought in the war, and second that he was destitute:

> I have no real nor personal estate, nor any income whatever, my necessary bedding and wearing apparel excepted, except two cows, six sheep, one pig. I am a laborer, but by reason of age and infirmity I am unable to work. My wife is sickly and rheumatic. I have five children, viz: Joseph,

aged nineteen, an idiot from birth; Thomas and Nathan, fifteen, twins; James Sullivan, eight; Susan, six. Without my pension I am unable to support myself and my family.

Perhaps Martin exaggerated his helplessness (many claimants did), but the court found his total worth to be only $52 and therefore worthy of a pension.[25]

So at the age of fifty-seven, Joseph Plumb Martin started receiving $96 a year, far more money than he ever got as a soldier, and the first significant recompense for his service. In 1797, he had been granted one hundred acres of "bounty-land" in the "military district" of Ohio, but possessing neither the resources nor the desire to move his family that far, he sold his rights to a speculator. (During the war, Congress and nine states, having little money, had tried to attract soldiers with promises of land; the idea was not only to raise an army for free, but also to place seasoned soldiers in western regions, where they might be called upon again to fight Indians.) Martin's brief encounter with his bounty land was common, and it made him bitter. After losing both his land bounty and his farm, he wrote:

When the country had drained the last drop of service it could screw out of the poor soldiers, they were turned adrift like old worn-out horses, and nothing said about land to pasture them upon. Congress did, indeed, appropriate lands under the denomination of "Soldier's lands," in Ohio state, or some state, or a future state, but no care was taken that the soldiers should get them. No agents were appointed to see the poor fellows ever got possession of their lands; no one ever took the least care about it, except a pack of speculators, who were driving about the country like so many evil spirits, endeavoring to pluck the last feather from the soldiers.[26]

Yet however neglectful the country had been in the past, the mood was changing. During the military fervor accompanying the War of 1812, Revolutionary veterans, formerly scorned, suddenly found themselves celebrated as true American patriots. Starting in 1818, more than a third of a century after the fact, some soldiers were finally granted pensions. But why should they have to prove their indigence before receiving any money? Martin and others wanted not pity but respect, and of course the money that would affirm their newfound esteem.

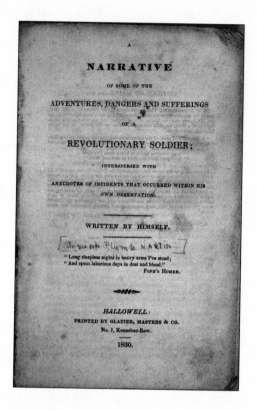

Figure 44. Title page of Joseph Plumb Martin's memoir. "Great men get great praise; little men, nothing," Martin wrote, but his narrative helped common soldiers get their due.

In 1828, Congress took another giant step to mend its ways. Henceforth, any soldier, whether an officer or a private, would not have to prove he was poor in order to earn a pension. There was one hitch, however: this only applied to those who had served from 1778 to the end of the war.

No longer disparaged, veterans continued to push for more. What about all the others who had served their country, but for lesser tours of duty?

It was during this period, when aging soldiers were fighting for recompense and recognition, that Joseph Plumb Martin wrote and published his account, *A Narrative of Some of the Adventures, Dangers and Sufferings of a Revolutionary Soldier, Interspersed with Anecdotes of Incidents that Occurred Within His Own Observation*, which he hoped would further the interests of veterans. Once again, in his own way, he would contribute to history, and as he did, he would place his own life in historical context, right at the heart of the nation's favorite story.

Writing was not new to Martin. He had been serving for years as his town's clerk, he had dabbled in verse, and he even liked to draw, a sign of his creative urge. Despite his lack of formal training, he possessed the requisite tools, as well as the compelling drive, to write his story.

Not unpredictably, Martin's modest memoir, printed anonymously on a local press and bound with wooden boards, made few waves in political or literary circles nationwide. Undoubtedly, it added to the old soldier's acclaim within his community, and that must have felt good. But for well over a century, the handful of extant copies were consulted only by scholars or antiquarians, who probably viewed Martin's memoir as little more than quaint.

Then, in the middle of the twentieth century, an official of the Morristown National Historical Park discovered the book in a private collection and showed it around to scholars. One of these, George Scheer, decided to annotate Martin's narrative and republish it. That was in 1962, perfect timing for a renaissance. In the decade to follow, and for several decades after that, historians began to shift their gaze sideways and downward, away from the familiar figures who had come to dominate the national narrative. A new breed of historians and storytellers, looking for everyday figures to represent everyday lives, has feasted on the detailed descriptions and musings of Private Yankee Doodle, as Scheer affectionately called him. Now, whenever the drama of the American Revolution is re-created for television documentaries, Private Joseph Plumb Martin is there on the screen, acted out by some fellow with a teasing grin who recites colorful snippets from the private's engaging narrative.[27]

"Great men get great praise; little men, nothing," Martin remarked in the wake of his harrowing experiences at Fort Mifflin. This is not as true as it used to be, although still more true than it should be.[28]

Stories change with time and appetite. No contemporary of the Revolution could possibly have imagined that Americans in the early twenty-first century would be more familiar with the wartime experiences of Private Joseph Plumb Martin than with the illustrious careers of many generals. Nor would they have guessed that the most powerful civilian of the time, the Financier, would be left out of the story altogether.

Those who have chronicled our nation's founding often imply—and their readers often assume—that history itself selects the appropriate cast for the story. In truth, we writers do, and, more frequently than we would care to admit, we do it while relying on an embarrassing array of default criteria: availability of sources, reader identification, narrative appeal, and national tradition.

But the default mode limits inquiry. It fosters the illusion that certain things happened, and no more; that a few people mattered, while the remainder did not; that history has set structures, with clear beginnings and pat endings.

The dynamic story of our nation's founding deserves a fuller treatment than that. There were so many people who threw their lives into the project, and so many aspects to the multifaceted drama. The style of our retelling ought to reflect this. It ought to suggest that the story is rich, the possibilities never ending—much in the spirit of our nation itself.

For history does go on, and the telling should go on as well. In these pages, I hope to have broadened the scope, but of course it could be broader yet. Other lead characters, with their diverse stories, could take the tale elsewhere: to the interface between religion and politics, for instance, hardly alluded to in these pages, but certainly a component of the sweeping tale. Or to the relationship between the emerging United States and the rest of the Atlantic world, not only European nations but also Africa, the Spanish and French empires in the Americas, the remnants of the British American Empire, and Native American nations linked to all of the above through trade. And of course there is so much more to be said about how enslaved Americans experienced the Revolution, not to mention persecuted loyalists, and also . . .

So the beat goes on. All history is revisionist history, evolving and adapting to new knowledge and changing sensitivities; any other approach is by definition doctrinaire, anathema to a free people. We define our nation by the way we characterize its beginnings, and nothing could be more "American" than this simple truth: everyone counts. Not until all the stories have been told can we sit back and say, "This is the way it was. This is who we are."

Notes and Sources

First, a note of thanks.

I dedicate this book to all those researchers and archivists and editors who, over the past two centuries, have uncovered and made public the exact words and deeds of our Founders. Although I have put in my time within musty archives and by dim micro-film machines, trying to decipher letters written by hand in the eighteenth century, research for a book of this scope would not have been possible without a long tradition of archival scholarship.

In the early decades of the nineteenth century, a small army of American scholars collected, transcribed, catalogued, and published writings from the Revolutionary generation. The patriotic printer Isaiah Thomas created the American Antiquarian Society to "encourage the collection and preservation of the Antiquities of our country . . . to improve and interest posterity." Jared Sparks focused on the letters of influential individuals such as George Washington, Benjamin Franklin, and Gouverneur Morris, while Jonathan Elliot published the works of politicians and statesmen involved in the political debates of the times. Peter Force, Benjamin Lincoln, and other diligent archivists presented to the public countless documents from the Founding Era's ubiquitous conventions and congresses. When veteran soldiers petitioned for belated pensions, decades after the War for Independence, government interviewers transcribed tens of thousands of their oral depositions.

After the Civil War, a renewed wave of patriotic fervor led local antiquarians in virtually every community within the original thirteen states to gather and publish letters and documents from the Revolutionaries, and to preserve physical memorabilia. During the first half of the twentieth century, scholars diligently processed and indexed these collections, and in recent decades teams of editors have cross-referenced and annotated these multifarious materials, as well as uncovering new ones. Meanwhile, a new breed of scholars has expanded the historical record by documenting the everyday lives of Revolutionary Americans who were once overlooked.

Today, the collected works for each of our most famous Founders include dozens of volumes apiece, while the writings, journals, and letters of several lesser known compatriots appear in book format as well. Thanks to digital technology, archivists have provided electronic access to the public records of the times, and now, with the tap of a key, documents of all kinds magically surface. With remarkable ease, historians can bypass multiple layers of interpretation that have accrued over time and go back to reproductions and transcriptions of a plethora of original sources, some hard copy and others electronic, as I have done while writing this book.

I am indeed grateful to the countless, unheralded lovers of history, strangers yet cohorts, who have allowed me to interact daily with real historical players from the Founding Era, the people who brought us a nation.

Note on Capitalization, Punctuation, and Spelling

While retaining the original spelling, I have altered capitalization and punctuation within quotations to conform to modern usage, for this makes the words and thoughts of the authors appear less archaic and more accessible. Although most scholars prefer to retain original capitalization, I see no useful purpose in this practice, which depends inordinately on idiosyncratic handwriting and has little if any significant effect on content. I have retained the original only for words that were generally capitalized at the time, such as Town, County, Country, Colony (referring to a specific political unit), Army, and Liberty. I have also retained it within political broadsides and advertisements, where authors might have been using capital letters to specific effect.

Similarly, I have taken liberties with punctuation to render original texts more accessible to modern readers. Here, there might be a stronger argument to retain the original, because punctuation can occasionally affect meaning, but this is rare and the effects minimal, while the benefits of increased readability are real and frequent.

Although altering the spelling would also make some passages easier to read, the change of words through time yields interesting nuances in its own right, which I don't wish to sacrifice. Retaining the original words alerts us to the possibility that a specific meaning or usage might have been somewhat different back then. True, spellings that appear strange to the eye might slow us down, as do unfamiliar capitalization and punctuation, but in this case, I think we benefit by taking just a little more time, reminding ourselves with each unique passage that English-speaking people in the past relied on a language that was very similar to the one we use today—yet slightly different.

Abbreviations

People

GW	George Washington	MOW	Mercy Otis Warren
HL	Henry Laurens	RM	Robert Morris
JL	John Laurens	TB	Timothy Bigelow
JPM	Joseph Plumb Martin	TY	Thomas Young
JW	James Warren	WW	Winslow Warren

Document Collections

APS	*American Political Society, Minutes*	*JSCC*	*Journal of the South Carolina Council*
BTR	*Boston Town Records*	*JPCM/CC*	Lincoln, *Journals of*
DFC	Madison, *Debates in Federal Convention*		*Provincial Congress of Massachusetts/County*
DHRC	Jensen, *Documentary History of the Ratification of the Constitution*		*Conventions*
		JPCSC	Hemphill, *Journals of Provincial Congress of South Carolina*
JFC	Elliot, *Journal of Federal Convention*	*LDC*	*Letters of Delegates to Congress*
JCC	*Journals of the Continental Congress*	*WTR*	Rice, *Worcester Town Records*

Research Libraries

AAS	American Antiquarian Society	NYHS	New York Historical Society
HSP	Historical Society of Pennsylvania	NYPL	New York Public Library
		PM	Pilgrim Museum
MHS	Massachusetts Historical Society	SC	South Carolina State Archives

To facilitate usage, all notes are listed in short form. Complete citations follow alphabetically by author in two sections: sources contemporary to the Revolutionary era and secondary sources.

Chapter 1: Facing East and West

1. GW, *Diaries*, 1:195; Cleland, *GW in Ohio Valley*, 80. See also GW to Dinwiddie, 5/29/54, GW, *Papers*, (Col) 1:110.

2. For Washington's journal of this expedition, see GW, *Diaries*, 1:130–61 or Cle-

land, *GW in Ohio Valley*, 1–28; for Dinwiddie's summons and the French reply, see Cleland, *GW in Ohio Valley*, 29–32.

3. Cleland, *GW in Ohio Valley*, 63; Dinwiddie to GW, 3/15/54, and GW to Dinwiddie, 3/20/54, GW, *Papers*, (Col) 1:75, 78

4. Ellis, *His Excellency*, 14.

5. Dinwiddie to Board of Trade, 6/18/54, GW, *Papers*, (Col) 1:114–15.

6. Contrecoeur to Duquesne, 6/2/54, GW, *Papers*, (Col) 1:114.

7. GW, *Diaries*, 1:195. For letters he wrote in the immediate aftermath of the encounter, see GW, *Papers*, (Col) 1:107–9. In his first letter to Dinwiddie, he devoted 1,200 words to his recompense before recounting the battle.

8. GW to John Augustine Washington, 5/31/54, GW, *Papers*, (Col) 1:118. On May 29, the day after the encounter, Washington wrote to Dinwiddie: "I have a constitution hardy enough to encounter and undergo the most severe tryals, and I flatter myself resolution to face what any man durst, as shall be prov'd when it comes to the test, which I believe we are upon the border's of." GW, *Papers*, (Col) 1:107–8.

9. GW, *Diaries*, 1:241.

10. Invoice to Robert Cary, 9/28/60, GW, *Papers*, (Col) 6:461–64.

11. GW to Charles Lawrence, 9/28/60, and GW to Robert Cary, 9/28/60, GW, *Papers*, (Col) 6:458–60.

12. HL to John Ettwein, 3/19/63, HL, *Papers*, 3:373–74.

13. *Pennsylvania Gazette*, 4/19/59; 5/11/58. Willing and Morris sold slaves like any commodity. In response to a "sin" tax of ten pounds per head on imported slaves, they joined with two dozen other Philadelphia firms to protest the unfair restraint of trade, as they viewed it. Scharf and Westcott, *History of Philadelphia*, 1:256.

14. Fritz, *Cast for a Revolution*, 8.

15. MacCracken, *Old Dutchess Forever*, 321–22; Maier, *Old Revolutionaries*, 125.

16. Nutt, *History of Worcester*, 56–58.

17. Adams to William Tudor, 3/29/17, Adams, *Works*, 10:248.

18. MOW, *History*, 1:47.

19. Fritz, *Cast for a Revolution*, 10.

20. Regan, *Pundit and Prophet*, 38–40; Fritz, *Cast for a Revolution*, 13–14, 42–43; MOW, *History*, 1:85.

21. Adams to Tudor, 3/29/17, Adams, *Works*, 10:244–46.

22. Adams, *Legal Papers*, 2:127–28. A few years later, Adams offered a public rendition of what Otis had said, adding his own rhetorical flair to that of his mentor: "I will to my dying day oppose, with all the powers and faculties God has given me, all such instruments of slavery on the one hand, and villainy on the other, as this writ of assistance is. . . . Let the consequences be what they will, I am determined to proceed. The only principles of public conduct that are worthy a gentleman, or a man are, to sacrifice estate, ease, health and applause and even life itself to the sacred calls of his country." Adams, *Legal Papers*, 2:139–41; reprinted from the *Massachusetts Spy*, 4/29/73.

23. Adams to Tudor, 3/29/1817, Adams, *Works*, 10:248.

24. Hutchinson, *History of Massachusetts-Bay*, 3: 63–64, 69. Hutchinson's perspective quickly became entrenched in Tory thought. "If his father was not appointed a Justice of the Superior Court," polemicists recited over and over, James Otis vowed "to set the Province in a flame if he died in the attempt." Oliver, *Origin & Progress of American Rebellion*, 28; *Boston Gazette*, Apr. 4, 1763; *Boston Newsletter*, Apr. 7, 1763.

25. Quincy, *Cases in Superior Court*, 412–13.

26. Tyler, *Smugglers and Patriots*, 25–63.

27. *South Carolina Gazette*, Sept. 5, 1761; HL, *Papers*, 3:79. Ashley Ferry was also called Shem Town or Butler Town.

28. Anderson, *Crucible of War*, 466; Oliphant, *Anglo-Cherokee Frontier*, 151.

29. *JSCC*, 1761–62, 102. One councilman, George Austin, was Laurens's business partner, while another, Egerton Leigh, would become the object of Laurens's wrath several years later.

30. Oliphant, *Anglo-Cherokee Frontier*, 178.

31. HL to John Ettwein, 7/11/61, HL, *Papers*, 3:75; Gadsden to Peter Timothy, 3/12/63, Gadsden, *Writings*, 55; Godbold and Woody, *Christopher Gadsden*, 30; HL, *Papers*, 3:275–355.

32. Godbold and Woody, *Christopher Gadsden*, 24–25, 41; Greene, "Gadsden Election Controversy," 469–92.

33. HL to Christopher Rowe, 2/8/64, and HL to Joseph Brown, 8/30/64, HL, *Papers*, 4:164–65 and 389–90.

34. Ibid.; Godbold and Woody, *Christopher Gadsden*, 34.

35. Muhlenberg, "Extract Account of Paxton Boys," 74–75.

36. Rawles, "Memoir," 41. "Pextang" referred to Paxtang Creek, a tributary of the Susquehanna River. This seems to have given rise to the name for Paxton Township, which in turn lent its name to the Paxton Boys.

37. Franklin, *Papers*, 11:27.

38. Muhlenberg, "Extract Account of Paxton Boys," 75.

39. David Rittenhouse, quoted in Hindle, "March of the Paxton Boys," 479.

40. Slaski, *Thomas Willing*, 97–99, 129–32.

41. Many of the sixty-three extant pamphlets are reprinted in Dunbar, *Paxton Papers*.

42. Young, *Memory of James Wolfe*, 18, cited in Hawke, "Eternal Fisher in Troubled Waters," 10.

43. Edes, "Memoir of Dr. Thomas Young," 15.

44. Jones, *Vermont in the Making*, 143–45; Edes, "Memoir of Dr. Thomas Young," 26. "Great land-jobbers" are the words of Thomas's brother, Joseph, but Joseph was describing Thomas's attitude.

45. Young, *Reflections on the Dispute*, 14–15.

46. Bellesiles, *Revolutionary Outlaws*, 22.

47. Ibid., 20–21; Jellison, *Frontier Rebel*, 12.

48. Edes, "Memoir of Dr. Thomas Young," 16–17; Anderson, "Who Wrote Ethan Allen's Bible?" Anderson claims that fewer than 100 of the 477 pages of the final

work—Ethan Allen, *Reason: The Only Oracle of Man*, published in 1784—were written by Allen.

49. GW, *Papers*, (Col) 7:242–46. See also 7:219–25, 415–17, and 511–13.

50. Greene, *Colonies to Nation*, 18.

51. GW to Stewart, 4/27/63, GW, *Papers*, (Col) 7:206.

52. GW to Robert Cary & Co., 8/10/64, GW, *Papers*, (Col) 7:323.

53. GW, *Papers*, (Col) 8:391. Blocked from the West, Washington did invest in a scheme to the southeast: forty thousand acres of wet, uninhabited terrain near the North Carolina border. After gaining title from the legislature, each of the ten "Adventurers for Draining the Dismal Swamp" (as the Dismal Swamp Land Company was initially called) agreed to contribute five slaves, who were to be charged with emptying out the water. They would log the swamp as they drained it, and then start farming. Washington himself surveyed the land, and he dutifully purchased new slaves to fulfill his commitment, but the project literally got bogged down, for the draining proved more difficult than anticipated, and Washington lost more money than he made. GW, *Papers*, (Col) 7:269–76, 300, 314; GW, *Diaries*, 1:319–26. For the complete story of this venture, see Royster, *Dismal Swamp Company*.

54. Wallace, *Life of Laurens*, 125–26. The British Army destroyed this home during the Revolutionary War. Laurens built a new one in 1784, but that was razed by the Union Army during the Civil War. In 1949 Mepkin Plantation became Mepkin Abbey, the home of Trappist monks.

55. HL, *Papers*, 3:459.

56. HL to Richard Oswald, 7/7/64; HL to John Ettwein, 3/19/63; HL to John Augustus Shubart, 12/31/63, HL, *Papers*, 4:334–35; 3:374; 4:117–18. For more on the land grants, see HL, *Papers*, 5:33–35 and 5:670–71.

57. For survey histories of the activities of these various companies, see Abernathy, *Western Lands*; Livermore, *Early American Land Companies*; Friedenberg, *Life, Liberty, and Pursuit of Land*.

Chapter 2: Liberty and Property—and No Stamps!

1. Morgan, *Prologue to Revolution*, 35–43.

2. *Boston Gazette*, 8/19/65; *Boston Post-Boy*, 8/26/65; Hoerder, *Crowd Action*, 97.

3. *Boston Post-Boy*, 8/26/65; Hoerder, *Crowd Action*, 98.

4. Francis Bernard to Lord Halifax, 8/15/65, Morgan, *Prologue to Revolution*, 107. Deacon Elliot also tried to take down the display, only to be "advis'd to the contrary by the populace, lest it should occasion the demolition of his windows." *Boston Gazette*, 8/17/65.

5. *Boston Post-Boy*, 8/26/65; Hutchinson, *History of Massachusetts-Bay*, 3:87; Rowe, *Diary*, 89.

6. Bernard to Lord Halifax, Aug. 15, 1765, in Morgan, *Prologue to Revolution*, 107–8.

7. *Boston Gazette*, 9/16/65.

8. Ibid.; Young, *Liberty Tree*, 347.

9. Hutchinson to Richard Jackson, 8/30/65, Morgan, *Prologue to Revolution*, 108–9; *Boston News-Letter*, suppl., 9/5/65; Hutchinson, *History of Massachusetts-Bay*, 90; Gordon, *History of Independence*, 1:178.

10. Nash, *Urban Crucible*, 222; Nash, "Prerevolutionary Urban Radicalism," 20.

11. *Pennsylvania Gazette*, 10/10/65, reprinted in *Boston Gazette*, 10/21/65; Wharton to Franklin, 10/13/65, in Franklin, *Papers*, 12:315–16. See also Franklin, *Papers*, 12:269–70, 353; Hutson, "Philadelphia's White Oaks," 3–25.

12. *Pennsylvania Gazette*, 10/10/65, reprinted in the *Boston Gazette*, 10/21/65; Morgan and Morgan, *Stamp Act Crisis*, 250–52; Oberholtzer, *Robert Morris*, 10–13.

13. Morgan and Morgan, *Stamp Act Crisis*, 251.

14. Willing, *Letters and Papers*, 34.

15. HL to Mathew Johnson, 5/30/64, HL, *Papers*, 4:295; Wallace, *Life of Henry Laurens*, 58–59 and 502–3; HL to Mathew Johnson, 5/30/64, HL to George Appleby, 11/9/64, and HL to the Earl of Albemarle, 10/10/64, HL, *Papers*, 4:295, 499, and 467.

16. HL to Joseph Brown, 10/11/65, HL, *Papers*, 5:25.

17. *South Carolina Gazette*, 10/31/65; Walsh, *Charleston's Sons of Liberty*, 36–37; McDonough, *Gadsden and Laurens*, 68–69; HL, *Papers*, 5:27; HL to William Fisher, 2/27/66, HL, *Papers*, 5:77.

18. HL to Joseph Brown 10/28/65, HL, *Papers*, 5:29–32 and 35–40. A public account of the incident appears in *South Carolina Gazette*, 10/31/65.

19. HL to William Fisher, 2/27/66, HL, *Papers*, 5:78; HL to John Laurens, 1/4/76, quoted in HL, *Papers*, 5:32. Teasingly, friends of the family started referring to James as "Liberty." (HL to John Lewis Gervais, 1/29/66, HL, *Papers*, 5:55.)

20. *South Carolina Gazette and Country Journal*, 2/11/66. The declarations of the Stamp Act Congress are reprinted in Morgan, *Prologue to Revolution*, 62–63.

21. HL to James Grant, 2/17/66, quoted in Godbold and Woody, *Christopher Gadsden*, 62.

22. Bull to Henry Conway, 2/6/66, quoted in Maier, "Charleston Mob," 176.

23. Black population estimate from Webster, "Voyage to Charleston, 1765," cited in Donnan, *Documents of Slave Trade*, 4:415. This estimate might have been high, but not terribly so; in 1790 the first federal census recorded the proportion of blacks at about two-thirds. Purvis, *Revolutionary America, 1763 to 1800*, 171–72.

24. Wood, "Liberty Is Sweet," 157–58, 177.

25. Ibid., 158, 177–78.

26. Ibid., 158–59,

27. HL to John Lewis Gervais, 1/29/66, HL, *Papers*, 5:53–54.

28. HL to George Dick, 6/?/64, HL, *Papers*, 4:299.

29. Edes, "Memoir of Dr. Thomas Young," 26.

30. McAnear, "The Albany Stamp Act Riots," 490. The rest of this discussion is based on Van Schaack's testimony, confirmed by contemporary newspaper accounts, as presented in McAnear's article.

31. Colonial Albany Social History Project Web site.

32. Leake, *John Lamb*, 3–4.

33. Morgan, *Prologue to Revolution*, 155.

34. *Boston Gazette*, 8/19/65.

35. Hutchinson to Pownall, 3/8/66, Morgan, *Prologue to Revolution*, 124.

36. Morgan, *Prologue to Revolution*, 155.

37. Rowe, *Diary*, 95.

38. *Boston Gazette*, 5/26/66. This is one of several vivid descriptions to appear in the Boston papers. The quotations in the following paragraphs are also taken from this issue.

39. Gibbes, *Documentary History*, 1:11; *Boston Post-Boy*, 6/2/66.

40. HL to William Fisher, 2/27/66, in HL, *Papers*, 5:77–78.

41. Oberholtzer, *Robert Morris*, 13.

42. Mark, *Agrarian Conflicts*, 138; Countryman, "Out of the Bounds of the Law," 49; Governor Moore to Secretary Conway, 4/30/66, O'Callaghan and Fernow, *Documents Relative to Colonial History of New York*, 7:825.

43. Edes, "Memoir of Dr. Thomas Young," 12; Kim, *Landlord and Tenant*; Montresor, "Journals"; TY to John Wendell, 12/15/66, MHS, Photostat Collections.

44. GW to Robert Cary, 9/20/65, and Capel and Osgood Hanbury to GW, 3/27/66, GW, *Papers*, (Col) 7:398–402, 457.

45. Mason to Committee of Merchants in London, 6/6/66, Mason, *Papers*, 1:65–72. This letter is reprinted in Morgan, *Prologue to Revolution*, 158–63.

Chapter 3: A Perfect Sense of Their Rights

1. MOW, *Poems, Dramatic*, 219.

2. For the Warren home in Plymouth, see Brown, *Mercy Warren*, 38, and Anthony, *First Lady*, 49–50.

3. *Boston Evening Post*, 5/13/65; quoted in Fritz, *Cast for a Revolution*, 58–59, and Galvin, *Three Men of Boston*, 83.

4. MOW, "Private Poems," 206.

5. HL to William Freeman, 10/9/67, HL, *Papers*, 5:48.

6. HL to James Habersham, 9/5/67, HL, *Papers*, 5:296-297.

7. HL to James Grant, 8/12/67, and HL to James Habersham, 9/5/67, HL, *Papers*, 5:279, 298.

8. HL, *Papers*, 5:287–88, n. 7; HL to James Habersham, 9/5/67, HL, *Papers*, 5:296; Leigh, *Man Unmasked*, HL, *Papers*, 6:472.

9. HL, *Appendix to High Court*, HL, *Papers*, 7:8–9; HL to Thomas Smith, 8/8/69, HL, *Papers*, 7:117. Leigh, like Gadsden, had once been his friend and was even family, having married Laurens's niece. Years later, Leigh would disgrace the family by fathering a child with his wife's sister, thereby concluding the ongoing battle for honor between the two men in Laurens's favor.

10. HL to Richard Oswald, 4/27/68, HL, *Papers*, 5:669; cited in McDonough, *Gadsden and Laurens*, 87.

11. In the wake of the Stamp Act fiasco, George Grenville had been replaced as prime minister first by the moderate Marquis of Rockingham and then by William Pitt, known for championing the American cause, but when Pitt, recently dubbed the Earl of Chatham, became incapacitated by illness, his chancellor of the Exchequer, Charles Townshend, effectively seized the reins of his ministry. Townshend's ascension to power signaled a return to the tough policies reminiscent of the Grenville administration. To balance the budget, Pitt had suggested taxing the profits of the East India Company and taking control of India, which the company then claimed as its own, but in his absence, this attack on corporate power was summarily rejected. Instead, Townshend proposed, and Parliament approved, a multifaceted program that started, strangely enough, with a tax cut for landed gentry in England. This pleased the MPs' constituencies but angered colonists in America, who rightfully suspected they would have to foot some of the bill. For a succinct treatment of British politics that resulted in the Townshend measures, see Jensen, *Founding of a Nation*, 215–28.

12. TY to John Wendell, 11/23/66, MHS, Photostat Collections.

13. TY to Abigail Dwight, 2/13/67, MHS, Sedgwick Collection, Sedgwick 2, box 2.

14. TY to John Wendell, 12/15/66, MHS, Photostat Collections.

15. *Boston Gazette*, 4/27/67.

16. Ibid., 5/4/67.

17. Cary, *Joseph Warren*, 28.

18. *Boston Gazette*, 7/6/67. For the Young-Warren exchange, see *Boston Gazette*, 5/25/67 through 7/27/67; Hawke, "Eternal Fisher in Troubled Waters," 14; Cary, *Joseph Warren*, 28–30.

19. Edes, "Memoir of Dr. Thomas Young," 8.

20. Boston Sons of Liberty to John Wilkes, 6/6/68, and Young to Wilkes, 9/6/69, MHS, *Proceedings*, 47:191 and 209.

21. Wilkes to Boston Sons of Liberty, 7/19/68, MHS, *Proceedings*, 47:192.

22. Young to Wilkes, 7/6/69, MHS, *Proceedings*, 47:202. Although only three of the letters are extant, in the first of these Young wrote, "Having once before presumed to write you a private letter . . ." *Proceedings*, 202. Judging from the tone of the letters, there could possibly have been many more.

23. John Dickinson to James Otis, 12/5/67, *Warren-Adams Letters*, 1:3.

24. Fritz, *Cast for a Revolution*, 77.

25. TY to Hugh Hughes, 9/15/70, MHS, Misc. Bound Documents.

26. Ibid., 7/30/69, Huntington Library; Henry, "Young and the Boston Committee," 219–21.

27. For the meeting with Bernard, see MOW, *History*, 1:59.

28. *Boston Evening-Post*, 9/28/67, writing under the name "Britano Americus." For confirmation of Young's various pseudonyms, see Maier, *Old Revolutionaries*, 107.

29. Ibid., 10/12/67.

30. *South Carolina Gazette*, 10/3/68; reprinted in HL, *Papers*, 6:122–23 and Walsh, *Charleston's Sons of Liberty*, 31–32.

31. HL to Richard Oswald, 9/10/70, HL, *Papers*, 7:360.

32. HL to Grant, 10/1/68, HL, *Papers*, 6:119–20.

33. Schlesinger, *Colonial Merchants*, 110–12.

34. *Pennsylvania Gazette*, 10/20/68.

35. Ibid., 5/12/68.

36. Schlesinger, *Colonial Merchants*, 128; Jensen, *Maritime Commerce*, 179; Merchants of Philadelphia, Papers, vol. 62.7.

37. Thomson, Papers, 62:174–78. The agreement of March 10, which finalized the agreement of February 6, is reprinted in Mason, *Papers*, 1:100–101.

38. *Pennsylvania Gazette*, 3/9/69.

39. Gough, *Christ Church*, 48–51.

40. Thomson, Papers, 62:180–85, 220–25; *Pennsylvania Gazette*, 8/31/69 and 5/10/70.

41. W.E. Woodward, *George Washington: The Image and the Man* (New York: Boni and Liveright, 1926), 152–53.

42. GW to George Mason, 4/5/69, GW, *Papers*, (Col) 8:177–80; Mason, *Papers*, 1:96–98.

43. Mason, *Papers*, 1:105.

44. Ibid., 1:103–5.

45. Van Schreeven et al., *Revolutionary Virginia*, 1:69; Washington, *Diaries*, 2:152.

46. Van Schreeven et al., *Revolutionary Virginia*, 1:73; Lossing, *Field-Book of Revolution*, 2:484.

47. Van Schreeven et al., *Revolutionary Virginia*, 1:73–77; Mason, *Papers*, 1:109–12.

48. Maier, "Charleston Mob," 183; Maier, *From Resistance to Revolution*, 118; Gadsden, *Writings*, 83–84.

49. HL to Daniel Grant, 4/27/70, HL, *Papers*, 7:286.

50. HL to Matthew Robinson, 6/1/70, and HL to Lachlan McIntosh, 5/10/70, HL, *Papers*, 7:290 and 7:300.

51. HL to Henry Humphreys, 5/19/70 and 6/8/70, HL, *Papers*, 7:298. Emphasis in the original.

52. HL to Matthew Robinson, 6/1/70, HL, *Papers*, 7:300.

53. HL to Samuel Johnston, 8/13/70, HL, *Papers*, 7:321; HL, *Papers*, 7:322–23; *Gazette*, 8/23/70.

54. HL to Richard Clarke, 8/25/70, HL, *Papers*, 7:329.

55. HL, *Papers*, 7:411; *Gazette*, 12/13/70.

Chapter 4: A Violent Turn

1. *Boston Gazette*, 9/4/69.

2. Thomas Hutchinson to Francis Bernard, 9/5/69, cited in Galvin, *Three Men of Boston*, 184; *Boston Chronicle*, 9/7–11/69; *Boston Gazette*, 9/4/69 and 9/25/69; John Adams, *Works*, 2:219.

3. *Boston Chronicle*, 9/14–18/69.

4. Ibid.

5. Ibid., 9/ 7–11/69 and 9/14–18/69; *Boston Gazette*, 9/18/69.

6. TY to John Wilkes, 9/6/69, MHS, *Proceedings*, 47:209; Galvin, *Three Men of Boston*, 186.

7. *Boston Gazette*, 9/25/69; Samuel Adams to John Smith, 12/20/65, Samuel Adams, *Writings*, 1: 380–86; John Adams, *Works*, 2:219.

8. MOW to James Otis, 9/?/69, MOW Letterbook, MHS, cited in Fritz, *Cast for a Revolution*, 85.

9. Fritz, *Cast for a Revolution*, 85; Adams, *Works*, 2:226–27.

10. Adams, *Works*, 2:228; Rowe, *Diary*, 199, 201.

11. MOW, "Private Poems," 213–14.

12. TY to Hugh Hughes, 7/30/69, Huntington Library; Henry, "Young and the Boston Committee," 220. Hugh Hughes was the brother of Philadelphia's John Hughes, Benjamin Franklin's friend, whose political career was ruined when he accepted an appointment as stamp distributor in 1765 (see ch. 2).

13. Tyler, *Smugglers and Patriots*, 138–69.

14. TY to Hughes, 3/22/70, Huntington Library.

15. New England Papers, Sparks Manuscripts 10, 3:56, cited in Maier, *Old Revolutionaries*, 107.

16. *Boston Gazette*, 9/11/69.

17. TY to Hughes, 1/29/70, Huntington Library.

18. Hutchinson, *History of Massachusetts-Bay*, 3:192.

19. TY to Hughes, 3/22/70 and 5/11/70, Huntington Library.

20. *Boston Gazette*, suppl., 2/19/70.

21. *Boston Gazette*, 9/11/69.

22. Adams, *Works*, 2:228.

23. Adams, *Legal Papers*, 3:112; Zobel, *Boston Massacre*, 192.

24. Linder, Boston Massacre Trials, Trial of Captain Preston.

25. Hutchinson, *History of Massachusetts-Bay*, 3:197.

26. *Boston Gazette*, 3/12/70.

27. Hutchinson, *History of Massachusetts-Bay*, 3:198.

28. Warren, *History*, 1:94.

29. Linder, Boston Massacre Trials, Summation of John Adams. "Teague," denoting an Irish clan, was used by colonists as a slur on Irish people.

30. *Boston Gazette*, 3/12/70.

31. Fischer, *Paul Revere's Ride*, 377.

32. Cook, *Long Fuse*, 149.

33. TY to Hughes, 7/30/69, Huntington Library.

34. Frothingham, *Joseph Warren*, 157; Zobel, *Boston Massacre*, 233; Tyler, *Smugglers and Patriots*, 154–58; TY to Hughes, 7/26/70, Huntington Library. John Rowe also described Young's procession: "July 24. This afternoon 'The Body' as they are called met & just before some of them proceeded through the streets with Dr. Young at their head with three flags flying, drums beating & a French horn." *Diary*, 205.

35. Wells, *Samuel Adams*, 1:366; Edes, "Memoir of Dr. Thomas Young," 28; TY to Hughes, 9/15/70, MHS, Misc. Bound Documents.

36. Schlesinger, *Colonial Merchants*, 225–26; Jensen, *Founding of a Nation*, 365–66.

37. *Boston Gazette*, 3/11/71; Loring, *Hundred Boston Orators*, 24–25.

38. Egnal, *Mighty Empire*, 224; Holton, *Forced Founders*, 91.

39. GW to William Crawford, 9/17/67, GW, *Papers*, (Col) 8:26–29.

40. Crawford to GW, 9/29/67, GW, *Papers*, (Col) 8:39.

41. GW, *Papers*, (Col) 8:30; GW, *Diaries*, 2:51–52,

42. Mason, *Papers*, 1:8. Franklin's group, known at the time as the Walpole Company after its most prominent British member, was later called the Vandalia Company, the name of the new colony it hoped to create.

43. Washington's account of the expedition is reprinted in GW, *Diaries*, 2:286–328, and Cleland, *GW in Ohio Valley*, 240–69.

44. GW, *Diaries*, 2: 296–98; Cleland, *GW in Ohio Valley*, 251, 254.

45. GW, *Diaries*, 2: 304; Cleland, *GW in Ohio Valley*, 258–59.

46. GW, *Diaries*, 2: 316; Cleland, *GW in Ohio Valley*, 265.

47. GW, *Papers*, (Con) 1:93–94. Of the 200,000-acre bounty land from 1754, Washington received about 23,000 acres, along with 4,000 additional acres he acquired through trade. In addition, at the close of the French and Indian War, veteran field officers were entitled to 5,000 acres. (Privates received only 50 acres.) In addition, Washington purchased another 8,000 acres from other veteran officers, 3,000 coming from his bankrupt neighbor John Posey.

48. Kay, "North Carolina Regulation," 95–97.

49. Kars, *Breaking Loose Together*, 138; Lee, *Crowds and Soldiers*, 53.

50. Wells, *Samuel Adams*, 1:367.

51. Perhaps Hutchinson was only passing on a rumor and Young didn't go after all, but even so, the rumor itself is significant: if any patriot from Boston could be associated in the public mind with the Regulators, Thomas Young was the man. If Young did in fact go, why would he have returned to Boston so soon? Once in Regulator country, he probably would have received a cool welcome. A few months earlier, as the nonimportation movement was beginning to unravel, some leading Boston patriots had traveled to other New England port towns, such as Salem, Providence, and Newport, only to be greeted by a chorus of boos from local patriots, who resented their intrusions and claimed that Boston merchants had been the first to cheat on nonimportation. Tyler, *Smugglers and Patriots*, 164. This sort of reaction was likely to have been even more pronounced in North Carolina, where prominent Sons of Liberty from the coastal regions had actively opposed the Regulators from the beginning. In this context, angry backcountry farmers would not likely have offered a hero's welcome to a meddling Son of Liberty from Boston, nor would they have given him a platform for political preaching. However much he supported their cause, there was not much Thomas Young could do to help—at least not there.

52. Lee, *Crowds and Soldiers*, 87, 269–70; Kay, "North Carolina Regulation," 103.

53. Kars, *Breaking Loose Together*, 201–3.

54. One of the writers, "Leonidas," addressed Governor Tryon directly, demanding a "direct and satisfactory" answer to a series of rhetorical questions. *Massachusetts Spy*, 6/27/71. If we judge by the inflammatory language (contrasting "industrious hus-

bandmen" with "extortioners, traitors, robbers, and murderers") and the knowledge of local events in North Carolina (reference to a trial that had not been publicized elsewhere), Leonidas might well have been Thomas Young. When a number of "Gentlemen" at the King's Arms tavern in Newbern, North Carolina, got hold of the issue with Leonidas's letter, they took immediate offense. They called a special meeting of concerned citizens, which issued the following resolution: "*Resolved*, That the Chairman be requested to direct the sheriff of the county to give orders that the paper called the *Massachusetts Spy*, No. 17, be publicly burnt under the gallows by the common hangman, on Wednesday next, as an open testimony of the utter abhorrence and detestation in which that infamous production, and its still more infamous authors, are held by the people of this government." *Massachusetts Spy*, 8/29/71.

55. Jellison, *Frontier Rebel*, 38; Bellesiles, *Revolutionary Outlaws*, 82.
56. Jellison, *Frontier Rebel*, 52; Bellesiles, *Revolutionary Outlaws*, 78.
57. Bellesiles, *Revolutionary Outlaws*, 89, 97.
58. Jellison, *Frontier Rebel*, 53.
59. Bellesiles, *Revolutionary Outlaws*, 212.

Chapter 5: Politics and Tea

1. Oberholtzer, *Robert Morris*, 292.
2. Flexner, *Indispensable Man*, 51–55; Ellis, *His Excellency*, 61.
3. HL to John Lewis Gervais, 5/29/72, in HL, *Papers*, 8:353.
4. *Massachusetts Spy*, 3/26/72. For the complex history of the play's various manuscript versions and publications, see Richards, *Mercy Otis Warren*, 86–89.
5. Fritz, *Cast for a Revolution*, 105; MOW to Samuel Allyne Otis, 12/22/72, MOW Letterbook, MHS.
6. Gordon, *History of Independence*, 1:312–13. Numerous other historians for more than two centuries have followed Gordon's lead in attributing the idea to James Warren.
7. TY to Hughes, 8/31/72, MHS, Misc. Bound Documents.
8. Ibid.
9. Brown, *Revolutionary Politics*, 59–64. The "Boston Pamphlet" is reprinted in *BTR*, 95–108, and S. Adams, *Writings*, 2:359–68. Excerpts appear in Greene, *Colonies to Nation*, 179–82. "Depravity of mankind" appears in TY to Hughes, 8/31/72, MHS, Misc. Bound Documents. For Warren's harsh words about Young, see ch. 3 above.
10. *Boston News-Letter*, 11/26/72.
11. *Boston Gazette*, 11/30/72.
12. TY to Hughes, 12/21/72, MHS, Misc. Bound Documents.
13. TY to Hughes, 1/29/70 and 3/2/70, Huntington Library.
14. TY to Hughes, 12/21/72, MHS, Misc. Bound Documents.
15. Brown, *Revolutionary Politics*, 94–99; Bushman, "Massachusetts Farmers," 80. The original replies are in Boston Committee of Correspondence, Minute Book. The

replies were generally recorded in the minutes of their respective towns, but not all of these minutes are extant, and the surviving minutes of the BCC are not necessarily complete, so there might well have been more. For the number of towns sending representatives to the General Court, see Patterson, *Political Parties*, 34.

16. Moynihan, *History of Worcester*, 61.

17. Adams, *Diary and Autobiography*, 3:265–70; Moynihan, *History of Worcester*, 61–62; *WTR*, 138–40; Lincoln, *History of Worcester*, 66–67.

18. Brooke, *Heart of the Commonwealth*, 144.

19. *WTR*, 199–202.

20. *WTR*, 87, 131, 162, 180; Nutt, *History of Worcester*, 56–57; Moynihan, *History of Worcester*, 65.

21. Nutt, *History of Worcester*, 58–59; Izard, "Andrews-Bigelow Site."

22. *WTR*, 203.

23. Ibid., 205.

24. Johnson, *Worcester in War for Independence*, 41. For Chandler and Paine genealogies, see Nutt, *History of Worcester*, 76–78, 200.

25. Adams to JW, 11/4/72, *Warren-Adams Letters*, 1:12.

26. Adams, *Works*, 2: 299.

27. MOW to Catharine Macaulay, 6/7/73 [or 6/9/73], MOW Letterbook, MHS, 1:1–2.

28. MOW to Catharine Macaulay, 12/29/74, MOW Letterbook, MHS, 1:6.

29. Abigail Adams to MOW, 7/16/73, *Adams Family Correspondence*, 1:84–85.

30. MOW to John Adams, 10/11/73, *Warren-Adams Letters*, 2:402–3.

31. *Boston Gazette*, 5/24/73.

32. Ibid., 7/19/73.

33. Brown, *Mercy Warren*, 47.

34. *Boston Gazette*, 11/29/73.

35. Drake, *Tea Leaves*, 172.

36. For Young's early advocacy of throwing the tea overboard, see Labaree, *Boston Tea Party*, 141–42, 295 n. 31; Upton, ed., "Proceeding of Ye Body," 299; Drake, *Tea Leaves*, 44, 172; Bancroft, *History of United States*, 4: 274.

37. *Boston Gazette*, 12/6/73; Frothingham, *Joseph Warren*, 263; Upton, "Proceeding of Ye Body," 292–93.

38. Labaree, *Boston Tea Party*, 133.

39. Abigail Adams to MOW, 12/5/73, *Adams Family Correspondence*, 1:88–89.

40. Labaree, *Boston Tea Party*, 134; John Andrews to William Barrell, 12/1/73, Andrews, "Letters," 325.

41. Birnbaum, *Red Dawn at Lexington*, 29. For the genesis of this tale, see Raphael, *Founding Myths*, 52–53.

42. Upton, "Proceeding of Ye Body," 297–98. According to another firsthand account, "Mr. Samuel Adams cried out that it was a trick of their enemies to disturb the meeting, and requested the people to keep their places." Drake, *Tea Leaves*, 70. "An Impartial Observer" reported in both the *Boston Evening Post* and the *Boston Gazette*

of December 20 that after the first "war-whoop" from the doorway, "silence was commanded, and a prudent and peaceable deportment again enjoined." A similar report appeared in the December 23 issue of the *Massachusetts Gazette and Boston Weekly News-Letter*.

43. Drake, *Tea Leaves*, 71–72.

44. Thatcher, *George R. T. Hewes*, 261–62; Drake, *Tea Leaves*, 95; Lossing, *Field-Book of Revolution*, 1:499.

45. Adams to JW, 12/17/73, *Warren-Adams Letters*, 2:403–4.

46. Adams, *Diary and Autobiography*, 2:86. For statistics on tea shipments to Boston, as well as to New York, Philadelphia, and Charleston in the autumn of 1773, see Labaree, *Boston Tea Party*, 335.

47. TY to John Lamb, 5/13/74, Leake, *John Lamb*, 84.

Chapter 6: The First American Revolution

1. Haldimand to Lord Dartmouth, 12/28/73, quoted in Labaree, *Boston Tea Party*, 155.

2. *Boston Gazette*, 1/24/74; Oaks, "Philadelphia Merchants," 121–22; Drake, *Tea Leaves*, 365; Labaree, *Boston Tea Party*, 158.

3. John Adams to JW, 12/22/73, *Adams, Papers*, 2:3; *Boston Gazette*, 3/21/74; Butterfield, *Adams Family Correspondence*, 1:102. "Tuskurarine Race" refers to the Tuscarora Indians, one of the six nations of the Iroquois Confederacy, whom the tea-dumping patriots impersonated. A "Favonian breeze" refers to Favonius, the Roman god of a gentle west wind. Amphitrite is a Greek sea goddess.

4. James Tilghman Jr. to GW, 4/7/74, GW, *Papers*, (Col) 10:23–24. The handful of letters that did not focus on land dealt with the estate of GW's stepson, John Custis.

5. John Adams to JW, 12/22/73, Adams, *Papers*, 2:3.

6. APS, Minutes; Lovell, *Worcester in the Revolution*, 21–26.

7. APS, Minutes; *WTR*, 214–15; Boston Committee of Correspondence, Correspondence and Proceedings, reel 2, letter 495; Lincoln, *History of Worcester*, 77–78; Lovell, *Worcester in the Revolution*, 27–29.

8. Hersey, *Col. Timothy Bigelow*, 8–9. Although Hersey states this incident occurred on 3/7, this or a similar confrontation could also have taken place at the 5/20 or 6/20 meetings (see below).

9. Raphael, *First American Revolution*, 32–33, 41–42.

10. APS, Minutes; *WTR*, 224–27.

11. *WTR*, 230–33; *Boston News-Letter and Massachusetts Gazette*, 6/30/74; *Boston Gazette*, 7/4/74. Spelling here is in accordance with Rice in *WTR*.

12. TY to John Lamb, 5/13/74, Leake, *John Lamb*, 84.

13. TY to John Lamb, 6/19/74, Leake, *John Lamb*, 89.

14. *BTR*, 177–78; Rowe, Diary, 277.

15. Foner, *Labor and the American Revolution*, 130; Brookhiser, *Gentleman Revolutionary*, 20.

16. GW to Fairfax, 6/10/74, GW, *Papers*, (Col) 10:96–97.

17. GW to James Wood, 2/20/74, and GW to William Preston, 2/28/74, GW, *Papers*, (Col) 9:490, 501. See also letters of 2/17 and 2/28 (483, 501).

18. GW to Bryan Fairfax, 7/20/74 and 8/24/74, GW, *Papers*, (Col) 10:130, 156.

19. Ibid. These words, penned to an aristocratic neighbor who had been siding with British policies, signal Washington's cognizance of the ironic use of the term "slavery" in the colonists' complaints.

20. APS, Minutes; Salisbury Family Papers; Newfield, *Worcester on Eve of Revolution*, 86. Salisbury also ordered up new supplies of "barr lead," "gun locks," and "bullets—25 to the pound."

21. Wroth, *Province in Rebellion*, 877–80; Lincoln, *JPCM/CC*, 627–31.

22. APS, Minutes; *WTR*, 234, 238–39; Lincoln, *History of Worcester*, 83; Lovell, *Worcester in Revolution*, 38. Today, if you go to the clerk's office in the Worcester City Hall and ask to view volume 4, page 21, of the Town Records, you will see the horizontal lines, the spiraling loops, and several finger-size smudges of ink drawn sloppily across the yellow, aging paper. The only words peeking out through all the markings are "some evil minded," an appropriate summation for the mood of the day. On the third and final page of the Protest (page 23), the signatures have been crossed out, but this time the lines are all different: some straight, others looped, and each with a slightly different stroke. This was not the work of one man. From the visual evidence, we can safely surmise that each of the Protestors was called forth to strike his own name from the record.

23. Paine to Thomas Gage, 8/28/74, Wroth, *Province in Rebellion*, document 154, 528–31.

24. Newfield, *Worcester on Eve of Revolution*, 39.

25. The full story of Paine's resignation, with citations, appears in Raphael, *First American Revolution*, 75–79.

26. Gage to Dartmouth, 8/27/74, Gage, *Correspondence*, 1:366.

27. TY to Samuel Adams, 8/19/74, Adams, Papers, NYPL; Wroth, *Province in Rebellion*, 808, 812; Raphael, *First American Revolution*, 82, 237.

28. Wroth, *Province in Rebellion*, 689–92; Boston Committee of Correspondence, Correspondence and Proceedings, reel 1.

29. Undated letter from Joseph Clarke, in Trumbull, *History of Northampton*, 346–48.

30. Gage to Dartmouth, 9/2/74, Gage, *Correspondence*, 370.

31. TY to Samuel Adams, 9/4/74, Adams, Papers, NYPL.

32. Gage to Dartmouth, 9/2/74, Gage, *Correspondence*, 1:372.

33. Stiles, *Literary Diary*, 479–81.

34. John Adams, *Diary and Autobiography*, 2:160.

35. APS, Minutes.

36. Parkman, Diary.

37. Lincoln, *JPCM/CC*, 635–37.

38. Parkman, Diary; Raphael, *First American Revolution*, 130–38.

39. Lincoln, *JPCM/CC*, 638–40.

40. Ibid., 641–44.

41. Elizabeth Adams to Samuel Adams, 9/12/74, Adams, Papers, NYPL. Although Mrs. Adams's letter is dated 9/12, Young's letter to Samuel Adams the following week, cited below, clarifies the date, as does John Andrews to William Barrell, 9/13/74, Andrews, "Letters," 360.

42. TY to Samuel Adams, 9/20/74, Adams, Papers, NYPL.

43. TY to John Lamb, 10/4/74, Lamb, Papers.

44. Ibid.

45. *New York Gazeteer*, 9/8/74, and *Boston Evening-Post*, 9/19/74, cited in Wells, *Samuel Adams*, 2:250.

46. Young's letter is reprinted in Willard, *Letters on the American Revolution*, 32–33.

47. TY to Samuel Adams, 10/11/74, Adams, Papers, NYPL; Edes, "Memoir of Dr. Thomas Young," 27. There is some chance that the two Whitworth incidents, poorly documented, should be conflated into one, but in any case, Young certainly had a penchant for personal confrontation.

48. Simon Pease to Joshua Winslow, 11/3/74, Winslow Papers, MHS.

49. Andrews to Barrell, 10/6, Andrews, "Letters," 373–74.

50. Ibid., 8/29, 348.

51. Judd, Diary, vol. 2 (1773–1782), entry for 9/7/74.

52. *WTR*, 244; Lincoln, *History of Worcester*, 91–92; Lovell, *Worcester in the Revolution*, 50; Nutt, History of Worcester, 538.

53. APS, Minutes.

54. John Pitt to Samuel Adams, 10/16/74, Adams, Papers, NYPL. For additional evidence of the rift between western radicals and the Boston leadership, see Raphael, *First American Revolution*, 172–77, 248–49.

55. Wroth, *Province in Rebellion*, 81–82.

56. Lincoln, *JPCM/CC*, 28–29. Italics appeared in the official minutes.

57. Ibid., 30.

Chapter 7: Going Continental

1. MOW, *History*, 1:147; Rakove, *Beginnings of National Politics*, 38–39; JW to John Adams, 7/14/74, Adams, *Papers*, 2:106, and *Warren-Adams Letters*, 1:26.

2. JW to John Adams, 7/14/74, Adams, *Papers*, 2:107, and *Warren-Adams Letters*, 1:27.

3. John Adams to JW, 6/25/74, Adams, *Papers*, 2:100; MOW to John Adams, 7/14/74, Adams, *Papers*, 2:108, and *Warren-Adams Letters*, 1:28–29; MOW to Abigail Adams, 8/9/74, *Adams Family Correspondence*, 1:139.

4. Joseph Warren to Samuel Adams, 8/15/74 and 8/21/74, in Frothingham, *Joseph Warren*, 339–44.

5. Adams, *Diary and Autobiography*, 2:114; *Pennsylvania Packet*, 2/14/74.

6. *JCC*, 1:25–26.

7. John Adams, *Diary and Autobiography*, 2:134–35.

8. Silas Deane to Elizabeth Deane, 9/7/74, *LDC*, 1:35; Joseph Reed to [Charles Pettit?], 9/4/74, quoted in Rakove, *Beginnings of National Politics*, 45.

9. GW to Bryan Fairfax, 8/24/74, GW, *Papers*, (Col) 10:155.

10. Robert McKenzie to GW, 9/13/74, GW, *Papers*, (Col) 10:161; Diary of GW 9/28/74, 3:280; Adams, *Diary and Autobiography*, 2:140-141; John Adams to Joseph Palmer, 9/27/74, and John Adams to William Tudor, 10/7/74, Adams, *Papers*, 2:173, 187–88; Samuel Adams to Joseph Warren, 9/25/74, Adams, *Writings*, 3:159.

11. GW to Robert McKenzie, 10/9/74, GW, *Papers*, (Col) 10:171–72.

12. Adams, *Diary and Autobiography*, 2:117; Silas Deane to Elizabeth Deane, 9/10/74, *LDC*, 1:61–62; Thomas Lynch to Ralph Izard, 10/26/74, *LDC*, 1:247.

13. The Continental Association appears in *JCC*, 1:75–80. A complete text is reprinted in Greene, *Colonies to Nation*, 247–50.

14. *Pennsylvania Gazette*, 12/7/74.

15. Schlesinger, *Colonial Merchants*, 500.

16. RM to James Duff, 2/26/75, Morris Papers, NYPL.

17. HL to JL, 12/12/74, HL, *Papers*, 10:2–3.

18. Ibid., 3.

19. Ibid., 1/4/75, 10:15.

20. Ibid., 1/18/75, 10:28.

21. JL to HL, 12/3–4/74 and 1/20/75, HL, *Papers*, 9:646 and 10:33.

22. HL to JL, 1/22/75, HL, *Papers*, 10:41.

23. JL to HL, 12/3–4/74, HL, *Papers*, 9:647.

24. HL to JL, 2/6/75, HL, *Papers*, 10:57.

25. Greene, *Colonies to Nation*, 248–49.

26. MOW, *History*, 1:151–54.

27. Force, *American Archives*, 1:1261; Moore, *Diary of American Revolution*, 9–10. See also Oliver, *Origin & Progress of American Rebellion*, 154–55. Oliver added, "And in the month of February following, this same *Dunbar* was selling provisions at *Plimouth*, when the mob seized him, tied him to his horse's tail, & in that manner drove him through dirt & mire out of the Town, & he falling down, his horse hurt him."

28. MOW to John Adams, 1/30/75, *Warren-Adams Letters*, 1:37.

29. John Adams to MOW, 3/15/75, *Warren-Adams Letters*, 1:43.

Chapter 8: Blows Must Decide

1. Fairfax Independent Company to GW, 10/19/74, GW, *Papers*, 10:173.

2. Resolutions of the Fairfax County Committee, GW, *Papers*, 10:236; George Mason to GW, 2/17–18/75, GW, *Papers*, 10:265–69, and Mason, Papers, 1:220–24.

3. "Remarks on Annual Elections for the Fairfax Independent Company," Mason, *Papers*, 1:229–31.

4. George Mason to GW, 2/18/74, Mason, *Papers*, 1:224, and GW, *Papers*, 10:268; King George III to Lord North, 11/18/74, in Commager and Morris, *Spirit of 'Seventy-Six*, 1:61; Middlekauff, *Glorious Cause*, 262.

5. Van Schreeven et al., *Revolutionary Virginia*, 2:366–67.

6. Wirt, *Patrick Henry*, 121–23.

7. James Parker to Charles Stuart, 4/6/75, quoted in Hample, "Liberty or Death Speech," 308. The letter was originally published in *Magazine of History*, Mar. 1906, 158. For more on Patrick Henry's speech, see Raphael, *Founding Myths*, chapter 8.

8. Van Schreeven et al., *Revolutionary Virginia*, 2:374–75.

9. GW to Lord Dunmore, 4/3/75, GW, *Papers*, 10:320–22.

10. Lord Dunmore to GW, 4/18/75, GW, *Papers*, 10:337–38.

11. MOW, *History*, 1:157.

12. Wroth, *Province in Rebellion*, document 458, 1555; TB to William Henshaw, 3/1/75, Henshaw Family Papers, box 1, folder 3, AAS. Three weeks later, in the face of revamped patriot pressure, Wheeler was forced to apologize for his wavering. His recantation of 3/21 is also in the Henshaw Family Papers.

13. Wroth, *Province in Rebellion*, document 671, 1969. Dr. Benjamin Church, a member of the Provincial Congress's Committee of Safety, was the likely source of this intelligence. Three days earlier, an intelligence report stated that "Twelve pieces of Brass Cannon mounted, are att Salem and lodged near the North River, on the back of town." Wroth, *Province in Rebellion*, document 670, 1968.

14. JW to MOW, 4/6/75, *Warren-Adams Letters*, 1:44.

15. Andrews, "Letters," 401.

16. Lincoln, *JPCM/CC*, 135.

17. French, *General Gage's Informers*, 15; "General Gage's Instructions, of 22d February, 1775, to Captain Brown and Ensign D'Bernicre," and "Narrative, &c.," MHS, *Collections* 4 (1916): 204–18.

18. JW to MOW, 4/6/75, *Warren-Adams Letters*, 1:44–45.

19. Andrews, "Letters," 402; Lincoln, *JPCM/CC*, 142–43. See also *Massachusetts Gazette and Boston Post-Boy*, 4/10/75.

20. Spy report of 4/15/75, Wroth, *Province in Rebellion*, document 683, 1981; French, *General Gage's Informers*, 23–24.

21. Thomas, *History of Printing*, 1:180–81; Nutt, *History of Worcester*, 245.

22. Fischer, *Paul Revere's Ride*, 93–94.

23. Fischer, *Paul Revere's Ride*, 90. The following section, unless otherwise noted, follows Fischer's detailed account of the warnings on the night of 4/18, the militia mobilization during that night and the next morning, and the Battles of Lexington and Concord.

24. For the full story of the Concord cannons, and how they might have contributed to Gage's march on Concord, see Bell, "Behold, the Guns Were Gone!"

25. Fischer, *Paul Revere's Ride*, 249.

26. Wade and Lively, *This Glorious Cause*, 9.

Chapter 9: *Rage Militaire*

1. Lincoln, *History of Worcester*, 97.

2. Scheide, "Lexington Alarm," 3–4, 17.

3. Martin, *Narrative*, 6–7. The news arrived in New Haven, ten miles to the east of Milford, around noon on 4/21, and presumably in Milford shortly thereafter.

4. Martin, *Narrative*, 8–9.

5. MOW to Mrs. Bowen, 4/?/75, MOW Letterbook, MHS, cited in Fritz, *Cast for a Revolution*, 131; MOW to Catharine Macaulay, 8/24/75, Gilder-Lehrman Institute, New York City.

6. MOW to JW, 5/3/75, Warren Family Letters, Pilgrim Museum.

7. TY to William Heath, 4/26/75, William Heath Papers, 1:205, MHS.

8. Samuel Ward to Henry Ward, 6/22/75, *LDC*, 1:535. See also John Adams to Abigail Adams, 5/29/75 and 7/7/75, *LDC*, 1:416 and 1:603; *Pennsylvania Journal*, 7/5/75, cited in Hawke, "Eternal Fisher in Troubled Waters," 24.

9. Goodrich, *Lives of the Signers*, 235.

10. RM to General Lee, 7/12/75, Morris MSS, Misc., HSP, quoted in Ver Steeg, *Robert Morris*, 13.

11. *Massachusetts Spy*, 5/3/75, quoted in Schlesinger, *Colonial Merchants*, 232.

12. Royster, *Revolutionary People at War*, 25–53.

13. Drayton, *Memoirs*, 1:222.

14. HL, *Papers*, 10:114.

15. HL to Johann Rodolph Von Valltravers, 5/22/75, and HL to JL, 5/15/75, HL, *Papers*, 10:134 and 10:119–20.

16. HL to Von Valltravers, 5/22/75, and HL to James Laurens, 5/24/75, HL, *Papers*, 10:134 and 10:139.

17. Drayton, *Memoirs of the American Revolution*, 1:252–53. Laurens was reading the report from the General Committee, at which he himself had presided.

18. Hemphill, *JPCSC*, 36–37; Drayton, *Memoirs*, 1:254.

19. HL to JL, 6/8/75, with enclosure, HL, *Papers*, 10:172–79.

20. Ibid., 5/24/75, 10:139–40.

21. Van Schreeven et al., *Revolutionary Virginia*, 3:5 and 3:55.

22. Ibid., 3:55 and 3:6.

23. GW to the Albemarle Independent Company, 5/3/75, GW, *Papers*, 10:350.

24. Pickering, *Plan of Discipline*, 9–10, quoted in Florence, "Minutemen for Months," 76–77.

25. JW to John Adams, 5/5/75, *Warren-Adams Letters*, 1:47.

26. Florence, *Militiamen for Months*, 78.

27. Ibid., 75.

28. Lincoln, *JPCM/CC*, 231.

29. JW to John Adams, 6/18/75, *Warren-Adams Letters*, 1:60.

30. John Adams to JW, 6/27/75, *Warren-Adams Letters*, 1:67.

31. Cash Accounts for June, 1775, GW, *Papers*, (Col) 10:369–70; GW to Martha

Washington, 6/18/75, GW, *Papers*, (Rev) 1:4. A cartouche box was for carrying powder or cartridges.

32. Massachusetts Provincial Congress to GW, 7/3/75, GW, *Papers*, (Rev) 1:53.

33. Wade and Lively, *This Glorious Cause*, 171; MOW to John Adams, 7/5/75, *Warren-Adams Letters*, 1:72. Historian Justin Florence, after examining numerous diaries and letters, concludes that most soldiers attributed little importance to Washington's assumption of command, mentioning it only briefly if at all in their writings. *Militiamen for Months*, 62.

34. GW to Lund Washington, 8/20/75, and GW to Lee, 8/29/75, GW, *Papers*, (Rev) 1:336, 372.

35. The tension between Washington and the "people's army" he commanded is explored in Anderson, "Hinge of the Revolution," 21–48.

36. Mason to [Mr. ———— Brant?], 10/2/78, Mason, *Papers*, 1:434; McDonnell, "Popular Mobilization in Virginia," 955–56.

37. McDonnell, "Popular Mobilization in Virginia," 965–70; McDonnell, *Politics of War*, 111.

38. McDonnell, "Popular Mobilization in Virginia," 966; Fielding Lewis to GW, 11/14/75 and Lund Washington to GW, 12/3/75, GW, *Papers*, (Rev) 1:372 and 1:479.

39. Hemphill, *JPCSC*, 49.

40. HL to Fletchall, 7/14/75, HL, *Papers*, 10:214–18.

41. Fletchall to HL, 7/24/75, and William Thomson to HL, 7/29/75, HL, *Papers*, 10: 245–46, 255.

42. RM to Charles Lee, 8/21/75, quoted in Ver Steeg, *Robert Morris*, 201.

43. Stephenson, "Supply of Gunpowder," 277.

44. GW, *Papers*, (Rev) 1:289, 468; Franklin, *Papers*, 22:163–67.

45. John Adams to Horatio Gates, 4/27/76, *LDC*, 3:587.

46. *JCC*, 12/2/76, 3:396.

47. GW to John Hancock, 9/21/75, GW, *Papers*, (Rev) 2:28.

48. Council of War, 9/11/75, GW, *Papers*, (Rev) 1:451.

49. GW to Arnold, 9/14/75, GW, *Papers*, (Rev) 1:455–59.

50. General Orders, 9/5/75, GW, *Papers*, (Rev) 1:415.

51. Royster, *Revolutionary People at War*, 23–24.

52. Although there is no direct corroboration in the journals of the expedition, the notion that Bigelow climbed Mount Bigelow, and hence bequeathed its name, has been a part of local tradition since at least the early nineteenth century. When Major Return Jonathan Meigs passed by the mountain on 11/17, he reported trying to climb it with Captain Oliver Henchett, but they failed to reach the peak because "we were too late in the day." Roberts, *March to Quebec*, 178. Bigelow passed the mountain shortly before Meigs. He too was undoubtedly tempted to ascend it, and it seems quite plausible that he did.

53. Roberts, *March to Quebec*, 210.

54. Ibid., 75.

55. Bigelow, *Bigelow Family Genealogy*, 1:78, quoted in Desjardin, *Howling Wilderness*, 82.

56. Greenman, *Diary*, 18–19.

57. Timothy Bigelow to Anna Bigelow, 10/28/75, Crane, *Services of Colonel Timothy Bigelow*, 14. Bigelow, in the advance party, reached the Canadian settlements several days before Greenman.

58. Roberts, *March to Quebec*, 677.

59. Ibid., 701. For more on those who were reluctant, including other names, see pages 231, 374, and 429.

60. Ibid., 702. Captain Simeon Thayer reported the pressures exerted on men who evidenced a disinclination to fight: "Dec. 28. Some of the soldiers took 4 men that refus'd to turn out, and led them from place to place with halters round their necks, exposing them to the ridicule of the soldiers, as a punishment due to their effeminate courage." Ibid., 273–74.

61. Greenman, *Diary*, 48.

62. Ibid., 24; Roberts, *March to Quebec*, 154, 157.

Chapter 10: Liberty for All?

1. Josiah Smith to James Poyas, 5/18/75, quoted in Olwell, *Masters, Slaves, and Subjects*, 229, 238; Alden, "John Stuart Accuses William Bell," 320. Olwell suggests that the elliptical reference to "N*****s" instead of "Negroes" marked an attempt, however feeble, to keep this news from the slaves themselves. "Canadiens" refers to the French Acadians, over one thousand in number, who were expelled from Nova Scotia and sent to South Carolina in 1756.

2. Thomas Hutchinson to Council of Safety, 7/5/75, HL, *Papers*, 10:205–7.

3. HL to JL, 6/23/75, HL, *Papers*, 10:191.

4. Lord Campbell to Lord Dartmouth, 8/31/75, and Narrative of George Milligen, 9/15/75, Davies, *Documents of American Revolution*, 11:111.

5. HL to JL, 8/20/75, HL, *Papers*, 10:321; Davies, *Documents of American Revolution*, 11:110–11.

6. Davies, *Documents of American Revolution*, 11:96–97.

7. Ibid., 11:95.

8. HL to JL, 8/20/75, HL, *Papers*, 10:321–22.

9. Ibid., 7/30/75, 10:358.

10. Facsimile of original broadside from Tracy W. McGregor Library, University of Virginia, reproduced in Kaplan and Kaplan, *Black Presence in American Revolution*, 74. Dunmore had drafted his proclamation one week earlier, but he waited until his forces prevailed in a skirmish at Kemp's Landing before publishing it.

11. Edmund Pendleton to Richard Henry Lee, 11/27/75, quoted in Pybus, *Epic Journeys*, 9.

12. Lund Washington to GW, 12/3/75, GW, *Papers*, (Rev) 2:480. Lund was speaking of white bonded servants as well as black slaves. If white servants escaped, he said, slaves would follow. Harry Washington's age, the description of him as a "fine fellow, and the approximate date of his flight from Mount Vernon come from the *Book of Negroes*, book 1, part 2. See also Pybus, *Epic Journeys*, 3, 5, 20, 218.

13. *Maryland Gazette*, 12/14/75, cited in Wood, "Dream Deferred," 185. Pybus questions the story, repeated frequently at the time and since, that the black recruits wore uniforms with this inscription. *Epic Journeys*, 11.

14. Quarles, "Lord Dunmore as Liberator," 494; Frey, *Water from the Rock*, 63; GW to Joseph Reed, 12/15/75, and GW to Richard Henry Lee, 12/26/75, GW, *Papers*, (Rev) 2:553 and 2:611.

15. Mullin, *Flight and Rebellion*, 134; Holton, *Forced Founders*, 158–60.

16. Quarles, *Negro in American Revolution*, 15. Washington's order was actually issued by Horatio Gates, the recently appointed adjutant general. "All Orders transmitted through him from the Commander in Chief, whether written, or verbal, are to be punctually, and immediately obey'd." GW, *Papers*, (Rev) 1:78–79.

17. Council of War, 10/8/75, GW, *Papers*, (Rev) 2:125.

18. General Orders, 11/12/75, GW, *Papers*, (Rev) 2:354.

19. GW to John Hancock, 12/31/75, and General Orders, 12/30/75, GW, *Papers*, (Rev) 2:623 and 2:620.

20. GW, *Papers*, (Rev) 2:625.

21. Lincoln, *History of Worcester*, 99.

22. Zilversmit, *First Emancipation*, 111. The Assembly eventually passed the buck to Congress, wary that there might be "an impropriety in our determination on a question which may ... be of extensive influence, without previously consulting your Honors." Congress made no reply and the abolition bill was never revived.

23. HL and the Council of Safety to Richard Richardson, 12/19/75, HL, *Papers*, 10:576. For more on the raid on Sullivan's Island, see Moultrie, *Memoirs of American Revolution*, 1:113–115; David Ramsay, *History of South Carolina*, 1:50–51; Olwell, *Master, Slaves, and Subjects*, 239–41; Wood, "Dream Deferred," 178–79.

24. HL and the Council of Safety to Stephen Bull, 1/20/76, HL, *Papers*, 11:50.

25. Stephen Bull to HL, 3/14/76, HL, *Papers*, 11:163, or Gibbes, *Documentary History*, 1:268.

26. Council of Safety to Stephen Bull, 3/16/76, HL, *Papers*, 11:172.

27. Patrick Tonyn to David Taitt, 4/20/76, Davies, *Documents of American Revolution*, 12:108–9.

28. Hemphill, *JPCSC*, 256–57.

29. George Galphin to HL, 2/7/76, HL, *Papers*, 11:93–97.

30. Henry Stuart to John Stuart, 8/25/76, Davies, *Documents of American Revolution*, 12:197. With the usual land route cut off by patriots, Stuart had to sail around Florida and land at Mobile. The following description of the council at Chota is based on this letter.

31. Davies, *Documents of American Revolution*, 12:192. The chiefs later claimed they had been tricked into signing the Sycamore Shoals Treaty without a clear understanding of its terms, and American courts invalidated the agreement because it had been made by private parties rather than the government. Most of the white farmers who had moved into the disputed area, however, simply remained where they were, even without valid claims.

32. Calloway, *American Revolution in Indian Country*, 184; Davies, *Documents of American Revolution*, 12:198, 200.

33. Davies, *Documents of American Revolution*, 12:199.

34. Ibid., 12:202.

35. Ibid., 12:203.

36. Adams, *Familiar Letters*, 149–50.

37. John Adams to Abigail Adams, 4/14/76, Adams, *Familiar Letters*, 155.

38. John Adams to James Sullivan, 5/26/76, Adams, *Papers*, 4:208–12.

Chapter 11: Independence

1. Commager and Morris, *Spirit of 'Seventy-Six*, 1:281.

2. JW to John Adams, 11/14–15/75, *Warren-Adams Letters*, 1:181–84.

3. Ibid., 11/15/75, 1:184. A few weeks earlier, Mrs. Warren wrote to Adams directly, claiming that moderates in Congress, "if left to themselves," would not complete "certain important public accounts . . . till the close of the Millenium." MOW to John Adams, 10/?/75, Adams, *Papers*, 3:270, or Warren Family Letters, Pilgrim Museum.

4. Jefferson to John Randolph, 11/29/75, Commager and Morris, *Spirit of 'Seventy-Six*, 1:283.

5. Commager and Morris, *Spirit of 'Seventy-Six*, 1:282.

6. RM to unknown, 12/9/75, *LDC*, 2:470.

7. From Benjamin Rush's *Autobiography*, cited in Commager and Morris, *Spirit of 'Seventy-Six*, 1:285.

8. Paine, *Common Sense*, 69.

9. Ibid., 70.

10. Ibid., 75.

11. Ibid., 76–77.

12. Ibid., 83, 86.

13. Young to John Wendell, 11/23/66, MHS, Photostat Collections.

14. James Bowdoin to MOW, 2/28/76, *Warren-Adams Letters*, 1:209.

15. GW to Joseph Reed, 1/31/76, GW, *Papers*, (Rev) 3:228.

16. HL to JL, 2/22/76, HL, *Papers*, 11:115. See also HL to William Manning, 2/27/76, HL, *Papers*, 11:128.

17. Jensen, *Founding of a Nation*, 649–50.

18. John Adams to Horatio Gates, 3/23/76, *LDC*, 3:431.

19. Jensen, *Founding of a Nation*, 663.

20. The Buckingham instructions are reprinted in Maier, *American Scripture*, 226–29.

21. Selby, *Revolution in Virginia*, 95.

22. Ibid., 97.

23. Ryerson, *Revolution Is Now Begun*, 180–86.

24. Franklin, *Papers*, 22:148.

25. Rosswurm, *Arms, Country, and Class*, 90. For the identification of "Elector" as Thomas Young, see Hawke, "Eternal Fisher in Troubled Waters," 25.

26. *JCC*, 5/10/76, 4:342.

27. Ibid., 5/15/76, 4:358.

28. Marshall, *Diary*, 70–72.

29. John Adams to JW, 5/20/76, *Warren-Adams Letters*, 1:250.

30. *Pennsylvania Gazette*, 5/22/76.

31. Ibid., 5/15/76.

32. Edward Shippen Jr. to Jasper Yeates, 5/23/76, quoted in Hawke, *In the Midst of Revolution*, 146; Marshall, *Diary*, 74.

33. Marshall, *Diary*, 76–77; Ryerson, *Revolution Is Now Begun*, 227.

34. John Adams to John Lowell, 6/12/76, quoted in Hawke, *In the Midst of Revolution*, 165.

35. *JCC*, 6/7/76, 5:425.

36. Thomas Jefferson's Notes of Proceedings in Congress for 6/7–10/76, *LDC*, 4:158–65.

37. "Instructions to the Delegates of Charles County, Maryland," Force, *American Archives*, 6: 1019; Samuel Chase to John Adams, 6/28/76, Adams, *Papers*, 4:351 and *LDC*, 4:305. For instructions from other Maryland counties, see Force, *American Archives*, 6:933, 1017–21.

38. Maier, *American Scripture*, 47–96, 217–34. The instructions from the New York mechanics are reprinted in Raphael, *Founding Myths*, 304–5.

39. John Adams to Samuel Chase, 7/1/76, *LDC*, 4:347; Proceedings in Congress, *LDC*, 4:359.

40. Caesar Rodney to Thomas Rodney, 7/4/76, *LDC*, 4:387–88.

41. Gadsden to Samuel Adams, 4/4/79, Gadsden, *Writings*, 163.

42. "June 2, Sunday—Went to Christ's Church, hiss'd the Minister for praying for the King as in the Littany," Charles Willson Peale, Diary, quoted in Hawke, *In the Midst of Revolution*, 143; Gough, *Christ Church*, 141.

43. RM to Silas Deane, 6/5/76, *LDC*, 4:146–48.

44. John Adams to Abigail Adams, 7/3/76, Adams, *Familiar Letters*, 193.

45. Ibid.

46. Thomas Jefferson to Henry Lee, 5/8/1825, Jefferson, *Writings*, 10:343.

47. McCullough, *1776*, 135; GW, *Papers*, (Rev) 5:245–46.

48. McCullough, *1776*, 137; *New York Gazette*, 7/22/76.

49. *Massachusetts Spy*, 7/24/76. Reprinted in Lincoln, *History of Worcester*, 103.

50. *JCC*, 7/4/76, 5:516.

51. RM to Joseph Reed, 7/21/76, *LDC*, 4:511–12.

52. RM to Silas Deane, 8/11/76, *LDC*, 4:657; Abernathy, *Western Lands*, 159–60. On 9/12, Morris told Deane that if he pursued the "trade plan" he had outlined, "it will reward you beyond any other pursuit." *LDC*, 5:147.

53. HL to JL, 8/14/76, HL, *Papers*, 11:228, 234.

54. Ibid., 11:224-225.

55. Ibid., 11:234.

56. Marshall, *Diary*, 81.

57. MOW to John Adams, 3/10/76, and MOW to John Adams, 10/?/75, Adams, *Papers*, 4:50 and 3:268, or Warren Family Letters, Pilgrim Museum; MOW to Colonel James Otis, 1775, Warren Family Letters, Pilgrim Museum; MOW to John Adams, 4/3/76, Adams, *Papers*, 4:108–9, or Warren Family Letters, Pilgrim Museum.

Chapter 12: Battle Lines

1. Schecter, *Battle for New York*, 4.

2. JPM, *Narrative*, xii, 16–17.

3. Ibid., 16.

4. Washington, *Papers* (Rev), 6:315; JPM, *Narrative*, 34.

5. JPM, *Narrative*, 41, 36.

6. GW to John Hancock (President of Congress), 9/16/76, GW, *Papers* (Rev), 6:313.

7. Nathanael Greene to Nicholas Cooke, 9/17/76, Greene, *Papers*, 1:300; Schecter, *Battle for New York*, 186; Washington, *Papers* (Rev), 6:316.

8. JPM, *Narrative*, 23, 26.

9. Washington, *Papers* (Rev), 6:288.

10. GW to Hancock, 9/25/76, GW, *Papers* (Rev), 6:393–400. The following quotations also come from this letter.

11. JL to HL, 12/3–4/74, HL, *Papers*, 9:647.

12. Ibid., 8/14/76, 11:226.

13. HL to Hope & Co., 8/17/76, and JL to HL, 8/14/76, HL, *Papers*, 11:248 and 11:227–29.

14. Hatley, *Dividing Paths*, 193; Calloway, *American Revolution in Indian Country*, 197.

15. Drayton to Francis Salvador, 7/24/76, Gibbes, *Documentary History*, 2:29.

16. HL to Hope & Co., 8/17/76, HL, *Papers*, 11:248; Williamson to Drayton, 8/22/76, Gibbes, *Documentary History*, 3:32: HL to Williamson, 9/3/65, and HL to James Laurens, 9/27/76, HL, *Papers*, 5:2 and 11:271–72. Historian Tom Hatley notes that three thousand head of cattle that accompanied the soldiers, together with all the horses and mules, added "a variation on scorched earth" as they devoured the forage. "Where we encamped," one of the soldiers recalled after the war, in "one night the beeves destroyed the whole of it even to the stumps, and destroyed the grass to the bare ground." Hatley, *Dividing Paths*, 219.

17. Cited in Hatley, *Dividing Paths*, 199–200.

18. Hatley, *Dividing Paths*, 195.

19. In the words of John Stuart, "The Cherokees are rather divided. A great number of them for the purpose of obtaining permission to return to their towns have patched up a peace with the rebels, while a far greater number of them have moved

near one hundred miles lower down the river where they have built a large town and made considerable settlement, and although threatened by the rebels with destruction are not intimidated." John Stuart to Lord George Germain, 12/4/78, Davies, *Documents of American Revolution*, 15: 284–85.

20. JL to HL, 8/14/76, HL, *Papers*, 11:229.

21. JL to Martha Laurens, 8/17/76, HL, *Papers*, 11:255–56.

22. *Pennsylvania Evening Post*, 4/22/76; Edes, "Dr. Thomas Young," 41.

23. Rosswurm, *Arms, Country, and Class*, 101, 104.

24. The Pennsylvania Constitution of 1776, passed on September 28, is reprinted in Greene, *Colonies to Nation*, 339–45.

25. Marshall, *Diary*, 98.

26. RM to Silas Deane, 6/5/76, *LDC*, 4:146.

27. GW to Lund Washington, 9/30/76, GW, *Papers*, (Rev) 6:441–42.

28. JPM, *Narrative*, 47. Help was on the way, however minimal: on September 20, the Secret Committee of Commerce ordered Robert Morris, one of its members, "to write to the Continental Agents in Connecticut & Rhode Island to get 600 tents made up with all possible expedition & send them as fast as made to Genl. Washington." Secret Committee Minutes, 9/20/76, *LDC*, 5:207.

29. JPM, *Narrative*, 51.

30. Ibid., 54–55.

31. GW to Greene, 11/16/76, and Greene to GW, 11/18/76, GW, *Papers* (Rev), 7:165 and 7:176.

32. Schecter, *Battle for New York*, 255; McCullough, *1776*, 244; Charles Lee to Horatio Gates, 12/13/76, Commager and Morris, *Spirit of 'Seventy Six*, 1:500.

33. JPM, *Narrative*, 57–58.

34. Charles Lee to GW, 11/30/76, GW, *Papers*, (Rev) 7:235. Although Lee resisted submitting to GW, he insisted that because he was second in command, other generals must submit to him. Only four days earlier, he had scolded General William Heath for presuming that he enjoyed a "command separate from and independent of any other superior—that General Heath and General Lee are merely two Major Generals, who perhaps ought to hold a friendly intercourse with each other." This was not the case, Lee insisted. With Washington gone, Lee stated firmly, "I of course command on this side the Water [Hudson River]. . . . For the future I will and must be obey'd." Charles Lee to William Heath, 11/26/76, GW, *Papers*, (Rev) 7:218.

35. GW to Samuel Washington, 12/18/76, GW, *Papers* (Rev), 7:371.

36. Commager and Morris, *Spirit of 'Seventy Six*, 1:505.

37. RM and Benjamin Franklin to Silas Deane, 10/1/76, *LDC*, 5:279.

38. Committee of Secret Correspondence Statement, 10/1/76, *LDC*, 5:273. Emphasis appears in Franklin, *Papers of Benjamin Franklin*, 22:637.

39. RM to Deane, 9/12/76, *LDC*, 5:147; RM to Bingham, 12/4/76 and 4/25/77, *LDC*, 5:572–73; 6:651.

40. *JCC*, 6:1027.

41. RM to Silas Deane, 12/20/76, *LDC*, 5:622.

42. Ibid., 5:627; Oberholtzer, *Robert Morris*, 293.

43. *JCC*, 6:1042 and 6:1032.

44. RM to William Bingham, 12/4/76, *LDC*, 5:574; Tinkcom, "Revolutionary City," 128; Marshall, *Diary*, 105.

45. Fischer, *Washington's Crossing*, 192–201.

46. GW to Hancock, 12/20/76, GW, *Papers* (Rev), 7:382.

47. Ibid., 7:385.

48. Joseph Reed to GW, 12/22/76, GW, *Papers* (Rev), 7:414.

49. Fischer, *Washington's Crossing*, 202–3, 208–9.

50. *JCC*, 6:1043–46.

51. Executive Committee to GW, 12/28/76, *LDC*, 5:686–87.

52. GW to Hancock, 12/29/76, GW, *Papers* (Rev), 7:477.

53. GW to RM, 12/31/76, GW, *Papers* (Rev), 7:497.

54. RM to GW, 1/1/77, GW, *Papers* (Rev), 7:508.

55. GW to Hancock, 1/5/77, GW, *Papers* (Rev), 7:521.

56. Ibid., 7:523.

57. MOW to JW, 12/29 and 12/31/76, Warren Family Letters, Pilgrim Museum.

Chapter 13: Home Rule—First Drafts

1. *Pennsylvania Evening Post*, 3/15/77, quoted in Brunhouse, *Counter-Revolution in Pennsylvania*, 27.

2. *Pennsylvania Evening Post*, 4/10/77; Brunhouse, *Counter-Revolution in Pennsylvania*, 28, 30, 239, note 47.

3. For confirmation that Young was the creator of the name "Vermont," consider the 1786 petition of Ethan Allen, Thomas Chittenden, and Joseph Fay to the Vermont Assembly for the relief of Young's family. Young deserved official recognition, they said, "having pointed out the system to be pursued to establish Government by a separate jurisdiction & to whom we stand indebted for the name of Vermont." Quoted in Edes, "Dr. Thomas Young," 53.

4. Quoted in Edes, "Dr. Thomas Young," 44–45; Evans, Early American Imprints, 1:15649.

5. Adams to Lee, 6/29/77, *LDC*, 7:264.

6. Edes, "Dr. Thomas Young," 12; Duane to Livingston, 6/28/77, *LDC*, 7:260; *JCC*, 6/30/77, 8:511, 513.

7. *Independent Chronicle* (Boston), 7/17/77, quoted in Edes, "Dr. Thomas Young," 49.

8. Main, *The Sovereign States*, 147–51.

9. Greene, *Colonies to Nation*, 339–45.

10. Main, *Sovereign States*, 162.

11. Mason, *Papers*, 1:277–78

12. Ibid., 1:284.

13. Ibid., 1:288.

14. There were two notable exceptions: the 1579 Union of Utrecht, which formed

the basis for the Dutch Republic, and the Iroquois Confederacy, a long-lasting bond between six Indian nations that allowed for shared sovereignty. Certainly, people like Benjamin Franklin were familiar with the broad principles of the Iroquois Confederation; less certain is the willingness of Franklin and others to follow the intellectual and institutional leadership of a people whom they regarded as less civilized than themselves. There was one historic example of a brief confederation in British North America. More than a century past, back in 1643, four New England colonies (Massachusetts Bay, Plymouth, Connecticut, and Hartford) had entered "into a firm and perpetual league of friendship and unity for offense and defense, . . . and for their mutual safety and welfare." Mathews, "Franklin's Plans for Colonial Union," 396. For a while the confederation performed its common mission of fighting Indians, but the new colonies of Rhode Island and Maine were denied membership for religious and political reasons, and the largest colony, Massachusetts Bay, balked at picking up the lion's share of the bill. After King Philip's War in 1675 and 1676, the confederation fell apart.

15. Franklin, *Papers*, 22:122–23.

16. *JCC*, 5:425.

17. Ibid., 5:433.

18. Dickinson's draft appears in *LDC*, 4:232–50.

19. The committee draft of July 12 appears in *JCC*, 5:546–54.

20. The final draft of the Articles of Confederation appears in *JCC*, 9:907–25, and Greene, *Colonies to Nation*, 428–35.

21. Freeman, *George Washington*, 4:554.

22. Ferguson, *Power of the Purse*, 26.

23. RM to Silas Deane, 12/20/76, and RM to John Jay, 1/12/77, *LDC*, 5:623 and 6:87.

24. Ver Steeg, *Robert Morris*, 5, 201.

25. RM to William Bingham, 4/25/77; RM to Jonathan Hudson, 6/18/77 and 6/24/77; RM to William Whipple, 9/4/77, *LDC*, 6:651; 7:207 and 7:248; 6:603.

26. HL to JL, 2/3/77, HL, *Papers*, 11:294.

27. Charles Thomson's Notes of Debates, 7/24–25/77, *LDC*, 7:371–75.

28. John Adams to Abigail Adams, 8/19/77, Adams, *Familiar Letters*, 292; HL, *Papers*, 10:xxi; see also 11:xvi–xvi for a similar letter.

29. HL to John Lewis Gervais, 9/5/77, HL, *Papers*, 11:487.

30. Oberholtzer, *Robert Morris*, 14. It remains unclear who exactly had done the "offering," and we have only Mary's word to go on.

31. Mires, *Independence Hall*, 24.

Chapter 14: In Victory and Defeat

1. *WTR*, 294.

2. *Massachusetts Spy*, 4/17/77 and 5/22/77; *WTR*, 298–303; Lincoln, *History of Worcester*, 105–6; Crane, *Colonel Timothy Bigelow*, 39–43.

3. Middlekauff, *The Glorious Cause*, 372.

4. *WTR*, 302.

5. Nutt, *History of Worcester,* 561; APS, Minutes; Lincoln, *History of Worcester,* 106.

6. Crane, *Colonel Timothy Bigelow,* 43.

7. Ibid., 44.

8. Morton and Spinelli, *Beaumarchais,* 110.

9. Crane, *Colonel Timothy Bigelow,* 46; Hannah Winthrop to MOW, 11/11/77, *Warren-Adams Letters,* 2:451.

10. Freeman, *George Washington,* 4:500.

11. JL to James Laurens, 10/25/76, HL, *Papers,* 11:277.

12. HL to John Lewis Gervais, 8/9/77, HL, *Papers,* 11:428.

13. JL to HL, 8/13/77, HL, *Papers,* 11:453.

14. Royster, *Revolutionary People at War,* 225; HL to Gervais, 10/8/77, HL, *Papers,* 11:547.

15. Massey, *John Laurens,* 76–77.

16. HL to JL, 10/8/77, HL, *Papers,* 11: 548–49.

17. HL to Gervais, 10/8/77, HL, *Papers,* 11:547.

18. JPM, *Narrative,* 59–61.

19. Ibid., 88–92.

20. Ibid., 91–92.

21. Ibid., 95.

22. Ibid., 100.

23. Ibid., 101.

24. GW to HL, 12/23/77, HL, *Papers,* 192.

25. JL to HL, 12/23/77, HL, *Papers,* 190.

26. JPM, *Narrative,* 104, 114; GW to Nathanael Greene, 2/12/78, GW, *Writings,* 10:454–55.

27. TB to General Heath, 4/7/78, quoted on the Timothy Bigelow genealogical Web site, http://www.bigelowsociety.com/rod/coltim4.htm, posted January 8, 2000, consulted May 1, 2007.

28. Chevalier du Plessis to HL, 2/8/78, HL, *Papers,* 12:425; Massey, *John Laurens,* 88–89; JL to HL, 3/9/78 and 2/9/78, HL, *Papers,* 12:530 and 12:430.

29. JL to HL, 1/23/78, HL, *Papers,* 12:330.

30. Ibid., 12/23/77, 12:191.

31. HL, *Papers,* 12:359–62.

32. JL to HL, 1/3/78, HL, *Papers,* 12:244–45.

33. Lesser, *Sinews of Independence,* 54–73.

34. JL to HL, 6/1/78, HL, *Papers,* 13:390.

35. JPM, *Narrative,* 127.

36. Ibid., 127.

37. Ibid., 127, 131.

38. Ibid., 132–33. While textbooks today conflate the subject of Martin's account with a real and identifiable woman from Carlisle, Pennsylvania, we have no clue as to

her actual identity. We do know there were many others like her, women who joined with men in battle, firing cannons and hauling water in buckets and generally performing their fair share of physical labor on behalf of the Continental Army. For the origins of the Molly Pitcher legend, see Raphael, *Founding Myths*, 27–44.

39. JPM, *Narrative*, 130.

40. JL to HL, 6/30/78 and 7/2/78, HL, *Papers*, 13:532–37, 543–45.

41. Ibid., 8/22/78, HL, 14:202.

42. Greene to GW, 8/31/78, Greene, *Papers*, 2:502.

43. JPM, *Narrative*, 150, 153.

Chapter 15: Falling Apart

1. *WTR*, 315–17.

2. Ibid., 288, 317; Minutes, APS, at AAS.

3. MOW, *Poems, Dramatic*.

4. Zagarri, *Woman's Dilemma*, 101; JW to John Adams, 6/13/79, *Warren-Adams Letters*, 2:105.

5. JW to Samuel Adams, 10/25/79, *Warren-Adams Letters*, 2:59–60.

6. RM to James Duane, 9/8/78, *LDC*, 10:607; *JCC*, 12/9/78, 12:1205.

7. Wallace, *Henry Laurens*, 346; Charles Thomson to Committee of Congress, 9/6/79, *LDC*, 13:460.

8. HL to Committee of Congress, 9/1/79, HL, *Papers*, 15:159.

9. Mason, *Papers*, 2:399–409; 2:414–22.

10. Abernathy, *Western Lands*, 228.

11. Mason, *Papers*, 2:595–98.

12. Mason, Jefferson, and Wythe to Clark, 1/3/78, Mason, *Papers*, 1:410.

13. Abernathy, *Western Lands*, 196–97.

14. Clark to Mason, 11/19/79, Mason, *Papers*, 2:555–88.

15. GW to Sullivan, 5/31/79, GW, *Writings*, 15:189–93.

16. Dearborn, *Revolutionary War Journals*, 159.

17. Cook, *Journals of Sullivan Expedition*, 90–91, 112–13.

18. Young, *Forgotten Patriot*, 12–13; RM to Bradford, 10/8/76, *LDC*, 5:321.

19. Rosswurm, *Arms, Country, and Class*, 178.

20. *Pennsylvania Gazette*, 6/2/79.

21. Statement of July 7, printed in the *Pennsylvania Gazette*, 12/15/79.

22. Peale, *Selected Papers*, 1:318–19.

23. Silas Deane, quoted in Rosswurm, *Arms, Country, and Class*, 191; *Pennsylvania Gazette*, 7/28/79.

24. Rosswurm, *Arms, Country, and Class*, 192.

25. Morris, *Papers*, 1:214; Rosswurm, *Arms, Country, and Class*, 195–97.

26. Rosswurm, *Arms, Country, and Class*, 206.

27. Marshall, *Diary*, 223.

28. Sellers, *Charles Willson Peale*, 178.

29. Rosswurm, *Arms, Country, and Class*, 211–17; Alexander, "Fort Wilson Incident," 602–10.

30. HL to John Adams, 10/4/79, HL, *Papers*, 15:182.

31. Alexander, "Fort Wilson Incident," 607–8; Rosswurm, *Arms, Country, and Class*, 217–27; Smith, *James Wilson*, 136–39.

32. Thacher, *Military Journal*, 184–85.

33. JPM, *Narrative*, 172.

34. Greene to Benoni Hathaway, 1/6/80, Greene, *Papers*, 5:243; Lesser, *Sinews of Independence*, 144–69.

35. JPM, *Narrative*, 182.

36. Ibid., 182–86.

37. GW to Jonathan Meigs, 5/26/80, and GW to Trumbull, 5/26/80, GW, *Writings*, 18:424–25.

38. GW to Reed, 5/28/80, GW, *Writings*, 18:434–35.

39. JL to HL, 1/14/78, HL, *Papers*, 12:305.

40. GW to HL, 3/20/79, GW, *Writings*, 14:267; HL to JL, 2/6/78, HL, *Papers*, 12:413; Ramsay to William Henry Drayton, 9/1/79, Gibbes, *Documentary History*, 2:121.

41. Massey, *John Laurens*, 157; GW to JL, 4/26/80, GW, *Writings*, 18:300.

42. JL to HL, 5/25/80, HL, *Papers*, 15:300.

43. James Custer to HL, 6/?/80, HL, *Papers*, 15:301–2. See also JL to HL, 5/25/80, HL, *Papers*, 15:300.

44. Samuel Massey to HL, 6/12/80, HL, *Papers*, 15:305–6.

45. Ibid., 15:305, and note 3.

46. HL to Richard Henry Lee, 8/1/80, HL, *Papers*, 15:320–3.

47. HL, Journal and Narrative of Capture and Confinement in the Tower of London, HL, *Papers*, 15:330–5.

48. MOW to WW, 3/25/80, Warren Family Letters, Pilgrim Museum.

49. HL, *Papers*, 15:344, 623–24.

50. WW to MOW, 4/28/81, cited in Warren, "Young American's Adventures," 253.

51. Warren, "Young American's Adventures," 252.

52. Hamilton to James Duane, 9/3/80, Hamilton, *Papers*, 2:400–18.

53. James Lovell to Elbridge Gerry, 11/20/80, *LDC*, 16:364.

54. Ibid., 9/5/80, 16:20.

55. Jensen, "Idea of National Government," 370.

56. JW to Samuel Adams, 12/4/80, *Warren-Adams Letters*, 2:152.

57. JPM, *Narrative*, 196.

58. Lesser, *Sinews of Independence*, 193; Secretary of Commonwealth, *Massachusetts Soldiers and Sailors*, 2:27; Wright, *Continental Army*, 214.

59. GW to Henry Knox, 7/28/80, GW, *Writings*, 19:275.

60. GW, General Orders, 2/18/81, GW, *Writings*, 21:241.

61. Nutt, *History of Worcester*, 59; Washington County, Town of Montpelier Web

site, http://www.rootsweb.com/~vermont/WashCoTownMontpelier.html (consulted Sept. 9, 2005).

62. *WTR*, 377–86.

63. The list of recruits appears in Nutt, *History of Worcester*, 562. Twelve of twenty-one appear in *Massachusetts Soldiers and Sailors*, and ten of these listings record occupations. "List of Voters for the Year 1779 in Worcester," Worcester Society of Antiquity, *Proceedings*, 16 (1899): 451–52.

64. Circular letter to New England and New York, 1/20/80, GW, *Writings*, 21:130.

65. GW to the President of Congress, 1/23/81, and GW to Commissioners for Redressing the Grievances of the New Jersey Line, GW, *Writings*, 21:136 and 21:147; Freeman, *George Washington*, 5:247–49.

66. GW to JL, 4/9/81, GW, *Writings*, 21:439.

Chapter 16: Endgame

1. William Pierce to St. George Tucker, 7/20/81, cited in Frey, *Water from the Rock*, 133.

2. Casualty statistics are from Peckham, *Toll of Independence*, and Symonds, *Battlefield Atlas*.

3. Symonds, *Battlefield Atlas*, 93.

4. Phillips, *Cousins' Wars*, 162, 638; Greene to Samuel Huntington, 12/28/80, Greene, *Papers*, 7:9, quoted in Hoffman, *Uncivil War*, 107–8.

5. Pybus, *Epic Journeys*, 45; GW, *Writings*, 22:14. Pybus (45–46) argues that Lund's list, which includes the name of "Harry, a man about 40 years old, valuable, a horseler," was prepared in 1783, with an eye to laying claims to the British for lost property. Harry Washington apparently fled five years earlier (see chapter 10).

6. *JCC*, 2/7/81, 19:126.

7. RM to President of Congress, 3/13/81, RM, *Papers*, 1:17–19.

8. Jensen, *New Nation*, 60.

9. RM, *Papers*, 66–72; *JCC*, 5/26/81, 20:545–48.

10. RM to Benjamin Harrison, 1/15/82, RM, *Papers*, 4:46.

11. Reed to Greene, 11/1/81, RM, *Papers*, 1:21.

12. RM, *Papers*, 1:70.

13. GW to Comte de Rochambeau, 6/13/81, and GW to Board of War, 6/28/81, GW, *Writings*, 22:208 and 22:280.

14. GW, *Writings*, 22:102–3, 388; Freeman, *George Washington*, 5:300.

15. GW, *Diary*, 3:409; Freeman, *George Washington*, 5:308–9.

16. GW to President of Congress, GW, *Writings*, 23:14; RM to GW, 8/28/81, RM, *Papers*, 2:147.

17. RM, *Papers*, 2:158–59.

18. Ibid., 2:173; GW to RM, 9/6/81, RM, *Papers*, 2:205.

19. RM, *Papers*, 2:172.

20. JPM, *Narrative*, 222–23.

21. General Orders, 7/22/80, GW, *Writings*, 19:224.

22. JPM, *Narrative*, 230.

23. Ibid., 241–42.

24. Freeman, *George Washington*, 5:377.

25. Massey, *John Laurens*, 125; Hamilton, *Papers*, 1:602–4.

26. GW to Cornwallis, 10/18/81, GW, *Writings*, 23:237.

27. JPM, *Narrative*, 240–41.

28. Freeman, *George Washington*, 5:388.

29. Massey, *John Laurens*, 201.

30. HL, *Papers*, 15:436.

31. Ibid., 15:456–57.

32. JPM, *Narrative*, 248.

33. Ibid., 255–58.

34. GW, *Writings*, 23:271, 297, 302, 347, 352, 356, 359, 361, 365, 367, 390, 443, 447, 477; GW to Greene, 11/16/81, GW, *Writings*, 23:347.

35. Freeman, *George Washington*, 5:513; Mackesy, *War for America*, 524–25.

36. Zeisberger, *Diary*, 1:79–81.

37. Brackenridge, *Narratives*, 9–12.

38. William Irvine to GW, 7/11/82, *Washington Papers*, Library of Congress, 4:387–88; GW to William Irvine, 8/6/82, GW, *Writings*, 24:474.

39. GW to Sullivan, 5/31/79, GW, *Writings*, 15:189–93; Cook, *Journals of Sullivan Expedition*, 8.

40. JL to HL, 3/9/78, HL, *Papers*, 12:532.

41. Massey, *John Laurens*, 208; Klein, *Unification of a Slave State*, 107.

42. Massey, *John Laurens*, 205.

43. Greene to Henry Lee, 6/6/82, Massey, *John Laurens*, 219.

44. JL to Greene, 3/9/82, Greene, *Papers*, 10:473; Greene to Henry Lee, 4/22/82, in Massey, *John Laurens*, 216.

45. Hamilton to JL, 8/15/82, Hamilton, *Papers*, 3:145.

46. Massey, *John Laurens*, 227.

47. Peckham, *Toll of Independence*, 96.

Chapter 17: Settling Up

1. HL to Franklin, 5/16/82, HL, *Papers*, 15:501.

2. *JCC*, 9/17/82, 23:584.

3. HL to Adams, 11/12/82, HL, *Papers*, 16:55.

4. *JCC*, 20:651–52.

5. Morris, *Peacemakers*, 383.

6. Ibid., 375–77.

7. Adams, *Diary and Autobiography*, 3:80–82; HL to Gervais, 4/4/84, HL, *Papers*, 16:403; "Preliminary Articles of Peace: November 30, 1782," Avalon Project at

Yale Law School, http://www.yale.edu/lawweb/avalon/diplomacy/britain/prel1782 .htm (consulted Sept. 23, 2007).

8. HL, *Papers*, 16:73–74, 264–68; Pybus, *Epic Journeys*, 61.

9. HL to Oswald, 8/16/83, HL, *Papers*, 16:267.

10. Ver Steeg, *Robert Morris*, 166–67.

11. *JCC*, 24:291.

12. Luzerne to RM, 1/18/83, RM, *Papers*, 7:319.

13. RM to President of Congress, 1/24/83, RM, *Papers*, 7:368.

14. *JCC*, 24:285–86.

15. Ibid., 24:294–97.

16. Ibid., 24:307–9. After delivering his speech, Washington endeavored to read a letter that indicated Congress's commitment to paying the soldiers, but as he fumbled with his papers, he confessed (the words are not exact): "Gentleman, you must pardon me. I have grown grey and now find myself growing blind." Freeman, *George Washington*, 5:435. Starting in the second quarter of the nineteenth century and continuing ever since, Americans have been told that Washington staged his confession on purpose, that he carried the day because of the pity he instilled by this passing remark, and even, in many tellings, that his little ploy came before, not after, his formal presentation. This interpretation does the commander in chief, who sought respect rather than sympathy, a great injustice. George Washington carried the day because of a masterful performance, starting with his initial response and continuing through his persuasive address.

17. G. Morris to John Jay, 1/1/83, and G. Morris to Knox, 2/7/83, RM, *Papers*, 7:256 and 7:417–18.

18. JW to JA, 10/27/83 and 1/28/85, *Warren-Adams Letters*, 2:230, 248.

19. GW to President of Congress, 3/19/83, GW, *Writings*, 26:238.

20. *JCC*, 24:242.

21. For the various accounts, some quoted below, see GW, *Writings*, 26:401–12; Wilson, *Loyal Blacks*, 60 n. 35.

22. Wiencek, *Imperfect God*, 257.

23. GW to Harrison, 5/6/83, GW, *Writings*, 26:401.

24. *Book of Negroes*, book 1, part 1.

25. GW to Parker, 4/28/83, GW, *Writings*, 26:364.

26. *Book of Negroes*, book 1, part 2.

27. Nova Scotia Archives and Record Management, Halifax, researched by Cassandra Pybus. This portion of the *Book of Negroes* does not appear on the Black Loyalists Web site.

28. Boston King's complete narrative is reprinted in Carretta, *Unchained Voices*, 351–66.

29. Pybus, *Epic Journeys*, 63–64: Wilson, *Loyal Blacks*, 65.

30. RM to President of Congress, 5/1/83 and 5/3/83, and RM to GW, 5/29/83, RM, *Papers*, 7:777, 789, and 8:131.

31. For a detailed account of the Philadelphia mutiny, see RM, *Papers*, 8:215–38.

32. JPM, *Narrative*, 275–82.

33. *WTR* (1784–1800), 439.

34. Town of Montpelier website, http://www.rootsweb.com/~vermont/WashCoTown Montpelier.html (consulted Oct. 19, 2007).

35. *WTR* (1784–1800), 423.

36. Freeman, *George Washington*, 5:460–61.

37. *Rivington's New-York Gazette*, 11/26/83.

38. GW to Henry Knox, 12/3/83, GW, *Writings*, 27:258; *Rivington's New-York Gazette*, 12/3/83.

39. GW, *Writings*, 27:254.

40. The resignation, dated 12/21/83, is in GW, *Writings*, 27:284–85.

41. GW, *Writings*, 26:483–96.

Chapter 18: Desires and Discontents

1. GW, *Writings*, 27:285.

2. GW to Parker, 9/12/83, GW, *Writings*, 27:150–51; GW, *Diary*, 4:157.

3. GW to Fielding Lewis, 2/27/84, GW, *Writings*, 27:346.

4. GW to Augustine Washington, 6/6/80, GW, *Writings*, 19:135.

5. GW to James Duane, GW, *Writings*, 27:133–40; GW, *Diary*, 4:28.

6. GW, *Diary*, 4:22.

7. Ibid., 4:58.

8. GW to RM, 2/1/85, GW, *Writings*, 28:55.

9. Quoted in Slaski, *Thomas Willing*, 336.

10. RM to Congress, 3/8/83, RM, *Papers*, 7:525–530. The intriguing "window tax," a simple method of assessing wealth, was first proposed by Gouverneur Morris in 1780 (7:537).

11. JW to Gerry, 11/16/83, Gardiner, *Study in Dissent*, 171.

12. Quoted in Young, *Robert Morris*, 168.

13. RM, *Papers*, 8:343.

14. MOW to WW, 8/22/84, Warren Family Letters, Pilgrim Museum, 2:181.

15. Ibid., 9/12/82, 2:123.

16. Ibid., 11/10/84, 2:197.

17. Ibid., 2:198; MOW to Elbridge Gerry, 6/6/83, Gardiner, *Study in Dissent*, 162.

18. MOW to Gerry, 6/6/83, Gardiner, *Study of Dissent*, 163.

19. Davies, *Macaulay and Warren*, 255.

20. MOW to George Warren, 3/7/85, Warren Family Letters, Pilgrim Museum, 2:217.

21. Quoted in Davies, *Macaulay and Warren*, 235–36.

22. Sarah Vaughan to Catherine Livingston, 5/20/85, quoted in Davies, *Macaulay and Warren*, 229.

23. MOW to WW, 11/10/84, Warren Family Letters, Pilgrim Museum, 2:198.

24. MOW to George Warren, 3/24/85, Warren Family Letters, Pilgrim Museum, 2:219.

25. HL, *Papers*, 16:504, 522.

26. HL to William Bell, 2/7/85, HL, *Papers*, 16:535–36.

27. Nadelhaft, *Disorders of War*, 145, 156–57.

28. Edgar, *South Carolina*, 246.

29. HL to Michael Hillegas, 4/14/86, HL, *Papers*, 16:645–46.

30. HL to John Lewis Gervais, 5/5/84, HL, *Papers*, 16:451.

31. HL to Hamilton, 4/19/85, HL, *Papers*, 16:553–55.

32. HL to Jacob Read, 7/16/85 and 9/15/85, HL, *Papers*, 16:579–80, 597.

33. HL to Read, 9/15/85, HL, *Papers*, 16:597.

34. HL to Hamilton, 4/19/85, HL, *Papers*, 16:554–55

35. JW to Adams, 4/30/86, *Warren-Adams Letters*, 2:272–73.

36. Feer, *Shays's Rebellion*, 95, 176–79; Szatmary, *Shays' Rebellion*, 39.

37. Feer, *Shays's Rebellion*, 60; Szatmary, *Shays' Rebellion*, 29–31; Lincoln, *History of Worcester*, 116.

38. *Worcester Magazine*, 39:2 (Dec. 1786) 473–75, quoted in Colton, "Unwilling to Stain the Land."

39. Lincoln, *History of Worcester*, 118–21.

40. *JCC*, 31:893–96.

41. Szatmary, *Shays' Rebellion*, 83–84; JW to John Adams, 5/18/87, *Warren-Adams Letters*, 2:293.

42. *JCC*, 31:895.

43. MOW to John Adams, 12/?/86, Warren Family Letters, Pilgrim Museum, 2:268.

44. Moynihan, "Meetinghouse vs. Courthouse," 45; Rice, *Worcester Town Records* (1784–1800), 128.

45. Szatmary, *Shays' Rebellion*, 57–59, 123–26.

46. GW to Knox, 12/26/86, GW, *Writings*, 29:122.

Chapter 19: New Rules

1. *JCC*, 31:893.

2. *Massachusetts Centinel*, 8/7/84, quoted in Jensen, *New Nation*, 124.

3. Caughey, *McGillivray*, 91–92.

4. *DHRC*, 1:180, 184.

5. Ibid., 1:187.

6. Madison, *DFC*, 17–18.

7. The official records are sparse, neglecting all debate and transcribing only the formal motions. There was one other copious note taker, Robert Yates, but he was not quite so thorough, and he departed less than halfway through. Several others took notes during particular sessions, and one, William Pierce of Georgia, jotted down his personal impressions of each of the delegates.

8. GW, *Diaries*, 5:156.

9. Madison, *DFC*, 5/28, 26–27; Elliot, *JFC*, 1:141.

10. Madison, *DFC*, 5/29, 28; Elliot, *JFC*, 1:143.

11. George Mason to George Mason Jr., 5/20/87, Mason, *Papers*, 3:880.

12. Madison, *DFC*, 5/29, 29.

13. Ibid., 5/30, 34–36; Elliot, *JFC*, 1:150–51.

14. Lee to Mason, 5/15/87, Mason, *Papers*, 3:877.

15. *DHRC* 1:226.

16. Madison, *DFC*, 5/30, 36–38; Elliot, *JFC*, 1:151, 475–76.

17. Madison, *DFC*, 6/1, 46, and 6/16, 125.

18. Ibid., 7/24, 357–58.

19. Ibid., 6/1–6/2, 48–51.

20. Ibid., 5/31, 39–41.

21. Ibid., 6/4, 64.

22. Ibid., 9/17, 653–54.

23. Ibid., 9/17, 655.

24. Ibid., 9/15, 651, and 8/31, 566.

25. Ibid., 9/17, 657.

26. Ibid., 9/15, 652.

27. Ibid., 9/17, 656.

28. Ibid., 9/17, 658–59.

29. Ibid., 5/29, 34–35. Luther Martin complained, justifiably, that men who were "nationalists" cast off that name "because they thought the word might tend to alarm," and he carefully elucidated the incongruity: "Although now, they who advocate the system [the proposed Constitution] pretend to call themselves *federalists*, in convention the distinction was quite the reverse. Those who opposed the system were there considered and styled the *federal party*, those who advocated it *anti-federal*." Elliot, *JFC*, 1:362; emphases in original. Other opponents, often anonymous, also tried to recapture the label, calling themselves "The Republican Federalist" (aka James Warren), "A Democratic Federalist," "A Federal Farmer," and so on, but these names didn't stick.

30. *DHRC* 2:95–97,100, 104.

31. Ibid., 2:111.

32. Ibid., 2:112–17; 13:294.

33. Ibid., 13:346-351; Mason, *Papers*, 3:991–93; GW to Madison, 10/10/87, *DHRC* 13:358.

34. *DHRC* 13:337; GW to David Stuart, 10/17/87, *DHRC* 13:385.

35. *DHRC* 2:602.

36. Ibid., 2:670–708.

37. Ibid., 2:709–25.

38. MOW to Abigail Adams, 9/22/87, *DHRC* 4:16.

39. MOW to Catharine Macaulay, 8/2/87, Warren Family Letters, Pilgrim Museum, 2:276; MOW to Macaulay, 9/28/87, *DHRC* 4:23.

40. *DHRC* 4:349, 5:834.

41. Ibid., 5:1071; Raphael, *First American Revolution*, 217.

42. *DHRC* 5:1032–33.

43. Ibid., 6:1109–14.

44. TY to John Wendell, 11/23/66, MHS Photostat Collections.

45. *DHRC* 6:1118, 1384; JW to John Adams, 5/18/87, *Warren-Adams Letters*, 2:293.

46. *DHRC* 6:1381–82

47. Ibid., 5:702.

48. Ibid., 6:1462.

49. Ibid., 6:1479–87.

50. Ibid., 16:272–91.

51. Freeman, *George Washington*,135; GW, *Writings*, 29:507–8; GW, *Diaries*, 5:335.

52. Jefferson to Madison, 12/20/87, *DHRC* 8:250–51.

53. RM to Horatio Gates, 6/12/88, *DHRC* 10:1613.

54. *DHRC* 10:1476–77.

55. Ibid., 10:1572–75; 1538–40; 1550–56.

56. GW, *Diaries*, 5:349–52.

57. GW to C. C. Pinckney, 6/28/88, GW, *Writings*, 30:9–10.

58. Hopkinson, *Grand Federal Procession*; "Order of Procession," broadside printed by Hall and Sellers, 1788; Van Horne, "Federal Procession of 1788."

59. Waldstreicher, *Perpetual Fetes*, 100–101.

60. *DHRC* 14:181.

61. Ibid., 16:274, 466–69; Hamilton, Madison, and Jay, *Federalist Papers*, vii.

62. Gillespie, *Ratifying the Constitution*, 316–28;

63. Jefferson to Alexander Donald, 2/7/88, *DHRC* 8:353–54.

64. *JCC*, 34:523.

65. GW to Henry Lee, 9/22/78, GW, *Writings*, 30:97–98.

66. GW, *Writings*, 30:83, 295–96.

67. Rakove, *Original Meanings*, 334.

68. For a compilation of the proposed amendments, see Bailyn, *Debate on Constitution*, 2:536–76.

69. *DHRC* 16:281–82.

Chapter 20: Lives and Legacies

1. MOW to Gerry, 3/24/91, Gardiner, *Study in Dissent*, 246.

2. Ibid.

3. MOW to Adams, 5/8/89, Regan, *Pundit and Prophet*, 376; Knox to MOW, 7/9/89, *Warren-Adams Letters*, 2:317; Adams to MOW, 5/29/89, *Warren-Adams Letters*, 2:314; MOW to Knox, ?/?/89, MOW, Letterbook, MHS.

4. Fritz, *Cast for a Revolution*, 238.

5. Regan, *Pundit and Prophet*, 384; MOW to WW, 5/18/91, Warren, Letterbook, MHS.

6. Fritz, *Cast for a Revolution*, 238.

7. Regan, *Pundit and Prophet*, 386.

8. MOW, *History*, 3:423, 431.

9. Ibid., 3:435–36.

10. Brunhouse, *Counter-Revolution in Pennsylvania*, 221–27.

11. RM to Sylvanus Bourne, 3/30/95, Gilder-Lehrman collection.

12. Young, *Forgotten Patriot*, 198–251; Oberholtzer, *Robert Morris*, 317–57. The Walnut Street Gaol, famous at the time, bordered Prune Street as well and was sometimes denoted by that name.

13. Bouton, *Taming Democracy*, ch. 10.

14. Kohn, "Decision to Crush the Whiskey Rebellion," 573.

15. GW, *Writings*, 35:214–38.

16. GW to Burgess Ball, 9/25/94, Cleland, *Washington in Ohio Valley*, 369–71; GW, *Writings*, 34:37.

17. Kohn, "Decision to Crush the Whiskey Rebellion," 584; GW, *Writings*, 28–37.

18. HL, *Papers*, 16:745–51.

19. Wallace, *Henry Laurens*, 423.

20. HL, *Papers*, 16:762, 795–801.

21. Ibid., 16:782.

22. Edes, "Dr. Thomas Young," 53.

23. The 1793 Vermont Constitution is on the Web at: http://vermont-archives .org/govhistory/constitut/con93.htm (consulted Sept. 9, 2008).

24. Izard, "Andrews-Bigelow Site"; Crane, "Chapter in War of Revolution," 196.

25. JPM, *Narrative*, xiv–xv; Taylor, *Liberty Men and Great Proprietors*, 247–48.

26. JPM, *Narrative*, 283.

27. Ibid., vii–viii.

28. Ibid., 95.

Full Citations for Sources Contemporary to the Revolutionary Era

Adams Family Correspondence, L. H. Butterfield, ed. Cambridge, MA: Belknap Press, 1963.

Adams, John. *Diary and Autobiography*, L. H. Butterfield, ed. Cambridge, MA: Belknap Press, 1961.

Adams, John. *Legal Papers of John Adams*, L. Kinvin Wroth and Hiller B. Zobel, eds. Cambridge: Harvard University Press, 1965.

Adams, John. *Papers of John Adams*, Robert J. Taylor, ed. Cambridge, MA: Belknap Press, 1977–.

Adams, John. *Works of John Adams*, Charles Francis Adams, ed. Boston: Little, Brown, 1850–56.

Adams, John, and Abigail Adams. *Familiar Letters of John Adams and his Wife Abigail Adams, during the Revolution*. New York: Hurd and Houghton, 1876.

Adams, Samuel. Samuel Adams Papers. NYPL, Bancroft Collection.

Adams, Samuel. *The Writings of Samuel Adams*, Harry Alonzo Cushing, ed. New York: G. P. Putnam's Sons, 1904.

American Political Society [APS]. Minutes. AAS.

Andrews, John. "Letters of John Andrews of Boston, 1772–1776." MHS, *Proceedings* 8 (1864–65), 316–412.

Bailyn, Bernard, ed. *The Debate on the Constitution: Federalist and Antifederalist Speeches, Articles, and Letters During the Struggle over Ratification*. New York: Library of America, 1993.

Book of Negroes (roster of former slaves traveling to Canada in 1783). Black Loyalists Web site, Canada's Digital Collections, http://epe.lac-bac.gc.ca/100/205/301/ic/cdc/blackloyalists/index.htm (consulted Sept. 6, 2008).

Boston, City of, Record Commissioners. *Boston Town Records, 1770 through 1777* [*BTR*]. Boston, 1887.

Boston Committee of Correspondence. Correspondence and Proceedings. NYPL, Bancroft Collection.

Boston Committee of Correspondence. Minute Book. NYPL, Bancroft Collection.

Boston Pamphlet. MHS online, "The Coming of the American Revolution," http://masshist.org/revolution/doc-viewer.php?old=1&mode=nav&item_id=649.

Brackenridge, Hugh Henry, ed. *Narratives of a Late Expedition Against the Indians, with an Account of the Barbarous Execution of Col. Crawford and the Wonderful Escape of Dr. Knight and John Slover from Captivity, in 1782*. Philadelphia: Francis Bailey, 1783; repr. New York: Garland Publishing, 1978.

Carretta, Vincent, ed. *Unchained Voices: An Anthology of Black Authors in the English-Speaking World of the Eighteenth Century*. Lexington: University of Kentucky Press, 1996.

Caughey, John W., ed. *McGillivray of the Creeks*. Norman: University of Oklahoma Press, 1938.

Cleland, Hugh, ed. *George Washington in the Ohio Valley*. Pittsburgh: University of Pittsburgh Press, 1955.

Colonial Albany Social History Project, "Sons of Liberty Constitution" (Albany), http://www.nysm.nysed.gov/albany/solconst.html (consulted Sept. 7, 2008).

Commager, Henry S., and Richard B. Morris, eds. *The Spirit of 'Seventy-Six: The Story of the American Revolution as Told by the Participants*. Indianapolis and New York: Bobbs-Merrill, 1958.

Cook, Frederick, ed. *Journals of the Military Expedition of Major General John Sullivan against the Six Nations of Indians in 1779*. Auburn, NY: Knapp, Peck, and Thomson, 1887.

Davies, K.G., ed. *Documents of the American Revolution 1770–1783*. Dublin: Irish University Press, 1976.

Dearborn, Henry. *Revolutionary War Journals of Henry Dearborn, 1775–1783*, Lloyd A. Brown and Howard H. Peckham, eds. Chicago: Caxton Clus, 1939.

Donnan, Elizabeth, ed. *Documents Illustrative of the History of the Slave Trade in America*. New York: Octagon, 1965.

Drake, Francis S., ed. *Tea Leaves: Being a Collection of Letters and Documents relating to the Subject of Tea to the American Colonies in the year 1773*. Boston: A.O. Crane, 1884.

Drayton, John. *Memoirs of the American Revolution*. Charleston: A.F. Miller, 1821.

Elliot, Jonathan, ed. *Debates in the Several State Conventions on the Adoption of the Federal Constitution . . . together with the Journal of the Federal Convention* [*JFC*]. New York: Burt Franklin, 1888.

Evans, Charles, and Roger Bristol. *Early American Imprints, Series I: 1639–1800*. AAS.

Force, Peter, ed. *American Archives, Fourth Series: A Documentary History of the English Colonies in North America from the King's Message to Parliament of March 7, 1774, to the Declaration of Independence by the United States*. New York: Johnson Reprint Co., 1972 (first published 1833–46).

Franklin, Benjamin. *Papers of Benjamin Franklin*, Leonard W. Labaree and William B. Willcox, eds. New Haven: Yale University Press, 1959–.

Gage, Thomas. *Correspondence of General Thomas Gage*, Clarence E. Carter, ed. New Haven: Yale University Press, 1931.

Gadsden, Christopher. *The Writings of Christopher Gadsden*, Richard Walsh, ed. Columbia: University of South Carolina Press, 1966.

Gardiner, C. Harvey, ed. *A Study in Dissent: The Warren-Gerry Correspondence, 1776–1792*. Carbondale: Southern Illinois University Press, 1968.

Gibbes, R.W., ed. *Documentary History of the American Revolution*. New York: Appleton, 1855.

Gordon, William. *The History of the Rise, Progress, and Establishment of the Independence of the United States of America*. Repr. Freeport, NY: Books for Libraries Press, 1969 (first published in 1788).

Greene, Jack, ed. *Colonies to Nation, 1763–1789: A Documentary History of the American Revolution*. New York: W.W. Norton, 1975.

Greene, Nathanael. *Papers of General Nathanael Greene*, Richard K. Showman, ed. Chapel Hill: University of North Carolina Press, 1976.

Greenman, Jeremiah. *Diary of a Common Soldier in the American Revolution, 1775–1783*; Robert C. Bray and Paul E. Bushnell, eds. De Kalb: Northern Illinois University Press, 1978.

Hamilton, Alexander. *Papers of Alexander Hamilton*, Harold C. Syrett, ed. New York: Columbia University Press, 1961.

Hamilton, Alexander, James Madison, and John Jay. *The Federalist Papers*, Clinton Rossiter, ed. New York: Penguin, 1961.

Hemphill, William E., ed. *Extracts from the Journals of the Provincial Congress of South Carolina, 1775–1776* [*JPCSC*]. Columbia: South Carolina Archives Department, 1960.

Hopkinson, Francis. *Account of the Grand Federal Procession, Philadelphia, July 4, 1788*. Philadelphia: M. Carry, 1788.

Hutchinson, Thomas. *The History of the Colony and Province of Massachusetts-Bay.* Cambridge, MA: Harvard University Press, 1936.

Jefferson, Thomas. *Writing of Thomas Jefferson,* Paul Leicester Ford, ed. New York: G.P. Putnam's Sons, 1899.

Jensen, Merrill, et al., eds. *Documentary History of the Ratification of the Constitution* [*DHRC*]. Madison: State Historical Society of Wisconsin, 1976–.

Journal of the South Carolina Council, 1761–1762 [*JSCC*]. Columbia: South Carolina Archives.

Journals of the Continental Congress, 1774–1789 [*JCC*]. Library of Congress, American Memory, http://memory.loc.gov/ammem/amlaw/lwjclink.html (consulted Sept. 7, 2008).

Judd, Jonathan Jr. Diary. Forbes Library, Northampton, MA.

Lamb, John. John Lamb Papers. NYHS.

Laurens, Henry. *Appendix to the Extracts from the Proceedings of the High Court of Vice-Admiralty in Charlestown, South-Carolina.* Charleston: David Bruce, 1769.

Laurens, Henry. *The Papers of Henry Laurens,* Philip M. Hamer, ed. Columbia: University of South Carolina Press, 1968–2003.

Leigh, Egerton. *The Man Unmasked.* Charleston: Peter Timothy, 1769.

Letters of Delegates to Congress [*LDC*]. Library of Congress, American Memory, http://memory.loc.gov/ammem/amlaw/lwdglink.html (consulted Sept. 7, 2008).

Lincoln, William, ed. *The Journals of Each Provincial Congress of Massachusetts in 1774 and 1775, and of the Committee of Safety, with an Appendix, containing the Proceedings of the County Conventions* [*JPCM/CC*]. Boston: Dutton and Wentworth, 1838.

Linder, Douglas, ed. "The Boston Massacre Trials." http://www.law.umkc.edu/faculty/ projects/ftrials/bostonmassacre/bostonmassacre.html (consulted Sept. 7, 2008).

Loring, James Spear, ed. *The Hundred Boston Orators Appointed by the Municipal Authorities and other Public Bodies, from 1770 to 1852.* Boston: John P. Jewett & Co., 1853.

Madison, James. *Notes of Debates in the Federal Convention of 1787* [*DFC*]. New York: W.W. Norton, 1987. Because Madison's notes are published in diverse places, I've added dates to each citation for easy reference.

Marshall, Christopher. *Extracts from the Diary of Christopher Marshall, 1774–1781,* William Duane, ed. Albany, NY: Joel Munsell, 1877.

Martin, Joseph Plumb. *Private Yankee Doodle: Being a Narrative of Some of the Adventures, Dangers and Sufferings of a Revolutionary Soldier,* George F. Scheer, ed. Boston: Little, Brown, 1962 (originally published in 1830 at Hallowell, Maine, under the title *A Narrative of Some of the Adventures, Dangers and Sufferings of a Revolutionary Soldier, Interspersed with Anecdotes of Incidents That Occurred Within His Own Observation*). Although there are other modern editions of Martin's *Narrative,* I cite Scheer's because it is well annotated.

Mason, George. *Papers of George Mason,* Robert A. Rutland, ed. Chapel Hill: University of North Carolina Press, 1960.

Merchants of Pennsylvania. "Papers of the Merchants of Philadelphia." Sparks Manuscripts, Houghton Library, Harvard University.

Montresor, John. "Journals of Captain John Montresor." New York Historical Society, *Collections* 14 (1881): 362–83.

Moore, Frank, ed. *The Diary of the American Revolution.* New York: GW Square Press, 1967.

Morgan, Edmund S., ed. *Prologue to Revolution: Sources and Documents on the Stamp Act Crisis, 1764–1766.* Chapel Hill: University of North Carolina Press, 1959.

Morris, Robert. *The Papers of Robert Morris, 1781–1784,* E. James Ferguson, ed. Pittsburgh: University of Pittsburgh Press, 1973.

Morris, Robert. Robert Morris Papers. NYPL.

Moultrie, William. *Memoirs of the American Revolution.* New York: D. Longworth, 1802.

Muhlenberg, Reverend Henry Melchior. "Extract Account of the March of the Paxton Boys against Philadelphia in the Year 1764," Hiester H. Muhlenberg, tr. *Collections of the Historical Society of Pennsylvania* 1 (1853).

New England Papers. Sparks Manuscripts, Houghton Library, Harvard University.

O'Callaghan, E.B., and B. Fernow, eds. *Documents Relative to the Colonial History of New York.* New York: Weed, Parsons, 1856–87.

Oliver, Peter. *Origin & Progress of the American Rebellion,* Douglass Adair and John A. Schutz, eds. Stanford: Stanford University Press, 1961.

Paine, Thomas. *Common Sense.* Repr. in *Thomas Paine Reader.* Michael Foot and Isaac Kramnick, eds. New York: Penguin, 1987.

Parkman, Ebenezer. Diary. AAS.

Peale, Charles Willson. *Selected Papers of Charles Willson Peale and his Family,* Lillian B. Miller, ed. New Haven: Yale University Press, 1983.

Pickering, Timothy. *An Easy Plan of Discipline for a Militia.* Boston: S. Hall, 1776.

Quincy Jr., Josiah. *Reports of Cases Argued and Adjudged in the Superior Court of Judicatur of the Province of Massachusetts Bay, between 1761 and 1772.* Boston: Little, Brown, 1865.

Ramsay, David. *The History of the American Revolution.* Philadelphia: R. Aitken & Son, 1789.

Ramsay, David. *History of South Carolina.* Trenton: Isaac Collins, 1785; Charleston: D. Longworth, 1809.

Rawles, William. "A Memoir of William Rawles," T.J. Wharton, ed. *Memoirs of the Historical Society of Pennsylvania* 4:1 (1840).

Rice, Franklin P., ed. *Worcester Town Records from 1753 to 1783* [*WTR*]. Worcester, MA: Worcester Society of Antiquity, 1882.

Rice, Franklin P., ed. *Worcester Town Records (1784–1800)* [*WTR (1784–1800)*]. Collections of Worcester Society of Antiquity, vol. 8.

Roberts, Kenneth, ed. *March to Quebec: Journals of the Members of Arnold's Expedition.* New York: Doubleday, 1947.

Rowe, John. *Letters and Diary of John Rowe*, Anne Rowe Cunningham, ed. Boston: W.B. Clarke, 1903.

Salisbury Family Papers. Manuscript Collection, AAS.

Secretary of the Commonwealth. *Massachusetts Soldiers and Sailors of the Revolutionary War*. Boston: Wright & Potter, 1898.

Stiles, Ezra. *The Literary Diary of Ezra Stiles*, Franklin B. Dexter, ed. New York: Charles Scribner's Sons, 1901.

Thacher, James. *A Military Journal During the American Revolutionary War, from 1775 to 1783 . . .* Boston: Richardson & Lord, 1823.

Thomas, Isaiah. *History of Printing in America*. Repr. New York: B. Franklin, 1967 (first published in 1810).

Thomson, Charles. Charles Thomson Papers. Sparks Manuscripts, Houghton Library, Harvard University.

Upton, L.F.S., ed. "Proceeding of Ye Body Respecting the Tea." *William and Mary Quarterly*, third series, 22 (1965): 287–300.

Van Schreeven, William J., Robert L. Scribner, and Brent Tarter, eds. *Revolutionary Virginia: The Road to Independence, A Documentary Record*. Charlottesville: University Press of Virginia, 1973.

Wade, Herbert T., and Robert A. Lively, eds. *This Glorious Cause: The Adventures of Two Company Officers in George Washington's Army*. Princeton: Princeton University Press, 1958.

Warren-Adams Letters. Boston: Massachusetts Historical Society, 1917.

Warren Family Letters and Papers. Pilgrim Museum (PM), Plymouth, MA.

Warren, Mercy Otis. *History of the Rise, Progress and Termination of the American Revolution*. Boston: Manning and Loring, 1805.

Warren, Mercy Otis. Letterbook. Massachusetts Historical Society (MHS).

Warren, Mercy Otis. *Poems, Dramatic and Miscellaneous*. Boston: T. Thomas and E.T. Andrews, 1790.

Warren, Mercy Otis. "The Private Poems of Mercy Otis Warren," Edmund M. Hayes, ed. *New England Quarterly* 54:2 (June 1981).

Washington, George. *The Diaries of George Washington*, Donald Jackson, ed. Charlottesville: University Press of Virginia, 1976–79.

Washington, George. *The Papers of George Washington*, W.W. Abbot and Dorothy Twohig, eds. Charlottesville: University Press of Virginia, 1983–. The volumes are numbered in separate series: Colonial (Col), Revolutionary War (RW), Confederation (Con), Presidential (P), and Retirement (Ret).

Webster, Pelatiah. "Journal of Pelatiah Webster's Voyage to Charleston, 1765," T.P. Harrison, ed. Southern Historical Association, *Publications*; reproduced in *Publications of the South Carolina Historical Society*, 1898.

Willard, Margaret Wheeler, ed. *Letters on the American Revolution, 1774–1776*. Boston and New York: Houghton Mifflin, 1925.

Willing, Thomas. *Willing Letters and Papers*, Thomas Willing Balch, ed. Philadelphia: Allen, Lane & Scott, 1922.

Winslow Papers. MHS.

Wroth, L. Kinvin, ed. *Province in Rebellion: A Documentary History of the Founding of the Commonwealth of Massachusetts, 1774–1775.* Cambridge: Harvard University Press, 1975.

Young, Thomas. *A Poem Sacred to the Memory of James Wolfe.* New Haven: James Parker, 1761.

Young, Thomas. *Some Reflections on the Dispute Between New York, New Hampshire, and Col. John Henry Lydius of Albany.* New Haven, CT: Benjamin Mecom, 1764. Evans, *Early American Imprints* 1:9889.

Zeisberger, David. *Diary of David Zeisberger, a Moravian Missionary among the Indians of Ohio,* Eugene F. Bliss, tr. and ed. Cincinnati: Historical and Philosophical Society of Ohio, 1885.

Full Citations for Secondary Sources

Abernathy, Thomas P. *Western Lands and the American Revolution.* New York: D. Appleton-Century, 1937.

Alden, John R. "John Stuart Accuses William Bull." *William and Mary Quarterly,* third series, 2 (1945).

Alexander, John K. "The Fort Wilson Incident of 1779: A Case Study of the Revolutionary Crowd." *William and Mary Quarterly,* third series, 31:4 (Oct. 1774).

Anderson, Fred. *Crucible of War: The Seven Years' War and the Fate of Empire in British North America, 1754–1766.* New York: Knopf, 2000.

Anderson, Fred W. "The Hinge of the Revolution: George Washington Confronts a People's Army." *Massachusetts Historical Review* 1 (1999) 21–48.

Anderson, George Pomeroy. "Who Wrote Ethan Allen's Bible?" *New England Quarterly* 10 (1937) 685–96.

Anthony, Katharine. *First Lady of the Revolution: The Life of Mercy Otis Warren.* New York: Doubleday, 1958.

Bancroft, George. *History of the United States of America, from the Discovery of the Continent.* Boston: Little, Brown, 1879 (first published 1834–1874).

Bell, J.L. "Behold, the Guns Were Gone! Four Brass Cannon and the Start of the American Revolution." Early American History Summer Seminars, MHS, 2001.

Bellesiles, Michael A. *Revolutionary Outlaws: Ethan Allen and the Struggle for Independence on the Early American Frontier.* Charlottesville: University Press of Virginia, 1993.

Bigelow, Patricia. *Bigelow Family Genealogy.* Flint, MI: 1986.

Billias, George A. *Elbridge Gerry: Founding Father and Republican Statesman.* New York: McGraw-Hill, 1976.

Birnbaum, Louis. *Red Dawn at Lexington.* Boston: Houghton Mifflin, 1986.

Bouton, Terry. *Taming Democracy: "The People," the Founders, and the Troubled Ending of the American Revolution.* New York: Oxford University Press, 2007.

Brooke, John L. *The Heart of the Commonwealth: Society and Political Culture in*

Worcester County, Massachusetts, 1713–1861. Amherst: University of Massachusetts Press, 1989.

Brookhiser, Richard. *Gentleman Revolutionary: Gouverneur Morris, the Rake Who Wrote the Constitution*. New York: Free Press, 2003.

Brown, Alice. *Mercy Warren*. New York: Charles Scribner's Sons, 1896.

Brown, Richard D. *Revolutionary Politics in Massachusetts: The Boston Committee of Correspondence and the Towns, 1772–1774*. New York: W.W. Norton, 1976.

Brunhouse, Robert L. *The Counter-Revolution in Pennsylvania 1776–1790*. Diss., University of Pennsylvania, 1942.

Bushman, Richard L. "Massachusetts Farmers and the Revolution." *Society, Freedom, and Conscience: The American Revolution in Virginia, Massachusetts, and New York*. New York: W.W. Norton, 1976.

Calloway, Colin. *The American Revolution in Indian Country*. Cambridge, UK: Cambridge University Press, 1995.

Cary, John. *Joseph Warren: Physician, Politician, Patriot*. Urbana: Illinois University Press, 1961.

Colton, Richard. "'Unwilling to Stain the Land': Conflict and Ambivalence in Shays' Rebellion," Springfield Armory, National Historical Site, Jan. 25, 2007.

Cook, Don. *The Long Fuse: How England Lost the American Colonies, 1760–1785*. New York: Atlantic Monthly Press, 1995.

Countryman, Edward. "'Out of the Bounds of the Law': Northern Land Rioters in the Eighteenth Century," in Alfred F. Young, *The American Revolution: Explorations in the History of American Radicalism*. De Kalb: Northern Illinois University Press, 1976, 37–70.

Crane, Ellery B. "A Chapter in the War of the American Revolution." Worcester Society of Antiquity, *Proceedings* 25 (1909–1911).

Crane, Ellery B. *Services of Colonel Timothy Bigelow in the War of the American Revolution, including his 15th Regt. Massachusetts Line in the Continental Army*. Worcester, MA: Blanchard Press, 1910.

Davies, Kate. *Catharine Macaulay and Mercy Otis Warren: The Revolutionary Atlantic and the Politics of Gender*. Oxford: Oxford University Press, 2005.

Desjardin, Thomas A. *Through a Howling Wilderness: Benedict Arnold's March to Quebec*. New York: St. Martin's, 2006.

Dunbar, John R. *The Paxton Papers*. The Hague: M. Nijhoff, 1957.

Edes, Henry H. "Memoir of Dr. Thomas Young, 1731–1777," *Publications of the Colonial Society of Massachusetts Transactions 1906–1907* 11 (1910): 2–54.

Edgar, Walter. *South Carolina: A History*. Columbia: University of South Carolina Press, 1998.

Egnal, Marc. *A Mighty Empire: The Origins of the American Revolution*. Ithaca: Cornell University Press, 1988.

Ellis, Joseph. *His Excellency: George Washington*. New York: Knopf, 2004.

Feer, Robert A. *Shays's Rebellion*. Diss., Harvard University, 1958; New York: Garland, 1988.

Ferguson, E. James. *The Power of the Purse: A History of American Public Finance, 1776–1790*. Chapel Hill: University of North Carolina Press, 1961.

Fischer, David Hackett. *Paul Revere's Ride*. New York: Oxford University Press, 1994.

Fischer, David Hackett. *Washington's Crossing*. New York: Oxford University Press, 2004.

Flexner, James Thomas. *Washington: The Indispensable Man*. Boston: Little, Brown, 1974.

Florence, Justin. "Minutemen for Months: The Making of an American Revolutionary Army before George Washington, April 2–July 2, 1775." *Proceedings of the American Antiquarian Society* 113:1 (2003).

Foner, Philip S. *Labor and the American Revolution*. Westport, CT: Greenwood Press, 1976.

Freeman, Douglas Southall. *George Washington: A Biography*. New York: Scribner's, 1951.

French, Allen. *General Gage's Informers*. New York: Greenwood Press, 1968.

Frey, Sylvia R. *Water from the Rock: Black Resistance in a Revolutionary Age*. Princeton: Princeton University Press, 1991.

Friedenberg, Daniel. *Life, Liberty, and the Pursuit of Land*. Buffalo: Prometheus Books, 1992.

Fritz, Jean. *Cast for a Revolution: Some American Friends and Enemies, 1728–1814*. Boston: Houghton Mifflin, 1972.

Frothingham, Richard. *Life and Times of Joseph Warren*. Boston: Little, Brown, 1865.

Galvin, John. *Three Men of Boston*. New York: Thomas Y. Crowell, 1976.

Gillespie, Michael Allen, and Michael Lienesch. *Ratifying the Constitution*. Lawrence: University Press of Kansas, 1989.

Godbold Jr., E. Stanly, and Robert H. Woody. *Christopher Gadsden and the American Revolution*. Knoxville: University of Tennessee Press, 1982.

Goodrich, Charles. *Lives of the Signers of the Declaration of Independence*. Hartford, CT: R.G.H. Huntington, 1841.

Gough, Deborah Mathias. *Christ Church, Philadelphia: The Nation's Church in a Changing City*. Philadelphia: University of Pennsylvania Press, 1995.

Greene, Jack P. "The Gadsden Election Controversy and the Revolutionary Movement in South Carolina." *Mississippi Valley Historical Review* 46 (Dec. 1959): 469–92.

Hample, Judy. "The Textual and Cultural Authenticity of Patrick Henry's 'Liberty or Death' Speech." *Quarterly Journal of Speech* 63 (1977).

Hatley, Tom. *Dividing Paths: Cherokees and South Carolinians through the Revolutionary Era*. New York: Oxford University Press, 1995.

Hawke, David. "Dr. Thomas Young: Eternal Fisher in Troubled Waters." *New York Historical Society Quarterly* 54 (1970): 7–29.

Hawke, David. *In the Midst of Revolution*. Philadelphia: University of Pennsylvania Press, 1961.

Henry, Bruce. "Dr. Thomas Young and the Boston Committee of Correspondence." *Huntington Library Quarterly* 39 (1976): 219–21.

Hersey, Charles. *Reminiscences of the Military Life and Sufferings of Col. Timothy Bigelow.* Worcester, MA: Henry J. Howland, 1860.

Hindle, Brooke. "The March of the Paxton Boys." *William and Mary Quarterly,* third series, 3:4 (Oct. 1946): 462–86.

Hirschfeld, Fritz. *George Washington and Slavery: A Documentary Portrayal.* Columbia: University of Missouri Press, 1997.

Hoerder, Dirk. *Crowd Action in Revolutionary Massachusetts, 1765–1780.* New York: Academic Press, 1977.

Hoffman, Ronald, Thad W. Tate, and Peter J. Albert, eds. *An Uncivil War: The Southern Backcountry during the American Revolution.* Charlottesville: University Press of Virginia, 1985.

Holton, Woody. *Forced Founders: Indians, Debtors, Slaves, and the Making of the American Revolution in Virginia.* Chapel Hill: University of North Carolina Press, 1999.

Hutson, James H. "An Investigation of the Inarticulate: Philadelphia's White Oaks." *William and Mary Quarterly,* third series, 28:1 (Jan. 1971): 3–25.

Izard, Holly V. "The Andrews-Bigelow-Lincoln-Court Mills Site." Worcester Historical Museum, 2001.

Jellison, Charles. *Ethan Allen: Frontier Rebel.* Syracuse, NY: Syracuse University Press, 1983.

Jensen, Arthur. *The Maritime Commerce of Colonial Philadelphia.* Madison: State Historical Society of Wisconsin, 1963.

Jensen, Merrill. *The Articles of Confederation: An Interpretation of the Social-Constitution History of the American Revolution, 1774–1781.* Madison: University of Wisconsin Press, 1940.

Jensen, Merrill. *The Founding of a Nation: A History of the American Revolution, 1763–1776.* New York: Oxford University Press, 1968.

Jensen, Merrill. "The Idea of a National Government during the American Revolution." *Political Science Quarterly* 58:3 (Sept. 1943).

Jensen, Merrill. *The New Nation: A History of the United States during the Confederation 1781–1789.* New York: Knopf, 1950.

Johnson, Donald E. *Worcester in the War for Independence.* Diss., Clark University, 1953.

Jones, Matt Bushnell. *Vermont in the Making, 1750–1777.* Cambridge: Harvard University Press, 1939.

Kaplan, Sidney, and Emma Nogrady Kaplan. *The Black Presence in the Era of the American Revolution.* Amherst: University of Massachusetts Press, 1989.

Kars, Marjoleine. *Breaking Loose Together: The Regulator Rebellion in Pre-Revolutionary North Carolina.* Chapel Hill: University of North Carolina Press, 2002.

Kay, Marvin L. "The North Carolina Regulation, 1766–1776: A Class Conflict." In

Alfred F. Young, ed., *The American Revolution: Explorations in the History of American Radicalism*, 71–124. De Kalb: Northern Illinois University Press, 1976.

Kim, Sung Bok. *Landlord and Tenant in Colonial New York: Manorial Society, 1664–1775*. Chapel Hill: University of North Carolina Press, 1978.

Klein, Rachel N. *Unification of a Slave State: The Rise of the Planter Class in the South Carolina Backcountry, 1760–1808*. Chapel Hill: University of North Carolina Press, 1990.

Kohn, Richard H. "The Washington Administration's Decision to Crush the Whiskey Rebellion." *Journal of American History* 59:3 (Dec. 1972): 567–84.

Labaree, Benjamin W. *The Boston Tea Party*. New York: Oxford University Press, 1964.

Leake, Isaac. *Memoir of the Life and Times of General John Lamb*. Albany: Joel Munsell, 1857.

Lee, Wayne I. *Crowds and Soldiers in Revolutionary North Carolina: The Culture of Violence in Riot and War*. Gainesville: University Press of Florida, 2001.

Lesser, Charles H. *The Sinews of Independence: Monthly Strength Reports of the Continental Army*. Chicago: University of Chicago Press, 1976.

Lincoln, William. *History of Worcester, Massachusetts, from its Earliest Settlement to September, 1836*. Worcester: Charles Hersey, 1862.

Livermore, Shaw. *Early American Land Companies*. New York: Octagon, 1968.

Lossing, Benson. *The Pictorial Field-Book of the Revolution*. New York: Harper & Brothers, 1852.

Lovell, Albert A. *Worcester in the War of the Revolution: Embracing the Acts of the Town from 1765 to 1783 Inclusive*. Worcester: Tyler & Seagrave, 1876.

MacCracken, Henry N. *Old Dutchess Forever!* New York: Hastings House, 1956.

Mackesy, Piers. *The War for America, 1775–1783*. Cambridge: Harvard University Press, 1965.

Maier, Pauline. *American Scripture: Making the Declaration of Independence*. New York: Vintage, 1998.

Maier, Pauline. "The Charleston Mob and the Evolution of Popular Politics in Revolutionary South Carolina, 1765–1784." *Perspectives in American History* 4 (1970).

Maier, Pauline. *From Resistance to Revolution: Colonial Radicals and the Development of American Opposition to Britain, 1765–1776*. New York: Knopf, 1972.

Maier, Pauline. *Old Revolutionaries: Political Lives in the Age of Samuel Adams*. New York: Knopf, 1980.

Main, Jackson Turner. *The Sovereign States, 1775–1783*. New York: Franklin Watts, 1973.

Mark, Irving. *Agrarian Conflicts in Colonial New York, 1711–1775*. New York: Columbia University Press, 1940.

Massey, Gregory D. *John Laurens and the American Revolution*. Columbia: University of South Carolina Press, 2000.

Mathews, Lois K. "Benjamin Franklin's Plans for a Colonial Union, 1750–1775." *American Political Science Review* 8 (Aug. 1914).

McAnear, Beverly. "The Albany Stamp Act Riots." *William and Mary Quarterly*, third series, 4:4 (Oct. 1947): 486–98.

McCullough, David. *1776*. New York: Simon & Schuster, 2005.

McDonnell, Michael A. *The Politics of War: Race, Class, and Conflict in Revolutionary Virginia*. Chapel Hill: University of North Carolina Press, 2007.

McDonnell, Michael A. "Popular Mobilization and Political Culture in Revolutionary Virginia: The Failure of the Minutemen and the Revolution from Below." *Journal of American History* 85 (1998).

McDonough, Daniel J. *Christopher Gadsden and Henry Laurens: The Parallel Lives of Two American Patriots*. Sellinsgrove, PA: Susquehanna University Press, 2000.

Middlekauff, Robert. *The Glorious Cause: The American Revolution, 1763–1789*. New York: Oxford University Press, 1982.

Mires, Charlene. *Independence Hall in American Memory*. Philadelphia: University of Pennsylvania Press, 2002.

Morgan, Edmund S., and Helen M. Morgan. *The Stamp Act Crisis: Prologue to Revolution*. Chapel Hill: University of North Carolina Press, 1953.

Morris, Richard B. *The Peacemakers: The Great Powers and American Independence*. New York: Harper & Row, 1965.

Morton, Brian, and Donald Spinelli. *Beaumarchais and the American Revolution*. Lanham, MD: Lexington Books, 2003.

Moynihan, Kenneth J. *A History of Worcester, 1674–1848*. Charleston, SC: History Press, 2007.

Moynihan, Kenneth J. "Meetinghouse vs. Courthouse: The Struggle for Legitimacy in Worcester, 1783–1788." In Martin J. Kaufman, ed., *Shays' Rebellion: Selected Essays*. Westfield, MA, 1987.

Mullin, Gerald W. *Flight and Rebellion: Slave Resistance in Eighteenth-Century Virginia*. New York: Oxford University Press, 1972.

Nadelhaft, Jerome J. *The Disorders of War: The Revolution in South Carolina*. Orono: University of Maine Press, 1981.

Nash, Gary B. "Social Change and the Growth of Prerevolutionary Urban Radicalism." In Alfred F. Young, ed., *The American Revolution: Explorations in the History of American Radicalism*, 3–36. De Kalb, IL: Northern Illinois University Press, 1976.

Nash, Gary B. *The Urban Crucible: Social Change, Political Consciousness, and the Origins of the American Revolution*. Cambridge: Harvard University Press, 1979.

Newfield, Lillian E. *Worcester on the Eve of the Revolution*. Master's thesis, Clark University, 1941.

Nutt, Charles. *History of Worcester and Its People*. New York: Lewis Historical Pub. Co., 1919.

Oaks, Robert Francis. "Philadelphia Merchants and the American Revolution, 1765–1776." Diss., University of Southern California, 1970.

Oberholtzer, Ellis P. *Robert Morris: Patriot and Financier*. New York: Macmillan, 1903.

Oliphant, John. *Peace and War on the Anglo-Cherokee Frontier*. Baton Rouge: Louisiana State University Press, 2001.

Olwell, Robert. *Masters, Slaves, and Subjects: The Culture of Power in the South Carolina Low Country, 1740–1790*. Ithaca: Cornell University Press, 1998.

Patterson, Stephen E. *Political Parties in Revolutionary Massachusetts*. Madison: University of Wisconsin Press, 1973.

Peckham, Howard H. *The Toll of Independence: Engagements and Battle Casualties of the American Revolution*. Chicago: University of Chicago Press, 1974.

Phillips, Kevin. *The Cousins' Wars: Religion, Politics, and the Triumph of Anglo-America*. New York: Basic Books, 1999.

Purvis, Thomas L. *Revolutionary America, 1763 to 1800*, Almanacs of American Life Series. New York: Facts on File, 1995.

Pybus, Cassandra. *Epic Journeys of Freedom: Runaway Slaves of the American Revolution and their Global Quest for Liberty*. Boston: Beacon Press, 2006.

Quarles, Benjamin. "Lord Dunmore as Liberator." *William and Mary Quarterly*, third series, 15 (1958).

Quarles, Benjamin. *The Negro in the American Revolution*. Chapel Hill: University of North Carolina Press, 1996 (first published in 1961).

Rakove, Jack. *The Beginnings of National Politics: An Interpretive History of the Continental Congress*. New York: Knopf, 1979.

Rakove, Jack. *Original Meanings: Politics and Ideas in the Making of the Constitution*. New York: Knopf, 1996.

Raphael, Ray. *A People's History of the American Revolution*. New York: The New Press, 2001.

Raphael, Ray. *The First American Revolution: Before Lexington and Concord*. New York: The New Press, 2002.

Raphael, Ray. *Founding Myths: Stories That Hide Our Patriotic Past*. New York: The New Press, 2004.

Regan, Mary Elizabeth. *Pundit and Prophet of the Old Republic: The Life and Times of Mercy Otis Warren, 1728–1814*. Diss., University of California, Berkeley, 1984.

Richards, Jeffrey H. *Mercy Otis Warren*. New York: Twayne Publishers, 1995.

Rosswurm, Steven. *Arms, Country, and Class: The Philadelphia Militia and the "Lower Sort" during the American Revolution, 1775–1783*. New Brunswick: Rutgers University Press, 1987.

Royster, Charles. *The Fabulous History of the Dismal Swamp Company: A Story of George Washington's Times*. New York: Knopf, 1999.

Royster, Charles. *A Revolutionary People at War: The Continental Army and American Character, 1775–1783*. Chapel Hill: University of North Carolina Press, 1979.

Ryerson, Richard A. *The Revolution Is Now Begun: The Radical Committees of Philadelphia, 1765–1776*. Philadelphia: University of Pennsylvania Press, 1978.

Scharf, J. Thomas, and Thompson Westcott. *History of Philadelphia*. Philadelphia: L.H. Everts, 1884.

Schecter, Barnet. *The Battle for New York: The City at the Heart of the American Revolution*. New York: Penguin, 2002.

Scheide, John H. "The Lexington Alarm." *Proceedings of the American Antiquarian Society*, Apr. 1940, repr. AAS, 1941.

Schlesinger, Arthur M. *The Colonial Merchants and the American Revolution, 1763–1776*. New York: Frederick Ungar, 1957.

Selby, John E. *The Revolution in Virginia, 1775–1783*. Williamsburg: Colonial Williamsburg Foundation, 1988.

Sellers, Charles C. *Charles Willson Peale*. New York: Charles Scribner's Sons, 1969.

Slaski, Eugene R. *Thomas Willing: Moderation during the American Revolution*. Diss., Florida State University, 1971.

Smith, Charles Page. *James Wilson: Founding Father*. Chapel Hill: University of North Carolina Press, 1956.

Stephenson, Orlando W. "The Supply of Gunpowder in 1776." *American Historical Review* 30:2 (Jan. 1925).

Stuart, Nancy Rubin. *The Muse of the Revolution: The Secret Pen of Mercy Otis Warren and the Founding of a Nation*. Boston: Beacon Press, 2008.

Symonds, Craig L. *A Battlefield Atlas of the American Revolution*. Nautical & Aviation Pub. Co., 1986.

Szatmary, David. *Shays' Rebellion: The Making of an Agrarian Insurrection*. Amherst: University of Massachusetts Press, 1980.

Taylor, Alan. *Liberty Men and Great Proprietors: The Revolutionary Settlement of the Maine Frontier, 1760–1820*. Chapel Hill: University of North Carolina Press, 1990.

Thatcher, Benjamin Bussey. *Traits of the Tea Party; Being a Memoir of George R. T. Hewes, One of the Last of Its Survivors*. New York: Harper & Brothers, 1835.

Tinkcom, Harry M. "The Revolutionary City, 1765–1783." In Russell F. Weigley, ed., *Philadelphia: A 300-Year History*. New York: W.W. Norton, 1982.

Trumbull, James R. *History of Northampton, Massachusetts, from its Settlement in 1654*. Northampton: Gazette Printing Co., 1902.

Tyler, John W. *Smugglers and Patriots: Boston Merchants and the Advent of the American Revolution*. Boston: Northeastern University Press, 1986.

Van Horne, John C. "The Federal Procession of 1788." Carpenters' Hall, http://www.ushistory.org/carpentershall/history/procession.htm (consulted Dec. 12, 2007).

Ver Steeg, Clarence. *Robert Morris: Revolutionary Financier*. New York: Octagon Books, 1972.

Waldstreicher, David. *In the Midst of Perpetual Fetes: The Making of American Nationalism, 1776–1820*. Chapel Hill: University of North Carolina Press, 1997.

Wallace, David Duncan. *The Life of Henry Laurens*. New York: G.P. Putnam's Sons, 1915.

Walsh, Richard. *Charleston's Sons of Liberty: A Study of the Artisans, 1763–1789*. Columbia: University of South Carolina Press, 1959.

Warren, Charles. "A Young American's Adventures in England and France during the Revolutionary War." MHS, *Proceedings for 1932–1934*, Boston, 1940.

Wells, William V. *The Life and Public Services of Samuel Adams*. Boston: Little, Brown, 1865.

Wiencek, Henry. *An Imperfect God: George Washington, His Slaves, and the Creation of America*. New York: Farrar, Straus & Giroux, 2003.

Wilson, Ellen Gibson. *The Loyal Blacks*. New York: G.P. Putnam's Sons, 1976.

Wirt, William. *Sketches of the Life and Character of Patrick Henry*. Philadelphia: James Webster, 1818.

Wood, Peter. "The Dream Deferred: Black Struggles on the Eve of White Independence." In Gary Y. Okihiro, ed., *In Resistance: Studies in African, Caribbean, and Afro-Ameircan History*. Amherst: University of Massachusetts Press, 1986.

Wood, Peter H. "'Liberty Is Sweet': African-American Freedom Struggles in the Years before White Independence." In Alfred F. Young, ed., *Beyond the American Revolution: Explorations in the History of American Radicalism*. De Kalb: Northern Illinois University Press, 1993.

Wright Jr., Robert K. *The Continental Army*. Washington, DC: Center of Military History, United States Army, 1983.

Young, Alfred F. *Liberty Tree: Ordinary People and the American Revolution*. New York: New York University Press, 2006.

Young, Eleanor. *Forgotten Patriot: Robert Morris*. New York: Macmillan, 1950.

Zagarri, Rosemarie. *A Woman's Dilemma: Mercy Otis Warren and the American Revolution*. Wheeling, IL: Harlan Davidson, 1995.

Zilversmit, Arthur. *The First Emancipation: The Abolition of Slavery in the North*. Chicago: University of Chicago Press, 1967.

Zobel, Hiller B. *The Boston Massacre*. New York: W.W. Norton, 1970.

Image Credits

Figure 1. Map: British North America, 1754. Library of Congress, American Memory online. "The American Revolution and Its Era: Maps and Charts of North America and the West Indies, 1750–1789" (http://memory.loc.gov/ammem/gmdhtml/armhtml/armhome.html).

Figure 2. Philadelphia in the 1760s. National Archives online, "Pictures of the Revolutionary War" (http://www.archives.gov/research/american-revolution/pictures/).

Figure 3. "A View of the Year 1765," engraving by Paul Revere. Courtesy, American Antiquarian Society.

Figures 4 and 5. Mercy Otis Warren and James Warren, by John Singleton Copley. Photograph © 2009 Museum of Fine Arts, Boston.

Figure 6. The Boston Massacre, by Henry Pelham. Courtesy, American Antiquarian Society.

Figure 7. The Boston Tea Party, as portrayed in 1793. The Granger Collection, New York. 0009361.

Figure 8. A New England town meeting. The Granger Collection, New York. 0064464.

Figure 9. "The Bostonians paying the exciseman, or tarring and feathering," British cartoon from 1774. National Archives online, "Pictures of the Revolutionary War" (http://www.archives.gov/research/american-revolution/pictures/).

Figure 10. Worcester town records, October 4, 1774: the first call for a new and independent government. Courtesy, Worcester City Clerk David J. Rushford and Ashley Cataldo.

Figure 11. Convention of Worcester County blacksmiths pledges to enforce the Continental Association. Courtesy, American Antiquarian Society.

Figures 12–15. The battles of Lexington and Concord, by Amos Doolittle and Ralph Earl. Chicago History Museum.

Figure 16. "Bloody Butchery by the British Troops," broadside by Ezekiel Russell. Courtesy, American Antiquarian Society.

Figure 17. "The Virginia Colonel": George Washington in 1772, by Charles Willson Peale. National Archives online, "Pictures of the Revolutionary War" (http://www.archives.gov/research/american-revolution/pictures/).

Figure 18. Dunmore's Proclamation to free slaves. Tracy W. McGregor Library of American History, Special Collections, University of Virginia Library.

Figure 19. "List of Negroes that went off to Dunmore." Library of Virginia.

Figure 20. Patrick Henry's call to increase slave patrols. Library of Congress.

Figure 21. Title page from Thomas Paine's *Common Sense*. The Granger Collection, New York. 0023659.

Figure 22. The Declaration of Independence, broadside by John Dunlap. USHistory .org online (http://www.ushistory.org/Declaration/document/dunlap.htm).

Figures 23 and 24. Committee of Safety musket and tricorn hat. Military History, Smithsonian Institution. Online exhibit, "The Price of Freedom: Americans at War" (http://americanhistory.si.edu/militaryhistory/exhibition/flash.html).

Figure 25. James Pike's powder horn. Chicago History Museum.

Figure 26. Thomas Young's broadside to the people of Vermont, April 11, 1777. Courtesy, American Antiquarian Society.

Figure 27. Title page of the Articles of Confederation and Perpetual Union between the States. The Granger Collection, New York. 0035072.

Figure 28. John Laurens, miniature by Charles Willson Peale. Independence National Historical Park.

Figure 29. British bombardment of Fort Mifflin. The Granger Collection, New York. 0013193.

Figure 30. George Washington in 1779, by Charles Willson Peale. The Granger Collection, New York. 0007292.

Figure 31. "The Soldiers in the Field doing duty," cartoon from 1777. Reproduced by permission of The Huntington Library, San Marino, California, from *The Downfall of Justice* (Danvers, Massachusetts: E. Russell, 1777).

Figure 32. "One for forty" banknote from Virginia. The Granger Collection, New York. 0010827.

Figure 33. Robert Morris and Gouverneur Morris, by Charles Willson Peale. Courtesy of the Pennsylvania Academy of the Fine Arts, Philadelphia. Bequest of Richard Ashhurst.

Figure 34. A cancelled "Morris note." Princeton University Library, Rare Books and Special Collections.

Figure 35. Henry Laurens, by John Singleton Copley. The Granger Collection, New York. 0050044.

Figure 36. American peace commissioners in Paris, by Benjamin West. The Granger Collection, New York. 0023432.

Figure 37. "A map of the United States of America agreeable to the peace of 1783." Library of Congress, American Memory online. "The American Revolution and

Its Era: Maps and Charts of North America and the West Indies, 1750–1789" (http://memory.loc.gov/ammem/gmdhtml/armhtml/armhome.html).

Figure 38. Robert Morris, by Charles Willson Peale. Wikimedia Commons (http://commons.wikimedia.org/wiki/Image:Robert_morris_portrait.jpg).

Figure 39. Mary Morris, by Charles Willson Peale. National Archives online, "Pictures of the Revolutionary War" (http://www.archives.gov/research/american-revolution/pictures/).

Figure 40. "Looking Glass for 1787," cartoon by Amos Doolittle. Library of Congress, American Treasures online (http://www.loc.gov/exhibits/treasures/trt050.html).

Figure 41. Winslow Warren in 1785, by John Singleton Copley. Photograph © 2009 Museum of Fine Arts, Boston.

Figure 42. Title page from Mercy Otis Warren's *History of the Rise, Progress and Termination of the American Revolution*. Courtesy, American Antiquarian Society.

Figure 43. George Washington in 1795, by Gilbert Stuart. Wikimedia Commons (http://commons.wikimedia.org/wiki/Image:George_Washington_1795.jpg).

Figure 44. Title page from Joseph Plumb Martin's *Narrative of Some of the Adventures, Dangers and Sufferings of a Revolutionary Soldier*. Courtesy, American Antiquarian Society.

Index

Note: Page numbers in italics indicate images and illustrations.